Commercial Real Estate Analysis for Investment, Finance, and Development

Commercial Real Estate Analysis for Investment, Finance, and Development, a fully revised fourth edition of the authors' leading textbook, presents the foundations of real estate investment analysis with the rigor of general finance and economics. This book introduces the essential building blocks of the field: market assumptions, valuation, financial analysis, and development. Drawing from extensive academic and industry experience, the authors approach the investment analysis process using a combination of theory and practical tools in a discussion tailored to advanced students.

Topics include value concepts, mortgage analysis, financing alternatives, option value, leverage and risk analysis, as well as institutional and capital market trends. Additionally, the new edition addresses climate risks, alternative property types, and the impact of technology on real estate as an asset class. New supplemental online resources complement the book's conceptual and quantitative study questions, chapter summaries, and other useful pedagogical features.

Combining a practical grounding in economics and finance with updated tools and resources, this edition of *Commercial Real Estate Analysis for Investment, Finance, and Development* provides a new generation of professionals the foundation and tools they need to excel as investment managers, advisers, and analysts. Ideal for graduate studies in real estate, finance, and business, this textbook prepares students for the real-world complexities and challenges of commercial real estate.

For access to additional, online chapters and other Instructor and Student Resources, please visit: www.routledge.com/cw/geltner-miller

The American Real Estate Society (ARES) Real Estate Thought Leadership Collection Series

The American Real Estate Society promotes the global dissemination of research representing the forefront of critical thought in real estate, with findings applicable to all areas of industry, policy, education, and practice. ARES publishes a broad range of real estate topics within an international scope, including finance, economics, investment, business, development, housing, sustainability, and environmental and urban studies. ARES publications provide insider access to the latest high-level real estate research, case studies, reports, analyses, pedagogies, and reviews. These constitute an up-to-the-minute resource of interest and relevance to business decision-makers, academic researchers and educators, industry professionals, and emerging real estate leaders.

ARES publishes six, peer-reviewed, academic journals in partnership with Routledge, Taylor & Francis that provide relevant and timely research of interest to real estate academics and practitioners worldwide: The *Journal of Real Estate Research* (JRER), *Journal of Housing Research* (JHR), *Journal of Real Estate Literature* (JREL), *Journal of Real Estate Portfolio Management* (JREPM), *Journal of Real Estate Practice and Education* (JREPE), and *Journal of Sustainable Real Estate* (JOSRE). For more information visit: www.aresnet.org/page/ARES-Journal-Info#rjer

Conference

ARES hosts an academic and professional conference each spring in a unique travel destination that attracts real estate researchers from around the globe. The event features formal paper presentations, panels and roundtables, exhibitions, and social and networking events.

Membership

Membership in ARES includes a subscription to the journals, discounted conference registration, and many other benefits. For more information visit: www.aresnet.org/page/Benefits

ARES
American Real Estate Society

For more information: www.routledge.com/The-American-Real-Estate-Society-ARES-Real-Estate-Thought-Leadership/book-series/ARES

Commercial Real Estate Analysis for Investment, Finance, and Development

Fourth Edition

David M. Geltner, Norman G. Miller, Alex van de Minne,
Piet Eichholtz, Thies Lindenthal, and Lily Shen

Routledge
Taylor & Francis Group
NEW YORK AND LONDON

Designed cover image: Shutterstock

4th edition published 2026
by Routledge
605 Third Avenue, New York, NY 10158

and by Routledge
4 Park Square, Milton Park, Abingdon, Oxon, OX14 4RN

Routledge is an imprint of the Taylor & Francis Group, an informa business

Third edition published by Mbition 2014

ISBN: 978-1-041-08119-7 (hbk)
ISBN: 978-1-041-07639-1 (pbk)
ISBN: 978-1-003-64383-8 (ebk)

DOI: 10201/9781003643838

Typeset in Times New Roman
by Newgen Publishing UK

For access to the online chapters and other Instructor and Student Resources, please visit: www.routledge.com/cw/geltner-miller

Dedication

This book is dedicated to our parents,
our spouses, and our children,
and to all the students we have known who
wanted to know not just what, but why.

Contents

*PART IV Real Estate Development (Chapters Available Online Only; ***Link to Access Online Chapters Below)*

PART V Mortgages from an Investment Perspective

PART VI Macro-Level Real Estate Investment Analysis

*** For access to the online chapters and other Instructor and Student Resources, please visit: www.routledge.com/cw/geltner-miller

PART VII Other Selected Topics

*** For access to the online chapters and other Instructor and Student Resources, please visit: www.routledge.com/cw/geltner-miller

Preface

WHAT THIS BOOK IS ABOUT

What is real estate? You could say that it is land. In that sense, real estate is the quarter of the earth's surface on which all 8 billion human beings live. Or you could say it is built space, the structures in which we live, work, and play, that shape and define our cities, and shelter our dreams. Or you could say that real estate is one-third of the value of all capital assets in the world, over $60 trillion worth of assets in the United States alone. Real estate is important, regardless of what line of work you are in.

But think a bit more about what real estate is. Perhaps most obviously, it is not called "real" for nothing. Real estate is real. It is earth, wood, plaster, bricks, glass, concrete, and steel. Like any major aspect of the real world, real estate can be studied academically from several different perspectives, bringing to bear several different academic and professional disciplines. So, if you ask someone, *What is real estate?* The answer you get will likely depend on the profession of the person you are asking. While an architect will describe real estate from an aesthetic and functional perspective, an engineer will describe it from a physical structural perspective. An environmental scientist will describe it from an ecological perspective, and a lawyer will describe it as a bundle of rights and duties associated with "real property," that is, land and the permanent structures on it. All of these answers would be correct, and a complete study of real estate requires a very comprehensive *multidisciplinary* approach.

Yet this book, while not ignoring these various perspectives, is not intended to be a complete multidisciplinary text. In order to provide sufficient depth and rigor to our study, this book concentrates on one of the major disciplines for studying real estate. The discipline we will be using is that of economics. Indeed, we need to be more precise even than that. Within the economic study of real estate, there are two major branches: urban economics and financial economics. The former is the branch of economics that studies cities, including the spatial and social phenomena relevant to understanding real estate. The latter is the branch that studies capital markets and the financial services industry. These are the two major branches of economics we will be using in this text because they are the most relevant for understanding commercial property from an investment perspective. Our major emphasis, however, will be on the second of these two branches, the financial economic aspects of real estate.

Why is the financial economic study of real estate so important? To answer this question, let's go back to our original question, *What is real estate*? Just as the architect's or engineer's answer to this question emphasizes the physical (bricks and mortar), and the lawyer's answer emphasizes the legal (bundle of rights), the successful real estate business professional's answer is likely to emphasize the financial economic aspects. The investor's fundamental answer to the question is, *Real estate is potential future cash flows.* The nature of these cash flows, their magnitude, timing, and risk, will fundamentally be determined in the rental market, which is where urban economics comes in. But whatever the specific nature of the potential stream of future cash flows generated by real estate, any such stream is, more generally, nothing more and nothing less than what is called a capital asset. And capital assets trade in capital markets. So that is where financial economics takes over.

Capital markets determine the opportunity costs and values of investments and capital assets, and allocate the flow of financial capital (aka "money") to and among the underlying physical assets, which in turn produce the future real benefit flows that are the defining characteristic of capital assets. But perhaps more to the point for those with a more public policy or urban planning perspective, financial capital ultimately determines what real estate assets will be built, where, and when, in an entrepreneurial capitalist society such as that of the United States and many other countries. The physical structures and aesthetic characteristics studied by the engineer or architect would not and cannot exist in reality without the financial capital to command the resources to produce them. Therefore, the academic discipline that studies financial capital allocation and decisions is of vital importance to any real estate professional. As noted, this discipline is financial economics.

Once again, we should be more precise. Within the discipline of financial economics, two major fields are typically covered in the core curriculum in graduate-level business schools: corporate finance, and investments. Corporate finance concentrates on applications relevant to the financial and strategic management of large corporations whose equity is usually traded on the stock exchange. The investments field studies applications relevant to individuals and institutions making investment decisions about the wealth they own or manage. Both of these fields are relevant to analyzing commercial property from an investment perspective. Indeed, more so than in the classical (or "mainstream") presentations of these two fields, in real estate, the topics and applications addressed in corporate finance and investments are more closely interwoven. In real estate, we need to integrate these two fields that have grown apart in the mainstream literature and pedagogy. Indeed, in recent years, the growth and development of the private equity sector of the investment industry has brought even "mainstream" investments and corporate finance closer together. But real estate was there first.

To make this integration, we must address a number of features that make real estate unique—different from both the typical corporate finance and the securities investments contexts. For example, most commercial property is not held by publicly traded, taxed corporations. It may be held directly by taxed individuals or tax-exempt institutions, or it may be held by real estate investment trusts (REITs), which are publicly traded corporations that are not taxed at the corporate level. Rarely is commercial property actually owned (as opposed to rented) by the taxed corporations that dominate the stock market, and such "corporate real estate" will not be a major focus of this text, as it is generally not considered part of the real estate investment industry. Commercial property assets themselves also differ from the underlying assets held by the typical publicly traded, taxed corporation in that there is almost always a well-functioning market for trading commercial property ownership, that is, investment property (property that produces income for non-user owners). The productive physical assets of most corporations (machines, laboratories, factories) are not usually traded in so well-established and liquid a market as the commercial property market. In this respect, real estate assets are more like the assets studied in the mainstream investments field, primarily stocks and bonds. But the commercial property market is not as liquid or efficient in its operation as the securities markets dealt with in mainstream investments. (When was the last time you went online and ordered the sale of half of your ownership of 1000 North Main Street "at market" before close of business that day?) Another fascinating difference between real estate and the mainstream corporate and securities environment is the simultaneous existence of two parallel asset markets in which real estate trades. Commercial properties are traded directly in the private property market, and they are traded indirectly in the stock market through the equity shares of REITs and other real estate firms.

These and other differences require a specific, real-estate-oriented treatment and synthesis of the topics covered in mainstream corporate finance and investments. This treatment can be, and needs to be, consistent with, integrated with, and built on the mainstream financial economic fields. A seamless intellectual continuum should exist from the typical finance course taught in the MBA core to the typical graduate course in Real Estate Finance or Real Estate Investments, an intellectual continuum from "Wall Street" to "Main Street." After all, since capital and information flow freely between these loci in the real world, real estate investment knowledge and practice should be built on the same principles that underlie the corporate and securities world. Unfortunately, many investment courses in universities do not cover real estate in any depth, aside from noting that REIT markets exist. This is why the study of real estate via financial economics provides unique and desirable expertise for anyone wanting a complete picture of the investment universe.

The real estate treatment we need must also present an intellectually coherent framework, rigorous from an academic perspective, built on a few solid underlying concepts and principles, not a hodgepodge of vaguely connected, *ad hoc* methodologies and rules of thumb. The advanced real estate investments student needs such a solid framework of fundamental principles and rigorously grounded analytical tools that remain relevant in a fast-changing world. Such an elegant framework must include practical procedures and methodologies that can be applied directly to help answer typical real estate investment decision-making questions in the real world. Built on fundamental economic principles, such methods will allow the student to apply creatively the real estate investment analysis framework they learn in academia to the infinite variety of situations they will no doubt encounter in the real world.

The purpose of this book is to present such a framework, a corpus of principles, methods, and knowledge, at a level that the typical graduate student can readily understand (with a little time, effort, and study, of course). Our intention and hope is that, whether you are pursuing an MBA, MRE, CRAA, MCP, or other, whether or not you already have some background in mainstream finance or in real estate or in urban economics, you will find this book useful.

One final point: We know that some people claim that real estate is too complex, or lacking in hard data, to study "scientifically"—that it is an art, not a science. The implication is that we can do no better than to support real estate decision-making with purely ad hoc analytical techniques. In effect, the implication of this claim is that real estate decision-making should be "shot from the hip," or based on vaguely articulated intuition, even though this decision-making governs one-third of the world's assets.

But by now, in the twenty-first century, such an attitude truly is ignorance. We can do much better than "seat-of-the-pants" decision-making. Yes, real estate is complex, data are less than perfect, and decision-making will always be somewhat of an art and require good judgment. Real estate is neither rocket science nor heart surgery, and we will never outgrow our need to always apply common sense. But both financial and urban economics are highly developed, sophisticated fields of study. They contain a very impressive corpus of knowledge and toolkit of methodology, as rigorous as any branch of the social sciences. They encompass a long history and a vast body of scientific literature, both at the theoretical and empirical levels, and have several Nobel laureates to their credit. Quantitative data in real estate are getting better and more widespread all the time. Financial and urban economics are out there waiting to be applied to real estate investment decision-making. We hope readers of this book will transform insights into impactful decisions that shape the future of our cities, maximize productive use of capital, and improve the professionalism of the industry. We challenge you not only to learn, but to lead.

Organization of the Book

This book is designed to be useful for several types of students, in several types of graduate courses (as well as advanced or honors undergraduates). The most typical users will be business students who already have some basic finance background, or urban studies or real estate students who already have (or will elsewhere receive) a background in urban economics. With this in mind, students should be able to use this book somewhat flexibly.

In general, as is typical of textbooks, this book progresses from basic underlying concepts and principles to more specific and specialized considerations and applications. However, we would characterize the structure of this book as being more akin to a spiral than a straight line. This is because everything is related to everything else. We start at an introductory level, touching several aspects, then circle back around again as we progress deeper into the subject matter. The result is some degree of repetition, but in different contexts or different levels of depth. This keeps the treatment always more practical and broad-minded, and also facilitates use of the book by specific chapters or parts without necessarily having to use the entire book in chapter order, thereby giving the book flexibility to be relevant to a broad range of students.

With this in mind, the book is organized into seven Parts that fall into two major halves. The first half consists of the first three Parts, 15 chapters, and is the printed portion of the book. This is the most basic material, the "core" of the subject matter, fundamental topics that tend to be more abiding even as the world changes. These 15 chapters will probably cover most or all of the subjects in a basic one-semester graduate course in Real Estate Investments, including for students with little or no previous background in many of the key topics. The second half of the book consists of the remaining four Parts, 14 chapters, focusing on more advanced or specialized topics that in our opinion are very important and in some respects are "cutting-edge" as of the mid-2020s. The second half of the book is entirely online, in digital form only. This format will enable easy access for readers of the first half of the book (the printed half) and will also facilitate rapid updating of the cutting-edge material as advancements are made in the field during the mid- to late 2020s. A more detailed description of each of the seven Parts follows.

Part I. This Part consists of four chapters that introduce the most basic foundations of real estate investment, including such key topics as the Time Value of Money, the basics of Discounted Cash Flow (DCF) valuation, and the Net Present Value investment decision rule. It is here that we first elaborate the key economic principles underlying rigorous real estate investment analysis: opportunity cost, market equilibrium, and wealth maximization.

Part II. In this Part we introduce the nuts and bolts of real property income analysis, the fundamental source of real estate investment value. Part II focuses on the numerators of the DCF valuation model. The six chapters in this Part focus on the terminology of real estate income, the determinants of rent at the market level and property level, the forecasting of rent at both those levels, and the basics of leases and leasing strategy.

Part III. This Part completes the basic investment analysis framework by focusing on the denominators of the DCF valuation model, and by extending the framework beyond the property asset level to the investor level. Thus, not only how to know what to invest in, but also how to finance the investment. This includes in-depth and rigorous consideration of the effect of leverage, the nature and use of mortgages (including basic mortgage terminology and payments and yield computation), and the sophisticated consideration of income tax effects and their interaction with debt financing. Part III also introduces key concepts that are uniquely important in real estate investment, including the distinction between "market value" and "investment value," and the consideration of inefficiencies in the relevant asset market.

Part IV. This Part begins the online portion of the book. It includes three chapters specifically focusing on land value and the real estate development process. These closely related topics (land derives its value from its development potential; the economics of development are based on land value) are obviously of great importance in the real world, yet are relatively under-studied in most traditional real estate finance and investment courses. Land value and real estate development (RED) are cutting-edge topics from an intellectual perspective, relatively sparsely treated in the academic literature. Here we present a rigorous foundation for their study from an economic and investment perspective, as always, based on opportunity cost, market equilibrium, and wealth maximization.

Part V. The three chapters in Part V focus on mortgages in more depth and breadth than what was covered in Part III. The book delves into different types of mortgages, the basics of mortgage payments, yields and values, and the analysis and underwriting of commercial mortgages in particular.

Part VI. This Part presents the basics of what we call macro-level real estate investment analysis. By that we mean that we depart from the focus earlier in the book on individual property assets and individual investment decisions. Here, we focus on concepts and methods for dealing with real estate from a "top-down" perspective, that is, from a perspective encompassing aggregates of many individual properties, such as portfolios, funds, and REITs. Part VI thus complements the earlier Parts (which present a more "bottom-up" view). The four chapters in Part VI deal with many of the more recent developments in the institutional real estate investment industry. They cover topics such as modern portfolio theory and capital markets equilibrium pricing theory as these relate to real estate, unique characteristics of real estate investment performance data as an "asset class," and the indexing of commercial (investment) property prices and investment returns.

Part VII. This final Part of the book includes four chapters on selected topics that are important and not treated elsewhere in the book. Here we cover real estate investment trusts (REITs), international real estate investing, considerations of sustainability and climate change risk, and a brief synthesis of technology in real estate investment.

A final word on how this book "reads" is in order. Economics is a very technical subject with a heavy emphasis on analysis and quantitative techniques (i.e., *lots of math and formulas).* Because this is an economics text, we can't get around this, even though we know it makes this subject tough for many students. We do sympathize, however, and we have tried to address the problem in several ways.

First, we have tried to clarify concepts intuitively whenever possible, and we have tried to present lots of simple numerical examples. Second, we have tried to identify sections of the text that are particularly advanced or difficult from an analytical or technical perspective and to set these aside to some extent. They are indicated by a preceding asterisk (*) in their section numbers. Less advanced or more "analytically challenged" students may want to skim these sections and not worry too much about the analytical details. While the points covered in these sections are important (or we would have left them out altogether), the overall implication of the point is more important than the technical details.

Finally, we have tried to systematize the presentation of all the material in this book, so as to clarify the underlying structure of the knowledge presented here. The concepts and tools presented in this book are essentially all based on a few simple foundational economic principles, including especially (as noted above): market equilibrium, opportunity cost, and wealth maximization. This gives this material an underlying unity. If you look carefully, we hope you will see not only utility, but also some beauty and elegance in the material presented in this book.

FEATURES IN THE FOURTH EDITION

We continue to be very gratified by the reception of this book since its first edition was published in 2000. Its increasing use by leading graduate programs, both in the United States and other countries, has confirmed our original belief that the real estate industry and its Academy are ready for the more advanced and economically rigorous treatment that is the hallmark of this text. With over 1250

Google Scholar citations as of 2024, this book continues to be the most cited text in the field of real estate finance and investments.

A lot has happened in the dozen years since the Third Edition of this text was written, and our knowledge about real estate investment, as well as the relevant data and analytical and computational toolkit, has grown greatly. This Fourth Edition features the most comprehensive update and revision of the text since its original publication. The 30 chapters and eight Parts of the 3e have been comprehensively reviewed, updated, edited, and reorganized into the 29 chapters and seven Parts of this 4e, as described above. Three of the chapters are entirely new, focusing on forecasting, sustainability, and technology. And as noted, the book has been divided into two halves, the printed half and an online half described above. We think this modernizes the book for the 2020s. This enables the printed portion of the book to be more compact with a lower price point than would otherwise be possible, while including most of the material that most introductory courses will want to teach. The new chapter structure places the financial economics basics up front. We think this improves a hallmark of this text, which is that it includes introductory material sufficient to serve the needs of beginner students who have no background in either financial or urban economics. Yet the text continues to carry the reader all the way through to the cutting-edge with the most sophisticated and rigorous treatment of real estate analytics and investment.

This Fourth Edition also represents a significant "passing of the torch" especially from the original co-authors (Geltner and Miller) to a new generation of pre-eminent real estate scholars, the other members of the substantially expanded co-authorship team (though Geltner and Miller have continued to be involved in this Edition at a high level).

Online Resources: For both students and instructors, there are now a plethora of slides, videos, spreadsheets, and other supplemental materials that are available online for users of this text. These are in addition to the 14 online chapters of the text itself, the second half of the book. Some of the supplemental material is helpful for solving concepts presented in the text. Others go beyond the text and are merely supplemental resources. We expect to continue to add to these resources over time. Many will be valuable in your toolbox, so please take the time to review these supplements.

With all these improvements, we are very excited about this new edition. It is our hope that it will be used even more widely around the world, and that through its wise use by our very intelligent and thoughtful readers, the efficiency and quality of real estate investment and development around the world will be improved as a result, for the betterment of humankind.

Cambridge, Massachusetts
San Diego, California
West Hartford, Connecticut
Maastricht, Netherlands
Cambridge, England
Clemson, South Carolina
November 2024

About the Authors

David Geltner is Professor Emeritus of Real Estate Finance at the Massachusetts Institute of Technology. He taught real estate investments for 13 years at the University of Cincinnati, and for 20 years at MIT where he held leadership positions in the Center for Real Estate and the Master of Science in Real Estate Development degree program. He is the recipient of the David Ricardo Medal of the American Real Estate Society, the James Graaskamp Award of the Pension Real Estate Association, and the John Quigley Medal for Advancing Real Estate and Urban Economics of the American Real Estate and Urban Economics Association. Geltner was the lead author of the prior three editions of this textbook.

Norm Miller, PhD is an Emeritus Professor at the University of San Diego and the University of Cincinnati, and Vice-President of the Homer Hoyt Institute, a think tank of global urban economic scholars and industry research directors. He is a housing, finance and capital markets expert. He started the *Journal of Sustainable Real Estate* and served as the President of the American Real Estate Society. See www.linkedin.com/in/norm-miller-8167935/ Contact at nmiller@sandiego.edu

Alex van de Minne received his PhD from the University of Amsterdam in 2015. After which, he tried his luck on the other side of the pond in the United States. Since then, he held both academic and industry positions in renowned institutes, including MIT, Moody's, Real Capital Analytics, and the Federal Reserve of Philadelphia.

Piet Eichholtz is Professor of Finance and Real Estate at Maastricht University, where he chaired the Finance Department. His academic work, which is published internationally in academic and practitioner journals, focuses on real estate sustainability and climate risk, (long-term) real estate investment performance, REITs, and international real estate investment. His teaching in real estate and finance has won numerous awards and he is one of the initiators of the Global Real Estate Leaders Program. Besides his academic career, Eichholtz is an active entrepreneur, having started several companies. He also serves and served in advisory and non-executive roles with institutional investors and property developers.

Thies Lindenthal is the Grosvenor Professor of Real Estate Finance at the Department of Land Economy, University of Cambridge, England, and a professorial fellow at Pembroke College.

His research interests are twofold: First, he analyzes property investments in the very long term, tracking rents, prices, and returns for up to 500 years. The second research line focuses on applied machine learning techniques to utilize high-dimensional "Big(ish)" data. Put differently, he uses images and other data that are too complex for spreadsheets to better understand property values, household preferences, and decisions made by very human and not always rational agents.

Lily Shen, PhD Lily Shen is an Associate Professor of Real Estate Finance at Clemson University and a visiting scholar at the Federal Reserve Banks. After witnessing the 2008 financial crisis, she dedicated her career to advancing real estate research aimed at fostering more resilient financial systems. Leveraging her experience in Silicon Valley, she has been at the forefront of integrating AI into real estate teaching and research. Her work has been featured in *The Economist*, *The Washington Post*, and published in leading academic journals, including the *Journal of Financial and Quantitative Analysis*, *Management Science*, and the *Journal of Urban Economics*.

Part I

Real Estate Investment Foundation, Time Value of Money, and NPV Decision Rule

Two major branches of economics underlie the rigorous study of real estate: financial economics and urban economics. Part I introduces the most basic tools and principles of financial economics that are relevant for real estate at the micro-level of individual property investments. (Part II will introduce you to the relevant urban economics.) Why is financial economics so important and useful? The most fundamental characteristic of real estate is that it is long-lived. After all, land underlies all real estate, and land "lives" forever, practically speaking. When we combine this longevity with the fact that real estate can generally produce benefits for some people, we arrive at the essence of why financial economics is important for understanding real estate. Financial economics is the branch of economic science that focuses on capital markets, that is, markets for capital assets. Capital assets are claims to potential future benefit flows that can be measured in monetary terms. Real estate assets are, therefore, capital assets. One cannot understand real estate without knowledge of financial economics.

The heart of financial economics is the systematic study of how markets for capital assets function and thereby determine the prices of such assets, giving monetary value to such things as real estate assets. Fundamentally, financial economics is concerned with how capital markets weigh the timing, risk, and other attributes of the possible future cash flows from different types of assets to determine what they are worth in the market today, that is, at what price they trade or could be traded.

We start Part I with an introduction and overview (Chapter 1), situating real estate in the context of the broader capital markets and giving the reader some perspective on the role of real estate as an investment asset class. Chapter 2 presents the major mathematical formulas used in converting multiyear cash flow streams to present value and computing returns on investments, the essential tools in the study and practice of financial economics as applied to real estate. Chapter 3 presents the fundamentals of the measurement of investment performance. Finally, in Chapter 4, we will introduce the backbone of most of this book: a discounted cash flow model for real estate investment at the micro-level, that is, the level of individual-specific real estate investment assets.

DOI: 10.1201/9781003643838-1

1 Introduction to Commercial Real Estate Investment

CHAPTER OUTLINE

LEARNING OBJECTIVES

After reading this chapter, you should understand:

- The basic structure and functioning of the investment industry.
- The nature of investor objectives, constraints, and concerns.
- The major types of investment products and vehicles and the difference between an underlying asset and an investment product.
- The major similarities and differences in the investment products based on real estate as opposed to other classical industrial or service corporations as underlying assets.
- The four major traditional investment asset classes and their characteristic differences.
- The investment performance of the major asset classes in recent decades at a broad-brush and general level.
- Some of the major historical trends and events that have influenced real estate investment performance in recent decades.

What is better than starting a book on commercial real estate investment by defining "investment" and "commercial real estate"? Unless you have had quite some exposure to real estate investment, this chapter will provide some helpful background. This chapter will not go into any deep academic theories or methods. Still, we will present some fundamental information practitioners deal with daily, directly or indirectly, in the investment business. This chapter is divided into three major

DOI: 10.1201/9781003643838-2

sections. The first discusses the investment industry, beginning with the most fundamental underlying consideration—investors' objectives and concerns. The second section presents real estate as one investment asset class among several alternatives. It compares real estate investment performance to the other major asset classes at a broad-brush level. This chapter ends with a brief history of recent real estate investment trends.

1.1 THE INVESTMENT INDUSTRY

Why do we invest? Moreover, what do we mean by the investment *industry*? In this case, the term *industry* refers to a branch of economic activity or trade. In this sense, the investment business is a major industry in the United States in which much value is added and income earned. An introduction to some aspects of this industry is a perfect place to begin a serious study of commercial real estate as an investment, and that is the purpose of this first section of this chapter. We start with the most fundamental element in this industry: the *investors*.

1.1.1 INVESTOR OBJECTIVES AND CONCERNS

Investors buy and sell capital assets, thereby making up both the demand and supply side of the capital markets. Through the process of buying and selling, investors determine the market values of capital assets, that is, the prices at which these assets trade. In deciding the prices at which they are willing to trade, investors consider the fundamental characteristics of the asset's future cash flow prospects. All other things equal, an investment with a higher prospective future cash flow or less risk in its cash flows will be more in demand and, therefore, higher priced. Investors also consider the nature of the capital markets in which the assets trade and how the functioning of those markets may affect the prices at which assets can trade, as well as the cost and timeliness of such trading.

With this in mind, consider the question: *why do people invest*? Investment is the act of putting money aside that would otherwise be used for current consumption expenditure. Why would someone do that? At the individual level, people may find themselves with more money than they currently need for consumption, or they may have a future objective for which they are willing to sacrifice some current consumption.

Consider a dual-income couple in their 20s. They may want to save for a down payment on a house. This might involve an investment horizon of 3 to 5 years. Now consider a couple in their mid-30s. They may want to begin saving for their children's college tuition. This might involve a horizon of 10 to 15 years. Another couple in their mid-40s might want to save for retirement, with an investment horizon of over 20 years. Finally, consider a retired couple in their 60s or 70s. They may have assets they have accumulated over their working lives. They may want to begin drawing current income out of these assets or even draw down the principal value of the assets to bolster their spendable income during their retirement years.

All of these individuals may differ not only in their investment time horizons but also in their preferences for risk-taking in their investments. Virtually all investors would prefer a safe investment to a risky one, other things being equal. However, other things are not equal; in particular, investments vary in their risk and trading characteristics, with riskier assets generally offering higher returns on average in a well-functioning capital market. (They have to; otherwise, no one would buy them.) Some investors are willing to take on more risk in order to expect a higher return on average over time. Other investors prefer the opposite. What are the major **investment objectives** and **constraints/concerns** most investors face? At a fundamental level, it is useful to distinguish two different and mutually exclusive types of investment objectives:

- The **growth** (or **savings**) **objective** implies a relatively long time horizon with no immediate or likely intermediate need to use the cash being invested.

- The **income** (or **current cash flow**) **objective** implies that the investor has a short-term and ongoing need to use cash generated from the investment.

Investors with a growth objective can put money away for a relatively long period of time. The investment only needs to pay out cash if and when it is sold, and it need not be sold anytime soon. For example, many start-up companies will not generate cash to pay investors for many years. However, once the start-up establishes a foothold in the market, its potential upside can be enormous. Suppose the investment does generate income in the meantime. In that case, this might be plowed back into the enterprise to maximize the growth of the accumulated capital over the investment time horizon. This objective is typical of young to middle-aged individuals, wealthy individuals of all ages, and institutions such as pension funds of growing companies that expect to experience more cash inflow than outflow liabilities for many years into the future. Many endowments or sovereign wealth funds are also in this category for much of their investment.

On the other hand, investors with an income objective need to consider how much cash the investment will generate initially and how this cash flow stream may change over time. Typically, an investor with a current income objective would tend to look for an investment with a high current cash payout rate, that is, the fraction of investment value that is typically paid out to the investor each year (e.g., in the form of interest coupons, dividends, or net rental payments). Investors with an income objective typically include retired individuals and institutions such as endowment funds, pension funds, or life insurance companies with a greater number of retired members or policyholders than current contributors.

All investors have either a savings or an income objective. Sometimes, the same investor may have both objectives for different parts of a wealth portfolio. However, in addition to these objectives, investors face one or more of a set of typical constraints or concerns. The following list summarizes the major constraints and concerns that affect most investors:

- **Risk:** The possibility that future investment performance may vary over time in a manner that is not entirely predictable when the investment is made. Investors dislike risk and will purchase risky assets only if they offer a discount in price (a premium in their expected long-run average return).
- **Liquidity:** The ability to sell investment assets quickly at full value and without much affecting the price of the assets. Investors like liquidity. Other things being equal, investors will pay more for (or, equivalently, accept lower returns from) more liquid assets. Liquidity allows investors to move capital in or out of the investment and respond to news and perceived opportunities in a timely manner.
- **Time Horizon:** The future time over which the investor's objectives, constraints, and concerns are relevant. Investors' time horizons obviously affect both their ability to bear risk and their need for liquidity or tolerance for illiquidity. For example, an investor with a short investment horizon might not be interested in investing in an asset with low liquidity.
- **Investor Expertise** and **Management Burden:** How much knowledge, ability, and desire does the investor have to manage the investment process and assets?
- **Investor Size:** How "big" the investor is regarding the amount of capital available or in need of investment. Larger investors may face lower costs per dollar invested due to economies of scale, and they may face a broader range of alternatives. They may also face a greater ability to hire professional managers, both for their investments in general and for the operation of any assets they own. On the other hand, larger investors may face greater pressure as they must invest large sums at once. In some respects, they may have less liquidity, as the weight of their capital may tend to influence asset prices when they move it around.
- **Capital Constraint:** Whether the investor faces an absolute constraint on the amount of capital they have available to invest or can obtain additional capital relatively easily if good investment opportunities are available (e.g., from stockholders or depositors). A capital constraint

means that the investor may sometimes have to forego investing in profitable opportunities, and it means that anything they do invest in prevents them from investing in something else. Such investors need to ensure they are ordering their priorities correctly to choose the best overall combination of investments available to them at a given time.

A key implication of the range of differing investment objectives and constraints is that *investors are heterogeneous*—they have different personal goals and lifestyles, are at different points in their life cycles, and have different amounts of wealth and earned income. The ideal investment for one investor will not be the same as the ideal investment for another investor. Furthermore, many investment decisions are not made by individuals but by institutions: banks and life insurance companies; funds, such as pensions, endowments, sovereign wealth, and mutual funds; and investment intermediaries, such as private equity investment management funds. Like individuals, investment institutions are also a heterogeneous lot. They have different constituencies, different liabilities and spending needs, and different levels or types of expertise, and they are subject to varying types of regulations and legal constraints. Institutions also come in all sizes, from small to very large. All of this affects their investment objectives and constraints, as described previously.

One implication of investor heterogeneity is that it lays the foundation for a market in investment products. Different products can be tailored to various objectives and constraints, and heterogeneity means that some investors will want to buy what or when other investors want to sell. This creates an active market, thereby creating liquidity.

1.1.2 General Structure of Investment Products and Vehicles

A fundamental point that relates the investment industry to the broader economy and society is that beneath investment products (possibly many layers of them) lie underlying physical or productive assets that generate profits and cash flow by adding value to the economy. At a broad-brush level, the investment industry matches *heterogeneous investors* (sources of financial capital) with *heterogeneous productive assets* (physical capital). This is done by developing investment institutions, products, and vehicles. In this system, it is useful to distinguish underlying assets from investment products or vehicles. Underlying assets refer to the directly productive physical capital, such as a corporation that designs and produces phones. Such a corporation is, in fact, a collection of physical, human, and legal assets and relationships organized into a system that can produce net cash flow over time through the production and sale of goods or services. In contrast to underlying assets, investment products or vehicles are typically (though not necessarily) one or more levels removed from the underlying assets, but they are based on the underlying assets. While investment products and vehicles are not themselves directly productive in the physical as opposed to purely financial sense, they have direct or indirect claims on, and sometimes commitments to, the directly productive underlying physical assets. Investment vehicles may or may not have governing authority over the underlying assets. And the investment products (the investment industry) add value by matching and connecting sources and uses of capital.

The best way to understand this system is to look at a picture. Exhibit 1-1 schematically depicts how the investment industry works in the classical and traditional structure of the U.S. industry, using a fictitious industrial corporation, ABC Widgets Corporation, as the underlying asset. The box at the bottom of the diagram depicts ABC Widgets, the underlying asset, a collection of physical and human resources that generates a cash flow stream by producing and selling widgets. For the investment industry, underlying assets such as ABC Widgets Corporation are the "raw material" on which investment products are based. The "finished products" are vehicles where investors can directly place their money or financial capital.

The first layer of investment products is those based most directly on the cash flow of the underlying asset. This layer would be represented by common stocks and corporate bonds issued by the

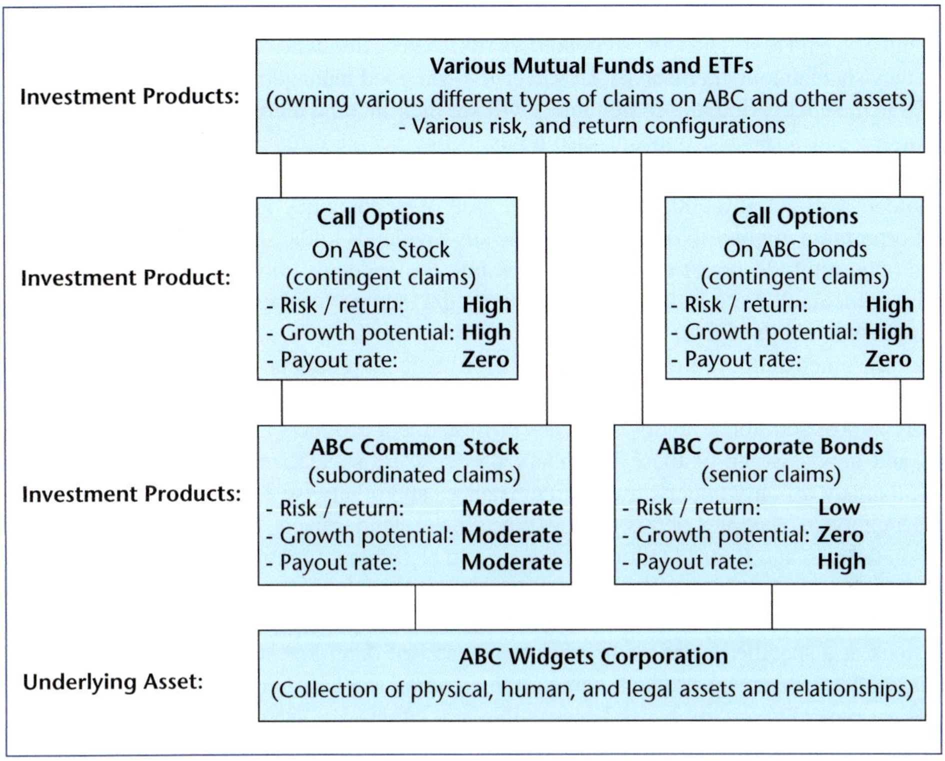

EXHIBIT 1-1 Underlying Assets versus Investment Products, an Example from Traditional Corporate Finance.

underlying corporation. In traditional corporate finance for large industrial and service corporations, these basic investment products are usually publicly traded in a relatively liquid secondary market, such as the stock exchange. In essence, the claims to ABC's cash flows are partitioned into two investment product classes with different risk and return characteristics.

ABC corporate bonds are senior claims, meaning that they will be paid first and are for a fixed contractual amount with a finite expiration or maturity. All of these features make ABC bonds relatively low risk for most investors. Only in extreme cases where ABC might have to file for bankruptcy are the bondholders in trouble. Traditional bonds provide a relatively high payout rate (compared to other investment products). On the flip side, the company's performance is not reflected in the value of the bond. In other words, the bondholders cannot benefit from higher sales.

By contrast, ABC's common stock is the residual (subordinated) claim on ABC's cash flow, with no contractual guarantee of the amount the stockholders will receive. ABC's stock represents the equity in the ABC Corporation, perpetual-lived claims with governing authority over the corporation, and they present the typical investor with more risk but the prospect of higher returns on average over the long run than ABC's bonds. If ABC is a large, well-established firm, then its stock may be viewed as having moderate investment risk. Such a firm typically pays regular dividends, providing stockholders with at least some income from their investment, with the bulk of their return coming in the form of expected growth in share price over time. The amount of dividend the corporation gives to its investors generally depends on (1) the current cash flow the corporation is generating, and (2) how much of this cash flow is retained with the purpose of re-investing it in its own business. (For example, to buy new / more efficient machinery.)

Let us elaborate a bit further on the differences between subordinated claims (stock) and senior claims (bonds) with a stylized example. Say that ABC produces a cash flow of $70,000 that it can distribute among its shareholders and bondholders. Of this, $50,000 is reserved for the bondholders, which must be paid first. Thus, the shareholders "only" get a dividend of $20,000 ($70,000–$50,000), which they share among themselves. However, if—via good management—the income increases to $80,000 in the next period, the shareholders will see their income increase from $20,000 to $30,000, or an increase of 50%. The opposite also holds. If the income reduces to $60,000, the shareholder must bear that loss, not the bondholders. Note that irrespective of the company's performance, the bondholders will get $50,000. (Other than in case of delinquency and/or bankruptcy, of course.) ABC Corporation might also decide not to give any dividends to the shareholders. In this case, ABC sees an opportunity to invest its earnings back into the company so that it might reap the benefits (via higher income) in the future. In this scenario, the income for the shareholders is zero now, but the growth potential is higher.

Since the nineteenth century, this first level of investment products—stocks and bonds—has been the mainstay of corporate finance and the investment industry in the United States. However, since the early 2000s, additional layers and types of investment products have been developed based on stocks and bonds. Some of these secondary products are specialized claims, such as contingent claims, that pay off only under certain circumstances and otherwise expire worthless.

The archetypal examples of this product type are the standardized "call and put options," publicly traded on the Chicago Board Options Exchange and elsewhere. Options are an example of a derivative investment product in that they are derived from other products, in this case, common stocks. For example, an ABC call option would allow its holder to purchase a certain number of shares of ABC stock at a specified price on or prior to a specified date. For such a product, the underlying asset is another investment product, namely the common stock or bonds of ABC Corporation. Call options are typically very high risk because they are effectively levered to a high degree, and they may end up being worthless if the underlying asset's share price never rises above the exercise price at which the option allows the purchase of the stock. The expected return on long positions in call options is very high, but that is because the risk is very high, and there is no income at all while holding the option.

Other investment products that have become very important in recent decades are mutual funds and exchange-traded funds (ETFs). A typical mutual fund or ETF is a diversified pool of stocks and/or bonds. Such funds allow investors to invest indirectly in many different stocks or bonds simply by purchasing a share in the fund. Mutual funds and ETFs are pretty varied, with different objectives and different risk and return profiles.

Yet another significant development in recent decades has been the increasing importance of private equity. That is, companies that are temporarily or permanently removed from (or not yet in) the publicly traded stock market. The firms are held privately, often by funds that have numerous investors. Private equity allows firms to avoid some of the constraints of the public stock exchanges. Although the stock market's liquidity is very valuable, the public arena sometimes subjects firms to herd behavior on the part of investors that may result in the undervaluation of the firm. Or the firm may become burdened by the informational and regulatory requirements of the public exchange. Sometimes, greater value or management flexibility can be unlocked by taking the firm private. In other cases, start-up firms that are just incubating or building up their value may be able to thrive better with private equity, and at least for a while, until they have the scale and track record that can make for a successful initial public offering (IPO). Private equity plays a large and important role, including in real estate. Still, it entails less liquidity and transparency and sometimes, in some respects, less informational efficiency than the public stock exchanges.

Going back to our simple stylized example, the main point of the system of investment products built upon the underlying asset of ABC Widgets Corporation, as depicted in Exhibit 1-1, is to allow investors with different risk and return objectives to be satisfied investing, directly or indirectly, in the *same underlying asset*. By defining different types of claims on future cash flows, ABC Widgets can offer investors products with very different risk and return characteristics, indeed, risk and return characteristics that can be quite different from those of the underlying asset itself. ABC Widgets' future cash flow stream may be a perpetual, low-risk, slightly variable stream, while its bonds are very low-risk, finite-lived, fixed streams; its stock shares are moderate-risk, perpetual assets with substantial price volatility; and its call options are very high-risk, short-lived "bets." An investor in a mutual fund owning some shares of ABC will barely notice the individual or unique effect of ABC on his returns.

We see how investor heterogeneity drives the investment industry. We also see how the entire system is built ultimately on underlying physical assets, which produce cash flow streams from producing and selling goods and services. These are the "raw materials" in the investment industry. This is where real estate comes into the picture.

1.2 THE COMMERCIAL REAL ESTATE INVESTMENT INDUSTRY

What do we mean by "commercial real estate," and how does it relate to the investment industry? More broadly speaking, why do we need a separate real estate investment book instead of a more "mainstream" investment textbook?

1.2.1 Defining Commercial Real Estate

Real estate is land, and all things permanently attached to it. The "thing" attached to the land is typically called the building, "improvements," or the "structure." When purchasing real estate, you also acquire certain (property) rights. More specifically, you get the right to control, occupy, develop, improve, exploit, pledge, lease, and sell the real estate.[1] The focus of this book is, however, on *commercial* real estate. With commercial real estate, we refer to **investable** property with the purpose of creating a cash flow. This is different from owner-occupied housing. Owner-occupied housing is, in the first place, an asset that provides consumption benefits and may or may not provide investment returns. Investable real estate means that the property is or could be sold regularly on the market. For example, a small family-owned retail store or bed and breakfast would probably not change hands often, meaning it is not traded and thus not investable.[2]

As such, we identified almost 100 billion square feet of investable commercial real estate in the United States in 2020, worth approximately $18 trillion. The major "food groups" in commercial real estate are apartment, industrial, retail, and office. With apartments, we mean income-producing rental units, not owner-occupied housing. While our main focus is on multi-family apartment buildings, in principle, single-family rental homes and mobile homes, or manufactured housing, can also be forms of investment property. Other large niches exist as well, like hotels and healthcare (the latter is also known as medical office). Exhibit 1-2 gives the distribution of the different property types in the United States over two dimensions in 2020. The first (Exhibit 1-2A) gives the percentage by square footage. We find that 20% of all the square feet of real estate is retail, for example. The second (Exhibit 1-2B) gives the percentage breakdown by dollar value. At first glance, the two seem to be very similar. Indeed, retail is worth 18% of all US real estate by dollar value. However, two exceptions are also visible: Industrial and Healthcare. Industrial properties account for 28% of all square footage but only 15% of the total dollar value. For healthcare properties, we see the opposite happening. Only 3% of all the square feet of real estate is occupied by healthcare, whereas it represents a whopping 16% of the total dollar value. Square foot prices cause this. Industrial warehouses tend to be large properties but with low dollar-per-square-foot values, whereas healthcare / medical offices are smaller, higher

[1] Fee simple absolute in the United States is the highest form of private ownership, although public oversight via various land use regulations overlays the real estate market.

[2] According to CoStar, 70% of all commercial real estate is investable by this definition. However, it should be noted that this 70% is based on the *total value* of real estate, not the *number* of properties. By the number of properties, the investable market is considerably smaller. This is because many smaller (i.e., lower value) properties are also not investable by this definition.

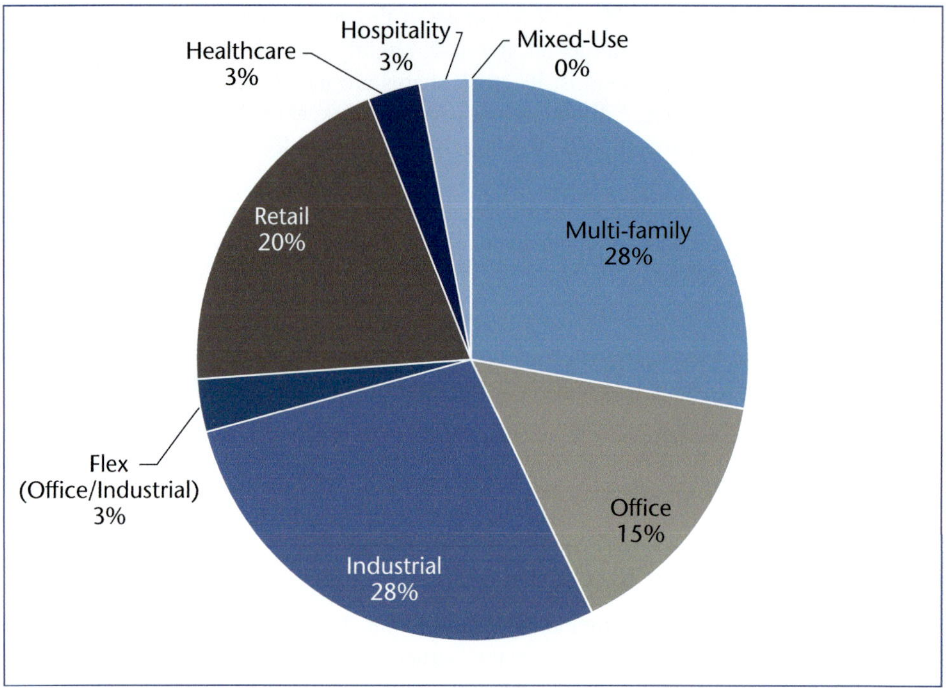

EXHIBIT 1-2A US Commercial Property by Total Amount of Square Feet in 2020. Total is 97B Square Feet.

Source: CoStar.

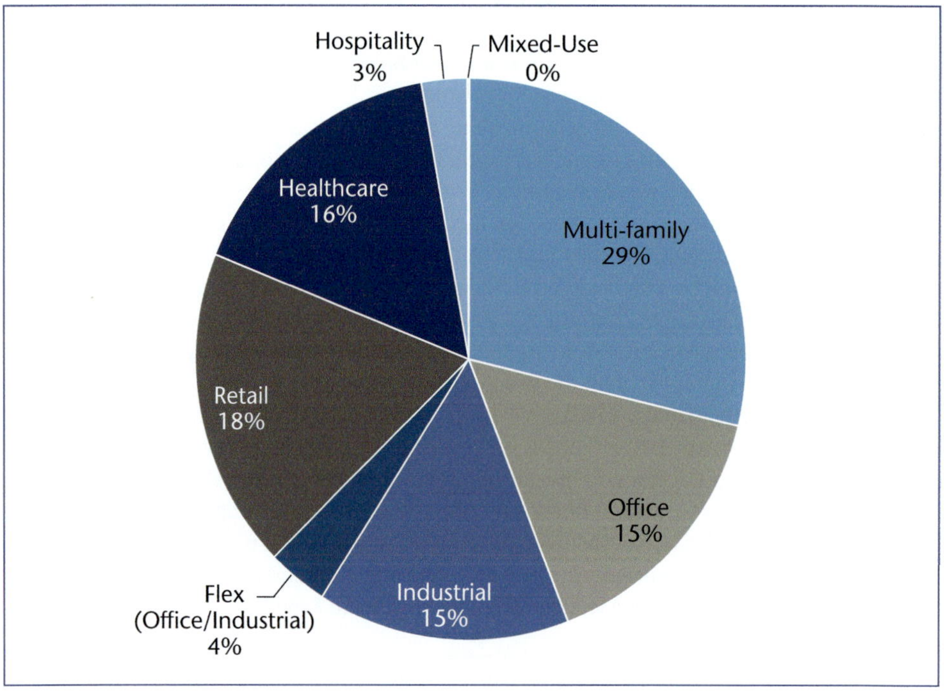

EXHIBIT 1-2B US Commercial Property by Dollar Value in 2020. Total is $18 trillion.

Source: CoStar.

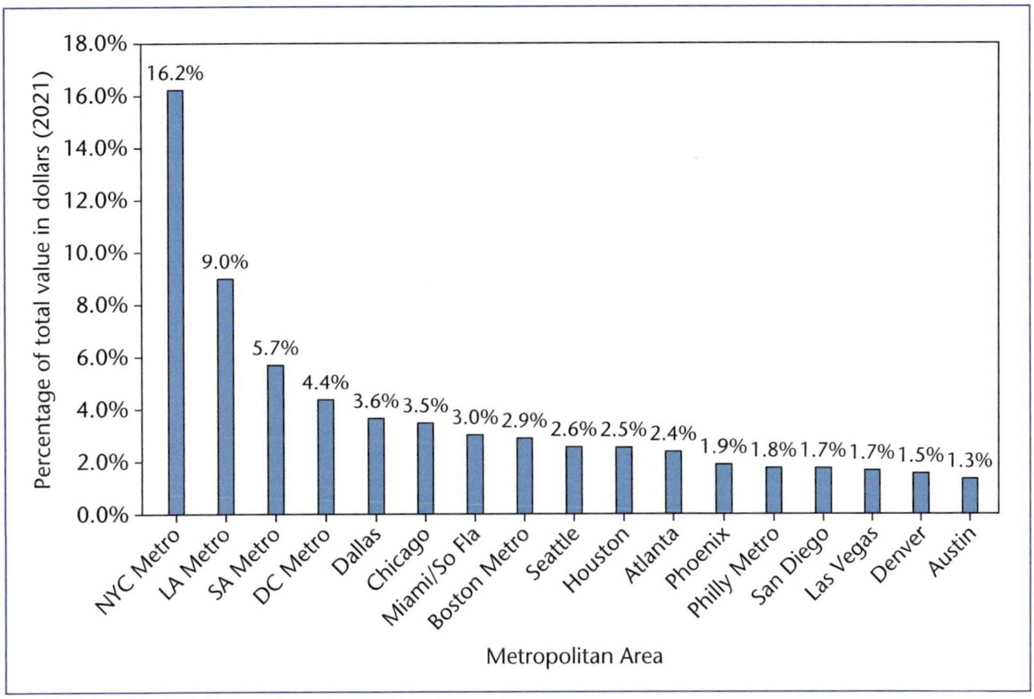

EXHIBIT 1-3 US Commercial Property by Metropolitan Area, as a Percentage of the Total Dollar Value of the Real Estate in the US.

Source: Own calculations, using data from Real Capital Analytics/MSCI.

dollar-per-square-foot properties. Why there are large differences per square foot for these different property types will be one of the main topics throughout this book. And keep in mind that these are snapshots as of 2020. Real estate is a very dynamic field, evolving all the time.

Another defining feature of commercial property is that it concentrates on large cities. In Exhibit 1-3, we plot the distribution of commercial real estate values for a selection of large metropolitan areas as a percentage of the total real estate value in the U.S. Note that we have approximately 150 such metro areas in the United States. However, New York alone contains 16% of the total US commercial property market value, with Los Angeles a distant second at 9%. San Francisco and the Washington DC metro area follow in third and fourth with 5.7% and 4.4% respectively. The top nine metro areas (including Seattle in Exhibit 1-3) already contain over 50% of all the real estate value in the United States. In other words, the top 9 largest metro areas (out of 150) have 50% of all the commercial real estate (in dollar value). Even though we use American data here, you will find a similar pattern worldwide.[3]

Exhibit 1-4 gives a sense of the size (the $18 trillion mentioned before) of the commercial real estate market in the United States around 2020. The categories on the left of the pie chart, roughly between 8 and 12 o'clock, give all the real estate categories, including real estate debt (i.e., the mortgage). If you combine all the real estate debt and equity, real estate represents over a third of all assets in the United States. This is larger than the entire stock market valuation at that same time. Single-family housing

[3] This curious phenomen can be found in completely other fields as well and is known as Zipf's law. Zipf's law (also known as the rank/size rule) states that when a list of measured values is sorted in decreasing order, the value of the nth entry is often approximately inversely proportional to n. For example, we know that the most common word in the English vocabulary "the" can be found twice as much when analyzing text compared to the second most common word "of." In cities globally we find that the second largest city in a country has half the population of the largest city, the third city has a third of the population of the largest city, etc. If you are interested in why this would happen, see (among others) Gabaix, X. 1999. "Zipf's Law for Cities: An explanation." *Quarterly Journal of Economics* 114(3): 707–738.

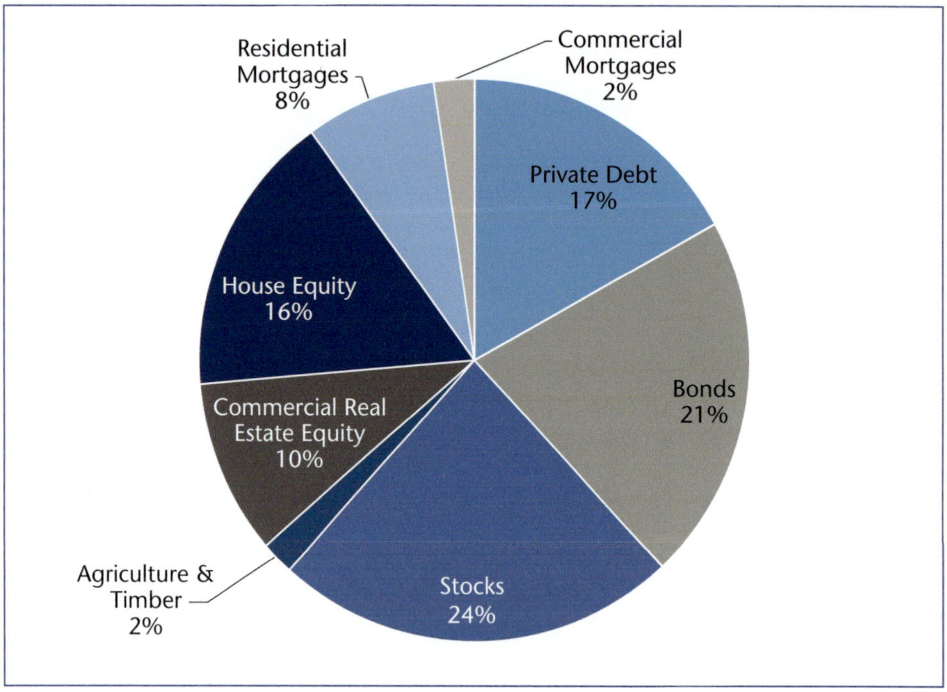

EXHIBIT 1-4 U.S. Investable Capital Market Around 2020, Totaling Around $140 trillion.

Source: Own calculations using data from SIFMA, Nareit, Zillow, NASDAQ, FRED, Statistica, and cqexecutive.

(equity) takes the lion's share of this combined real estate value with $23 trillion. Including single-family housing in this pie chart is slightly misleading, as you cannot invest in this category. True, as of writing, investors are purchasing single-family housing en masse in the United States. However, the intent is to change it to rent-producing (i.e., commercial) real estate, not to house its employees, for example. There is about $10 trillion of residential mortgage debt on these properties. We find about $14 trillion of equity for commercial real estate with $4 trillion in mortgage debt.

1.2.2 Investing in Commercial Real Estate and Why It's Different from "Mainstream" Investment

Real estate is distinguished from what is often termed "mainstream" investment. This typically refers to securities that are publicly traded. Although large quantities of real estate also end up being securitized in one way or the other, and such real estate securities (such as REITs and MBS) are important aspects of the securities markets. Other (non-real estate) private asset markets may include infrastructure, commodities, agriculture, timber and mining assets, and transport vehicles (ships and planes). Some of these other privately traded assets are similar to or overlap with real estate and are sometimes managed together with real estate as "real assets." However, this book focuses on income-producing (or potentially income-producing) real-built property (including the development thereof). We will also use the term "commercial real estate" or "commercial property" to refer to our subject. In this section, we will introduce you to three major ways to invest in commercial property: (1) directly, (2) indirectly through listed REITs, and (3) indirectly through real estate debt, as portrayed structurally in the diagram in Exhibit 1-5.[4]

[4] Additional alternative means of investment in real estate, such as via crowdfunding, blockchain-based "tokens," derivatives, and other possibilities may offer intriguing opportunities in the future, but as of this writing remain on the fringe of the industry

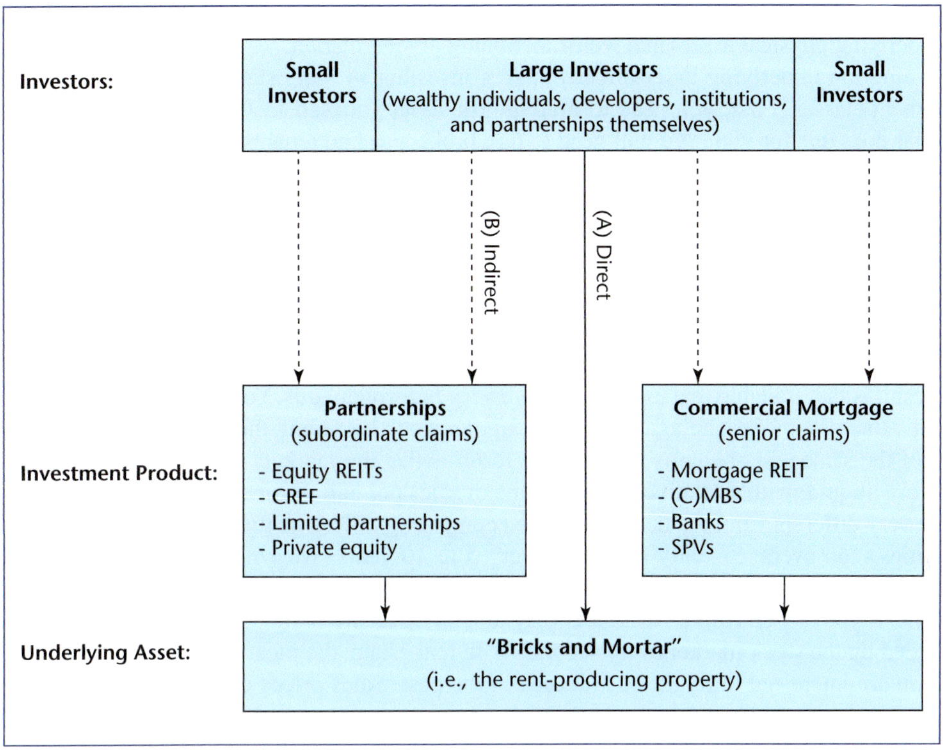

EXHIBIT 1-5 Example of the Investment System in Real Estate.

Let's begin by considering the most basic way to invest in real estate, direct investment in real property, and consider the similarities and differences between Exhibit 1-5 and "mainstream" investment as described earlier in Exhibit 1-1. Real estate investment and mainstream investment share a few attributes. There is an underlying asset called the *property*; there is income/dividend called *rent*;[5] and there is debt, called a *mortgage*. The basic principle of investment stays the same: You invest money now in the hopes of getting your capital back plus a return later. However, there are also many differences between real estate and other types of investments. In Exhibit 1-5, we provide a simplified overview of how real estate investment is structured.

Arguably, the largest difference between mainstream investment and real estate investment is that it is possible to *own the underlying physical asset directly*. This is indicated by the solid line (A) in Exhibit 1-5, which links the underlying asset at the bottom with the investors represented by the box at the top of the diagram. Note that this box is divided into two types of investors: large and small. Underlying physical assets are large entities, typically worth millions of dollars each. It is generally not possible for small individual investors who are not very wealthy to own whole commercial properties directly. However, it is possible for wealthy individual investors and investment institutions (such as pension funds or life insurance companies) to own large commercial properties or portfolios of properties directly. And there is a market in which such underlying physical assets trade directly, namely, the private property market. This is a key difference between the investment

[5] As you will find out in Chapter 5 and Part II of this book, this statement is not completely true. Managing a property is costly. Thus, the cash flow received by the investor will be less than the rent received via tenants. In this case, comparing a company's earnings to the rent received in a real estate investment is more appropriate. However, given that this is the introductory Chapter, we keep it simple and ignore semantics.

system for real estate and that for typical industrial and service corporations: the direct tradability of the underlying physical assets in a well-functioning private market.

Owning the underlying asset directly makes investing in real estate very different from other investment classes. First, you need to **manage the asset yourself** instead of simply investing in a firm that does this for you. You will need to hire brokers to find tenants for your asset, make necessary repairs to the property, pay taxes on time, and ensure it is cleaned every so often, among many other things discussed in this book. Thus, investing directly in real estate has a heavy management burden. However, this also allows skillful and entrepreneurial investors to specialize and achieve high returns.

A related important difference between direct real estate investment and "mainstream" investment is that whole assets are typically traded rather than homogenous common shares.[6] (While firms are very different from one another, one share of the same firm is identical to another.) The practical result is that tradable real estate assets are very **heterogeneous.** You cannot readily observe the market value of a real estate asset like you can of a stock by seeing the price at which an identical share of the same asset recently traded. One result is that the markets trading real estate assets are relatively illiquid, with a relatively low volume of sales per unit of time. For example, one property can be very different from the next, even when comparing offices on the same street. And individual properties – on average – only sell once every 5 to 10 years. We will come back to these topics multiple times, but in short, this means it is more difficult to find the "true" value of real estate. For example, if you buy an Apple stock, it is easy to look up its price. Indeed, hundreds of Apple stocks are traded on the stock market every second. With real estate, the most recent sales price of a property you are interested in might be a decade in the past. Sales prices of other properties that were sold more recently might not be comparable to your property.

Thus, how should you evaluate the price of a property you are interested in? Obviously, this book will help overcome this hurdle, but it is still fair to say that purchasing real estate includes hefty search costs and less certainty about current market value. It is, therefore, not surprising that, on average, a real estate deal takes 8 months.[7] (Compare that to stocks, where, with the help of apps like Robinhood, you can make a deal with a click of a button!)

Real estate **transaction costs** include brokers' fees (which help find and negotiate the deal) and costs associated with legal fees. In some jurisdictions, there are also transaction taxes, which can seriously increase the deal's cost. Apart from any transaction taxes, the transaction costs will depend on the transaction size and typically range between 2% (large deal) and 10% (small deal) of the initial purchase price. These high transaction costs come with further drawbacks: It makes quick buying and selling of real estate nearly impossible, as you need time to offset the initial 2%–10% in transaction costs.[8]

With all the above issues, you might wonder why investors would be interested in purchasing real estate. Indeed, compared to buying stocks and bonds, you have low liquidity, high transaction costs, and a high management burden. However, certain investors are interested in real estate *because* of the management burden. More to the point, one person's "burden" is another's "opportunity." *You* can make the decisions that will affect your return on the asset level. In other words, you have direct control over the investment/asset. Real estate management requires skill and expertise, but it can be a source of profit or a separate and complementary business.

Of course, many investors need more specialized expertise or time, but want real estate risk/return exposure. They need to be able to invest in real estate without the management burden associated with holding it directly. For this, we have **indirect investment** in real estate. (Revisit the dashed

---

[6] This may change over time if real estate tokenization takes hold as another ownership format.

[7] Source: MSCI / RCA, consulted between 2005 and 2016.

[8] Quick buying and selling is impossible anyway due to the long selling process of 8 months described in the previous paragraph.

line (B) in Exhibit 1-5.) For example, indirect investors in real estate equity are often interested in real estate's ability to diversify an investment portfolio that otherwise consists largely of traditional corporate stocks and bonds. Various real estate (passive) equity investment products have been developed over the years. Some of the most prominent include real estate limited partnership units (RELPs), private equity (open and closed-end funds), private real estate investment trusts (REITs), commingled real estate funds (CREFs or unit trusts), and perhaps, someday, real estate tokens. These investment vehicles are similar to corporate stock, providing their investors with an ownership interest in the underlying asset. However, these real estate equity vehicles differ from corporate stock; in some cases, they have somewhat limited governance authority over the assets and are not traded in liquid public exchanges.

Now we turn to the second way to invest in real estate, as indicated in Exhibit 1-5, listed real estate investment trusts (REITs). This is the closest real estate can get to the stock market and mainstream investment. Listed REITs will be discussed in more detail in Chapter 26. In short, these real estate investment companies are listed on the public stock exchange. Given that REITs' assets are (mostly) in real estate, purchasing their stock gives you exposure to the real estate market. If property prices collapse, so will REITs' stock prices, and vice versa. The pro of holding REITs is thus that the market is liquid (you can buy and sell the stock at any time) and that you are relieved of the management burden of the underlying asset while still being exposed to real estate risk/return. You can also invest in real estate (indirectly) as a small investor this way. As of writing, REITs are holding over $1 trillion in real estate in the US, making the listed REITs among the bigger players in the property market. Obviously, if you *want* management authority on the asset level, then holding listed REITs is not for you. Another downside of REITs is that their stock values tend to be more volatile than the privately held real estate market in the short run. This is caused by stock market "noise." By this, we mean that traders on the stock market are easily spooked by random events and respond immediately to them. Later, investors might find out that the event did not impact the property market, and stock values go back up again. Short-term and random volatility will not prevail in direct real estate investment due to the long holding and negotiation period. Some investors do not appreciate the stock market's high levels of (visible and short-term) volatility and, therefore, prefer holding real estate. Some derivative trading (like in the aforementioned call options) is also possible for larger REITs.[9]

Finally, consider the third major way to invest in real estate, as indicated in Exhibit 1-5: real estate debt. This includes private "whole loan" products and securitized debt that is often publicly traded, like bonds on the stock exchange. Exhibit 1-6 provides some data on who originated debt in the commercial property market in the United States over a selection of years. The percentages are based on the total dollar amount of the loans originated by different lenders. First, you will notice that a large share of the mortgages are originated by a category denoted "MBS," which stands for (residential) mortgage-backed securities. For commercial (income-producing) property, "MBS" mostly refers only to debt on multi-family rental apartment properties. (There are also much larger amounts of single-family home MBS, which are beyond the scope of this book.) The general idea of all mortgage-backed securities is that many mortgages are pooled into one entity (called a Special Purpose Vehicle, SPV), which issues relatively small denomination securities based on the mortgage pool. The securities are sold to investors in the "secondary market." These ultimate investors can be anyone, from various institutions to individuals (usually via funds). Mortgage-backed securities are generally rated in terms of their default risk by bond credit rating agencies, and the higher grades of the securities are typically traded in the bond market. MBS is for apartment/residential real estate only. In the United States, as of the early 2020s, the apartment MBS industry is dominated by

[9] Note that REITs themselves invest directly in real estate. (See the solid line at the bottom of Exhibit 1-5.) In other words, if you have a career working for a REIT, you are directly investing real estate. It is the shareholders of that REIT who are indirectly investing in real estate.

government agencies that effectively guarantee the cash flow to the investors, reducing the risk of investing in these MBS considerably.

If we disregard residential real estate for a moment, you will find a smaller bar called "CMBS." CMBS stands for **commercial mortgage-backed security**. CMBS is very similar to MBS, but the difference is that there is no government guarantee for the ultimate investors. By the early 2020s, the CMBS label in Exhibit 1-6 refers to securities based on non-residential properties. Different classes of securities are usually issued from the same underlying mortgage pool. Some classes are riskier than others, and different classes have different typical maturities. This allows a variety of risk and return patterns to be created for the different (C)MBS classes based on the same underlying pool of mortgages. This way, investors with different risk preferences and investment horizons can be served.

In total, 37% of all loan originations are held on banks' balance sheets. This number would be close to 50% if we omit apartments. Local banks represent the biggest group within this cohort. As mentioned earlier, commercial property is complex to price due to the lack of sales and the heterogeneity of CRE. As a result, a large part of the business is based on mutual knowledge and trust between investors and banks with local market knowledge (often called "relationship lending"). This is doubly so for the real estate development industry (construction loans are a special category and are not included in Exhibit 1-6).

Another way to invest indirectly in debt as an investor is by buying stock of a **mortgage REIT** ("mREIT"). An mREIT functions very similar to the aforementioned REITs and provides similar benefits. The main difference is that mREITs issue debt for commercial property instead of owning real estate equity. MREITs can also invest in mortgage-backed securities. We find that 4% of all mortgage originations were done by such mREITs in 2021. Mortgage REITs are often highly

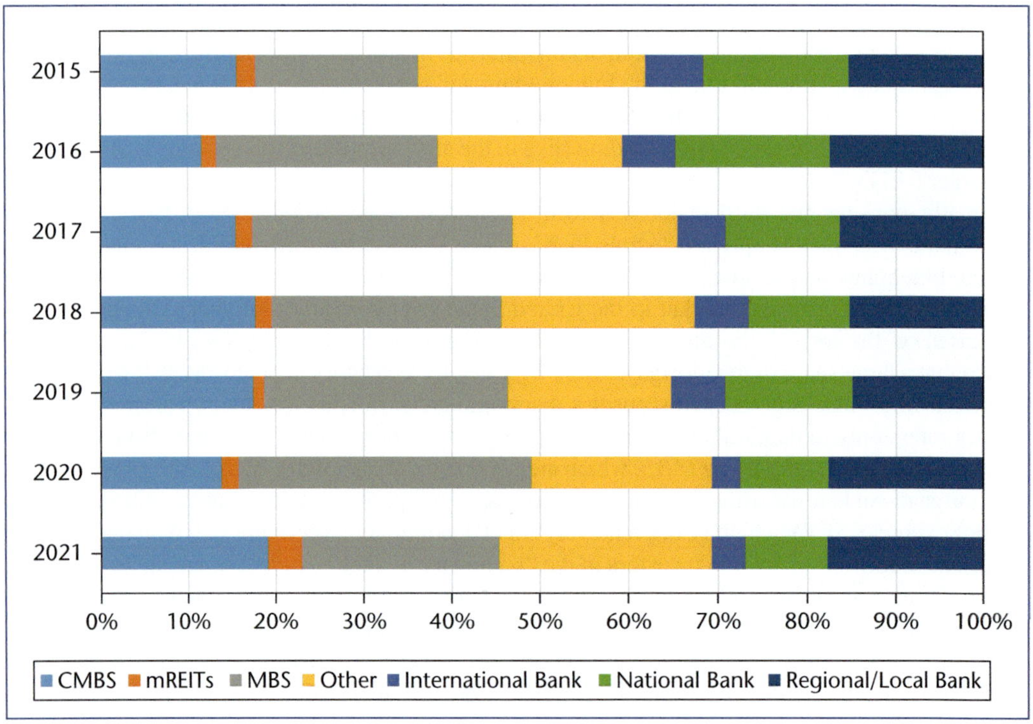

EXHIBIT 1-6 Type of Lender at Origination for a Selection of Years. The Percentage is Based on the Total Dollar Amount.

Source: Real Capital Analytics (now MSCI).

levered, which can cause their investment performance to differ significantly from the underlying mortgages they own. The other category consists of loans from individuals, insurance funds, pension funds, and other types of lenders.

Let us now summarize the modern real estate investment system depicted in Exhibit 1-5. The defining characteristic of this system is that the underlying assets are real properties. Real property is unique, presenting risk and return characteristics that are not quite like those of the whole industrial and service corporations that form the underlying assets in traditional corporate finance. Unlike typical corporate finance, real estate underlying physical assets trade directly in a well-functioning, albeit private, asset market. The investment industry creates investment products and vehicles that enable a variety of risk and return patterns to be carved out of the same underlying assets so that heterogeneous investors can be better served and capital can flow more efficiently and effectively to real estate. As always, equity and debt products are prominent in the investment system.

1.3 HOW HAS REAL ESTATE PERFORMED HISTORICALLY?

Do you recall what we said about the importance of having different types of underlying physical assets to offer greater quantity, variety, and range of alternatives to heterogeneous investor groups? We noted that commercial real estate is a unique class of underlying assets. In the remainder of this chapter, we want to put ourselves in the shoes of investors, scanning the big picture of the investment universe available to them to see the nature and role of real estate as one of several major investment asset classes. We will review the major asset classes' historical, empirical investment performance. To simplify matters at this broad-brush level, we will consider the main traditional form of institutional real estate investment, that is, the direct unlevered investment in large-scale commercial property (the so-called "core" of private real estate investment portfolios). See the Text Box 1.1 as well for the definition of "core."

TEXT BOX 1.1 DIFFERENT RISK AND RETURN CATEGORIES IN REAL ESTATE

Real estate brokers and investors typically subdivide real estate investments into the following categories: (1) core, (2) core plus, (3) value-added, and (4) opportunistic. In short, "core" is the safest investment, and "opportunistic" is the riskiest investment, with the other types between those two. These terms refer in part to the type of physical real estate assets (size, age, quality, location) but also to some extent to the "style" of investing on the part of the investing institution (degree of leverage, nature of leasing and capital improvement strategy, etc). Suppose a real estate fund or property is advertised as "core," for example. In that case, it will attract a specific type of investor with a low-risk appetite and typically a need for current income as well as relatively strong liquidity (ease of resale). However, there is not a single clearly agreed-upon definition of these brackets. Every investor and broker may have a slightly different definition. Roughly speaking, the categories are constructed as follows (as of the early 2020s);

- **Core real estate**: Returns come from current income; total return target 6–9%; low risk (compared to other real estate); little debt used (50% LTV or less); long hold possible (10 years or more) but good resale ability if necessary. Archetypal properties would be large, relatively new "trophy" properties in first-or second-tier city CBDs with solid economics; properties fully leased, ideally to AAA tenants.

- **Core plus real estate**: mix of current income and growth (price appreciation), total return target 8–12%, moderate risk, 50–60% LTV, 5–7-year hold. Stabilized buildings generating steady rents.
- **Value-added**: some income return, expected significant price appreciation; target total return 12%–18% return with accompanying risk; often 60–70% LTV, 5–7-year horizon. Modestly performing property and anticipating improved asset management can raise rent and value, for example, through capital improvements and/or leasing strategy.
- **Opportunistic**: (AKA "opportunity funds") Highest expected return from capital gains; total return target of 15–20% or more, but with substantial risk. Often highly levered albeit at high rates, complex capital stack; short holds (5 years or less). Undermanaged assets require substantial rehabilitation and repositioning. It often includes land speculation or development projects and may include investment in operating companies in addition to direct real estate.

LTV stands for Loan-to-Value or the debt as a percentage of the total purchase value. See Chapter 12 for more details.

1.3.1 Four Major Investment Asset Classes

Traditionally, four major asset classes are identified in the core of the investment universe for portfolio planning.

- Cash (T-bills)
- Stocks
- Bonds
- Real estate

Although classification at this level is necessarily somewhat stylized and simplified, these four classes make a helpful taxonomy for several reasons. First, each presents unique characteristics regarding the objectives and constraints concerning investors. Second, substantial empirical historical data are publicly available regarding the investment performance of each of these asset classes, including time series of periodic total returns. Third, each of these four classes is large enough in magnitude to support substantial capital flow into or out of the asset class without significant disruptions to markets and industries. Fourth, each of these asset classes is "investable." In other words, asset markets and investment vehicles exist, enabling passive institutions and/or individuals to buy and sell assets in each of these classes.[10] Exhibit 1-4 shows that total commercial real estate equity was worth $14 trillion in the US (excluding mortgages), the stock market was worth $34 trillion, and the bond market was worth $30 trillion in 2020. In addition, the combined value of Treasury bills of 1 year or less was $3.5 trillion in 2022.

Exhibit 1-7 presents a qualitative characterization of the typical investment performance expectations of each of the four asset classes. The table qualitatively describes each asset class along with its investment performance and constraints/concerns, as laid out previously.

[10] Other, less "investable," asset classes can be defined conceptually, such as "human capital" and small, privately held businesses. But it is difficult to invest in such other classes, and difficult to quantify their magnitude.

EXHIBIT 1-7
Characteristics of the Major Investment Classes

Investment Objective	Stocks	Real Estate*	Long-Term Bonds+	Cash (T-bills)
Return	High	Moderate	Moderate to Low	Low
Income (as % of return)	Low	Moderate	High	None
Growth (as % of return)	High	Moderate	None	None
Investment Concern	**Stocks**	**Real Estate***	**Long-Term Bonds+**	**Cash (T-bills)**
Risk	High	Moderate	Moderate to Low	Low
Liquidity	High	Low	Moderate	High
Time Horizon	short	Long	Moderate	Short
Investor Expertize and Management Burden	Small	Large	Small	Small
Investor Size	Small	Large	Small	Small
Capital Constraint	Small	Large	Small	Small

Notes:
* "core" real estate, unlevered (without a mortgage).
+ 10 year AAA corporate bonds (*Fred*)

Exhibit 1-7 clarifies what we mean by saying that each asset class offers investors unique investment performance attributes. All four classes differ substantially from the others in what they provide for investors. Together, they present a wide range of possibilities.

Real estate has an important role in the overall picture as one of these four major asset classes. In particular, in the risk and return dimensions, investment in real estate tends to fall between stocks at one extreme and cash (or short-term bonds such as T-bills) at the other extreme. In this regard, real estate is much like long-term bonds. Unlike bonds, however, real estate provides some capital growth and relatively good inflation protection. On the other hand, the contractual and finite nature of bond cash flows enables investors who can buy and hold bonds to maturity without having to sell them in the bond market to greatly reduce the risk in their investment (at least in nominal terms).[11] The other defining features of real estate are also shown in Exhibit 1-7: You'll have little liquidity and a high management burden.

Another important and defining characteristic of the four major asset classes is that they do not all "move together" in their investment performance. That is, they do not always tend to all do well, or all do poorly simultaneously. The correlation among their periodic returns is generally only moderately positive. This means that investors can diversify their portfolios by allocating across the four asset classes.

1.3.2 Historical Investment Performance

Exhibit 1-8 presents a broad-brush historical, empirical picture of the investment performance of the four asset classes since 1978 in the United States. The exhibit shows what one dollar of investment at the end of 1978 would have grown to by the end of each of the following years in each of the four asset classes. Exhibit 1-8 assumes that any income generated by the investment was plowed

[11] Real estate investors with a long-term and flexible holding horizon can also greatly reduce the risk. Most of the return for such investors will come in the form of relatively stable and predictable real estate rents. Such investors may also be able to take advantage of the greater degree of asset price predictability in the real estate market (see Chapters 8 and 9). Note also that real estate is fairly categorized as low to moderate risk only without substantial leverage (see Chapter 12).

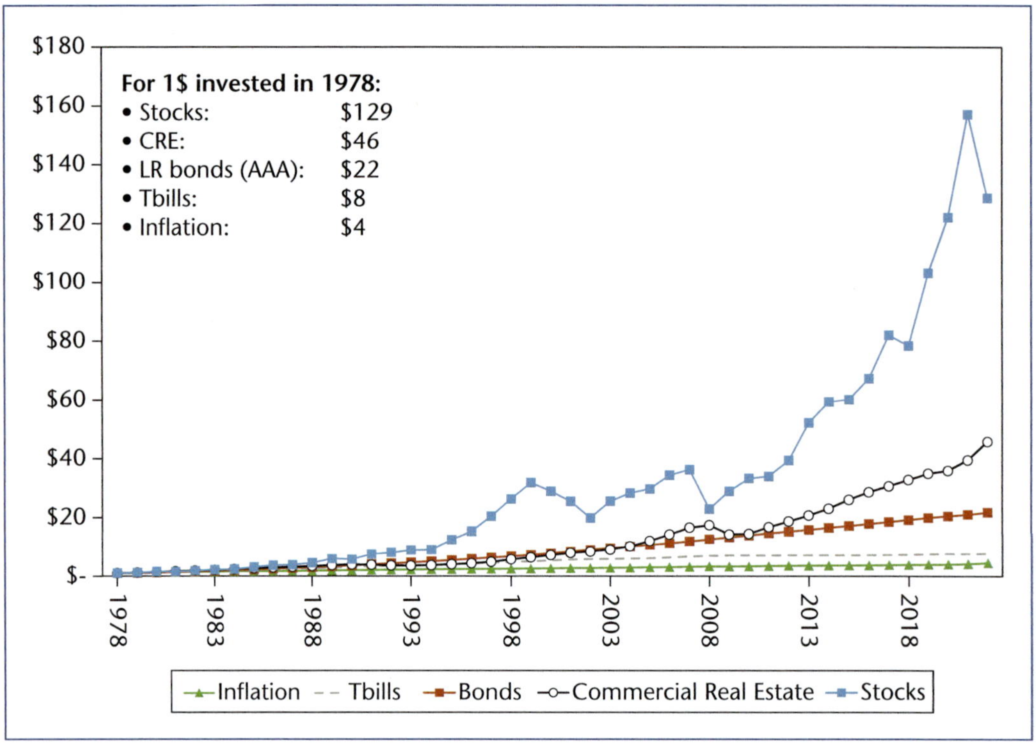

EXHIBIT 1-8 Forty four-year Historical Performance of Major Investment Classes Compared to Inflation. 1$ was Invested in 1978 in Each Category.

back into the investment, so the values shown represent the compounded accumulation of the total returns. In addition to the four asset classes, Exhibit 1-8 shows the effect of inflation by tracing inflation, or more accurately, the Consumer Price Index (CPI), indicating the number of dollars necessary each year to purchase what one dollar could have bought in 1978.

Over the historical period shown in Exhibit 1-8, the champion performer was the stock market. For every dollar invested in 1978, the investor in the stock market would have $129 by 2022. A similar investment in real estate would have grown to $46, while an investment purely in long-term bonds would have grown to $22. U.S. Treasury bills provided the lowest return, that is, a continuously rolled-over re-investment in the short-term notes of the government, like a typical money market fund. Such an investment would have grown to only $8 per dollar of original investment. All four asset classes "beat inflation"; that is to say, they provided their investors with a positive "real" return, increasing the purchasing power of their invested dollars. The CPI indicates that it would have taken $4 to buy in 2022 what $1 would have bought you at the beginning of 1978.[12]

[12] Quantitative performance histories such as those portrayed in Exhibit 1-9 must be interpreted cautiously. It is difficult to measure investment performance in a way that is exactly comparable across asset classes, and there is always a question of what "index" best represents the specific investments or opportunities faced by a given investor. The numbers in Exhibit 1-9 are based on the following indexes. For the stock market, we have used the Standard & Poor's 500 Index, which consists of 500 relatively large stocks. For bonds, we have used an index of AAA Moody's corporate bond rates with a maturity of 20 years or longer. Both the stock and bond index returns, as well as the Treasury bill returns, are available on FRED. The real estate returns shown here are based on NCREIF total returns. One issue is that the price appreciation is based on appraised values, which can contain a lag and can be too smooth (Chapter 24).

EXHIBIT 1-9
Historical Statistics on Annual Returns, 1978–2022

	Average Total Return	Standard Deviation
Inflation	3.50%	2.69%
Tbills	4.82%	3.98%
Bonds	7.30%	3.16%
Commercial Real Estate	9.32%	6.99%
Stocks	13.02%	16.46%

Exhibit 1-9 summarizes the 1978–2022 annual investment performance history shown in Exhibit 1-8, using some basic statistical measures. The first column of Exhibit 1-9 indicates the average annual total return, the growth in investment value from both capital value appreciation and income paid out to the investor (such as dividends, interest, or rent). The second column indicates the annual standard deviation in these yearly total returns during the 45-year history considered. This standard deviation measures the variability across time in the returns, also known as the volatility of the investment. This is a primary way to measure the risk in the investment asset class. Volatility is reflected in the "bumpiness" or propensity for "up and down" movement or cycles in the historical charts of index values. In line with Exhibit 1-7, we find that stocks outperformed commercial real estate but were riskier investments as well (as measured by the volatility of the returns). Exhibit 1-10 provides the income yield for the stock market (dividend) and commercial real estate between 1978 and 2022. The average cash payout rate on the stock market was 3%, whereas it was 4.5% for commercial real estate.

While the historical results shown in Exhibit 1-8 and Exhibit 1-9 are broadly consistent with the relative total return expectations noted in Exhibit 1-7, it is essential to realize that investment performance is always risky to some extent. This means that performance, in both absolute and relative terms comparing across the asset classes, varies over time in never perfectly predictable ways. For example, commercial real estate performance in the late 1980s and early 1990s was abysmal. Even long-run corporate AAA bonds performed better during this period; see Exhibit 1-11A. The main reason was already established in the mid- to late 1980s. Tax incentives resulted in a building boom of historic proportions. The development industry converted financial capital into physical structures, especially office buildings, shopping malls, and hotels. Much of this development was driven or supported by tax incentives that distanced the investor from the underlying economic costs and benefits of the physical real estate that was being built, resulting in many bad projects that found themselves with few tenants. Furthermore, the savings and loan and commercial banks that financed much of the new construction operated in an environment of "moral hazard," in which government deposit insurance divorced their source of capital from the risks of their investment.

In 1986, a sweeping tax reform act removed virtually all of the special tax incentives from which real estate had benefited. Also, by the late 1980s, the inflation rate was down sharply, and inflation appeared to be under control, undercutting the "inflation fear" source of real estate investment demand. By the late 1980s, the extent of overbuilding in the space market was becoming apparent, as was the financial crisis in the overextended savings and loan industry, which had loaned vast sums in commercial mortgages backed by economically weak building projects. The commercial real estate asset market began to falter. The stock market drop and economic recession of 1990 were the straws that broke the camel's back (even though it was a mild and short-lived recession). Amid crumbling financial institutions awash with bad mortgages, the bottom fell out of the commercial property market in the early 1990s. Traditional sources of capital for commercial real estate, such as banks, life insurance companies, and pension funds, dried up completely. Indeed, the capital flow from such sources turned negative, with lenders refusing to refinance loans that came due and even

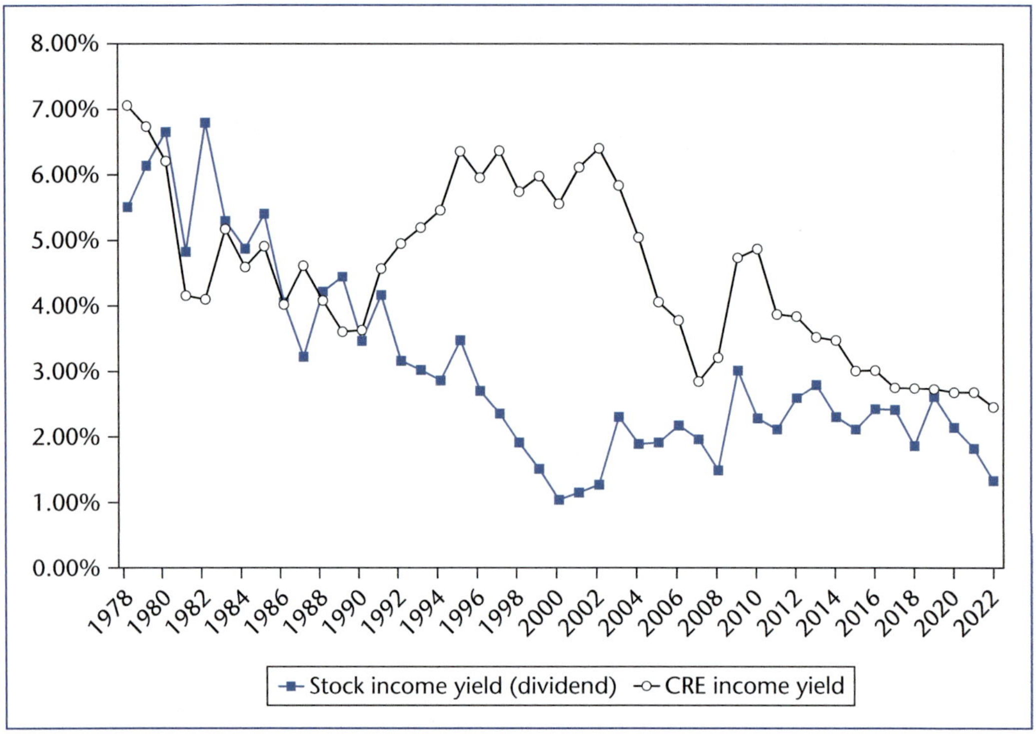

EXHIBIT 1-10 Income Yield for Both the Stock Market and Commercial Real Estate (CRE), 1978–2022.

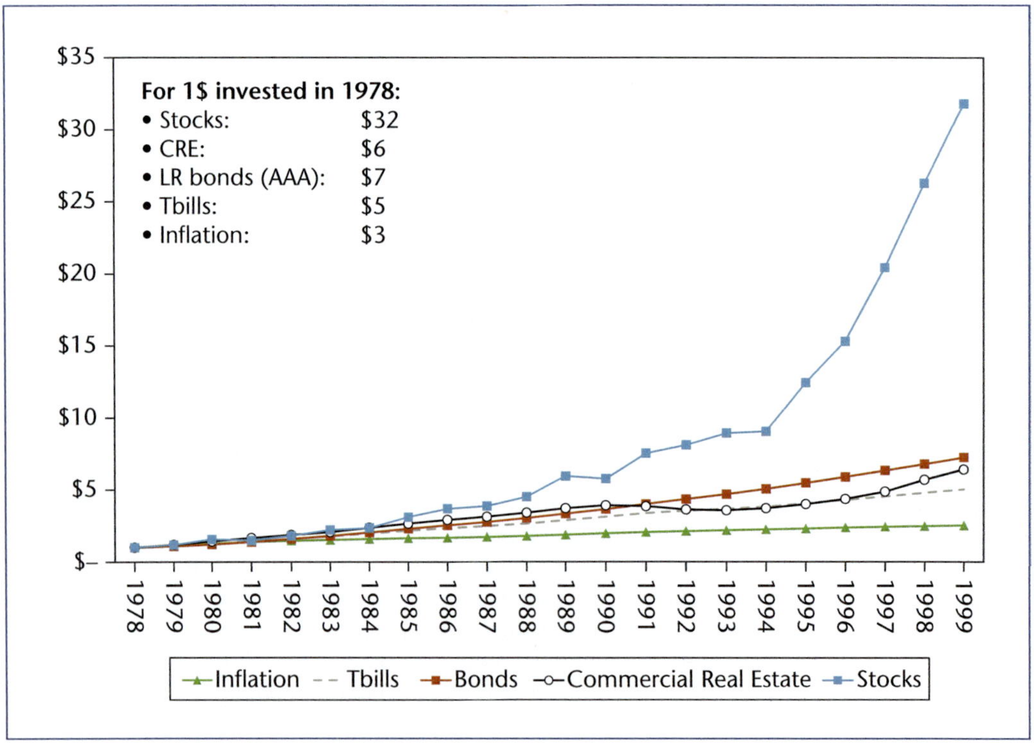

EXHIBIT 1-11A Performance of Major Investment Classes Compared to Inflation 1978–1999.

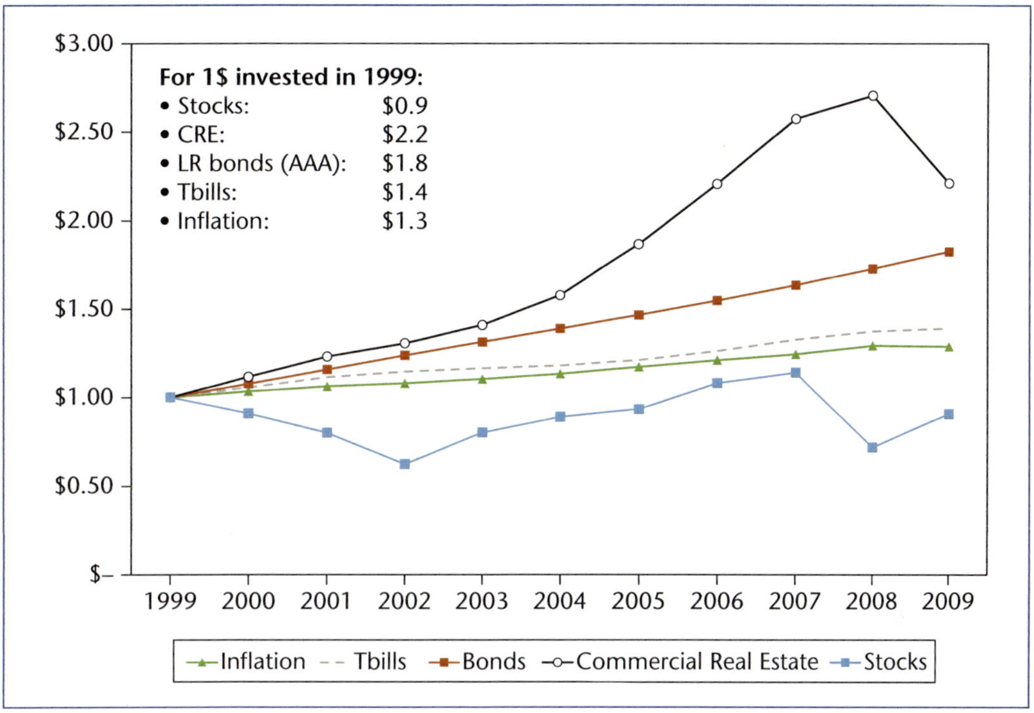

EXHIBIT 1-11B Performance of Major Investment Classes Compared to Inflation 1999–2009.

trying to sell existing mortgages. Commercial real estate asset prices fell 30 to 50% in just 2 years in most of the major property markets, the largest drop in property values in the United States since the Great Depression. (In contrast, the housing market was not hit nearly so hard then, except for a few overheated cities.)

The bottom for commercial properties was finally reached in 1992 and 1993, accompanied by an influx of new capital entering the real estate market. The money came first from opportunistic "vulture funds" and "grave-dancers" financed by wealthy individuals. This was followed rapidly by the public capital markets as a new source of money in the form of an unprecedented expansion of the REIT industry and the development of an entirely new industry in the form of commercial mortgage-backed securities (CMBS). In 1993 alone, 50 new REITs issued initial public offerings (IPOs) of stocks, raising over $9 billion, more than three times the largest previous annual total. During this period, it was not uncommon to be able to buy large new commercial properties for a small fraction of their construction cost (although such properties were often largely devoid of tenants!).

Commercial real estate recovered in the mid-1990s (Exhibit 1-11A) and was even the star performer throughout most of the 2000s (Exhibit 1-11B). In contrast, it was the stock market's turn to underperform gravely. A single dollar invested in the stock market in 1999 would yield $0.9 in 2009, performing worse than even inflation. The remarkable development of securitization in the public capital markets as a source of real estate investment money during the 1990s powered the recovery of the commercial property investment market during most of the remainder of that decade (until 1998) and greatly changed the real estate investment industry. The development of both the debt and equity sides of this market was stimulated by government actions. For example, the CMBS industry had its roots in the **Financial Institutions Recovery, Reform, and Enforcement Act of 1989 (FIRREA),** passed by Congress to bail out the savings and loan industry. FIRREA set up the Resolution Trust Corporation (RTC), a government corporation charged with rapidly selling huge quantities of bad commercial mortgages that the government had taken from defunct banks and thrifts. FIRREA also imposed risk-adjusted capital requirements on financial institutions, providing them an incentive to hold assets in a publicly traded ("securitized") form, such as CMBS, rather than as whole loans. Necessity being the mother of invention, the means to tap the public debt market was found via the CMBS vehicle. By the mid-1990s, the traditional sources of capital, especially the pension funds and commercial banks, were also back in the real estate investment business in a big way. With the long economic boom of the 1990s, excess supply in the space markets was gradually filled up with tenants, further bolstering the confidence of conservative investors. The commercial property market was fully recovered by the end of the decade.

The early years of the new century were very good for commercial and investment real estate asset markets, even though a comparatively mild national recession in 2000–2001 cut badly into demand for many types of commercial space usage and undercut rents in most space markets. After a substantial fall in REIT prices during 1998–2000, which had relatively little impact on the private property market, REIT shares soared with the bursting of the high-tech "dot.com bubble" in 2001 and a resulting counter-flow of investors into an asset class that provided cash flow, dividends, and tangible assets—the opposite of many of the ephemeral dot.com stocks that had recently crashed. More broadly, the mainstream professional investment establishment on Wall Street seemed finally to be recognizing both direct private investment in real estate as well as REITs and CMBs as legitimate elements in the core of the institutional investment portfolio. The bursting of the dot.com bubble seemed to erase the stigma of real estate being an "informationally inefficient" asset class (and the memory of the early 1990s real estate crash), just as it erased the idea that the "informationally efficient" stock market could not be susceptible to "irrational exuberance" with its attendant corrections. The resulting boost in investor demand for real estate kept asset prices up, even as underlying space markets tumbled, and property income declined.

Obviously, a lot happened after this period as well. First, we experienced the **Great Financial Crisis** of 2007. Even though the origin of the crisis is still ill-understood,[13] the result was a global financial crisis and economic recession more severe in the United States than any since the Great Depression and a general collapse in prices across all asset classes. Investors panicked (with reason) and fled risk of any kind for the safe harbor of U.S. Treasury bills (whose yields actually went slightly negative for a time as their prices were bid up!). Commercial property was not at all immune. On a calendar year basis, commercial property prices dropped 35% from the end of 2006 to the end of 2009 (a 28% loss after accounting for income generated by the properties during that period), completing commercial real estate's third major asset market pricing cycle in a half-century (with prior bottoms in 1975 and 1992). This latest crash was steeper and faster than the previous ones, and even the NCREIF (National Council of Real Estate Investment Fiduciaries)[14] Property Index rammed its valuations down much harder and quicker than in the 1990s. (In late 2008 and early 2009, NCREIF member fund managers and accountants sometimes overruled appraisers in making property valuation reports for the index, as the appraisers had little hard price evidence to work from amid virtually paralyzed markets for large properties.)

Even though the economy recovered soon afterward, in early 2020, COVID-19 hit. Property prices initially plateaued but soon increased considerably. The long-run ramifications of COVID-19

---

[13] Arguably the most widely accepted explanation is that commercial banks (after the "recourse rule" was introduced) were more or less forced to invest heavily in complex financial products with AAA ratings. (Even though this rating, especially in hindsight, was questionable.) After prices of such products dropped, the same banks stopped investing in business and consumer loans to maintain their capital "cushion." The real crisis began after businesses and consumers were unable to obtain credit.

[14] Established over 40 years ago, the National Council of Real Estate Investment Fiduciaries (NCREIF) serves the institutional real estate investment community as its Data Central. NCREIF produced the first property-level return index, the NCREIF Property Index (NPI), dating back to 1978. NCREIF properties tend to be large, class A "core" properties. Even though they do not represent the overall real estate market per se, their data is very detailed, making it a popular database nonetheless.

on commercial real estate are still open for debate. On the one hand, technological innovations increased the ease of working from home. As a result, businesses need less office space. On the other hand, there is more demand for warehouses to distribute goods ordered via the same technological innovations (spearheaded by Amazon.com). There is also evidence that households moved out of dense urban centers and to suburban areas. This could indicate better real estate returns for housing and retail in said suburban areas moving forward. Again, as of writing in the early 2020s, it is hard to predict the impact of COVID-19 on property values. However, the main point we are trying to get across is that the timing of the investment in real estate really matters.

1.4 CHAPTER SUMMARY

This chapter has presented some basic background information about commercial real estate assets as an investment class. We highlighted the similarities and differences between real estate and the other major traditional investment asset classes, particularly stocks and bonds. We noted important recent developments in the public capital markets, the REIT and CMBS industries, and the current major sources of capital. We put this information in some historical context and provided some summary quantification of typical investment performance in recent decades based on empirical evidence. You should now have a working knowledge of the basic commercial real estate investment products and vehicles and the recent history that sets the stage for today's real estate investment world. This knowledge will be useful as you pursue subsequent chapters in this book or undertake a career in the industry.

KEY TERMS

- Investment objective
- Growth (savings) objective
- Income (current cash flow) objective
- Risk
- Liquidity
- Time horizon
- Investor expertise
- Investor management burden
- Investor size
- Capital constraint
- Investor heterogeneity
- Underlying asset
- Investment product (vehicle)
- Passive investors
- Commingled real estate funds (CFREFs)
- Private REITs (real estate investment trusts)
- Private markets
- Commercial mortgage-backed securities (CMBS)
- Financial, Institutions Recovery Reform, and Enforcement Act (FIRREA)

STUDY QUESTIONS

In Your Own Words

1.1 What distinguishes commercial real estate from owner-occupied housing?
1.2 Name the four major property types in commercial real estate introduced in the chapter.

1.3 Why do healthcare properties generally command higher prices per square foot compared to industrial properties, despite being smaller in size?
1.4 What is the main reason for the high concentration of commercial real estate value in large U.S. cities?
1.5 What does "CMBS" stand for, and how does it function in the real estate market?
1.6 How does investing in REITs provide liquidity compared to direct real estate ownership?
1.7 What are the three major ways to invest in commercial real estate as outlined in the chapter?
1.8 Why is real estate considered a less liquid investment compared to stocks?
1.9 What are some of the common transaction costs associated with direct real estate investment?

Check Your Knowledge

1.10 What is the most fundamental characteristic of real estate compared to other asset classes?
A) It is easily converted into cash through a highly liquid market
B) It has a relatively short life span, necessitating frequent turnover
C) It is a long-lived asset that often appreciates over extended periods
D) It is primarily transacted through cash purchases due to its high value
1.11 Which of the following asset classes generally has the highest risk?
A) Cash
B) Bonds
C) Real estate
D) Stocks
1.12 Why is real estate considered less liquid than stocks or bonds?
A) Real estate deals are simpler to negotiate
B) Real estate assets are heterogeneous and take longer to sell
C) Real estate can be sold instantly with low costs
D) Real estate prices fluctuate less frequently
1.13 Which of the following investment vehicles gives indirect ownership of real estate?
A) Common stock
B) Mutual funds
C) REITs
D) Corporate bonds
1.14 What role do commercial mortgage-backed securities (CMBS) play in real estate investment?
A) They offer liquidity to small investors in commercial properties
B) They securitize pools of mortgages backed by commercial properties
C) They offer guaranteed returns from commercial real estate
D) They are used exclusively for residential real estate investment
1.15 Which investor is most likely to choose an income-focused real estate investment?
A) A young couple saving for their child's education
B) A wealthy entrepreneur in their 30s
C) A retired couple looking for steady cash flow
D) A start-up company owner looking for growth
1.16 Why might a real estate investor prefer direct ownership over investing in a REIT?
A) Direct ownership offers higher liquidity
B) Direct ownership eliminates management responsibilities
C) Direct ownership provides control over the property and decisions
D) Direct ownership involves less risk than REITs

1.17 How do inflation and real estate investments typically interact?
   A) Real estate provides protection against inflation due to increasing property values
   B) Inflation has no effect on real estate investments
   C) Inflation decreases the value of real estate over time
   D) Real estate value is negatively correlated with inflation

Chapter Case: Investment Decision at Yoshida Capital

Yoshida Capital, a medium-sized investment firm, is exploring opportunities to expand its portfolio into commercial real estate. The firm currently focuses on stocks, bonds, and some residential real estate, but is considering a diversification strategy to enter the commercial real estate market.

The company's team is evaluating two commercial properties located in two different cities:

1. City Center Office Complex in New York City
   - Type: Class A office building
   - Price: $150 million
   - Annual Expected Rent: $12 million
   - Transaction Costs: 8% of the purchase price
   - Market: Highly competitive with high demand but also subject to fluctuations due to remote work trends.
2. Industrial Warehouse in Houston, Texas
   - Type: Distribution center
   - Price: $45 million
   - Annual Expected Rent: $3.5 million
   - Transaction Costs: 6% of the purchase price
   - Market: Houston is growing as a logistics hub with increasing demand for warehouse space due to e-commerce growth, but the market can be more volatile with fluctuating oil prices.

Yoshida Capital must decide which investment will provide the best long-term return while considering the risks associated with each market.

1. Which property has higher transaction costs as a percentage of the purchase price?
   A) City Center Office Complex
   B) Industrial Warehouse
   C) Both properties have the same transaction costs
   D) Transaction costs are not relevant to the decision
2. What market factor makes the Houston Industrial Warehouse an attractive investment?
   A) The presence of Class A office buildings
   B) Growth of e-commerce fueling demand for logistics hubs
   C) Lower expected rental income
   D) Stability in the oil market
3. Which property has a higher expected annual rental income as a percentage of its purchase price?
   A) City Center Office Complex
   B) Industrial Warehouse
   C) Both properties have the same rental income ratio
   D) Rental income is not a factor in the decision
4. Which factor might make the Houston Industrial Warehouse a riskier investment than it initially appears?
   A) Oversupply of office spaces

B) Dependence on the volatile oil market
C) Excessive demand for residential housing
D) Too much liquidity in the real estate market

5. How do transaction costs affect the overall profitability of a commercial real estate investment?
   A) They have no impact on profitability
   B) They increase short-term costs, reducing initial profitability
   C) They increase long-term profitability
   D) They only impact the rental income
6. What is one major reason Yoshida Capital might favor the Industrial Warehouse over the City Center Office Complex?
   A) Higher transaction costs
   B) Greater market demand due to e-commerce growth
   C) Lower rental income
   D) Stronger demand for office space in New York
7. Why would Yoshida Capital be concerned about the liquidity of the City Center Office Complex?
   A) It is located in a remote area
   B) There is excess demand for industrial space
   C) Remote work trends may reduce the demand for office space
   D) New York real estate is highly liquid

2 Present Value Mathematics for Real Estate

CHAPTER OUTLINE

LEARNING OBJECTIVES

After reading this chapter, you should understand:

- The basic formulas and procedures for converting typical real estate future cash flows and risk patterns to present values, given the appropriate discount rates.
- The origin or derivation of these formulas, in such a way that you can apply them with some flexibility to new situations.
- How to invert the present value formulas to compute the implied return or the time until a future value is received.

DOI: 10.1201/9781003643838-3

In the previous chapter, we complained that pricing commercial real estate (CRE) is not as straightforward as pricing stocks, for example. In order to understand how we *would* price CRE, you first need a fundamental understanding of the time value of money, how to measure returns (Chapter 3), and how to combine this in a discounted cash flow model (Chapter 4). This chapter will focus on explaining the time value of money and how you can mathematically express it. If you find yourself wondering at some point in this chapter how all this math relates to real estate, don't worry; you'll find out in the next two chapters! We guarantee you that the time value of money is very fundamental to understanding and quantifying the value of real estate.

If someone offered you a choice between $10,000 today or $10,000 1 year from now, which would you choose? It is a fundamental fact of financial economics that dollars at one time are not equivalent to dollars at another time. This is not just because of inflation. Due to the real productivity of capital and due to risk, future dollars are worth less than present dollars, even if there is no inflation. In real estate investment analysis, we constantly need to compare dollars at different points in time. Present value mathematics consists of the formulas, procedures, and techniques for making such comparisons and evaluations. This chapter will present some of the most basic and commonly used of these tools.

Please keep in mind that the focus of this chapter is on the mechanics—the formal mathematical formulas. In order to know how to use these formulas properly in real estate investment analysis, you need to know the right numbers to plug into the formulas. This requires combining economics with mathematics, which we will explore in later chapters.

For the purposes of this chapter, present value formulas can be grouped into two classes: single sums and multiperiod cash flows. The single-sum formulas are the most basic building blocks, as the multiperiod formulas are all built up as sums of the single-sum formulas. So we will begin this chapter with single-sum formulas, and then advance to multiperiod formulas in the second half.[1]

2.1 SINGLE-SUM FORMULAS

Single-sum formulas refer to situations in which only two points in time are considered. Typically, one of these two points is the present. A single cash flow or monetary value is posited at one of the two points in time, and the task is to determine the value it equates to at the other point in time.

2.1.1 Single-Period Discounting and Growing

The simplest sort of present value problem is single-period discounting or growing. Let's go back to the choice between $10,000 today versus 1 year from today. We no doubt agree that we would all choose the $10,000 today. But suppose the choice is $10,000 today versus $11,000 in 1 year, or $12,000, and so on. Clearly, there is some value greater than $10,000 that we would prefer to take in 1 year. How high that "indifference point" is depends on several things. For example, we would want to consider how much interest we could earn on a 1-year deposit in a bank. If we could earn 5 percent simple interest on a 1-year certificate of deposit (CD), then $10,500 in 1 year would be equivalent to $10,000 today, because $10{,}000 \times 1.05 = 10{,}500$. However, we might require a promise of more than $10,500 in a year in exchange for our $10,000 today if we view the future promise as being more risky than a bank CD. In effect, we might want more than a 5 percent expected return to

[1] If you are already familiar with these formulas and procedures, you can safely skip this chapter. The only thing we do here that is a little different from the typical coverage is that we present the underlying geometric series formula from which the regular multiperiod (annuity and perpetuity) present value formulas are derived. This will give the reader some additional depth and flexibility and enable us to show how to develop formulas for the present values of buildings with long-term leases, a common problem in commercial real estate.

get us to forgo the present cash. Suppose we wanted a 10 percent expected return "risk premium" on top of the 5 percent we could earn at the bank for a total expected return of 15 percent in order to entice us to forgo our \$10,000 today in exchange for a cash sum promised next year. Then \$11,500 is our indifference point because

$$\$10{,}000 + (15\% \times \$10{,}000) = \$11{,}500$$

or equivalently

$$\$10{,}000 \times (1 + 0.15) = \$11{,}500$$

Now, suppose that we know our expected return percentage (say, 15 percent, as in the previous example) and that we know the amount that is being promised 1 year from now. So, the question is, how much are we willing to forgo today in exchange for the promised sum in 1 year? We can find this present value by simply inverting the previous formula and solving for the present value rather than for the future value. For example, if \$11,500 is being offered in 1 year, then we could determine that we are willing to pay \$10,000 today by dividing the expected future amount by one plus the expected return, as follows:

$$\$10{,}000 = \frac{\$11{,}500}{1+0.15}$$

Assuming that 15 percent is our required expected return (opportunity cost of capital), any offer of more than \$11,500 next year would be preferred over holding on to our \$10,000 today, while any offer of less than \$11,500 would be rejected in favor of keeping our \$10,000 today.

In the previous example, the \$10,000 amount is the *present certainty equivalent*, often more simply referred to as the **present value**, of the *future expected sum* (or **future value**) of \$11,500 in 1 year, based on a simple annual expected return of 15 percent. In general, if we let PV represent the present value, FV represent the future value, and r represent the simple expected return, then the formula for discounting future values to present value is:

$$PV = \frac{FV}{1+r} \tag{1a}$$

and the corresponding formula for growing a present value to its future equivalent is:[2]

$$FV = (1+r)PV \tag{1b}$$

Using formula (1a), you could answer the question of how much cash in the present would equate to \$10,000 promised money in 1 year, under the 15 percent required return assumption of the previous numerical example. The answer would be PV = \$8,695.65 = \$10,000/1.15. When solving for present value given the future value, the problem is one of **discounting** rather than **growing**, and

[2] This is the first of many formulas you will encounter in this chapter. Most people don't like memorizing formulas and rely on spreadsheet software that offers these formulas in an intuitive manner. We offer spreadsheet examples, for all of the problems presented in this chapter on the website accompanying this book. We also prepared a spreadsheet with all formulas used in this chapter and for the odd-numbered study questions at the end of this chapter, which cover all of the types of problems presented here.

the required expected return percentage in the denominator acts as the **discount rate**. Discounting is merely the inverse of growing.

2.1.2 Single-Sums over Multiple Periods of Time

The problem in the previous section involved only a single period of time, with the return or discount rate expressed as a simple rate per the amount of time in that period. For example, if everything in the earlier numerical example were the same except that the waiting period between the present cash and the future payment were 2 years instead of 1 year, then the formulas would still apply only we would have to interpret the 15 percent return as a simple biennial rather than annual return, that is, a return over 2 years instead of 1 year.

Now, suppose there is more than one period of time between the time of the *PV* amount and the time of the *FV* amount, yet we want to express the return per unit of time in each period. For example, suppose the future payment is promised in 2 years and we want to obtain 15 percent simple annual return *each* year. If you put, say, \$100 in a 1-year CD at 15 percent simple annual interest, you would have \$115 = (1.15 × \$100) after 1 year. If you took that \$115 and put it in another 15 percent CD again the second year, your \$115 would grow to \$132.25 = (1.15 × \$115) after the second year. In other words, \$100 growing at 15 percent simple annual interest compounded annually for 2 years is

$$(1.15)(1.15)100 = (1.15)^2\, 100 = 132.25$$

Note that this is more than the \$130 you would have if you simply took the original \$15 interest and multiplied it by two. This is because you earn interest on interest (or return on return) whenever the interest or return is compounded (that is, computed and credited to the principal in the account). This process is known as **compounding** or compound growth.

It is easy to see by extension of this reasoning that if we were dealing with 3 years instead of two, we would have

$$(1.15)(1.15)(1.15)100 = (1.15)^3\, 100 = 152.09$$

So, by inductive reasoning, we can see that the general formula for equating present and future value across multiple periods with compounding once per period is given by

$$PV = \frac{FV}{(1+r)^N} \tag{2a}$$

for discounting a future sum to present value and:

$$FV = (1+r)^N\, PV \tag{2b}$$

for compounding a present sum forward to its future equivalent, where *r* is the simple interest or discount rate (or expected return) *per period*, and *N* is the number of periods between the present and the future time when the future sum is to be received.

The previous formulas are the building blocks for classical present value and mortgage mathematics. In modern practice, these formulas are normally applied using a spreadsheet. For example, the right-hand side of (2a) would be keyed in a spreadsheet as $FV/(1 + r)^N$, where *FV*, *PV*, *r*, and *N* represent the cell addresses of the relevant future sum, present value, simple interest rate per period, and number of periods, respectively.

In case you need to solve for the compound growth rate or the length of time until the future value will be received, the previous formulas can be algebraically inverted to solve for r or N:

$$r = \left(\frac{FV}{PV}\right)^{1/N} - 1 \tag{2c}$$

$$N = \frac{\ln(FV) - \ln(PV)}{\ln(1+r)} \tag{2d}$$

where ln(·) refers to the natural logarithm.

2.1.3 Simple versus Compound Interest

From the discussion in the previous section, you can see that there is more than one way to define how the **interest rate** (or equivalently, the rate of return, or the discount rate) is measured per period when there is more than one period between the *PV* cash flow and the *FV* cash flow. For example, go back to the example in the previous section in which we started out with \$100 in the present and grew this to \$132.25 after 2 years. We saw how this growth could be expressed as a per annum (or annual) rate of 15 percent, using annual compounding, because $(1 + 0.15) \times (1 + 0.15) = 1.3225$. But it would also be possible to take the total return increment over the 2 years, the 32.25 percent, and simply divide this by two and express the return as 16.125 percent per annum. This latter definition is called simple interest, because it does not include the effect of compounding.

The important point to remember is that how we define the interest or return per period does not affect the actual dollars that we have at the two points in time. The definition is merely a matter of convention. Whether we call it 15 percent per year compounded annually, or 16.125 percent per year simple interest, it is still \$132.25 starting out from \$100 2 years earlier. You do have to be careful to understand the definition being used in a given context, and you must be consistent (e.g., don't compound simple interest in formulas to compute future sums).

2.1.4 Effective versus Nominal Rates

In the example in the previous section, the compound interest rate was computed assuming the interest was compounded once per year (annual compounding). But, in fact, interest may be compounded at any **frequency**. Often, interest is compounded more frequently than once per year. For example, suppose 7.5 percent semiannual interest were compounded over a year (i.e., twice). After 1 year, you would have (1.075)(1.075) = 1.155625 times whatever amount you started with. As you can see, 7.5 percent compounded semiannually would be equivalent to a little over 15.56 percent simple annual interest or interest compounded annually. Nevertheless, in terms of the conventions of measurement and quoting of interest rates, the 7.5 percent compounded semiannually would usually be referred to as 15 percent per annum interest, compounded semiannually. The term **effective annual rate** (or **EAR**) would be used to refer to the 15.5625 percent actual yield.

In real estate applications, cash flows often occur at monthly intervals. For example, rents and mortgage payments are usually scheduled at monthly intervals. As a result, monthly interest rates are often actually applied in calculations, but rates are quoted in what is called nominal per annum terms. Under the convention of quoting rates in nominal per annum terms, the simple per-period rate (which is the rate that is actually applied in calculations) is multiplied by the number of periods in a year for the purpose of quoting the rate in per annum terms. For example, a simple interest rate of 1 percent per month would typically be referred to as a 12 percent per annum rate (i.e., the nominal per annum rate), even though the effective rate or EAR is $(1.01)^{12} - 1 = 12.6825\%$. The EAR is defined as the actual annual yield corresponding to the nominal rate defined previously, given the simple per-period rate compounded at the end of each period. The relationship between effective and nominal rates is shown in the following formulas:

$$EAR = (1 + i/m)^m - 1 \tag{3a}$$

$$i = m\left[(1 + EAR)^{1/m} - 1\right] \tag{3b}$$

where i is the nominal annual rate, m is the number of compounding periods per year, and $i/m = r$ is the actual simple interest rate being applied per compounding period. In the previous example, we had $i = 12.00\%$, $EAR = 12.6825\%$, $r = 1.00\%$, and $m = 12$. The nominal annual rate i is sometimes referred to as the **equivalent nominal annual rate (ENAR)**.

As a result of this naming convention, when applying the present value and future value formula (2) described previously, one usually works in nominal terms by expanding the simple per-period interest rate compounded once per-period (r) and the number of basic periods of time (N) as follows, consistent with the earlier definitions:

$$r = i/m$$

$$N = m \times T$$

where i is the nominal annual rate of interest (e.g., 12 percent in the previous example), m is the number of compounding periods per year (e.g., 12 in the example of monthly compounding), and T is the length of time between when the PV and FV cash flows occur *measured in years*. Recast in nominal per annum terms (allowing for a compounding frequency different from yearly), the present value formulas for single sums become as follows:

$$PV = \frac{FV}{\left(1 + \frac{i}{m}\right)^{mT}} \tag{4a}$$

$$FV = PV\left(1 + \frac{i}{m}\right)^{mT} \tag{4b}$$

$$i = m\left[\left(\frac{FV}{PV}\right)^{1/(mT)} - 1\right] \tag{4c}$$

$$T = \frac{\ln(FV) - \ln(PV)}{m\ln(1 + i/m)} \tag{4d}$$

Spreadsheet financial formulas typically require as direct inputs the rate per period (r) and the number of periods (N). In order to work in nominal annual terms, the user must therefore have the spreadsheet calculate r and N from i, m, and T in other cells of the worksheet, and have these other cells serve as the inputs to the present value formulas.

2.1.5 Bond Equivalent and Mortgage Equivalent Rates

As noted, rent is usually collected monthly and mortgage payments are usually made monthly, so nominal rate (i, or the ENAR, using the earlier labels) based on the previous formulas with $m = 12$ is the most common way interest rates or yields are quoted in real estate. Nominal rates defined this way are sometimes referred to as **mortgage equivalent rates**.

Meanwhile, over on Wall Street, traditional corporate bonds and long-term government bonds are designed to pay interest semiannually, that is, twice per year.[3] In fact, classical bonds had coupons corresponding to each of the promised semiannual interest payments, which the bondholder would clip off and turn in at a bank to receive the payment in cash. Because of this, in the bond market, rates are typically quoted with $m = 2$ in formula (3). Nominal rates based on $m = 2$ are thus referred to as **bond equivalent** or **coupon equivalent rates.**

Thus, real estate rates and bond rates are quoted in different ways. This was fine as long as Wall Street and Main Street did not interact very directly. But nowadays, many mortgages are combined in pools and sold in the bond market, and bond market yields largely determine mortgage market yields. People dealing with mortgages need to be able to convert readily between mortgage equivalent and bond equivalent yields. This is done by *equating the effective annual rate (EAR)*. For example, we noted that a bond equivalent rate of 15 percent corresponds to an EAR of 15.5625 percent, found by plugging $i = 0.15$ and $m = 2$ into formula (3a). Now plug this 15.5625 percent EAR into formula (3b) with $m = 12$ to find that the mortgage equivalent rate of 14.551655 percent corresponds to the bond equivalent rate of 15 percent. Mortgage equivalent rates are lower than their corresponding bond equivalent rates because the increased frequency of compounding results in faster growth. If the mortgage equivalent rate were 15 percent, this would correspond to a bond equivalent rate of 15.4766 percent and an EAR of 16.07545 percent. (Plug $i = 0.15$ and $m = 12$ into formula (3a) to obtain the EAR, which you then plug into formula (3b) with $m = 2$.) As always, this type of operation is easily done using financial spreadsheets by changing the value in the "periods per year" input, without the need to memorize the formulas—see the questions at the end of this chapter.

2.1.6 Continuously Compounded Interest Rates

The extreme limit of frequent compounding of interest is **continuous compounding**. Many bank accounts, CDs, and other financial instruments employ continuous compounding, and many interest rates are quoted in continuously compounded terms. Continuous compounding is also mathematically convenient for many types of analyses, especially those involving advanced mathematics, and so is often used in sophisticated studies.[4] In continuous compounding, the interest is literally compounded every instant.

Computing continuously compounded interest rates and continuously compounded growth or discounting is easy using the natural logarithm and the base of natural logs (the latter is known by the mathematical symbol e, which stands for a value approximately equal to 2.7183, and is available as a special key on most business calculators and in all spreadsheet software). The continuously compounded equivalents corresponding to the various forms of formulas (2) or (4) are shown as formula (5), where T is the amount of time in years (including fractional parts of a year) between the

[3] The terms *semiannual* and *biannual* are equivalent, both referring to twice per year. The term *biennial* is different, referring to once every 2 years.

[4] Continuous compounding enables one to convert complex multiplicative expressions into simple additive expressions using natural logs. Additive expressions are much easier to work with mathematically. For example, if r_t is the simple rate of return in period t, then at the end of two periods, $FV = (1 + r_1)(1 + r_2)PV$, but if r_t is the continuously compounded rate of return in period t, then $\ln(FV) = \ln(PV) + r_1 + r_2$, where $\ln(\cdot)$ is the natural logarithm. The ending log value is simply the beginning natural logarithm value plus the sum of all the continuously compounded periodic returns.

PV and *FV* cash flows, and *k* is the *per annum* continuously compounded rate (of growth or discount, i.e., the continuously compounded interest rate).

$$PV = FV/e^{Tk} \tag{5a}$$

$$FV = PVe^{Tk} \tag{5b}$$

$$k = \frac{\ln(FV) - \ln(PV)}{T} \tag{5c}$$

$$T = \frac{\ln(FV) - \ln(PV)}{k} \tag{5d}$$

2.2 MULTIPERIOD PROBLEMS

The formulas described in Section 2.1 are the basic building blocks. They deal with only one future cash flow. Of course, real estate is a long-lived asset that typically produces cash flows for many periods, or indeed infinitely into the future. The present value of any stream of discrete cash flows can be computed using the previous formulas by simply computing the present value of each future sum and then adding all these present values together. For example, suppose \$10,000 will be received in 2 years and another \$12,000 will be received in 3 years. Suppose the interest rate applicable to the payment 2 years from now is 10 percent, and the rate applicable to the payment in 3 years is 11 percent (all compounded annually). Then, the present value of the future cash flow stream consisting of these two payments is \$17,038.76, computed using formula (2) as follows:

$$PV = \frac{\$10,000}{(1+0.10)^2} + \frac{\$12,000}{(1+0.11)^3} = \$8,264.46 + \$8,774.30 = \$17,038.76$$

Of course, such a procedure gets tedious when there are many future cash flows. This is one reason it is often useful in real estate investment analysis to be able to express the present value of a multiperiod future cash flow stream using a simplified formula. Another reason is that such simplified formulas may enable interesting relationships to become apparent. For example, they can reveal the basic nature of the relationship among the current yield or income return, the expected average future **growth rate** of the cash flows, and the discount rate or required expected total return on a long-lived commercial property with a regular pattern of cash flow generation.

Relatively simple formulas for present value relationships can usually be found if the future cash flow stream has a regular pattern. While the cash flow streams of real buildings will not usually be so regular, they can often be well approximated (or "modeled") by regular patterns that enable simple present value formulas to be computed. These simple multiperiod formulas are the subject of this section of this chapter.

2.2.1 Geometric Series Formula

In the real world, cash flow streams often all occur at equal intervals of time, and all change over time at a constant rate (even if that rate is zero). Such a regular stream of cash flow is known as an **annuity** if the stream has a finite life (a finite number of cash flows), or a **perpetuity** if the stream is infinite. Many important real estate cash flows are of this type (such as mortgages and leases). Other real estate cash flows can be reasonably approximated by annuities or perpetuities (e.g., the net cash flow from an apartment building may be modeled as a constant-growth perpetuity). So, these are very important.

In order to explain how to value annuities and perpetuities, we think it is best to begin with first principles: a mathematical formula known as the **geometric series formula**. If you understand the geometric series formula, you will have a greater depth of knowledge that will give you more flexibility to solve a wider range of real estate problems in the real world. For example, you will be able to develop a simple analytical formula for the value of a building that rents out its space in long-term leases, a typical and fundamental situation in commercial real estate. This will enable you to analyze such issues as the optimal lease term, or the trade-off between lease term and rent levels or the rent growth rate. So bear with us a moment as we delve into some classical mathematics. At first, this may seem complicated and abstract, but we will soon get to a very simple formula that you will be able to apply in a variety of practical real estate situations.

Suppose we have a sum consisting of N terms, each of which is exactly d times the value of the preceding term, and whose first term has the value a. Another term for d is the **common ratio**. Label the value of this sum S.

$$S = a + ad + ad^2 + \ldots + ad^{N-1}$$

Now multiply this sum by the common ratio, d:

$$Sd = ad + ad^2 + ad^3 + \ldots + ad^N$$

Now subtract Sd from S:

$$S = a + ad + ad^2 + \ldots + ad^{N-1}$$

$$-Sd = -ad - ad^2 - \ldots - ad^{N-1} - ad^N$$

The intermediate terms all cancel out in the subtraction, leaving:

$$\begin{aligned} S - Sd &= a - ad^N \\ &= (1-d)S = a(1-d^N) \end{aligned}$$

Thus,

$$S = a(1-d^N)/(1-d) \tag{6a}$$

Formula (6a) is the geometric series formula. It says that the sum of the series equals the first term times the quantity one minus the common ratio raised to the power of the number of terms, all divided by the quantity one minus the common ratio.

Now note that if $d < 1$, then $d^\infty = 0$, so if the series is infinite (as in a perpetuity), then the value of the sum simplifies to

$$S = a/(1-d) \tag{6b}$$

These simple formulas can be used to address a wide range of real estate problems. Some of the most important examples are discussed in the following sections.

2.2.2 Present Value of a Level Annuity in Arrears

Perhaps the most widely used application of the geometric series formula is to compute the present value of a **level annuity** in arrears, which is a series of equal payments made at the *end* of every period starting one period from the present. This type of cash flow stream defines the classical mortgage, with monthly payments. For example, a 30-year mortgage is a level annuity in arrears with $N = 360$.

To see how this problem is an example of the geometric formula, let's take a specific example. Suppose there are 240 payments left on a mortgage that has monthly payments of \$1,000 each. How much is the mortgage worth today if the opportunity cost of capital (discount rate) is 12 percent per year (actually, 1 percent per month) and the next payment on the mortgage is due 1 month from now?

We can set up this present value as the sum of a sequence of present values of single-sums, using formula (2a):

$$PV = \frac{\$1,000}{1.01} + \frac{\$1,000}{1.01^2} + \frac{\$1,000}{1.01^3} + \ldots + \frac{\$1,000}{1.01^{240}}$$

Here, the first term is $a = \$1,000/1.01$. The number of terms is $N = 240$. And the common ratio is $d = 1/1.01$, because each term is that factor times the previous. Now if we substitute these values of a, d, and N into the geometric formula (6a) we arrive at

$$PV = \frac{a(1-d^N)}{1-d} = \frac{(\$1{,}000/1.01)\left[1-(1/1.01)^{240}\right]}{1-(1/1.01)}$$

$$= \frac{\$1{,}000\left[1-(1/1.01)^{240}\right]}{0.01} = \$90{,}819$$

This famous case of the geometric formula is often written as

$$PV = PMT\frac{1-1/(1+r)^N}{r} \tag{7a}$$

or alternatively as

$$PV = PMT\left(\frac{1}{r} - \frac{1}{r}\frac{1}{(1+r)^N}\right)$$

where PMT is the level cash flow payment amount, and r is the effective simple interest rate *per payment period.*

The ratio of the present value of the annuity to the amount of each payment, PV/PMT, is often referred to as the "annuity factor," or the "present value interest factor for an annuity" (PVIFA).[5] As we can see from formula (7a), the annuity factor is a function only of the interest rate r and the number of payment periods N: $[1 - 1/(1 + r)^N]/r$. You multiply the periodic payment amount by this factor to arrive at the present value of the cash flow stream.

Keep in mind that the underlying formula that is equivalently expressed in (7a) is

$$PV = \frac{PMT}{1+r} + \frac{PMT}{(1+r)^2} + \frac{PMT}{(1+r)^3} + \ldots + \frac{PMT}{(1+r)^N} \tag{7}$$

---

[5] For constant-payment mortgages, this is also known as the mortgage constant, the ratio of the mortgage payment to the initial principal loan amount.

From this expansion, we can see that the annuity formula is an application of the geometric series formula, with $a = PMT/(1 + r)$ and $d = 1/(1 + r)$. We also see how formula (7) is built up as a series of applications of formula (2). It should be clear that an underlying assumption is that the simple effective interest rate per payment period (r) is being compounded at the end of every payment period. Thus, for example, if the payment period is monthly and $r = 1\%$, then the nominal interest rate would typically be quoted as 12 percent, and the effective annual rate would actually be 12.6825 percent, based on formula (3a).

Expressed in terms of the nominal annual rate, the annuity formula becomes

$$PV = PMT\frac{1-\left(\dfrac{1}{1+\dfrac{i}{m}}\right)^{Tm}}{\dfrac{i}{m}} \tag{7b}$$

where the variables are all defined as before.

2.2.3 Present Value of a Level Annuity in Advance

Sometimes the cash flows arrive at the *beginning* of each period, rather than at the end. This is particularly common for rent payments in long-term leases. For example, suppose a 20-year ground lease has a fixed net rent of \$1,000 per month paid at the beginning of the month. What is the value of this lease when it is signed if the opportunity cost of capital is 12 percent per year (1 percent per month)? We have

$$PV = \$1,000 + \frac{\$1,000}{1.01} + \frac{\$1,000}{1.01^2} + \ldots + \frac{\$1,000}{1.01^{239}}$$

This is the same as the previous problem only multiplied by 1.01. Here, the first term is $a = \$1,000$, but otherwise this problem is identical to the previous one (N is still 240, the number of terms on the right-hand side, or the total number of payments, and the common ratio, d, is still 1/1.01). So, the lease is worth

$$\begin{aligned} PV &= \frac{a\left(1-d^N\right)}{1-d} = \frac{(\$1,000)\left[1-(1/1.01)^{240}\right]}{1-(1/1.01)} \\ &= \left(\frac{1.01}{0.01}\right)\$1,000\left[1-(1/1.01)^{240}\right] = \$91,728 \end{aligned}$$

To convert formula (7a) to give present value with payments in advance, you simply multiply the right-hand side of (7a) by the factor $(1 + r)$, or equivalently by $(1 + i/m)$, to remove one period's discounting from the present value calculation. Thus, the annuity present value formula for payments in advance is given by formula (8a) (keeping in mind that $r = i/m$ and $N = mT$ in the usual convention).

$$PV = PMT\left(1+r\right)\frac{1-1/\left(1+r\right)^N}{r} \tag{8a}$$

The annuity formula is much more commonly used assuming payments in arrears than in advance. Spreadsheet software formulas typically provide an optional indicator to convert present value formulas to payments in advance, with the default being for payments in arrears.

2.2.4 Present Value of a Constant-Growth Annuity in Arrears

The annuities we have just considered were level payment annuities; that is, all their periodic cash flows were equal. Now let's relax that assumption by allowing all the periodic cash flows to grow (or shrink) at a constant rate. That is, each cash flow is the same multiple of the previous cash flow. The present value of such a stream of cash flow will also be an application of the geometric series formula. For example, consider a 10-year lease providing for annual payments at the end of each year. The initial rent is \$20/SF, but that rent will grow at a rate of 2 percent per year each year thereafter. What is the present value of the lease, per SF, assuming an opportunity cost of capital of 10 percent per year?

To solve this problem, first set up the underlying present value problem as a series of formula (2) type single-sums:

$$PV = \frac{\$20}{1.10} + \frac{(1.02)\$20}{1.10^2} + \frac{(1.02)^2\,\$20}{1.10^3} + \ldots + \frac{(1.02)^9\,\$20}{1.10^{10}}$$

This allows us to see that the first term is a = \$20/1.10, the number of terms on the right-hand side (number of periodic payments) is $N = 10$, and the common ratio is $d = (1.02/1.10)$. Plug these values into formula (6a) to get

$$PV = \frac{a\left(1-d^N\right)}{1-d} = \frac{(\$20/1.10)\left[1-(1.02/1.10)^{10}\right]}{1-(1.02/1.10)}$$
$$= \$20\frac{1-(1.02/1.10)^{10}}{0.10-0.02} = \$132.51$$

So, the lease is worth \$132.51/SF.

This case of the geometric formula is referred to as the **constant-growth annuity**, and is often written as

$$PV = CF_1\frac{1-\left[(1+g)/(1+r)\right]^N}{r-g} \qquad (9)$$

where CF_1 is the value of the *initial* cash flow (periodic payment), g is the growth rate *per period* in the cash flows, and r is as always the discount rate per payment period. Note that in the special case where $g = 0$, the constant-growth annuity formula collapses to the level payment annuity formula, as it should.

2.2.5 Present Value of a Constant-Growth Perpetuity

Now consider an infinite sequence of cash flows, a perpetuity in which each periodic payment is a constant ratio times the previous payment. For example, suppose an apartment building has 100 identical units that rent at \$1,000 per month with building operating expenses paid by the landlord equal to \$500 per month. On average, there is a 5 percent vacancy. You expect both rents and operating expenses to grow at a rate of 3 percent per year (actually, 0.25 percent per month). The opportunity cost of capital is 12 percent per year (actually, 1 percent per month). How much is the property worth?

Once again, to solve this problem we first set it up as a fundamental series of single-sums based on formula (2). The initial monthly net cash flow is 500 × 100 × 0.95 = \$47,500. Thus, the underlying present value problem is

$$PV = \frac{\$47,500}{1.01} + \frac{(1.0025)\$47,500}{1.01^2} + \frac{(1.0025)^2\,\$47,500}{1.01^3} + \ldots$$

This allows us to see clearly that the first term is $a = 47,500/1.01$ and the common ratio is $d = 1.0025/1.01$. As this is a perpetuity, we apply the simpler version of the geometric formula (6b) instead of (6a), so we have

$$PV = \frac{a}{1-d} = \frac{\$47,500/1.01}{1-(1.0025/1.01)} = \frac{\$47,500}{0.01-0.0025} = \$6,333,333$$

The building is worth \$6,333,333.

This case of the geometric formula is written in general notation as

$$PV = \frac{CF_1}{r-g} \tag{10}$$

with the variables defined as before, and it is referred to as the **constant-growth perpetuity** formula.

2.2.6 Some Basic Economic Implications of the Perpetuity Formula

The constant-growth perpetuity formula is often taught in introductory finance as a famous and simple way to compute the fundamental value of a share in a company's common stock. The formula is referred to as the *Gordon Growth Model*, in which CF_1 is the current annual dividend payment per share, g is the expected long-term average annual growth rate in the company's dividends (presumably the growth rate in the company's earnings per share), and r is the stock market's required expected annual total return from investing in the stock (including consideration of how risky the stock is). For example, if a company currently pays \$1 per share in quarterly dividends (\$4/year), has a track record of providing consistent long-term average growth in dividends of 5 percent per year, and the market requires an average annual total return (including both dividends and capital gain) of 12 percent, then the stock should be worth \$4/(0.12 – 0.05) = \$4/0.07 = \$57.14 per share.

In general, the constant-growth perpetuity model represents a basic way to understand the value of any infinitely lived income-producing asset, as a relationship among the current level of net cash flow produced by the asset, the likely long-term average rate of growth in that cash flow, and the expected annual total return required by investors in the asset. As such, this model is broadly applicable to commercial property and provides a basic understanding of the cap rate, defined as the current annual income divided by the value of the property. For example, the constant-growth perpetuity model reveals that the apartment building described earlier would have a cap rate of 9 percent (12%–3%) (this is $r - g$ on a per annum basis). In other words, the apartment would sell for a price approximately 11 times its annual net income (that is, 1/0.09). In fact, the building's annual net income is \$570,000 (\$47,500 × 12). Dividing this by the \$6,333,333 estimated value implies the cap rate of 9 percent. Thus, the perpetuity model reveals that the cap rate for a building like this equals investors' expected total return minus their expected annual long-term growth rate in the building's net income.

*2.2.7 Introducing Long-Term Leases

While some types of commercial real estate, such as apartment buildings or flexible office spaces, do not make much use of long-term leases, many types of commercial property use leases that last several years or more. For example, leases in office or warehouse buildings are often 3 to 10 years long, traditionally. Within each lease, once the lease is signed, the cash flows specified in the lease have relatively low risk because the tenant is contractually obligated to make the lease payments—from the perspective of the risk of the rental cash flows, once the lease is signed, it is much like a loan to the tenant, or a bond issued by the tenant. On the other hand, prior to the signing of any given lease, the cash flows that the building can earn under such future leases are less certain, which makes them more risky, for it is not known exactly what rent a landlord will be able to charge. Furthermore, within each lease the growth rate in the rent will often be known for certain, while between leases the growth rate will depend on conditions in the rental market.

Thus, to model the cash flows of a building subject to long-term leases, we need to consider two different growth rates and two different discount rates. One set of rates applies *within* leases (the **intralease rates**), and the other set of rates applies *across* leases (the **interlease rates**). At first glance, this would seem to complicate the present value calculation greatly. However, the geometric series formula enables us to obtain a relatively simple formula for the present value of such a building. The present value calculation is broken down into two steps. Each lease is a constant-growth annuity whose present value as of the time of lease signing can be determined using formula (6a), and the building as a whole is a constant-growth perpetuity whose value can be determined using formula (6b). In effect, the building is a "perpetuity of successive annuities."

Consider the following example: A space will be leased out in 10-year leases successively in perpetuity. The leases have annual rent payments at the beginning of the years. Each lease will be for a constant rent once that lease is signed, but new leases will be signed at rent levels reflecting annual growth in market rent. This growth is expected to be 1 percent per year, but this is an uncertain, risky growth expectation. So the expected rent in each successive lease will be 1.01^{10} times the previous lease's rent, although this is not guaranteed. Once a lease is signed, the opportunity cost of capital for computing the PV of that lease as of the time of its signing is 6 percent per year, reflecting the relatively low risk of the contractually fixed rental payments. However, between leases or prior to lease signings, the opportunity cost of capital is 11 percent per year, reflecting the greater risk associated with not knowing for certain what the future market rent will be. The initial lease is expected to be signed (and first rent received) 1 year from now, with an annual rent of $10/SF. What is the value of this property per SF?

In the first step of solving this problem, we compute the present value of the first lease when it is signed, as a level annuity in advance. We have $a = 10$, $N = 10$, $d = (1/1.06)$:

$$PV(\text{Lease 1}) = \frac{a(1-d^N)}{1-d} = \frac{\$10(1-1/1.06^{10})}{1-1/1.06}$$
$$= \$10\left(\frac{1.06}{0.06}\right)(1-1/1.06^{10}) = \$78.02/\text{SF}$$

The present value of this first lease as of today is this expected value at signing (1 year from now) computed above, divided by 1.11 (because this is a risky value—we do not know for sure the lease will be signed with a rent of $10/SF). Thus, the present value of the first lease as of today is $78.02/1.11 = $70.29/SF. This is the value of the first term in the perpetuity of successive annuities that represents the present value of the property as a whole. Thus, this is the value of *a* in the perpetuity formula (6b) for calculating the building's value.

In the second step of solving this problem, we need to identify the common ratio, d, to apply in the perpetuity problem. In this case, $d = (1.01/1.11)^{10}$, because there are 10 years (the lease term) between each expected lease signing, and we expect market rents to grow at a rate of 1 percent per year in this rental market. In other words, if we let PVL_j represent the value of the jth lease at the time of its signing, then the perpetuity that represents the building value is given by the following infinite series of single-sums:

$$PV(building) = \frac{PVL_1}{1.11} + \frac{(1.01)^{10}\, PVL_2}{1.11^{11}} + \frac{(1.01)^{20}\, PVL_2}{1.11^{21}} + \ldots$$

Note that the larger interlease discount rate of 11 percent is used here because we are discounting *across leases*, that is, across time prior to the signings of the future leases we are evaluating—this is in contrast to the computation of the values, at signings, of each lease, in which the smaller intralease discount rate is applied in the annuity formula. Thus, the value of the property is

$$PV(building) = \frac{a}{1-d} = \frac{PVL_1/1.11}{1-(1.01/1.11)^{10}} = \frac{\$70.29}{1-(1.01/1.11)^{10}} = \$115.05/\text{SF}$$

So, the building is worth \$115.05/SF.

Note that this is a substantially different value than if we employed the simple constant-growth perpetuity formula to the initial \$10/SF rent level as if there were no long-term leases: $PV = CF_1/(r - g) = \$10/(0.11 - 0.01) = \$10/0.10 = \$100/\text{SF}$.

The use of long-term leases, while delaying the growth in cash flow to only once every 10 years, reduces the risk of the cash flows sufficiently in this case so that the present value of the space is substantially greater than it would be if only short-term leases were employed. The ability to apply the underlying geometric series formula flexibly *as* in this problem, enables one to analyze questions involving long-term leases, such as the trade-off between lease term, rental level, and building value.

TEXT BOX 2.1 SUMMARIZING THE PRESENT VALUE OF GEOMETRIC CASH FLOW STREAMS

All of the previous problems have really only used a single underlying formula, the geometric series formula (6). The general procedure has been to set up the underlying present value problem as a sequence of single-sums, so that it is clear what is the first term on the right-hand side of the equation (the value a), what is the common ratio between those terms (d), and what is the number of terms (N). In complex problems, such as when more than one long-term lease is involved, this procedure should be applied in more than one step, building up the overall present value problem. The following list summarizes the application of formula (6) to the basic simple cases:

- For the level perpetuity or annuity, $d = 1/(1 + r)$ where r = interest rate per period.
- For constant-growth perpetuity or annuity, $d = (1 + g)/(1 + r)$.
- For cash flows in arrears (at the end of periods), $a = CF_1/(1 + r)$.
- For cash flow in advance (at beginning of periods), $a = CF_1$.
- For annuities, N = number of periods.
- For perpetuities, N = infinity and d must be <1 (so, $d^N = 0$).

2.2.8 How to Convert Annuities to Future Values

All of the previous examples were present value problems in which we were converting a future cash flow stream to present value. In some cases, it is useful to do the reverse: convert a stream of cash flows into a future value as of a terminal point in time, by growing the cash flows to the terminal point. In fact, this can still be done using the same geometric formula. For example, consider the future value of an annuity of \$100/month in arrears (paid at the ends of the months) for 12 months at 12 percent per annum (compounded monthly, actually 1 percent per month). As always, the first step is to set the problem up as a sequence of single-sums based on formula (2), in this case formula (2b). Here we have

$$FV = \$100(1.01)^{11} + \$100(1.01)^{10} + \ldots + \$100$$

So the first term is $a = 100\ (1.01)^{11}$, the number of terms is $n = 12$, and the common ratio is $d = 1/1.01$. Thus,

$$FV = \frac{\$100(1.01)^{11}\left[1-(1/1.01)^{12}\right]}{1-(1/1.01)} = \$1,268.25$$

In general, the future value problem simply represents $(1+r)^N$ times the present value problem. For example, if the following gives the present value:

$$PV = \frac{CF_1}{1+r} + \frac{CF_2}{(1+r)^2} + \ldots + \frac{CF_N}{(1+r)^N}$$

then multiplying both sides of the equation by $(1+r)^N$ will give the future value as in formula (11):

$$\begin{aligned}(1+r)^N PV &= (1+r)^N \frac{CF_1}{1+r} + (1+r)^N \frac{CF_2}{(1+r)^2} + \ldots + (1+r)^N \frac{CF_N}{(1+r)^N} \\ &= CF_1(1+r)^{N-1} + CF_2(1+r)^{N-2} + \ldots + CF_N = FV\end{aligned} \quad (11)$$

2.2.9 Solving for the Cash Flows

If the present value can be expressed as a function of a single periodic payment amount, such as the level payment in an annuity or the initial cash flow in a growth annuity or perpetuity, then it is straightforward to invert the present value formula to solve it for the cash flow. For example, the following formula inverting (7a) tells the level payment amount (*PMT*) that is required to produce a given present value, given the number of payments and the interest rate:

$$PMT = PV\frac{r}{1-1/(1+r)^N} \quad (7c)$$

For example, a borrower wants a 30-year, monthly-payment, fixed-interest mortgage for \$80,000. As a lender, you want to earn a return of 1 percent per month, compounded monthly. You agree to provide the \$80,000 up front (i.e., at present), in return for the commitment by the borrower to make 360 equal monthly payments in the amount of \$822.89 each, starting with the first payment due in 1 month. The required monthly payment of \$822.89 is found as

$$\$822.89 = \$80,000\frac{0.01}{1-1/(1.01)^{360}}$$

2.2.10 Solving for the Number of Payments

Similarly, it is possible to invert the previous formulas to find the number of payments or length of time required for a given cash flow stream to produce a given present value. For example, to find the number of specified level payments required to pay off a given amount at a given interest rate, formula (7) can be solved for *Tm*:

$$Tm = -\frac{\ln\left(1-\frac{i}{m}\frac{PV}{PMT}\right)}{\ln\left(1+\frac{i}{m}\right)} \tag{7d}$$

where ln(·) is the natural logarithm. In the case of the growth annuity, formula (9) is solved for *N*:

$$N = \frac{\ln\left(1-\frac{PV}{CF_1}(r-g)\right)}{\ln\left(\frac{1+g}{1+r}\right)} \tag{9a}$$

2.2.11 Combining the Single Lump Sum and the Level Annuity Stream: Classical Mortgage Mathematics

The typical calculations associated with classical mortgage mathematics can be solved using one or the other or a combination of the single-sum formulas described in Section 2.1 and the annuity formulas just described. This is because the classical mortgage is constructed as an annuity with the contractual principal as the *PV* amount.[6] To calculate the monthly payments on a loan of a given amount, you simply apply the annuity formula solved for the payment as in (7c). To calculate how much you can borrow given a specified level of monthly payments for a specified number of years, you apply the present value annuity formula (7a). To calculate the remaining outstanding loan balance (*OLB*) at any point in time (i.e., after a given number of payments), the annuity formula also applies. The *OLB* equals the present value of the remaining loan payments discounted at the loan's contractual interest rate, so you apply the annuity formula (7a) to determine the *PV* with *N* equal to the number of payments not yet made. The *PV* amount so determined equals the *OLB* on the loan. In other words, after *q* payments have been made on a loan that has a monthly payment amount of *PMT* and originally was for *T* years at a rate of *i*, the *OLB* is given by

$$OLB = PMT\frac{1-\left(\frac{1}{1+\frac{i}{m}}\right)^{(Tm-q)}}{\frac{i}{m}} \tag{7e}$$

[6] Note that the contractual principal of a loan is not necessarily exactly equal to the amount of cash the borrower will receive from the lender at the time the loan is disbursed. This is due to the possible presence of discount points of prepaid interest or loan application fees and other expenses that may be taken out of the loan disbursement. Nevertheless, the borrower's debt obligation at the time the loan is taken out equals the entire contractual principal amount.

For example, the \$80,000, 12 percent, 30-year mortgage we noted earlier with the monthly payments of \$822.89 would have an outstanding loan balance after 10 years of payments equal to \$74,734.39, based on the following calculation:

$$\$74{,}734.39 = \$822.89\frac{1-1/(1.01)^{240}}{0.01}$$

The classical mortgage is "fully amortizing," meaning that the regular monthly payments completely and exactly pay off the entire contractual principal over the course of the maturity of the loan. But many loans are not fully amortizing. They may amortize, for example, at a 30-year rate but have a maturity of only 10 years, which means that the outstanding loan balance is due after 10 years. An extreme version of this would be a loan that does not amortize at all, also known as an interest-only loan. Interest-only loans are common, particularly among commercial mortgages.

In the case of partially amortizing or non-amortizing loans, the cash flow stream from the mortgage consists of the combination (or sum) of an annuity plus a single lump sum payment at the end. The annuity portion consists of the interest plus any partial amortization, while the single sum at the end consists of the remaining principal at the time of maturity of the loan. In the case of an interest-only loan, the annuity is purely interest (each payment equaling the per-period simple interest rate times the contractual principal), while the single-sum liquidating payment at the end equals the entire contractual principal amount.

Using our previous labels and formulas (i.e., *FV* represents the single-sum amount and *PMT* represents the regular periodic payment amount), a wide variety of mortgages can be represented by the following formula:

$$PV = \left(\frac{PMT}{(1+r)} + \frac{PMT}{(1+r)^2} + \ldots + \frac{PMT}{(1+r)^N}\right) + \frac{FV}{(1+r)^N} \quad (12)$$

where, as always, $r = i/m$, the simple per-period interest rate, and $N = Tm$, the total number of periods in the maturity of the loan. In formula (12), the first part on the right-hand side in the parentheses is the annuity part, and the last term on the right is the single sum. For example, a 12 percent interest-only loan for \$80,000 would have $PMT = \$800$ and $FV = \$80{,}000$, which would give $PV = \$80{,}000$ at the 12 percent nominal annual rate ($r = 12\%/12 = 1\%$), for any loan term (any value of N).

2.3 CHAPTER SUMMARY

This chapter has presented the major formulas and procedures that are most useful for the calculation and analysis of the present value of the types of cash flow streams most commonly found in commercial real estate. Included in this are the important inverses of the present value formulas, that is, formulas for calculating implied returns, terminal values, and the time (or number of payments) until a certain present or future value is achieved. We have focused on the formal mechanics of the basic formulas, leaving the economic reasoning and analysis necessary for the correct application of these formulas largely to be covered in later chapters.

KEY TERMS

- Single-sum formulas
- Present value

- Future value
- Discounting
- Growing
- Discount rate
- Interest rate
- Compounding
- Growth rate
- Compounding frequency
- Effective annual rate (EAR)
- Equivalent nominal annual rate (ENAR)
- Mortgage equivalent rate
- Bond equivalent (coupon equivalent) rate
- Continuous compounding
- Annuity
- Perpetuity
- Geometric series formula
- Common ratio
- Level annuity
- Constant-growth annuity
- Constant-growth perpetuity
- Interlease rate
- Intralease rate
- Internal rate of return (IRR)

STUDY QUESTIONS

In Your Own Words

2.1 How does the choice between simple and compound interest affect the present value of a future cash flow?

2.2 What is the significance of the effective annual rate (EAR) when comparing investments or loans with different compounding frequencies?

2.3 Why is the Gordon Growth Model, used in stock valuation, similar to the constant-growth perpetuity formula used in real estate?

2.4 What is the difference between a level annuity in arrears and a level annuity in advance, and how does it affect their present values?

2.5 Given that all other factors are the same, how should you set up your financial calculator to correctly calculate the present value for a level annuity in advance?

Check Your Knowledge

2.6 What is the present value of an offer of $15,000 1 year from now if the opportunity cost of capital (discount rate) is 12% per year using simple interest?

A) $13,393
B) $13,500
C) $16,392
D) $16,800

2.7 What is the future value of $25,000 that grows at an annual interest rate of 11% per year for 2 years?
A) $27,750
B) $22,523
C) $ 30,803
D) $ 20,291

2.8 You are considering two real estate offers, which offer has the higher present value?
Offer A: A payment of $15,000 in 2 years, with a 12% annual discount rate, compounded annually.
Offer B: A payment of $14,000 in 2 years, with an 11% annual discount rate, compounded annually.
A) Offer A (12% discount rate, $15,000)
B) Offer B (11% discount rate, $14,000)
C) Both have the same present value
D) Cannot be determined without more information

2.9 What is the future value of $20,000 that grows at a nominal annual interest rate of 12% per year, compounded monthly, for 2 years?

2.10 What is the corresponding effective annual rate (EAR) of an 8% nominal annual interest rate compounded semiannually, monthly, and continuously? Based on your answers, discuss how the compounding frequency affects the EAR.

2.11 If the bond equivalent rate is 10%, what is the corresponding mortgage equivalent rate? Conversely, if the mortgage equivalent rate is 10%, what is the corresponding bond equivalent rate? Explain how these rates are related.

2.12 You invested $15,000 in a lake property and received a cash flow of $30,000 after 5 years. Calculate the following:
a. What annual interest rate, compounded annually, was earned on the investment?
b. What nominal annual rate, compounded monthly, was earned on the investment?
c. What continuously compounded rate was earned on the investment?

2.13 You are borrowing $80,000 for 25 years at 10% nominal annual interest compounded monthly. How much must your monthly payments be if you will completely pay off the loan over the 25-year period (i.e., what is the level payment annuity with a present value of $80,000)?

2.14 A tenant offers to sign a lease paying a rent of $2,500 per month, in advance (i.e., the rent will be paid at the beginning of each month), for seven years. At 9% nominal annual interest compounded monthly, what is the present value of this lease?

2.15 A building is expected to require $1 million in capital improvement expenditures in five years. The building's net operating cash flow prior to that time is expected to be at least $20,000 at the end of every month. How much of that monthly cash flow must the owners set aside each month in order to have the money available for the capital improvements, assuming the equal monthly contributions placed in this "sinking fund" will earn interest at a nominal annual rate of 6%, compounded monthly?

2.16 A landlord has offered a tenant a 10-year lease with annual net rental payments of $30/SF in arrears. The appropriate discount rate is 8%. The tenant has asked the landlord to come back with another proposal, similar in every way except with rent that steps up annually at a rate of 3% per year, in return for a lower starting rent. What should the landlord's proposed starting rent be?

2.17 An apartment building can be well represented as producing net rent of $10/SF annually in arrears, with expected annual growth over the long run of negative 1% per year (that is, a decline of 1% per year). Use the constant-growth perpetuity formula to estimate the apartment building's value (per SF) if the required annual expected total return from the investment is 10%.

2.18 A 100,000-SF space is expected to rent in five-year fixed-rent leases successively in perpetuity (annual payments at the beginning of the years). You expect the first lease will be signed one year from now, with the first rent payment to be received at that time. The second lease will begin five years after that, the third five years later, and so on. The rent in each lease is constant, but between new lease signings the rent is expected to grow at a rate of 2% per year. The rent on the first lease is expected to be $20/SF per year. To compute the present value of each lease as of the time of its signing, use a low discount rate of 8% per year, reflecting the fact that the cash flows under the lease are contractually fixed. However, prior to the signing of each lease, the amount of the rent for that lease is uncertain and risky, so a 12% rate is appropriate for discounting lease values back to present value prior to lease signings. Use the level annuity formula embedded in a constant-growth perpetuity formula to compute the present value of this 100,000-SF space. (Hint: Recall the $S = a\,(1 - d^n)/(1 - d)$ geometric sum formula. This is a level annuity in advance embedded in a constant-growth perpetuity.)

Chapter Case: Anna's Real Estate Investment Strategy Using Present Value Mathematics

Anna, a young and promising real estate analyst, recently started her studies in a prestigious real estate program. With her newfound knowledge in present value mathematics, she is eager to apply these concepts to her own real estate investment plans.

Her goal is to double her current investment of $200,000 and determine how long it will take to reach $400,000 with a 10% annual interest rate under different compounding scenarios. She first considers annual compounding to see how long it will take to double her investment, then evaluates how more frequent compounding impacts her investment's growth.

1. How many years will it take for $200,000 to double to $400,000 at 10% interest compounded annually?
   A) 5.5 years
   B) 6.93 years
   C) 7.27 years
   D) 8 years
2. If the nominal annual interest rate is 10% and is compounded monthly, what is the effective monthly interest rate?
   A) 0.83%
   B) 0.75%
   C) 1%
   D) 10%
3. How many years will it take for $200,000 to double to $400,000 at 10% nominal interest compounded monthly?
   A) 6.93 years
   B) 6.96 years
   C) 7.27 years
   D) 7.5 years
4. How many years will it take for $200,000 to double at 10% interest compounded continuously?
   A) 6.93 years
   B) 7.27 years
   C) 7 years
   D) 8 years

5. Which compounding method results in the fastest growth for Anna's investment?
   A) Annual compounding
   B) Monthly compounding
   C) Quarterly compounding
   D) Continuous compounding
6. If Anna increases her initial investment to $400,000, how will this affect the time required for her investment to double ($800,000) under any compounding scenario?
   A) The time to double increases
   B) The time to double decreases
   C) The time to double remains the same
   D) The time to double depends on the compounding method
7. What is the primary benefit of compounding more frequently, such as monthly or continuously, compared to annually?
   A) It increases the nominal principal
   B) It increases the overall growth rate by applying interest more often
   C) It decreases the investment period
   D) It lowers the interest rate
8. What happens to the time required to double an investment if the interest rate is increased from 10% to 12%?
   A) The time increases
   B) The time decreases
   C) The time stays the same
   D) It depends on the amount of the investment
9. What is the future value of Anna's $200,000 investment after 10 years if it grows at an annual rate of 10% compounded annually?
   A) $541,482
   B) $487,500
   C) $537,012
   D) $518,748

3 Measuring Investment Performance

The Concept of Returns

CHAPTER OUTLINE

LEARNING OBJECTIVES

After reading this chapter, you should understand:

- What do we mean by investment returns, and how do we quantify both period-by-period total returns and IRRs?
- The two major components of the total return and why they are important.
- The characteristic features of the main types of returns and when it is best to use each type.
- What is meant by risk in investment, how to quantify risk, and how it relates to returns.
- How to account for inflation in return measures.

Now that you are equipped with some basic background information and tools from the two preceding chapters, you are ready to begin mastering the basic building blocks of real estate investment analysis, beginning in this chapter with a consideration of how return and risk are measured. Of course, the problem of measuring investment performance is common to all types of investment, not just real estate, so much of what we will cover in this chapter is identical to what you will find in any introductory corporate finance or investments textbook. Here, we will make sure the application of these concepts to real estate is made clear, and we will cover some considerations and conventions that apply uniquely or particularly to real estate investment analysis.

DOI: 10.1201/9781003643838-4

3.1 INVESTMENT RETURNS: BASIC DEFINITIONS AND CLASSIFICATION

Recall from Chapter 1 that underlying the variety of investors and investment goals are two fundamental objectives: income and growth (or savings). We also noted several typical constraints and concerns investors have, including, most prominently, the question of *risk* in the investment. What we want to do now is to build on these concepts to define a way to *quantify investment performance:* How well is the investment doing for the investor? To this end, the concept of investment **returns** is very useful. Returns are the measure of investment performance, both at the micro-level of individual properties and at the macro-level within the context of an overall investment strategy (the big picture of real estate as an asset class among others in the capital markets). Indeed, we will see how this concept may be defined and measured in a way that enables us to quantify not only the overall average investment performance over time but also the amount of risk in the investment.

Return is how we measure profit in an investment endeavor. In essence, the return on investment is *what you get minus what you started out with, expressed as a percentage of what you started out with.* For example, if you invest $100 and end up with $110 a year later, you have made a 10 percent return. If you end up with only your original $100, you have a zero percent return; if you end up with only $95, you have a return of negative 5 percent.

Investors typically quantify return measures by looking backward or forward in time.

1. Looking backward in time, **ex-post** (i.e., realized, historical) returns are used to measure past performance, which is useful
   - to estimate future performance (to the extent the future can be predicted from the past);
   - to judge the past performance of investment advisors or managers, and/or;
   - to understand the current investment environment and "mood," as it is a product of recent past experience.
2. Looking forward in time, **ex-ante** (i.e., expected) returns are used to quantitatively express future performance expectations, which are directly relevant for making investment decisions in the present, for these decisions will have their wealth impact for the investor as a result of what transpires in the future.

3.1.1 Two Fundamental Types of Return Measures

It is useful to distinguish two major types of return measures: **period-by-period** (or **periodic**) **returns** and **multiperiod returns**. We will consider each of these in turn.

Periodic returns are usually quantified as simple **holding period returns (HPR)**. They measure what the investment grows to *within* every single period of time, assuming that all cash flow (or asset valuation) occurs only at the *beginning* and *end* of the period of time (i.e., no intermediate cash flows). Periodic returns are measured separately over each of a sequence of regular and consecutive (relatively short) periods of time (typically daily, monthly, quarterly, or annually). For example, in 2008, the return on the S&P 500 index of stocks was a most disappointing negative 37 percent, but in 2009, it bounced back nicely with a very pleasing 26.5 percent return, followed by a 15.1 percent return in 2010. Periodic returns can be averaged across time to determine the **time-weighted return (TWR)**, so called because a given rate of return that is earned over more periods or during a larger fraction of the overall time interval will figure more strongly in the overall average return.

The second general type of return measure, the multiperiod return, gives a single inherently multiperiod return number for a relatively long-term period of time during which there can be cash flows into or out of the investment at intermediate points in time. The **internal rate of return (IRR)** is the most widely used multiperiod return measure. Unlike period-by-period returns, the IRR can be computed without knowing the capital value of the investment at intermediate points in time. This makes the IRR more convenient to compute for real estate investments that are not regularly and frequently reappraised (or "marked to market"). Although the multiperiod IRR usually covers more than 1 year, it is generally quoted as a per annum (i.e., per-year) rate. For example, we might determine that a certain investor earned a 12 percent return per year over the 3 years from the beginning of 2011 through the end of 2013. The IRR is a **money-weighted** (or dollar-weighted) **return** because it reflects the effect of having different amounts of money invested or returned at different periods of time during the overall lifetime of the investment.

3.1.2 Advantages and Disadvantages of Periodic and Multiperiod Return Measures

Modern real estate investment analysis widely uses both period-by-period and multiperiod return measures. Each type of return measure has several advantages and disadvantages, or strengths and weaknesses, for different applications.

In real estate, period-by-period returns are more relevant at the macro-level and in examining portfolios of investments. Periodic returns allow real estate investment performance to be quantified using the same type of metric that is used for the main components of most institutional portfolios, stocks, and bonds. Investment classes that do not have good measures of their periodic returns are traditionally considered marginal or "noncore" components of such portfolios. Periodic returns also facilitate the measurement of the risk in investment performance by quantifying the variability of returns over time (asset "volatility"). For macro-level and portfolio analysis, real estate performance must be compared with other types of assets over the same interval of time, both regarding risk and return, and it is important to observe the **co-movement** of returns for different assets. That is, we need to know how different asset classes tend to move either together or differently over time. Periodic returns allow this type of analysis to be done. Similarly, periodic returns are particularly useful for tracing asset markets' historical ups and downs, identifying turning points, and discerning time trends in the markets.

Period-by-period returns are also more appropriate for evaluating or comparing the performance of investment managers without control over the timing of capital flows into or out of their investments. This is because periodic returns and the time-weighted averages computed from them are insensitive to the timing of capital flows into or out of the investments whose returns are being measured. (This is not true of money-weighted returns.) Many investment managers or institutions lack control over capital flow timing. For example, a pension fund must invest all the money that flows into it from active employee member contributions each year, even if that comes in at unexpectedly high rates, which can create problems and delays in deploying the capital. Pensions must also draw out sufficient money each year to pay the pension benefit liabilities they face for retired members, and an unexpected increase in the number of retirees may affect investment timing decisions that affect return performance. These are functions of demographics and employment policies of the pension plan sponsor and are not under the control of the investment manager.

On the other hand, the IRR is the classical measure of investment return at the micro-level for individual properties and development projects. For this purpose, the IRR has two great advantages. First, it does not require knowledge of the market values of the investment asset at intermediate points in time. (This contrasts with the periodic return, which cannot be computed without such intermediate asset value knowledge.) In real estate, the typical investment is held for several years, and we typically do not know the exact capital value of the investment asset except at the beginning and end of the investment holding period when the property is bought and sold. However, we do know the cash flows generated by the asset each period, which is what we need to compute the IRR. In such circumstances, a money-weighted multiperiod return such as the IRR may be the only type of total return that can be quantified.

The other advantage of the IRR is just the opposite of that of the TWR regarding the effect of the timing of capital flow. Just as there are times when one does not want the return measure to be influenced by the timing of capital flow into or out of the investment, there are times when one wants precisely this. In particular, a money-weighted, purely internal return measure such as the IRR will give a fairer and more complete picture of the performance of an investment manager who *does* have responsibility and control over the timing and amounts of cash flow into and out of the investment vehicle.

In the remainder of this chapter, we will develop your understanding of each of these two types of return measures in greater depth, with particular emphasis on real estate investment applications.

3.2 PERIODIC RETURNS

In traditional real estate investment analysis, and even today, for most individuals and partnerships that invest in commercial properties, periodic returns are seldom computed. Yet modern real estate investment at the institutional level could not function without the widespread use of periodic returns. These types of returns are the bread and butter of the world of Wall Street. The ability to compute real estate periodic returns is fundamental to linking Wall Street and Main Street, a seminal development of the last decades of the twentieth century in the real estate investment industry. Periodic returns for real estate are necessary to elevate real estate to the status of an investment asset class that can compete in the multi-asset institutional portfolio alongside the classical investment classes of stocks and bonds, asset classes for which a wealth of periodic return data exist.

There is another reason for learning how to relate the periodic return measure to real estate in some depth, even at the micro-level. Because of the simplicity of its definition and construction, the simple HPR is a powerful conceptual tool and an elegant pedagogical device. It can be very useful for understanding the nature of real estate investment performance. For all these reasons, in this section, we will formally present the periodic return measure and, in some depth, relate its computation to a basic definition of investment risk.

3.2.1 Formal Definition of the Periodic Return

It is time to introduce the most widely used quantifiable definition of the period-by-period return, the simple holding period return, and describe how this return measure may be broken out into various components that are separately important to investors.

The most basic and **complete** measure of periodic return is called the **total return** because it includes both the change in the asset's capital value during the period and any income paid out by the asset to the investor during the period. We will use the symbol r_t to refer to the total return during period t. (The periods most commonly used for real estate period-by-period returns are quarters, although you might also find monthly or annual periods.) The formula for the total return during period t is:

Equation 1

$$r_t = \left[\frac{(CF_t + V_t - V_{t-1})}{V_{t-1}}\right]$$

Where:

- CF_t represents the net amount of cash flow or income paid out to the investor in (owner of) the asset during period t.
- V_t represents the market value of the capital asset as of the end of period t. Likewise, V_{t-1} gives the value of the capital asset in the previous period. Thus, $V_t - V_{t-1}$ (sometimes also referred to as ΔV_t) is the (dollar-amount) change in capital value at t.

Note that equation (1) can also be written as:

$$r_t = \left[\frac{(CF_t + V_t)}{V_{t-1}}\right] - 1$$

In formula (1), the assumption is that CF_t occurs entirely at the end of period t. The HPR assumes a passive, zero cash flow investment *within* each period of time, with valuations at the beginning and end of each period. It is as though the assets were bought at the beginning of each period and sold at the end. The lack of cash flow prior to the period's end may not exactly match reality, however. For example, a stock may pay out its quarterly dividend in the middle of the calendar quarter. In practice, the periods used for computing the sequence of periodic returns are defined as intervals of time short enough so that the exact timing of the cash flow within the period makes little numerical difference. Usually, quarterly or shorter intervals will do the trick in this regard. If not, approximations, such as time-weighted investment, are typically employed, which will be described shortly.

TEXT BOX 3.1 NUMERICAL EXAMPLE OF PERIOD-BY-PERIOD RETURN COMPONENTS IN REAL ESTATE

Say that property A has a value of $1,000,000 in 2022 ($V_{t-1}$). The value grew to $1,010,000 in the current year (V_t). Finally, the cash flow generated by this property is $100,000 ($CF_t$). How do we compute the current yield (y_t), appreciation return (g_t) and total return (r_t)?

- y_{2023}: **current yield**: $\frac{\$100{,}000}{\$1{,}000{,}000} = 10\%$
- g_{2023}: **appreciation return**: $\frac{\$1{,}010{,}000 - \$1{,}000{,}000}{\$1{,}000{,}000} = 1\%$
- r_{2023}: **total return**: 10% + 1% = 11%

The period-by-period total return can be divided into two components: the income return and the appreciation return. These are relevant for the two major types of investment objectives we noted in Chapter 1: income and growth.

The income return, which is also often referred to as the **current yield** (or "cash yield" or "cash-on-cash"), we will label y_t for period t and define it as:

Equation 2

$$y_t = \frac{CF_t}{V_{t-1}}$$

Thus, the income return equals the cash flow paid out to the asset owner during period t as a fraction of the asset's value at the beginning of the period. Various other labels, such as **capital return**, capital gain, price-change component, or growth, are also used to depict the appreciation return. We will symbolize it by g_t for period t, as given by

Equation 3

$$g_t = \frac{V_t - V_{t-1}}{V_{t-1}}$$

Thus, the appreciation return is the change in the asset market value during period *t* as a fraction of the asset market value at the beginning of period *t*.

Note that the income and appreciation return components sum to the total return during the period:

Equation 4

$$r_t = y_t + g_t$$

Thus, the income and appreciation return represent components of the total return. Clearly, *the income return component is more directly relevant to investors' income objectives, while the appreciation return component is more directly relevant to the growth objective.*

The total return is the most important measure of the periodic return because it is more complete than either the growth or income component alone. Furthermore, converting growth into yield or vice versa within the total return is generally possible. Still, it *is impossible to increase the sum of the two components (*the total return). For example, to convert growth into yield, one sells a portion of the investment, thereby "cashing out" some or all of the capital gain. To convert yield into growth, one reinvests some or all of the received income, either in the same asset or in a different asset.

The total return is thus the fundamental statistic for measuring period-by-period investment returns. However, it is important to realize that in the case of direct investment in real property assets, it may be more difficult or expensive to convert between yield and growth than is the case with investments in financial securities such as stocks and bonds (or REITs). For example, it may be difficult or unwise to reinvest income from a property back into improvements in that property, as the property may not need improvement or improvement of the property would not yield sufficient future payback in the form of rental increases or building operating expense reductions. (Of course, income from the property could be invested in other assets.) Similarly, it may be difficult or impossible to sell a part of a property or a partial interest in a property in order to convert capital gain into realized income. (Another possibility would be to borrow against the increased equity the property provides due to a gain in value, increasing the risk of the remaining investment.) Because conversion between yield and gain is more difficult or costly for real estate assets, investors often are more concerned about the individual return components in the case of real estate assets than they are for financial securities such as stocks.

The formulas given previously make it clear that in order to calculate the period-by-period returns and components, one must know (or estimate) the value of the property at the beginning and end of each period of time, with the periods defined as fairly short intervals, such as years or quarters. While most individual investors do not go to the trouble or expense to reappraise and record property values so frequently, institutional investors and fiduciaries such as pension funds may indeed require frequent reappraisals for the purpose of "marking to market" the values of investors' assets and indeed to enable the tracking of the period-by-period returns. Indices of period-by-period capital returns may also be computed statistically using transaction price data from a large sample of individual properties, at least some of which are bought and sold each period.[1] As a result, a growing amount of period-by-period return data is available for real estate.

[1] Examples of price indices in the United States include the MSCI / RCA CPPI (Commercial Property Price Index), CoStar Commercial Repeat-Sales Index (CCRI), and an appraisal-based index available from NCREIF. MSCI also produces price indices outside of the United States. The development of such indices is not straightforward, as we will discuss in Chapter 24. (Online portion of this book.)

3.2.2 Time-Weighted Investment

The simple HPR formula described earlier, which assumes all cash flow occurs at the ends of the periods, works well enough in the securities market where public asset price quotes enable periodic returns to be computed typically on a monthly or daily frequency. In fact, it usually works fine as a very close approximation, even for quarterly returns, a common frequency for some major real estate indices. However, the longer the period, the greater the inaccuracy caused by the fact that not all cash flows actually occur only at the ends of the periods. A method is needed to deal with *intermediate* cash flows (e.g., monthly cash flows within quarterly periodic returns).

The general approach to address this problem is to compute the internal rate of return (IRR) within each period, assuming the asset was bought at the beginning of the period and sold at the end, with other cash flows occurring whenever they actually occurred within the period. As the exact computation of the IRR is inconvenient, in practice, this approach is implemented for our present purposes by adjusting to the simple HPR, known as time-weighted investment. This involves the replacement of the simple V_{t-1} denominator in the HPR formula with a time-weighted denominator. The time-weighted adjustment to the HPR formula is shown in formula (5), for the return within each period (the subscript *t* is omitted for simplicity).

Equation 5

$$r = \frac{End\,Value - Begin\,Value + \sum CF_i}{Begin\,Value - \sum w_i CF_i}$$

where $\sum CF_i$ refers to the sum of all cash flows occurring within period *t*, and w_i is the proportion of period *t* remaining at the time when cash flow *i* was received by the investor. (Note that cash flow from the investor to the investment is negative; cash flow from the investment to the investor is positive.)

For example, consider an asset worth \$100 at the beginning of the calendar quarter, still worth \$100 at the end of the quarter, and paying out \$10 to the investor only at the end of the quarter's first month. The simple HPR for the quarter would be computed as (100 - 100 + 10)/100 = 10.00%. The exact IRR for the quarter is 10.70 percent (not annualized), computed as;

$$0 = -100 + \frac{10}{\left(1 - \frac{IRR}{mo}\right)} + \sum_{j-2}^{3} \frac{0}{\left(1 + \frac{IRR}{mo}\right)^j} + \frac{100}{\left(1 + \frac{IRR}{mo}\right)^3}$$

- IRR per month (mo) = 3.45%
- IRR per quarter = $(1.0345)^3 - 1 = 10.70\%$

The HPR computed with the time-weighted denominator will give a comparable answer (at $r = 10.71\%$), computed as;

$$r = \frac{\$100 - \$100 + \$10}{\$100 - \left(\frac{2}{3}\right) x \$10} = \frac{\$10}{\$93.33} = 10.71\%$$

3.2.3 Real versus Nominal Returns

To fully understand the meaning of the return measures we have just described, you need to understand the role of **inflation** in return measures and the difference between a real and a nominal return.

Inflation is the gradual loss of purchasing power of the dollar (or any currency unit) as prices of the same goods and services rise over time. When we speak about inflation, we usually refer to general inflation, which describes the rise in prices across an average "market basket" of all economic goods and services.[2] The most widely employed measure of general inflation in the United States is the Consumer Price Index (CPI), published monthly by the Bureau of Labor Statistics (BLS). If the CPI rises from 150 in December 2023 to 155 in December 2024, we would say there was 3.33 percent inflation in 2024 (as (155–150)/150 = 0.0333). This means that on average (or for the "average" consumer), prices are 3.33 percent higher in December 2024 than they were a year earlier. Put another way, the real purchasing power of the dollar shrank by 3.33 percent in 2024. It requires $1.0333 in 2024 to buy what $1.00 bought in 2023.

What may matter most to investors is the **real return**, defined as the return net of inflation. A real return is a return measured in constant-purchasing-power dollars. On the other hand, returns are generally observed and reported using "current" dollars, that is, dollars of whatever purchasing power prevails at the time when the dollars are transacted. Returns in current dollars are often called **nominal returns**, distinguishing them from real returns. Thus, nominal returns include inflation, while real returns are adjusted for inflation so that they reflect the actual purchasing power return net of inflation. Returns are normally quoted and reported in nominal terms unless stated otherwise or when it is obvious from the context. It is then up to the user of the return information to make the inflation adjustment.

Let's go back to our hypothetical example in which the CPI at the end of 2023 is 150, and at the end of 2024 is 155, so there was 3.33 percent inflation during 2024. Suppose a property that was worth $1,000,000 at the end of 2023 (in current 2023 dollars) is worth $1,020,000 at the end of 2024 (in current 2024 dollars). The property also generated $80,000 in net cash flow during 2024 (assuming all of this cash flow occurred at the end of the year). In nominal terms, the total return would be computed as:

$$r_{2024} = \frac{\$80,000 + (\$1,020,000 - \$1,000,000)}{\$1,000,000} = 10.00\%$$

The 10 percent nominal return includes an 8 percent income component and 2 percent price appreciation (capital gain). To estimate the real return, we divide the 2024 dollar amounts by the ratio of the 2024 to 2023 cost of living, 1.0333, to express all components of the return in dollars with the same purchasing power, namely year 2023 dollars. The computation of the real returns is shown in a separate Text Box 3.2.

TEXT BOX 3.2 EXAMPLE OF REAL ESTATE VERSUS NOMINAL RETURNS

2023 Property value	= $1,000,000
2024 Cash flow from property	= $80,000
2024 Property value	= $1,020,000
2024 Inflation	= 3.33%

[2] Obvious items in this basket of goods are things like food and beverages. However, it also includes the cost for recreational activities, health care costs and even housing costs. In fact, housing costs (mostly rent) are approximately a quarter of the total basket. This can create a reinforcing loop if you peg the rent to the CPI. Rents can go up because inflation went up, because rent went up, etc.

What is the **total return (r) in real terms in 2024**?

- $\text{Real g} = \frac{\$1,020,000/1.0333}{\$1,000,000} - 1 = -1.29\%$
- $\text{Real y} = \frac{\$80,000/1.0333}{\$1,000,000} - 1 = +7.48\%$
- $\text{Real r} = \frac{\$1,100,000/1.0333}{\$1,000,000} - 1 = -1.29\% + 7.48\% = +6.46\%$

The nominal total return is 10 percent, compared to a real total return of **6.46 percent**. It is also common to use a shortcut in which you subtract the inflation from the total return (or individual components). In that case, you would get 10% – 3.33% = **6.66%**.

You should note several points about this computation. First, the real growth or appreciation is negative, reflecting a real depreciation (negative appreciation) of 1.29 percent; the property value would have had to increase to $1,033,300 just to keep pace with inflation. Second, the real total return is some 3.55 percent less than the 10 percent nominal return. This difference is greater than the 3.33 percent inflation because of the effect inflation has not only on the $1,000,000 base capital as of the beginning of the period but also on the incremental earnings represented by the $80,000 income and $20,000 nominal capital gain. Third, note that the effect of inflation is much smaller in the income return component than in the appreciation return component or total return in percentage terms. This is because the income is generally at least an order of magnitude smaller than the property value when measured in dollar terms over a short time interval (such as a year). Thus, inflation is often ignored in the current yield component of real estate investment. Fourth, note that the commonly used shortcut of simply subtracting the inflation rate from the nominal appreciation or total return gives approximately correct answers to the nearest whole percent (as long as the amount of inflation is small and/or the holding period is short).

Finally, you should note that inflation can be negative during periods of deflation when the currency's purchasing power increases over time. All of the previous procedures still apply, only with negative percentages for inflation (subsequent CPI levels lower than prior levels). Note that real returns will always be below nominal returns when experiencing any inflation and the other way around when experiencing deflation.[3]

3.2.4 Measuring Risk in Returns

One of the things investors are most concerned about when making investments is *risk*. As real estate is well known to involve risk, understanding how risk is related to returns is a basic part of understanding real estate investment. In traditional real estate investment analysis, risk measurement is largely ignored quantitatively and addressed mostly qualitatively, with **due diligence** inquiries about what could go wrong that could affect returns.[4] However, such an approach will not suffice in the modern institutional investment environment. We need to be able to quantify the risk in real estate investment in a way comparable to how risk is measured in the other major investment asset

[3] We should also note that there are other measures of inflation that some users may prefer, such as the producer price index, PPI, which is a measure based more on wholesale prices paid by businesses.

[4] Due diligence involves research into the property, the leases, the maintenance contracts, market conditions, financing terms and what the best and worst cases might be. These tasks are critical for all investors and generally occur prior to acquisition.

classes. In recent decades, this has begun to be done with increasing sophistication, based on the use of real estate periodic returns data.

In principle, we can think about investment risk and define it formally in various ways. For example, one intuitive definition would be that risk is the probability that the investors will lose all of the capital they invest. For example, if you take out a mortgage to buy a property, and later you cannot make the mortgage payments and the bank forecloses on your loan and fails to sell the property for more than you owe on the loan, then you would have lost all the capital you put into the property. This, however, is a rather extreme and narrow definition of risk, relevant only to the specific problem of default risk on levered investments. We might also consider risk as the possibility of losing *any* of the original invested capital. For example, if you pay $100,000 for a property free and clear of any debt, and a year later the property has earned $5,000 in net income, but you cannot then sell the property for more than $90,000, then you would have lost 5 percent of your investment value (at least on paper, as of that point in time). Or we could define risk as some combination of the probability of loss and the likely severity of loss if it occurs.

All of these notions of risk are related to the range in the possible future returns that the investment might earn or to the degree of deviation or dispersion of those returns around the ex-ante expected return. The most widely used statistical measure to quantify such dispersion is known as the **standard deviation** of the probability distribution of future return possibilities. This measure of investment risk is also known as **volatility**. The greater the standard deviation in the possible return (for a given future time horizon), the greater the risk is. Thus, a good general way to think about and quantify risk in investments is depicted in Exhibit 3-1. The horizontal axis represents all the possible values that the return on some investment could have over a given future time horizon. The vertical axis measures the probability associated with each possible future return value.

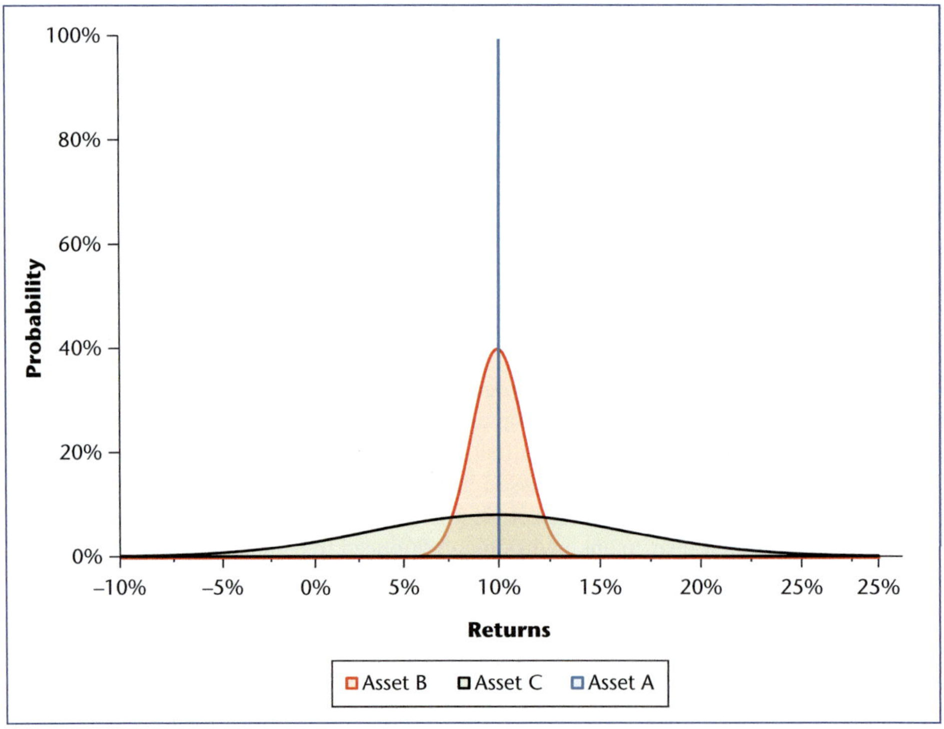

EXHIBIT 3-1 Risk and Expected Return as Future Return Probability Distributions: Three Assets.

If the future return could be known exactly in advance, then there would be only one point on the horizontal axis, the known inevitable future return, which would have a probability of 100 percent. In this circumstance, the subsequently realized return (ex-post) would certainly exactly equal the expected return (ex-ante). This would be a *riskless* asset and is depicted in Exhibit 3-1 for the asset labeled A, which has a sure return of 10 percent. The standard deviation of the probability distribution of asset A's return is zero.

The asset labeled B depicts an investment asset with a small amount of risk. The future return is unknown for certain in advance; there is some range of possible values. The ex-post realized return will not necessarily exactly equal the ex-ante expectation. For asset B, the expected return is again 10 percent, but now the standard deviation is 1 percent. The probability distribution pictured in Exhibit 3-1 has the typical bell shape of what is called the normal (or Gaussian) distribution. Most analysts consider that this shape is not a bad approximation of the general shape of the typical return distributions of real estate and other major capital assets.[5]

The normal distribution is symmetrical, which means the realized returns are as likely to be above as below the mean or expected value, which is also the single most probable value. With the normal distribution, there is about a two-thirds chance that the realized return will lie within one standard deviation of the mean. So, in the case of asset B, there is only about one chance in three that the realized return would fall outside the 9 to 11 percent range. Although no extreme return value is completely ruled out by the normal distribution, as you can see in the graph, there appears to be effectively no chance of asset B's return falling below 7 percent or above 13 percent during the given time interval covered in this example.

The asset labeled C in Exhibit 3-1 depicts a riskier investment asset. The expected return is again 10 percent, but now the standard deviation is 5 percent, implying a one-third chance that the return could fall below 5 percent or above 15 percent. We see that the effective outer range of future possibilities appears to extend from 3 percent (a loss) to + 23 percent. There is only a 1 percent chance that the realized return would lie beyond this range.

To place this quantitative measure of investment risk in some practical perspective, there is good evidence that the standard deviation of the return distribution of a typical individual real estate investment (say, a fully leased income property) is more than 15 percent per year. A diversified portfolio of many individual real estate assets would have a smaller standard deviation but probably still be around 10 percent per year or more, depending on how the returns are measured. (See the feature at the top of this page.) This compares to annual volatility of around 30 percent for a typical individual stock and more than 15 percent for diversified investments in large stocks as represented by an index such as the S&P 500.[6]

TEXT BOX 3.3 HOW VOLATILE IS COMMERCIAL REAL ESTATE IN REALITY?

Volatility is a very basic measure of the risk of assets from an investment perspective. It is very easy to observe empirically and measure the volatility of assets that are traded as securities on public exchanges, such as stocks and bonds (including REITs). Measuring the volatility of rarely (and privately) traded assets is much more difficult, such as commercial properties.

---

[5] But it is only an approximation. Actual returns (in many types of investments, including real estate) tend to have "fat tails," with more probability of extreme events (especially on the downside) than is indicated by the normal distribution. An example of this are the MSCI CPPIs (commercial property price indexes) which are based on a repeat sales model (Chapter 24.4 for more details on such indices) with a t-distribution. The t-distribution—indeed—allows for such "fat tails."

[6] Some recent historical quantitative evidence on volatility was presented in Chapter 1. As point of interest, the standard deviation of all equity REITs' (total) returns between 1972 and 2022 was 18.4 percent (source: Nareit).

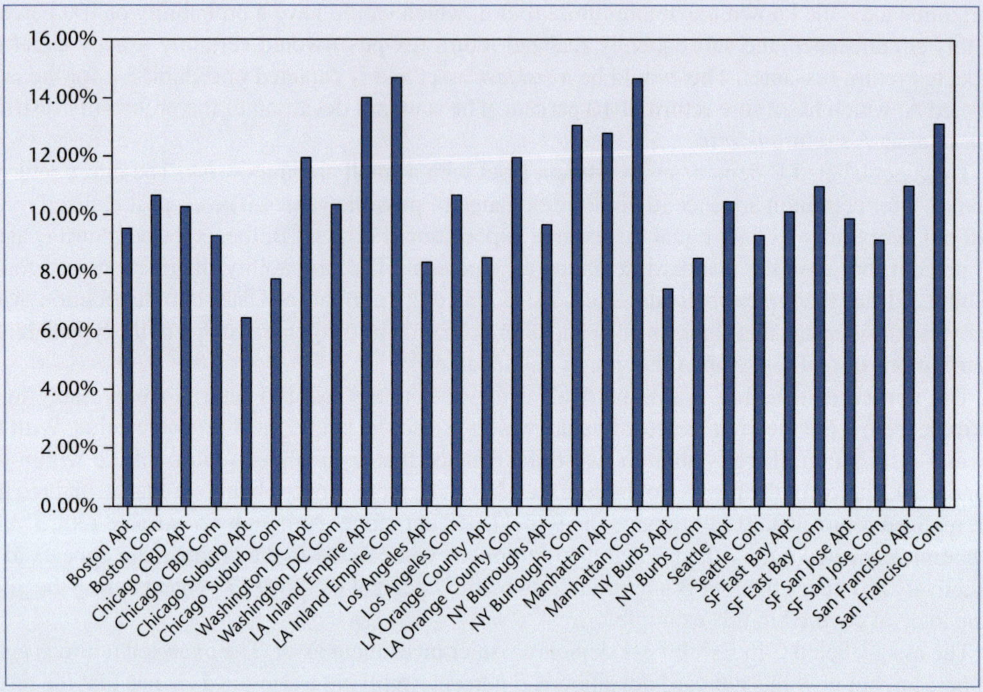

EXHIBIT 3-2 Annual Total Return Volatility of CRE for a Selection of Markets.

Source: Calculation our own, MIT PDP and MSCI/RCA Apt is for apartment buildings, and Com combines office, retail, and industrial. Data used is between 2000 and 2020.

Nevertheless, research undertaken in the academic community starting in the late 1980s and, more recently, large electronic databases of commercial property transaction prices, such as those compiled by CoStar Group and MSCI, have given us a pretty clear idea about the quantitative magnitude of real estate volatility measured in a manner roughly comparable to that of stocks and bonds.

In Exhibit 3-2, we give the annual total return volatility for a selection of markets. The total return indices are provided to us by the MIT price dynamics platform. These total return indices are constructed using the MSCI CPPIs and income data from NCREIF. Glancing at Exhibit 3-2, you will find that total return volatility can differ quite substantially from one market to the next (and for a given span of time).[7] For example, the total return volatility for apartments in Los Angeles is 8 percent, but in the neighboring Inland Empire the volatility for the same property type is 14 percent. The average total return volatility over all these markets is 10 percent. At this point, we should be cautious about assuming that precise historical volatility measurements such as those in Exhibit 3-2 will remain stable over time.

In summary, the average annual total return volatility is approximately 10 percent for a well-diversified portfolio of private properties.[8] However, as noted earlier, the exact return

[7] Based on historical data, we tend to find that supply constrained markets such as LA Inland Empire, Manhattan, San Francisco tend to have higher volatility than elastic markets where adding new supply is easier, such as Chicago suburbs, although this also depends on the property type.

[8] Individual properties can run into good fortune or bad fortune (or good or bad management) relative to the market as a whole in which the property is situated. A property might lose its anchor tenant, for example, even though the market is

volatility depends on the market and property one invests in. As with many aspects of real estate investment, volatility is not an exact science. A final point about volatility in real estate investment that we should mention here is that, to a much greater degree than public securities assets such as stocks, real estate market values exhibit inertia and cyclicality. This creates some degree of predictability in property markets, more so than in securities markets. Predictability means that asset returns are positively autocorrelated, which means that volatility tends to be relatively greater over longer investment horizons up to a point. On the other hand, the predictable component of volatility is arguably not an investment "risk," at least not in the same way that unpredictable future value movements are, as investors should be able to manage what can be predicted.

In principle, we are thus able to quantify both the expected return and the risk in that return for investments by using statistics about the probability distributions of their future return possibilities. The mean of the distribution represents the expected return, and the standard deviation of the distribution represents the risk. The main point to understand in this definition of risk and return is that risk is defined by the range or deviation of the possible future return outcomes around the prior expectation of the return, which may be thought of roughly as a best guess (that is, an unbiased guess, neither optimistic nor pessimistic). Therefore, this definition of investment risk raises an interesting corollary: the more risky (higher standard deviation) the asset, the greater the "upside" possibility. That is, given two assets with the same expected return; the riskier asset will typically have a greater chance of returning a larger profit than the less risky asset could. This may partly explain why more trading and investor interest surrounds more volatile assets.

A final note on total return volatility is whether it is driven more by changes in income or asset values. In a normal market, lease income is somewhat predictable, and asset values are the primary driver of return volatility. To understand why, please revisit equation (2) in this Chapter. The income return is computed by dividing the income of a property by the asset value (of the previous period). The issue is that periodic income (such as annual or quarterly) is typically only a small fraction of asset values. Hence, a large swing in income will not translate into a large swing in return (i.e., return volatility). For example, say that we have an income of \$100,000 on an asset worth \$2,000,000 in the previous period. This gives an income return of 5 percent (= \$100,000 / \$2,000,000). Next, assume that a large tenant left in the subsequent period, reducing the income by 20 percent to \$80,000. If the property value remained the same,[9] the income return would only be reduced to 4 percent (\$80,000 / \$2,000,000). Thus, a large swing of 20 percent of income only reduces the return by 1 percentage point (from 5 percent to 4 percent). In contrast, a drop in asset values by a similar magnitude of 20 percent (to \$1,600,000) would translate directly into a 20 percent decrease in return. (See equation (3) in case of doubt.)

3.2.5 Relationship between Risk and Return

Investors are *risk averse,* some more than others. For example, suppose two assets are available to investors, both identical in every respect (including, in particular, the fact that they have the same

doing fine or run into a major unexpected repair, or include a theater tenant that faces a government closure during a health scare. This "idiosyncratic" risk can be diversified away by having a large portfolio. In reality, it is difficult in real estate to diversify in all markets, and as a result the actual property-level volatility will be approximately 2 percentage-points higher compared to the general market volatility.

[9] This assumption might seem unrealistic at first. Indeed, property values are fundamentally related to how much rent they can generate. However, as will find out in future Chapters, the most important price determinant is *expected future rents*. In this case, a loss of one tenant in the short run will not impact property values erratically if one expects to find a new tenant in its place soon.

expected return ex-ante), except that asset *A* is less risky (has a lower standard deviation of return). In contrast, asset *B* is riskier (as depicted in Exhibit 3-1). No investor would want to buy asset B when faced with this choice, and indeed, any investor holding B would prefer to sell it and buy *A*. Thus, the price of asset *A* would be bid up, and the price of *B* would be bid down. This process would act to increase the expected return on *B* and decrease the expected return on A (relative to the prices one would have to pay to obtain them).[10] In equilibrium (that is, when supply and demand balance for both assets), the riskier asset must offer a higher mean return (ex-ante) than the less risky asset.

This is perhaps the most fundamental point in the financial-economic theory of capital markets: that expected returns are (and should be) greater for more risky assets. This point is depicted in Exhibit 3-3. This same point is also described algebraically in the following equation:

Equation 6

$$E\left[r_t\right] = r_{f,t} + E\left[RP_t\right]$$

Where:

- $E\left[r_t\right]$ gives the expected total return of a given asset over future periods T.
- $r_{f,t}$ is the return one could earn during period *t* from investing in a riskless asset (such as U.S. government Treasury bonds). This is also known as the **risk-free rate**. Note that the holding period matters, so if the expected holding period is ten years, one would use a 10-year Treasury bond as the risk-free rate. (See Chapter 11 for a more detailed discussion on how to measure the risk-free rate.)
- $E\left[RP_t\right]$ represents the expected **risk premium** that investors require on an ex-ante basis for investing in the given asset. The expected risk premium is proportional to the amount of risk investors perceive to be involved in investing in the given asset.

In Exhibit 3-3, risk (as perceived in the investment marketplace) is measured on the horizontal axis, and expected total return (ex-ante, going forward) is measured on the vertical axis. The idea is that investors can achieve a sure return equal to the rate labeled r_f by investing in a riskless asset. This **risk-free interest rate** compensates investors for the pure **time value of money**, the fact that investors are allowing someone else (in this case, the government) to use their money for some period of time. Risky assets must offer a higher expected return in order to compensate investors for taking on additional risk when they buy these assets. The difference between the risk-free interest rate and the expected return on a risky asset is the expected **risk premium**, which is seen in the graph to be proportional to the amount of risk in the asset.

The picture presented in Exhibit 3-3 might be called financial economics in a nutshell. It is the single most important idea to remember from this book. It is an idea that is so simple and obvious that it never evokes arguments from students in an academic setting, yet it seems to be much more difficult for people to keep in mind when they get out in the real world. People investing in real estate commonly believe, implicitly if not explicitly, that they are getting a higher ex-ante return *without* assuming greater risk. We will see how the risk/return trade-off depicted in Exhibit 3-3 enters at a fundamental level into almost every aspect of investment analysis and decision-making as the later chapters of this book unfold. So, always keep Exhibit 3-3 in mind.

[10] We will have more to say about the link between asset prices and returns in the following chapters. Suffice it to say here that a lower price for an asset implies, other things being equal, a higher expected return for the investor. The key point of this section is reinforced in Video 1 in the online supplements for this chapter.

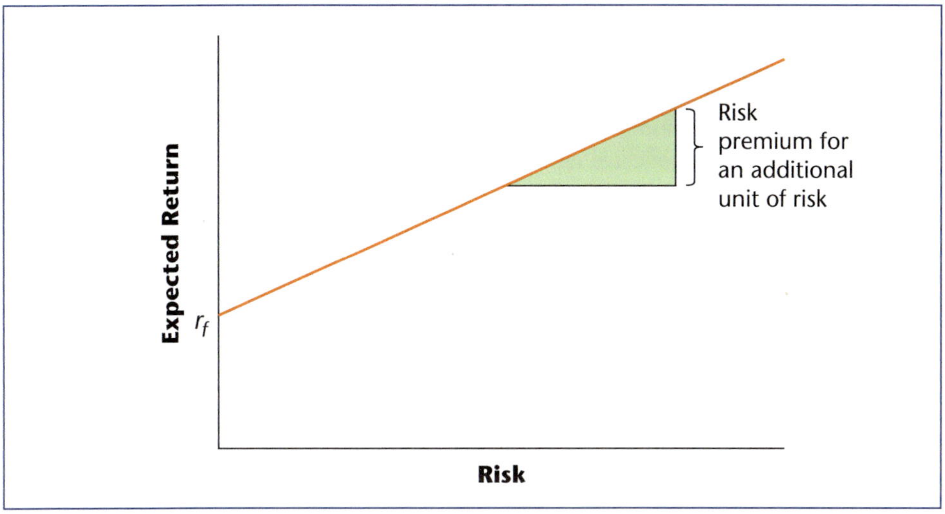

EXHIBIT 3-3 Financial Economics in a Nutshell: Risk and Return.

3.2.6 Summarizing Periodic Returns: Synthesizing the Three Ways to Break Down the Total Return

This is perhaps a good time to pause, step back, and synthesize some of what we have learned about periodic returns. The HPR is an elegant measure of investment performance, capturing a rich depth of attributes that matter to investors in a simple way that allows quantitative measurement. Notice in particular that we have identified three different ways in which the periodic or time-weighted average total return can be broken down into two components: income plus growth, risk-free rate plus risk premium, and real return plus inflation premium. These are summarized here (note we dropped the subscript t and expectations sign for readability):

$$r = y + g$$

$$r = r_f + RP$$

$$r = R + (i + iR) \approx R + i$$

Where:

- i refers to the inflation rate.
- R provides the total return.

3.3 MULTIPERIOD AND MONEY-WEIGHTED RETURNS

Suppose you want to know the return earned over a multiperiod span of time, expressed as a single average annual rate. There are two widely used approaches for computing such a measure. One is simply to take the average of the periodic returns across the time span in question. This will produce a *time-weighted* average return (TWR). The other approach is to compute an inherently multiperiod return, most often the IRR, which is a *money-weighted* average return. These two approaches will be discussed in this section.

3.3.1 Time-Weighted Average Return

The average of consecutive period-by-period returns across time is referred to as a time-weighted average return for the overall interval of time. The term *time-weighted* comes from the fact that, for example, if the periodic returns are 10 percent, 10 percent, and 13 percent in each of three consecutive years, then the arithmetic average return across the three periods is 11 percent per year (the 10 percent is weighted twice as much as the 13 percent). As noted, the time-weighted average return is *independent of the magnitude of capital invested at each point in time.* It is, therefore, *not affected by the timing of capital flows into or out of the investment.*

We can compute the time-weighted average return from a series of periodic returns in two ways. The simple or **arithmetic average** indicates the central tendency of the individual periodic returns. It is computed as the sum of the individual periodic returns divided by the number of periods. In contrast, the **geometric average** reflects the effects of **compounding** or the earning of return on return. This is also referred to as **chain-linking** the returns. In the previous example, the arithmetic and geometric mean would be computed as follows:

Arithmetic mean:

$$11.00\% = \frac{10\% + 10\% + 13\%}{3}$$

Geometric mean:

$$10.99\% = (1.10\ x\ 1.10\ x\ 1.13)^{\frac{1}{3}}$$

(In this example, there is little difference, but the two measures can be significantly different in practice.)

Each of these methods of computing the time-weighted average has some advantages and disadvantages that make it more appropriate than the other for certain purposes. The following attributes characterize the arithmetic mean:

- The arithmetic mean is *always* at least as great as the geometric mean (e.g., if the geometric mean is negative 5 percent, the arithmetic mean might be negative 4 percent); the more so, the greater the volatility in the periodic returns series. The two measures are equal only if there is no volatility at all (constant return).
- The arithmetic mean has “superior statistical properties” in the sense that it provides the best estimator of the true underlying return tendency each period and, therefore, provides the best forecast of the return for any one future period (assuming that the future is governed by the same underlying return-generating process as the past).
- The arithmetic mean return components (income and appreciation) sum to the arithmetic mean total return.

These attributes of the arithmetic mean can be contrasted with the following attributes of the geometric mean:

- Because the geometric mean reflects the compounding of returns, it better represents the average growth rate per period during the overall time span so as to reflect the relation between the amount of value the investor ends up with and the amount they started with (assuming reinvestment).

- The geometric mean is independent of the volatility of the periodic returns (given the beginning and ending values of the investment). The geometric mean return components (income and appreciation) do not sum to the geometric mean total return. (A complicated "cross-product" term involving the interaction of the two components is left out of the compounding of the individual components.) Indeed, the geometric mean income return is of questionable economic meaning, although the geometric mean appreciation return can represent the average growth in asset value or price.

Considering the previous attributes, it is not surprising that the arithmetic mean is most widely used in forecasts of future expectations and in portfolio analysis. On the other hand, because of the geometric mean's direct relation to the ending value as a multiple of the beginning value, it is unsurprising that the geometric mean is most widely used in historical performance measurement and in the evaluation of investment managers. For this purpose, it is also an advantage of the geometric mean that it is more independent of the volatility of the periodic returns.[11] In general, the geometric mean tends to be used more often by practitioners and accounting professionals. In contrast, the arithmetic mean tends to be used more often by academics and economists.[12] The arithmetic and geometric means are more similar:

- the less volatility there is in the periodic returns and
- the more frequent the returns (the shorter the return periods)

In the extreme, if there is no volatility at all (constant returns), or the length of the return periods approaches zero (continuous compounding), the arithmetic mean will exactly equal the geometric mean across time.

3.3.2 Internal Rate of Return (IRR)

The IRR is the classical and traditional measure of investment performance in real estate. It is needed in two situations. Since investments in real property are usually held for a long period of time, several years at least, most property owners want to avoid going to the expense of regularly appraising the value of their property when they are not planning to sell it. Thus, calculating the period-by-period returns necessary to compute a time-weighted average at the micro-level of individual properties and deals is often impossible. In contrast, the IRR can be calculated easily with data that the property owner will almost always have available. It requires only (1) the price the property was bought for, (2) the cash flow generated by the property during each period since it was bought, and (3) an estimate of what the property is currently worth (or what it was sold for).

The IRR is also useful because it is a money-weighted average return, as contrasted with a time-weighted average. As noted earlier, a money-weighted return reflects the effect of the magnitude of capital invested during each period. As a result, it captures the effect of capital flow *timing*. If an investor tends to enter an investment just before it does well and exit the investment just before it does poorly, the IRR earned by that investor will improve accordingly, above the geometric TWR on the underlying investment. The reverse occurs if the timing is unfavorable. Thus, if measuring the effect of capital flow timing on the investment performance is *appropriate*, then the IRR is a

[11] For a given geometric mean performance, the arithmetic mean will be larger the greater is the volatility in the periodic returns. Thus, an investment manager can score a higher arithmetic mean simply by holding in more volatile assets.

[12] Academics are prone to avoid the whole issue of geometric versus arithmetic means by simply working with continuously compounded returns (log differences), in which the distinction between the two types of means effectively disappears. (The sum of the log differences divided by the number of return periods is the same as the log of the ratio of ending to beginning value levels divided by the length of time between them.)

better measure than the TWR. Similarly, suppose it is *inappropriate* to include such effects (such as when the manager being evaluated does not have responsibility or control over timing). In that case, the IRR is not an appropriate performance measure. In the real world, many situations are somewhat ambiguous in this regard. An investment manager may have some influence over capital flow timing but not complete freedom. In classical investment analysis in the securities industry, the time-weighted average return has generally been considered more appropriate in most investment management situations. However, each case may be considered on its own merits.

The formal definition of the IRR is as follows. Let PV represent the amount invested in year 0 (e.g., 2023) and let CF_t refer to the cash flow in year t (e.g., $t = 1$ refers to 2024, $t = 2$ refers to 2025, and so on). It is important to note that the cash flow during intermediate years may be generated either from the operation of the asset or partial sales, that is, the disposition of part of the asset. Intermediate cash flows may also reflect subsequent investments after the initial purchase or construction of the property (for example, capital improvement expenditures are negative cash flows from the investor/owner's perspective). The sign of cash flows must be defined consistently. For instance, cash outflows (from the investment to the investor) are positive, while cash inflows (from the investor to the investment) are negative. Now define an investment holding period or "horizon" such that in year T the investment is assumed to be wholly liquidated (i.e., sold). Then CF_T includes both any net operating cash flow during year T as well as the "salvage" value or net sale proceeds from the final disposition of the property (this latter cash flow is usually referred to as the "reversion" in real estate parlance). Then, the IRR is defined by the following equation:

Equation 7

$$PV = \frac{CF_1}{1+IRR} + \frac{CF_2}{(1+IRR)^2} + \ldots + \frac{CF_T}{(1+IRR)^T}$$

In general, **solving equation (7) algebraically is impossible** when trying to determine the IRR analytically. It is necessary to solve the equation "numerically," that is, by trial and error.[13] For some patterns of cash inflows and outflows across time, it will be mathematically impossible to compute an IRR (the IRR will not exist), or the IRR may not be unique (more than one value may solve the equation). Such cases are pretty rare in practice for real estate investments, as they occur most often when there is more than one reversal of sign in the cash flow stream.

This may occur in redevelopment or turnaround projects, for example, in which an initial investment is followed by positive cash flow that is then followed by large cash outflows for redevelopment and then more positive cash inflow after the redevelopment.[14]

To better understand how the IRR is a money-weighted average return across the time span it covers, consider our previous numerical example in which we postulated three consecutive years in which an investment produces periodic returns of 10 percent, 10 percent, and 13 percent. We noted previously that this gives the investment a time-weighted average return of 11 percent. Now, suppose you put $100 into the asset, earning these returns at the beginning of the first year. At the end of the first year, you would have $110, and by the end of the second year, your investment would have grown

---

13 In Excel, you can also use the "goal seek" function under "data -> what-if analysis" to automatically form a Monte-Carlo simulation that will numerically find the IRR. Video 2 in the online supplements to this chapter demonstrates the IRR in Excel.

14 The problem may also arise in computing IRRs realized by investors in funds that draw in and pay out cash over time. In such cases, while a unique IRR may not be determinable, there will often (though not always) exist only one IRR that is reasonable. In any case, a reasonable "cost of capital" can always be posited by the analyst and a single net present value (NPV) determined for the project at that capital cost. (More about this in future chapters.) Also, various types of "adjusted IRRs" have been developed in the financial management literature to facilitate computation of an explicit return, although any of these require additional assumptions that inevitably involve some subjectivity and judgment.

another 10 percent to $121 (equal to $110 x [1 + 10%]). At that point in time, suppose you decide to put an additional $200 of new capital into the asset. So, you have $321 in the investment at the beginning of the third year, when it earns 13 percent. You end up with $362.73 at the end of the third period ($321 x [1 + 13%]). Your cash flows are—$100 at the beginning of year 1,—$200 at the beginning of year 3, and + $362.73 at the end of year 3. This cash flow stream can be computed using the previous formula for an IRR of 11.69 percent. The IRR is higher than the time-weighted return because more capital was invested during the year when the higher (13 percent) periodic return was earned.

On the other hand, suppose instead of investing more at the beginning of year 3, you had disinvested part of your capital at that point in time, say, by selling half of your $121 investment. Then, the cash flow stream would have been — $100 at time zero, + 60.50 two years later, and + 68.37 at the end of year 3. This stream has an IRR of 10.60 percent, which is not only less than the IRR with the previously considered favorable cash flow timing but also less than the underlying investment's time-weighted return of 11 percent.

Finally, suppose you were completely passive after your initial $100 investment, taking nothing out and putting no more into the investment. Your cash flow stream would then have been — $100 at time zero and + $136.73 at year 3 (100 × 1.10 × 1.10 × 1.13). This stream has an IRR of 10.99 percent, exactly equal to the geometric mean time-weighted average return for the underlying investment during those three years.

The IRR is referred to as an *internal* rate because it includes only the returns earned on capital *while it is invested in the project* (or with the manager who is being evaluated). Once capital is withdrawn from the investment, it no longer influences the IRR. This is, in fact, what makes the IRR a money-weighted return.

It is also important to note that the IRR gives a measure of the total return that was achieved by the investment: from initial income flow, subsequent growth (or decline) in income flow, and finally, capital value appreciation (or decline) as reflected in the sale price (or terminal value) of the asset at the end. The IRR reflects both the initial cost of the investment, and any subsequent capital invested, as the IRR is based on *net* cash flows in each period. It is a purely cash flow-based measure that does not differentiate between investment and return on or return of investment. The IRR does not indicate *when* the return was generated within the overall span of time covered by the return (e.g., would the return per annum have been higher or lower if the asset had been held half as long?). It is, therefore, not useful for computing statistics such as co-movements among assets or volatility of returns across time.

Some other aspects of the IRR may help to build your intuition about it, particularly in relation to the time-weighted return. First, as we saw in the previous example, *if there are no intermediate cash flows, the IRR will exactly equal the time-weighted geometric mean return* (no cash placed into or taken out between the beginning and end of the investment). Second, there is a special theoretical case of regularity in which the IRR and periodic return are the same. Suppose (1) regular intermediate cash flows grow at a constant rate every period, and (2) the asset value always remains a constant multiple of the current periodic cash flow. Then, the IRR will exactly equal the sum of the initial cash yield rate plus the growth rate ($IRR = y + g$), and the IRR will exactly equal both the arithmetic and geometric time-weighted mean return ($IRR = r$).[15] (The growth rate, g, here applies identically to both the cash flows and the asset capital value.) This special case is equivalent to a constant-growth perpetuity, which, as we will see in Chapter 4, has a present value of $PV = CF_I/(r — g)$, and a current yield equal to the inverse of the constant multiple: $y = CF_1/PV$. The regularity conditions described in this paragraph can be a simplification and stylization of an investment in a typical income-generating property, in which case the mathematical equivalencies noted here are convenient and insightful.

[15] The combination of constant-growth cash flows and constant-multiple asset value implies that the periodic returns are constant across time, so there is no volatility, allowing the arithmetic and geometric means to equate in the periodic returns.

TEXT BOX 3.4 A NOTE ON IRR TERMINOLOGY

In the real estate appraisal business, the IRR is often called the "total yield." In real estate investment and appraisal, the expected IRR looking forward into the future when investing is often called the "going-in IRR." In the bond business, the IRR is simply called the bond yield. The yield to maturity (YTM) is the IRR, assuming the bond is held to maturity.

3.4 CHAPTER SUMMARY

This chapter has continued to develop your basic set of tools and building blocks for real estate investment analysis by defining investment returns in some depth and detail. We defined two types of returns at a specific, quantitative level: periodic returns (the HPR), which underlie time-weighted average returns (TWR), and money-weighted multiperiod returns (in particular, the IRR). The strengths and weaknesses, and the major uses, of each of these types of returns were described. We also showed how the periodic return could be used to define components of return, as well as investment risk, in a way that can be measured quantitatively, such as the volatility or range of variability, in these returns over time. The next chapter will use what we have presented here to show how real estate investments can be analyzed and evaluated quantitatively at the *micro,* or individual asset level.

KEY TERMS

- Returns
- Ex-post
- Ex-ante
- Period-by-period (periodic) returns
- Multiperiod return
- Holding period return (HPR)
- Time-weighted return (TWR)
- Internal rate of return (IRR)
- Money-weighted return
- Co-movement
- Total return
- Income return
- Appreciation return
- Current yield
- Capital return (gain, growth)
- Inflation (CPI)
- Real return
- Nominal return
- Standard deviation
- Volatility
- Risk premium
- Risk-free interest rate
- Time value of money
- Arithmetic average return
- Geometric average return
- Compounding return

STUDY QUESTIONS

In Your Own Words

3.1 Describe the two fundamental types of return measures.

3.2 Explain the difference between time-weighted and dollar-weighted multiperiod return measures.

3.3 In what situations is it most advantageous to use periodic returns? When does it make sense to use multiperiod return measures?

3.4 Describe three ways to break the total nominal return down into two components. Provide formulas and label your variables.

3.5 Now, consider two different assets: an apartment building in the city and a raw land parcel on the fringe of the metropolitan area. The raw land generates no income but incurs 1% of its value annually in property taxes, while the apartment has a current yield (cap rate) of 8%. Given that the raw land is also more volatile and riskier than the apartment, which asset is likely to have a higher appreciation return? Prove, using basic algebra and investment logic, that the raw land must have an ex-ante expected appreciation rate at least 9% higher than the apartment building. (Hint: Refer to your answer to Question 3.4.)

3.6 What is wrong with the following statement: "Time-weighted average return is particularly well-suited to measuring real estate investment performance for investors who actively try to time the market when buying and selling properties"?

3.7 Explain the difference between arithmetic and geometric time-weighted average returns.

Check Your Knowledge

3.8 A commercial building has the potential to deliver either a 20 percent gain or a 5 percent loss over the next year, with both outcomes equally likely. What is the mean (expected) return of the investment?

A) 5%
B) 7.5%
C) 10%
D) 15%

3.9 Using standard deviation, quantify the risk of the property investment with potential returns of a 20 percent gain or a 5 percent loss, assuming both outcomes are equally likely.

A) 5%
B) 10%
C) 12.5%
D) 15%

3.10 The real estate investment advisor to the Tired Old Firemen's Pension Fund is faced with a possible property acquisition that will cost $4,200,000. The advisor feels that in one year, this property will face the following subjective probabilities. There is a 25 percent chance for an optimistic scenario or "upside" outcome, in which case the property will be worth $5,000,000. There is a 25 percent chance of a pessimistic scenario or "downside" outcome, in which case the property would be worth $3,750,000. And there is a 50% chance of an expected scenario or "most likely" outcome, in which case the property will still be worth $4,200,000 next year. Using simple HPRs, compute the following.

a. The expected appreciation return
b. The standard deviation of the possible appreciation return, (Note: If you use Excel on this, use STDEVP rather than STDEV because this is not a sample—it is your complete subjective probability distribution. The range on which to apply STDEVP would include four cells, two for the "most likely" outcome.)

3.11 In the fourth quarter of 2024, the NCREIF Property Index (NPI) total return for the Bay metropolitan area was 4.47% (this is a quarterly return, not per annum). This was based on 165 properties having, as shown in the following table, an aggregate appraised (market) value of \$10,254,210,187 at the beginning of the quarter and \$10,209,681,774 at the end of the quarter. The drop in appraised value does not imply a decrease in property values in this case, as investors sold partial ownership interests in properties (partial sales) in the index generating aggregate proceeds of \$414,134,757. The properties produced \$160,072,817 in net operating income and absorbed \$81,264,596 in capital improvement expenditures during the quarter. Using the data provided and the NCREIF return formulae given in the chapter, answer the following questions.

NPI Data for Bay Metropolitan Area (End of Quarter)

	Total Return	Income (NOI)	Capital Exp. (CI)	Market Value	Partial Sales (PS)
2024 Q3				\$10,254,210,187	
2024 Q4	4.47%	\$160,072,817	\$81,264,596	\$10,209,681,774	\$414,134,757

What would the quarterly total return for the Bay metropolitan area have been if the NPI used the simple HPR formula (with just the beginning asset value in the denominator) instead of a time-weighted investment value in the denominator? (Note how little difference this would make in basis points, even multiplying by four to factor up to annual from quarterly rates.)

3.12 The following table gives the NPI total return for a three-year (12-quarter) period for San Francisco and Boston.

YYQ	San Francisco	Boston
2023.1	0.0024	0.0141
2023.2	0.0098	0.0050
2023.3	0.0082	0.0078
2023.4	0.0156	0.0296
2024.1	0.0325	0.0429
2024.2	0.0181	0.0248
2024.3	0.0427	0.0421
2024.4	0.0655	0.0309
2025.1	0.0301	0.0439
2025.2	0.0361	0.0393
2025.3	0.0520	0.0433
2025.4	0.0487	0.0447

Compute the following quarterly statistics for both cities to the nearest basis point, and answer the subsequent questions. (Hint: We suggest using a spreadsheet.)

a. The arithmetic average return (use the AVERAGE function in Excel)

b. The standard deviation of the return ("volatility," use STDEV in Excel)

c. The geometric mean return (you can use the Excel statistical function GEOMEAN, but you have to add unity to each return in the series, and then subtract unity from the GEOMEAN result, or just apply the geometric mean return formula directly by compounding the returns in the spreadsheet)

d. Why are the arithmetic means higher than the geometric means?

e. Based on the geometric mean, and factoring up to a per annum rate, by how many basis points did Boston beat San Francisco during this period?

3.13 A popular real estate investment option for institutional investors is an "open-end" fund, also called a commingled real estate fund (CREF). In this type of fund, investors can add or withdraw money based on the appraised value of the fund's assets, which are regularly updated. For example, if the fund's assets are worth $10 million and you invest $100,000, you own 1% of the fund, meaning you are entitled to 1% of the net income and proceeds from sales.

Now, let's consider a scenario where an investor places $200,000 in the fund at the end of 2024, giving you two units (or shares). Over the next three years, here's what happens: In 2025, the fund pays $5,000 per unit from rental income, and at the end of the year, the value of each unit is reappraised to $98,000. In 2026, the fund pays $10,000 per unit from rental income, and at the end of the year, the value of each unit rises to $112,000. In 2027, the fund pays $7,000 per unit from rental income, and at the end of the year, the fund is sold, and each unit is worth $118,000 in cash proceeds.

Use a calculator or spreadsheet to answer the following questions. Report your answers to the nearest basis point.

a. Assuming that appraised value accurately reflects market value (opportunity cost) of the assets at intermediate points in time, what are the period-by-period total returns for each of the three years the investment was held (2025, 2026, and 2027)?
b. Based on these period-by-period returns, what is the geometric average annual total return during the three-year holding period of the investment (2025–2027)?
c. What is the internal rate of return (IRR, per annum) of the investment over its 3-year holding period?
d. Which of these two average returns over the 3-year life of the investment tells exactly what the profit would have been per original dollar invested if the investor had taken the cash paid out plus proceeds from liquidating his units at the end of each year and used all (and only) this cash to immediately purchase units (and fractions thereof) in the fund again for the following year (i.e., so that there was no cash flow into or out of the investment except at the beginning and end of the 3-year period)?

3.14 Suppose that the investor in the above question at first was cautious, buying only one unit at the end of 2024. Then a year later, he felt that the market would rebound in 2026 after its poor performance in 2025. So he made an additional capital contribution to buy one more unit at that time. Then, with the great performance of the fund in 2026, he decided to cash out one of his units at the end of 2026 (assuming the fund would purchase the unit back for its appraisal-based value as of the end of 2026).

a. Calculate the investor's IRR.
b. Why is this IRR higher than that calculated in the previous question, and also higher than the mean period-by-period return to the fund over the 2025–2027 period?
c. Why is the time-weighted HPR a better measure for judging the performance of the fund, and the IRR a better measure for judging the performance of the investor in this case?
d. Under what conditions would the IRR not be a fair measure of the investment decision maker's ex-post performance?

Chapter Case: Kai Realty Select Fund

Kai Realty Select Fund is a private equity real estate investment fund that specializes in acquiring commercial properties on behalf of its wealthy investor clients. The fund follows an investment strategy focused on acquiring properties in high-growth urban areas. While these properties are expected to generate steady rental income, they are located in volatile markets, and inflation rates are rising.

At the end of 2025, the fund acquired a property for $11,250,000, anticipating both stable rental income and property value appreciation over time. At the end of 2026, the property was sold for $12,500,000, and it generated $950,000 in net cash flow during that year. During 2026, inflation was 3.5%, and the yield on government bonds stood at 5%.

The management team is evaluating whether this specific investment aligns with the fund's objectives by assessing key performance metrics such as income return, appreciation return, risk-adjusted return, and the impact of inflation.

Choose the correct answer and discuss whether this investment meets the fund's investment objectives based on your answer.

1. What is the nominal income return for the property in 2026?
   A) 7.56%
   B) 8.44%
   C) 6.73%
   D) 9.23%
2. What is the nominal appreciation return for the property in 2026?
   A) 5.67%
   B) 11.11%
   C) 9.83%
   D) 7.34%
3. What is the nominal total return for the property in 2026?
   A) 11.11%
   B) 19.56%
   C) 15.12%
   D) 10.25%
4. What is the ex-post risk premium for the property in 2026, based on the yield on government bonds?
   A) 14.56%
   B) 19.56%
   C) 10.67%
   D) 8.44%
5. What is the real appreciation return for the property in 2026, adjusting for inflation using the definition?
   A) 7.61%
   B) 2.09%
   C) 7.35%
   D) 6.00%
6. What is the continuously compounded nominal total return for the property in 2026?
   A) 11.23%
   B) 12.01%
   C) 17.86%
   D) 13.78%
7. What is the continuously compounded nominal appreciation return for the property in 2026?
   A) 10.54%
   B) 6.78%
   C) 5.51%
   D) 5.67%
8. If Kai Realty Select Fund is concerned about market volatility, which type of real estate investment would provide more stability?
   A) Properties focused on appreciation

B) Properties generating steady income returns
C) High-growth commercial properties
D) Speculative land investments

9. The yield on government bonds during 2024 is expected to be 5%. What role does this bond yield play in evaluating the real estate investment?
   A) It serves as a benchmark for assessing the investment's risk-free return
   B) It measures the property's volatility relative to the bond market
   C) It reduces the property's nominal appreciation return
   D) It increases the fund's overall risk tolerance
10. How would rising inflation most likely impact the real return on the 2024 property investment?
   A) It would increase the property's nominal return
   B) It would reduce the real purchasing power of the investment returns
   C) It would have no impact on the real return
   D) It would reduce both the nominal and real return
11. Which of the following strategies might Kai Realty Select Fund adopt to protect against rising inflation?
   A) Investing only in fixed-income real estate assets
   B) Adjusting rental agreements to include inflation-linked rent increases
   C) Reducing the property's holding period to minimize exposure
   D) Holding the property in a low-growth area

4 Micro-Level Valuation of Real Estate

DCF and NPV

CHAPTER OUTLINE

LEARNING OBJECTIVES

After reading this chapter, you should understand:

- The relationship between investor return expectations and asset prices.
- The (Discounted Cash Flow) DCF valuation procedure and how to use it.
- The relationship between DCF and ratio shortcut procedures such as direct capitalization.
- The NPV investment decision rule (including the hurdle rate).

At the micro-level of real estate investment activity, the level at which deals are made, the primary question can usually be summed up as: *How much is the asset worth*? Each side in a potential deal will almost always be willing to "do the deal" at some price. So, the question boils down to, at what price? In this chapter, we want to answer this question in a way that gives you a solid basis from which you can use your reasoning abilities to deal with the range of situations the real world may present. To do that, we begin with the link to the fundamental investor objectives and concerns we discussed and learned how to quantify in Chapter 1. As always, we will be guided by the three fundamental economic principles that thread their way through this book: (1) Opportunity cost, (2) Market equilibrium, and (3) Wealth maximization.

DOI: 10.1201/9781003643838-5

4.1 RELATION BETWEEN RETURN EXPECTATIONS AND PROPERTY VALUES IN THE ASSET MARKET

One main aim of this book is for real estate investors to fundamentally understand the asset *value* of a property. What is the *price* one should pay for a real property? However, the previous chapter concerned different definitions of *returns*, and we made a big deal about how earning returns is the objective of investment. What is the relationship between asset values on the one hand and returns on the other?

In order to understand fundamentally what is going on at the micro-level in most real estate activity, we need to establish the link between the expectation of returns, which motivates investors, and the prices or values of assets, which is the issue they are most directly grappling with in the day-to-day business of real estate investment. In essence, this "missing link" can be summed up in the following precept:

> *The prices investors pay for properties determine their expected returns because the future cash flow the properties can yield is independent of the price investors pay for the properties today.*

To make this point more concrete, consider the following simplified example. (Video 1 in the Chapter 4 online supplements folder also provides a demonstration.) Suppose it is reasonable to expect that a certain property can produce a net rental income of $10,000 in the upcoming year and will be worth $105,000 at the end of the year. If we pay $100,000 for the property today, our expected total return at the time of purchase is 15 percent. This is determined as the $10,000 rent plus the $5,000 capital gain ($105,000 less the $100,000 price we paid), expressed as a fraction of the amount invested (i.e., the price we paid). On the other hand, if we pay $105,000 today, the expected return is only 9.52 percent ($10,000 plus no capital gain, divided by the $105,000 investment amount). If we could get the property today for $95,000, our expected return would be 21.05 percent over the coming year ($10,000 rent plus a $10,000 gain in investment value from $95,000 to $105,000, as a fraction of the $95,000 initial investment).

Thus, the expected return is inversely related to the asset's price because the expected future cash flows from the asset (including those from the resale) remain the same, no matter how much you pay today for the asset. They remain the same because they are determined by factors that are independent of how much you pay today for the asset. Future rents are determined by supply and demand in the space market. The resale price you can reasonably expect is determined by the future rents the next buyer can expect going forward and by the opportunity cost of capital (the next buyer's required expected return) at the time of your resale. Neither of these factors—the equilibrium in the space market nor that in the capital market—is influenced by the price you pay today for the property.

In the classroom, this precept may seem terribly elementary and obvious. Students never argue against it when we teach it in an academic environment. But out there in the real world, a kind of "fog of war" descends over the field of the deal-making battle. There is often pressure to close a deal, making participants susceptible to wishful thinking or optimistic framing. *"The seller won't budge below $10 million. I know the first year's income will be $1 million, and I know my fund's target return is 12 percent, so it must be reasonable to expect that the property will be worth $10,200,000 a year from now (as that will give me the 12 percent return)."*

This type of reasoning is so tempting and so easy to slip into in the heat of battle that it is not at all uncommon. Indeed, it is sometimes even put forth as an explicit principle of real estate investment, known as the **Greater Fool Theory**. According to this theory, you don't need to worry about paying too much for a property because, even if you have been foolish and paid too much, it is unlikely that you are the stupidest person in the market. Thus, you can always count on finding a greater fool who will pay at least that much again and rescue your ex-post return! In truth, we cannot deny that it may sometimes be possible to "luck out" in this manner. But if you have gone to the trouble to get this far in this book, you probably already agree that the Greater Fool Theory is hardly a sound, systematic basis for making good real estate investment decisions.[1]

Apart from its hazards at the individual level, widespread application of the Greater Fool Theory would lead, by definition, to a disconnection between asset prices and the underlying fundamental cash flow generation potential of those assets. Such a disconnection is the definition of an asset price "bubble," in which prices grow over time only because each buyer expects such growth, unrelated to the underlying physical productive potential of the assets. Most finance students have heard about the famous Tulip Bulb Bubble in seventeenth-century Holland, in which the equivalent of hundreds of thousands of dollars was paid for single tulip bulbs. Closer to hand, many practitioners regard the pricing of many real estate assets attained during 2007 as reflecting some sort of bubble. Of course, bubbles have a tendency to burst. When they do, it is the practitioners of Greater-Fool-Theory investing who get burned, who prove themselves to have been the greatest fools after all.

4.2 A DISCOUNTED CASH FLOW MODEL FOR REAL ESTATE

Understanding the time value of money, returns, and the link between asset values and expected returns, we can now focus on developing a **discounted cash flow model** (or **DCF** for short) for real estate. DCF is probably the single most important quantification procedure in micro-level real estate investment analysis. The goal of the DCF is to provide us with an asset value, ergo, the price we should be paying for our property of interest. (See also Video 2 in the Chapter online Supplements.) In essence, the procedure consists of three steps:

1. Forecast the expected future cash flows.
2. Ascertain the required total return.
3. Discount the cash flows to present value at the required rate of return.

Mathematically, these three steps can be summarized in the following equation, letting V represent the value of the property today:

Equation 1

$$V = \frac{E_0[CF_1]}{(1+E_0[r])^1} + \frac{E_0[CF_2]}{(1+E_0[r])^2} + \ldots + \frac{E_0[CF_{T-1}]}{(1+E_0[r])^{T-1}} + \frac{E_0[CF_T]}{(1+E_0[r])^T}$$

where:

- CF_t = Net cash flow generated by the property in period *t*.
- $E_0[r]$ = Expected average multiperiod total return (per period) as of time zero (the present), the opportunity cost of capital (OCC) for this investment, expressed as the going-in IRR.[2]

[1] We will refine this point in Chapter 9. Uncertainty surrounding exactly how much any real estate asset is worth can make it rational for a subsequent buyer to indeed be influenced to some extent by what the previous price was. And there is growing evidence in the field of "behavioral economics" that even seasoned and professional business people are psychologically prone to make systematic mistakes, such as "anchoring" value estimates onto prior prices. However, this does not change the fundamental rationality and sensibleness of the principle enunciated here, which states that it is best to base value estimation primarily on the asset's objective capability to generate operating net cash flow.

[2] Note here that we assume the same *r* in every period. In practice, one could vary the *r* by time and/or by perceived risk. For example, the residual value of the property at time *T* might be considered less certain and a higher *r* could be used. We will expand upon these variations later in the chapter.

- T = The terminal period in the expected investment holding period, such that CF_T would include a terminal valuation (TV), such as the net **resale value** of the property at that time, in addition to normal operating cash flow.

To clarify the basic mechanics of this procedure, consider the following simple numerical example. The subject property is an office building with a single lease. Suppose the present time is the end of the year 2023. The building has a 6 year net lease that provides the owner with \$1,000,000 at the end of each year for the next three years (2024, 2025, 2026). After that, the rent increases to \$1,500,000 for the following three years (2027 through 2029), according to the lease. At the end of the sixth year (2029), the property can be expected to be sold for ten times its then-current rent, or \$15,000,000. Thus, the investment is expected to yield \$1,000,000 in each of its first three years, \$1,500,000 in each of the next two years, and finally, \$16,500,000 in the sixth year (consisting of the \$1,500,000 rental payment plus the \$15,000,000 "reversion" or sale proceeds). In this way, we have quantified an expectation of the multiperiod future cash flow stream this property can generate.

Now suppose that, after considering the relative risk and current expected returns of real estate versus stocks and bonds and of this particular office building versus other types of real estate, you figure that 8 percent per year would be a reasonable expected total return for an investment in this property. The 8 percent remains fixed throughout the holding period. In other words, 8 percent is the opportunity cost of capital (OCC) for this property, what you could expect to earn from other investments of similar risk to this building; in effect, it is the equilibrium expected return in the market for this type of property. Then, the market value of the property is found by applying the DCF formula (1) as follows:

$$\$15{,}098{,}000 = \frac{\$1{,}000{,}000}{(1.08)^1} + \frac{\$1{,}000{,}000}{(1.08)^2} + \frac{\$1{,}000{,}000}{(1.08)^3} + \frac{\$1{,}500{,}000}{(1.08)^4} + \frac{\$1{,}500{,}000}{(1.08)^5} + \frac{\$16{,}500{,}000}{(1.08)^6}$$

We see that the property's estimated market value is \$15,098,000 as of the present time (year 2023). This price (\$15,098,000) will yield an expected average total return of 8 percent for the buyer. If the price were less than this, say, \$14 million, the buyer would get an ex-ante (going-in) return greater than 8 percent (namely, 9.6 percent at the \$14 million price, computed as the IRR on the \$14 million investment, assuming the given expected future cash flow stream). This would be a better deal for the buyer but a lousy deal for the seller, assuming the 8 percent going-in IRR well reflects capital market expectations for returns on this type of investment. If the price were greater than the indicated value, say, \$16 million, then the expected return for the buyer would be less than 8 percent, indeed only 6.8 percent at the \$16 million price, and this would presumably be a bad deal for the buyer and a good deal for the seller.

Now that we understand the basic procedure or mechanics of the DCF, it is our job to find the parameters used in the DCF formula (1). More specifically, we need the following four inputs;

1. Prediction of the future net cash flows (CF) for every year t.
2. Estimate the current OCC (r) in the market for the property.
3. Determine the resale year T.
4. Predict the resale price (aka reversion cash flow) of our property in year T (which we have labeled TV, for terminal value)

After we find these inputs, we can discount the cash flows to the present value, which will be our estimate of the property's market value, using the DCF formula (1). Predicting cash flows will be the topic of Chapters 8 and 9, and finding the correct return requirement (the OCC) is the subject of Chapter 11. But before we delve deeper into the procedure, let us first introduce a couple of "simplifications" or "shortcuts" to the DCF in the remainder of this Chapter. These shortcuts are widely used in practice. The shortcuts are (1) using a single (blended) discount rate for all the components of the net cash flows, (2) using a single cash flow growth parameter instead of predicting separate cash flows for every year, and (3) employing the Gordon Growth Model to obtain the resale price.

4.2.1 A Single (Blended) Discount Rate (r)

In the DCF valuation procedure, the discount rate converts future dollars into their present value equivalents. This requires accounting for both the time value of money and the risk in the expected future cash flows. Recall from Chapter 3 that the total return (which we labeled r) can be broken into a risk-free interest component and a risk premium component: $r = r_f + RP$. The risk-free interest rate component accounts for the time value of money, and the risk premium component accounts for the risk. This means that a higher discount rate should be applied to more risky cash flows because such cash flows effectively have a higher cost of capital in the asset markets.

One application of this principle to commercial property investment analysis relates to properties with long-term leases signed by high-credit tenants, particularly many office and industrial buildings. Cash flows within signed leases are fixed contractual obligations of the lessee (tenant) and, therefore, do not subject the landlord to rental market risk (except in the case of tenant default). Such projected cash flows should thus typically be discounted at a lower rate within the lease (that is, after the signing of the lease). The relatively low discount rate used to convert cash flows across time within leases may be called the **intralease discount rate**. Conversion of projected future cash flows or values to present value across time prior to when the future values are contractually fixed would be made using a **higher interlease discount rate** that reflects the property's rental market risk. The interlease discount rate would normally apply to determine the present value of both the future long-term leases not yet signed (discounted to present from the time of their projected future signing) and the residual or reversion cash flows representing projected proceeds from future resale of the property.

To clarify this point, let us extend our previous numerical example of the office building. Suppose that the existing net lease in the building expires at the end of the sixth year, but we wish to do a ten-year DCF valuation. Suppose further that our expectation as of today about the net rent this property can earn for the four years following the expiration of the existing lease (years 7 through 10) is $2 million per year and that we expect the property would sell at the end of year 10 for $20 million net. Thus, the 10-year expected cash flow projection for this property is given in the table in Exhibit 4-1.

The first six of these annual cash flows are relatively low risk because they are already contracted for with an existing tenant. The last four cash flows, corresponding to years 7 through 10, reflect our expectations about the most likely annual rent that would be signed at the end of year 6 (beginning of year 7) for a multiyear lease beginning at that time. Once that lease is signed, the risk within the years covered by the lease will be low, like the risk in the first six cash flows.

Because of this, the four annual $2 million expected cash flows from the second lease, covering years 7 through 10, should, in principle, be discounted at the low intralease discount rate back to a

EXHIBIT 4-1
Hypothetical Office Building Net Cash Flows

Year		1	2	3	4	5	6	7	8	9	10
CF_t	$	1$	1$	1$	2$	2$	2$	2$	2$	2$	22

"future present value" as of the beginning of year 7 (the time the second lease is expected to be signed, six years from now). Once the "future present value" of the second lease is calculated as of its signing, then this amount should be discounted back to time zero at the higher interlease discount rate.

With this more sophisticated perspective, assuming the OCC relevant for the intralease discount rate is 7 percent, and the interlease rate is 9 percent, we arrive at a present value of $18,325,000 as our value estimation for our office property, as follows:

$$\$18,325,000 = \sum_{t=1}^{3} \frac{\$1M}{(1.07)^t} + \sum_{t=4}^{6} \frac{\$1.5M}{(1.07)^t} + \frac{\left(\sum_{t=1}^{4} \frac{\$2M}{(1.07)^t}\right)}{(1.09)^6} + \frac{\$20M}{(1.09)^{10}}$$

Even though the above formula is technically sound, we should pause and point out that allowing for time-varying discount rates is rarely done in current practice. Applying a single **blended OCC** to all the property's projected net cash flow is more typical. Why would this be?

For one thing, many buildings with long-term leases have many different spaces, all with leases that expire at different times. It gets tedious and time-consuming to apply the approach described in the preceding section rigorously. Another consideration is that it is often unclear what the different discount rates should be. For one thing, property net cash flows may not be entirely fixed even during periods covered by leases. The leases may be "gross leases" that only fix the rental revenue, exposing the landlord to risk in the property's operating expenses (see Chapter 10 for more details on such leases). The leases may also include a percentage or indexed rent, which will vary according to future contingencies (Chapter 10). There may also be some risk of tenant default. Uncertainty over the correct discount rates takes some of the motivation out of the desire to be methodologically correct. Finally, if a property has a pattern of lease expirations over time that is typical for buildings of its type, then one may apply a single blended IRR rate as a legitimate shortcut. The legitimacy of this shortcut depends on the rate having been derived from observation of the values of buildings similar to the subject property so that the blended rate indeed represents the opportunity cost of capital, that is, the expected return on investments of comparable risk.

To see how this works, let's return to our numerical example. We can compute a single blended rate of return that discounts the ten expected future cash flows in Exhibit 4-1 to the "correct" present value of $18,325,000 simply by computing the IRR for this cash flow stream. The IRR is 8.57 percent. If our building were typical of a class of similar buildings regarding the time and risk pattern of its lease expirations and cash flows, then we would tend to observe a blended rate of around 8.5 percent being widely applied in the market, as a shortcut to value buildings such as ours, using the DCF procedure. We could then take that blended rate observed in the market and apply it to our building's projected future cash flows to arrive at the same value estimation of $18,325,000, as follows:

$$\$18,325,000 = \sum_{t=1}^{3} \frac{\$1M}{(1.0857)^t} + \sum_{t=4}^{6} \frac{\$1.5M}{(1.0857)^t} + \sum_{t=7}^{10} \frac{\$2M}{(1.0857)^t} + \frac{\$20M}{(1.0857)^{10}}$$

As noted, the use of separate, explicit interlease, and intralease discount rates is limited in current DCF valuation practice. We have introduced the concept here partly for pedagogical reasons, to deepen your understanding of the fundamental sources of commercial property value, and to build your intuition about applying the DCF technique. How precisely it is necessary or possible to match discount rates with different risks in the cash flow components is always a judgment call. In the real world, separate rates are typically used only when special circumstances exist, such as when a building has a long/short master lease or other atypical lease expiration pattern.

4.2.2 Cash Flow Growth Rate (g) and the Direct Capitalization Shortcut

Note that one input in the DCF formula (1) is the expected cash flows in every year up through the terminal year T. An existing building may have a lease roll that can be used to estimate future cash flows based on aggregating the individual lease terms for each year. But it is often useful in practice to simplify by forecasting the net cash flows in the formula denominators by applying a single constant growth rate, a parameter we will label g. Thus, the expected future cash flows in equation (1) are replaced by:

Equation 2

$$E_0\left[CF_t\right] = CF_0\left(1 + E_0\left[g\right]\right)^t$$

where;

- CF_0 = the cash flow in period 0 (the time of purchase)
- g = the constant growth rate (effectively a long-run average rate)
- t = year of interest

Note that a buyer will know the cash flow when purchasing the property. It seems rather obvious that this would be the first thing a buyer would like to know. Thus, CF_0 is considered a given here.[3] The only parameter one then needs to estimate is g. For example, if the cash flow is \$1 million when we purchase the property (CF_0), and the expected annual growth rate (g) is 5 percent, we would expect the cash flows in year 5 to grow to \$1M x $(1.05)^5$ = \$1.28M. Note that this is equivalent to \$1M x (1.05) x (1.05) x (1.05) x (1.05) x (1.05) = \$1.28M.

The actual procedure for estimating this expected growth rate will be discussed in later Chapters. But why do we make this simplification? And is it realistic? The short answer is no. In the real world, cash flows will go up and down depending on where you are in the cycle, the length of the contracts in the property, and, more generally, how strong the local space market is. However, we find that cash flow rates tend to be more stable in the *long run*, making them easier to predict. Predicting a specific cash flow for each specific year will often be very difficult beyond initial lease terms and, therefore, often not realistic in practice. Note that other fields face similar issues. For example, climatologists have difficulty knowing the exact temperature a month from now. However, understanding the seasonal average or general direction of temperature over several decades (i.e., climate change) is well established.

To exemplify this, see Exhibit 4-2, where you can find the cash flow growth[4] for offices in the United States between 2010 and 2022. One line gives the year-over-year change in cash flows, and the other two show rolling averages for five and 10 years, respectively. Note that the specific year-over-year growth can be very erratic, even though this depicts a broad national aggregate. For example, in 2010, we find a negative 10 percent change in cash flows. This is followed up in the next year (2011) by a positive 4 percent change in cash flows, a difference of 14 percentage points. Could you realistically see this coming? On the other end of the extreme, the 10-year rolling average has been relatively stable in this period, meandering between 4 percent and 6 percent. This indicates

[3] Per usual, things are never this simple. The issue is that the property you are buying might not have a typical cash flow for that market segment at the time of purchase. For example, a large tenant might have left just prior to purchasing the property, temporarily reducing the rent collected, or the previous landlord might have done a "bad deal" and negotiated a rent with one of the tenants that is lower compared to the market average. You will need to correct the cash flow in year 0 first, before any forecasting can be done. This will be discussed in detail in Chapter 9.

[4] More specifically, we look at the growth of Net Operating Income (NOI). This accounting construct is not exactly the same as net cash flow but is closely related, and will be introduced and treated in detail in Chapter 5.

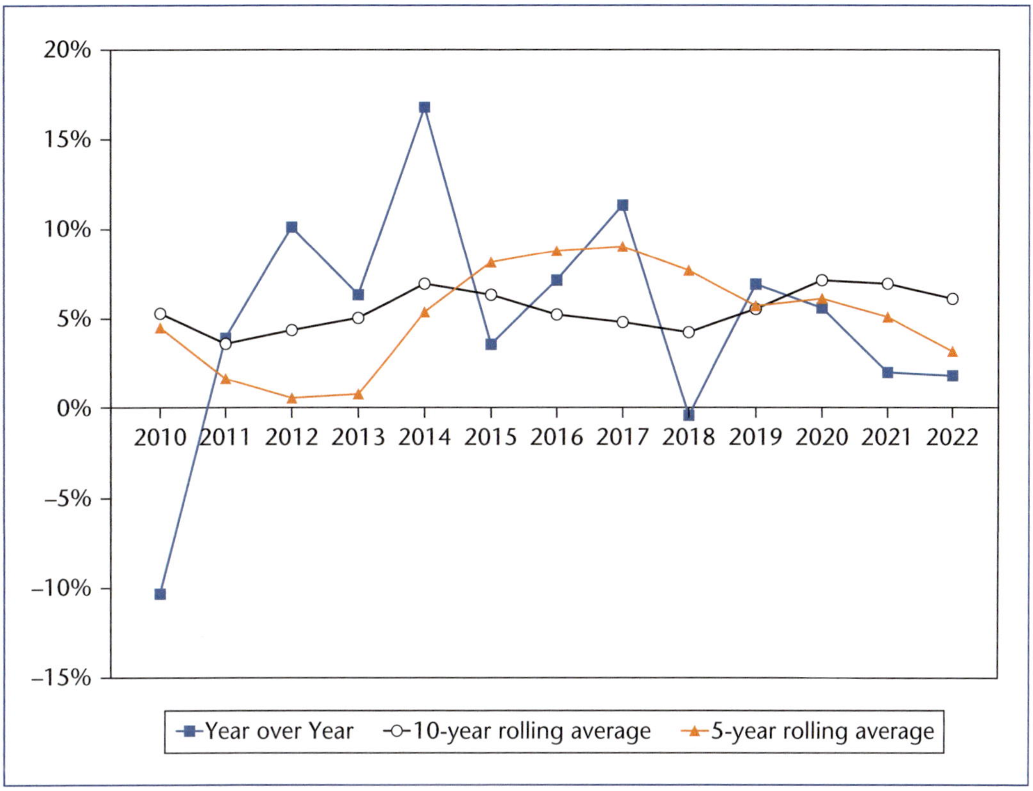

EXHIBIT 4-2 Realized Long-run Cash Flow Growth for Office in the US. Year Over Year Versus a 10-year Rolling Average.

Source: NCREIF.

that real estate cash flows are **mean-reverting** to a long-run average. Individual property cash flows can be even more difficult to predict (although in-place long-term contracts associated with vintage leases may provide some predictability; see Chapter 9 as well).

You might be wondering how we can ensure that the cash flows will revert to some average in the future. What if we are wrong and the long-run average changes? What if I only want to keep the property for two years, not giving the cash flows enough time to mean revert? Also, note that the timing of the cash flows *does* matter in a DCF. Earlier cash flows get more "weight" compared to later ones. In other words, spikes in cash flows early on will increase the present value of an otherwise similar property that has its spike in cash flows in later years. Thus, even though the long-run average cash flow growth was identical between the two properties, the first property will have a higher value. Considering all this uncertainty, why even bother with prediction? And why simplify the forecast to a single parameter *g* if this is unrealistic?

To answer these criticisms, you should understand that we consider the unpredictable cash flow volatility as *risk*. Put differently, if you know *exactly* with no uncertainty what the cash flows will be for the coming T years, there is no (cash flow) risk. This is seldom the case for real estate investments, except occasionally for only a few upcoming years. The key point to remember is that such risk is captured by the denominator of the DCF, particularly by the opportunity cost of capital (r, the discount rate). The standard risk-adjusted discount rate version of the DCF formulation does not try to explicitly quantify risk in the cash flow numerators of the present value equation. Other things equal, the more unsure you are about the future of the cash flows, the higher total return you should demand, *lowering* the value of the property. Hence, we do the best we can with the tools and information at our disposal in predicting the average cash flow growth (which we will provide in Chapters 8 and 9), and the riskiness is then subsequently captured by the return requirement. It's crucial to understand the difference between the forecast (numerator of DCF) and risk (denominator of DCF) in this sense. We will come back to this principle a few times throughout this book.

In the final year of the DCF, we have two distinct cash flows. First, we have the operating cash flow (essentially the cash generated by the property through leasing activity) in the final year, and second, the reversion cash flow. The reversion cash flow is essentially the net **sales price** of the property in year T. As noted, the net sales price can more generally be considered as the **terminal value** (***TV***), effectively an **exit value** (***EV***) as well. Suppose the property is not sold in the terminal year of the DCF analysis. In that case, you can equally well think of the reversion component as the predicted market value of the property at that time, an estimate of what the property *could* sell for if the owner chooses to sell it (i.e., the opportunity cost of the property at that time). In the latter case, the reversion component would not actually be a cash flow. Still, it would be a potential or possible cash flow, effectively part of the value of the property nonetheless. Even though both cash flow components happen in the final period, they are treated very differently. This is so both in how tax and debt interact with each component (Chapters 12 and 13) and by how each component is calculated. Before we show how to compute the terminal reversion value in period T, we first need to discuss the concept of **perpetuity**.

In real estate (and other fields in finance), we assume that the property will generate cash flows in perpetuity. This might seem very unrealistic. What examples are there of investments that generate cash flows ad infinitum? The oldest—still paying—perpetuity is a bond from the Dutch Water Works, issued in 1624 and currently owned by the New York Stock Exchange. 400 years is a long time, but not per se infinite. However, there are two things to consider when investing in real estate.

First of all, real estate *is* a very long-lived asset. Building structures are very long-lived as physical capital goes, and land is even longer-lived. Buildings get demolished, but typically, something new will be put in their place. Empty malls are refurbished into self-storage units, micro-fulfilment centers, and pickleball complexes, and mothballed offices might become student housing. Cities badly damaged during the Second World War, such as London, Berlin, Rotterdam, Tokyo, and Shanghai, bounced back and became real estate hot spots again. Carthage was completely dismantled, stone-by-stone, by the Romans, and they even spread salt on the ground so no crops could grow. Yet a few decades later, Carthage was rebuilt and became the second-largest city in the Western Roman Empire (Tunis, the current capital of Tunisia, is still located nearby). Commercial real estate tends to be located in central areas in large, complex cities. Dismantling such large, complex societies, which took centuries to build, has proven to be very difficult.

Secondly, the DCF will put less weight on future cash flows to such an extent in the present value computation (assuming $g < r$, see Chapter 2 as well) that you needn't worry about the concept of perpetuity that much from a purely technical or mathematical point of view. For example, take $CF_0 = \$1M$, $g = 2\%$, and $r = 8\%$. The value of the property is subsequently the sum of all the discounted cash flows (which go to perpetuity!). We can use the following equation (essentially combining equations (1) and (2)) to compute the value of the individual cash flows in every year t:

$$CF_t = \frac{\$1M(1.02)^t}{(1.08)^t}$$

In Exhibit 4-3, we plot the value of the discounted cash flows between one year (t = 1) from now and (T =) 200 years in the future in the blue-shaded area. The black line gives the cumulative sum of the present value of this investment. We find a value of exactly \$17 million for this investment (see right axis) after holding this property for 200 years. More importantly, cash flows in the far future hardly add up to anything. More specifically, if we kept T at 60 – and assumed the property would *not generate any cash flows* after this year – the value of the property would already be \$16.5 million. Thus, the next 140 years only add \$500,000 to the value of the property. In short, even though the concept of perpetuity seems unrealistic initially, it is not as far-fetched or impactful as one might think.

Now that we have a better grasp of perpetuity, let's go back to the terminal value (*TV*) and the terminal year of the analysis (*T*). To begin with, remember how to value our investment (in this case, real estate). It is the sum of all the remaining discounted cash flows. Thus, if the property were to be marketed in year 10 ($T = 10$), the value of the property at that time would be the sum of the discounted cash flows between year 11 and the next time it would be sold. And at that next time, it would be the value from then to the following time of sale. And so on, in perpetuity. In effect, because the DCF valuation is always forward-looking from the point in time of the valuation, the property's present value at any time is a perpetuity. So, how do we compute the discounted cash flows all the way to perpetuity? You might think that just running your investment through a large enough number of years (like T = 200 as in Exhibit 4-3) will approximate pretty well for going to perpetuity. This is true. But this is where we can use the simplification and the shortcut we are suggesting. By using our simplifying assumption of the constant growth rate (*g*), we can invoke the mathematical formula of the present value of a constant growth perpetuity, introduced in Chapter 2. This simple mathematical formula collapses the infinite series perpetuity equation into a very elegant formula, as we will show below. This mathematical formula underlies a famous valuation (or "capitalization") model widely used in investments, known as the **Gordon Growth Model** (**GGM**). And the GGM is closely related to the very popular real estate valuation shortcut known as "direct capitalization," or applying a so-called "cap rate" to value an income property in one step.

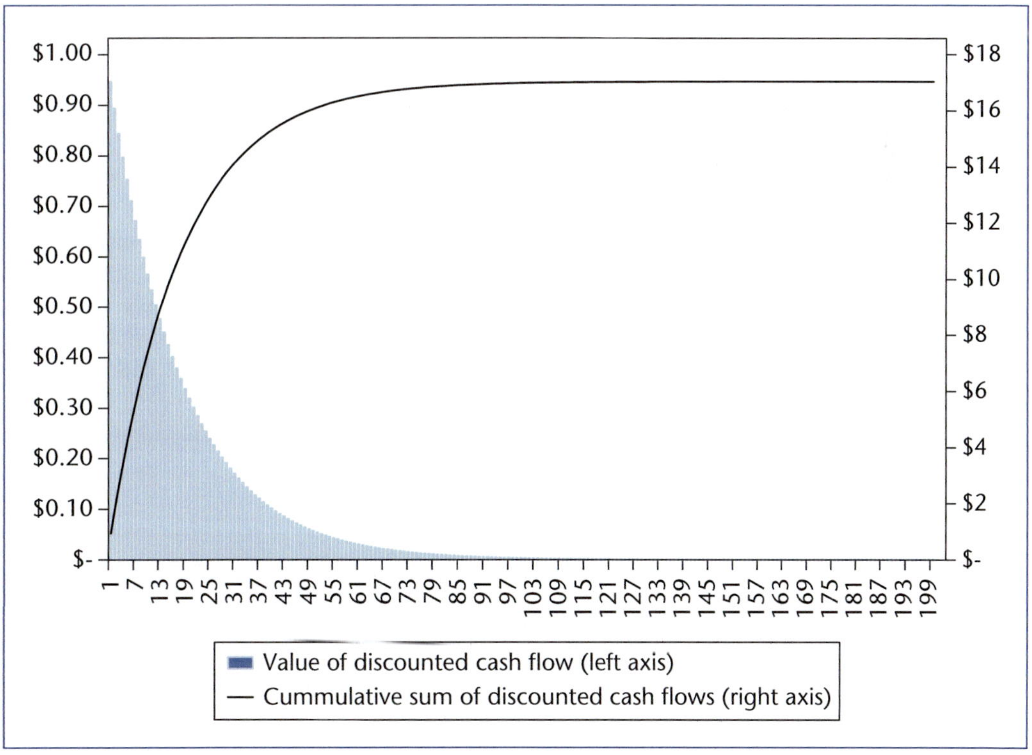

EXHIBIT 4-3 Discounted Cash Flows from Year 1 to Year 200. With $g = 2\%$, $r = 8\%$, and $CF_0 = \$1M$. All Numbers in the Exhibit are in Millions of Dollars.

The GGM is a simple formula that gives the value of the discounted cash flow model that goes to perpetuity. The formula is as follows:

Equation 3

$$GGM; V = \frac{CF_1}{(r-g)}$$

The GGM formula makes a lot of intuitive sense. A long-lived asset, be it a stock or a property, will be more valuable; other things being equal: the greater its initial net cash flow, the greater the expected growth in its cash flows (and hence in its future value). It will be less valuable if it has a greater opportunity cost of capital (which will be a function of interest rates and the perceived investment risk in the asset).

At this point, we already have all the components for our shortcut property valuation at our disposal. In order to find the value of the investment *now*, we need the cash flow in period 1 (*note, not period zero*), the cost of capital (r), and cash flow growth expectation (g). To see how the GGM works in practice, let us consider two properties called A and B. Both properties have a cash flow in year one of $1 million. Both properties also have the same OCC, namely 8 percent. However, the cash flow for property A is not expected to grow in the foreseeable future ($g = 0\%$). In contrast, property B's cash flow is expected to grow at 3 percent annually ($g = 3\%$). Intuitively, you would expect property B to be more valuable. Indeed, this property will generate more cash flow for the investor. Luckily, the GMM accounts for this by lowering the denominator and increasing V. More specifically, property A will have a value of $1M/(8% – 0%) = $12.5M. Whereas property B will be worth $1M/(8% – 3%) = $20M, a whopping difference of $7.5 million. Likewise, a lower OCC and higher starting cash flow will increase property values *ceteris paribus*.

Note that equation (3) is expressed as the value *now*. When we use the formula in this way, it is the real estate valuation shortcut known as *direct capitalization*. That is, we value the property today by dividing its first year's (year 1, that is, the upcoming year) net cash flow by an appropriate "capitalization rate," or "cap rate," for short. It is important to note that, in contrast to typical mainstream finance terminology, what is referred to as the capitalization rate or cap rate in typical real estate practice in the United States is *not* the same thing as the discount rate r in the multiperiod DCF formula (the total return OCC), as the real estate **"cap rate" is instead $r - g$**, the total return OCC *minus* the long-run expected growth rate. (The typical practice is a little more nuanced than this because the numerator is usually defined as the net operating income rather than the net cash flow, but for now, you can ignore this difference and note that in this context, $r - g = y$, the current cash yield rate of the property, as described in Chapter 3.) In practice, the cap rate is often estimated empirically by observing sales of comparable properties in the property market and comparing their sales prices (V or PV) with their observed (or estimated) upcoming year's net cash flow (or net income), CF_1. More detail on how to empirically estimate the cap rate is provided in Chapter 11. (And see Video 3 in Chapter 4 online Supplements for more perspective.)

Since $V = CF_1 / (r - g)$, therefore:
$(r - g) = CF_1 / V$.

Thus, the direct capitalization method becomes, in effect, a way to estimate the current market value of a property by comparison to the observed prices of the sales of similar properties in the market.

Just as direct capitalization is an often-used simplification to shortcut the multiperiod DCF valuation (in effect, by assuming the constant growth rate), so it can also be used to estimate the terminal value within the multiperiod formulation of the DCF, this will be useful in those cases when one does not wish to use the full shortcut of current value direct capitalization as described above. This will be in cases where one does not wish to assume a constant cash flow growth rate in the near term, for example, to reflect more precisely the cash flows under existing contractual leases. Thus, one wants to use the multiperiod DCF valuation equation (1). However, we can still use the shortcut direct capitalization formula to estimate the reversion value of the property in the terminal period, *TV*. In that case, we will be using the perpetuity formula to find the expected sales price of the property in the *future*. Thus, the procedure would be as follows. First, specify the terminal period of the analysis (*T*). Next, compute the cash flow in *T+1*. Subsequently, divide that cash flow by r-g (or, in effect, by the projected "going out" cap rate at that future point in time). This will provide us with the expected sales price of the property in period *T*. The terminal value (*TV*) is thus given by;

Equation 4

$$TV = \frac{CF_{T+1}}{(y)}$$

Where in this case, y represents the estimate of the cap rate as of year *T*, the so-called "terminal cap rate" or "going-out cap rate." Finding the going-out cap rate will be discussed at length in Chapter 11.

It is important to note that we will not be able to have much certainty about the sales price in T years for typical horizon years used in practice in multiperiod DCF valuation, such as ten years in the future. The GGM will give us an *expected* sales price, but nothing is certain. Indeed, suppose we are using the multiperiod approach rather than simple direct capitalization. In that case, it is because we have wanted to specify more precisely the cash flows in the intervening years, and this would probably suggest that we have more confidence in predicting those cash flows (perhaps because existing leases at least partly govern them) than in predicting the going-out terminal value of the asset. In effect, the reversion value may realistically be more uncertain, hence riskier from an investment perspective, than the prior operational cash flows. Now, recall that the uncertainty about the future sales price is captured by the OCC discount rate in the denominator (r_V) as applied *to* the terminal value ***(TV)***! The discount rate r_V appropriate to the *TV* may be different than, and probably larger than, the discount rate *r* applied to the earlier operational cash flows *CF*. To summarize, in order to find the value of a property, we discount the operational and reversal cash flows by employing the following DCF;

Equation 5

$$V = \sum_{t=1}^{T} \underbrace{\frac{CF_0(1+g)^t}{(1+r)^t}}_{operational} + \underbrace{\frac{TV}{(1+r_V)^T}}_{reversion}$$

Where TV (= terminal value = sales price) is calculated separately as in equation 4. In practice, as noted, often a single blended discount rate is used for both *r* and r_V, in the form of a so-called "going-in IRR." Practitioners often do not know how to confidently differentiate between the appropriate discount rate for the operational cash flows and the reversion cash flow. The formula above (typically with the blended $r = r_V$) will be the one we will use in principle throughout this book, with a few additions and elaborations here and there as we progress. However, truly understanding equation (5) is an important first step.

4.2.3 The Multiperiod Analysis Horizon Date (T)

As noted, it is often necessary or desirable to conduct the multiperiod DCF analysis described in equation (1) or (as somewhat simplified) in equation (5) rather than the simpler direct capitalization approach of equation (3). This is typically the case for one of three reasons. The property may have an existing long-term contractual lease structure or tenancy that is atypical to warrant explicit modeling of the contractual cash flows for several years. And/or the purpose of the DCF analysis may be to satisfy the requirements of a lender or other investor that requires such a more exact treatment of the cash flows through to some multiperiod horizon (typically 5 to 10 years). The third reason will be if the cash flows in the subject property are expected to grow at variable or atypical rates during several of the upcoming years.

Whenever such a multiperiod DCF analysis is to be conducted, it becomes necessary to pick the final period in the analysis horizon. This is effectively modeled as if it would be the period in which you will sell the property, though in reality, the property need not necessarily be sold in that year, and there is generally no reason to pre-commit to a resale date. Also, changing the final period does not impact the value of the investment now. Effectively, the terminal period of the DCF is simply the horizon period of the multiperiod analysis. In practice, it is often, though not always, the end of year 5, 7, or 10.

It is interesting to note that in traditional income property appraisal terminology, the direct capitalization approach often corresponds to what is called the "market method" or the "price comparison" method of property valuation, as the cap rate is often estimated by observing the sales prices and net incomes of comparable properties that have sold in the relevant market. In contrast, the multiperiod DCF approach often corresponds to what appraisers call the "income method" of property valuation, which is based on an analysis of the income the property can generate and the capitalization of that income. Of course, in theory, the property has one "true" market value. So, in theory, both methods should give the same present valuation.

4.3 SORTING OUT SOME TERMINOLOGY: DISCOUNT RATE, OCC, IRR

This might be a good moment to pause and reflect on the symbol *r* we have been using throughout the book so far and to clarify some terminology that often confuses students at this point. We have been using three different words to describe the symbol *r* in the context of DCF, namely, (1) discount rate, (2) opportunity cost of capital (OCC), and (3) Internal Rate of Return (IRR). It is important to note that even though these terms are related, there are important differences from a definitional point of view, and the same symbol can give our valuation formulas different practical meanings depending on the circumstances and context. Consider the following elaborations of the definitions.

- **Discount rate**. The discount rate is simply a mechanical term. It is a mathematical rate we use to translate value amounts across time. In our DCF formula, we use the discount rate to reduce future cash flows to present values. We saw in Chapter 2 that it is also possible to grow present values to future values. As a mechanical device in such mathematical formulas, *r* does not necessarily have any specific economic meaning.
- **Opportunity Cost of Capital (OCC)**. What can give *r* more economic meaning is when it represents the OCC. In this context, the OCC is the expected return in the market for assets or investments of similar risk and duration characteristics to the subject property being valued in the DCF analysis. In other words, the OCC is the equilibrium expected return in the relevant sector of the capital market where such assets are traded. It is, therefore, the expected return that the investor requires for the investment to be "fair" because it is what the investor is giving up, on an expectational basis, by investing in the subject property instead of investing in another similar such asset, since the investor has the *opportunity* to alternatively invest in another such asset in the market. Real estate properties are indeed unique, but they are usually not so unique as to negate the usefulness of the conceptual construct of the OCC. If, in our DCF valuation formula, we specify the discount rate, *r*, to indeed equal the OCC, then the present value the formula gives us will be our estimate of the *market value* of the asset (presuming the specified cash flows also are good estimates that would be typical in the market).

- **Internal Rate of Return (IRR)**. The IRR is similar to the discount rate in the sense that it does not have an economic meaning per se. It is merely a mathematical definition of a particular way to define the "return" on an investment in a multiperiod context where there may be intermediate cash flows while the investment is held. As described in Chapter 3, the IRR is a particularly useful and appealing way to define the total return for individual real estate investments. It does not require intermediate valuations of the asset, and it counts all cash flows equally, whether return on or return of invested capital. It reflects the timing of when capital is invested (money-weighted return), which can be important in real estate investment. **The IRR is defined as the discount rate that equates all the future cash flows to the present value** and, equivalently, vice versa, equates the present value to all the future cash flows. In itself, the IRR in a DCF formula does not necessarily equal the OCC because the present value in a DCF analysis may not be the market value of the asset. Similarly, the present value in a DCF valuation will not be the asset's market value if the IRR implied by that present value is not equal to the OCC.

As noted in Chapter 3, the IRR may be used either *ex-ante or ex-post*. In the former case, it is the forward-looking expected return (in the sense of probability of an expectation across future possibilities). In the DCF and asset valuation context, this use is often referred to as the "going-in IRR" (as in "going into" or "entering into" the investment). In its *ex-post use, the IRR would be the backward-looking actually realized historical IRR over some past horizon* or a lifetime of an investment. The term "going-out IRR" can refer to such *ex-post* usage in the context of DCF analysis. However, in a forward-looking *ex-ante* DCF analysis, the term "going-out IRR" can also refer to the expected return of the subsequent buyer of the property in the resale in the terminal period of the analysis (the going-in IRR of that subsequent buyer).

In a DCF valuation of a property, the discount rate, the OCC, and the going-in IRR will all be the same *if* the present value in the DCF analysis is the *market value* of the property. In this situation, the discount rate used in the DCF is equal to the (blended) OCC, where the OCC reflects market evidence on the total return required for an investment with similar risk. If a buyer over- or underpays for a property, the IRR and discount rate will differ from the OCC.

A simple numerical example will serve to illustrate these points. Recall the example 6-year DCF from early in Section 4.2, in which the OCC is taken to be 8 percent, which, given the operating and reversion cash flows, yields a present value of approximately \$15 million:

$$\$15\ million = \frac{\$1{,}000{,}000}{(1.08)^1} + \frac{\$1{,}000{,}000}{(1.08)^2} + \frac{\$1{,}000{,}000}{(1.08)^3} + \frac{\$1{,}500{,}000}{(1.08)^4} + \frac{\$1{,}500{,}000}{(1.08)^5} + \frac{\$16{,}500{,}000}{(1.08)^6}$$

In the formula, 8 percent is obviously the discount rate that mathematically yields a present value of \$15 million. In this example, presumably, 8 percent is the equilibrium expected return in the capital market for investment in assets of similar risk to the subject, measured as a blended IRR. Therefore, assuming that the cash flows are unbiased estimates of what the future will bring, \$15 million is the approximate present market value of the subject asset. Similarly, and equivalently, if we could know directly by some other means that the asset's current market value is \$15 million, then the formula tells us that 8 percent is the OCC, reflecting the current equilibrium in the market and the risk in the asset. If an investor pays \$15 million for the asset today, they face a going-in IRR of 8 percent (this is an *expectation*, not a guarantee!). A potential buyer might like to pay less and be looking at an expected return (going-in IRR) greater than 8 percent. They might offer the seller \$14 million, which would provide them with a 9.6 percent going-in return:

$$\$14\ million = \frac{\$1,000,000}{(1.096)^1} + \frac{\$1,000,000}{(1.096)^2} + \frac{\$1,000,000}{(1.096)^3} + \frac{\$1,500,000}{(1.096)^4} + \frac{\$1,500,000}{(1.096)^5} + \frac{\$16,500,000}{(1.096)^6}$$

In that case, 9.6 percent is obviously (mathematically) the discount rate in the formula and is (therefore) the IRR at the $14 million price. But 9.6 percent is not the OCC, and $14 million is not the market value of the asset, and the seller would be ill-advised to take that offer. "Market value" is often referred to as "fair value" (meaning a fair price for both sides, buyer and seller). It is the value the seller should be able to expect to sell the property for in a reasonable amount of time in the current market, as it represents the equilibrium pricing in that market. This is equivalent to the professional appraisal definition of "market value" as being equal to the "most probable price," which is the price that reflects the most typical buyer and seller requirements.

4.4 THE NPV INVESTMENT DECISION RULE

Up to now, we have been focusing on DCF as an analytical methodology that helps value properties and investments and analyze their return characteristics (for example, by computing IRRs implied by given prices). This is largely an exercise in "positive economics," essentially, descriptions of what is. But now, let us turn to an exercise in "normative economics," essentially a description of what "should be."

Recall that at the outset of this book (in the Preface), we highlighted three fundamental and common-sense principles of economics that we said would thread their way through pretty much this entire book: Opportunity cost, Market equilibrium, and Wealth maximization. Hopefully, it is obvious to you how those first two principles are deeply underlying the DCF valuation and analysis tools we have been describing. But what about that third principle, wealth maximization? Now, we want to bring the wealth maximization principle into play to put forth an investment decision rule that is very famous and widely espoused in financial economics (particularly, the sub-field of capital budgeting). This is the so-called "Net Present Value Rule," or NPV for short. Here is the rule:

1. Maximize the NPV across all mutually exclusive alternatives.
2. Never choose an alternative that has NPV < 0.[5]

Following this rule, combined with careful (realistic) application of the DCF valuation procedure (by using the correct OCC as the discount rate), would protect the seller in the previous example from making the mistake of agreeing to the buyer's offer of $14 million. Giving up an asset worth $15 million in return for receiving $14 million cash would have a *negative* NPV: $14 – $15 = – $1 million. The rule would also clarify and quantify the value of the deal from the buyer's perspective. If they *could* get the asset for $14 million, then the deal would be worth NPV = $15 – $14 = + $1 million. In that case, the first part of the rule would help the potential buyer to choose between that possibility and a mutually exclusive alternative that gains an asset worth $5 million for a price of $4.5 million.[6]

[5] The second part of the rule (never choose investments that have NPV < 0) is encompassed in the first part of the rule. It is virtually always possible to do something with NPV = 0 no matter how much money you have available to invest (including the possibility of "doing nothing," e.g., buying Treasury bills), so that there is practically always a zero-NPV alternative that is mutually exclusive to any investment. Hence, maximizing the NPV across mutually exclusive alternatives logically implies never doing a deal with NPV < 0.

[6] Note that this is in spite of the fact that the second project offers a "profitability ratio" of 0.5/4.5 = 11% while the first project only offers a 1/14 = 7% ratio. The key point here is that, the two investments are mutually exclusive: you must do

The beauty of the NPV rule lies in its elegance, simplicity, and intuitive appeal. The power of the NPV rule derives from the fact that it is based directly on the fundamental **wealth maximization** principle. In effect, the NPV rule says nothing more and nothing less than "Maximize your wealth." The corollary to this is that any rule other than the NPV rule will violate the wealth maximization principle. In effect, if you do not follow the NPV rule, you will be "leaving money on the table."

To clarify the link between the DCF valuation procedure and the NPV decision rule, it may be helpful to express the NPV for the typical commercial property investment decision as follows:

$$\textit{IF}\text{ buying: NPV} = \text{V} - \text{P}$$

$$\textit{IF}\text{ selling: NPV} = \text{P} - \text{V}$$

Where: V = Value of property at time zero (e.g., based on DCF)

P = Sales price of property (in time-zero equivalent $)

This makes it easy to see that the NPV rule simply says that you should maximize the value of what you are getting minus the value of what you are giving up, assuming these values are computed in an "apples versus apples" manner, adjusting for time and risk. The role of the DCF procedure is to make the necessary adjustments for time and risk.

4.4.1 NPV Rule Corollary: Zero NPV Deals Are OK

The following corollary to the NPV decision rule is often overlooked in practice:

Zero-NPV deals are OK!

A deal does not need a large positive NPV to make sense. Zero-NPV deals are not zero-profit deals because if the discount rate accurately reflects the opportunity cost of capital, it includes the expected return on the investment. This return is the normal amount of "profit" required for an investment of this nature. Zero NPV simply means that no supernormal profit is expected. A zero-NPV deal is only "bad" if it is mutually exclusive with another deal with a positive NPV.

Related to this point, notice that if the NPV is defined based on the market value of the asset in question, then the NPV on one side of the deal (e.g., that of the seller) is just the negative (or opposite sign) of the NPV on the other side of the deal (e.g., that of the buyer). Market value, which we will label MV for short, is, by definition, the price at which the property is expected to sell in the current asset market. This is, therefore, also the price a buyer must expect to pay to obtain the property. Thus, from this perspective:

$$\text{NPV(Buyer)} = \text{V} - \text{P} = \text{MV} - \text{P}$$
$$\text{NPV(Seller)} = \text{P} - \text{V} = \text{P} - \text{MV} = -\text{NPV(Buyer)}$$

Now, if both the buyer and the seller apply the NPV rule, they both require NPV > 0. However, as we saw in the earlier equations, this requirement can only be satisfied simultaneously on both sides of the deal if NPV = 0. That is

(i) $\text{NPV(Buyer)} \geq 0 \rightarrow -\text{NPV(Seller)} \geq 0 \rightarrow \text{NPV(Seller)} \leq 0$
(ii) $\text{NPV(Seller)} \geq 0 \rightarrow -\text{NPV(Buyer)} \geq 0 \rightarrow \text{NPV(Buyer)} \leq 0$
(iii) and (ii) together $\rightarrow \text{NPV(Buyer)} = \text{NPV(Seller)} = 0$

Thus, as long as we evaluate the NPV based on market values, we would expect a zero NPV.

In practice, investment decision-makers often only like to do deals that appear to have a substantial positive NPV. However, this desire may be unrealistic when the deal is evaluated from a market value perspective. The impression of widespread achievement of large positive NPVs may be more illusory than real in typical commercial real estate investing. Fundamentally, this is because real estate assets usually trade in well-functioning markets, where there is plenty of competition among potential buyers and sellers and among different but similar properties.

Several factors may make it appear that real estate investments have large positive NPVs when in actuality they do not. For example, the discount rate or cost of capital may be taken to be the cost of borrowed funds, which is lower than the full opportunity cost of capital because it ignores the higher risk (hence higher required return) equity component. Another common mistake is that cost components are left out of the equation. For example, the investor's own time and resources spent finding the deal and managing the project, or the property ownership responsibility, may be left out of the analysis or not fully priced. In development projects, the true opportunity cost of the land may be ignored in the NPV calculation or included only at its historical cost rather than the current market value. Yet the use of the land is clearly an opportunity cost of the development (due to the irreversibility of the construction project). The value of that opportunity cost is the current market value of the land, including the effect of any permitting, assemblage, or improvements the developer has added, which may be considerably greater than the land's historical cost. (See part IV of this book online.)

The fact that the expected NPV of a typical real estate investment deal is approximately zero has an important practical implication. It suggests that if you analyze a deal and find that it offers a large positive NPV based on market values (relative to the amount of investment involved), you should first double-check your analysis and information. An apparently large positive NPV would typically imply that either you or the opposite party in the transaction has made a serious mistake. Make sure it is not you![7]

4.4.2 Choosing among Alternative Zero-NPV Investments

How can an investor decide among alternative deals if they all seem to present an NPV of zero, evaluated honestly? There are two major answers to this question. The first concerns the difference between "market value" and "investment value." This difference will be discussed in depth in Chapter 14. The point here is that it is possible for NPV to be substantially positive for a given investor for a given deal when evaluated from that investor's personal investment value perspective, even when the assets are priced fairly at a market value such that the NPV of the deal is zero from a market value perspective. This normally requires that at least one party on one side of the deal has some unique ability to profit from the real estate that is being traded.

---

one or the other; you cannot do both. This type of absolute mutual exclusivity arises, for example, between two alternative ways to develop the same land parcel, or between developing the land today versus waiting and developing it next year. With this absolute type of mutual exclusivity, the wisdom of the NPV rule is obvious: would you rather have $1,000,000 or $500,000? But hold on, you say, the first project uses up $14,000,000 of my capital; the second project only $4,500,000, leaving me with $9,500,000 more still available to invest. You may have a good point there, for example, if you face a rigid capital availability constraint and have other positive NPV opportunities available, or if the flexibility provided by retaining more liquidity would be valuable. Considerations such as these can be difficult to quantify. The NPV rule is best when comparing alternatives that are not too different in scale and nature. As always, reason and common sense must be given the last word.

7 The conditions under which it would be reasonable to expect a large positive NPV are discussed in Chapter 14. An obvious filter that is widely employed in practice is to ascertain how long an apparent bargain has been available in the market. One would not expect substantially positive NPV opportunities, measured on the basis of market value, to wait around very long in a well-functioning market. By definition, such opportunities should get snapped up quickly. If you have found a deal that is abnormally good-looking but has been available for quite a while, your suspicions should rightly be raised. Presumably, a lot of other people have shied away from the deal for some reason. What is the reason? That reason is probably that the deal does not really present an NPV bargain.

The second way investors may rationally decide among alternatives with equal (zero) NPVs is similar to the kinds of investment decisions that investors in the stock market must make all the time. In the stock market, it is taken as virtually self-evident that the efficiency of the market gives transactions a zero NPV from a market value perspective. Investors typically have other objectives and constraints besides maximizing NPV, which leads them to select some stocks over others. For example, in real estate, investors may have portfolio objectives, such as increasing exposure to some types of properties or decreasing exposure to other types (e.g., for diversification purposes). Or investors may feel that they know more than the market does about a given asset's long-term value or worth. In real estate, certain investors may feel that they have greater expertise or ability or can operate more efficiently in some real estate markets or in managing certain types of real estate assets. There may be synergies between a given property and other properties the investor owns. (Recall that, unlike investors in the stock market, investors in direct property markets can obtain operational control and responsibility for the assets they invest in. This brings both opportunities and potential burdens that must be considered regarding the specific assets available.) Investors may also have target investment amounts and property sizes (this may reflect a desire to minimize administrative costs or overhead of the macro-level investment entity). They may prefer doing business with certain parties, either on the opposite side of the deal or as joint venture partners with them. Credibility matters, and a reputation for closing as promised matters greatly in the market. Another consideration is that while two alternatives may realistically present the same (zero) NPV, the quality of the information about one of the alternatives may be better, thereby presenting the investor with less uncertainty. All of these provide reasons to choose one available asset over another when they both present equal (zero) NPVs.

Some assets also better fit investors' preferences for return attributes (income vs. growth) or their perception of their strengths and capabilities as asset managers or property operators. Supplemental Chapter 4A, online, provides a way to parse or "attribute" the expected going-in investment return (IRR) in a manner that may help distinguish between alternative investments. This can help investors match investment opportunities with their preferences.

Finally, it should be remembered that just because the expected (and average or typical) NPV of a real estate investment is zero, this does not imply that you can assume that the NPV is zero without doing an honest and conscientious "due diligence" analysis. Real estate assets are not homogeneous securities traded in highly efficient exchanges where the dissemination of public information and the trading of private information are highly regulated. Both buyers and sellers sometimes make pricing mistakes. In the direct property markets of real estate investments, the old expression *caveat emptor* still applies to a greater degree than in the securities markets.

4.4.3 Hurdle Rate Version of the Decision Rule

An alternative version of the NPV decision rule—preferred by many decision-makers— expresses the decision rule in terms of the investment's expected and investor's required return (typically a single blended IRR rate) rather than in terms of its NPV. The IRR version of the investment decision rule is as follows:

1. *Maximize the difference between the project's expected IRR and the required return.*
2. *Never do a deal with an expected IRR less than the required return.*

As always, the required return is the total return, including a risk premium reflecting the riskiness of the investment (i.e., the OCC of the investment), the same as the discount rate that would be used in the DCF analysis of the market value of the investment described in Section 4.2. This required return is referred to as the **hurdle rate**. The first part of the rule ensures that projects with the highest returns will be selected first. The second part ensures that no projects will be selected that do not at least cover their opportunity cost of capital on an ex-ante basis. Note also that if your hurdle rate is too high relative to the market, you will always be outbid, suggesting you will have a zero-asset portfolio.

The formal process of using the hurdle rate decision rule is to first look at all cash flows generated by the investment. This includes CF_0 and the subsequent growth (g) over a period of – typically – 10 years. In the final year, you also have a reversion cash flow for selling the property (using the "cap rate" method discussed earlier). The asking price for which the property is on the market is treated as a large negative cash flow in year 0. Subsequently, you can compute the IRR of this investment. The hurdle rate decision rule says that if the IRR of the investment is higher than the pre-set hurdle rate, one should purchase the property.

In most typical circumstances, when applied properly, the IRR version of the investment decision rule will give the same decision result as the NPV version of the rule. That is, if the investment under consideration passes the NPV test with NPV ≥ 0, then it will also pass the IRR test with IRR ≥ $E_0(r)$, where $E_0(r)$ = OCC. However, in practice, we find that there can be differences between both approaches, mostly caused by the fact that the hurdle rate is not always based on the property-specific OCC, *even though it should be*! For example, management might set a firm-level hurdle rate of 8 percent based on the corporate average cost of capital. Any investment that exceeds this hurdle would then be considered desirable by management. However, this does not take into account the fact that the subject property of the analysis might be riskier than the corporate average and that, thus, investment in a property providing, say, even a 9 percent going-in IRR might still be a negative NPV investment. Setting the hurdle rate as the property-specific OCC can help overcome this problem.

Even if the hurdle rate is specifically chosen per property and is based on the property's OCC, you can still get a different outcome from the NPV and hurdle rate decision rules in specific circumstances. These differences occur when rank-ordering matters, which is problematic if you have mutually exclusive investments. In that case, the scale of the alternative projects matters. One project may present a higher percentage return but provide less actual money value (added wealth). Mutual exclusivity occurs if the investor cannot do both projects being compared: implementing one project rules out the possibility of implementing the other. The most obvious example of mutual exclusivity in real estate is that of real estate development on a given land site when comparing two alternative developments of the same site.

For example, say that you inherited a plot of land. After careful analysis, you find that you could develop either but not both of two distinct projects, called Project A and Project B. You cannot develop both projects on this one piece of land, so you must pick one. Now, further assume that the OCC and thus your hurdle rate for both projects is 10%. Project A is a \$15 million investment presenting a 15 percent going-in IRR, while Project B is a \$5 million investment presenting a 20 percent going-in IRR. The NPV of project A is:

$$1.15(\$15\text{M})/1.10 - \$15\text{M} = \$17.25\text{M}/1.10 - \$15\text{M} = +\$682{,}000.$$

The NPV of project B is:

$$1.20(\$5\text{M})/1.10 - \$5\text{M} = \$6\text{M}/1.10 - \$5\text{M} = +\$455{,}000.$$

Project A is generally preferable (wealth maximizing), even though it presents a smaller IRR.[8]

[8] Suppose the investor has a total of \$15 million of equity capital available to invest. With Project B, she could still invest \$10 million in Treasury bonds (or in the stock market, for example). With project A, she has blown all her capital. But investments in Treasury bonds (or in stocks) are generally zero NPV, leaving her wealth unchanged. To maximize her wealth, she must put all \$15 million into Project A.

Another consideration is that, even though the IRR rule is usually valid when properly applied, it is not uncommon in practice for the IRR rule to be misapplied, in that investors seek the project that presents the highest IRR without considering possible differences in risk. The NPV rule is less susceptible to this weakness, as it forces an explicit determination of the opportunity cost of capital (the discount rate).

TEXT BOX 4.1 DO INVESTORS USE THE HURDLE RATE RULE INSTEAD OF THE NPV RULE?

Sometimes, investors claim they use the hurdle rate rule instead of the NPV rule. If this is really true, then they are not maximizing their wealth. As successful investors in the long run are, virtually by definition, those who maximize their wealth, it is probably not entirely accurate that these investors use the hurdle rate rule instead of the NPV rule. It is likely that they routinely employ the hurdle rate rule. Still, in those rare circumstances in which the hurdle rate and NPV rules would give a different answer, the most successful investors probably implicitly apply the NPV rule instead due to its wealth implications. Although it is intuitive to think in terms of returns, ignoring the NPV can lead to muddled thinking. When you focus uniquely on the return, allocating your money to investments that provide the highest return is tempting. But this may be unwise if the high-return investments are also of greater risk or prevent you from making larger investments that would actually increase your present wealth more. Note that it is also tempting for sponsors or managers to sell property too early in order to achieve a higher IRR, even though that IRR exceeds the required rate of return and would continue to do so if held. The NPV or absolute payback ratio might be maximized by holding longer. The reason for an early sale might be (1) a promise must be kept on the maximum term of the investment fund, (2) the sponsor might have an incentive contract that provides a greater share of the profit if the IRR exceeds a specified hurdle, and (3) the sponsor wants to brag about beating the required rate of return so that they have an easier time raising capital on the next fund. It is a mathematical characteristic of the IRR that, for a given amount of monetary profit, it is easier to score a higher IRR for shorter holding periods due to the fact that the IRR is measured on a per annum basis.

4.5 CHAPTER SUMMARY

This chapter presented the basic concepts and procedures for commercial property valuation and investment analysis at the micro-level: the level of individual properties or projects. In this chapter, we started with the concept of investment returns (investment profits) from Chapter 3. We related the returns investors are interested in to the asset values they grapple with in micro-level deals. We presented the multiperiod DCF method as the basic tool in this process and showed how DCF relates to the widely-used shortcut of direct capitalization. Finally, we related asset valuation to investment decision-making by considering the NPV rule. We tried to point out how the three fundamental common-sense economic principles of opportunity cost, market equilibrium, and wealth maximization underlie and elucidate all of these procedures when and if they are correctly applied.

KEY TERMS

- Returns and values
- Expected cash flows (numerators)

- Greater Fool Theory
- Discounted cash flow (DCF)
- Opportunity cost of capital (OCC)
- Going-in IRR
- Intralease discount rate
- Interlease discount rate
- Reversion cash flow
- Expected returns (denominators)
- Blended IRR
- Unbundled cash flows
- Direct capitalization
- Discount rate
- Net present value (NPV)
- Market value
- Hurdle rate
- Cap rate

STUDY QUESTIONS

In Your Own Words

4.1 What is the Greater Fool Theory? How can the multiperiod DCF valuation procedure help to protect investors from falling victim to this theory?

4.2 What is wrong with the following statement: Property X is worth $10 million in the market today because it produces $1 million of annual net income, and cap rates in the relevant property asset market are currently 10 percent.

4.3 What is the approximate relationship among the cap rate, the discount rate, and the long-run average growth rate in property cash flow and value? Write down the formula, then answer the following questions:

a. Write the investor's required return as the sum of the risk-free rate plus a risk premium to establish the approximate relationship between the cap rate, interest rate, risk premium, and growth rate in property cash flow.

b. How are cap rates affected by interest rates? Does an increase in the risk-free rate imply higher cap rates? (Hint: There is no mention of "all else equal.")

c. Many analysts have taken to defining the spread between the cap rate and the risk-free rate as a risk premium. What is wrong with this practice? Under what conditions does this lead to the perception of a high-risk premium being incorporated into property values, when in fact the opposite is true?

4.4 Why is a zero-NPV deal OK? Where is the profit for the investor in a deal in which NPV = 0?

4.5 Why is the NPV of the typical deal zero when evaluated from a market value perspective?

4.6 Describe at least two other considerations besides NPV that can allow investors to choose among alternative investments that have the same NPV.

4.7 Describe at least two problems that can be encountered in using the hurdle rate version of the NPV investment decision rule, and how those problems can be resolved.

Check Your Knowledge

4.8 In the NPV investment decision rule, what should investors prioritize?

A) Maximizing total rent

B) Maximizing net present value (NPV) across all alternatives

C) Minimizing opportunity costs
D) Maximizing transaction costs

4.9 What does the term "opportunity cost of capital" (OCC) represent in the context of real estate valuation?
A) The initial investment price
B) The cost of equity capital
C) The expected return from the next best alternative investment with comparable risk
D) The cost of financing through debt

4.10 An office building in Greenville has a cap rate of 9% and a long-run average growth rate in property cash flow of 2% annually. What is the approximate discount rate (r) that should be applied to this property?
A) 9%
B) 11%
C) 10.32%
D) 12%

4.11 Which of the following is a limitation of using a single blended discount rate in the DCF model?
A) It applies only to short-term leases.
B) It cannot differentiate between cash flows of varying risk.
C) It always underestimates the terminal value of a property.
D) It requires predicting detailed cash flows for every year.

4.12 The following table shows two 10-year cash flow projections (in $ millions, including reversion) for the same property. The upper row is the projection that will be presented by the broker trying to sell the building, and the bottom row is the realistic expectations. Suppose that it would be relatively easy for any potential buyers to ascertain that the most likely current market value for the property is about $10 million.

Year	**1**	**2**	**3**	**4**	**5**	**6**	**7**	**8**	**9**	**10**
Presented	$1.0000	$1.0300	$1.0609	$1.0927	$1.1255	$1.1593	$1.1941	$1.2299	$1.2668	$14.7439
Realistic	$1.0000	$1.0100	$1.0201	$1.0303	$1.0406	$1.0510	$1.0615	$1.0721	$1.0829	$12.1399

a. What going-in IRR (blended rate) will equate the presented cash flow projection to the observable $10 million present value (as of year 0)?
b. What rate will equate the realistic projection to that same present value?
c. What is the most likely amount of "disappointment" in the ex-post rate of return earned by an investor who buys this property believing the broker's cash flow projection (i.e., the difference in presented versus realistic return)?

4.13 The buildings in a certain warehouse market are characterized by net cash flow projections like the one shown in the following table, based on net leases of five years' duration. In this market, properties are typically evaluated using a going-in IRR of 10.50 percent (blended rate). Thus, the typical property sells for a cap rate of about 8.25 percent. You have the opportunity to purchase a property with these same typical cash flow projections, at the typical cap rate or going-in IRR. However, your building is entirely covered by a 10-year lease with a AAA-credit tenant who can borrow money at 6 percent.
a. How much is this lease worth?
b. Assuming that the appropriate interlease and reversion discount rate is 12 percent, what is your NPV from this deal?

Ten-Year Cash Flow Projection ($ millions)

Year	1	2	3	4	5	6	7	8	9	10
Operating	$1.0	$1.0	$1.1	$1.1	$1.2	$1.2	$1.3	$1.3	$1.4	$1.4
Reversion										$14.0
CF	$1.0	$1.0	$1.1	$1.1	$1.2	$1.2	$1.3	$1.3	$1.4	$15.4

4.14 You are evaluating two investment opportunities, Blue Ridge Apartments (A) and Green Valley Towers (B). Their projected cash flows (including reversion) are shown in the following table for property A and property B.

a. If both properties sell at a cap rate (initial cash yield) of 10 percent, what is the expected total return on a 10-year investment in each property?

b. If the 10 percent cap rate represents a fair market value for each property, then which property is the riskier investment (and how do you know)?

c. What is the annual growth rate in operating cash flows for each building during the first nine years?

d. How is this growth rate related to the cap rate and the investor's expected total return (IRR) in each property?

Annual Net Cash Flow Projections for Two Properties ($ millions)

Year	1	2	3	4	5	6	7	8	9	10
A	$1.0000	$1.0100	$1.0201	$1.0303	$1.0406	$1.0510	$1.0615	$1.0721	$1.0829	$12.1399
B	$1.0000	$0.9900	$0.9801	$0.9703	$0.9606	$0.9510	$0.9415	$0.9321	$0.9227	$9.9573

Chapter Case: Summit Heights Commercial Plaza

Summit Heights Commercial Plaza is a well-located mixed-use property that Kai Property Group is evaluating for a potential long-term investment. The property is composed of retail and office spaces in a prime business district, making it attractive due to its steady rental income streams and potential for appreciation in value. The building is currently listed with an asking price of $260,000.

Summit Heights Commercial Plaza currently has stable tenant occupancy with several long-term leases in place. The property is expected to generate future net cash flows of $25,000 per year for the first five years (at the end of each year), with an anticipated increase of 20% after the fifth year. This would result in cash flows of $30,000 per year for the following five years. Kai Property Group expects to sell the property at the end of 10 years for 10 times the net cash flow at that time, leading to a projected sale price of $300,000.

1. What is the Present Value of Summit Heights Commercial Plaza if the required return is 12%?
   A) $141,824
   B) $221,749
   C) $248,075
   D) $266,099
2. What is the NPV if Kai Property Group purchases the building at the seller's current asking price of $260,000?
   A) –$118,176
   B) $11,925
   C) –$11,925
   D) $6,099

3. Four interns at Kai Property Group are discussing what a negative NPV means. Who is correct?
   A) Alice: "A negative NPV means the investment will exceed the required return."
   B) Brian: "A negative NPV means the investment falls short of the required return."
   C) Catherine: "A negative NPV means the investment will break even."
   D) David: "A negative NPV means the investment has no future cash flows."
4. Four interns are trying to figure out what it means when an investment has a "zero NPV." Who has the right interpretation?
   A) Alice: "A zero NPV means the investment has zero profit."
   B) Brian: "A zero NPV means the investment covers only its opportunity cost and does not generate supernormal profits."
   C) Catherine: "A zero NPV means the investment will result in a financial loss."
   D) David: "A zero NPV means the investment does not have any return on capital."
5. What is the IRR if Kai Property Group buys the property for $260,000?
   A) 12.5%
   B) 13.0%
   C) 11.24%
   D) 12.00%
6. By what percentage does the property value change if the required return drops from 12% to 11%?
   A) The value decreases by 6.36%
   B) The value increases by 6.36%
   C) The value decreases by 1%
   D) The value increases by 1%
7. If the cash flow growth increases to 25% in year 6 to $31,250, instead of the original assumption of 20%, what is the resulting property value?
   A) $250,000
   B) $254,656
   C) $248,075
   D) $260,000
8. What is the effect of increasing cash flow growth from 20% to 25% after year 5?
   A) Property value decreases by 2.65%.
   B) Property value remains the same.
   C) Property value increases by 2.65%.
   D) Property value becomes negative.
9. How does an increase in the terminal capitalization rate affect the resale price of Summit Heights Commercial Plaza at the end of year 10?
   A) It increases the terminal value.
   B) It decreases the terminal value.
   C) It has no effect on the terminal value.
   D) It decreases the operating cash flows.

Part II

Nuts and Bolts of Property Income Analysis

Just as financial economics is the primary branch of economics useful for studying the real estate asset market, so urban economics is the primary academic discipline for rigorously studying the space market. The space market is where and how rents are determined. It, therefore, underlies the cash flow numerators of the DCF asset valuation model presented in Chapter 4. That model allows you to see how important those numerators are for asset value and, hence, for success or failure in investment performance. Now, here in part II, we will drill down into those numerators in a concrete and practical fashion. We will focus on how rent is determined and why and how it varies over time and space. And then, considering that it is the *net* cash flows that matter, we will consider such topics as what costs are associated with owning real estate. How are leases structured? And other topics to give you a solid grasp of dealing with the fundamental cash flows that matter at the property level.

The plan of attack is as follows. First, we will discuss the nuts and bolts of real estate cash flow proformas (cash flow projections) in Chapter 5. In Chapters 6 and 7, we go over fundamental concepts of urban economics, which will answer questions about what drives rent. Subsequently, we provide tools and perspectives to forecast rent and net cash flow growth, in Chapters 8 and Chapter 9. Finally, Chapter 10 will review leases and leasing considerations and how to compute the effective rent.

DOI: 10.1201/9781003643838-6

5 Income Definitions for Commercial Real Estate

CHAPTER OUTLINE

LEARNING OBJECTIVES

After reading this chapter, you should understand:

- The components and basic structure of the typical commercial property investment cash flow proforma.
- The difference between operating expenses and capital expenditures.
- Distinguish between rent roll, net operating income, and property-before-tax cash flow.
- The exact formula for computing the expected sales price.

Chapter 4 laid out the basic framework for investment valuation at the micro-level. This chapter will focus on individual cash flow items used in the DCF, discounted cash flow, and proforma. We will decompose all income and expense items associated with commercial real estate investment at the asset level in detail.

All of the discussion in this chapter is at what may be called the "property-before-tax" (PBT) level (also referred to as the "asset level"). That is, we are examining cash flows and valuation at the property level, as distinguished from the level of the owner of the property equity and as distinguished from the portfolio (or "macro") level. The PBT level is most appropriate for analyzing the market

DOI: 10.1201/9781003643838-7

value of property assets. Thus, the analysis here does not consider funds borrowed against the property, debt service payments, or income taxes, which are matters to be treated in subsequent chapters.

5.1 THE PROFORMA

Arguably, we can view the **proforma** as being the single most important document when analyzing a commercial real estate investment decision. The proforma presents the fundamentals of what we described in the DCF evaluation in the previous chapter. Recall that the DCF evaluation process consists of (1) forecasting all cash flows and (2) applying the correct discount rate. The proforma is essentially the numerator in that DCF evaluation, the forecasted net cash flows, based on a detailed list of all the income and expenses a specific property is expected to generate. The DCF also provides the data for calculating several important financial ratios, which will be discussed later.

The Latin origin of the word proforma means "for form." This suggests that this cash flow forecast document may be produced more for appearance's sake or as a formality than as a serious step in analysis and evaluation. Indeed, we would be less than honest if we did not admit that this is often the case in practice, as lenders and outside investors will typically require a proforma before a deal can be considered. But the proforma, or the cash flow forecast that makes it up, should be taken seriously. Going through the exercise of trying to estimate unbiased, realistic forecasts of a property's future cash flow generation potential is fundamental to sound decision-making. With this in mind, let's look at the nuts and bolts of a typical real estate proforma.

As noted in Chapter 4, cash flows are typically projected for a reasonably long period of time (5 to 10 years is the most common). This is because real properties are long-lived, and most investors hold properties for long periods (in part, in order to minimize the effect of transaction costs on returns). Even if the owner expects to sell the property shortly, the property's resale value (i.e., the price any potential buyer would be willing to pay for it) fundamentally depends on the property's ability to generate operating income over the long term. Hence, a long horizon is still necessary for a solid evaluation. Long-horizon forecasts also have the salutary effect of forcing the analyst to grapple with difficult issues regarding where the rental market is headed. (Most of the value of most buildings is derived from the building's earning potential after the current leases expire.)

EXHIBIT 5-1
Typical Line Items in a Proforma for Income Property

1. Operating Cash Flows (t = 1,...,T)

Cash flow item	Abbreviation	Item
Potential gross income	(PGI)	(a)
(*rent p. SF x rentable SF*)		
– Vacancy allowance	- (vacancy)	(b)
(*vacancy rate (%) x PGI*)		
= Effective gross income	(EGI)	(c)
+ Other income	(OI)	(d)
– Operating expenses	(OpEx)	(e)
= Net operating income	(NOI)	(f)
– Capital expenditures	(CapEx)	(g)
= Property before-tax cash flow	(PBTCF)	(h)

2. Reversion Cash Flows (T)

Cash flow item	Abbreviation	
Property value at time of sale	(TV)	(i)
– Selling expenses		(j)
= Property before-tax cash flow	(PBTCF)	(k)

The importance of completing the proforma construction exercise is particularly obvious in the case of commercial properties with long-term leases. However, it may also be useful for apartment properties, as it makes explicit the long-term rental-and-expense growth rate assumptions that underlie the property's value.

As noted in an earlier Chapter, two categories of cash flows should be represented in a complete proforma for real estate investment analysis: the **operating cash flows** and the **reversion cash flows**. The former refers to cash flows that result from the normal operation of the property and, therefore, accrue to the owner of the property regularly throughout the period the property is held as an investment. In contrast, reversion cash flows occur only at the time of, and due to, the sale of all or a portion of the property asset. The term "reversion" reflects the basic idea that the return of the original capital invested in the asset should occur when the value "reverts back" to the investor upon the sale of the asset (though effects such as asset market changes and building structure depreciation make this conception less precise and less certain than in the case, for example, of the par value of a long-term coupon bond). The table in Exhibit 5-1 shows, in general form, the typical line items in a proforma for an income-producing property.

5.2 OPERATING CASH FLOW ITEMS

Next, we will discuss each operating cash flow line item (items a – h, in Exhibit 5-1). It will also provide some averages or typical percentage values of all the line items to get a sense of the relative importance of each item. (Of course, every property is unique, and leases will vary as to who pays what, so please take the numbers with a grain of salt.)

5.2.1 POTENTIAL GROSS INCOME (ITEM A, EXHIBIT 5-1)

The top line item in the operating cash flows is the primary potential source of property revenue, the cash it could earn if it were fully rented. This item is typically labeled potential revenue or **potential gross income (PGI)**. In practice, this item is also often called the **rent roll**, especially in multi-tenant properties with long-term leases. This is because, in such properties, the current PGI is often enumerated by explicitly listing each lease and potentially leasable space in the property. The PGI is determined by multiplying the amount of rentable space (e.g., square feet) by the rent per unit of space (e.g., rent per SF). In the case of apartment properties (or hotels), the apartment unit (hotel room) itself is often the spatial unit used. For example, the rent roll for a building with 100 similar apartment units could be calculated by multiplying the average expected rent per unit times the 100 units in the building.

Note that the rentable area (RA) is generally less than the gross area (GA) of a building due to common areas for lobbies, elevators, staircases, building equipment areas, etc. As described more fully in the text box regarding building area measurement, commercial property in the United States has an RA/GA ratio of approximately 90 percent (sometimes called the "efficiency ratio"). So-called "assignable space" (which is what the office tenant can use to actually house employees) averages only some 80 percent of RA, a vital consideration when relating required RA to the number of employees.

TEXT BOX 5.1 WHAT SQUARE FOOTAGE?

When investing in real estate, understanding definitions of (and procedures for measuring) building floor areas is critical. When two parties have different standards in mind, errors can cost significant sums of money. Making things worse is that building code definitions can vary from one country to another. Arguably, the most important of such codes in the United States is developed by BOMA (The Building Owners and Managers Association), which has been publishing such standards since 1915. Some of their most important definitions are;

- **Construction Gross Area (CGA)**. CGA is used for estimating construction costs or maintenance costs and is a sum of all occupiable and nonoccupiable spaces – such as balconies, terraces, entry alcoves, roofs, and colonnades. It also includes exterior covered spaces that are part of the building's occupiable space. Construction Gross Area represents the largest square footage calculation since it includes all areas.
- **Gross Area (GA).** GA is like the CGA except that it excludes the nonoccupiable spaces mentioned above. Given that it includes *all* occupiable spaces, the square footage of staircases, elevators, restrooms, (load-bearing) columns, and lobbies are still part of the GA.
- **Rentable Area (RA)**. RA is a term used in the BOMA to identify the portion of a floor or building for which a tenant will pay rent. It is loosely defined as the sum of the tenant's area and the tenants' share of the common or shared spaces (amenity and service areas). The RA will exclude outer walls/columns[1], staircases, (vertical) shafts, and elevators.
- **Usable Area (UA).** Very similar in definition to the rentable area, but excludes the service areas (restrooms, electrical closets, data closets, etc.). As such, UA is always smaller than RA. The UA is important as it is used to compute the efficiency ratio; see below. Corridors and lobbies are still included in the UA.
- **Net Assignable Area (NAA)**. Simply stated, NAA is the sum of spaces that can be specifically assigned to people or programs. Excluded from NAA are the building service area, corridors, lobbies, circulation area, and mechanical area that are required for the building's operation.

The difference in square footage between the Gross Area and Rentable Area is typically around 10%, with a great deal of variation based on design. Subsequently, the **efficiency ratio** is calculated by dividing the Net Rentable Area by the Usable Area. According to BOMA, the typical efficiency ratio for large office buildings in the US was 80%–92% between 2006 and 2019. On average, the efficiency ratio will be slightly lower for more affordable multifamily properties, as there tends to be less shared space and higher for high-rise, high-amenity apartment units.

5.2.2 Vacancy Allowance (item b, Exhibit 5-1)

Generally, we cannot realistically expect a property to always be fully leased and generate its entire PGI every year. (Chapter 9 will provide more details on why.) The second line item in Exhibit 5-1, the vacancy allowance, accounts for the expected effect of vacancy in the property's net cash flow. This line item is usually quantified in one of two ways. For properties with many short-term leases, such as apartment buildings, the vacancy allowance is typically accounted for as a percentage of the PGI. For example, suppose the average tenant remains in an apartment for 5 years, and the average apartment unit is vacant for three months between tenants. Then the total cycle for a unit is 63 months (60 months occupied, followed by 3 months vacant), so the average apartment is – therefore – vacant 3/63, or 4.8 percent, of the time, which could be rounded off to 5 percent. The vacancy

[1] Columns inside the building are typically still included in the square footage "assigned" to the tenant. In other words, columns inside your space are not subtracted from the lease, and the tenant will pay rent for the space the column occupies!

allowance in the proforma would be computed as 5 percent of the potential gross revenue projection each year.

The second method of computing the vacancy allowance is to explicitly forecast the likely vacancy period associated with each rental unit or space in the building, considering the expiration of each lease currently in the building, the typical lease term, and the likelihood of tenant renewal. This method is more appropriate for buildings with long-term (i.e., multiyear) leases or buildings that currently have substantial vacancy that is expected to be filled over some projected schedule.

There may also be a collection allowance in addition to the vacancy rate. For example, based on historical trends, about 0.5% to 1.5% of tenants cannot fulfill their lease obligation because of bankruptcy.[2] This is not unusual for start-ups and lower-credit tenants, so some extra percentage of lost rent should be included in the vacancy loss above, which could be described as the vacancy and collection allowance.

5.2.3 Effective Gross Income (item c, Exhibit 5-1)

Subtracting the vacancy allowance line-item amount (in money terms) from the PGI provides a projection of what is often referred to as the **effective gross income (EGI)** for the property in the proforma each year. To understand the typical gap between PGI and EGI per square foot, we plot the historic averages for NCREIF properties in Exhibit 5-2.

5.2.4 Other Income (item d, Exhibit 5-1)[3]

Many properties have other sources of earning income besides the rental of their space for the occupancy of tenants; for example;

- Revenue from operating vending machines or laundry machines in apartment buildings.
- Revenue from parking operations, billboard, or antenna rental in office or retail buildings.
- Revenue generated by smaller retail operations (like kiosks or newsstands) in a mall.
- Excess electricity generated by solar panels on the roof of the building is being sold back to the grid.

These sources of income are typically referred to as **other income**, represented by the third line item in Exhibit 5-1. The amount of other income generated by properties is very idiosyncratic. For some properties, like super regional shopping malls, other income as a proportion of EGI can be very high, and for others, it is negligible. A famous example of the first is the Empire State Building in New York, whose observation deck generates more income than all the rents collected in the property itself *combined.*

5.2.5 Operating Expenses (item e, Exhibit 5-1)

The next major category in the proforma is **operating expenses (OpEx)**. This heading will include several regularly occurring, specific expense line items associated with the ongoing operation of the property. You can look at these costs as mandatory, given that you need them for the property to function on a day-to-day basis. Typical major categories include property management and administration, utilities, insurance, regular maintenance and repair, and property taxes. Income taxes are

---

[2] Source: CoStar. This is for non-residential properties.

[3] Some examples exist where EGI is calculated as: EGI = PGI – vacancy – *other income*. EGI is not a formal term in GAAP accounting, hence some leeway exists on where "other income" goes. We will keep "other income" below EGI going forward.

not included in the operating expenses because they are attributable to the owner/investor, not the property itself.

It should also be noted that for investment analysis purposes, property management expenses should be identified and charged as an operating expense (i.e., above the NOI bottom line), *even if the owner/investor will be managing the property itself.* The time and energy of whoever is performing this job reflect the **property management opportunity cost**. In the case of owner/managers (or "self-management"), it is important not to confuse the return on the financial capital invested in the property with the return on human capital or labor invested in property management. After all, investment in other forms of capital, such as stocks or bonds, would not generally require management input on the part of the investor. So, comparisons among investment alternatives will be biased in favor of real estate if this cost is not subtracted from the real estate yield.

In general, the cost of property management in cases of self-management can be quantified by the opportunity cost defined by the fee that a professional property manager would charge to manage the subject property. This is often in the range of 5 percent to 10 percent of the EGI per year for small properties. Due to economies of scale, management costs are usually lower on a percentage basis for larger properties. For example, management costs of large-scale class A or prime office properties are typically in the 2 percent to 3 percent range.

It is often useful to describe a property's operating expenses in terms of either **fixed** or **variable costs** (or, some line items may be best described as a combination of the two). Fixed expenses, in principle, are unaffected by the level of occupancy in the building. They will remain at the same level (at least in the short run, say, for a year or so) no matter how vacant or full the building may be. Property taxes and insurance charges are typically in this category. Variable expenses occur in direct proportion (more or less) to the occupancy level. For example, in a half-vacant building, utility expenses may be only a little over half what they would be when the building is full.

Class A properties often have so-called **net leases** (also called **triple-net** or **NNN** leases) in which the tenants pay all or most of the operating expenses. Other leases partially reimburse some or all operating expense line items (see Chapter 10 for more details). For example, landlords and tenants often negotiate **expense stops**, in which tenants pay all operating expenses above an agreed-upon base level, which typically reflects the level of operating expenses per square foot when the lease is signed. When operating expenses are expected to be reimbursed by tenants, these reimbursements will typically appear as additional positive cash flow line items in the proforma, as positive inflows in the landlord's favor, partially offsetting the operating expense outflows.

5.2.6 Net Operating Income (item f, Exhibit 5-1)

The **net operating income (NOI)** results from subtracting the operating expenses from all the previously discussed sources of revenue (rental revenue net of vacancy allowance, other income, and expense reimbursements). NOI is the most widely used indicator of the property's net cash flow or operating profit generation ability. This is even though a more complete and accurate measure of net cash flow would subtract necessary capital improvement expenditures routinely made on the property. However, because of the irregular and discretionary nature of the timing of many capital improvement expenditures, the NOI is typically a more stable and easily quantified number than the actual net cash flow after capital expenditures. As a result, in common usage, NOI is often treated as virtually the same thing as the property's net cash flow, and property investment current yield or income return measures (such as the cap rate) are often quantified as the current NOI divided by the current property value. While convenient and often sufficient, such a practice does risk ignoring the potentially important impact of capital improvement expenditures on the actual net cash yield of the asset.

5.2.7 Capital Improvement Expenditures (Item G, Exhibit 5-1)

This brings us to the next line item in Exhibit 5-1, **capital improvement expenditures (CapEx)**. In general, this item refers to major expenditures providing long-term improvements to the physical quality of the property, required to maintain or add to the value of the property. Examples would be replacing or upgrading the heating, ventilation, and cooling (HVAC) system; replacing a roof; adding a parking lot or repaving an existing one; adding new landscaping; or other such investments.

In addition to capital improvements to the building as a whole, capital expenditures are often associated with signing specific long-term leases. Such **leasing costs** include **tenant improvement expenditures (TIs)** reimbursed to the tenants and **leasing commissions** paid to leasing brokers (including tenant reps). TIs are a major category of capital expenditures in many buildings with long-term leases. This refers to customized physical improvements, including finishings, partitioning, and decorations, provided at the time of lease signing to the space the tenant will occupy. To some extent, these may be viewed as **concessions** the landlord offers the tenant to get the tenant to sign the long-term lease. In the United States, it is not uncommon for the landlord to incur some level of TI expenditures, even just to get an existing tenant to stay and sign a new lease when their existing lease expires. TIs may be managed and paid for directly by the landlord, or the landlord may simply provide the tenant with an allowance amount, which the tenant then spends as they deem fit. The tenant may also pay for some TIs in some cases, which do not, therefore, enter into the property cash flow proforma. When tenants require unique TIs that most tenants would not need, it adds risk to the owner since such TIs may need to be removed prior to re-leasing. Generic TIs needed by all tenants present less risk to the landlords, and such considerations may affect rent-setting policies.

Leasing costs are typically negligible for apartment properties. Indeed, TIs hardly exist in the rental apartment market due to the short-term nature and low present value of the leases, and leasing commissions are usually nonexistent because households do their own apartment searching and finding. The breakdown of capital expenditures is more evenly distributed between the two major categories of leasing commissions and building improvements for office, retail, and industrial properties.

From a cash flow timing perspective, the characteristic of capital improvement expenditures that distinguishes them from regular operating expenses is that capital expenditures occur less frequently, at irregular intervals of time. General capital expenditures are also characterized by considerable *flexibility* and *discretion* on the property owner's part as to exactly when to make the expenditure and how much to spend. At the same time, leasing costs are linked to the dates when leases expire. In the property management business, projected capital expenditures will typically be presented in a separate proforma as part of a capital budget for the property. However, capital expenditures must be consolidated into the overall property cash flow proforma for investment analysis purposes.

Even though the NOI is often thought of as the operating bottom line in property-level analysis, it is important to recognize that capital expenditures are, in fact, not a minor or trivial determinant in the net cash flow of the property for most property types. On average, over the long run, capital improvement expenditures typically equal 1 percent to 2 percent of the property value per year (typically around 10 percent to 20 percent of the NOI). This percentage will, of course, tend to be less in new buildings and greater in middle-aged buildings. Very old buildings may be nearing redevelopment and so do not warrant major capital improvement expenditures.

It is also important to recognize that accounting procedures vary as to what is classified as a capital improvement instead of an operating expense. For example, as noted, commissions paid to leasing brokers are often classified as capital improvement expenditures, even though such expenditures do not alter the physical structure and are generally not rare or discretionary, and they are typically financed from the cash flow generated by the building. GAAP accounting rules allow some discretion in the treatment of capital expenditures. At one extreme, some landlords treat almost all capital

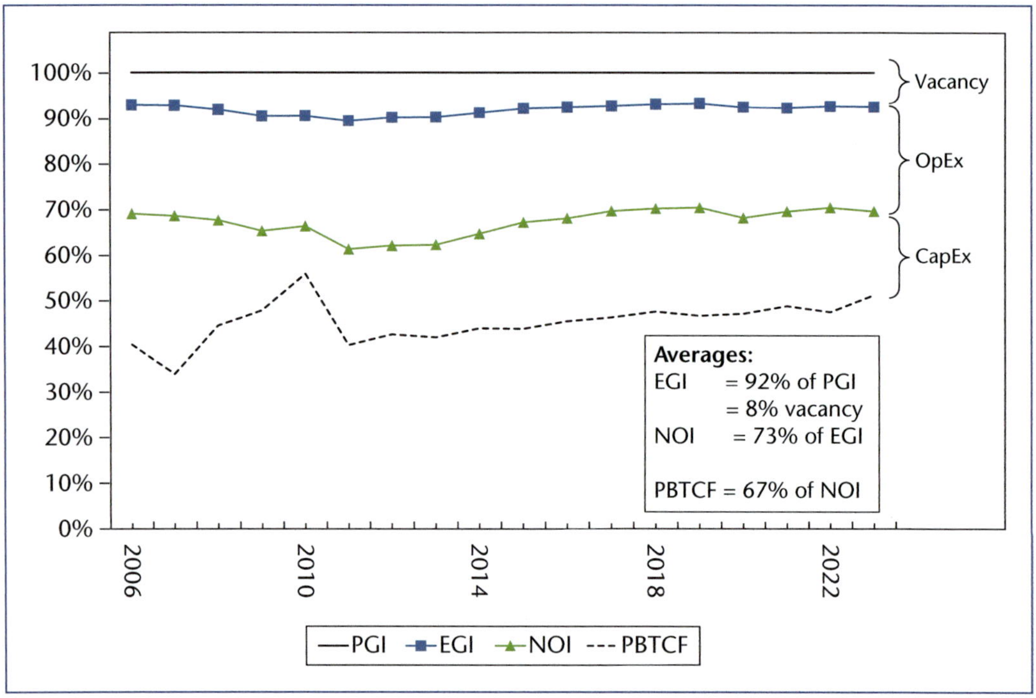

EXHIBIT 5-2 Average Breakdown of the Different Line Items (2006Q1–2022Q2).

Source: NCREIF.

expenditures as current expenses (taken out above the NOI "bottom line"). But more generally, in accrual accounting, capital expenditures are amortized (as a form of depreciation expense) over some specified lifetime of the given improvement.

5.2.8 Property before-tax Cash Flow (item h, Exhibit 5-1)

As noted, viewing the NOI as the bottom line of cash flow available for distribution from building operations can be somewhat misleading. The more realistic picture of the free-and-clear cash flow available to the owners of the property (before debt service and income taxes are taken out) is represented by the NOI less the capital improvement expenditures. We label this the property-before-tax cash flow (PBTCF) in Exhibit 5-1, thus representing the overall operating bottom line for the property asset.

5.2.9 Overview of Operating Cash Flow Items

In order to get a sense of how large these line items are on average, we provide a full breakdown of the individual components in Exhibit 5-2, expressed as a fraction of the top-line PGI (source: NCREIF). Of course, every property is different, and things change over time. This is especially true for CapEx, given its flexible and discretionary nature. Therefore, these averages cannot simply be copied into your proforma. Still, they will help understand the typical cost of owning real estate, at least for the generally high-quality properties held by institutional investors represented by NCREIF in the United States.

At the top of Exhibit 5-2 we have the Potential Gross Income (PGI). In other words, how much income could a property, in theory—if fully occupied—generate? Compared to the PGI, the

Effective Gross Income (EGI) is 8% lower on average due to vacancy. About 27% of EGI is spent on operating expenses (OpEx), resulting in a net operating income (NOI) of 73% of EGI and 67% of PGI, according to NCREIF. Finally, the Capital Improvement Expenditures (CapEx) in the NCREIF population of properties are 33% of NOI, giving a property-before-tax cash flow (PBTCF) 67% of NOI and 45% of PGI.

One interesting anecdote can be found around the Global Financial Crisis of 2007–2009. During that time, CapEx spending dropped dramatically. Indeed, the difference between PBTCF and NOI is only 10 percentage points in 2009 and 2010. During a time of crisis, fewer units are rented out (i.e., fewer TIs and leasing commissions), and investors opt to postpone major renovations. In contrast, OpEx has been relatively flat. This further exemplifies the difference between OpEx (mandatory to keep "the lights on") and CapEx (discretionary, for a time).

As noted earlier, these numbers are simply raw averages for a specific subset of commercial property (i.e., the NCREIF properties). However, it serves as an important insight that owning real estate is *expensive*. Of all the rent a property could generate (PGI), less than half (PBTCF) goes to the property owners (including both equity and debt investors). This is before considering income taxes and debt service, which the property owner may owe, which will be discussed in a later Chapter. The key point is that not all the rent you pay is pocketed by the landlord; far from it!

5.3 REVERSION CASH FLOW ITEMS

In addition to the operating cash flows described above, reversion cash flows must be included in the proforma in any year when all or part of the property asset is expected to be sold. (See the second part of Exhibit 5-1.) In most cases of simple property investment, reversion cash flows will appear only in the last year of the proforma, as the entire property is expected to be sold at once. (It gets more complicated in the case of multiple-asset investments in which there may be a planned selling schedule for some of the properties.) Indeed, for investment analysis purposes, a proforma for use in DCF valuation should always include reversion cash flows in the last year of the proforma, if not before, even if there are no plans to sell the property at that time. Otherwise, a major part of the property's value will be left out of the analysis. At the property-before-tax level, the reversion cash flows consist simply of the expected resale price of the property at the projected future point in time, net of selling expenses (such as brokers' fees and transaction costs).

5.3.1 Property Value at Time of Sale (Item I of Exhibit 5-1)

In Chapter 4, we discussed that the best and most widely used method for forecasting the property's resale price is to apply direct capitalization to the end of the proforma projection period via the cap rate method. However, in that Chapter, we kept the terminology neutral. We stated that to compute the value, you had to divide the "net income" (one period ahead) by the (empirical) cap rate. By now, you are more aware of the different definitions of income. Thus, to be more precise, with "net income," we meant the property's **Net Operating Income**.

To find the property value at the time of sale, the analyst projects the NOI of the property one more year beyond the proforma horizon. For example, in a 10-year analysis, the NOI would be projected for an 11th year. The year-11 NOI would then be divided by a projected **reversion cap rate** (also known as the **going-out cap rate**, **terminal cap rate,** or **resale cap rate**) to forecast the expected market value of the property at the time of reversion at the end of the 10th year. If the NOI projection is realistic, and the cap rate assumption is realistic, then this should provide a realistic projection for the selling price. Thus, the terminal value TV is given by;

$$TV_{t=10} = \frac{NOI_{t=11}}{y^{exit}}$$

where the going-out cap rate is provided by y^{exit}, some useful considerations and methodologies for projecting the going-out cap rate will be discussed in Chapter 11. Note that cap rates are, therefore, NOI-based. In words, cap rate = NOI/V. Or NOI = cap rate × V. You can also compute the property value *now* using the cap rate method by dividing the NOI in year one by the **going-in cap rate**. This direct capitalization approach to property valuation is useful as a quick back-of-the-envelope exercise. However, the more complete multiyear DCF approach is preferred for investment analysis purposes. Simple up-front direct capitalization doesn't include the effect of CapEx. It can ignore the important present value of money cash flow timing effects, such as from vintage leases or major vacancies. It also tempts the analyst to short-cut around the important fundamental exercise of medium to long-term rental market forecasting (see Chapter 4).

We already discussed why we would rather use NOI-based capitalization instead of PBTCF-based direct capitalization. PBTCF can differ substantially from one period to the next, somewhat serendipitously, due to the random or discretionary timing of improvements. NOI is more stable and makes comparisons between properties easier. The text box will provide some further discussion, including real empirical data, to drive home this point.

TEXT BOX 5.2 COMPARING CAP RATES TO INCOME YIELDS, AND OTHER FORMS OF DIRECT CAPITALIZATION.

The PBTCF divided by the value of the property is denoted the **income yield** or **net cash yield** and can be quite different from one property to the next, due to the nature of CapEx. To exemplify this, we provide the average cap rates and income yields for different property types (between 2000 and 2023) in Exhibit 5-3. We also give the average standard deviation of said cap rates and income yields, which gives a sense of the spread of cap rates and income yields.

Comparing the average cap rates to net cash yields reflects our previous point that PBTCF is reduced below NOI by the subtraction of CapEx (while the yield rate has the same denominator: the property asset value). The gap between the cap rate and income yield is lowest for industrial properties. This is because a single tenant occupies many such properties with long (NNN) contracts in specialized industries. As a result, leasing turnover is low (with corresponding low leasing costs), and the property does not need new tenant improvements

EXHIBIT 5-3

Average and Standard Deviation (Cross-sectional and Longitudinal) of NOI-based Cap Rates and PBTCF Yields in the US for Different Property Types Between 2000 and 2023

PropType		Average	Standard Deviation
Apartment	cap rate	5.08%	1.72%
	income yield	3.84%	5.76%
Industrial	cap rate	5.93%	5.76%
	income yield	4.59%	8.31%
Office	cap rate	6.41%	3.32%
	income yield	3.82%	9.66%
Retail	cap rate	6.39%	2.98%
	income yield	4.92%	8.85%

Source: NCREIF.

regularly. Often, such tenants also do their own CapEx; generally, only a little CapEx is required (think of simple warehouse space, for example). Cap rates were highest for office properties during this period, indicating that this market was riskier (r) and/or had little growth potential (g) compared to the other property types. It should be noted that NCREIF office properties are skewed toward high-end prime properties.

Exhibit 5-3 also provides the standard deviation (cross-sectional and longitudinal) of the cap rates and income yields for this population of properties. Note that the standard deviation is 3 to 4 times larger for income yields than cap rates. This relates to the point made throughout this Chapter on the discretionary and more temporally variable nature of CapEx. As a result, it is difficult to compare income yields or PBTCF between properties for any given period. A more subtle point to consider can be found by glancing at Exhibit 5-2 again. What you find there is that PBTCF is not that much more volatile *over time* compared to NOI, and both NOI and PBTCF mostly follow each other. (Except for around the GFC.) This is because the differences in CapEx even out over a large sample of properties. In other words, most of the standard deviation in CapEx across properties is driven by idiosyncratic differences, not longitudinal changes.

Another shortcut valuation procedure is to apply a **gross income multiplier (GIM)** to the effective gross income (EGI) of the property rather than applying the cap rate to the net operating income. With the GIM, you could say that properties trade for "20 times the rent," for example. The GIM is particularly useful for valuing small properties where one can estimate the gross revenue with relative ease and reliability, based simply on observation of the prevailing gross rents in the relevant space market, combined with knowledge about the size and rentable space in the subject building. Information on the building's operating expenses and, hence, net income may be more difficult to obtain or viewed with more suspicion, as its only source may be the current property owner who is trying to sell the building.

Both the cap rate and the GIM are examples of **ratio valuation**, in which a single year's income or revenue (normally the current or upcoming year) from the property is multiplied (or divided) by a ratio to arrive at an estimate of the current asset value of the property. Note that throughout this book, we will be employing the cap rate method to determine the terminal value of the property. We do this mostly because in the US the investment industry typically uses this method and there is empirical data about it. However, the GIM method might be more applicable in other countries or institutional settings.[4]

Getting terminal values using the cap rate method helps protect the investor against temporary real estate market bubbles and the Greater Fool fallacy.[5] In the first place, by placing the reversion fairly far into the future (e.g., 10 years), the reversion value component's relative magnitude in the property's overall present value is sharply reduced. (It is usually well below one-half the total present value.) This serves to mitigate the effect of mistakes or bias in the projected reversion value, such as the reflection of the current asset market cycle (e.g., a possible bubble?) in the reversion amount being circularly reflected back in the derived present value of the property. Second, by using projected direct capitalization based on NOI, the reversion forecast is based on a projection of the

---

4 One example is the Netherlands, where the so-called "gross yield" (i.e. the GIM) is a very popular alternative to the "net yield" (i.e. the cap rate).

5 According to this theory, you don't need to worry about paying too much for a property because, even if you have been foolish and paid too much, it is unlikely that you are the stupidest person in the market. Thus, you can always count on finding a greater fool who will pay at least that much again and rescue your ex-post return! (See Chapter 4.)

fundamental ability of the property to earn operating cash flow in the rental market rather than a simple extrapolation of the current investor's purchase price of the property.

5.3.2 Selling Expenses (Item J of Exhibit 5-1)

Certain costs are associated with selling a property. For example, in most cases, you will need an engineering firm to assess the property's condition. You might also want to have an appraised value of the property before you list it. This will allow you to set a realistic asking price. Brokers are needed to advertise the property and find a potential buyer. Brokerage fees vary with the size of the deal but could run 1% to 8% of the selling price, depending on the size and type of property. Finally, even after you sell the property, you will face other closing costs. These relate to legal fees (attorneys must review the contract) and title clearance. Average selling costs are between 2.5% and 10% of the sales price. The exact percentage depends largely on the size and complexity of the property. Larger buildings will have a relative (i.e., %) lower cost to sell.

5.3.3 Property-Before-Tax Cash Flow (Item K of Exhibit 5-1)

Note that we discussed the PBTCF before when discussing the bottom line of the operating cash flows. In the proforma, the reversion cash flow will also state its own PBTCF, which is simply computed by subtracting the selling expenses from the property sales value at time T. As before, being a property-before-tax amount, this represents the asset value not considering any debt or income taxes.

5.4 CIRCLING BACK: COMBINING THE DCF WITH THE PROFORMA

Now that we have learned all the line items on a proforma, how does this relate to the DCF valuation discussed in the previous Section of this book? To understand the relationship between the two, we start at the top (PGI) of the real estate proforma and work our way down (PBTCF).

The main line item we will forecast in future chapters is the *Potential Gross Income (PGI)*. In essence, the PGI, over time, captures changes in rents and thus reflects the demand and supply of space in the market. Understanding what underlies supply and demand for real estate space and how this can change over time is, therefore, an important topic in future Chapters. The EGI in year 0 is a given, as it is easy to observe the current income.[6] Finding the correct PGI is a bit more involved because of the effect of vintage leases and vacancy in the current year. You would need to estimate the market rents per square foot (or unit) and multiply by the size of your property. Chapter 9 will provide more details on this topic. After estimating the appropriate growth parameter *g* (Chapter 8), you can calculate the PGI in the upcoming years.

In Exhibit 5-4, we assume a year 0 PGI of $100,000, and the expected rental growth is 3%. As such, you can formulate expectations of the PGI in subsequent years. For example, in year 2, the PGI is expected to grow to ($100,000 x $(1.03)^2$ =) $106,090, etc. The forecasting does not end there, though. You also need to forecast;

- Vacancy rate
- Operating Expenses (OpEx)
- Capital Expenditures (CapEx)

[6] An obvious exception being developments, where no current rents are in place. See Part IV of this book for how to deal with such a scenario.

EXHIBIT 5-4

Pro Forma Line Items of Operating Cash Flows

INPUTS

PGI year	$
0	100,000
g	3.00%

	Operating Cash Flow Items	Year 1	2	3	4	5	6	7	8	9	10
(i)	*PGI*	$ 103,000	$ 106,090	$ 109,273	$ 112,551	$ 115,927	$ 119,405	$ 122,987	$ 126,677	$ 130,477	$ 134,392
(ii)	*Vacancy*	$ 5,150	$ 5,305	$ 5,464	$ 5,628	$ 5,796	$ 5,970	$ 6,149	$ 6,334	$ 6,524	$ 6,720
(iii)	*OpEx*	$ 20,600	$ 21,218	$ 21,855	$ 22,510	$ 23,185	$ 23,881	$ 24,597	$ 25,335	$ 26,095	$ 26,878
(iv)	*NOI*	$ 77,250	$ 79,568	$ 81,955	$ 84,413	$ 86,946	$ 89,554	$ 92,241	$ 95,008	$ 97,858	$ 100,794
(v)	*CapEx*	$ 15,450	$ 15,914	$ 16,391	$ 16,883	$ 17,389	$ 17,911	$ 120,000	$ 19,002	$ 19,572	$ 20,159
(vi)	*PBTCF*	$ 61,800	$ 63,654	$ 65,564	$ 67,531	$ 69,556	$ 71,643	$ (27,759)	$ 76,006	$ 78,286	$ 80,635

Where;

- NOI = Net Operating Income = (i) – (ii) – (iii)
- PBTCF = property-before-tax cash flow = (iv) – (v)

Note: The underlying Excel file can be found online.

With these line items, you can easily compute the remaining ones, i.e., NOI and PBTCF. For now (and purely for illustrative purposes), we assume that OpEx is 20% of PGI in all years, and vacancy is 5%. Capital Expenditures are always 20% of NOI, except in year 7, when we plan to renovate the lobby. The expected price tag for that (including other forms of regular CapEx that we incur that year) is $120,000. As a result, we experience a negative cash flow of $28K in year 7. Note that we ignore other income, given its highly idiosyncratic nature. However, if the other income is an important contributor to your property's total cash flow, you would obviously have to forecast other income as well.

The reversion cash flow can now also be computed. First, calculate the NOI in year 11 in your Excel file. Secondly, divide this cash flow by the going-out cap rate. For illustration, we assume a going-out cap rate of 8%. The terminal value will now be $\frac{\$103,818}{0.08} = \$1,297,719$. If the selling costs are 5% of the transaction price, we get a PBTCF of the reversion cash flows of about $1,232,833 (= $1,297,719 x (1 – 0.05)).

Now that we have prepared all the cash flow line items, how much should we pay for this property and its expected stream of income? As you recall from the previous section of this book, we must sum the discounted cash flows to find the value of this property. Specifically, we must discount the *property-before-tax cash flow (PBTCF)* at the appropriate discount rate *r*. Again, the opportunity cost of capital represents the total return one can typically expect to achieve in the asset market on a similar investment. The PBTCF represents the actual return received by the investor and is, therefore, the line item that we need to discount. Assuming a capital cost of 8.60%, we find a property value of $937K (rounded); see Exhibit 5-5.

A few common mistakes to be on the lookout for are: (1) do not forget to add the discounted reversion cash flow (approximately the $540 thousand in Exhibit 5-5) to the total sum, (2) make sure you are summing the discounted cash flows, and not accidentally the "normal" cash flows. If done

EXHIBIT 5-5
Discounting the Operational and Reversion PBTCF using a Discount Rate of 8.60%

Cash	Year										Reversion
Flow Items	**1**	**2**	**3**	**4**	**5**	**6**	**7**	**8**	**9**	**10**	**10**
PBTCF	$ 61,800	$ 63,654	$ 65,564	$ 67,531	$ 69,556	$ 71,643	$ (27,759)	$ 76,006	$ 78,286	$ 80,635	$ 1,232,833
PV(PBTCF)	$ 56,906	$ 53,972	$ 51,189	$ 48,549	$ 46,046	$ 43,671	$ (15,581)	$ 39,284	$ 37,258	$ 35,337	$ 540,264
Σ PV(PBTCF)			**$ 936,893**								

Where;

- PV(PBTCF) = the present value of the PBTCF in line (i). Calculated as $PV(PBTCF_t) = PBTCF_t/(1+0.086)^t$. Note that the reversion cash flow is discounted at the same rate (year 10) as the final year's operating cash flow.

correctly, you can now compute the value of commercial real estate. To summarize all the inputs needed to finalize a (before tax and debt) proforma, we need to find/estimate:

- PGI and vacancy in year 0
- Growth rate (g) of PGI, plus property-specific adjustments[7]
- Appropriate discount rate (r) for the PBTCF
- Estimates of OpEx, CapEx, and vacancy
- Going-out cap rate (y^{exit})
- Selling cost (% of sales price)

The main job of a real estate investor (and, by extension, this book) is finding these parameters.

5.5 CHAPTER SUMMARY

The previous sections have provided a general overview of the cash flow projection process. For typical properties with a 10-year proforma horizon, the implied present value or property valuation will be most sensitive to assumptions about the growth rate in future rents, the magnitude of the projected resale price (often a function of the assumption about the terminal cap rate), and the opportunity cost of capital that is applied as the discount rate, which will be discussed in Chapter 11. However, this is not the end of our journey. Finding all the necessary inputs and property-level adjustments is an arduous task, as the coming Chapters will detail.

KEY TERMS

- Proforma
- Operating cash flows
- Reversion cash flows
- Potential gross income (PGI)
- Rent roll
- Vacancy allowance

[7] With the danger of getting ahead of ourselves, the g parameter is typically for a market as a whole. However, your specific property might have some initial values that are "out of whack," like a high vacancy rate because a large tenant just left. As a result, your vacancy is expected to grow at a higher rate, etc. All of this will be discussed in great detail in Chapters 8 and 9.

- Effective gross income (EGI)
- Other income
- Operating expenses
- Property management opportunity cost
- Fixed costs
- Variable costs
- Net leases
- Expense stop
- Net operating income (NOI)
- Capital improvement expenditures
- Leasing costs
- Tenant improvement expenditures (TIs)
- Leasing commissions
- Concessions
- Property-before-tax cash flow (PBTCF)
- Reversion cap rate
- Going-out cap rate
- Terminal cap rate
- Resale cap rate
- Going-in cap rate

STUDY QUESTIONS

In Your Own Words

5.1 What is the main purpose of a real estate proforma statement?

5.2 What are the major categories of capital improvement expenditures? How do capital expenditures differ from regular operating expenses?

5.3 Why should you subtract management expenses before determining the property's NOI, even if you are managing the property yourself?

Check Your Knowledge

5.4 Why are capital expenditures not included in operating expenses?
 A) They occur less frequently, at irregular intervals of time.
 B) They are related to daily property maintenance.
 C) They are cash outflows for regular operations.
 D) They represent mortgage payments.

5.5 Why is Gross Income Multiplier (GIM) sometimes preferred for small properties or markets outside the U.S.?
 A) It is simpler and doesn't require detailed expense data.
 B) It is more accurate for high-value commercial properties.
 C) It includes capital expenditures in the calculation.
 D) It factors in operating income more comprehensively.

5.6 How are property taxes typically treated in a real estate proforma statement?
 A) As part of capital expenditures.
 B) As a recurring operating expense.
 C) As a non-operational expense.
 D) As an irrelevant expenditure.

5.7 A tenant has a gross lease with an "expense stop" of $2.75/SF. If the building has 200,000 SF of leasable space, reimbursable operating expenses of $750,000, and the tenant rents 25,000 SF, then how much does the tenant owe the landlord in expense reimbursements (the total dollar amount)?

5.8 You are a financial analyst constructing a multiyear proforma to value a potential property acquisition. As part of the analysis, you are considering the most likely scenario for a certain space for which the current tenant's lease will expire at the end of 2028. You estimate the following: the probability the existing tenant renews is 50 percent; if the tenant renews, you will need to spend an estimated $5/SF to upgrade the space; should the tenant not renew, it will take $15/SF to modernize the space for a new tenant; and you expect there will be 6 months of vacancy. Leases in this property are "triple-net" with the owner responsible for operating expenses associated with vacant space. Reimbursable building-level operating expenses are expected to be $5.50 in 2029, while market rent for triple-net leases is expected to be $14/SF. What is the expected property before-tax cash flow forecast (on a per square foot basis) you will put in the year 2029 of your proforma for this space?

5.9 Show a 10-year proforma projection of the operating NOI and net property-before-tax cash flow (PBTCF) for a three-unit apartment house in which (a) each unit currently (year 1) rents for $300/month; (b) rents are projected to grow at 3 percent per year; (c) the average tenant will remain three years, and then the apartment will be vacant an average of 3 months before the next tenant moves in; (d) operating expenses are currently estimated at $1,500 per unit per year (including management expenses), expected to escalate at 3 percent per year; (e) you anticipate needing to replace kitchen appliances for $1,000 per unit in year 3; and (f) you anticipate having to replace the single roof for $2,500 in year 5.

5.10 (Excel) You are evaluating the purchase of a 150,000-SF office building with a triple-net lease. The current contracted rent is $20/SF per year with no growth for the next 5 years. Rent is collected annually, with the first payment due in 1 year. Market rents for similar properties are $22/SF today and are expected to grow by 2.5% annually. In Year 6, the building will be released at the then-current market rent, with no further rent growth afterward. Before new tenants move in, there will be a 6-month vacancy, and tenant improvements (TIs) of $10/SF will be required at the end of year 6. At the end of year 10, the building will be sold at a price equal to 10 times the prevailing market rent at that time. Based on typical market conditions, the required return for this property is 12%. (Hint: With a triple-net lease, you can assume the rent equals the net operating cash flow.)

a. Develop a 10-year proforma that includes all projected cash flows from the property.
b. Calculate the NPV of the investment if the purchase price is $30 million. Assume a 12% required rate of return.
c. Calculate the IRR at the purchase price.
d. What is the cap rate at the $30 million purchase price?

5.11 You are a financial analyst constructing a multiyear proforma to value a potential property acquisition. As part of the analysis, you are considering the most likely scenario for a certain space for which the current tenant's lease will expire at the end of 2028. You estimate the following: the probability the existing tenant renews is 50 percent; if the tenant renews, you will need to spend an estimated $5/SF to upgrade the space; should the tenant not renew, it will take $15/SF to modernize the space for a new tenant; and you expect there will be 6 months of vacancy. Leases in this property are "triple-net" with the owner responsible for operating expenses associated with vacant space. Reimbursable building-level operating expenses are expected to be $5.50 in 2029, while market rent for triple-net leases is expected to be $14/SF. What is the expected property before-tax cash flow forecast (on a per square foot basis) you will put in year 2029 of your proforma for this space?

5.12 An apartment complex has 1,000 units, with an average of 100 units vacant at any given time. Each occupied unit generates $400 per month in rent, and the operating expenses for each occupied unit are $1,800 per year. Both rents and expenses are expected to grow at 3% per year. The required return for the investment is 12.5%, and the building's value is expected to remain a constant multiple of its net income (NOI).
   a. Calculate the Net Operating Income (NOI) for the first year.
   b. What is the NPV of a deal to buy the property for $25 million? (Hint: Use the perpetuity formula: $PV = CF_1/(r - g)$.)
   c. What is the IRR of the deal? (Hint: Just invert the perpetuity formula and solve for r.)

5.13 (Excel) Using the information from the previous question, perform a discounted cash flow (DCF) analysis in Excel instead of relying on the shortcut perpetuity formula. Create a 10-year cash flow projection with NOI growing at 3% per year. Calculate the sale price in year 10 as the NOI for year 11 divided by a 9.50% cap rate.
   a. Find the NPV using the =NPV(...) function, assuming an asking price of $25 million.
   b. How does your NPV result from the DCF approach differ from the cap rate approach used in the previous question? Compare the NPVs and explain your findings.

Chapter Case: Lakeview Plaza Acquisition

Dave Harrison, a senior director at Savannah Property Group (SPG), is evaluating the potential acquisition of Lakeview Plaza, a newly developed office building located in Orlando, FL. The property has a net rentable area of 200,000 square feet, and the current market rent is $5/SF annually. The seller has provided a list of the property's expected annual cash flows:

- The building is expected to be fully leased.
- A 1% collection loss must be accounted for based on historical data for similar properties in the area.
- The property taxes for the building are $100,000.
- The building is insured for hazard risks, with an annual insurance premium of $200,000.
- If an external property management firm is hired, the cost is $1.50/SF.
- Security costs are $0.50/SF.
- The building generates $200,000 annually from parking.
- The building also has a digital billboard, generating $100,000/year from advertisements.
- To prepare the building for leasing, 100 security cameras need to be installed, each camera costing $200 (including installation).

SPG plans to hold the building for 3 years and expects a 3% transaction cost based on the building's sale price at disposition.

Build a proforma for the Lakeview Plaza and answer the following questions.

1. What is the Potential Gross Income (PGI)?
   A) $500,000
   B) $1,000,000
   C) $1,500,000
   D) $990,000
2. What is the total deduction from the PGI for Vacancy and Collection Allowance?
   A) $5,000
   B) $10,000
   C) $15,000
   D) $20,000

3. What is the Effective Gross Income (EGI)?
   A) $1,260,000
   B) $1,270,000
   C) $1,290,000
   D) $1,300,000
4. How should parking fees and billboard advertisement revenue be categorized in the proforma?
   A) Fixed operating income
   B) Potential gross income
   C) Other income
   D) Variable operating income
5. What is the total operating expense?
   A) $500,000
   B) $600,000
   C) $700,000
   D) $300,000
6. What type of expense is the cost of installing security cameras?
   A) Operating expense
   B) Capital expenditure
   C) Variable expense
   D) Other expense
7. If SPG sells the property with a 10% going-out cap rate 3 years later, what will be the net reversion cash flow assuming the expected NOI in year 4 is $600,000?
   A) $6,000,000
   B) $5,820,000
   C) $180,000
   D) $582,000
8. SPG is considering whether to manage Lakeview Plaza internally or hire an external property manager. How could recognizing the opportunity cost of property management affect SPG's decision to manage the property internally?
   A) SPG will save money by eliminating property management fees, so opportunity cost does not impact their decision.
   B) Recognizing the opportunity cost may lead SPG to reconsider internal management, as their time and resources could be better used in more profitable ventures.
   C) Managing the property internally will always increase NOI, so opportunity cost is not relevant.
   D) Opportunity cost does not affect NOI or SPG's decision to manage the property internally.

6 Determinants of Rent I
Market Level

CHAPTER OUTLINE

LEARNING OBJECTIVES

After reading this chapter, you should understand:

- What determines land rents in a city.
- Why and how a freely functioning, competitive land market will lead to land being used at its "highest and best use" (i.e., most productive use).
- What determines the relative land values at different locations within a city and the relative growth rate of these values at different locations.
- The short- and long-run linkages among the real estate space market, asset market, and development industry that convert financial capital to new physical supply in the space market.
- How cycles or periods of imbalance between supply and demand can occur in the absence of perfect foresight.

The previous chapter relied on property before-tax (PBT) cash flow estimates when assessing investment performance and drafting proformas. This chapter will present basic urban economic principles that will help you compare income streams, actual and potential, across properties. Understanding

DOI: 10.1201/9781003643838-8

these principles is also fundamental to making the necessary *forecasts* of future income streams, which is such an important part of rational real estate investing.

First, a foundation of urban economics concepts will describe the distribution of urban rents and location values in cities. Understanding the determinants of urban rents allows us to think about future income streams in a structured way and to distinguish trends for different locations within a city. Second, we will link the space market to the asset market and the development industry, a dynamic link that is of vital importance in real estate investment performance. With location value being the major component in land value, it plays a key role in determining the shape of the long-run property supply function, which, in turn, governs the trend in rents.

6.1 SOME BASIC ECONOMIC PRINCIPLES OF URBAN FORM, LAND VALUE AND USE

The first general subject of this chapter is often called **urban form**. This term refers to the physical spatial characteristics of a city.[1] How big is the city spatially? What are its overall density and geographical dimensions? How does this density vary across different parts of the city? What are the patterns of the locations of different land uses, such as residential, commercial, and industrial, within the city? Where do people work, at home or in an office or a coffee shop or library? Where do high-income and low-income neighborhoods tend to be located, and what kind of transit do they use? Obviously, urban form and how it changes over time vitally affects land values and rents and, therefore, a whole range of real estate business decisions within any city.

6.1.1 Location and the Residual Nature of Land Value

Land is the most fundamental defining characteristic of real estate. Land derives its value from the fact that it is a necessary input or factor of production. The real estate value of land, therefore, comes from what is known as derived demand: people are willing to pay for land not because of the value land has in and of itself, but because land is necessary to obtain other things that have consumption or production value. Urban land value derives from the fact that land is necessary to construct buildings, and buildings are necessary or useful for most types of production of goods or services and for some types of consumption, such as housing, shopping, and many forms of entertainment and learning. What makes one urban land parcel worth more than another is primarily location. Indeed, when you buy a piece of urban land, you usually buy access to other points of attraction. In this section, we will introduce an important, though simplified, perspective on land value known as the **residual theory of land value**.

Let's begin with a specific example. A factory produces clothing by combining inputs from labor, machines, energy, and land. The machines actually produce the articles of clothing from the raw cloth, but labor and energy are needed to operate the machines and move the output. Land is necessary because the machines, people, and inventory take up space and need somewhere to locate. Indeed, where the factory is located will affect how profitable the manufacturing operation is because it will determine the costs of getting the raw material to the factory and the finished products from the factory to the ultimate points of retail sale. The cost of the labor and energy to operate the machines will also likely be affected by the location, based on accessibility to these other inputs.

Now consider all of these four basic types of inputs in the production process, known as production factors: land, labor, capital (i.e., physical capital, such as machines), and raw materials, including energy. All of these factors of production must be paid for by, and will therefore derive their value from, the value of the finished product. In dividing up the value of the finished product among the four factors of production, we can see that the defining characteristic of land that differentiates it

[1] The terms *urban spatial structure* and *urban morphology* are also used to describe this topic.

from the other three factors is that land is fixed in location, even in the long run. If you own a parcel of land, you can never move it to some other site where it might be able to earn more rent. The perspective of the residual theory of land value is that the three more mobile factors have to get paid first in order to keep them from "running away" if they don't get paid an amount equal to what they could earn elsewhere, something the land cannot do. The gross value of the production on the site, measured by the total revenue earned by the clothing factory, will, therefore, go first to the mobile inputs. Only **the residual**—what is left over after the mobile factors have been paid their necessary prevailing market costs—will be available to the landowner.

Suppose the factory in our example earns gross sales revenues of $10 million per year. The raw materials must be paid for first based on their market values, or else the sellers of those materials simply would not sell to this factory but rather take their goods elsewhere. Let's assume these raw materials cost $4 million, leaving $6 million of value to be added by the factory. Next, factory laborers must get paid the prevailing market wage, or else the workers will quit and take jobs elsewhere. Let's suppose all workers and other employees earn $5 million. This leaves $1 million per year in profit after subtracting the $9 million cost of goods sold.

But, in the long run, this profit must provide a return on investment to the financial capital that was contributed to establish the factory. In particular, the physical capital—the machines, plant, equipment, and the building—must be paid for in the form of a return on the financial capital that was invested. Otherwise, the financiers and investors who provided this capital will take it back (or, in the long run, they will not replace it when it wears out). Suppose the cost of building physical capital is $900,000 per year. You can think of this $900,000 per year as rent for machines that are leased or as an annual mortgage payment to pay off a loan of the financial capital invested in the plant and equipment. In the long run, all of this total $9,900,000 cost per year must be paid first to these more mobile factors before the landowner can get her share: only $100,000 per year, the "residual" that is left over after the other factors have been paid. This $100,000 is the maximum amount available from the factory operation to pay rent for the land itself, for the location and space that it provides for the production process.[2]

While we have used the example of a clothing factory, it should be easy to see that we could have picked any other type of factory. Indeed, any type of urban land use can be seen as producing some output of goods or services of value by combining some more mobile inputs with that of land (space and location). For example, a corporate headquarters office provides executive and control services for the rest of the corporation; a law office provides legal services for its clients; a shopping mall provides a convenient or stimulating environment for people to buy goods they need; and a house or apartment provides shelter and a conducive environment for the abode of a household.

The land is last in line to get paid among the inputs because it is "trapped"; it cannot go elsewhere. Of course, the residual theory of land value is a simplified model. The real world is a bit more complicated. But this model captures much of the essence of reality, at least in the long run, in a world where free markets govern the exchange of ownership.

There is a flip side of the coin from the perspective of the residual theory of land value. Land may get only, but it also gets *all* of the residual after the mobile factors have been paid their market values. In a well-functioning market system, competition among providers of mobile factors of production ensures that no such factor needs to be paid more than its market value. This means that, at least in the long run, land can receive as rents all of any increase in profit that would occur either from an increase in the market value of production (holding the market values of the mobile input

[2] How do the owners of the factory get their profits? They have not really been left out of the model. The factory owners would typically either be owners of the machines and/or the land, or they can be viewed as providing some of the labor, in the form of the managerial and entrepreneurship services necessary to run the business. Apart from their possible role as landowners, the factory owners are therefore part of the mobile factors of production that must be paid prior to the landowner, in the long run, or they will take their contributions elsewhere.

factors constant) or from a decrease in the cost of the mobile factors (holding the value of the output constant).

For example, if the factory in our previous example could sell its clothing output for $11 million instead of $10 million and the mobile factor costs remained the same, then the land could claim $1,100,000 annually. The same would occur if the costs of the mobile factors could be reduced to $8,900,000 instead of $9,900,000, holding the output value at $10,000,000.

How would the landlord capture the extra profit from the tenant? In the long run, the tenant's lease would expire, and the present tenant would then compete with other potential tenants for the land. That competition would lead the potential tenants to bid up their offered land rent to a level at which the tenants will just be making sufficient profit for themselves, that is, just covering their own costs, including normal profits. All other remaining revenues from production on the site would be included in the land rent offer.[3]

6.1.2 Competition, Equilibrium, and Highest and Best Use

While the residual theory of land value offers some important insight, economists note that it is a somewhat simplified perspective. In a well-functioning land market, competition exists both among providers of the mobile factors of production and among landowners. The residual theory considers the competition among the providers of the mobile factors, but it seems to ignore or discount the effect of competition among landowners. While each parcel of land is unique to some extent, a number of parcels are usually similar enough that they could substitute well for one another for the purposes of most potential users. So, there is competition in the land market among alternative sites. Similarly, while each potential land user may be unique in some respects, a number of potential users usually provide competition on the other side of the market as well. Of course, the long-lived nature of buildings means that land uses have limited flexibility to change quickly, and the time required to develop new projects is substantial. This allows temporary monopolistic rents to innovative land uses when local demand outstrips supply. In the long run, however, land use can and does change, so that the urban form we observe does tend to reflect basic economic forces and values.

Among the most powerful of economic forces is the tendency of markets to move toward equilibrium between supply and demand. Equilibrium is defined as the condition in which the market does not need to adjust the level of output any further because all consumers and producers are satisfied with the current level of consumption and production, given the current prices prevailing in the market (the equilibrium prices). A condition of market equilibrium that is relevant to the consideration of land value is reflected in a famous economic principle known as "Euler's Theorem." According to this theorem, each factor of production will be paid an equilibrium price (or wage) equal to its marginal product, that is, equal to the marginal value of what it contributes to the production process. This applies to land as well as to the mobile inputs to production. From the perspective of Euler's Theorem, land is not necessarily anymore "residual" than the other factors of production. In a sufficiently well-functioning land market, competition among landowners will drive the price of each land parcel to equal the value of its marginal contribution to the production process. But this raises the question: *Which production process*?—that is, to produce which good?

[3] The picture presented here is simplified by the assumption of "perfect competition." That is, we are assuming that there are sufficient numbers of potential tenants for the land competing with each other so that they bid away any excess profit. A more realistic rule of thumb that is often applied in the practice of valuing specific land parcels is to say that the land value is determined by the "second best" developer of the land. The very best developer (or tenant in the present model) for the land may have unique abilities to make profitable use of the site. This uniqueness could allow the very best user to capture and retain for themselves much or all of the value they add above the "second best" use for the site.

EXHIBIT 6-1
Highest and Best Use Example

	Site 1		Site 2	
	Clothing Factory	Grocery Store	Clothing Factory	Grocery Store
Revenues	$10,000,000	$4,600,000	$10,000,000	$5,000,000
Mobile Factor Costs	$9,900,000	$4,550,000	$9,990,000	$4,625,000
Residual (Land Rent)	$100,000	$50,000	$10,000	$375,000

To begin to answer this question, first consider another important characteristic condition of equilibrium in a well-functioning competitive market. In such a market, no participant on either side of the market can be made better off by a change away from the equilibrium without making someone else worse off. Indeed, with perfect markets, any benefits to gainers from a change away from the equilibrium could not offset the losses to the losers from that change.[4] This condition is known as Pareto optimality. In the case of the land market, such equilibrium will be reflected in the fact that each landowner will rent to the user who is willing to pay the highest rent for the land. Otherwise, at least in the long run, the dissatisfied landowners would kick out their current users and rent or sell to those who are willing and able to pay more. This maximizes the total rent earned by all the land (thereby maximizing the productivity of the society). Equivalently, from the perspective of the other side of the market, equilibrium is characterized by the condition that no land user would rather be located at a different place, given the cost of rent they would have to pay for another location. Otherwise, they would simply move to that other place and pay the rent charged there.[5]

Because of its importance, let us consider a bit more concretely what the concept of equilibrium in the land market means by extending our previous example of the clothing factory. Suppose there are two alternative potential uses for the site in question: the clothing factory or a grocery store. Let us further suppose that there are two possible locations, the one previously described, and an alternative site located a bit closer to most residences in the neighborhood but a bit farther from the main interstate highways. Exhibit 6-1 summarizes the revenues and mobile factor costs for each use at each site.

As described previously, the clothing factory at site one can earn revenues of $10 million per year, with mobile factor costs of $9.9 million, implying that the clothing factory could pay $100,000 per year in rent to the landowner at site one. The same factory at site two could still earn $10 million in revenue but would face $90,000 in additional transport costs getting the raw material to the factory and shipping out the finished product due to the greater distance from interstate-highway access. The result is that located at site two, the clothing factory would have only $10,000 residual left over with which to pay land rent.

The grocery store faces a somewhat different situation. While it, too, would experience lower transport costs by locating at site one, it would be less conveniently located to serve its retail customers in the residential neighborhood. Consequently, it would have to discount its prices and, therefore, would earn less revenue at site one. Indeed, the loss in revenue more than offsets the

[4] Suppose not. If one or more parties can be made better off without making anyone else worse off, then why would the market outcome not adjust to enable such "free" benefits to be captured? Until such adjustment is complete, the market is not in equilibrium.

[5] Once again, we are simplifying by describing "perfect markets." Pareto optimality in land markets requires not only perfect competition on both sides, but also a lack of locational externalities, also known as spillover effects. Externalities occur when what is done on one land parcel affects the value of adjacent or nearby land parcels. Such spillover effects can be either positive or negative. The existence of spillover effects in the real world is the major reason for land use control and regulation by communal authorities, such as zoning ordinances enacted by local governments.

delivery cost reduction for the grocery store. At site one, the grocery store would earn revenues of \$4.6 million with mobile factor costs (including delivery costs for receiving its merchandise) of \$4.55 million, leaving only \$50,000 residual available to pay rent. At site two, the grocery store would earn \$5 million in revenues, with \$4.625 million mobile factor costs, leaving \$375,000 to pay land rent.

The grocery store can pay more than the clothing factory for site two (\$375,000 vs. \$10,000 annual rent), while the clothing factory can pay more for site one (\$100,000 vs. \$50,000 annual rent). In the long run, both the factory and the store could move, and both the site one owner and the site two owner could remove any tenant (and redevelop the site). Therefore, only one result can be consistent with long-run equilibrium in the land market: the factory must be located at site one and the store at site two.

The equilibrium described in this example results in each location being used at its **highest and best use (HBU)**. This means that each site is used in the most productive way for that location. In this sense, productivity is represented by the *net* difference between the value of what is produced on the site and the costs of the mobile factors of production, that is, the land residual as we have defined it. Thus, equilibrium in the land market tends to result in land parcels being used at their highest and best use in the long run.[6]

6.1.3 Role of Transport Costs: The Bid-Rent Curve

Land rent and therefore land value differs from one place to another because the HBU residual value differs from one place to another, primarily as a result of differences in transportation costs. When the transportation costs faced by the users of the site are lower, the residual value is higher, other things being equal. For example, the clothing factory could make more profit located nearer to the highway where the delivery costs of both its inputs and outputs were lower. The grocery store could make more profit located nearer its customers, who then would not incur as much transportation costs getting to and from the store.

To understand the importance of transport costs, you must conceptualize these costs broadly. Transport costs include the costs of moving both inputs and outputs, costs borne both directly by the sellers and indirectly by the buyers. Transport cost is not limited to the direct monetary outlay for transportation, such as gasoline cost. For people, travel time is usually the most important component of transport costs. In our grocery store example, it is likely not gasoline cost but the value of the time lost in travel to and from the store that would force the store to discount its prices at site one. The implication is that land market equilibrium, the highest and best use of land, will be characterized by the *minimization of aggregate transportation costs* for the society as a whole.

The role of transport costs in determining HBU and land value leads to a key concept in classical urban economics, the **bid-rent curve** (or bid-rent function). The bid-rent is the maximum rent that a potential user would "bid," or be willing to pay, for a site or location. This bid-rent is essentially the same thing as the residual value discussed previously. Each potential user of land has a bid-rent curve (or function), which relates the user's bid-rent to the location of the land site, showing in particular how the bid-rent changes as a function of the user's distance from some central point. The central point is the point at which the transportation costs are minimized for that use, the point at which the bid-rent or residual value is maximized.

Each potential land use has its own bid-rent function. We might imagine the entrance to a nearby interstate highway as being the central point for the clothing factory because the highway reduces travel time and cost for its inputs and outputs. If site one is one mile from this highway entrance

[6] The social desirability of preserving undeveloped some land parcels can be represented in this model by recognizing that some parcels may have, due to their aesthetic or environmental qualities, a *direct* demand value (i.e., value in "consumption" as undeveloped land) exceeding any *derived* demand value in production, which they would have under development.

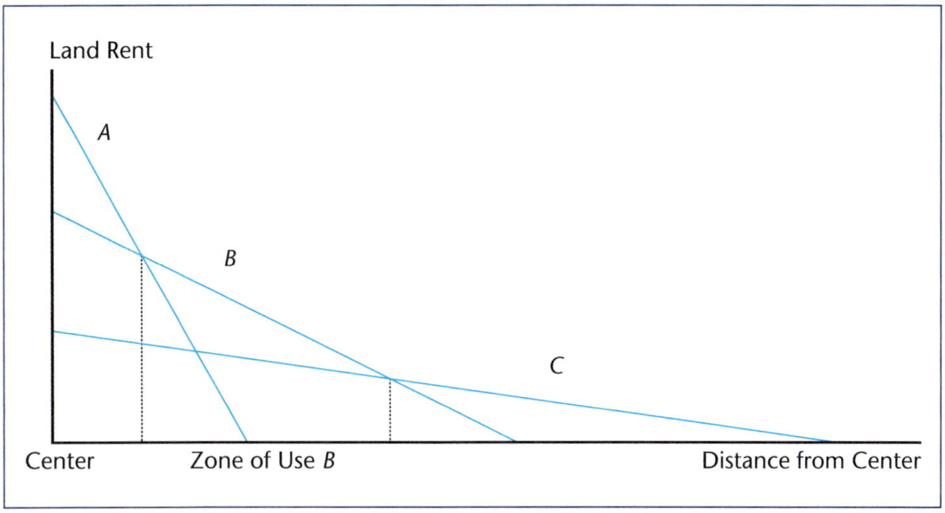

EXHIBIT 6-2 Bid-Rent Functions of Three Land Uses with Differing Productivity and Sensitivity to Transport Cost.

and site two is four miles from it, then the value of the bid-rent function for the clothing factory is \$100,000 at one mile and \$10,000 at four miles from this central point. The relevant central point for the grocery store would be different, perhaps the intersection of two arterial streets at the center of the residential neighborhood it serves. Suppose site two is at this intersection, and site one is three miles from it. The grocery store's bid-rent function would be valued at \$375,000 at site two and \$50,000 at site one.

Graphically, a bid-rent function is depicted on a chart with the vertical axis located at a central point and the horizontal axis representing distance from that point. Transportation costs are minimized at the central point, and the bid-rent is therefore maximized. The amount of the bid-rent at the central point (the height of the intercept on the vertical axis in the graph) depends on the inherent productivity or value of the land use when transportation costs are minimized. Land uses that are more productive (when transport costs are minimized) will have higher bid-rents at the central point. As you move away from the central point, the bid-rent falls as the transportation costs rise due to the less central location. The rate at which the bid-rent falls, the slope of the bid-rent function, depends on the magnitude of transportation costs in the production process of the given land use and on how sensitive these transportation costs are to distance from the central point. Land uses that are more sensitive to transport costs will have bid-rent curves with steeper downward slopes, bid-rents falling more quickly with distance from the central point.

This is depicted in Exhibit 6-2, which shows the bid-rent function for three different land uses, labeled *A*, *B*, and *C*. Use *A* has the greatest productivity when transportation costs are minimized and so has a higher bid-rent at the central point. Use *A* is also more sensitive to transport costs, perhaps, for example, because use A requires many people with a high value of time to commute to it every day. If they have to travel even just a little farther, on average, then use *A* will suffer a lot of loss in productivity or value generation. Use *C* has the lowest productivity in general but also the least sensitivity to transport costs, and so has the "shallowest" bid-rent function. Use *B* is between the other two in both respects. The result is that, *in equilibrium* in the land market, assuming all three uses have the same central point, use *A* will prevail closest to that center, being able to outbid the other uses, followed by use *B* a bit farther out from the center, followed by use *C* farthest out.

6.1.4 Summary of Basic Urban Land Value and Land Use Principles

The preceding section presented several of the basic economic principles of land value and use determination. Because the underlying demand for land is a derived demand, and other more mobile factors are required to produce value from land, land value is based on the residual available after the other factors (labor, capital, energy, etc.) have been paid their going market rates. This residual is strongly influenced by transportation costs, which, in turn, are strongly influenced by location, making land value largely a function of location. Different types of land uses have different productivities, different sensitivities to transportation costs, and different relevant geographical central points, that is, locations where their relevant transportation costs would be minimized. Therefore, different land uses have different residual values, or bid-rents, that they would be willing and able to pay for any given site. In long-run equilibrium in a well-functioning, competitive land market (when, in principle, even built structures can be changed through the development or redevelopment process), each land site will be used for its highest and best use, the use that can pay the highest bid-rent. This will tend to maximize the aggregate land value (residual value) and minimize the aggregate transportation costs of the society.

Finally, let's turn to the elephant in the room, the "death of distance" as a larger share of the workforce can and does work from home at least some days of the week. For them, commuting has become less of a burden or is even costless. Have the bid-rent functions flattened out, as a result, and centrality lost value? Without distance, will there even be any bid-rent curves? Each introduction of new modes of transportation—bicycle, public mass transportation, car—has lowered transportation costs and reshaped urban forms. Changed commuting patterns due to working from home are not any different in this respect, and demand for office space adapts accordingly. However, humans will remain social creatures, needing mentoring and collaboration time, so the death of the office is unlikely any time soon. Even in a world with completely flat bid-rent functions, such as with autonomous driving vehicles that let you work or play while in transit, there would still be "central places," locations of agglomeration where people would want to be and would congregate, even if fundamentally only because others are *there*. But such places would be more free to locate or spring up anywhere, irrespective of (nonexistent) transport costs. They would be fixed in location only because of the longevity of structures and the inertia of pre-existent patterns or else because of natural amenities or attractions. Within such centers land value would be high.

6.2 CLASSIC MONOCENTRIC CITY MODEL

The basic economic principles and concepts regarding land value and use described in the previous section have been combined in a very simple and elegant model of urban form known as the **monocentric city**. While this model greatly simplifies and abstracts from the complicated reality of modern cities, it captures enough of the essence to offer useful insights. Indeed, the monocentric model is a classic example of how theory, by simplifying reality, reveals important insights into the nature of that reality.[7]

In the monocentric city model, only one central point exists in the whole city, and this central point applies to all potential uses of the land. Indeed, in the simplest version of the model, which we will consider here, there is only one type of land use in the city, housing. The simple monocentric city is a circle of a certain radius extending out from the central point. The central point might be thought of as representing the downtown or central business district (CBD), to which all the

[7] The following discussion draws heavily from DiPasquale and Wheaton (1996), to which the reader is recommended for a more detailed and in-depth treatment of this topic. In general, the monocentric city model, as well as much of the location theory described in the previous section, has its origins in the theories developed by German economist Johann von Thünen early in the nineteenth century. While von Thünen focused on an agricultural state, much more recent extensions of the city model (of which the monocentric model described here is only a very simple version) have been attributed to such American economists as William Alonso, Edwin Mills, Richard Muth, and Dennis Capozza.

households must commute every day to produce some good that enables them to earn the income they must use to meet their housing costs, as well as all their other consumption needs. From this income, they also must pay the transportation costs for their daily commute. These transportation costs are, of course, a function of the distance of their houses from the CBD.

6.2.1 Circlopolis, the Quintessential Monocentric City

To make this model a bit more concrete, let us quantify a stylized example city we will call Circlopolis, which exists in the land of Agricolia. Outside the city, the land is farmed; inside the city, all land is residential, built to a density of two persons per acre, or 1,280 per square mile. The metropolitan population of Circlopolis is 1 million, which gives Circlopolis an area of 1,000,000/1,280, or 781 square miles. This determines the radius to the urban boundary, recalling that the formula for the area of a circle is π times the radius squared, so the radius is the square root of the area divided by π, which in this case is about 16 miles.

Now consider the annual rent for housing at the edge of the city, 16 miles from the center at the boundary between the urban and agricultural land use. In order to induce a farmer to sell his land to enable it to be converted from agricultural production to urban housing, you must pay the farmer the opportunity value of the land in its agricultural use. This would be the land's agricultural use residual (bid-rent), equal to the net profit per acre from agricultural production after all the mobile factors have been paid. Suppose this agricultural rent is $500 per acre per year. In addition, you must pay the annualized cost of building a house. Suppose there is one resident per house, and houses cost $50,000 to build, which can be paid for by a permanent mortgage at 10 percent per year, giving an annual construction cost rent of $5,000 per house. With two houses per acre, that makes the total annual housing rent per acre at the city edge $10,500, consisting of $10,000 to pay for the construction and $500 to pay for lost agricultural rent.

How does this real property rent change as we move from the urban boundary toward the city center? Residents of houses in more central locations will not have to pay as much for commuting costs, so they can pay more rent for housing and still maintain the same overall level of welfare. In fact, the *real property rent must rise as we approach the center at exactly the rate that the transportation costs fall.* This condition is required by equilibrium.

To see this, suppose this condition did not hold. Suppose, for example, that the real property rent rose by less than the decrease in transportation cost as you moved toward the center. Then, residents living closer to the center would be better off than those living farther out. This would cause everybody to want to move closer to the center. Demand would then outstrip supply for more central locations, while houses near the periphery would go searching for residents. Competition among residents bidding for centrally located lots and among landlords owning peripheral lots trying to find tenants would force the rent for the more centrally located lots up and the rents for the peripheral lots down until the relative levels were such that everybody was equally well off, considering both their housing rents and their commuting costs. A symmetrical argument would apply if housing rents rose more than the decrease in transportation costs as one moved closer to the center. In that case, everyone would want to live farther out, bidding up the rents there until the incentive for peripheral houses was eliminated. In equilibrium, therefore, the rents must be such that the total housing and commuting costs are the same across all distances from the center.

This tells us that the bid-rent curve for housing in Circlopolis must have a slope equal to the transportation cost per mile per acre. This slope is known as the rent gradient. It tells you how much the equilibrium real property rent per acre declines per mile of additional distance from the center of the city. *The rent gradient equals the transportation cost per mile per person times the number of people per acre.*

Suppose that in Circlopolis, the transportation cost per person is $250 per year per mile of distance from the CBD (round-trip commuting cost). Then, with two inhabitants per acre, the rent gradient must be $500 per mile. Housing located one mile from the urban boundary will rent for $250 more per year than housing on the boundary or $500 more per acre of land. By the time we get to the center of the city (16 miles from the edge), where there is no transportation cost, the housing rent will be $4,000 more per house (or per person), or $8,000 more per acre, than it is at the periphery. So, the total real property rent per year at the center will be some $18,500 per year, including $500 in agricultural opportunity cost rent, $10,000 in construction cost rent, and $8,000 in location rent (reflecting the location premium in the site). Note that the location rent per acre at the center exactly equals the transportation cost per acre at the periphery.

Now that we know the housing and transport costs for the inhabitants of Circlopolis, we can see how they are using their income. Suppose they have annual incomes of $50,000 each. They spend $9,250 per year on the combination of housing and transportation. (Recall that there are two persons in the form of two single-individual households per acre.) So, they must each be spending $40,750 per year on "other consumption" besides housing and transportation.[8] We have "backed into" this observation about other consumption expenditures, but in reality, the direction of causality may go both ways in the long run. How much the Circlopolites want to spend on other consumption (given their income level) also determines how much they have available to spend on housing and transportation, and this, in turn, will, in the long run, determine the size and density of Circlopolis. This can explain why we see such different densities in cities in different countries, since income levels and culturally based preferences for different types of housing and lifestyles differ widely across countries.

The simple monocentric city model represented by Circlopolis in the land of Agricolia is depicted graphically in Exhibit 6-3. The figure depicts a cross-section of real property rents from the agricultural hinterland just beyond the urban boundary through the center of the city.

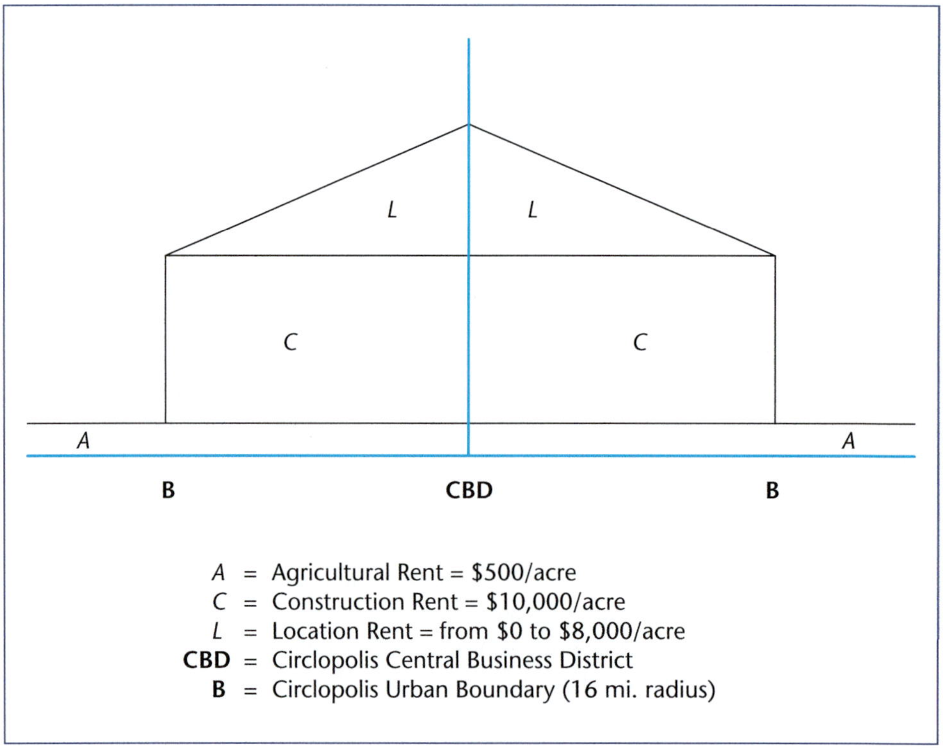

EXHIBIT 6-3 Cross Section of Real Property Rents in Circlopolis and Agricolia.

[8] In the magical city of Circlopolis, there are no taxes!

6.2.2 Using the Model: Four Principles of How Rents and City Size Change

The usefulness of the monocentric city model is that it reduces a very complex phenomenon, a city, down to a simple interaction among a few basic economic forces. This allows us to see easily what causes some of the essential features of the urban form. This, in turn, enables us to examine how rents and urban form may be affected by changes that can happen over time in an economy or society, such as growth in population or income or changes in transport costs. These changes can have very important effects on real estate opportunities. So let us now use the monocentric city model to examine these effects in our Circlopolis example by changing one variable at a time and seeing how this affects the land rents and urban form variables within the model.

Population: We begin by examining the effect of an increase in the population of Circlopolis, holding density and transportation cost per mile constant. With the density constant, the area of the city, and hence the radius, must expand. In particular, for every percent increase in population, the area must increase by an equal percent (for constant density), and the radius must increase by about half that percent.[9] The housing rent at the new periphery must equal the construction cost rent plus the agricultural rent, based on the same arguments as before, which have not changed. Likewise, the rent gradient as we move in from the new periphery must still be the same \$500 per mile (because transport cost and density are the same as before), again based on the same equilibrium argument. So, this means that population increase, holding density and other prices constant, must increase rents all over Circlopolis. This is depicted in Exhibit 6-4.

We can summarize the analysis up to now in an important principle:

Other things being equal, larger cities will have higher average location rents.

This basic principle, derived from such a simple model of urban form and land values, is no doubt a major reason that land prices, rents, and housing costs are so much higher in the nation's

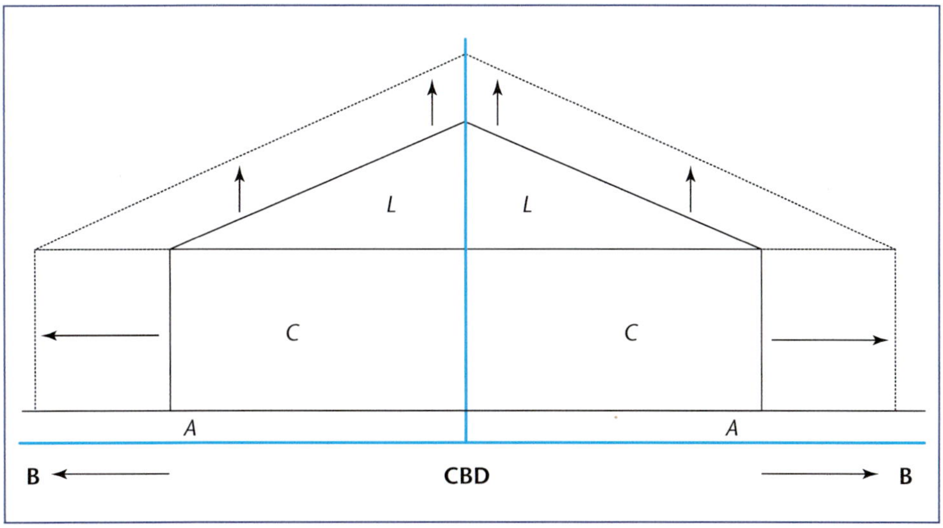

EXHIBIT 6-4 Effect of Population Growth with Density and Transport Cost Constant.

[9] If the area of the circle increases by p percent (that is, $AREA_{NEW}/AREA_{OLD} = 1 + p$), then

$$\frac{RADIUS_{NEW}}{RADIUS_{OLD}} = \frac{\sqrt{AREA_{NEW}/\pi}}{\sqrt{AREA_{OLD}/\pi}} = \sqrt{1+p} \approx 1 + p/2$$

for relatively small values of p. For example, if p = 10%, then the more exact value of $\sqrt{1.1} - 1$ is 4.9%.

largest cities, such as New York, Chicago, Los Angeles, and San Francisco. (For example, in 2020, the median house price in New York was $450,000, while in neighboring Hartford, it was $200,000.[10])

Perhaps this size principle seems intuitively obvious. But the monocentric city model allows you to deepen your understanding of why larger cities have higher rents. In particular, notice what caused the higher rents when we considered the growth in population in Circlopolis. In our simple model, we were holding density constant. Therefore, land rents (per acre of land) would tend to be higher in larger cities, even if such cities were no denser than smaller cities. This suggests that if larger cities are to keep rents per housing unit at the same level as those in smaller cities, then some combination of higher density and/or lower construction cost must prevail in larger cities. This, in turn, means that, if we hold rent per household constant across cities of different sizes, larger cities must be characterized by some combination of greater density and/or smaller housing units. The 500-square-foot efficiency apartment in Manhattan, stacked 40 on top of each other, might rent for the same as a 1,000-square-foot garden apartment in central Atlanta.

In fact, we can say more than this. We can see that what caused the higher rents in the population example was *not* the population per se, or even the area of the city, but the *length of the radius,* the distance of the urban boundary from the CBD. The rent gradient is fixed, based on transportation costs and density. The rent at the urban boundary is fixed, based on the agricultural opportunity cost and the building construction cost. Therefore, what governs the change in the average rent is the change in the distance each point finds itself from the urban boundary.

This is important because, for a given population and density, the radius of the city (i.e., the distance from the CBD to the urban edge) must be greater if the city cannot avail itself of an entire 360-degree arc. In reality, geographic constraints on the urban arc are quite common as, for example, with a city on a coastline or peninsula.[11] Most of the largest U.S. cities are on coasts or are cut by waterways or mountain ranges that effectively prevent the use of a large proportion of the arc around the CBD. This no doubt extends the radius of cities such as New York, Chicago, Los Angeles, and San Francisco, further adding to their tendency to support high rents.[12]

It is also interesting to note that if incomes were constant across cities of different sizes, then inhabitants of larger cities would either have to consume less housing (i.e., live in smaller houses and/or have less land per house) or spend more on transport costs, compared to residents of smaller cities. Either way, inhabitants of larger cities would have less economic welfare than inhabitants of smaller cities. Over time, such an imbalance in economic welfare between citizens of smaller and larger cities would not be tenable in an integrated economy. People would migrate from larger to smaller cities, *unless the larger cities offered higher incomes,* on average. But this is exactly what happens in the real world. Larger cities do tend to have higher average per capita incomes than smaller cities. Put the other way around, cities that are able to offer higher incomes tend to attract migration and over time, grow larger in population relative to other cities, until an equilibrium across cities is reached. The reality is that the average resident of New York or Los Angeles is, in fact, more productive than the average resident of Cincinnati or Cleveland, for example.

---

10 Estimates from ATTOM property data, available at www.attomdata.com.

11 The existence of lakes or unbuildable wetlands, slopes, or preserved open spaces or conservation land has the same effect of reducing the effective arc, even if the effect may occur at all points of the compass.

12 When the arc around which a city can expand is limited by, say, bodies of water or mountain ranges, the same total area must fit into a fraction of a circle. The radius equals $\sqrt{A/(\pi F)}$, where A is the area and F is the fraction (less than or equal to 1) of the full 360-degree arc around the CBD that can be used for growth. This is consistent with our point in Chapter 1 that a rising long-run marginal cost curve (increasing development costs including land cost), implying increasing real rents in equilibrium in the space market, would tend to occur in areas where land supply is constrained in the face of growing demand. Growing demand may be thought of as population growth in the present example. Keep in mind that the radius is the distance from the CBD to the edge of the developed urban area, for example, from Manhattan north up the Hudson Valley.

If we consider population changes within one city over time, then the monocentric city model can give some insight into how much, or how fast, rents may change over time, and how such changes may differ in different parts of the city. For example, it is not uncommon for a metropolitan area to increase 10 percent in population over a 10-year period, or indeed over a 5-year period in many Sunbelt cities. Holding density constant as before, such a population increase will result in approximately a 5 percent increase in the urban radius, from 16 miles to 16.8 miles in our Circlopolis example. All locations now have 0.8 mile additional location rent, or an increase in rent of $400 per acre per year.[13] Notice that the rent increase is constant across all the pre-existing points in the city, but the previous rent was higher for more centrally located points. This implies that the *percentage* increase in rent due to urban growth will be greater closer to the periphery of the metropolitan area. For example, at the old boundary, the rent grows from $10,500 per acre to $10,900 per acre, a 3.8 percent increase. At the center, the increase from $18,500 to $18,900 is only 2.2 percent. This difference is much more pronounced for the location rent component of the total real property rent.

Now suppose that instead of holding density constant, we held the area of the city constant, as might occur through regulatory or geographic constraints on land use (zoning, "green belts," islands, or mountains, for example). Not surprisingly, the model reveals that population growth would still result in higher land rents. But in this case, the reason is different. The radius is fixed, so the reason for the higher location rents cannot be the greater distance from the urban edge. However, with the radius fixed and the population growing, the density must increase. Now, recall that the land rent gradient in equilibrium must equal the difference in transportation cost per mile *per acre*. We are holding the transportation cost *per person* constant, but with more persons living per acre, the transportation costs per acre must increase. So, the rent gradient would increase. For example, if Circlopolis's population increased by 50 percent to 1,500,000, there would be three inhabitants per acre instead of two, and this would increase the rent gradient from $500 per mile to $750 per mile. The rent at the urban boundary would still be the same, but land rent everywhere else would increase due to the increased location premium. The new peak rent at the center would be $22,500 (including $12,000 per year of location rent) instead of the old center rent of $18,500 (a 22 percent increase). This is depicted in Exhibit 6-5.[14]

Thus, while population growth will always tend to increase land rents in a city, *how* the city grows will affect the nature and geographic distribution of those increases. This can be expressed in a second basic principle derived from the monocentric city model:

> *If a city grows by increasing area rather than density, property rent growth will be relatively greater closer to the periphery; but if a city grows by increasing density instead of area, property rent growth will be relatively greater the closer to the center of the city.*

It is likely that these two principles will continue to be important in the twenty-first century, but may play out differently in different regions. Some cities will impose growth boundaries and encourage more dense development, while others will sprawl with few land use controls. Metropolitan population growth in many cities in mature regions such as the United States and (even more in) Europe will likely be much slower in the next decades than in the nineteenth and twentieth centuries, but such growth will likely be a major factor in many emerging regions that are still undergoing substantial

---

[13] Recall that the additional rent occurs because there are more total people now in the city competing for (i.e., bidding for) the locations within the city, including some people who are farther from the center than anybody used to be when the periphery was not as far out. In order for all these competing citizens to be indifferent about their present location versus any other location (the characteristic of equilibrium), rents must settle at a level so that the people at the periphery are satisfied to live that far out considering the amount of location rent they are saving by doing so.

[14] Note, however, that in this example the rent *per person* would actually decline in the center, from $18,500/2 = $9,250/year, to $22,500/3 = $7,500/year. This is because in our simple model we kept construction cost the same per acre (increasing from 1.0 to 1.5 persons per room).

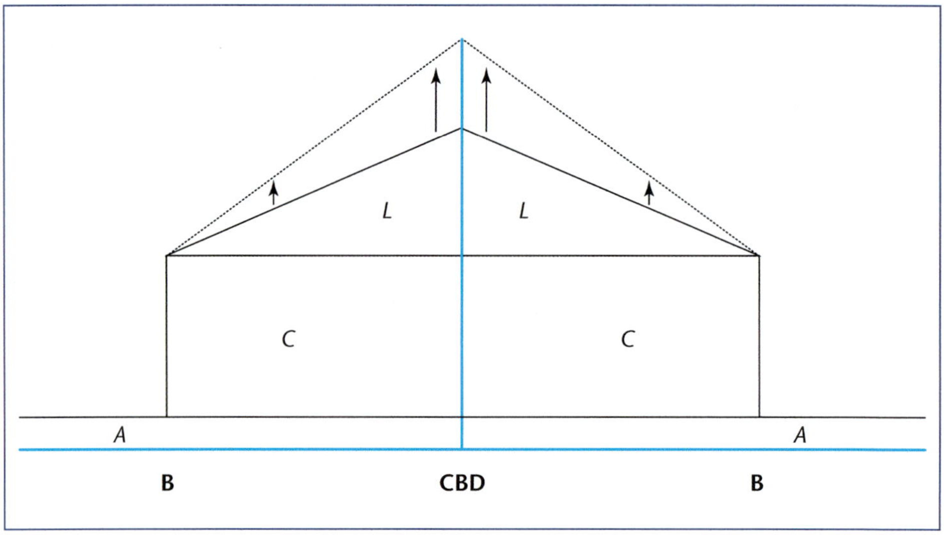

EXHIBIT 6-5 Effect of Population Growth with Area Constant.

urbanization. For example, West African cities are predicted to grow quicker in population than cities in China, which have grown at faster rates than the rest of the world since the 1990s. The tendency or ability to expand effective metropolitan geographic boundaries (commuting radius) may also vary as countries such as Nigeria, Saudi Arabia or India rapidly expand urbanized spatial areas. In contrast, mature U.S. or European cities with extensive exurban commuter sheds may already be near their effective limits (unless technological developments further reduce transport frictions, as discussed below).

Transport Costs: Population growth is not the only basic phenomenon that typically affects the modern city. A second important point to consider is what would happen as a result of a reduction in transport costs per person per mile, holding population and income constant. This could occur, for example, through improvements in transportation technology or infrastructure. In fact, the twentieth century witnessed almost continual improvements in these areas. It is likely that such improvements will continue well into the twenty-first century, especially if one considers the partial substitutability between telecommunications and transportation.[15] The advent of cell phones, laptop computers, the Internet, and other telecommunications developments will allow more flexible location and timing of work and shopping activity, which effectively reduces transport costs. Technological improvements in the automobile and mass transit, including greater fuel efficiency, greater safety and reliability, more efficient traffic control, and a more pleasant or productive travel environment (such as is provided by vehicle air-conditioning, stereo sound systems, cell phones, etc.), all act effectively to reduce transport costs.[16]

[15] Even in the absence of any reduction in transport cost per person-mile of movement, telecommunications and computing developments may allow a reduction in the number of commuting or shopping trips per capita per year, for example, by enabling people to work at home or shop on the Internet. This reduces transport costs per acre (per unit of time), at a given density and given distance from the central node. Transport cost per acre (per unit of time) is what affects the land rent gradient.

[16] As noted previously, we need to think of transport costs as not merely the monetary outlay for travel, but also all forms of "disutility" and inconvenience associated with travel. Even if average speeds do not increase (and travel time therefore does not decrease per mile), transport cost may fall if the disutility of the travel time decreases as a result of added comfort, productivity, or utility during the time traveling.

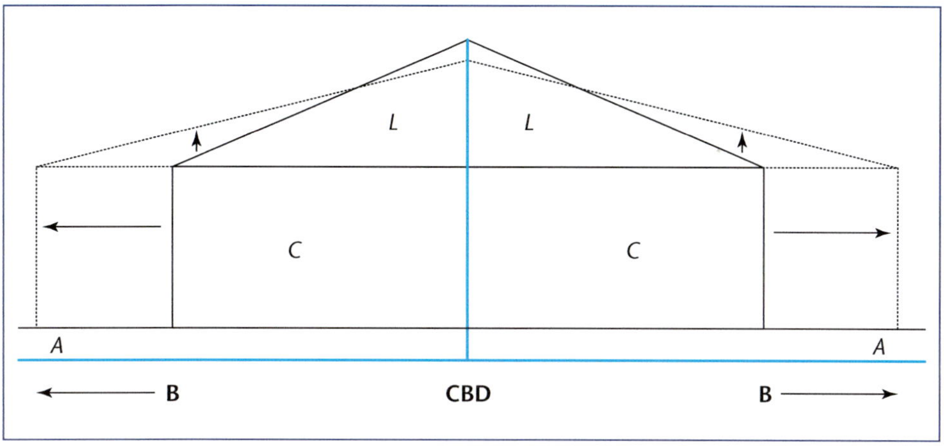

EXHIBIT 6-6 Effect of Transport Cost Reduction Savings Applied to Greater Purchase of Land.

We know that reducing transport costs per person per mile per year will reduce the rent gradient.[17] This can have various effects on land values and urban form. Exhibits 6-6 and 6-7 depict the two extreme alternatives. In the first case (6-6), the residents of Circlopolis have elected to spend at least some of the transport cost savings on purchasing more urban land. Such urban-density-reducing behavior might be reflected in the purchase of, for example, houses with larger lots farther out in the countryside, neighborhoods with more parkland and golf courses, or even shopping centers with more parking spaces. Such a density-reducing result of transport improvements would increase land rents near the periphery and reduce land rents at the center.

Indeed, the pure effect of a density reduction in the city, even without a reduction in transport costs, is to reduce the *absolute* land rents in the city's center.[18] Transport cost reduction will only magnify this reduction.

The second alternative possible effect of transport improvements occurs if the inhabitants of Circlopolis elect to keep their same level of residential density, that is, not to expand the spatial area of the city despite the transportation improvements. This would tend to happen only in cities that face severe physical or governmental constraints on spatial expansion (or perhaps in cultures where there is a positive preference for urban residential density, as might be the case, for example, in some Mediterranean countries or in Boulder, Colorado as an example). Then, the reduction in transport costs causes land rents to decline everywhere in the city (except on the very periphery). But even in this case, rents decline more for locations closer to the city's center, as depicted in Exhibit 6-7.

It may seem counterintuitive that a technological improvement that increases the overall welfare and productivity of society, namely, transport cost reduction, would result in an absolute *decrease* in total aggregate land value in the city, which is what is implied by the real rent reduction possibility

---

[17] Recall that the rent gradient is determined as the transport cost per mile per person times the density, and it would not make sense for transport cost reductions to increase the urban density. Therefore, transport cost reductions must reduce the rent gradient.

[18] This is because the location rent at the center of the city equals the rent gradient times the radius, and the rent gradient equals the transport cost per capita times the density. Thus, the rent gradient is directly proportional to the density, which is, in turn, inversely proportional to the area of the city. But the area of the city is not directly proportional to the radius, but rather to the *square* of the radius. Therefore, a decrease in density holding all else constant will result in a less-than-proportional increase in city radius, but a fully proportional reduction in rent gradient. For example, if density (and therefore rent gradient) were reduced by half, the radius would only increase by a factor proportional to the square root of two. Location rent at the center would be $\sqrt{2}/2$ times the previous location rent.

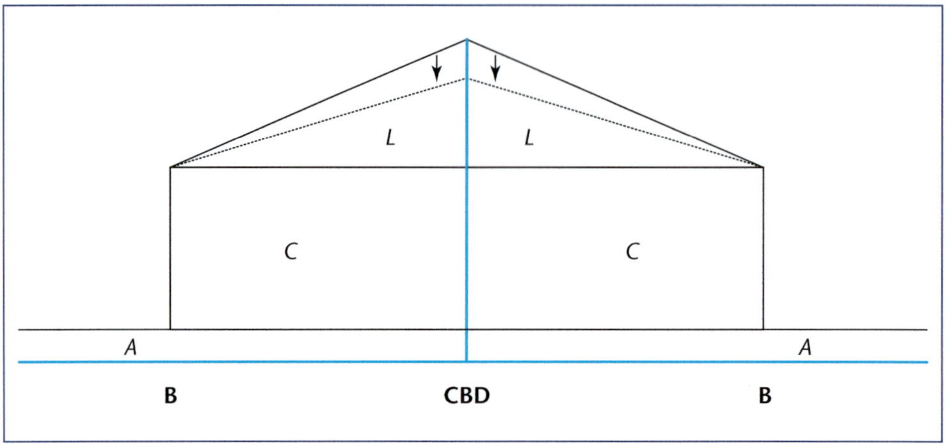

EXHIBIT 6-7 Effect of Transport Cost Reduction Savings Not Applied to Purchase of Land.

in the spatially constrained case depicted in Exhibit 6-7. To understand this, keep in mind that the value of urban land inside the urban boundary is due essentially to its location premium. This premium only exists because of each location's ability to save transport costs. As improved transport technology or infrastructure reduces those costs, the value of these savings is reduced.

More broadly, transport cost reductions reduce the value of the geographic centrality of location, making all locations more equal. Even if this results in an expansion of the urban area, this greater equality across locations must reduce the value of more central locations, at least relatively speaking.

This leads to a third important principle derived from the monocentric city model:

> *Declining transport costs (per person, per mile, or per year), holding population and income constant, will always reduce the value of location rent in the center of the city; the effect on the location rent near the periphery is generally ambiguous, depending on changes in density, but the overall result is certainly a flattening of rent gradients.*

This third principle can probably go a long way to explaining why we have not seen much increase in real rents over time in most U.S. cities during the twentieth century, despite tremendous population and income growth. It may clarify, especially how rents have typically declined in real (inflation-adjusted) terms in the central parts of many cities, including in the traditional CBDs, throughout the last half of the twentieth century.[19]

Once again, it is interesting to consider how Principle Three may play out differently in different regions in the twenty-first century. While technological progress (especially in the areas of telecommunications, computing, and the Internet) may affect all regions, rapidly developing countries such as China and India have much more potential for transport cost reductions than more mature regions due to infrastructure improvements (including mass transit) and rising automobile ownership, but only if these are not offset by greater densities and the resulting congestion, or perhaps more importantly, by the effect of more rapidly rising real incomes, as discussed below.

Income: The third and final phenomenon to examine is income growth, holding the population constant. Income growth is more pervasive than population growth, as some cities are not

[19] We noted in Chapter 1 that the LRMC (development cost, including land cost) curve in most U.S. cities appears to be only slightly upward-sloping, if at all, as evidenced by a lack of significant increase in real rents over time. Of course, many other factors are involved in real cities, including social and political considerations not contemplated in the monocentric city model.

growing in population. Still, per capita incomes have increased virtually everywhere and are likely to continue to do so, especially in rapidly developing regions such as Asia and Latin America. The effect of income growth is more complicated to examine because people can elect to spend their additional income in various ways, and income growth can have secondary effects on transport costs.

Normally, we would expect that people would elect to spend at least some of any additional income on purchasing more urban land (such as houses on larger lots, neighborhoods with more parkland and golf courses, more houses per capita—that is, smaller households due to people living on their own more, etc.). Thus, a rise in incomes would spread the city out spatially, reducing its density. While density reduction in general reduces the rent gradient, increasing the amount of unbuildable open space (parks, golf courses, etc.) reduces the "effective arc" of urban development, extending the urban radius without reducing the rent gradient, thereby increasing the central rent.[20] In any case, the effect will be to increase location rents near the periphery, similar to the case of transport improvements shown, for example, in Exhibit 6-6.

This city-expanding, potentially gradient-decreasing result of income growth would be further complicated (at least to some extent), however, by the indirect effect that higher incomes have on per capita transport costs. Recall that a major component of urban transport cost is the value of people's time wasted in traveling or commuting. This value per hour or per mile of travel is normally a positive function of per capita income. (Higher-income individuals are able and willing to pay more to save travel time because their opportunity cost of wasted time, in terms of forgone income, is greater, as is their ability to pay for leisure time.) So, this indirect effect of income growth will act (if density were held constant) to steepen the rent gradient, thereby offsetting, at least to some extent, the previously noted potentially gradient-decreasing effect of a rise in incomes.

Normally, we would expect at least some expansion in city area (hence, reduction in density) to result from income growth. However, if there are severe constraints on the ability of the city area to expand, then the transport cost effect of income growth would dominate. This would result in a steeper rent gradient and greater percentage increases in land rent nearer to the center of the city. This has probably not occurred in most U.S. cities but may have been a noticeable phenomenon in some other countries.

We can summarize this income effect in a fourth principle:

Increasing real income per capita (holding population constant) will tend to decrease rent gradients, with a possible result of absolute reductions in land rent at the center of the city, although a secondary transport cost increase effect (and/or increased open space reservation) due to higher incomes may mitigate this result or even reverse it, especially if the spatial expansion of the city is constrained.

6.2.3 Applying the Monocentric Model in PBT Forecasts

Although greatly simplified, the monocentric model of urban form we have examined here has clarified some basic and very important points about location rents in cities. Other things being equal, larger populations, or geographic constraints on the arc of growth which add to the radius of the city, will be associated with higher land rents. This, in turn, will require the city's inhabitants to spend larger amounts on the combination of transportation and housing costs, or else accept smaller houses in denser neighborhoods. In general, equilibrium among cities (reflecting the

---

[20] The key issue is whether the growth in real income changes the *percentage* of unbuildable land.

results of people's free ability to move among cities) means that larger cities in a country must be characterized by higher average per capita income levels for their citizens. Transportation improvements will tend to reduce the value of geographic centrality of location, tending to equalize land values throughout the city. Income increases have a more ambiguous effect, depending on how spatially constrained the city is and on the degree to which income increases result indirectly in an increase in transport costs.

Circlopolis may seem excessively simplified, too abstractly removed from the real world. But the beauty of a good academic theory lies precisely in its simplicity, in its ability to eliminate aspects of reality that are less important to the subject at hand, so that the aspects of reality that are more important can be clearly seen, and thereby understood. This is why the monocentric model—indeed, the monocentric model in its simplest form as presented here—holds such enduring value.

Almost everywhere in real estate there are "centers" and "peripheries." For a given real estate decision, the center that matters (and the associated periphery) may not be the downtown of a metropolis. The relevant center for an apartment development expected to house university students may be the location of the university campus. The relevant center for the clothing factory in our initial example might be a highway node. The point is, you can apply the monocentric model in a variety of ways to obtain useful insights.

Circling back to forecasting income estimates and practical questions, such as whether real rents for commercial properties will tend to increase over time in a growing city, or whether commercial property rents will tend to grow faster or slower in the long run than income from single-family homes, at first glance, many people would say, yes, commercial rents should grow in a growing city. But the monocentric city model should give you pause before answering so quickly. Commercial property tends to be located at or near central locations. We have seen in the monocentric city model two major conditions that can cause absolute real location rent levels to decline in central areas: transport improvements or (possibly) growth in real per capita income. If these phenomena dominate over the pure population growth effect, location rents in central areas, such as where most commercial buildings are built, could decline in absolute terms over the long run (after adjusting for inflation), even in a growing city. On the other hand, the monocentric model suggests that low-density housing rents might tend to grow over time, at least the land value component of their values, even in cities that are not growing in population. This is because low-density housing tends to be located near the periphery, where the monocentric model suggests location values tend to rise over time in a spatially expanding city.

The monocentric city model also has implications regarding long-run supply elasticity in the space market, and how this may tend to differ across cities, with implications in turn for long-range forecasting of the future growth in investment property rents. Recall from Exhibits 6-5 and 6-6 that larger and denser cities will tend to have higher location rents, and that cities with **physical supply constraints** such as coastlines, lakes or mountains will enhance these effects. Other things equal, this means that property values in such cities will tend to have a greater proportion of land value relative to building structure value, as building structure costs do not vary so much across cities. This means that the economic depreciation of the building structure will tend to have less relative impact on property values in larger denser cities, or ones with land supply constraints. And this in turn means that, other things equal, long-run growth in property-level rents will tend to be greater in cities with relatively constrained land supply. When you consider that the supply of built space can be constrained not only by physical characteristics but also, effectively, by **regulatory supply constraints** (local political constraints such as zoning), you can see how the monocentric model, broadly considered, holds deep implications for long-run rent forecasting for investment property, and how this can differ across cities.

TEXT BOX 6.1 WHAT HAPPENS IF DEMAND FALLS?

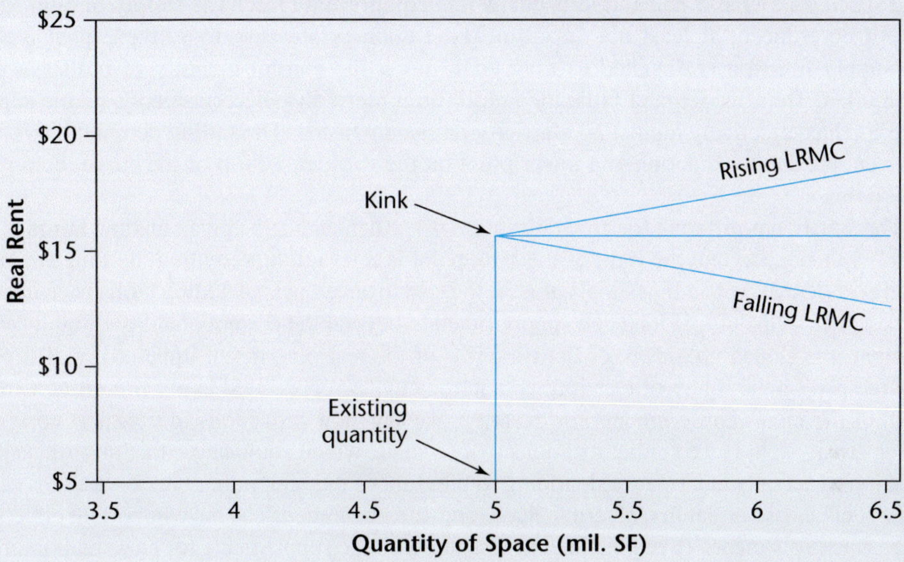

EXHIBIT 6-8

The monocentric model is essentially a static model; that is, it depicts the city at one point in time. We have nevertheless employed the model as a tool to gain some insight about how location rents may change over time, including in particular, the effect of increasing underlying demand for real estate due to population or income growth. But what happens if demand declines instead of growing? Sometimes cities lose population or employment, particularly in central areas.

In addition to the spatial economic considerations modeled in the monocentric city, in the long run, the growth (or lack thereof) in demand for real estate depends heavily on what happens to the so-called "**export sector**" (aka "basic sector") of the economic base of the metro area. The export sector consists of the industries and activities in which the city produces more value than what it consumes locally, the goods and services that it exports to other parts of the country and the world. If the export sector is growing, then the demand for real estate in the metro area broadly will be growing, although not necessarily in all areas or parts of the metro (as the monocentric model demonstrates).

The figure depicted here shows a simple model for understanding what can happen as demand for built space grows or shrinks in a given space market. The figure shows the supply function from a classical microeconomic model of a space market. As you probably know, in such a model, there is both a demand function and a supply function. The demand curve slopes downward to the right, and the supply curve slopes upward to the right. In this figure, we don't show the demand curve. But imagine a line sloping from the upper right toward the lower left. The level of that sloped demand line, how high it is in the graph, tells how much demand is in the market. The demand line will intersect the supply function that is shown in the figure at the equilibrium price and quantity in the market, that is, the equilibrium space rent and square footage (SF) of space occupied in the market. The higher the demand, the higher up and to the right that intersection (equilibrium) point will be on the supply function.

The interesting thing about the supply function for real estate is that it is "kinked", as depicted in the figure. The kink occurs at the current equilibrium rent and quantity of occupied space. But what if demand falls below that equilibrium level? The supply of built space cannot be reduced, at least not very quickly. Buildings are very long-lived. That is why the supply function is depicted as a vertical line at the current quantity of built space in the market. Thus, as demand falls, the equilibrium rent will fall very steeply, as the supply function has effectively almost no elasticity on the downside. The falling demand curve will intersect the supply function at a lower point on the vertical section of the curve, below the kink point.

The situation is different for growth in space usage demand in the given market. For that, the supply function beyond the right of the kink point is relevant, representing the long-run marginal cost (LRMC) of adding supply, that is, the cost to developers of adding built space into the market. The shape of that long-run supply function beyond the current quantity of built space, whether it is sloped up, down, or flat (in terms of the real rent, net of inflation), will depend in large part on the future of location rents in the city, as represented in our preceding exploration of the monocentric model. For example, we saw how reductions in transport costs and lower density could lead central locations to lose value, which could cause the long-run supply function to actually be downward-sloping to the right of the kink point. Other scenarios could make it either rise or flat in real terms. Such long-run phenomena can have important effects on real estate investments. (See the video in Chapter 6 online supplements for more elaboration.)

6.3 MARKETS IN EQUILIBRIUM: RENTS ARE INTERLINKED WITH ASSET VALUES AND SUPPLY

The current PBT income levels that we observe for a given building are largely based on the rents achieved in the local space market where the supply and demand for space meet. Going forward, neither supply nor demand is typically fixed or independent of the asset market and construction industry. For example, a stronger demand for space typically raises rents in the short run, which then translates into higher asset values. Those higher asset values induce more construction of new properties over time. On completion, the new supply will bring back rents to their long-run equilibrium values. When projecting PBT cash flows into the future, we cannot analyze the space market in isolation; we need to consider interdependencies with the capital markets and development.

6.3.1 Quadrant Model

Denise DiPasquale and Bill Wheaton have developed a graphic representation of the real estate system we just sketched.[21] This model consists of a quadrant graph, as shown in Exhibit 6-9. The quadrants depict four binary relationships that together complete the linkages between the space market, the asset market, and the development industry.

The quadrant graph is most useful for simultaneously examining the effect on the long-run equilibrium within and between the space and asset markets. The concept of long-run equilibrium in real estate involves allowing the markets sufficient time for the supply of built space to adjust to the

---

[21] Traditionally known as the "four-quadrant model" as labeled by the model's original authors, Wheaton & DiPasquale (1992), we shorten the name here, trying to reduce redundancy—after all, quadrants typically come in packs of four. A similar quadrant depiction of the link between the space and asset markets was presented by Fisher (1992).

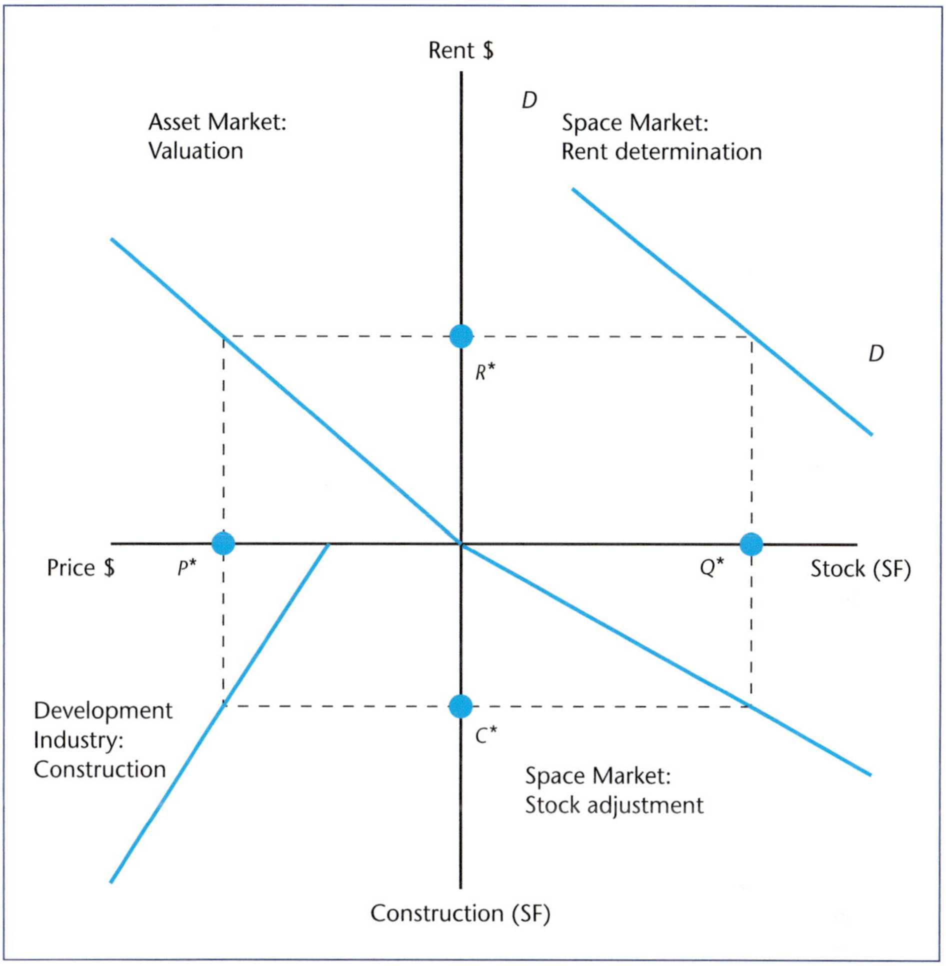

EXHIBIT 6-9 The DiPasquale-Wheaton Quadrant Diagram.

demand. Equilibrium in the quadrant graph is represented by a rectangle whose sides are vertical and horizontal connections between four points, one lying on each of the four binary-relationship lines in each of the four quadrants. Where the sides of this rectangle cross the four axes represents the equilibrium stock of built space, rent, asset prices, and rate of new construction in the market. In Exhibit 6-9, the rectangle is indicated by dashed lines, and the equilibrium prices and quantities are indicated by the points Q^*, R^*, P^*, and C^*. The northeast quadrant depicts the determination of rent in the space market. The horizontal axis in this quadrant is the physical stock of space in the market (e.g., in square feet), and the vertical axis is the rent (e.g., in $/SF per year). Thus, the axes of this quadrant are those of the classic price/quantity diagram in the space market, and the space usage demand function is represented in the northeast quadrant by the downward-sloping *DD* line. Suppose we draw a vertical line from the point on the horizontal axis representing the existing supply of space in the market (Q^*). In that case, the point at which that line intersects the demand function will tell us the current equilibrium rent, given the amount of space in the market. The equilibrium rent with Q^* amount of space in the market is R^*.

The northwest quadrant depicts the asset market valuation process, relating the equilibrium property prices (on the horizontal axis, in $/SF) to the current rent level (on the vertical axis shared with the northeast quadrant, also in $/SF). Note that in the quadrant diagram, the point in the center where the axes cross is the "origin" of all four graphs, so that in the northwest and southwest quadrants, the horizontal axis values increase as one moves from right to left.

The line in the northwest quadrant represents the cap rate or OAR (or its inverse, the price/earnings multiple). The steeper the line, the higher the cap rate (lower property price per dollar of current rent). By continuing a horizontal line from the current rent point R^* on the vertical axis to the cap rate line in the northwest quadrant and then drawing a vertical line down from that point to the price axis, we determine the property price (per SF) implied by the current rent. The point P^* represents the property price. Thus, the two top (or "northern") quadrants depict the short-run or immediate price link between the asset and space markets.

The two bottom (or "southern") quadrants depict the long-run effect of the real estate development industry by showing the impact of construction on the total stock of built space in the market. The southwest quadrant depicts the operation of the development industry—the physical asset production process. The relationship in the southwest quadrant is between property prices and the annual amount of construction activity (including rehabilitation and redevelopment as well as new development). The line in this quadrant relates a given level of property prices to a given rate of construction. The vertical (upside-down) axis represents the physical rate of construction in SF/year produced by the development industry. The further down the vertical axis you go, the greater the level of the construction activity.

The construction function line in the southwest quadrant is outward-sloping in Exhibit 6-9 (i.e., down and to the left), indicating that in the space market modeled by the diagram, higher property prices will stimulate a greater rate of new construction, as higher prices enable more costly sites to be developed, possibly at higher densities and/or development to proceed at a faster pace due to greater availability of capital. The outward slope of this line, therefore, represents rising long-run marginal costs in the supply of built space. Greater long-run supply elasticity (i.e., a flatter long-run marginal cost curve for real estate development) would be represented by a more steeply falling line in the southwest quadrant.[22] The construction function line intersects the property price axis at a positive value rather than at the origin because when the property price is below some threshold level, no construction will occur, as it would be unprofitable. A vertical line dropped down from the horizontal (asset price) axis at the current asset price P^* will intersect the construction function line at a point that corresponds on the downward vertical axis (drawing a horizontal line over to it) to the amount of new construction in the market per year (point C^*).

Finally, the southeast quadrant completes the long-run integration of the space and asset markets by linking the rate of construction to the total stock of built space available in the usage market. The line in the southeast quadrant relates the average rate of space construction per year to the total stock of space that can be indefinitely maintained in the market. It is not a continuation of, or related in any way to, the line in the northwest quadrant. The concept behind the southeast quadrant is that, in the long run, in the absence of new construction, older space will be removed from the stock as it "wears out" and old buildings are either abandoned and demolished or converted to other uses. Thus, on average, over the long run, a certain amount of new construction per year is necessary just to maintain a given stock of space available in the market. The greater the total stock, the greater the annual new-construction rate necessary just to maintain that stock in the long run (hence, the outward-sloping line from the origin). The line in the southeast quadrant thus links the C^* level of

[22] The line in the southwest quadrant is not exactly the same as the long-run-supply curve presented in Chapter 1, because the southwest quadrant determines the rate of construction per year, rather than the accumulated total stock of built space supplied in the market. The interaction of the two bottom quadrants fully depicts the long-run-supply function in the space market. The long-run-supply function "kink" described in the earlier text box does not appear in the quadrant diagram because this diagram shows purely long-run-steady-state relationships. However, the equivalent of the kink could be represented in the quadrant diagram by placing a kink in the stock adjustment line in the southeast quadrant at its corner of the initial rectangle, so that the line bends vertically up to the horizontal axis at Q^*.

construction activity to the Q^* level of total supply of built space. The quadrant picture thus depicts a **long-run steady-state equilibrium**.[23]

6.3.2 Using the Quadrant Diagram to Help Understand Boom and Bust in Real Estate Markets

Historically, real estate markets have been shaped by boom-and-bust periods in which either rents or prices have deviated from their fundamental values based on long-run equilibria in the space or asset market. Exhibit 6-10 provides an example of recurring property cycles in the city of Amsterdam. For 355 years, it shows the ratio of rents over prices: Whenever the ratio is low, properties are comparatively expensive as investors have to pay more to receive the rental cash flows (boom markets). In contrast, when rent-price ratios are high, asset prices have fallen relative to rents (bust markets). Most strikingly, the rent-price ratio returned to its long-run equilibrium value repeatedly throughout the centuries. Evidently, the space market, asset market, and development market were in balance—in the long run. For subperiods, however, deviations and corrections occurred again and again. In the next section, we will discuss some general patterns using the quadrant model.

First, consider the effect of an increase in demand for space usage, holding the real estate asset market constant. This is depicted in Exhibit 6-11A, where the demand function in the northeast quadrant moves out to the right, from D_0 to D_1. In the short run, there is no time for new space to be built in response to an unanticipated surge in usage demand, so unless developers and the capital markets have adequately anticipated the demand growth, rents might initially rise to levels that cannot be supported in the long-run equilibrium. This is indicated by the movement of rent on the vertical axis from the original level of R^* to a temporary high level of R_1, found by relating the original stock of space (Q^* on the horizontal axis) to the new demand function D_1. The long-run equilibrium effect of the growth in demand, however, results in rents that are not as high as the R_1 level. This suggests a run-up followed by a fallback in rents. The severity of this reversal and the extent to which decision-makers in the system anticipate it can determine the significance of any resulting "boom-and-bust cycle."

The rectangle traced in the dashed lines indicates the new long-run equilibrium based on the new D_1 demand function. The new equilibrium is represented by the points with the double asterisks, where the new rectangle crosses the axes. Note that while the new equilibrium rent (R^{**}) is above the old equilibrium rent (R^*), it is below the temporary R_1 rent level. The fact that R^{**} is above R^* indicates that this space market is characterized by at least a slightly upward-sloping long-run-marginal-cost function, that is, increasing real development costs (presumably reflecting land or location values increasing over time in real terms). Also, note that while the long-run equilibrium quantity of built space is higher than it was at the old demand level ($Q^{**} > Q^*$), the "absorption" (increased occupancy) of space is not so great as would have occurred if rents had been maintained at the old R* level. This is due to the effect of usage demand sensitivity to rent (i.e., price elasticity of demand), indicated by the slope of the demand function in the northeast quadrant.

A little experimentation with the quadrant graph will demonstrate an important point. The condition for the new equilibrium rectangle lying outside the old one due to growth in underlying usage demand (holding the capital market in the northwest quadrant constant) is that the asset construction function in the southwest quadrant must be outward-sloping (rising marginal costs). Rents, property

[23] For example, in a market where there are 100,000 apartment units, 1,000 to 2,000 units per year will likely be lost (generally older units) due to conversion into other uses, demolition to make way for other projects, or simple abandonment. So, to maintain 100,000 apartments in the market, 1,000 to 2,000 new units must be built per year. Similarly, an average construction rate of 2,000 to 4,000 new units per year will eventually support a steady-state stock of 200,000 units. This reveals how the quadrant diagram depicts long-run average relationships. In particular, the construction function in the southwest quadrant does not represent the amount of construction in any single year, but rather an average rate of construction maintained across a long span of time.

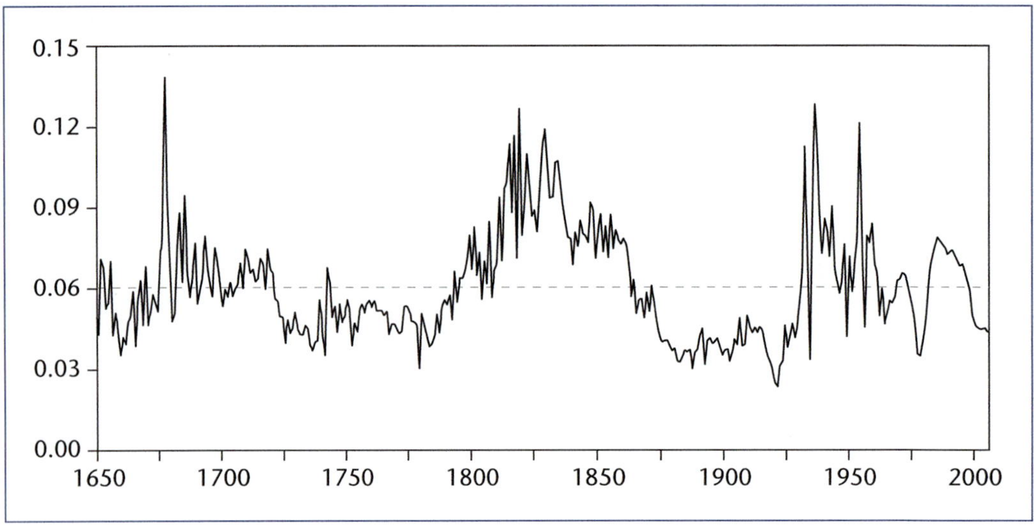

EXHIBIT 6-10 Rent-Price Ratio for Amsterdam, 1650–2005. (Ambrose et al., 2013, "House Prices and Fundamentals: 355 Years of Evidence," *Journal of Money, Credit and Banking* 45(2–3).)

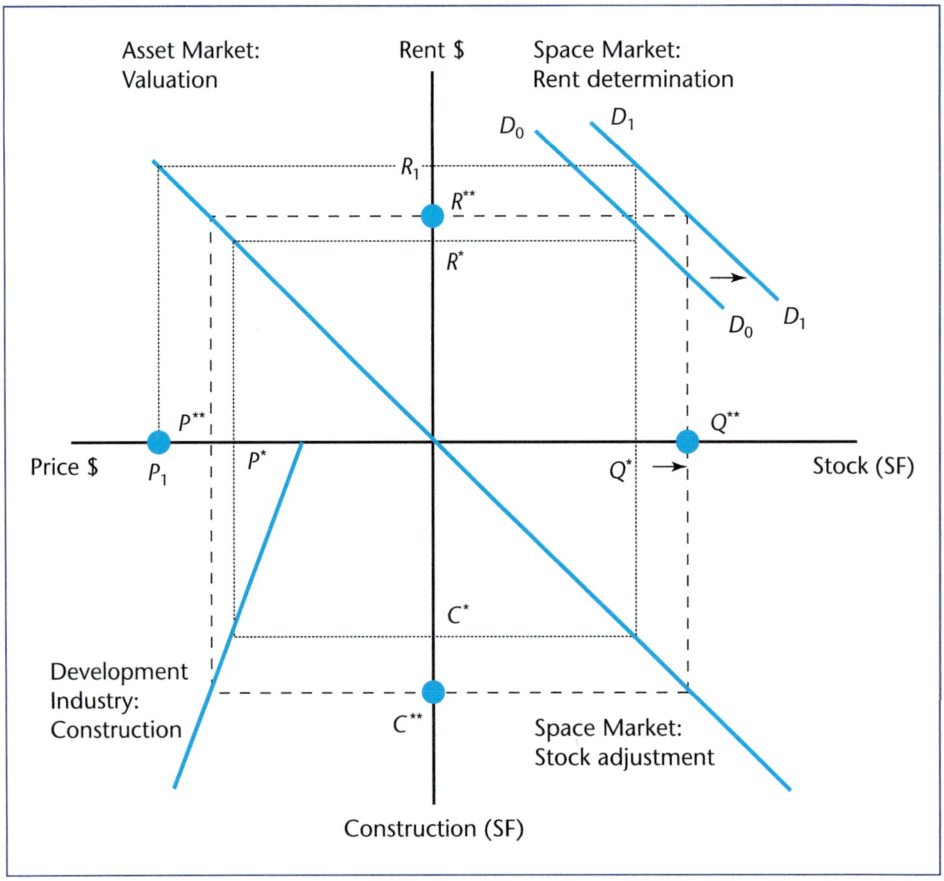

EXHIBIT 6-11A Effect of Demand Growth in Space Market.

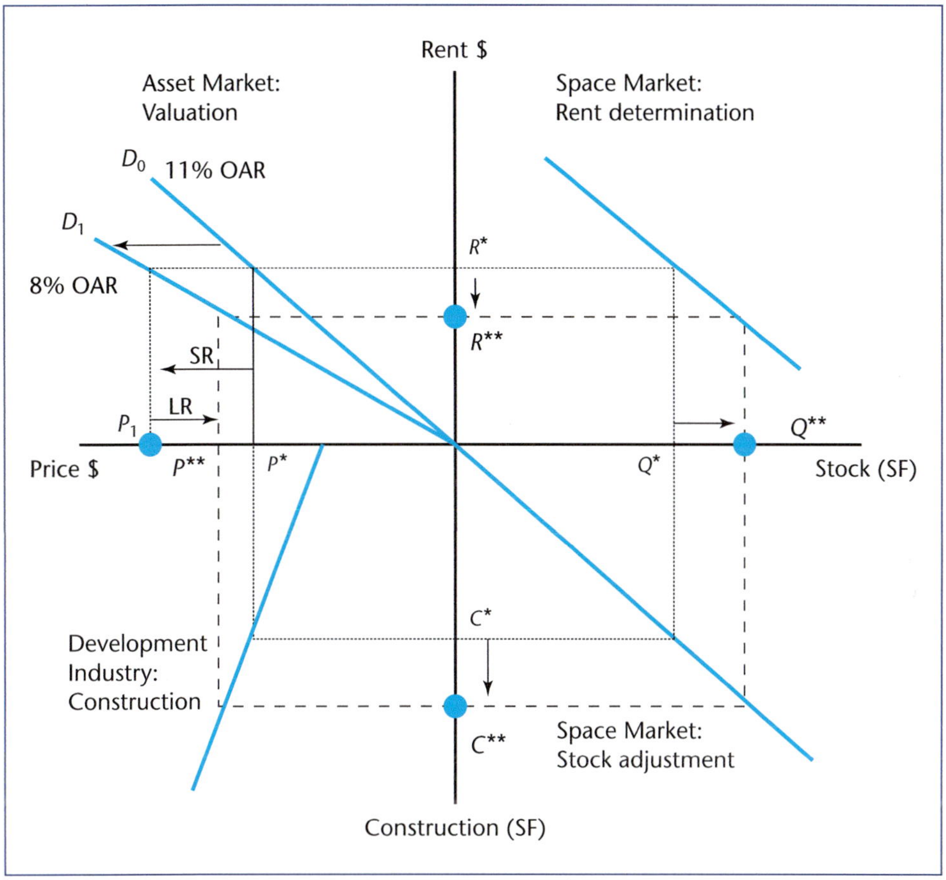

EXHIBIT 6-11B Effect of Demand Growth in Asset Market.

prices, and stock of space must all increase under these circumstances in response to rising usage demand in the northeast quadrant. However, the increase need not be proportionately the same across all of these variables. The amount of the increase will depend on the relative elasticities of supply and demand and the capital market's appetite for more investment in real estate, that is, on the shapes of the lines (or they could be curves) in the two upper quadrants.

The fundamental key to whether rents must rise with a growth in demand lies in the shape of the construction function in the southwest quadrant. If development costs are constant (completely vertical construction function in the southwest quadrant), then rents will remain constant in the long run, even with the growth in space usage demand. In that case, the long-run equilibrium rectangle will expand only to the right in its width dimension and only downward in its height dimension, that is, greater steady-state construction and stock of space but no greater rents or asset prices. Indeed, suppose the long-run marginal cost of development is declining in real terms (inward-sloping construction function in the southwest quadrant, bending down toward the vertical axis). In that case, the long-run result of an increase in usage demand will actually be lower rents and lower asset prices than before the usage demand grew. Because this result is somewhat counterintuitive and also seemingly belied by the initial short-run (but unsustainable) run-up in rent (to level R_1), it may not be properly anticipated by decision-makers in the real estate system, perhaps especially in the asset market and development industry, leading to initial gains followed by losses—a "boom-and-bust" result.

Next, consider the effect of an increase in demand for real estate investment assets among investors in the capital markets. By this, we mean a relative shift in preferences among investors so that they are willing to pay higher price/earnings multiples for real estate assets than they previously were. Such a shift might occur because investors now perceive real estate as less risky than other investment asset classes (such as stocks and bonds). Or perhaps investors for some reason don't mind or care about real estate's risk as much as they did previously (maybe because their investment holdings are more diversified). Or perhaps investors now tend to expect more future growth in real estate rents than they previously had been expecting, so they don't require as much current return. Or perhaps there is just a general increase in global liquidity (the amount of money available to invest, including some earmarked for real estate). The point is that, for some reason, investors are now willing to pay more for real estate assets per dollar of current real estate rental income than they were willing to pay before.

This type of capital market shift is indicated in Exhibit 6-11B by the movement down (to a shallower slope) of the valuation line in the northwest quadrant. For example, suppose that prevailing cap rates had been 11 percent on average, for typical properties in a given real estate market, and now they have moved down three points to 8 percent. This represents a substantial upward revaluation of property. Indeed, property values would rise some 37.5 percent if rents remained constant (from 1/0.11 to 1/0.08 per Euro of rent). And, of course, at first, rents would remain constant, holding supply and usage demand constant in the space market in the northeast quadrant. Thus, if investors are somewhat **myopic** and cannot foresee what the surge of financial capital into the real estate asset market will do to stimulate new construction, then property prices could rise temporarily to a level above what is sustainable in the long run. This is indicated in Exhibit 6-11B by the short-run rise in asset prices to the P_1 level from the original P^* level.

The new long-run equilibrium is found, as always, in a quadrant diagram, by the new rectangle connecting the four quadrants based on the new 8 percent OAR line in the northwest quadrant. This equilibrium is shown in Exhibit 6-11B by the dashed lines, which intersect the axes at the new equilibrium prices and quantities indicated by the double asterisks. Note that this new equilibrium involves a substantial increase in the amount of built space, which reflects the effect of a real estate development boom that brings the stock of space up to the new Q^{**} level. This is the **physical capital** result of the flow of **financial capital** into the real estate asset market (and development industry) caused by the shift in investor preferences toward real estate assets.

The new equilibrium involves lower rents ($R^{**} < R^*$) and, therefore, more use of space ($Q^{**} > Q^*$) than the original equilibrium, holding usage demand constant in the space market. The lower rents mean that the lower cap rates in the asset market do not result in as high a long-run rise in property prices as you might have thought at first, even with rising marginal development costs (outward-sloping construction function in the southwest quadrant). The new equilibrium property market prices of P^{**}, although possibly higher than the old P^* prices, may not be much higher, though the short-lived jump to P_1 may have been much higher. Again, we have the potential ingredients of a "boom and bust," but this time only in the asset market, as the effect on rents in the space market is purely downward pressure.

If development marginal costs decline (construction function bending down inward toward the vertical axis in the southwest quadrant), then this result is more extreme. Asset prices end up lower than they started out, even though cap rates are lower (higher asset price/earnings multiples) because the supply of space ultimately increases so much as to bring rents down so far (holding usage demand constant) that asset prices fall in spite of the lower cap rates. All of this occurs in a sustainable, steady state (i.e., with sufficient profit for all "players"). But again, the long-run result is somewhat counterintuitive and opposite to the initial short-run result, ingredients for potential overshooting and a "boom-and-bust" result that could expose some investors or developers to losses.

6.4 CHAPTER SUMMARY

This chapter presented the basic determinants of urban form and how cities are shaped and configured. Urban form is intimately linked to land values and basic real estate business activities such as building construction location and investment decisions. In this chapter, we described the fundamental economic principles and concepts that underlie the joint determination of land value and urban form. Concepts such as the residual value of land, bid-rent functions, land market equilibrium, the highest and best use principle, and rent gradients are basic to understanding how cities grow, develop, and change over time. These economic fundamentals, therefore, can be used to inform real estate business decisions. We also introduced a classic model of urban form that teaches through its elegance: the monocentric model.

The chapter also sketched the dynamic linkages among the markets for space, assets, and construction of new properties in what can be called the **real estate system**. We introduced the quadrant model as a simple visual tool for analyzing this system and showed how it can shed light on the traditional concept of the real estate cycle. Without perfect foresight by market participants, differences between short-run and long-run effects emerge as the system reaches (a new) equilibrium.

KEY TERMS

- Urban form
- Factor of production
- Residual theory of land value
- Mobile factors
- Highest and best use (HBU)
- Bid-rent curve (function) central point
- Transportation costs minimized
- Monocentric city
- Radius to the urban boundary
- Agricultural rent construction cost rent gradient
- Location rent (location premium)
- Physical supply constraints
- Regulatory supply constraints
- Export sector
- Kinked supply
- Quadrant model
- Real estate system

STUDY QUESTIONS

In Your Own Words

6.1 What is meant by a factor of production? Name four categories or types of production factors. How does land differ from the other factors?
6.2 Explain the residual theory of land value. Why is land value only the residual after other factors have been paid?
6.3 What does the following statement mean? Land value determines use, and at the same time, use determines value. Explain your answer.
6.4 Why are denser or more intensive land uses typically found closer to central locations?
6.5 Why is the classic monocentric city model a long-run equilibrium model?

6.6 Describe the two possible effects of population growth on both relative and absolute land values within a monocentric homogeneous city.

6.7 Describe the two possible effects of transportation cost reduction (per mile, per person) on both relative and absolute land values within a monocentric homogeneous city. Which one do you think dominates in the real world? Explain.

6.8 Describe the two possible effects of income growth on both relative and absolute land values within a monocentric homogeneous city, considering both direct and indirect effects. Which one do you think dominates in the real world? Explain.

6.9 The classic monocentric city model assumes that all commuting is into the city center. Consider a two-person household in which one person commutes to the city center while the other commutes in the reverse direction to the edge of the city.

   a. Draw the household's bid-rent function assuming round-trip commuting costs are the same in either direction.
   b. Now, assume that round-trip commuting costs are higher when commuting in to work in the CBD.

6.10 Describe each of the quadrants in the four-quadrant diagram. Set up the four-quadrant diagram, carefully labeling each quadrant.

Check Your Knowledge

6.11 A logistics center and a seasonal storage facility are bidding on a site near a highway intersection. The logistics center relies heavily on highway access, while the seasonal storage facility is less profitable and has minimal transportation needs. Which use is more likely to outbid the other for this location?

   A) The logistics center, due to its high reliance on transportation
   B) The storage facility, because it has lower profit margins
   C) Both uses would bid equally for the location
   D) Neither, as both would prefer other locations

6.12 What drives the "long-run supply elasticity" in the space market?

   A) Transport costs
   B) The construction industry's flexibility
   C) Landowner's income
   D) Population growth

6.13 Suppose the most productive use of a particular site is as a high-volume, upscale restaurant that can generate revenues of $600,000 per year. The operating expenses, including labor, food, and utilities (everything except rent) are $450,000 per year. The building can be built and equipped for $1 million, which can be paid for by a perpetual loan with interest of $100,000 per year. According to the residual theory, how much is the land parcel worth in terms of annual land rent?

6.14 A firm in industry A is making a location decision, and has narrowed the choice to two different locations, which we will call site 1 and site 2. The firm's revenue is independent of location and equals $5 million per year on each site. The firm's nonland production costs, however, differ at the two sites, being $4 million at site 1 and $4.5 million at site 2

   a. Assuming the land (rental) market is competitive, what is the firm's bid-rent for each site?
   b. Now, suppose a firm in industry B is competing for sites with an industry A firm. The industry B firm would have profits before land rent of $750,000 at site 1 and $650,000 at site 2. How is the land allocated, and what is the equilibrium land rent we would observe at each site?

6.15 Suppose user demand for space in a certain market grows from 4 to 5 million square feet (MSF) at \$10/SF net rent. Assuming property market cap rates remain constant at 10%, answer the following:
   a. Using a four-quadrant diagram, show the short- and long-run effects of this change in user demand. You may answer qualitatively or quantitatively, recognizing that specific quantitative answers depend on the shapes and slopes of the curves (i.e., the elasticities) in each quadrant.
   b. Explain how and why rents might "overshoot" the new long-run equilibrium level in the short run. What factors contribute to this overshooting, and how does forward-looking behavior by developers and investors affect the extent of this overshoot?

6.16 Suppose investor demand for real estate assets grows in the sense that prevailing cap rates (OARs) in the property asset market fall from 10% to 8%. Assuming that usage demand remains constant in the space market, answer the following:
   a. On a four-quadrant diagram, show the short- and long-run effects of this change in investor demand.
   b. Explain what factors might have caused investor asset demand for real estate to grow.

Chapter Case: Land Use in Urbantown

Urbantown is a monocentric city centered around a central business district (CBD) as its economic core. Natural barriers, including a lake to the west and a coastline to the south, limit outward expansion.

To improve connectivity, the government has invested in a light rail system and new highway intersections linking the suburbs to the CBD. These improvements attract logistics centers to highway intersections due to reduced transportation costs, while the CBD remains a prime location for high-density offices and luxury retail.

Urbantown's monocentric structure creates a "rent gradient," with the highest rents in the CBD, decreasing with distance largely due to transportation costs. Zoning regulations promote each area's "highest and best use," with the CBD supporting offices and luxury retail, and suburban areas designated for lower-density uses.

Based on Urbantown's urban structure, answer the following questions.

1. What does "bid-rent" represent, and how is it related to the residual value of land in Urbantown?
   A) It is the minimum rent a user is willing to pay for a location, unrelated to residual value.
   B) It is the average rent across all locations.
   C) It is the maximum rent a potential user would pay for a location, representing the residual value.
   D) It is the replacement cost of the land.
2. How do bid-rents create a "spatial equilibrium" in Urbantown?
   A) They prevent firms from moving by setting fixed rents for each location.
   B) They ensure firms are indifferent between locations because they earn zero profit after paying rent.
   C) They cap rent in certain areas to limit the number of firms.
   D) They encourage all firms to locate as close to each other as possible.

3. Imagine that transportation costs in Urbantown became negligible. How would this affect the bid-rent curves and the factors determining land value?
   A) They would remain steep, with transportation costs as the main factor.
   B) They would be flat, and site value would be determined by the highest and best use.
   C) They would have no specific shape.
   D) They would be vertical, unaffected by distance.
4. In Urbantown's CBD, high-rise office buildings and luxury retail occupy prime locations. How does the "highest and best use" principle determine land use in such high-demand areas?
   A) It ensures each location is used for the most productive purpose relative to its cost.
   B) It restricts land use changes to maintain zoning stability.
   C) It encourages all sites to be used for residential purposes.
   D) It prevents competition for high-value sites.
5. According to the monocentric city model, how do geographic constraints around Urbantown impact land rents compared to an otherwise identical city with no such barriers?
   A) Land rents are lower in Urbantown due to restricted growth.
   B) Land rents are higher in Urbantown because the geographic constraints limit outward expansion.
   C) Land rents are unaffected by geographic constraints.
   D) Land rents in Urbantown are lower only in the suburban areas.
6. Imagine if the geographic constraints limiting Urbantown's outward expansion disappeared, what would the monocentric city model say about the relative growth of land rents in the center versus the periphery as population or income grows?
   A) Land rent growth would be higher in the city center.
   B) Land rent growth would be the same throughout the city.
   C) Land rent growth would be greater at the city's periphery.
   D) Land rents would decrease uniformly across the city.
7. In Urbantown, if the location rent at the center is $6,000 per year per acre and the density is three people per acre, what is the annual transportation commuting cost per capita at the city's edge? If the annual transportation cost per mile from the CBD is $200, what is the radius of the city?
   A) Annual commuting cost per capita is $1,500, and the radius is 7.5 miles.
   B) Annual commuting cost per capita is $2,000, and the radius is 10 miles.
   C) Annual commuting cost per capita is $2,500, and the radius is 12.5 miles.
   D) Annual commuting cost per capita is $3,000, and the radius is 15 miles.

7 Determinants of Rent II

Property Level

CHAPTER OUTLINE

LEARNING OBJECTIVES

After reading this chapter, you should understand:

- The difference between land value and land rent, and the key determinants of land values in and around a city.
- Why uncertainty can result in higher land values but less land development in a city.
- Why it is sometimes more beneficial to wait on new development, even when feasible development options exist.
- Why different land uses and densities occur at different locations within a city.
- The impact of boundaries, whether by land use regulations or physical limits on land use density and value.
- Polycentric cities as overlapping monocentric patterns of land use and value.
- How neighborhoods or urban districts grow and mature and sometimes decline and rise again.
- The concept of property life cycle and its implications for real estate investors.
- The nature and cause of the major characteristics of urban form and how this can evolve.

The previous chapter presented just the basics, the bare bones of economic theory for understanding what shapes urban form and the pattern of land value changes over time and space within a city. The simple monocentric city model we explored then was not only very simple spatially, but it was essentially only a long-run or static model with little consideration of the dynamics of growth. This chapter presents some more advanced concepts and introduces some broader considerations that are important in real world cities. The first two parts of this chapter deal with real property asset value, as distinguished from the annual rents that were the focus of the previous chapter. This will clarify two very important concerns of real estate investors: growth expectations and uncertainty. The remainder of this chapter will then enrich the simple monocentric model of the previous chapter by introducing some important features of real-world cities, neighborhoods, and property investments.

DOI: 10.1201/9781003643838-9

7.1 FROM PROPERTY RENT TO PROPERTY VALUE: THE EFFECT OF RENT GROWTH EXPECTATIONS

Real property value is not the same thing as real property rent, although the two are closely related. Property value is the present value of the expected future rents the property could receive. Therefore, other things being equal, property value will be greater where rents are greater. But two other factors also affect property value in addition to the current level of rent the property can earn. The first factor is the expected future **growth rate** of the rents. The second is **uncertainty**, or risk, in the future level of those rents. In this section, we consider the effect of the first of these two factors.

A higher growth rate in future rents will increase the present value of those rents, thereby increasing property value, other things being equal. As we saw in Chapter 6, the location premium component of the equilibrium rents within a city can grow over time in real terms, and even more so in nominal terms given inflation. The potential for city expansion will cause the value of nonurban land just beyond the current boundary of the city to exceed the mere present value of future agricultural rents. This is because the present value of the expected future urban location rent premium is incorporated in the current undeveloped land value. The closer an external location is to the boundary of the city and the more rapidly that boundary is expanding toward that location, the greater will be this **growth premium** in the value of the nonurban land.

Indeed, even developed property within the urban boundary will be more expensive per dollar of current annual rent to the extent that the location rent premium is expected to grow. As a result of this growth premium, property will be more expensive (that is, it will sell at higher multiples of the current rent, or at lower "cap rate") in cities that are expecting greater future growth in rents. But should such growth expectations result in a delay of urban development? That is, will land be held undeveloped in anticipation of such future growth, even after it is profitable to develop the land?

Consider the simple numerical example as depicted in the table below. Suppose that growth in demand for a location suggests that by next year it will be possible to build a structure that will be 30 percent larger than the structure that would be optimal today. If building the smaller structure that is optimally sized for today's demand precludes building the larger structure that is expected to be optimal for next year's demand (i.e., no "expansion or conversion option"), and if investors require, say, a 20 percent expected return for land speculation, then the economics are as depicted in the table. Building today and building next year are mutually exclusive, and the present value today of waiting to build next year is $217 ($260/1.2), whereas the present value of building today is only $200. The land would sell for $217 today, and the rational landowner would choose to wait rather than develop immediately.[1]

EXHIBIT 7-1 HBU Numerical Example

Highest and Best Use (HBU)	Today (Known)	Next Year (Expected)
Value of Completed Built Property	$1,000	$1,300
Construction & Development Cost (Excluding Land)	$800	$1,040
Profit from Immediate Construction (Excluding Land)	$200	$260
NPV @ 20% Discount Rate (Expected Return)	$200	$217

But note that such optimal delay circumstances depend not just on the expectation of future growth in rent location premium, but that the evolution of the location premium will also imply a different optimal structure, in effect, an evolution of the highest and best use (HBU) of the location. It is only the expectation of an HBU evolution (in the absence of flexible structure expansion or conversion) that could make the delay of initial development a reasonable option. This is because, in the absence of such

[1] Implicit in this problem setup is the assumption that if the large structure costing $1,040 were built today, it would not be able to rent out sufficiently for a year, such that its value today would be less than $1,240.

an HBU evolution, building today does not forego the opportunity to take advantage of future rental growth, applying to the same fixed use (the same structure). Building today is not mutually exclusive with building next year from the perspective of taking advantage of the rental growth, since the structure you build today will generate that same rental growth as an identical one you would build next year.[2]

As a result, same use growth expectations alone provide neither an option premium in land value nor a reason to delay construction. This is the situation we face in the simple monocentric city model that we introduced in the previous chapter, where there is only one use in the urban development, namely, housing of a fixed density. But this situation is in contrast to the effect of volatility or uncertainty in growth expectations, the subject to which we turn in the next section.

7.2 EFFECT OF UNCERTAINTY ON SPECULATIVE LAND VALUE

Unlike the *expected* future location rent growth, the risk or uncertainty surrounding such growth does have implications for possible land speculation and delay of development, and hence can be a determinant of land value and city size. Mathematical techniques first applied by financial economists to valuing stock options have been used to analyze the effect of uncertainty on land values and urban form.[3] Professor Sheridan Titman was the first to point out that in the presence of uncertainty, it is rational for developers to wait longer than they otherwise would before starting construction, but that such uncertainty actually tends to increase land value.[4] This is because land provides its owner/developers with a **call option**. The owner of a land parcel has the *right without obligation* to develop the land at any time. When development is undertaken, this option is surrendered, the cost of construction is incurred, and in return the value of the developed property is obtained.[5]

This option-like characteristic allows the owner/developer to profit from uncertainty in the following way. Uncertainty in the real estate market can be thought of as the possibility of the occurrence of unexpected upswings and downswings in building values.[6] The option characteristic of land ownership allows the developer to take advantage of the "upside" of uncertainty while avoiding full exposure to the "downside." If and when an upswing occurs in the property market, the owner can choose to develop the property and make particularly large profits. If a downswing in the market occurs, the owner can simply choose not to develop for the time being, thereby avoiding potential losses. But once a structure is built, this optionality is lost; the property is now fully exposed to the downside (as well as the upside).

Capozza and Helsley (1990)[7] integrated this options-analysis approach into the classical monocentric city model and showed that uncertainty results in a smaller, denser city with higher rents than would prevail in the absence of uncertainty (other things being equal). The key reason for this is the **irreversibility of construction**. Once a structure is built on a land parcel, it is normally very difficult and expensive to remove or significantly alter it. In the analogy with stock options, once the option is exercised, you no longer have the option. The loss of the option is part of the cost of development (inherent in the land value).

Logically, if uncertainty gives value to options, then the optionality inherent in undeveloped (but developable) land will be more valuable the more uncertainty (or "volatility") there is in the

[2] Here, for simplicity we are ignoring the effect of long-term lease commitments.

[3] In fact, the option model has a number of applications in real estate that are of interest to commercial property investment analysts. Some of these applications will be described later in this book, primarily in Parts III and IV.

[4] See Titman (1985), "Urban Land Prices Under Uncertainty". *The American Economic Review* 75(3). The implication of option value theory for optimal development timing will be discussed in more depth in Part IV in the online portion of this book, where we will discuss the relationship of the "real options" literature to development decision making.

[5] The analogy with stock options is that upon surrendering the option and paying the "exercise price," you receive the underlying stock shares.

[6] The upswings and downswings are unexpected, not in the sense that people don't expect there to be upswings and downswings, but rather in the sense that these changes in the market cannot be perfectly forecasted.

[7] Capozza, D., and R. Helsley. 1990. "The stochastic city". *Journal of Urban Economics* 28: 187–203.

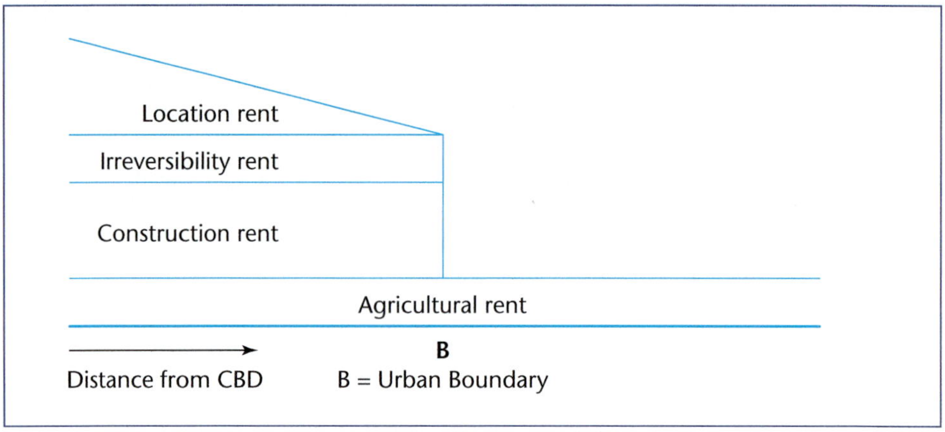

EXHIBIT 7-2 Components of Property Rent Outside and Inside the Urban Boundary, Under Uncertainty.

underlying real estate market. This is why, in the presence of uncertainty, it makes sense to wait longer than one otherwise would (that is, to wait for higher rents) to develop a parcel of land. Like surfers waiting for that perfect wave, developers will wait for some sign of an upswing in the market, or at least wait out any likely downswings.[8]

This is reflected in the fact that landowners demand a premium in the rent that the developed property must be able to charge (over and above the construction cost rent and the agricultural opportunity cost rent) before they are willing to develop raw land and thereby convert it to urban use at the boundary of the city. Capozza and Helsley labeled this extra rent the irreversibility premium. This premium is necessary because the present value of the urban rents must compensate not only for the construction cost and for the forgone agricultural rents, but also for the value of the call option that is being surrendered, the value of the fact that the landowner could wait and possibly develop the property even more profitably at a later date.

The implications of growth and uncertainty on property rent and value within the city and in the as yet unurbanized region just beyond the city boundary are shown in Exhibits 7-2 and 7-3, respectively. The property values depicted in Exhibit 7-3 are based on investor projections regarding the future levels of (and uncertainty surrounding) the property rent components shown in Exhibit 5-1, in particular regarding the behavior of the urban boundary over time. Each component in the property value has a corresponding component in the rents with the exception of the growth premium. This is because, as noted in the previous section, *expected* growth in location rent does not cause developers to delay development or demand a higher rent. However, as noted previously, there is a growth premium in the asset value, for this incorporates the present value of the expected future growth in location rents.[9]

Notice in Exhibit 7-3 that both the growth premium and the irreversibility premium in the undeveloped land value grow dramatically as the urban boundary approaches. For likely realistic situations, almost all of the market value of undeveloped land parcels just beyond the urban boundary of a growing city consists of these two premiums. The irreversibility premium associated

[8] The original Capozza-Helsley model has been further developed and explored. A contrasting view put forth by Steve Grenadier (2002) suggests that competition among landowners may drive away much of the option value (Grenadier, S., 2002. "Option exercise games: An application to the equilibrium investment strategies of firms." *Review of Financial Studies* 15(3). Also see Part IV in the online portion of this book for more discussion).

[9] Note that the rents modeled in Exhibit 7-2 are current "spot" rents, reflecting purely the current balance between supply and demand in the space market for the indicated locations in relation to the urban boundary. The rent one observes empirically in long-term leases does indeed often include a growth premium (depending on the lease terms; it is usually relatively small compared to the growth premium in land value).

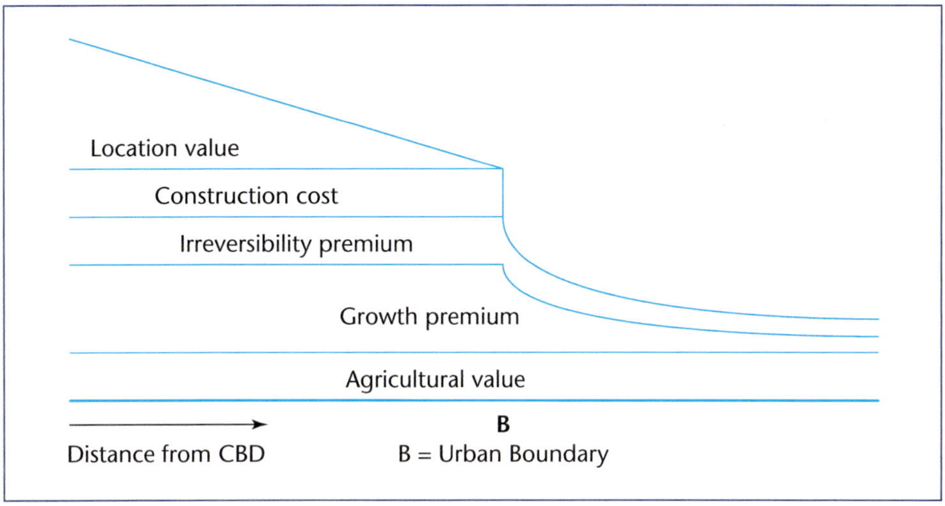

EXHIBIT 7-3 Components of Property Value Outside and Inside the Urban Boundary, Under Uncertainty.

with uncertainty will likely be a significant part of the total undeveloped land value near the boundary.

The growth and irreversibility premia represent what is often called the speculative value of undeveloped land. We can see from the discussion in this section that, in principle, such land value is based on real and rational considerations. While the irreversibility premium results in higher rents and higher urban densities, this is a rational response to uncertainty in real estate markets, leading to the efficient use of scarce construction capital, transportation resources, and land.

Depending on how fast the urban boundary is expanding outward, the growth and irreversibility premiums can cause undeveloped land values just outside the current boundary of urban development to grow at very high rates, making very high investment returns possible for speculative landowners. But such returns will also be quite risky and volatile, as a slight downturn in the urban growth rate can undercut the basis of the growth and irreversibility premiums that underlie the speculative land value.[10] Following the initial insights about the implications of option theory that were developed by Titman, Capozza, and others, subsequent scholarship provided a bit of a caveat. In principle, sufficient competition among developers holding potentially substitutable development sites may mitigate the option premium and the development delay effects

Extending the lessons of the simple monocentric city model we began in Chapter 6, we can summarize the effect of growth and uncertainty in a fifth principle, adding to the four already discussed in Chapter 6:

Faster urban growth and greater uncertainty in that growth will tend to increase urban property values, with the uncertainty also suggesting that a smaller, denser city with higher equilibrium rents is optimal, as rational development is postponed while landowner/developers wait for higher rents to compensate for greater option value given up in irreversible development. However, this effect is diminished the more competition there is among developers and substitutable development sites.

[10] During the 1990s and early 2000s, for example, with inflation less than 3% per year, average returns of 15% to 30% per year were typically expected by land speculators, and achieved returns were often much higher. However, in the housing collapse after 2006 prices of developable land parcels often collapsed by as much as 80 percent or more, sometimes at least temporarily down to virtually no value at all.

TEXT BOX 7.1 REALITY CHECK: HOW FAST DID URBAN RENTS GROW HISTORICALLY?

How well do these theories hold up when applied to long-run data on urban rents? A study tracing rents in seven western European cities (Amsterdam, Antwerp, Bruges, Brussels, Ghent, London, Paris) for up to 500 years offers mixed evidence: Despite rapid urban expansion and population growth, rental increases in the space markets were modest after accounting for inflation. The average annual growth rates in real terms were less than 40 basis points over half a millennium, even in economic superstar cities such as London and Paris. On the other hand, during the most dynamic urbanization era in Europe, when the Industrial Revolution allowed cities to grow exceptionally fast, rents did appreciate faster in all cities: Note in Exhibit 7-4 the shared upward trend between 1850 and 1900 that doubled real rents.

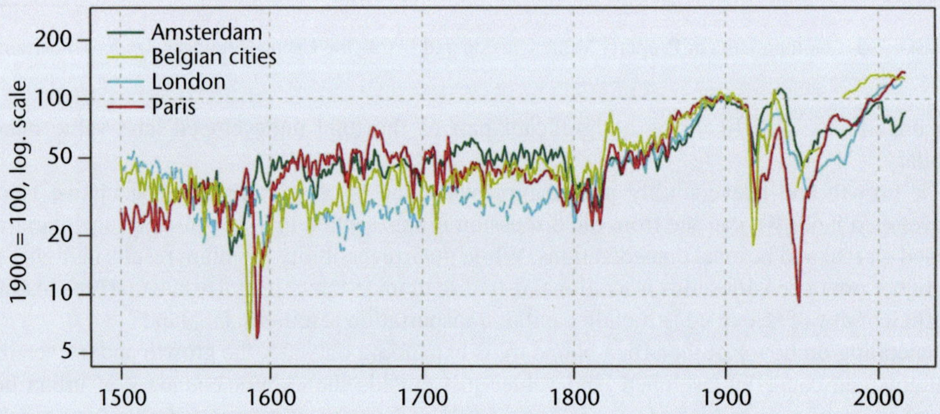

EXHIBIT 7-4 Real Urban Rent Indices for Western European Cities, 1500–2019.

Source: Eichholtz, P., Korevaar, M. and T. Lindenthal, "The Housing Affordability Revolution," SSRN Working Paper, 2025.

7.3 LET'S GET REAL: NEW TWISTS TO THE OLD MODEL

The classical monocentric city model provides a solid foundation for understanding urban spatial economics. However, real-world cities are far more complex and diverse than the simplified, homogeneous town of Circlopolis introduced earlier. With the fundamentals in place, we can now explore more realistic factors that shape urban environments.

7.3.1 Density Variations and Heterogeneous Land Use

In the simple monocentric city model, we assumed a single, homogeneous land use, such as housing of a uniform density, throughout the city. Real-world cities have a variety of land uses (e.g., housing, commercial, industrial, etc.) and a range of densities (e.g., high-rise, low-rise, spread-out). What is the most productive way for these various land uses to locate and distribute themselves within the city?

The answer to this question is easy to observe. In most cities, we observe denser, more intensive land uses closer to the center. Taller buildings, packed closer together, are found in or near central points (such as the CBD or other major transportation nodes where transportation costs are minimized). But you now have the tools to understand *why* this is the case and how this happens.

Freely functioning land markets result in denser development and more productive use of land located closer to central points where transportation costs are minimized. Such a result makes sense from the perspective of maximizing profits or incomes, because it minimizes the aggregate transportation costs of the society for the given production and consumption allocation. How such a result comes about in long-run equilibrium in the land market can be seen in Exhibit 6-2 in Chapter 6. Recall that this exhibit depicts the bid-rent curves of three different land uses around a single central point. The equilibrium land rent gradient around a central point will be determined by the highest bid-rent curve at each location, the "envelope" that traces out the highest bid-rent function over each point in space (horizontal axis). The more productive land use with the greatest sensitivity to transportation costs (use A in the exhibit) will outbid other land uses near the center. Other things being equal, denser development will indeed be more productive per acre, because greater density means that more labor and physical capital (structures and machines) are applied to the production process per acre of land. Also, recall from our discussion of the monocentric city that the rent gradient is proportional to density, other things being equal, because transportation costs per mile *per acre* are proportional to density. Thus, higher-density land uses will tend to be both more productive (at the central point) and characterized by steeper rent gradients.[11]

So it is not just a coincidence that the density of development tends to decline as one moves away from a geographically central point or transportation node. It is a reflection of the fundamental economic principle that in a production process, the input factors that are relatively scarce (and hence more expensive) should be used more sparingly and more productively. It is a basic fact of geometry (as well as geography) that central locations are scarcer than noncentral locations. If we combine this density result with the monocentric city model, we get the classical concentric ring model of urban form. First suggested by Ernest Burgess, of the famous Chicago School of Urban Geography, which flourished at the University of Chicago in the 1920s and 1930s, the concentric ring model is depicted in Exhibit 7-5. This model suggests that similar types of land uses will tend to be located at similar distances from the center of the city, resulting in concentric rings of similar land uses around the CBD. For example, denser, high-rise housing would tend to be located closer to the center than lower-density, low-rise housing.

The Burgess concentric ring model was a geographic model rather than an economic model like the monocentric city model. As such, Burgess's model was more complicated but less rigorous in some respects, including considerations other than just transportation costs and long-run equilibrium in the land market. In particular, the Burgess model considered the *dynamics of development,* including the effect of the chronological order in which different sections of the city are developed and the effect of the age of structures. His model also considered social factors characteristic of the United States in the twentieth century, such as the preference for greater lot sizes (lower residential densities) with increasing household income. In the Burgess model, the inner ring just outside the CBD was a transition zone or "gray area." This zone consisted of warehouses and industrial plants, uses that require good access to transportation, especially rail transport, which tended to be focused in or near the CBD at that time. This inner ring is viewed as a zone in transition, evolving into the expanding CBD at its inner edge and merging with low-income, high-density housing for the factory workers on its outer edge. As the city expands outward, this next ring consists of older and therefore less desirable houses than those in the outer, newest ring of the city, which consists of the lower-density middle- and upper-income housing.

---

[11] For an elegant, formal model of the real estate developer's decision regarding optimal density and maximum land bid price, see our simplified presentation of the Wheaton–DiPasquale Formula in Chapter 17 (in the online portion of the book).

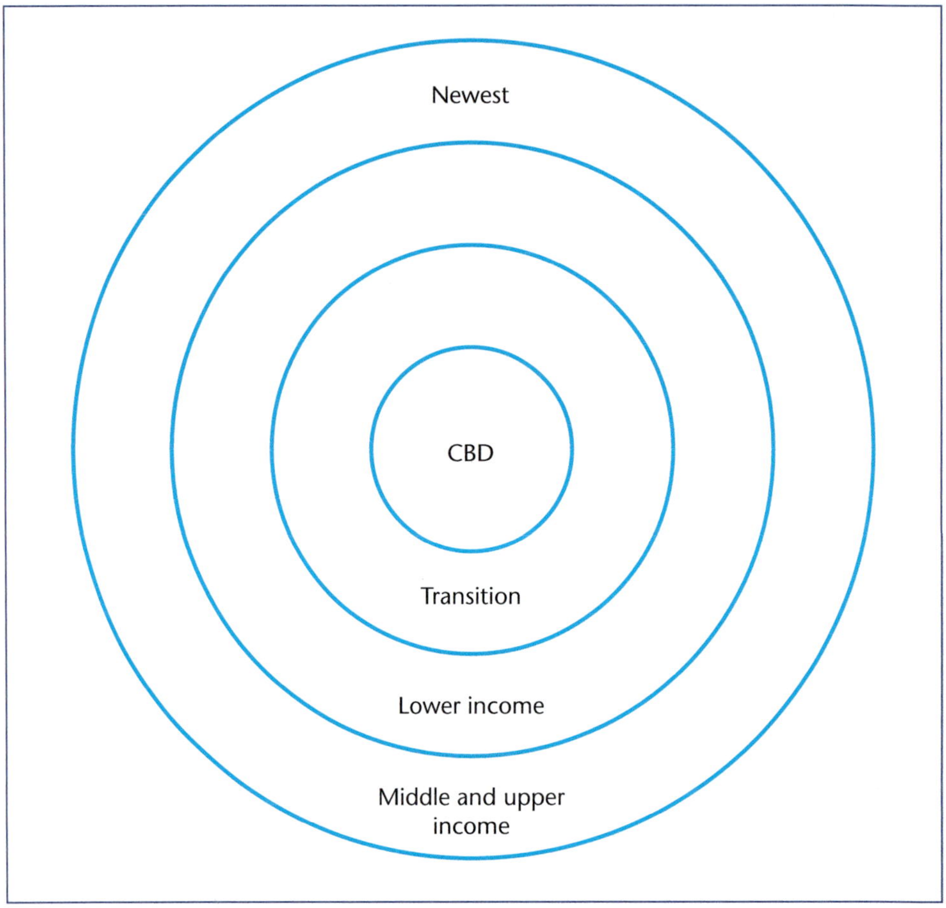

EXHIBIT 7-5 Concentric Ring Model of Urban Land Use Structure (Burgess).

The Burgess model explained many of the major features of the typical industrial city of mid-twentieth century America. Most notable was the tendency of higher-income residential neighborhoods to be located farther from the center. This is a somewhat curious phenomenon not found in many other countries. As noted in the previous chapter, higher-income households should have a higher value of time and therefore greater transportation costs per mile per person, leading to a steeper rent gradient. Higher-income households should also have a greater ability to pay for housing. These two facts by themselves would lead higher-income neighborhoods to tend to be located closer to the center of the city, as is indeed typical in the cities of many other countries. So how does it happen that higher-income residential neighborhoods tend to exist farther from the center in U.S. cities?

Here is a basic answer. Recall that lower densities reduce the transportation cost per acre and thereby reduce the rent gradient. If upper-income people desire enough larger lot sizes or have a strong enough preference for low-density neighborhoods, then this density effect can more than offset the transportation cost effect, resulting in an equilibrium location of higher-income households farther from the center. Furthermore, if higher incomes lead households to want to purchase newer houses, then this will also tend to force the higher-income neighborhoods farther from the center, at least in a city that has been growing rapidly for some time (as most twentieth-century cities were). This is because development proceeds from the center outward, leaving inner neighborhoods full of older housing stock. (Of course, in time that stock may be renewed, and if the city ceases population growth and household formation, eventually all neighborhoods could have similar-age housing structures.) Pollution from manufacturing, social and political issues related to crime, quality of education, and racial or ethnic diversity have also been factors affecting U.S. cities, which are characterized by municipal political boundaries that separate central cities and specific property uses from their surrounding newer suburbs.

While the concentric ring model captures some important elements of urban form, it also leaves much unexplained. Not long after Burgess came up with his model, another Chicago geographer suggested an alternative model, which is pretty much the opposite of the Burgess model. Homer Hoyt was not only a first-rate academic, but also a successful real estate investor and was famous for developing the **sector model of urban land use.**

According to the sector model, similar land uses do not all lie at a similar distance from the center of the city, but rather cluster along rays or in pie-shaped wedges emanating from the center. Again, the theory is based on the phenomenon of cities growing outward from their centers. Hoyt noted that once a particular type of land use becomes predominant in a particular direction from the center, or on a particular "side of town," then new development tends to continue that land use in the same direction outward from the center as the city grows. In East Coast cities like Boston and Philadelphia, it was established early on that the west side of town was the preferred location for upper-income residents. As these cities expanded in all directions, the west side retained its status as the fashionable and affluent area, continuing to grow outward from the city center.

The Hoyt "sector" model is depicted in Exhibit 7-6. Hoyt's theory was that some land uses are more compatible with each other and tend to be found in adjacent sectors. Thus, lower-income housing would more likely be found adjacent to industrial development than would high-

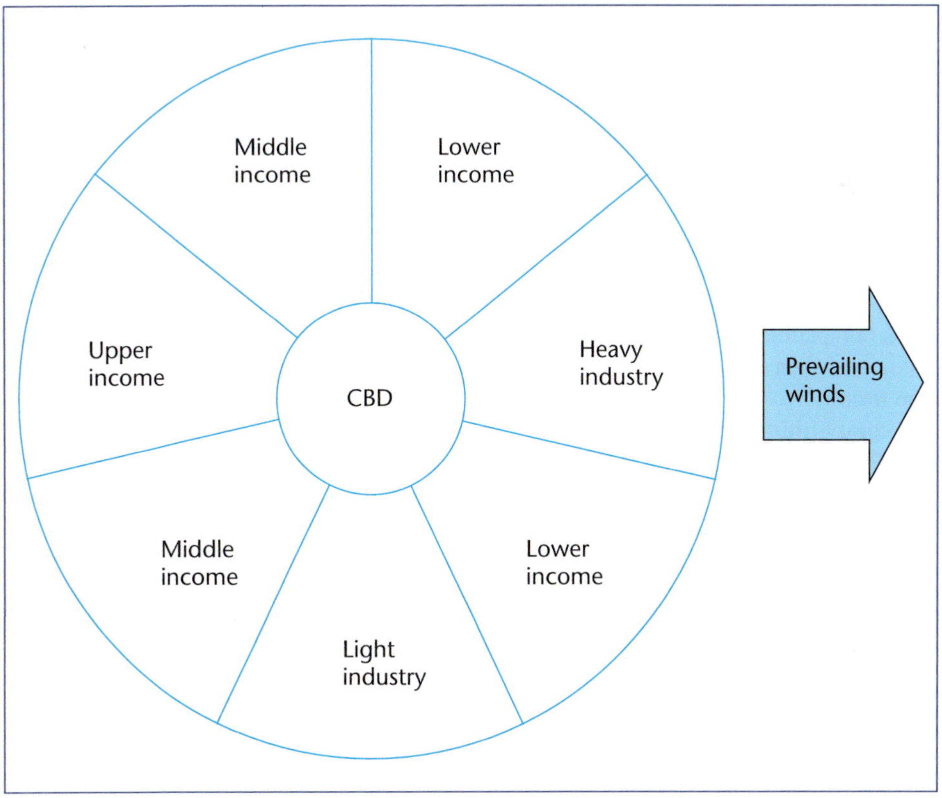

EXHIBIT 7-6 Sector Model of Urban Land Use Structure (Hoyt).

income housing. He also suggested an environmental cause of some location patterns, with high-income residential areas tending to be located upwind from heavy industrial zones, avoiding negative externalities

The concentric ring model and the sector model are diametrically opposite one another in their view of urban structure. Yet both clearly contain some essence of the truth. Most cities are partly explained by both perspectives.

7.3.2 Effect of Land Use Boundaries

Both the concentric ring model and the sector model of urban form and land use recognize that similar land uses tend to "clump together" in cities. For example, we speak of residential neighborhoods, commercial districts, and industrial zones. And we speak of high-income neighborhoods, middle-income neighborhoods, and low-income neighborhoods. In part, this is because similar land uses face similar transportation costs and locational needs. So, if one land use is the highest and best use at a particular site or location, that same general type of use will typically also be the highest and best use at nearby locations as well. Agglomeration economies and a preference for homogeneity may also play a role in some places. The natural tendency of similar land uses to coalesce is often reinforced by land use regulations in most cities, such as zoning regulations in U.S. cities. It is important to recognize that a natural consequence of districts that are relatively homogeneous in land use means that there will be land use *boundaries* between such districts. These *boundaries* affect the location rent and land value of the sites adjacent to them and nearby.

Certain types of land uses tend to be compatible and mutually supporting, bringing a synergy or increase in value to each district and use. Other types of land uses are incompatible and detract from the value of each other if they are located too closely. These are examples of what are known as spillover effects or locational externalities. For example, residential neighborhoods benefit from having shopping opportunities nearby so that the residents do not have to travel too far to shop. There is thus a benefit in having certain types of commercial districts (those with stores useful to the residents, such as grocery and convenience stores) near or within residential districts. On the other hand, heavy industrial zones—containing air or noise pollution generators, such as airports, or large commercial centers that generate high traffic volumes—are generally not compatible with most types of residential land use. Such land uses may reduce the value of nearby residential homes. One of the predominant arguments for zoning has been the minimization of negative externalities from alternative land uses, although zoning may have also been used for other unstated political and social reasons.

Both a freely functioning land market and well-crafted zoning regulations will tend to separate less compatible land uses and draw compatible uses together, at least over the long run.[12] Recognition of such differences underlies both the concentric ring and, especially, the sector model of urban form.

Even **compatible land uses** may have local boundary effects that differ from the general effect, however. For example, residents may generally prefer to be located closer to shopping opportunities, as long as they are not so close that traffic congestion and noise reduce the quality of residential life. It may be nice to have a convenience store a block or two away, but not so nice to have the store right next to your backyard. Similar points may be made about schools and churches, or even parks, if the park presents safety or privacy concerns. This is an example of a **negative locational externality**. As a result of boundary effects such as these, location rents often are depressed near a

[12] Because these spillover effects involve externalities, a type of market imperfection, a completely free laissez-faire land market will generally not result in optimal land use, although it may come pretty close. In theory, a profit-maximizing monopolist owning all the land might do a better job, as all the spillover externalities would be internalized. Zoning and community land use controls are ways to improve upon the laissez-faire result while reflecting broader social and political concerns of the community and avoiding the dangers of power concentration in the hands of a monopolist.

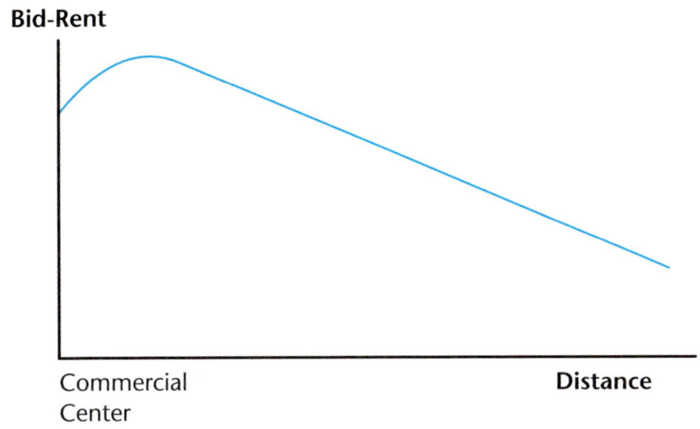

EXHIBIT 7-7 Effect of Negative Externalities Near a Land Use Boundary.

land use boundary, at least for one of the land uses (the one that is unfavorably affected, such as the residential use in the previous examples).[13]

This phenomenon is depicted in Exhibit 7-7, which shows the bid-rent function of a land use that benefits from accessibility to another land use at a boundary on the left edge of the horizontal axis of the graph. For example, the exhibit might depict the bid-rent of residential land use around a commercial center whose boundary is at the left edge of the graph. The bid-rent is lower near the land use boundary, then rises as distance eliminates the negative externality, then falls as further increasing distance reduces accessibility to the commercial center.

7.3.3 Polycentric Cities

Up to now, our discussion of urban form has focused largely on single central locations or "monocentric" cities. While most cities do have a single dominant center known as the central business district (CBD) or downtown, real-world cities also have other important centers (often referred to as **urban subcenters** in the urban economics literature). For example, most metropolitan areas of a million or more population in the United States have other **major activity centers (MACs)** besides the CBD, which serve metropolitan-wide needs, such as airports, major medical centers, and sports or educational complexes. In addition, traditional cities are sprinkled with **neighborhood business districts (NBDs)** or centers (NBCs), which serve the needs of local communities. In the last half of the twentieth century, all U.S. cities have also developed large regional shopping malls in the suburbs, serving large segments of the metropolitan area. By the late twentieth century, some of the largest suburban commercial centers, particularly those located on beltways and major interstate highway nodes, had developed into what Joel Garreau dubbed "edge cities," activity centers almost as large and multifaceted as many a traditional CBD.

Furthermore, some metropolises have never had a single very dominant CBD in the center. **Polynuclear cities** have not only subcenters, but also multiple major centers. Such cities range from

[13] While location rent may be depressed by location near the boundary, location value may in some cases actually be increased, if the neighborhood is growing, as sites adjacent to the existing commercial center, for example, may offer the prospect of conversion from residential to more valuable commercial use.

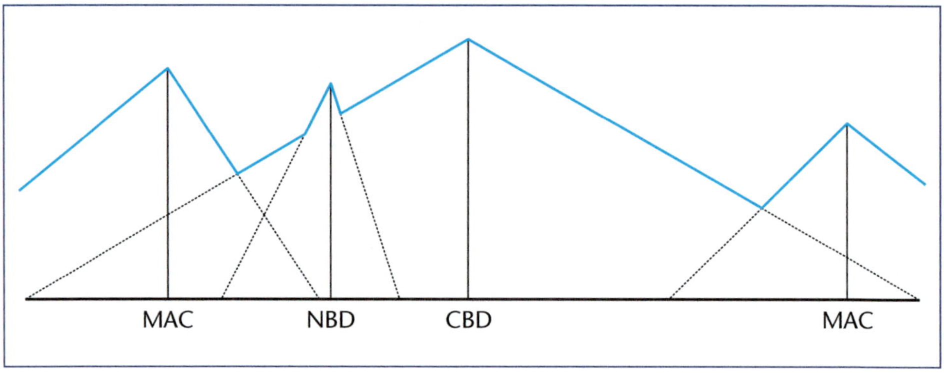

EXHIBIT 7-8 Rent Gradients in a Polycentric City.

"twins" such as Minneapolis-St. Paul, to multicentered conglomerates like the Los Angeles area, to clusters such as the Ruhr region in Germany or China's Pearl River delta.

Fundamentally, cities in the real world could never be perfectly monocentric because *different land uses have different and multiple central points* (locations where their relevant transportation costs are minimized). For example, recall the bid-rent example at the beginning of Chapter 6 regarding two land uses, a clothing factory and a grocery store. The clothing factory's central point (the maximum point of its bid-rent function) might be at the intersection of two interstate highways outside the center of town. The central point for the grocery store could be at the intersection of two commercial streets in the center of a residential neighborhood. Neither of these two central points is in the CBD of the metropolitan area. In fact, there might be several sites in the metropolitan area where either the factory or the store could be located with maximum productivity (minimum transport costs).

Thus, real cities are collections of major and minor central points within the metropolitan area. These tend to be related to one another in a more or less hierarchical manner. Land values and rent gradients are, as always, determined in equilibrium by the usage with the highest bid-rent curve at each location, leading to land being used at its highest and best use in the long run. This is depicted schematically in Exhibit 7-8 for a cross-section through a city that has a dominant CBD but also major outlying centers as well. The land rents (which determine and reflect the land uses) are given by the heavy solid lines, the highest bid-rent functions over each point.

A general effect of polycentrism and especially the type of "edge cities" that seem to be becoming more common in the twenty-first century in many countries is a flattening of the rent gradient. The development of multiple and mixed-use centers scattered throughout the metropolitan area has the effect of reducing the distance people need to travel, and this lowers transport costs per acre even without affecting transport costs per mile-traveled or reducing residential density. Along with the substitution of telecommunication and Internet/ computing for physical travel, polycentrism appears to be a major way cities are evolving to deal with what would otherwise be rising transportation costs. But keep in mind that a relatively flat bid-rent surface does not necessarily preclude high land (location) values *within* the central places, as physical agglomeration remains a valuable human phenomenon.

7.3.4 Neighborhood Dynamics and Life Cycle

The simple monocentric city model considers only transport costs in a long-run equilibrium in which there is complete flexibility to change the built structures on the land. The age of the built structures or of the neighborhoods of the city is ignored in this simple model. On the other hand,

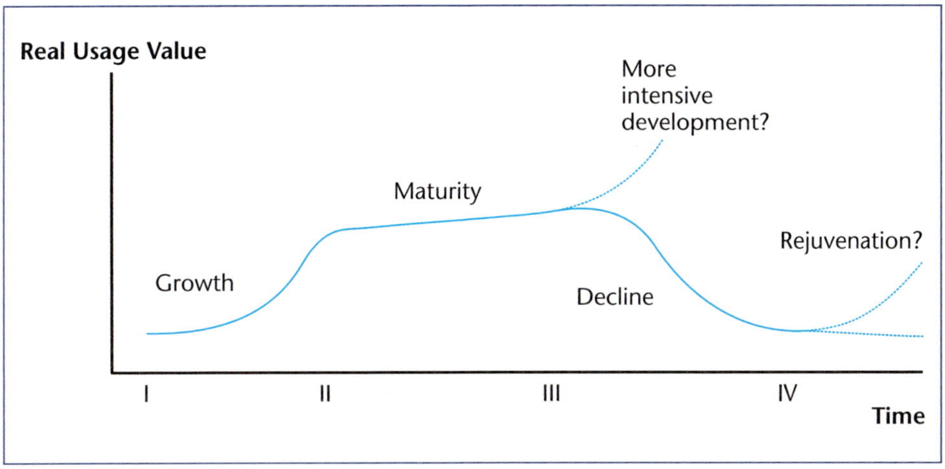

EXHIBIT 7-9 Neighborhood Succession Model.

both the Burgess and Hoyt models described previously recognized that land value and land use are indeed affected by the age of the built structures on the land. Older structures tend to be less productive, less desirable for users, and more expensive to operate or maintain. Yet even old structures usually have some value and tearing them down is costly. It is usually cheaper to build new buildings on undeveloped land, or land on which the existing buildings are so old or outmoded that they have almost no further value (and by the time buildings get that old, there may be a stigma attached to the neighborhood). Undeveloped land, by its nature, tends to be located near or beyond the existing periphery of the urban area. Thus, neighborhoods on or near the periphery of the metropolitan area tend to have structures that, on average are much newer than those in centrally located neighborhoods.

This unequal distribution of structural age in a city tends to be more pronounced in decades during and after major expansion, such as almost all U.S. cities experienced in the twentieth century. On the other hand, as we saw in Chapter 6, urban growth, especially if combined with growth in real incomes, should tend to increase the absolute value of all locations within the city. This includes the old, central neighborhoods, unless transportation cost reductions or social and political problems offset the advantages of centrality of location.[14]

This suggests a natural dynamic, or process of evolution, of neighborhoods within a city. Borrowing terminology from biology, this process is sometimes referred to as **neighborhood succession theory**. This theory differs from those we have previously examined in that it considers changes in land values and land uses in a single location (or part of a city, a neighborhood or district) across time. The previous models we have looked at focused on such changes across different locations within the entire city as of a single point in time. The typical life cycle of a neighborhood according to succession theory is depicted in Exhibit 7-9. Let us trace this model for a typical district, that of West Side in Anytown, USA.

At first, a bucolic agricultural zone just beyond the edge of the expanding urban area of Anytown, West Side experiences an initial growth phase characterized by rapidly rising usage and land values as the area becomes ripe for urban development. (Usage value refers to the value of the typical highest and best use—the HBU—in the area of the neighborhood.) This phase begins at point I in time, represented on the horizontal axis in Exhibit 7-9. The West Side area is initially developed with low-density housing and within a generation is fully built up with such new houses. As development

---

[14] In the long run, a stable city or one whose area is constrained would tend to have mixtures of new and old structures more evenly distributed across all neighborhoods or might even have more new structures in the inner neighborhoods.

is completed, West Side's growth period and rapid rise in usage value and undeveloped land value end, but the neighborhood enters a long period of maturity, in which values generally are maintained. Starting from point II in time, this mature period could continue indefinitely, with structures gradually being refurbished or replaced by new buildings as the original structures age, but the neighborhood retains its low-density residential character.

However, the evolution of the metropolitan area of Anytown as a whole may tend to put pressure on the West Side that could cause it to evolve in either of two possible directions away from this stable maturity. This occurs at point III in time in Exhibit 7-9.

The happier possibility is that land value in the West Side could rise again significantly. This might be caused by the expansion of the overall geographic area of the Anytown metropolis, which could give West Side a greater location premium as the neighborhood becomes, relatively speaking, more centrally located in the metropolitan area. Or West Side might evolve into a new subcenter within the metropolis, perhaps due to its proximity to a major hospital or university or airport, for example. This type of evolution would tend to change the HBU in West Side, making redevelopment to more productive land uses profitable in the neighborhood, such as development of higher-density housing and/or commercial buildings.[15] Zoning or other political constraints might be applied to hold off such redevelopment, maintaining the original density but now with higher-valued houses, making the neighborhood over time a more exclusive, upper-income area. The profit incentive would argue strongly for redevelopment, however. This might cause dissension within the neighborhood between those favoring and those opposed to rezoning and new development. But we might view such dissension as a "good problem," which (we can hope) would be resolved through a fair and democratic process.

Alternatively, the unhappy possibility would see West Side entering into a period of decline. The Anytown metropolitan area might evolve in a manner that reduces West Side's value. Various economic, geographic, and sociopolitical factors could cause such a decline. For example, intraurban transportation improvements could result in transport cost reductions that could reduce the location value of West Side. (Recall Exhibits 6-6 and 6-7 in Chapter 6.) As its structures age relative to newer neighborhoods, lower-income residents may move into West Side. Political boundaries based on historical accident may place West Side in a municipality with tax burdens that are high relative to income, with relatively poor-quality schools and social problems such as a high crime rate. Disinvestment may then ensue, in which West Side's buildings are allowed to age and deteriorate without capital replenishment. A negative spiral in terms of land value and property value could result, reflecting a lower-valued HBU for the area.

But this is not the end of the story. Of course, the decline could continue and gradually play out with West Side permanently stuck in a low-value status. However, it is also possible that in the decline in value lie the seeds of a turnaround. This is represented at point IV in time in Exhibit 7-9. With structures virtually completely deteriorated and property values depressed by the stigma of the neighborhood, redevelopment may now be rather inexpensive. If West Side has some favorable attributes that it can capitalize on, or if the Anytown metropolis evolves in a direction favorable for West Side, redevelopment or refurbishment of West Side could become profitable. For example, beginning in the 1970s and 1980s, many old, centrally located neighborhoods were revitalized through new investment (the term *gentrification* was coined). This process in the United States continued with greater momentum in the 1990s and early 2000s, especially in cities with growing economies attractive to large numbers of young, single professionals—centers of the knowledge-based

[15] Our previous discussion in Sections 7.1 and 7.2 of land value just beyond the boundary of an expanding city is relevant to the value of property in West Side in this circumstance. West Side is now just beyond the boundary of an expanding higher-density or higher-value (per acre) land use, for example, just beyond the boundary of an expanding Burgess model "ring," or polynuclear subcenter. In such a circumstance, much of the value of property in West Side will be due to the redevelopment option value of land ownership rather than the value of the existing structures on the land. This option-based land value will contain the growth and irreversibility premia described in Sections 7.1 and 7.2.

economy. In recent years, the aging of the baby boom generation in the United States has also led many well-to-do "empty nest" households to move into attractive inner city neighborhoods. Vibrant immigrant populations have also turned around many central city neighborhoods.

Rigorously quantifying neighborhood-life-cycle effects on location value is difficult because it requires a very long time series of historical data on property prices. However, a few scholars have attempted such analysis, and one of the longest-run histories of location value is that compiled by Professor Piet Eichholtz for the Herengracht canal in Amsterdam. Exhibits 7-10 and 7-11 present a property price index for the Herengracht extending over three centuries, from 1628 to 1974. This index is based on repeat-sales of the same structures, and reflects the usage value of the Herengracht location. That is, it is in effect an index of the value of the highest and best use property at the location of the Herengracht.[16] The index in Exhibit 7-10 has been adjusted for inflation and thus reflects the actual purchasing power of the usage value of the Herengracht location. It therefore depicts the history of the Herengracht neighborhood's life cycle as it has unfolded into the last half of the twentieth century.

The Herengracht was first developed in the early seventeenth century, when it was on the outskirts of the city. It was then, and remarkably has remained throughout its history, a fine address. The Herengracht is also interesting because it is a circumferential canal, with all points along the canal remaining at a similar distance from the historical center of Amsterdam, about a half-mile away. It is thus a sort of natural "Burgess ring." Furthermore, the buildings on the Herengracht have not changed very much, at least in their external appearances. The original structures, three- to five-story townhouses that touch one another, have remained, or at least their type has remained, albeit with many updates, improvements, and reconstructions.

Note that while there were ups and downs, often reflecting wars, plagues, or alternative periods of prosperity and growth of the Dutch economy, the real value of the Herengracht simply cycled around a flat trend for almost three centuries, until the early twentieth century. During this long period, the population and radius of Amsterdam grew only slowly, and the HBU of the Herengracht remained residential. The only substantial and sustained increase in the Herengracht's real location value during the period covered by the historical index (up to 1972) is seen to be a relatively sudden jump in the early to mid-twentieth century. This accompanied a great expansion in metropolitan Amsterdam that increased the centrality and therefore the location premium value of the Herengracht and altered its HBU from residential to commercial use. However, zoning regulations dampened the evolution of land use that would probably otherwise have occurred on the Herengracht during the mid- to late twentieth century.

The experience of the Herengracht is perhaps not typical of most neighborhoods, although it may be similar to many stable, fashionable neighborhoods in persistently successful cities. The Dutch are famous for the rigor and quality of their urban planning, and the Netherlands has had a generally successful economy since the Renaissance. With this in mind, it is interesting to note that the overall 347-year average annual gain in real location value on the Herengracht was only 0.56 percent. This value growth includes the effects of capital-improvement expenditures to develop or redevelop the structures and so is greater than the appreciation return that an investor would earn.[17] It is also interesting to note that the only substantial real gain in usage value after the canal's original development was associated with an evolution of the HBU. This is consistent with our discussion of land

---

[16] Exhibit 7-10 is taken from P. Eichholtz and D. Geltner (2004), "Four Centuries of Location Value: Implications for Real Estate Capital Gain in Central Places," *MIT/Maastricht Working Paper*. This index is based on *all* property sales transactions on the Herengracht, not just those of residential parcels, and therefore reflects the effect on value of a change in use of a building. As the cost of capital improvements is not subtracted from the index, while the sale prices do reflect the value of such improvements, in effect this version of the Herengracht index traces the value of the location HBU over time. This differs from the housing value Herengracht index published by Eichholtz in an earlier paper.

[17] Investors must pay for capital improvements, and this cost detracts from the returns that would otherwise be implied by the change in property price depicted in the index.

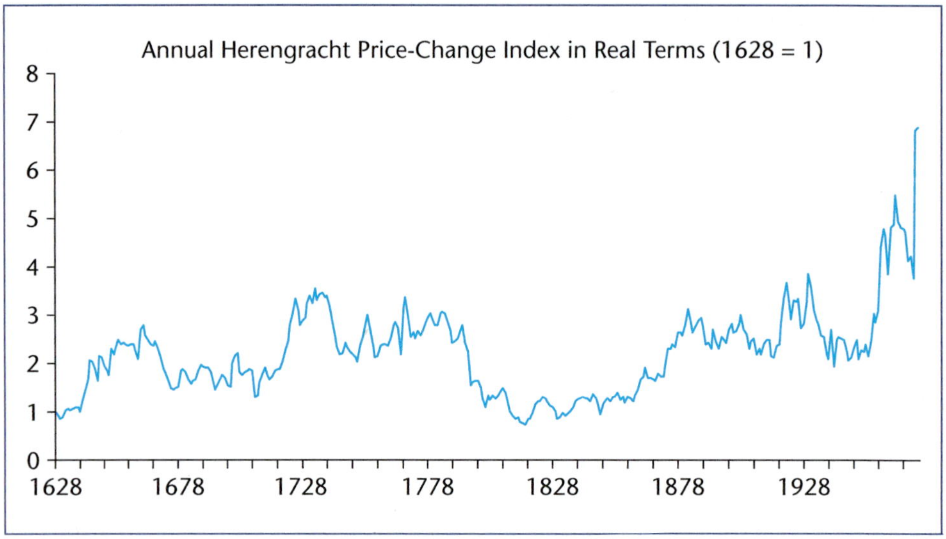

EXHIBIT 7-10 Herengracht Usage Value Index, 1628–1974.

Source: Eichholtz and Geltner 2004.

EXHIBIT 7-11

Summary Statistics of Herengracht Annual Repeat-Sale Price-Change Index

	Nominal			Real		
Period	**Mean**	**Standard Deviation**	**Signal/ Noise***	**Mean**	**Standard Deviation**	**Signal/ Noise***
1628–1974	1.28%	9.96%	2.20	0.56%	10.63%	2.35
1628–1699	1.00%	7.74%	1.04	0.59%	9.63%	1.29
1700–1799	0.13%	8.36%	1.94	-0.03%	10.35%	2.40
1800–1899	0.49%	8.09%	2.30	0.65%	8.95%	2.55
1900–1974	4.15%	14.61%	4.27	1.19%	13.70%	4.00

* Signal to Noise Ratio: Longitudinal standard deviation of estimated returns divided by the average standard error of the annual return estimates.

Source: Eichholtz and Geltner (2004).

value in Sections 7.1 and 7.2 earlier in this chapter. Major jumps in location value are associated with the advent and ultimately the exercise of the "real option" to develop or redevelop the land to a more productive use.

From the perspective of real estate investors, neighborhood succession theory holds an important implication. Succession theory suggests two things about the course of location (or usage) rents and values over time, and both of these are illustrated in our Herengracht example. First, location rents and values will tend to remain nearly constant, in real terms, over long periods of time, possibly indefinitely (once urban development has occurred in a neighborhood), even in successful locations. But second, the possibility exists of occasional, possibly relatively sharp or sudden changes in location rent and value, due to changes in the optimal role and function of the neighborhood within the metropolitan area (that is, changes in the neighborhood HBU). These changes may or may not be very easy to predict, and they can conceivably go in either a positive or a negative direction. As described in Section 7.2, to the extent that a change in location rent is predictable, it will be reflected in advance by corresponding changes in land values as defined by the redevelopment option value of the property ownership. Normally, there will be at least one, but perhaps only one, positive "pop" in such land value for any given location (the Herengracht has had two), occurring at (and just prior to) the time when that location is reached by an expanding urban boundary, when development of urban land uses first becomes feasible on the site.

TEXT BOX 7.2 NEIGHBORHOOD SUCCESSION IN PARIS AND AMSTERDAM

So far, we have analyzed the dynamic succession of neighborhoods through the lens of real usage value (Exhibit 7-9) or property prices (Exhibit 7-10). More relevant to property investors, however, are the total investment returns, which combine price appreciation, rental income, taxes and costs, all at the asset level. For Paris and Amsterdam, records of large portfolios of institutional investors offer rich evidence of the relative ebb and tide of realized property returns across the centuries but also across the city.[18] The maps below highlight how property yields vary spatially and temporally within cities, revealing pronounced investment dynamics. The "excess yields" indicate areas where the return on property investments either outpaces (colored in red) or lags behind (blue areas) the citywide medians.

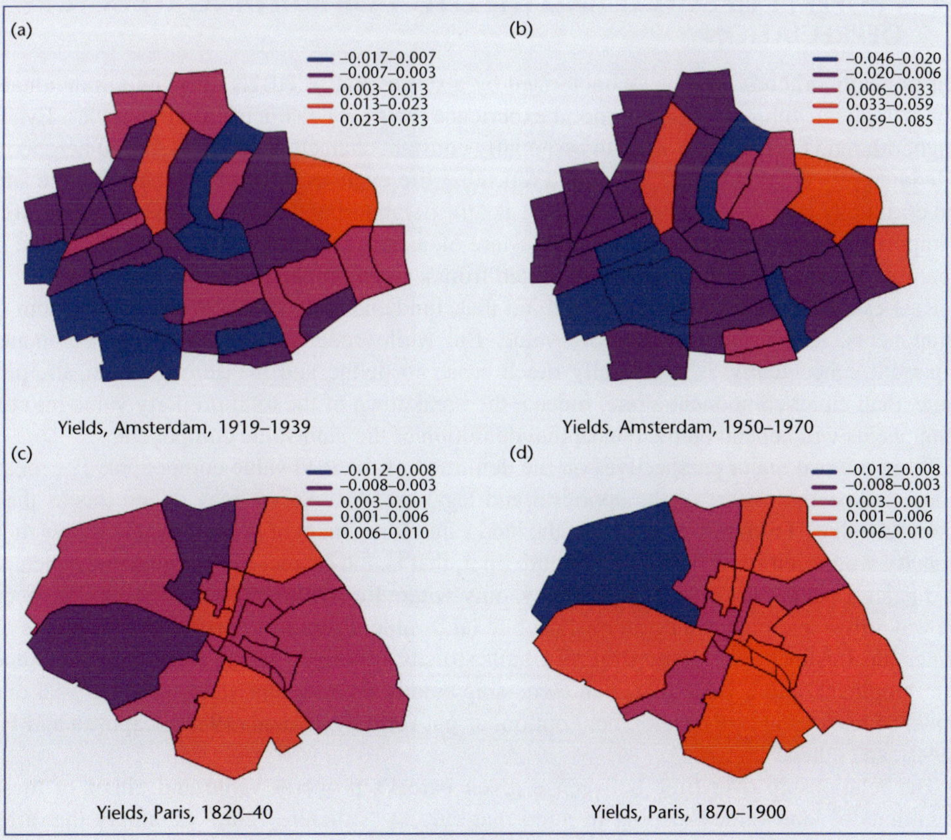

EXHIBIT 7-12 Median excess gross yields, by neighborhood.

[18] Eichholtz et al. (2021), "The Total Return and Risk to Residential Real Estate," *The Review of Financial Studies* 34

For Amsterdam, the variation within just a few blocks is striking. Here, high-value neighborhoods like the canal belt and museum areas consistently show lower income yields. This suggests these areas are stable in value and appeal, leading to high property values and low income yields. Conversely, areas like the neighboring working-class Jordaan, just a few meters off the prestigious Herengracht canal, offer higher yields, due to lower property prices relative to rental income. This spatial distinction in yields becomes more marked over time but maintains relative stability in ranking, meaning that, overall, high- and low-yield areas tend to remain in their respective categories. But some neighborhoods do change and rejuvenate more than others, indicating the importance of local conditions when assessing investment returns across a city.

For Paris, yields are more uniformly distributed, meaning the variation in yield values across different areas is less pronounced. This points to a more homogeneous property investment landscape in space in the French capital. However, note the yield shift in the northwest, indicating that property values and rental rates have changed here relative to the rest of the city—again a neighborhood deviates from the general trend.

7.4 PROPERTY LIFE CYCLE AND THE EFFECT OF BUILDING STRUCTURE DEPRECIATION

Just as neighborhoods may be characterized by a succession of HBUs over time, individual properties (or sites) within the neighborhood experience their own characteristic life cycles. Even if the neighborhood is very stable, with an essentially constant characteristic HBU for the neighborhood, individual properties will pass through a repeating life cycle as the built structure on the site ages and eventually is replaced or rehabilitated. Like the neighborhood life cycle, the **property life cycle** is important for real estate investors to be aware of, as it is fundamental to the nature of the investment returns that can realistically be expected from a given property.

Real estate investors should bear in mind that, fundamentally property value is the sum of two components: land value and structure value. But while understanding these two components is important conceptually, it is typically much easier to define and measure the sum, the property value, than either component alone. Indeed, the breakdown of the total property value into the two components will depend on the conceptual definition of the land value component.

There are two major perspectives on the definition of the land value component. The most traditional perspective is that of the appraisal and legal professions. We may define this as the "land appraisal value." From this perspective, the land value component of property value is how much the property would sell for if it had no structure on it, that is, the current market value of typical vacant land parcels similar to the subject property, only without a structure. A more recent perspective is the way urban and financial economists define land value. From this perspective, the value of land ownership (distinct from ownership of a built structure) derives purely from the development or redevelopment option value that such ownership entails. This is consistent with the "real options" model of land value as a development option, as put forth by Titman (1985), Capozza and Helsley (1990), and others.[19]

The relationship over time between a given parcel's property value and either of these two definitions of land value (keeping in mind that current "structure value" is simply the difference between the current property value and whichever definition of land value one prefers) is shown in the simple model of property life cycle presented in Exhibit 7-12. The exhibit presents a picture of

[19] This model will be presented in more depth in Chapter 16, in the online portion of this book.

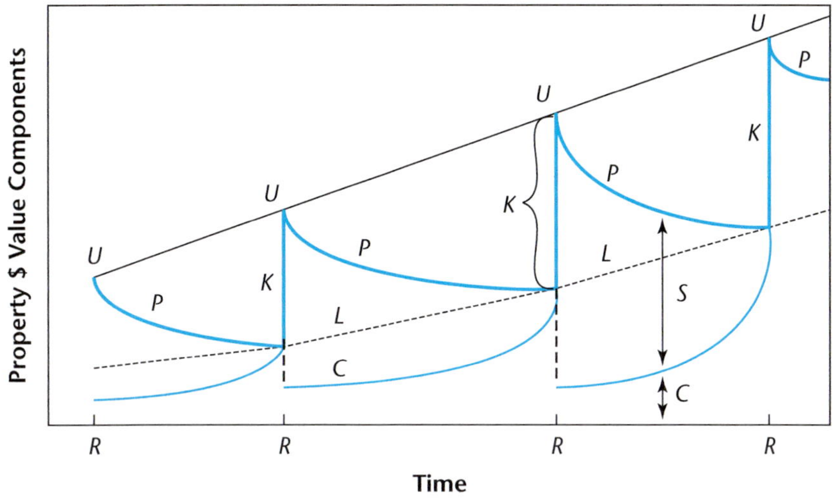

R = Construction/reconstruction points in time (typically 30–100 yrs between)
U = Usage value at highest and best use at time of reconstruction
P = Property value
S = Structure value
L = Land appraisal value (legal value)
C = Land redevelopment call option value (economic value)
K = Construction (redevelopment) cost excluding acquisition cost

EXHIBIT 7-13 Components of Property Value Over Time.

a single location in the city across an entire history of continuous time, which is represented on the horizontal axis.

The discrete points in time when construction or major reconstruction of the structure on this site takes place are represented by the *R* symbols along the time axis. At those points in time, the structure is built or rebuilt to best serve the HBU of the site as of that point in time. The value of the newly developed or redeveloped property just after each development may be seen as tracing out the evolution of the usage value of the site over time, based on its HBU (as if vacant). This trend, indicated by the solid line and the *U* symbols, is a good way to conceptualize the trend in the location value of the site.[20]

As depicted in Exhibit 7-13, the usage value of the site is growing continuously over time, as evidenced by the upward trend in the *U* values. Of course, this would not necessarily be the trend for any given site in the real world, especially if we measure value in real terms, that is, in dollars of constant purchasing power (i.e., net of general inflation). We have seen both in this chapter and the previous chapter how location value can either increase or decrease over time or remain constant for long periods.

[20] What we are calling "location value" reflects what the appraisal industry terms the "HBU as if vacant," the highest and best use to which the site would be developed if there were no existing structure on it. One should take care not to confuse this definition of location value with the value of the "location premium" component of property value described in our discussion of the monocentric city model in Chapter 6 and in Sections 7.1 and 7.2 of this chapter. While the two concepts are related, "location value" here (as usage value) would also include the value of the structure (when new). It should also be recalled that the simple version of the monocentric city model we were employing had only one urban usage of the land.

As noted, the market value of the property at any point in time consists of the **structure value** plus the land value. Just after reconstruction, structure value makes up the bulk of the property value. But the structure value declines over time as the building depreciates, due to the effects of physical, functional, and economic obsolescence. **Physical obsolescence** refers to the structure physically wearing out as, for example, its roof deteriorates and begins to leak. **Functional obsolescence** refers to the effect of changing technology and changing tastes or user requirements on the optimal physical design of a new structure for the relevant HBU. For example, major commercial structures may lose their "class A" status over a period of one or two decades if they are not "sustainable" enough to meet tenants' and investors' updated preferences. Finally, **economic obsolescence** refers to the fact that the nature of the structure may become unsuited to the HBU of the site as the HBU evolves over time. For example, the HBU may evolve from low-density to higher-density residential use, or from residential to commercial use, so a single-family home would no longer be an economical use of the site, even though the house may be fine physically and functionally.

The other component of the property value is the **land value** (labeled *L* or *C* depending on the definition). As noted, the economic land value component consists only of the value of the **redevelopment option**, including the growth and irreversibility premia described in Sections 7.1 and 7.2.[21] Defined this way, the land value component is very small just after redevelopment, because the building is then at the HBU for the site, so the profitability of further redevelopment, if any, is a long way off in the future.[22] Over time, the redevelopment option value component will grow if the structure depreciates physically or functionally, or if the HBU of the site, as if vacant evolves and changes over time away from that which the current structure can serve (this latter is economic obsolescence, as described above). As investments, call options are much riskier than their underlying assets (in this case, the usage value of the built property), and hence require a much higher expected return. Furthermore, all of that return must be earned in the form of appreciation of the option value, as the option itself pays no dividend. Thus, the curve of the *C* value in the exhibit traces out an expected exponential growth that is quite rapid between the reconstruction points in time.

On the other hand, the appraisal or legal definition of land value is much less exciting. It tends to be a roughly constant percentage of the usage value of the site, as indicated by the *L* curve in the exhibit. This conception of land value grows at a much lower rate (if at all), and with much less volatility than the economic definition of land value.[23]

The total of land value plus structure value equals the property value at any point in time, labeled P in the exhibit. The optimal time for redevelopment will not occur until the entire value of the site equals its land value component alone; that is, the current structure has become worthless as such due to the value of the redevelopment option on the site.[24] At such points in time, both definitions of

---

[21] As described in Section 7.1, the growth premium component of the land value reflects the expected value of the location premium in the future rent from a new or redeveloped structure, beyond the redevelopment point in time. Note, however, that the value of any location premium associated with the *current* structure is reflected in the structure value component of the property value, as opposed to the land value component, as these concepts are being defined here. This may appear to be inconsistent with the definition of land value in the context of the monocentric city model discussed in Chapter 6 and Sections 7.1 and 7.2. But in fact, structural depreciation and redevelopment were not included in the basic monocentric city model, so this is a fine point that was not contemplated in the definition of land value employed in that model. It should also be noted that the value of the current structure *as if* it would never be torn down represents an "opportunity cost" in any redevelopment of the site that would involve demolishing the existing structure. Even if this structure is no longer the HBU of the site, it would still typically be able to provide some future benefit flows. If the building is torn down, the future net cash flow it could have earned is forfeited.

[22] In financial option valuation terminology, the redevelopment option is *deeply* "out of the money" when the structure is new. This is because the value of the existing structure is part of the exercise price (or "strike price") of the option.

[23] Volatility is not depicted in Exhibit 7-13, which shows only the central tendency or expected trends over time. But recall from the residual theory of land value in Chapter 6 that most of the volatility in the property value will redound to the land value component.

[24] Note that this does not necessarily (or usually) imply that the existing structure could no longer earn positive net rents, only that such rents are insufficient to justify further delay of a more profitable redevelopment. The perspective taken

land value are the same, and this also equals the entire property value ($C = L = P$). In the exhibit, R is depicted as occurring when the old value of L or C equals the old value of P.

Typically, the structure value and the land value are bundled together and cannot be purchased separately.[25] Indeed, as noted, the breakout between these two components of property value at any point in time is practically and empirically difficult. But the combination of structure value and land value can be observed at any point in time as the total property value, the value of the bundle, P, indicated by the heavy line in the exhibit. The continuous change in P over time (between the reconstruction points) essentially determines the capital gain or loss that would be faced by an unlevered investor in the property during its period of operation between redevelopment events. The discontinuous jumps in property value at the points in time of the reconstructions reflect the injection of new capital into the property via the construction process, indicated by the K symbols in Exhibit 7-13. Therefore, these jumps do not in themselves represent a capital gain for any investor. It is important to recognize that the capital gain (or loss) experienced by an investor in the property is represented by the change in P only between reconstruction points, not across construction points, in Exhibit 7-13.

Exhibit 7-13 shows how **depreciation of the structure** renders the growth rate of the property value (P) generally less than the growth rate of the location or usage value (U). This result is guaranteed by the fact that the value of the newly redeveloped property includes the construction cost component (K), over and above the site acquisition cost component.

This leads to the Depreciation Principle that is of fundamental importance in real estate investment analysis:

Over the long run, the change in location value provides a theoretical ceiling to the investment capital gain of the unlevered investor in stabilized property (that is property that is fully operational).

As an example, suppose that redevelopment occurs once every 50 years, and at the time of redevelopment the old property (essentially just land value by then) is typically worth 20 percent of what the new, redeveloped property will be worth. This is equivalent to saying that site acquisition costs are 20 percent of the total project development costs. This means that during the 50 years between redevelopment events, built property value grows at an average rate of 3.2 percent per year *less* than the growth in location value of the site during that time.[26]

---

here is consistent with traditional appraisal practice of charging against the structure any loss in property value due to economic obsolescence or divergence of the existing structure from the HBU as if the site were vacant. It should also be noted that in some cases it may be optimal to hold a site for some time purely for speculation, before beginning redevelopment, even after the existing building on it becomes essentially worthless. The new HBU for the site may evolve further in a favorable direction. If you develop too soon, you may miss such opportunity. This is analogous to the fact that it is not always optimal to exercise a call option as soon as it is "in the money." Also, we are ignoring here the demolition cost for the existing structure. Demolition is an additional cost of redevelopment that can delay the optimal timing of construction.

[25] Some portion of the structure value may be "purchased" in the form of a long-term leasehold. The existence of long-term leaseholds encumbers the property to the potential detriment of the redevelopment option value component of the property value, possibly reducing the overall property value. See Dale-Johnson, D. (2001). "Long-term ground leases, the redevelopment option, and contract incentives." *Real Estate Economics* 29(3).

[26] Calculated as follows: $0.2 = 1 \times (1 + x)^{50} \rightarrow x = 0.2^{1/50} - 1 = -0.032$. If acquisition costs are 50% of development project value, and redevelopment occurs only every 100 years, then we have: $x = 0.5^{1/100} - 1 - -0.007$. Keep in mind that this refers to depreciation *only relative* to the evolution of the location value of the site, and applies on average over the entire property life cycle between redevelopment events. Although Exhibit 7-13 does not depict such a case, it is possible for property value to increase over time in real terms prior to redevelopment, if the land value component rises fast enough to more than offset the depreciation of the structure component. This will occur primarily only when either (a) the structure is nearly worthless, so that virtually the entire value of the property is in its redevelopment option value, or (b) there is a rapid positive change in the location value of the site.

The preceding principle regarding property value carries an implication for the rents that can be charged by a property owner between major redevelopment events. To the extent that rents remain an approximately constant percent of property value, rents must also grow at a rate less than (or decline at a rate greater than) that of the location value of the site. In fact, the more fundamental direction of causality flows in the other direction. Property value declines below that of the potential HBU (that is, the HBU as if the site were vacant) fundamentally because the rent that the market will bear for the existing structure falls further and further below the rent of the potential HBU. Even if the HBU remains constant, the building must compete against newer, less functionally obsolete competitors. Rental depreciation at the property level will be discussed in more depth in Chapter 9.

7.5 CHAPTER SUMMARY

This chapter and the previous chapter have taken you on an introductory tour through the inside of cities and into the basic structure of property value. The academic discipline primarily at work here, conducting these tours, has been urban economics, assisted ably by geography and, to some extent, sociology. The principles, tools, and insights raised in these tours are obviously important to making well-informed commercial property investment decisions. They relate especially to the ability to obtain a realistic impression of the long-run prospects for the space market relevant to particular locations. In the remaining chapters of Part II, we will zero in on the analysis of commercial property income at a less theoretical and more applied level.

KEY TERMS

- Growth premium
- Irreversibility premium
- Concentric ring model of urban form
- Sector model of urban land use
- Compatible land uses
- Negative locational externality
- Polycentric city
- Major activity center (MAC) neighborhood business district (NBD)
- Polynuclear city
- Neighborhood succession theory
- Property life cycle
- Structure value
- Physical obsolescence
- Functional obsolescence
- Economic obsolescence
- Land value
- Redevelopment option value
- Structural depreciation

STUDY QUESTIONS

In Your Own Words

7.1 How does the expected future growth rate of land rent affect the relationship between current land value and current land rent?

7.2 How does land provide its owner a "call option" that allows the owner to profit from uncertainty or volatility in future land rent?

7.3 How does uncertainty or volatility in future land rent affect current land value and land rent, all else being equal? As part of your answer, explain the notion of "value of waiting," why this leads to an "irreversibility" premium in land values, and the resulting implications for development timing and city size.

7.4 What are the fundamental determinants of (a) urban land value (i.e., inside the urban boundary) and (b) the value of undeveloped land just beyond the urban boundary? (Hint: Describe each component of land value, both inside and outside the urban boundary, as shown in Exhibit 7-2.)

7.5 Compare and contrast the Burgess concentric ring model with the Hoyt sector model of urban form. Which, if either one, do you think better describes most cities?

7.6 What is meant by the term "edge city"?

7.7 What does neighborhood succession theory say about how the rate land values or rents will tend to grow over time within a given neighborhood?

7.8 Discuss the effect of land use boundaries on bid-rents and land values. Give an example of two land uses with negative locational externalities for at least one of the uses when the two uses are adjacent to one another.

7.9 Can you think of a city with a tight growth boundary or one with none? What types of prices do you observe in these two cities for a typical 2,000 square foot home? Do you feel that density is important for a local government to control?

7.10 According to property life cycle theory, property value is the sum of the values of what two components? Describe each of these two components.

7.11 How do you know that property value must grow at a rate less than the growth rate in the location value of the site (on average over the long run between major redevelopment projects)?

7.12 When is it optimal (from an economic perspective) to demolish and redevelop a property?

7.13 Explain the difference in the evolution over time of *appraised (legal)* land value and *land redevelopment option (economic)* value of a site as illustrated in Exhibit 7-10.

7.14 (Dynamics of Urban Form) The simple monocentric city model presented in Chapter 6 is a long-run, static equilibrium model in which the past does not matter; in response to a change in income or population, the city is torn down and rebuilt in the new long-run equilibrium form. The explicit recognition in the current chapter of time (age) and the *durability* of real estate structures that depreciate over time means that a city is shaped by both its past and current market dynamics. Based on what you learned in this chapter about how cities grow as well as property and neighborhood life cycles, explain the economic logic underlying the following statements:

a. Cities tend to redevelop from the center outwards.
b. Older, growing cities offer significantly more redevelopment opportunities.
c. The density of housing falls with distance from the city center over time because of rising incomes and decreasing commuting costs, not because of a commuting cost housing consumption tradeoff. (Assume housing is a "normal" consumption good, the demand for which increases with income. Also, assume higher-income households demand higher-quality housing.)
d. Synthesize your answers to (a) through (c) and explain why many U.S. metropolitan areas are witnessing significant new housing construction at both the outer edges and the central city, with some redevelopment also taking place in so-called inner-ring suburbs.

Check Your Knowledge

7.15 According to the concentric ring model, where are high-density areas typically located?
   A) On the outskirts of the city.
   B) Near the city center.
   C) Outside the main urban boundary.
   D) Evenly spread throughout the city.

7.16 What effect does high uncertainty in rent growth have on development?
   A) It delays development.
   B) It accelerates development.
   C) It has no effect on development timing.
   D) It reduces development costs.

7.17 How does the "sector model" differ fundamentally from the "concentric ring model"?
   A) It organizes land use along linear pathways instead of circular zones.
   B) It explains city structures with less emphasis on social factors.
   C) It uses physical landmarks as central points of reference.
   D) It integrates a hierarchical zoning approach.

7.18 According to neighborhood succession theory, what marks the beginning of a neighborhood's maturity phase?
   A) Stability in land use and value.
   B) Decline in infrastructure quality.
   C) Rise in speculative land value.
   D) Increase in zoning restrictions.

7.19 In property life cycle analysis, what drives a jump in property value during redevelopment?
   A) Increased property taxes.
   B) Zoning flexibility.
   C) Depreciation rate.
   D) Capital injection from construction.

7.20 A downtown surface parking lot generates annual net cash flow of $180,000, and this is expected to grow indefinitely at 3% per year. Based on the current use and current capital market conditions, you feel that investors require a 12% return, which implies an initial income yield or cap rate of 9% (12% – 3%).
   a. What is the indicated current use value of the property? [Remember that value equals net rent divided by cap rate.]
   b. A developer recently paid $4.5 million for the site. What is the implied cap rate associated with this deal? Explain why the sale price differs significantly from the current use value you calculated in (a).

7.21 Consider two undeveloped land sites. At site 1, the highest and best use (HBU) is a warehouse that would cost $1 million to build (exclusive of land cost) and would then generate annual net rents of $150,000, which are expected to grow at 3% per year. At site 2, the HBU is an apartment building that can generate net rents of $800,000, projected to grow at 1% per year, with construction cost of $5 million. Suppose investors buying built properties (that is, properties already developed and in operation) require an initial annual return (in the form of current net income) of 12% minus the expected annual growth rate in the net income, as a percent of the investment cost. For example, they would want an initial yield or cap rate of 9% for the warehouse (12% – 3% = 9%). Suppose the land value for site 1 is $1 million and the land value for site 2 is $2 million. On which of these sites (1, 2, both, or neither) is it currently profitable to undertake construction? Show your reasoning.

Chapter Case: Lakeside Development in Seneca

Seneca is experiencing a surge of interest in its Lakeside District, a scenic area centered around Lake Keowee. This beautiful lake, known for its clear waters and lush surroundings, has become a prime location for both residential and commercial developments. Recognizing the area's potential, the Seneca city council recently enacted new zoning laws to guide development around the lake. These regulations aim to protect Lake Keowee's natural beauty while encouraging high-density residential and commercial projects closer to the downtown side of the lake, leaving other lakeside areas with lower-density requirements to preserve their appeal.

One of the major investors, Conklin Properties, has acquired two parcels of land around Lake Keowee. Parcel A is located on the downtown side, where high-density zoning has been proposed and expected to drive demand and rental prices upward. Parcel B, on the opposite side of the lake, falls under low-density zoning intended to maintain the area's quiet, natural environment. James Conklin, is now weighing its options for these two parcels, deciding whether to proceed with development immediately or hold off, considering potential market changes and the impact of zoning regulations.

Guide Conklin Properties' development decisions by answering the following questions:

1. Why might a property owner delay redevelopment despite current profitability?
   A) The structure is at peak depreciation.
   B) Agricultural use is more desirable.
   C) Growth expectations make future development more profitable.
   D) High interest rates prevent development.
2. Conklin Properties is considering the growth premium for Parcel A. This premium is primarily based on which of the following?
   A) Anticipated agricultural use value of the land
   B) Expected future increase in rents near downtown
   C) Speculative value from environmental protections
   D) Increased taxes from high-density zoning
3. The "call option" on Conklin's undeveloped land near Lake Keowee gives the company the ability to:
   A) Develop the land immediately without incurring any costs
   B) Delay development until market conditions are more favorable
   C) Decrease property value by reducing development obligations
   D) Deduct site acquisition costs from development expenses
4. How does the "usage value" of Parcel B change over time?
   A) It may increase or decrease depending on the surrounding urban context.
   B) It remains constant.
   C) It always decreases in high-density neighborhoods.
   D) It always decreases with location depreciation.
5. Around Lake Keowee, what factor is most likely to create a "boundary effect," where property values are influenced by the contrasting uses of high-density downtown development and quieter, low-density residential areas?
   A) Agglomeration economies
   B) Functional obsolescence
   C) Zoning regulations
   D) Structural obsolescence

6. Which of the following land use choices would best promote compatibility between high-density and low-density zones in the development around Lake Keowee?
   A) Placing high-density retail spaces directly next to low-density residential areas
   B) Using buffer zones like parks or green spaces between high-density hotels and low-density homes
   C) Expanding high-density zoning across the entire lakeside area
   D) Allowing industrial facilities next to low-density recreational areas

8 Forecasting The Space Market I

Real Estate Market Analysis

CHAPTER OUTLINE

LEARNING OBJECTIVES

After reading this chapter, you should understand:

- That forecasting rental trends and subsequent price trends are generally the most important outputs from market analysis.
- What a feasibility analysis is?
- That general real estate market analysis looks at trends within an entire market segment, geographically and by property type.
- That micro real estate decisions usually focus on a specific site or user.
- That submarkets may overlap and compete at the fringes.
- That available space is not the same as vacant space.
- That natural (equilibrium) vacancy is the point at which no rent pressure exists in either direction.
- That demand drivers vary by property type.
- That real estate cycles can be modeled as a function of demand, supply, vacancy, and profitability where values exceed costs and supply elasticity.
- That specific property types, such as data centers, surface parking lots, self-storage, and life science properties, have their own set of unique demand and supply drivers. All of these are emerging as potential niche markets for development and investment. (See online supplemental materials.)

The preceding chapters discussed the underlying economic and geographic forces that govern urban land values and location patterns. By now, you should clearly understand why rents can differ over space and time. This groundwork is essential on a practical level for the real estate investor, as it allows us to forecast the rental market. The forecast parameter was denoted *g* earlier in the DCF. As a reminder, this parameter is used to grow the potential gross income (PGI) from year 0 (often in practice at a constant rate as a simplification) for the duration of the holding period (10 years in our

DOI: 10.1201/9781003643838-10

illustrations). Arguably, forecasting future rental growth is both the most crucial exercise for the real estate investor and the most difficult to do.

In this Chapter and the next, we will discuss how rents relate to market fundamentals that are readily observable over long periods. Using such fundamental variables, we can forecast the space market and the resulting rents. The practical procedure laid out here is labeled a **real estate market analysis**. The objective of market analysis is the quantitative or qualitative characterization of the supply and demand sides of a specific space usage market relevant to a given property asset. This Chapter will focus on how you can use market analysis to forecast rent and price trends. We will provide examples for all major real estate types: multi-family, office, retail, and industrial. Chapter 9 will subsequently go into greater depth to show how this knowledge can be used to formally predict rental growth.

8.1 DEFINING THE SCOPE OF THE ANALYSIS

Real estate market analysis is performed for various purposes and in varying contexts to assist with different types of real estate decisions. Some market analyses focus on specific micro-level decisions. In contrast, others focus on broader and more general characterizations of real estate markets—specific micro-level analyses emphasize individual building sites or individual real estate users. For example, a developer might want to examine the feasibility of building a particular type of development on one or more specific sites or a specific type of building for one specific user. This is sometimes called "feasibility analysis" or "site analysis" for real estate development.

The second type of analysis (and the main focus of this Chapter), based on the general characterization of a real estate market, aims to quantify and forecast the supply of and demand for space, typically including forecasting future rents and vacancies in a particular geographic real estate **market segment**. Real estate space usage markets are segmented by both property type and geographic location. For example, an *office* building in *Hartford*, CT, does not compete for similar tenants with an *apartment* building in *Hartford* or an *office* building in *Orlando*, FL. Thus, the definition of a relevant real estate market typically specifies both a geographic scope and property type.

Geographically, market analysis typically focuses on the metropolitan level or even narrower, such as a quadrant or neighborhood of a metro area (e.g., the North Dallas Market or the South Atlanta Market). A metro region forms an overall functional market area that can be usefully subdivided into several submarkets. The CBD (or downtown) of the metropolitan area is typically considered one market area, and the suburbs are divided into several markets by geographic sector, sometimes including inner and outer rings. Typically, each market area has one or a few major transportation nodes and major activity centers. As a result, rent *levels* can vary considerably within a city (as predicted by the monocentric city model) as well as across different cities. However, it should be noted that rental *growth* is typically more similar within a given metro area for a given property type. This is because metro areas are, by definition, substantially integrated markets and sociopolitical phenomena characterized by the metro's economic base and property supply characteristics. Indeed, properties of the same type *within* a metro area will compete for similar tenants in the long run. For example, suppose the rents downtown become "too high" (than can be reasonably expected from market fundamentals). In that case, tenants will seek properties further away from the city center for a lower rent in the metro suburbs. This demand redirection will then "force" downtown rents to get back in line. At the margin, submarkets are linked and overlap.

This is exemplified in Exhibit 8-1, where we show office rents per square foot for the Boston and Los Angeles Metro Areas between 2006 and 2021. The black line provides the average (effective)[1] rents within the CBD, and the blue line gives the average rents outside the CBD area.[2] In both

[1] Effective rent will be introduced in Chapter 10 in more detail. In short, effective rent is defined as the rent tenants are paying after taking into account all incentives and rent-free periods. Note that the rental indexes shown in this section all depict nominal rents, not adjusted for monetary inflation.

[2] It should be noted that there is no official definition of CBD. For the Exhibit, we have defined the CBDs by drawing circles of radius 5km and 15km, respectively for Boston and Los Angeles, around the city halls. As a result, for example, we include Cambridge, the waterfront, and the Back Bay as part of the CBD for Boston.

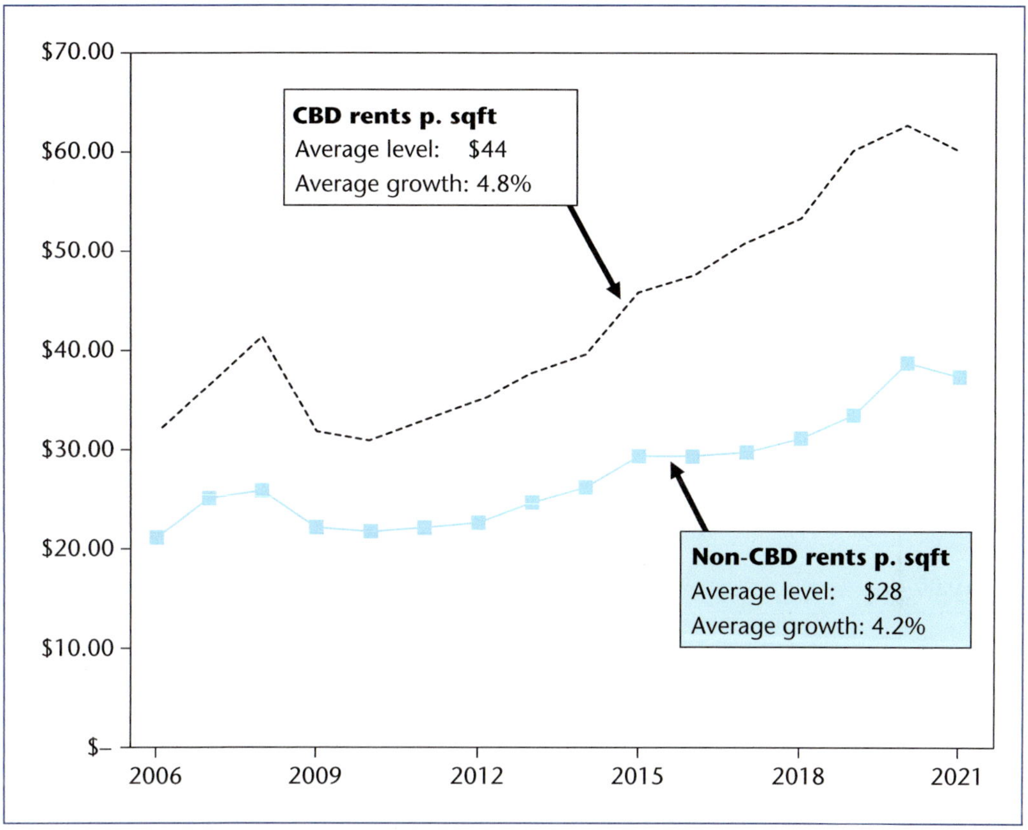

EXHIBIT 8-1A Office Rents Within the CBD and Outside of it for the Boston Metro Area.

Source: Own calculations using Compstak.

markets, CBD rents are always above non-CBD rents, although the difference in Los Angeles is minimal, at just $3 per square foot on average. In contrast, the difference between CBD and non-CBD rents per square foot is almost 60 percent on average in Boston, or $16 per square foot. The main explanation for the relatively flat rent gradient in Los Angeles is that this city is famously polycentric. As a result, there are multiple rent "spikes" over space. In Los Angeles, the difference in rental growth is also minimal. In Boston, rental growth in the CBD slightly outpaced non-CBD rental growth between 2006 and 2021, 4.8 percent to 4.2 percent, measured by the geometric mean growth rate (essentially, the ratio of the ending divided by the beginning value).

Keep in mind, however, that the market-wide averages depicted in the Exhibit do not necessarily tell the relevant story for any given individual building, although it is relevant information (as all buildings in a market directly or indirectly compete with each other to some extent). For example, the higher average CBD versus suburban rent growth in Boston was solely driven by the effect of *new* office buildings in the market. We will discuss the depreciation of rents in the next Chapter in great detail. For now, it suffices to note that younger buildings charge higher rents (other things equal). Thus, in the overall market average, rent will tend to increase if there is more development of new space in the market. If we omit new developments from our data, we find that rent growth was equal, at 3.9 percent in Boston's CBD *and* non-CBD areas. Boston's higher CBD rent growth reflected a greater change in composition (from old to new buildings), rather than by what is often referred to in real estate as "same-store growth" (even though in this case we're not talking about retail stores). (Some price indexes, such as those used in governmental GDP and inflation statistics, control for this consideration by use of various types of "*constant quality*" price indexing.)

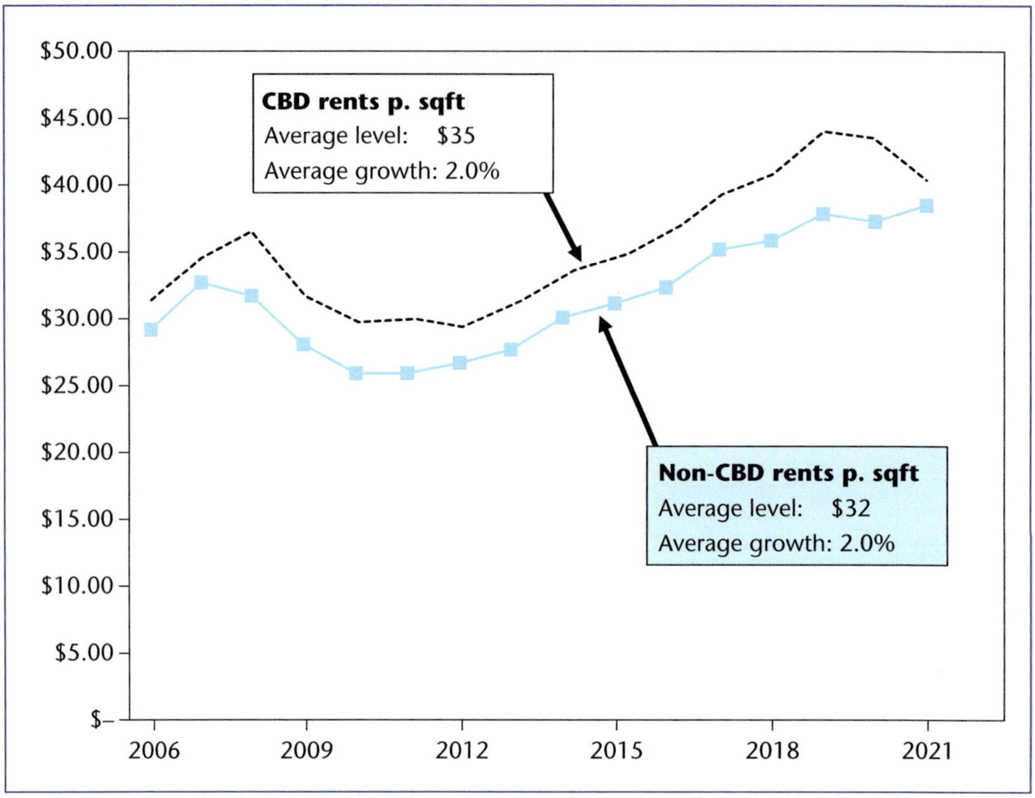

EXHIBIT 8-1B Office Rents Within the CBD and Outside of it for the Los Angeles Metro Area.

Source: Own calculations using Compstak.

Finally, it is important to note that space markets tend to segregate by property "quality," characterized by different rental price points. The market segments and the buildings within them are often labeled as "Class A," "Class B," or (sometimes) "Class C" (and others).[3] Class A properties are premium properties that tend to be newer, better located, have more amenities, or have better design and features. The exact definitions of such quality market segments are dynamic and fuzzy and may differ in different metros or regions. They also differ by property type; for example, industrial property is generally driven by different considerations than office or residential property. Such market quality segments are also related to one another in that there is typically a "trickle down" of older class A properties into Class B, and some potential tenants may want to move from one class to another (typically up to a higher class if and when rents are depressed). However, the quality market segments are very real in that different potential tenants and types of tenants are naturally at different price points in the rental market and require different quality segments.

In Exhibit 8-2, we return to the office market in Boston. Here, we show the average rent per square foot for A-class versus B-class buildings. We find that, indeed, A-class buildings tend to charge higher rents compared to B-class buildings. The average difference is $8 per square foot. However, like our discussion on the geographical differences, rental growth has been similar between the two property classes in our analyzed period. This will not always be the case, however.

Apart from geographical scope, the temporal range of the analysis must also be defined—that is, what period of time is to be covered. Historical analysis can give important insights into and a

[3] Many building owners and managers also use a plus or minus system, i.e. B+ or A- to provide subtle delineations in the quality categorization, while CoStar uses a 5 star system with 5 stars as equal to A and 4 stars equal to A-.

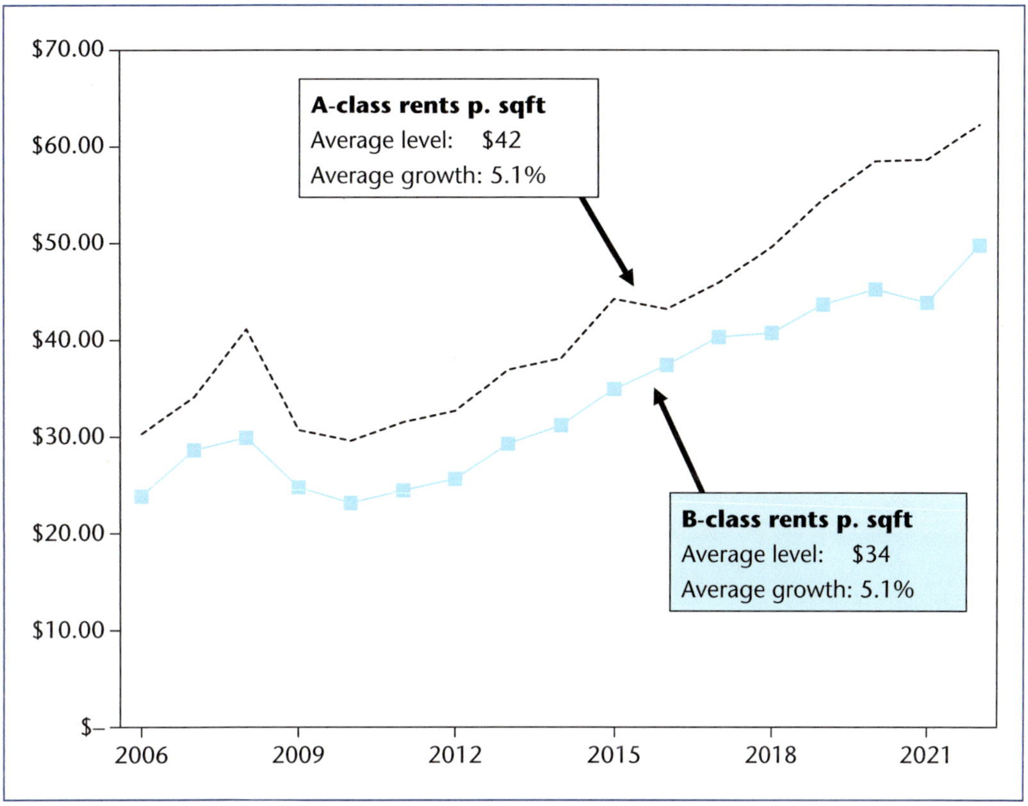

EXHIBIT 8-2 Office Rents per Square Foot for A and B-class Properties in the Boston Metro Area.

Source: Own calculations using Compstak.

perspective regarding the dynamics of a market. However, many market analysts also try to provide explicit future forecasts since decisions should be forward-looking in time. (You don't drive by looking in the rear-view mirror!) A 5- to 10-year future horizon is usually desirable, although data problems and random events often make forecasting much beyond three years rather unreliable. If the market tends to be cyclical (see Section 8.3), the length and stability of that cycle and the market's current position within the cycle should be considered. Some rental market cycles tend to be longer than 10 years, and it can be important to understand if one is likely to be near a peak or bottom.

In summary, a market analysis to forecast rental growth will typically be conducted at the metro level and focus on a target property type. Of course, not all the desired data will always be available, especially in smaller metro areas or for specialized property types. A widely-used solution is to increase the market breadth by adding neighboring metro areas or looking at different property types. Caution is advised, particularly for the latter (see Section 8.2.2). In extreme cases, there might be no readily identifiable "market use" for a given subject building if it is highly specialized or customized and possibly now obsolete. If little trading is happening, then analyzing supply and demand will only yield little (and noisy) information. In this situation, an investor would realistically be interested in the *investment value* rather than the *market value* of the building. (The difference in these two conceptions of value will be introduced in Chapter 14.) However, in most cases, the procedures laid out in the present and following chapters are sufficient for most typical investors in real assets.

8.2 THE STRUCTURAL APPROACH TO RENT FORECASTING

The typical general market analysis will focus on a few variables of the space market, or indicators, that quantitatively characterize both the supply and demand sides of the real estate space market and the balance between these two sides (the market equilibrium), fundamentally determining the market rent. Three physical variables, in particular, are very fundamental and relatively easy to observe: the amount of occupied space (or its change, referred to as "absorption"); the total stock of space both occupied and vacant (or its change, net "construction"); and the vacancy rate (percent of the stock that is not occupied). These physical variables, or their changes over time, are key to forecasting the economic variable that is of most interest to the real estate investor: the equilibrium market rent. One popular way to think about market equilibrium and rent is by considering the following three long-run (interdependent) structural relationships between the physical variables and the rent;

Equation 1

$$\text{Rent} = \text{f(Vacancy)}$$

$$\text{Occupied Space} = \text{f(Rent, Demand)}$$

$$\text{Construction} = \text{f(Rent, Vacancy)}$$

With f(), we mean "is a function of." As we will show in Section 8.3 and Chapter 9, once we understand/estimate these "functions," we can forecast our variable of interest: rent. The first relationship describes how vacancy drives rents; see Section 8.2.1 for a detailed discussion. The second relationship relates the total amount of space usage (in square feet or units) to the level of demand and the rent. For example, more space will be occupied if office employment grows in our market. When rents get high enough, the reverse might happen. Firms might choose to lease less space per worker or relocate to another city altogether. Finally, the third relationship in the set of equations in (1) relates the amount of new development to the likely profitability of new buildings, whose rent levels (+) and vacancy (–) can approximate.[4]

Note that we do not observe the *exact* nature of these relationships up front. More vacancies will likely mean lower rents; other things equal, but how much lower, and how soon? The functions in (1) may have different signs, sensitivities, and temporal lags in their right-hand sides. As you will see in the next Section, 8.2.1, these relationships also differ by market segment. Secondly, *almost* all variables are **endogenous**, meaning they impact each other. After all, they are all characteristics of the same market, the local space market. Consider the following physical identities (which are *calculated*, not estimated, as are the equations in (1)) that relate the variables in (1) back to each other;

Equation 2

$$OS_t = (1 - V_t)S_t$$

$$S_t = S_{t-1} + C_t$$

[4] Note that in the quadrant model of Chapter 6, profitability was approximated by using the cap rate in addition to the rent (that is, how much the asset market will pay per dollar of current rent). The three equations in setup (1) here are a simplification that is practical for purposes of forecasting market rent, as it is confined to space market variables. It is more difficult to forecast capital market variables such as cap rates.

Where;

- OS = occupied space (in square feet or units) in period t
- V = vacancy rate (%) in period t
- S = total stock (in square feet or units) in period t
- C = total amount of new development (in square feet or units) in period t

Thus, if you have 100 million square feet of office space and 5 percent vacancy, the occupied space (OS) will be (0.95 x 100m =) 95m square feet (first line of equation (2)). If we add another 5m square foot of office to this market, the new stock will be (100m + 5m =) 105m square foot (second line in equation (2)). You can flip these equations around if this is more convenient for you. For example, you can compute vacancy by $V_t = (S_t - OS_t)/S_t$, or total (net) construction by $C_t = S_t - S_{t-1}$.

Importantly, because some of these relationships involve lags in time (for example, construction takes time, and rents take time to adjust and might be constrained by existing leases), by combining the equations in (1) and (2), we can construct a mathematical system that allows the forecasting of rents for some period in the future based largely on these physical variables that can be observed relatively accurately today.

Let's provide a quick example to better understand how this would flow and how said variables are endogenous. Say the demand for office space in Seattle (WA) increases. As office workers move in, more office space will be occupied in the short run via the second relationship in equation (1). This will reduce the vacancy rate (first line of equation (2)) and, after some lag, increase rents (via vacancy in the first relationship in equation (1), as that relationship is a negative one with a lag). The higher rent and lower vacancy will, in turn, increase demand for real estate ownership because properties will now be more profitable. As a result, the stock of office square feet in Seattle will increase via new development (C), again, after a lag, per the third relationship in (1) and the second relationship in (2). This increase in space will then reduce vacancy, etc., until a new equilibrium is reached in the long run.

The attentive student will have noticed that these relationships are not (completely) new; the Quadrant Model of Chapter 6 depicts these relationships graphically, at a broad-brush and qualitative level. There are a few differences. As noted, we are here simplifying by ignoring the capital market role depicted by the cap rates in the northwest quadrant of the Quadrant Model. And the QM does not explicitly incorporate vacancy or specify temporal lags. These differences are because the QM focuses qualitatively on long-run equilibrium, whereas here, we are focused on quantitatively forecasting near to medium-term changes in rents and vacancy, the variables most directly affecting the economics of real estate investment and development decisions today. However, the key insights of Chapter 6 still apply, as indeed, the impact of demand on rent certainly depends on how elastically and quickly the "southern" quadrants of the QM will add to the supply of space in the rental market.

Obviously, these sets of equations are a simplified version of the real world. For example, we know that tax policies have increased construction in the past, at least in the U.S.[5] More development without more space demand will decrease rents in the long run. But despite (or perhaps because of) such simplification, the basic relationships in (1) and (2) have been employed quite successfully by some of the largest forecasting agencies (like CBRE) and are relatively easy to obtain for longer periods of time (via REIS and CoStar, for example). In such real-world industry practice, the equations are elaborated and calibrated based on much research, and future

[5] The most recent example in the U.S. is the "income and job act" of 2017, which essentially provided tax cuts for large private equity firms if they developed real estate in lower income neighborhoods. Another example are the generous tax shields introduced by the Reagan administration. In both cases new development was triggered beyond any initial increase in demand for space from tenants.

improvements will no doubt continue. For our pedagogical purposes here, it suffices to consider the simplified basics.

With that in mind, let us explore in more depth the following endogenous space market variables, which allow us to perform a market analysis that is relevant for near to medium-term forecasting;

- Rent
- Vacancy
- Construction

With these variables, we can also calculate other identities, that is, the occupied space and total stock. (As long as you have the total stock for one single period.) Note that one variable is missing above, *the demand for space*, entered in the second line of Equation 1. Demand for space is treated slightly differently because we assume this variable is **exogenous**. In contrast with the endogenous variables above, the demand for space is considered not to be impacted by the other variables in the system. The idea is that demand for space in a given location is governed by broad economic, technological, social, and demographic forces and trends external to (but relevant to) the given space market. As a result, in our example above for office space in Seattle, we started the paragraph by stating: "*Say, demand for office space in Seattle (WA) increases*." Thus, we treated the change in demand as a starting point, which provided an external shock to the system. Drivers of demand are very different for the different property types. Another difference between the demand for space and the other variables is that we – as the real estate investor – typically do not have to forecast it ourselves. As you will see, government agencies (like the BLS, Census Bureau, FRB, BEA), as well as private economic forecasting firms (such as Moody's, Oxford Economics, S&P Global, and others), provide such forecasts. Obviously, this might differ by country or for smaller market segments. (We will give some suggestions to deal with these situations in Chapter 9.)

In the next section, we will first detail the endogenous variables and their relationships with each other in a highly stylized way. We will follow that up with a discussion of the different drivers for demand by property type.

8.2.1 Rent, Construction, and Vacancy

The quantity of new construction starts and/or completions is a fundamental indicator of real estate markets. As described in Chapter 6, construction represents the addition of new supply to the stock of space available in the market. Of course, construction takes time, typically anywhere from a few months to build a simple house to a few years to build a large commercial complex. The new supply enters the market once the construction is complete and certified for occupancy, although pre-leasing may commit tenants in advance. In most markets, it is also essential to consider the demolition or conversion of older or obsolete structures and the construction of new buildings to arrive at the net addition of space supply in the market.

The second key market indicator is the stock of occupied space, or typically, more to the point, the change in that stock, which is referred to as absorption. Space absorption refers to the amount of additional space occupied per year. Absorption can be considered an indicator of the activity on the demand side of the space market, just as construction is an indicator of activity on the supply side. However, it is useful to distinguish between gross and net absorption in the market.

Gross absorption measures the total amount of space for which leases were signed during the year, regardless of where the tenants came from. This is a good measure of the volume of rental transaction activity and a very relevant measure of the demand for leasing brokerage services. However, some tenants would be moving from one site to another within the same market, so the signing of their lease would imply vacating one space in the market and occupying another in the same market. This would not mean a growth in the overall amount of occupied space in the market and thus would not signify growth in the overall demand for space.

A better measure of demand growth is **net absorption**, which is simply the net change in the amount of occupied space in the market. This is the more relevant number to compare to the net amount of construction completed during the same period of time. Comparing net construction completed to net absorption indicates whether demand and supply are growing at the same rate, with resulting implications for changes in the balance between demand and supply in the market. When net absorption exceeds net construction completions, vacancy declines in the market, and when construction exceeds absorption, vacancy rises. The relationship between the quantity of vacant space at the end of a period and the quantity of net construction completions and net absorption during the period is indicated by the following equation:

Equation 3

$$VS_t = VS_{t-1} + (C_t - A_t)$$

Where;

- VS = vacant space (in square feet or units) in period t
- C = net construction of space (in square feet or units) in period t
- A = net absorption of space (in square feet or units) in period t

The third key physical indicator is the vacancy rate (V), which refers to the percentage of the stock of built space in the market that is not currently occupied ($V_t = VS_t/S_t = 1 - OS_t/S_t$). To compute the vacancy rate, one must know two more fundamental quantities: the total stock of space in the market and the currently vacant space (or the occupied space, as $VS_t = S_t - OS_t$). For current and historical data, these quantities are determined by inventorying and surveying public records and landlords. They are often compiled by brokerage firms, consulting firms, or data firms that sell real estate market information. Note that there is also a difference between unoccupied space that is rented, possibly available via sublet, and vacant space not rented. This is simply a result of leases in place on space that is no longer needed. Space available in the sublease market is a leading indicator of vacant space.

To be more accurate, the vacancy rate should include all space that is currently unoccupied and available for occupancy, including space that may be currently under lease but available for subleasing.

Importantly, because vacancy is determined by both supply and demand acting together, the vacancy rate is an indicator that reflects the current balance between supply and demand in the market (the other is the current market rent level). Vacancy is thus an indicator of the current equilibrium in the space market rather than an indicator of either the supply or demand side alone. Vacancy rate data are usually more widely available and reliable than the other equilibrium indicator, rent levels, which may be affected by unknown lease terms.

It is important to remember that some vacancy is normal in a typical real estate market. Fundamentally, this is because it does not make economic sense for landlords to rent space to the first potential tenant that comes along, no matter what rent that tenant is offering to pay. Similarly, it does not make sense for tenants to rent space in the first building they find, no matter the rent or how suboptimal the location is. Both the space owner (landlord) and space user (tenant) suffer costs when tenants move (such as lost rent incurred by the landlord when the space is vacant and moving expenses incurred by the tenant who moves). This is why leases are typically signed by both parties for some period of time (especially in commercial property markets, where leases are often for multiple years). Therefore, for both the supply and demand sides of the market, profits will be maximized if firms take some time to search for better deals. This search time results in space being held vacant, waiting (in effect) for better deals to show up. Thus, zero vacancy in a market indicates suboptimal behavior on the part of decision-makers.

Another rational reason for vacancy in a market is growth in the demand side and the variable and unpredictable nature of that growth. Supply typically has to be added in a "lumpy" manner because buildings must be built of a specific size to be economical, considering construction and land costs. Because of the time it takes to build, construction decisions must be made without perfect information about the future balance of supply and demand in the market when the building is completed. This also leads naturally to some excess space being provided in the typical real estate market from time to time. It also suggests, in combination with our previous point about optimal search, that it may be profitable to maintain some inventory of available space. This "inventory model" of vacancy tends to be more important in markets where demand grows faster and with more volatility or ups and downs in the growth rate.

For these reasons, real estate markets are characterized by what is sometimes called a **natural vacancy rate**, which is the vacancy rate that tends to prevail on average over the long run in the market and which indicates that the market is approximately in a balance between supply and demand. When vacancy is below the natural rate, it is said that the market is a sellers' or landlords' market or that the rental market is tight, with demand exceeding supply in some sense. When the vacancy rate is above the natural level, the market is said to be a buyers' or tenants' market (or overbuilt), with the supply of available space exceeding the current level of demand. When vacancy is below the natural rate, rents will be driven up (and new development will tend to occur). When vacancy is above the natural rate, rents tend to be driven down.

The natural vacancy rate is not the same for all markets and may also change over time in a given market. As noted, it tends to be higher in faster-growing, more volatile markets and in markets with fewer regulatory or geographical constraints on new development. Whatever the natural vacancy rate (and it is usually challenging to know precisely what it is in any given market), the actual vacancy rate will tend to cycle over time around this natural rate. Exhibit 8-3 shows the U.S.'s average vacancy rate among NCREIF office properties during 1983–2023. Although such a national average does not reflect any one space market (and the natural vacancy is a market-specific concept), the exhibit nevertheless depicts the big picture of how the current equilibrium tends to cycle around the long-run equilibrium in space markets. The overall long-run average depicted in the Exhibit is 8.5 percent, but the current average cycled between less than 5 percent and over 13 percent, with peaks lagging after the ends of economic recessions (as occupancy tends to reflect employment, which tends to be a lagging effect of recessions).

The final, and in some respects, the most important market indicator is the current market rent, which refers to the rent level charged on typical new leases currently being signed in the market. Of course, rents on specific leases will vary according to the particular nature of the site and space being rented and to the lease terms. It is, therefore, important to try to control for such variations when measuring trends in rents across time. This makes reliable quantification of market rents rather difficult. It is also usually necessary to control for the effect of general inflation and to examine the trend in real rents. This is because real rents are what really matters (reflecting purchasing power or opportunity cost) and because real rents reflect the actual physical and economic balance between supply and demand in the space market. Another factor to remember is that asking rents, typically reported in landlord surveys, may differ from the effective rents being charged to new tenants. The concept of effective rent (discussed more fully in Chapter 10) includes the monetary effect of concessions and rent abatements that landlords sometimes offer tenants to persuade them to sign a lease. For example, a landlord may quote a rent of $15/SF but then provide the first year rent-free if the tenant signs a 5-year lease. Yet the rent may be reported in a survey or a casual inquiry as $15. Effective rents tend to be private information.

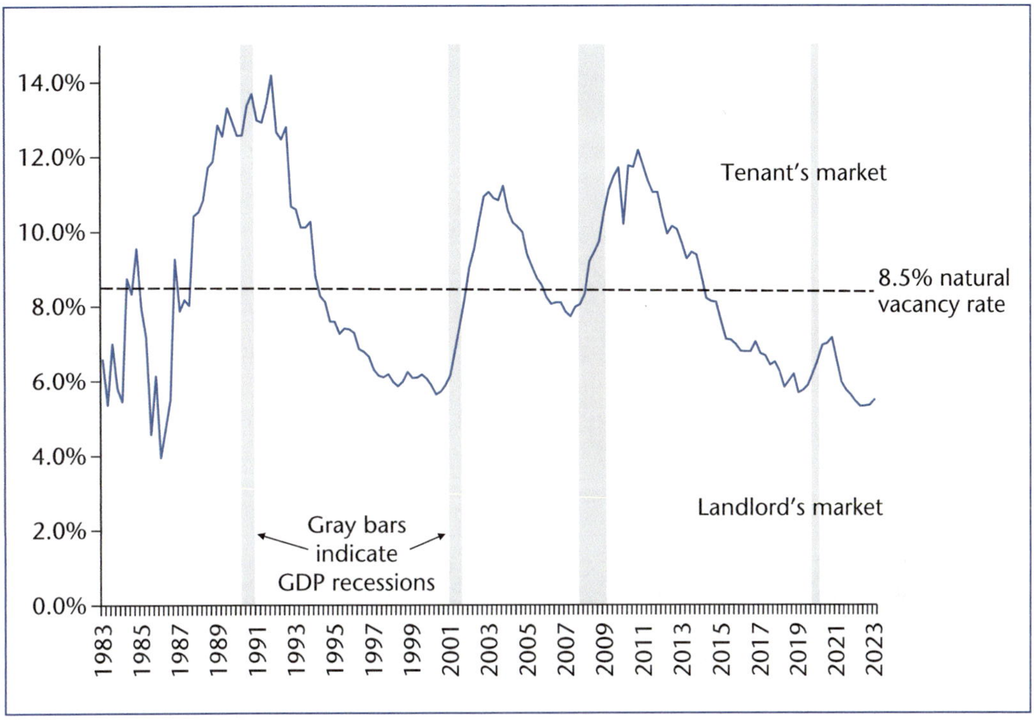

EXHIBIT 8-3 Average Reported Vacancy Among NCREIF Office Properties, 1983–2023. Recession periods are determined by a panel of experts at the NBER (National Bureau of Economic Research).

In Exhibit 8-4, we summarize office vacancy rates for three metropolitan markets: Boston, Los Angeles, and Atlanta. More precisely, we provide the vacancy rate (vacant space as a percentage of total stock), net construction (new development minus demolitions), and net absorption as a percentage of the total stock. (The construction and absorption percentages are expressed in the annual trailing average, even though the time periods on the horizontal axis are quarters. This allows you to understand the magnitude of annual growth rates.)

The three metropolitan office markets depicted in the figures were selected because they demonstrate the kind of variety that can exist across space markets. Los Angeles represents a very large and mature office market. While it may have large amounts of construction measured in absolute terms (its total stock of commercial office space is in the neighborhood of 500 million square feet according to CoStar Group, the source of the data in the figures), Los Angeles's growth in absorption and new construction is relatively small as a percent of the existing stock, averaging less than half a percent per year. Exhibit 8-4A reveals that Los Angeles has recently experienced three major down cycles in its office market, with negative net absorption (absolute decline in the amount of occupied space): after the dot. com bubble burst in the early 2000s, again after the financial crisis in 2008, and then after the outbreak of COVID-19.

Boston (Exhibit 8-4B) experienced higher construction growth and absorption rates on average compared to Los Angeles. The impact of the dot.com crash was more considerable in Boston. In contrast, the impact of the financial crisis and COVID-19 on absorption rates was smaller in Boston compared to Los Angeles. Speaking about the latter, one might be surprised that COVID-19 still impacts office absorption even after vaccines were developed (later in 2020). However, one should realize that COVID-19 coincided with a boost in telecommunication technologies, like Zoom. People were initially forced to work with such technologies and subsequently got used to them. This intersection caused the

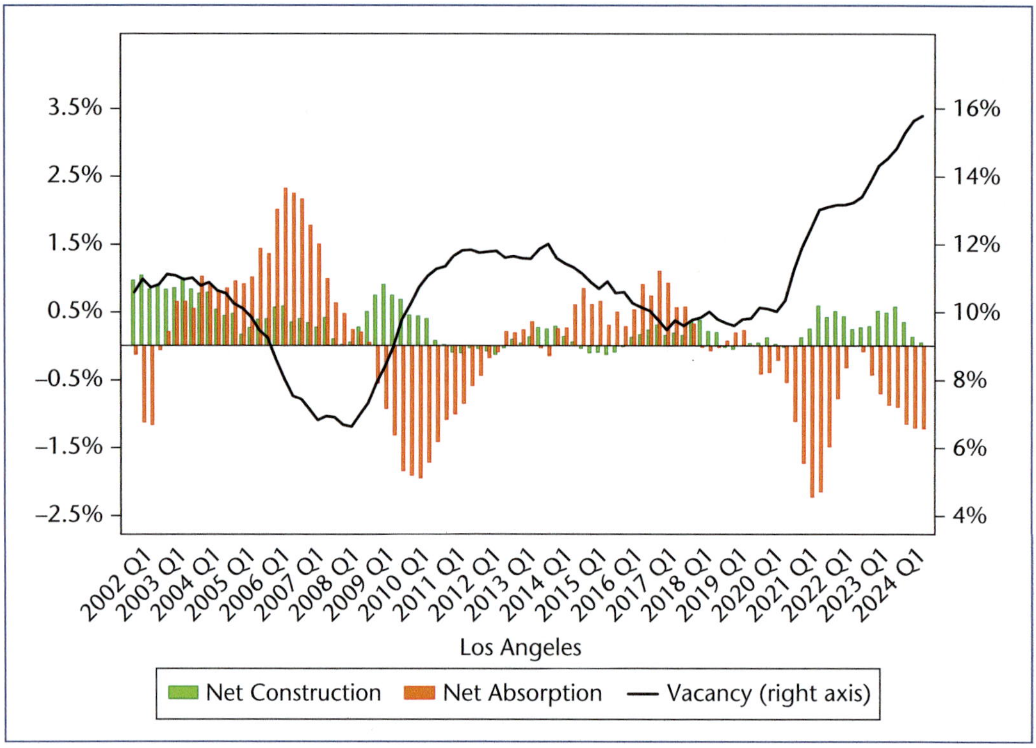

EXHIBIT 8-4A Net Construction Rate (1-year trailing average), Net Absorption Rate (1-year trailing average), and Vacancy Rate (right axis) for Office Los Angeles (CA).

Source: CoStar.

industry to change as much as it did. Thus, one could argue that this transition to WFH (work from home) would have been inevitable, but at a slower and more gradual rate.

However, what explains the difference in response to COVID-19 and WFH between Los Angeles and Boston? Recent research[6] has shown that there are two reasons why office markets are impacted differently by COVID-19. First, the industrial base of the city matters. In the sense that certain cities specialize in jobs that are easier to do from home (WFH). Employees in cities that employ more people in—for example—data analytics and sales will have a higher propensity to work from home. In contrast, legal or retail jobs are more challenging to perform from home. Thus, a city that mostly hires in the second group will tend to have fewer people working from home. The second reason pertains to differences in aggregate commuting time. Employees with high commuting costs will opt to work from home more often. Los Angeles is exactly such a city. The city is large, with relatively long commuting times. Thus, after the development of vaccines, at least some workers returned back to the office in Boston. In Los Angeles, the net absorption has never been positive since COVID-19. Unfortunately (for investors in office space in Boston), vacancy rates still skyrocketed in this city. The vacancy rates went from 7 percent pre-COVID, to 12 percent at the end of our sample (mid-2024). This was caused by high construction levels since COVID-19, not seen in 20 years. This construction boom was long overdue but ill-timed nonetheless. As shown in Exhibit 8-4B, Boston had seen considerable positive absorption between 2011 and 2020, while construction could not keep

[6] See the research paper called "The Price of Work-from-Home: Commercial Real Estate in the City and the Suburbs" by Ghosh, Rolheiser, Van de Minne, and Wang for more details on the impact of COVID-19 on property values.

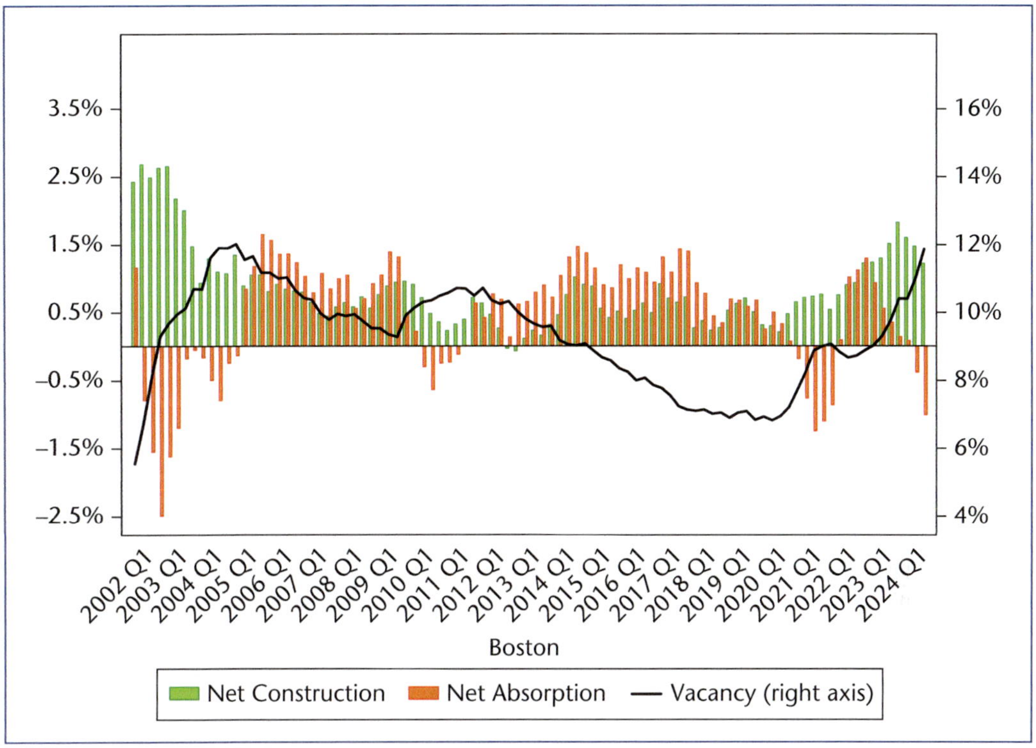

EXHIBIT 8-4B Net Construction Rate (1-year trailing average), Net Absorption Rate (1-year trailing average), and Vacancy Rate (right axis) for Office Boston (MA).

Source: CoStar.

up. An entire new office neighborhood (the South Boston "waterfront") was largely developed after 2020, which was planned pre-COVID.

Atlanta (Exhibit 8-4C) has tended to be the most rapidly growing of the three markets, with annual growth averaging over 1 percent of stock per year since 2000, exceeding 3 percent per year at the start of the sample. But Atlanta presents the highest vacancy rates. As noted, the natural vacancy rate tends to be greater in faster-growing cities that have relatively weak constraints on new supply, that is, where it is relatively easy and inexpensive for developers to build new space and where, therefore, the supply of space responds relatively quickly and elastically.

In Exhibit 8-5 we plot the office market real rent trends alongside the vacancy rates for the same metropolitan areas as before. The rents are effective new leases indexed to a value of 100 in each city as of 2000.[7] We only have data on effective rents until the end of 2022, a slightly shorter window than our previous vacancy data. The figures display "real rents," that is, net of general monetary inflation. Generally, the variation in both vacancy (similar to Exhibit 8-4, but for a shorter sample period) and rents appears strongly cyclical. However, some markets are more cyclical than others, and the cycle is not necessarily the same across the markets. For example, Boston's vacancy and real rent cycle is the most prominent (most amplitude) of all markets. Los Angeles had the least prominent vacancy cycle. Interestingly, Atlanta displayed the least cyclicality in office rents. The exhibit thus suggests that rents were less sensitive to vacancy in Atlanta. This would reflect greater price

[7] We estimated a pseudo repeated rent index using the Compstak data. For those interested in the technicalities, we estimated an OLS model with time, and building fixed effects, while controlling for the differences in unit sizes between the leases within the same building. The log of the effective rent per lease is the left-hand side variable. We exponentiated the time fixed effects to obtain our nominal index.

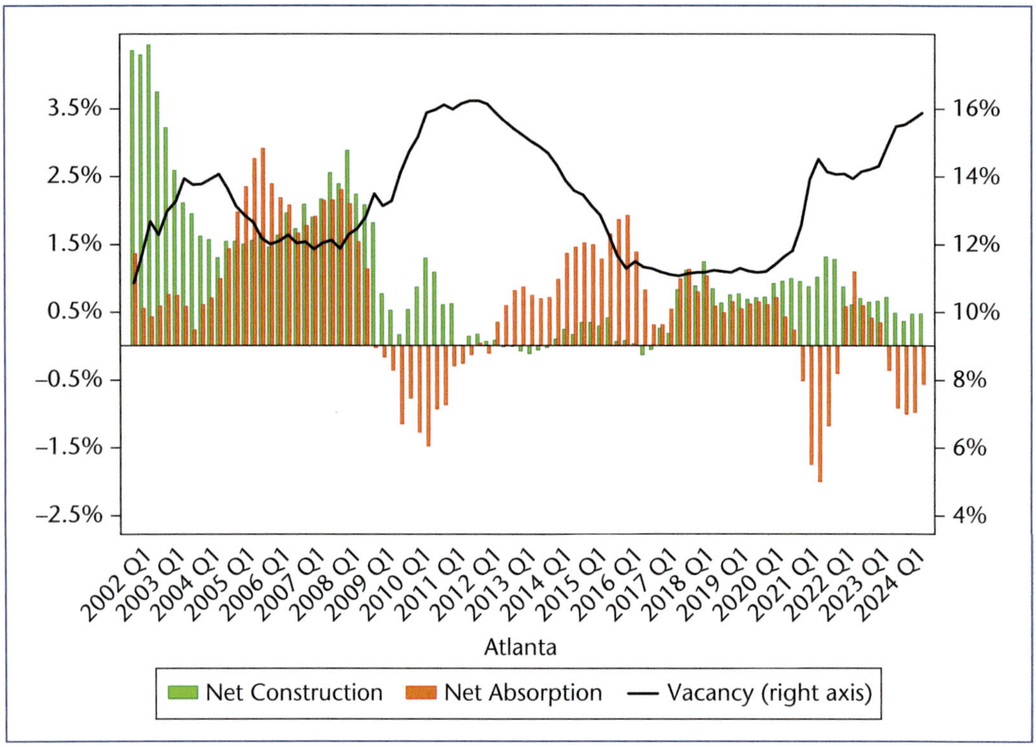

EXHIBIT 8-4C Net Construction Rate (1-year trailing average), Net Absorption Rate (1-year trailing average), and Vacancy Rate (right axis) for Office Atlanta (GA).

Source: CoStar.

elasticity of supply in Atlanta (i.e., a small increase in rents evokes a large and fast response in new development, thereby preventing rents from rising further in a growing market).

Exhibit 8-5 graphically displays the fundamental point noted earlier: rents tend to move inversely to vacancy, which is formulated by a negative relationship between the right-hand and left-hand sides of the first equation in (1). There is a clear (negative) relationship between rents and vacancy. It is also important to note that the rent cycle is lagged behind the vacancy cycle in time. This is due to lags in the responses in the variables, which will be discussed further later. For now, note that if we take the average vacancy over the 2000–2024 period covered in Exhibit 8-4, we would estimate the "natural" vacancy rate as about 11 percent in Los Angeles, 9 percent in Boston, and closer to 13 percent in Atlanta. In all markets, vacancy has risen in recent years due to COVID-19 and WFH. Some speculate that we will have new and higher natural vacancy levels because of COVID-19. As of writing (2024), it is too early to say.

The differences in the average effective rents (in 2022): $36/SF in Los Angeles, $49/SF in Boston, and $25/SF in Atlanta) reflect the basic principles of urban form introduced in Chapters 6 and 7. Atlanta faces the greatest availability of land, a full 360-degree development arc, and far lower density than Boston and Los Angeles, hence, a flatter rent gradient and lower central place location premiums. (Coastlines physically constrain both Boston and Los Angeles, and mountains further constrain LA while wetlands hamper Boston land availability, none of which constrain Atlanta.) Los Angeles is by far the largest of the three metros in population, which we noted in Chapter 6 tends to increase location premia. The fact that Boston has the highest average effective rent per square foot was alluded to earlier. Due to physical and (mostly) regulatory constraints, insufficient new construction was added to keep up with demand for a long time. More specifically, in Exhibit 8-6, we provide both the percentage of undevelopable land (as an estimate of physical space constraints)

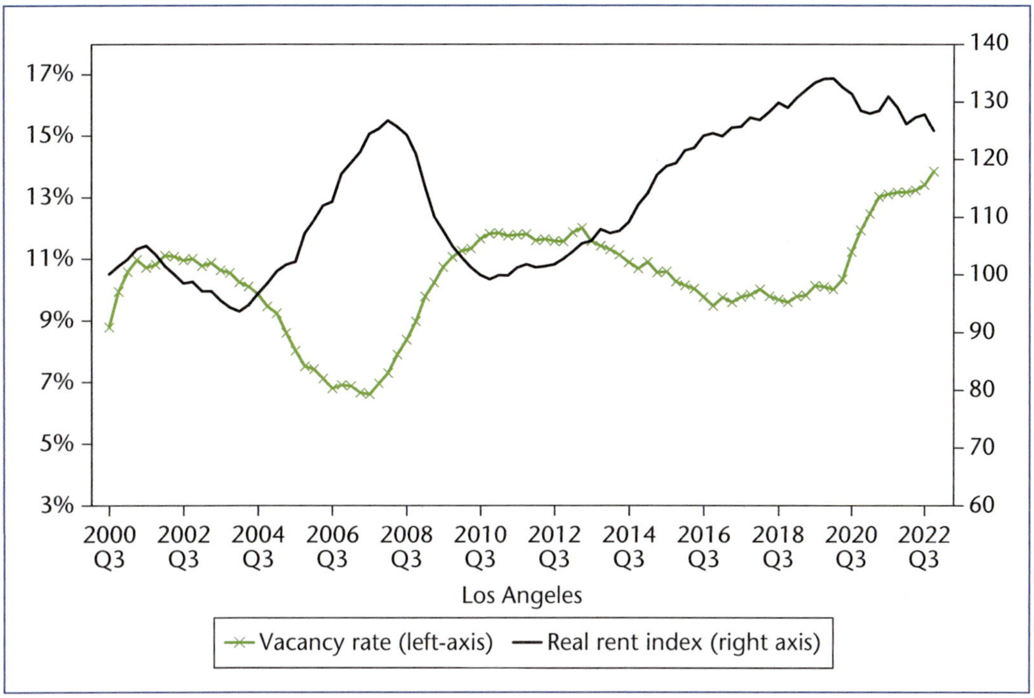

EXHIBIT 8-5A Real Rent and Vacancy Cycles for Los Angeles between 2000 and 2022.

Source: Own calculations using Compstak and CoStar.

and the Wharton Regulatory Index (based on a survey) for all three metros. A higher value for the regulatory index means that more stringent (local) regulation is hampering development. While both Los Angeles and Boston have a high share of undevelopable land, the Wharton Regulatory Index indicates that Boston had the highest regulatory constraints by far during the surveyed period. In fact, of all the MSAs surveyed by Wharton, only Providence (RI, a neighboring MSA) had a higher index score than Boston.[8]

As fascinating as it is to study the history of space markets, the main focus of the present chapter, as it is the main interest of potential real estate investors, is forecasting the *future* of such markets. The variables described in this section can be quite useful for that purpose. They can be combined and often added to other data to provide indicators for gaining insight into where a market is headed. For example, if you take the current amount of vacant space in the market, plus the amount of any new construction started but not yet complete, and divide that sum by 1/12th the annual net absorption, you get an indicator known as the **months supply** of available space. The formula is presented here:

Equation 4

$$Months\ Supply = \frac{Vacancy + Construction}{Net\ Absorption/12}$$

[8] We used the numbers found in Albert Saiz's "On Local Housing Supply Elasticity," available on SSRN. See Exhibit 8-6. Note that these numbers are from 2005–2010. More recent numbers show that regulatory constraints have eased in Boston. See the Wharton website for more recent surveys on metro-level regulatory constraints.

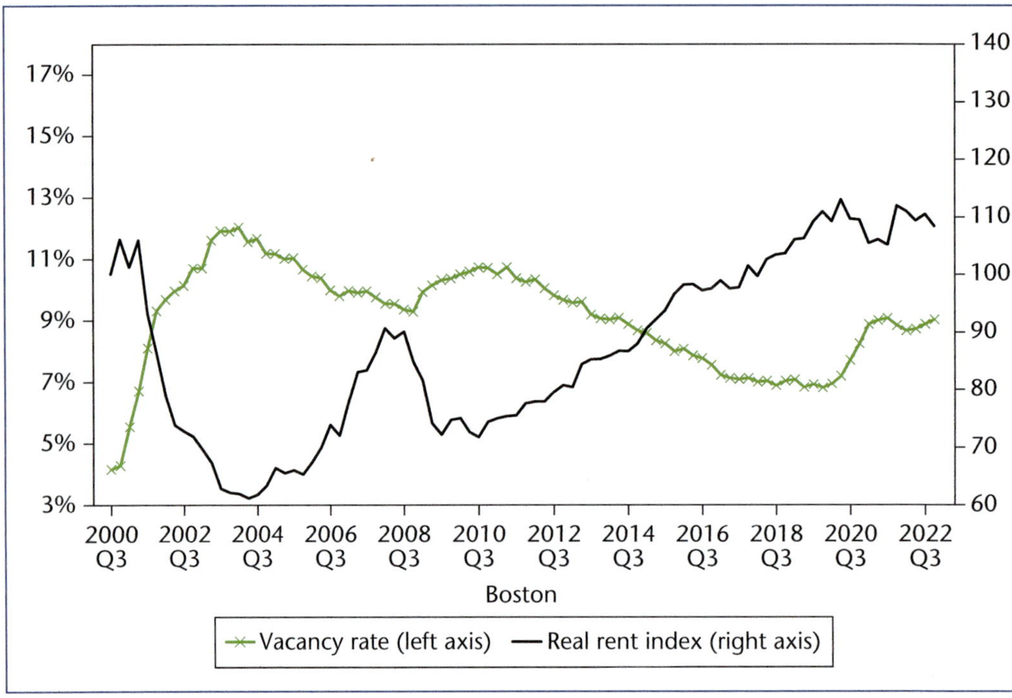

EXHIBIT 8-5B Real Rent and Vacancy Cycles for Boston between 2000 and 2022.

Source: Own calculations using Compstak and CoStar.

The months supply (MS) is an indicator of how long it will take (in months) for all of the vacant space in the market to be absorbed (driving the market down to a zero vacancy rate). For such interpretation of the MS formula, one would have to assume (1) the rate of new demand growth continues as indicated by the net absorption rate, and (2) there is no new construction in the market other than what has already been started. (The MS metric also does not explicitly consider pre-leased space in the new construction.) The idea is that the months supply metric can be compared to the length of time (in months) that it takes to complete the typical construction project. If the months supply is less than the construction time, then the market can support additional new construction. If (as we suggested earlier) it is not practical for the market to go all the way down to zero vacancy, or if there is likely to be demolition or abandonment of existing occupied space in the market, then the market can handle additional new construction, even when the months supply is somewhat greater than the average construction-project duration (the more so if some of the new construction is pre-leased). However, suppose the months supply extends far beyond the average construction project duration. In that case, the indication is that the market is oversupplied, and there will be continued downward pressure on real effective rents.

8.2.2 Drivers of Demand

All of the preceding text is relevant for all property types. For example, too much supply will *always* result in lower rents, no matter the market segment, due to the basics of how markets operate. (Although the *exact* impact can differ per market segment.) Likewise, if developers can profit when developing for a particular market segment, they will construct more square footage in said market. (Probably delayed, but eventually.) However, we find large differences between property types if we look at the typical (exogenous) drivers of demand. Next, we will discuss these drivers for every

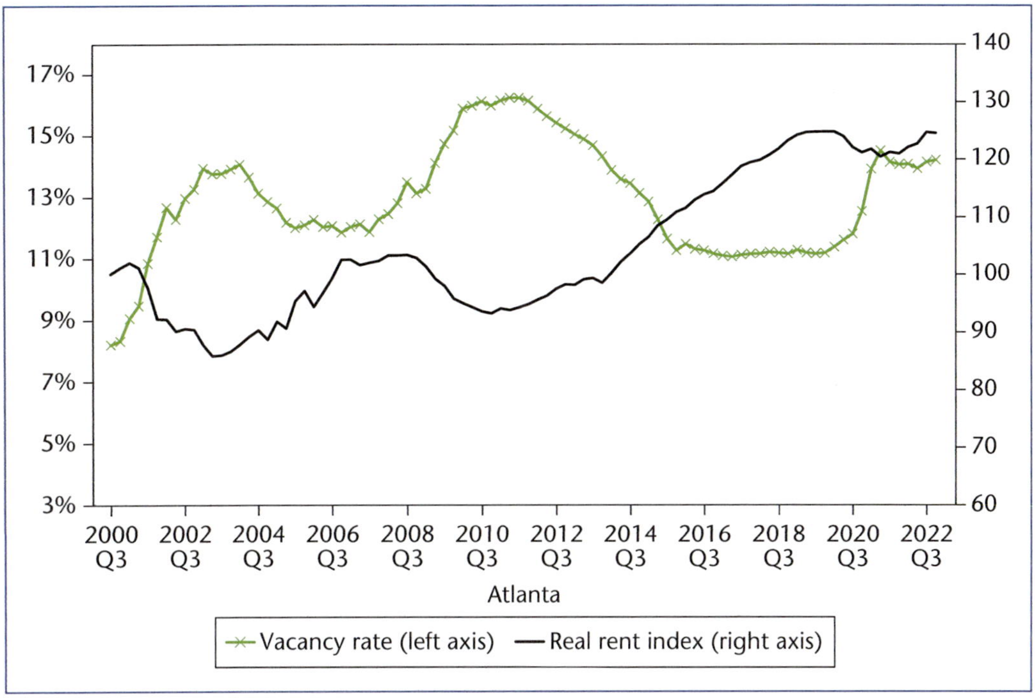

EXHIBIT 8-5C Real Rent and Vacancy Cycles for Atlanta between 2000 and 2022.

Source: Own calculations using Compstak and CoStar.

EXHIBIT 8-6

Share of Undevelopable Land and the Wharton Residential Urban Land Regulation Index (WRLURI) for our Three Metro Areas

Metro	%Undevelopable land	Regulatory Index
Los Angeles	53.43%	0.50
Boston	34.06%	1.67
Atlanta	4.30%	0.03

This data is from around 2005–2010.

Source: "On Local Housing Supply Elasticity" by Albert Saiz, available on SSRN.

major property type. (You can find a discussion of other, more specialized property types in the Appendix.) Let's start with the office market, as this was the focus of the previous section.

For the **office** sector, the main driver of demand for space is "simply" *office employment*. In the office space, employees are the "business" themselves that the firms supply. For example, attorneys give legal advice, and real estate investment managers produce proformas. If more legal advice is needed in the future, more office space must be supplied (or else the workers must squeeze together).

Governments typically track employment via surveys and subsequently tabulate it on a disaggregate level. The Bureau of Labor Statistics (BLS) does this in the United States. They define establishment-level types of activities via NAICS (North American Industry Classification System) codes. Codes starting with a five are associated with office work.[9] This primarily includes jobs in the

[9] Some will also argue that you must add NAICS code "92," which is associated with public administration. In the U.S. it is not uncommon for governmental agencies and municipalities to rent in the private sector.

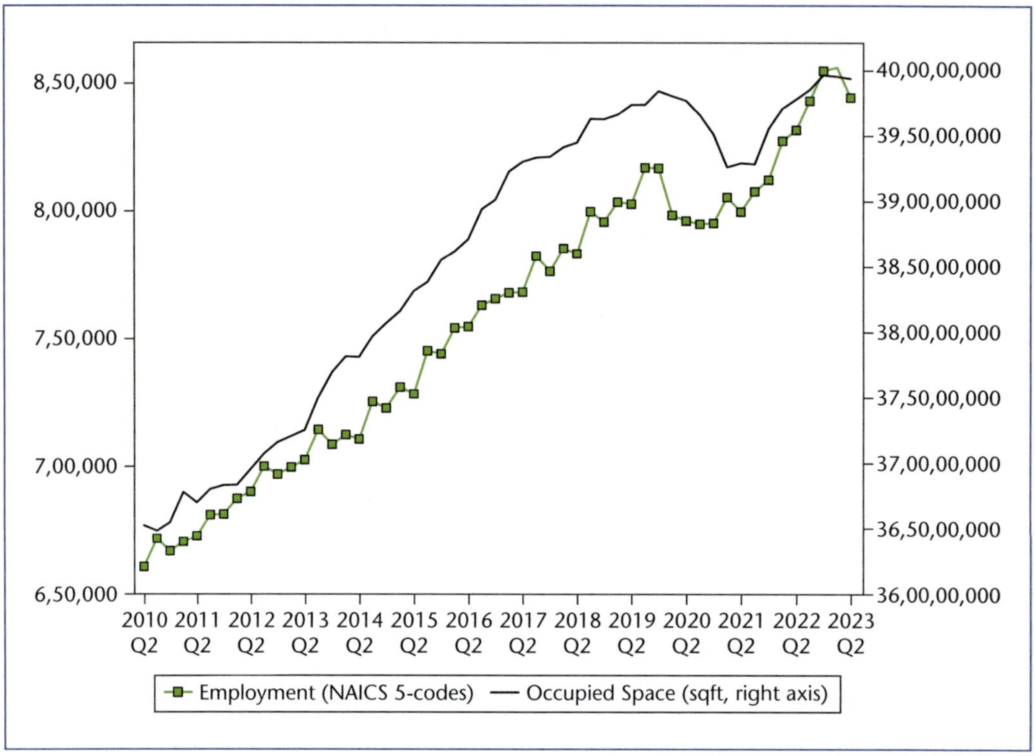

EXHIBIT 8-7A Office Employment (left-axis) and Occupied Space (right-axis) in Boston MSA, between 2010 and 2024.

Source: BLS and Costar.

FIRE industry (Finance, Insurance, and Real Estate). If we circle back to our earlier discussion, we do not expect construction, rents, or vacancy to impact employment in the office sector. In contrast, we assume it is the other way around.[10] In Exhibit 8-7, we display the total employment in the office sector (left axis), approximated by the 5-digit NAICS codes, and the occupied space (right axis) in square footage for the Boston MSA.[11]

Exhibit 8-7A shows that employment in the office sector and the occupied space (equation (2)) of office square footage grew at similar rates between 2010 and 2020. In the direct aftermath of COVID-19, office employment *and* the occupied space declined first. The negative impact on occupied space was slightly delayed, mainly because leases in the office sector are typically signed for 2 to 7 years (see Chapter 10). However, between 2021 and 2024, over 50,000 new office jobs were added to the region, resulting in office employment levels well above the previous peak. In contrast, the occupied space only increased to *match* the prior peak. There are two (not mutually exclusive) explanations for this phenomenon. First, some (new and old) employees now work from home (WFH). Second, firms occupy less office space per employee. Exhibit 8-7B provides the office space per employee for newly signed leases in Boston.[12] Between 2010 and 2020, the average square feet

[10] Although this assumption of exogeneity can be relaxed, as we will discuss in Chapter 9.

[11] Note that the Boston MSA includes all of Eastern Massachusetts, southeast New Hampshire (including its largest city Manchester), and Providence (RI).

[12] This is different from dividing the occupied space by the total amount of employees in Exhibit 8-7A for two important reasons: (1) these are newly signed leases, whereas total occupied space also contains leases signed years ago, and (2) this is the space that can be directly attributed to the tenant (net assignable area, see Chapter 5) instead of the gross area of the entire building.

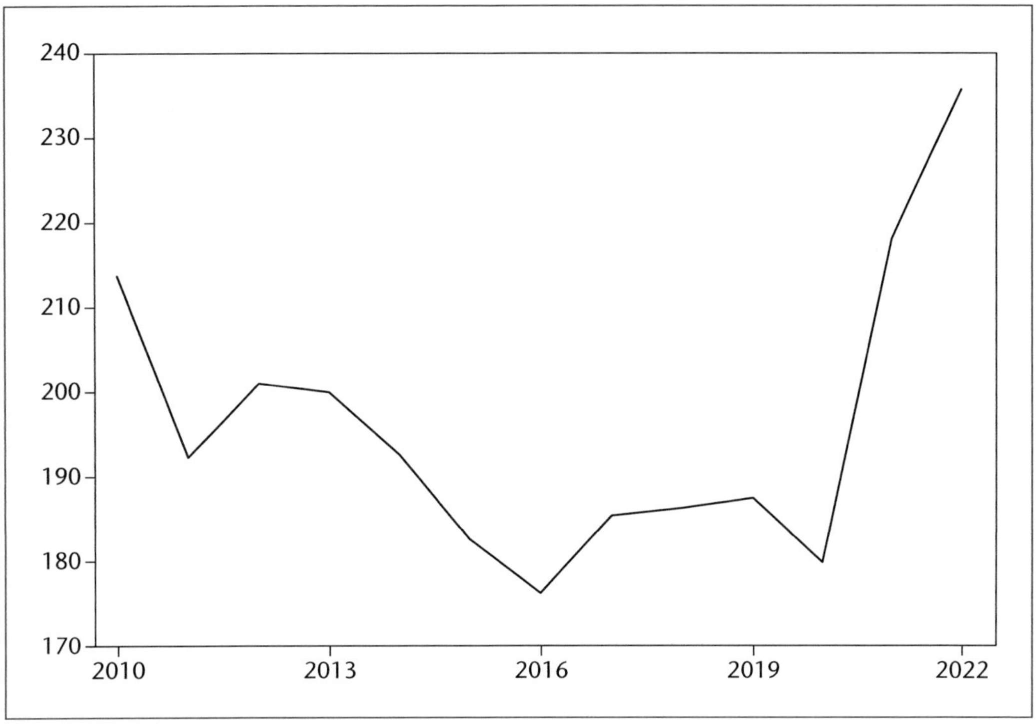

EXHIBIT 8-7B Square Foot per Employee (vertical axis) for Newly Signed Leases between 2010 and 2022 in Boston.

Source: Own calculations using Compstack.

per employee reduced at a steady rate from over 210 square feet to approximately 180 square feet on average in 2020. This period was conjoined with decreasing vacancy rates and higher (real) rent levels, resulting in employees huddling together. However, after COVID-19, the office usage per employee skyrocketed to over 230 square feet per employee, driven by lower real rents and excess office space. In other words, the relatively low uptick in occupied space after 2021 was not driven by firms renting less space per employee; quite the opposite! Indeed, if we take the census data, we find that one-fifth of all Bostonians worked from home in 2022. (This is higher than the U.S. average of 15 percent.) This will be an essential adjustment going into the future. If jobs are added in the office sector, we need to consider that not all of them will actually occupy space. As mentioned earlier, the propensity to WFH depends on the type of jobs and how commute-friendly the city is.

The demand for **housing** units, in general, is mainly driven by population and overall employment growth (not just office as before). In Section 8.1, we discussed how different property subtypes are still considered substitutes in the long run and that you can consider all office space for your market analysis. For housing units, this is more subtle. For example, housing can be targeted for specific age or income groups. Senior ("assisted living") housing, manufactured housing, and subsidized (sometimes referred to as "social") housing are such examples. Senior homes do not compete for the same tenants as manufactured houses and can, therefore, be considered a different market segment. Likewise, younger households prefer (rental) apartments over single-family housing. This is primarily due to the flexibility such homes provide (apartment leases are for 1 year only; see Chapter 10) and the simple fact that younger households do not have the purchasing power (yet) to own their own home. In the U.S. (source: Census Bureau in 2022), 64 percent of people 35 years or younger are renting. Lower-income households also prefer renting for similar reasons. This can happen in the social housing sector or the private market sector. Sixty-one percent of all people in the lower 25 percentile income-wise are renters in the United States (source: Census Bureau in 2022). Thus, investors in multi-family units will typically focus on forecasts of the number of younger families or blue-collar job growth. As with office space, if prices (rents) are relatively high, people will move together and occupy relatively fewer housing units.[13]

Fundamentally, the demand for **warehouse** space follows the need to store *inventory*. In recent decades, more goods have been shipped than ever before, in parallel with the growth of e-commerce. These goods are stored, transferred at specific points, and shipped directly to consumers and businesses (across states or even country lines). In contrast to the office market, in principle, using warehouse employment as a predictor of occupied space is not 100 percent kosher. The "business" that such firms supply is inventory space and distribution, not employees. The employees are just one of the factors used to achieve this goal. For example, firms can invest in automation to handle larger inventory quantities instead of increasing the workforce. E-commerce sales, truck tonnage by area, and port volumes are all indirect indicators of warehouse demand.

Unfortunately, data on inventory space can be challenging to obtain on a disaggregated basis. *Fortunately*, technology in the warehouse space, in the relatively long run, has been more or less fixed in the past decades. As a result, using employment in the warehouse space is still a valid approximation for the demand for space in this sector. The corresponding NAICS codes start with 48 or 49. This correlation is exemplified by Exhibit 8-8, which displays the growth (%) in occupied warehouse space and the (%) change in employment in this sector for the Dallas (TX) Metro Area. Indeed, Exhibit 8-8 shows high levels of co-movement between the increase in occupied warehouse square footage and employment. If we disregard 2020Q2 (the start of COVID-19), both grew by approximately 0.7 basis points per quarter, or almost 3 percent annually, between 2014 and 2024.[14]

Demand for **retail** space is driven primarily by retail sales or consumption of goods, not store workers. (This was the case for warehouse workers as well.) Unlike our data issue with warehouse inventory, sales data (or consumption data) is typically widely available. (Including forecasts.) For example, in the United States, the Census Bureau tracks sales on a disaggregated basis. The main challenge for retail space has been the (relative) increase in e-commerce in recent decades. With the aid of technology, e-commerce allows consumers to view an almost infinite variety of goods on platforms with transparent price comparisons. It also allows them to see how other consumers have reacted to the goods. The goods are then delivered to their doorstep, sometimes even on the same day.

The e-commerce sales as a percentage of total sales have increased from less than 1 percent in 2000 to 4 percent in 2010 to 16 percent in 2024 (source: Fred). Such e-commerce sales do not benefit the traditional retail space, although they benefit the warehouse space mentioned above. What makes it even more confusing is that many businesses operate both in-store retail and e-commerce. All of this means that you must be careful when using sales data (or even employment as an approximation); not all retail sales will translate into more demand for retail space. How e-commerce (as a percentage of total retail sales) will change going forward is still being determined.

---

[13] See for example the paper titled "Household formation, housing prices, and public policy impacts" by Börsch-Supan, A. "Household formation, housing prices, and public policy impacts." *Journal of Public Economics* 30(2) (1986): 145–164.

[14] The other subtype that falls under industrial space is *manufacturing*. The use of manufacturing space does *not* allow itself to be explained well by employment levels in the said industry. The main reason is the automation of jobs in manufacturing. For example, in the U.S., we find that the number of jobs in manufacturing has *decreased* in recent decades, even though the output of factories *increased* measured by real value during this same time period. Thus, expected output would be a better demand shock in this case. However, manufacturing space is typically developed and operated by the manufacturing firm itself, rather than by real estate investors, as these are highly specialized operations. The firms will make a separate NPV decision on whether to create extra manufacturing space (this relates to the concept of "investment value" we will introduce in Chapter 14). Sometimes a manufacturer might sell some types of manufacturing property to a tax-exempt investor (such as a pension fund) and rent it back on a long-term lease, primarily to minimize corporate income taxes. (Also known as a "sale/leaseback".) However, in such cases, the lease contracts are very long (at least 10 years); thus, the space market forecasting exercise is mostly moot.

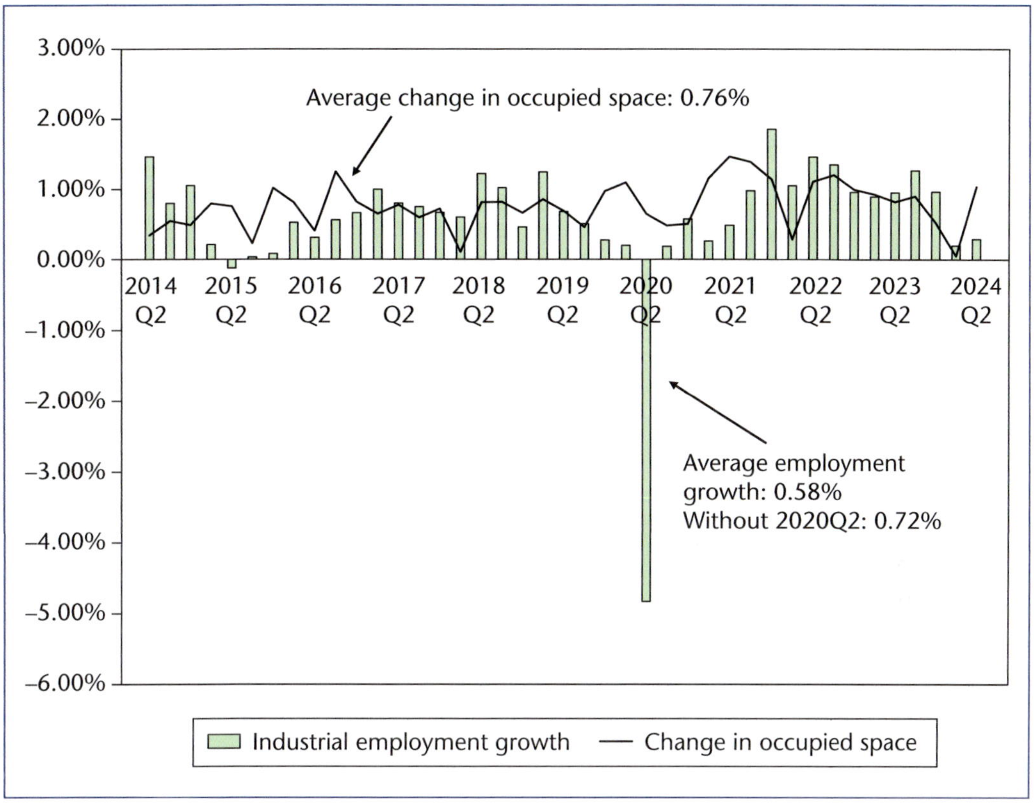

EXHIBIT 8-8 Change in Occupied Warehouse Space and Industrial Employment in Dallas (TX) Metro Area.

Source: Compstak and BLS.

Looking at the same Fred data as before, it seems e-commerce has stalled somewhat in the last few years. For example, e-commerce's percentage of total sales was 15 percent in 2020 (recall that it was 16 percent in 2024).

In this section, we provided the main (exogenous) drivers of demand for real estate space for the main property types. Employment growth is a good approximation of demand for space, although it is most appropriate for office space. Population growth is also a good predictor of the need for housing units for the housing market. Exhibit 8-9 provides a summary of the main drivers, plus some additional drivers that could be used as well in case of data limitations. For example, if retail sales are unavailable, changes in disposable income could also help predict said sales. We provide additional discussion on the demand for specialty property types (like hotels and self-storage) in the online supplemental materials corresponding to this Chapter.

*8.3 FORMAL MODEL OF SPACE MARKET EQUILIBRIUM DYNAMICS AND CYCLICALITY

The presentation of space market analysis in this chapter has been motivated especially by the importance of forecasting the future of the relevant space market for the real estate investor. The future determines the success of real estate investment, especially and most fundamentally, the future of the space market in which the investment property is located. To help the interested reader gain a basic familiarity with formal space market equilibrium forecasting, this section will present a simplified numerical example of a system of articulated supply, demand, and construction models

EXHIBIT 8-9

Summary of the Main Drivers of Demand for Different Real Estate Space

Property type	Demand driver
Single-Family (Owner-occupied)	**- Population**
	- Interest rates
	- Employment
Multi-Family (Rental)	**- Population**
	- Young population
	- Employment (*Blue color*)
Retail	**- Retail sales**
	- Disposable income
	- Retail employment
Office	**- FIRE employment**
Warehouse	**- Inventory**
	- Warehouse employment
	- Transportation employment

with price response elasticities and lags based on the earlier equations (1) and (2). Such a system of models is beneficial not only to help you get an idea of how more sophisticated real estate market forecasting is done and to derive some classical principles of real estate market dynamics, such as the potentially cyclical nature of many real estate space markets. (The general type examined here is often called a **stock-flow model**.) Formal modeling described here can allow a more rigorous and explicit quantitative forecast of future rents and vacancies and facilitate longer-term forecasts. This section also serves as a helpful conceptual basis for the forecasting analysis presented in Chapter 9, and as a sort of "bridge" connecting the Quadrant Model of Chapter 6 to the space market analysis tools discussed in both this and the next chapter.

Here, our simple dynamic model of a space market is represented by a system of six linked equations that reflect the relationship among supply, demand, construction, rent, and vacancy over time. The equations are linked because the output from each equation represents input in another equation, forming a complete representation of the market equilibrium over time across all six equations. The system will allow the simulation and forecast of rents, vacancy, construction, and absorption in the market each year.

The first two equations reflect the supply side of the market. Equation (1) is a model of the development industry, relating construction completions (new additions to the supply of space in the market) to rents prevailing in the market at the time when the construction projects are started.

Equation 5a

$$C_t = \begin{cases} \varepsilon\left(R_{t-L} - K\right), & \textit{if } R_{t-L} > K, \\ 0, \textit{otherwise} \end{cases}$$

C_t is the amount of new space completed in year t, and K is the replacement cost rent. R_{t-L} is the rent prevailing in the market in year $t - L$. Because construction takes time, there is a **lag** between when construction decisions are made (when the rents that trigger that decision are observed) and when new supply is completed. This lag is expressed in the model by the parameter L, which is the time it takes to complete the typical construction project in the market. There is also a "trigger rent" (like the replacement cost rent discussed in Chapter 7), above which new construction will start and below which no new construction will start. This trigger rent level is indicated by K, where values exceed the cost to create. The supply elasticity is reflected by the parameter *E*, which determines the amount of new construction started per dollar by which the current rent exceeds the trigger rent. Greater values of E indicate that development responds more elastically to rents; that is, more new supply will be built for each dollar that rents rise above the trigger level.

Equation (5b) states that the total stock of space supply in year *t*, labeled S_t, equals the previous year's stock, S_{t-1}, plus the new construction completed in year *t*. This equation is similar to the second line in Equation (2) before.

Equation 5b

$$S_t = S_{t-1} + C_t$$

Two more equations portray the demand side of the space usage market. Equation (3) is the demand model, relating the amount of space potential users would like to occupy, D_t, to the current rent level, R_t, and the current level of underlying need, N_t.

Equation 5c

$$D_t = \alpha - \eta R_t + \tau N_t$$

The measure of need reflects the fundamental sources of space usage demand discussed in the previous section. For example, for office markets, N_t might be measured by the number of office employees working in the market. The three parameters, α, β, and τ, calibrate the demand model. The parameter α is a constant or "intercept" for the model. The response sensitivity parameter η reflects the price elasticity of demand. In contrast, the parameter τ reflects the "technology" of space usage, reflecting the quantity of space usage demanded per unit of underlying need. For example, if N_t is the number of office employees, then η would represent the number of square feet per employee.

We assume it takes one year for space users to implement or realize the level of space usage demand they desire (due, for example, to the time required to find the necessary space and move into it or, in the case of reductions in space demand, to vacate space and get out of leases). So, equation (5c) equates the amount of space actually occupied at time *t*, OS_t, to the demand in the previous year, D_{t-1}. The previous year's demand is just the output of equation (3) applied in the previous period.

Equation 5d

$$OS_t = D_{t-1}$$

The fifth equation in the system defines the vacancy rate, V_t, as the fraction of the currently available stock of space that is currently unoccupied. This is similar to the second line in equation (2).

Equation 5e

$$V_t = (S_t - OS_t)/S_t$$

Note that the variables on the right-hand side of equation (5e) are outputs from equations (5b) and (5d).

Finally, the system is completed by equation (5e), which represents landlord- and tenant-rental-pricing behavior. Landlords are assumed to raise or lower rents in response to perceived contemporaneous vacancy rates. In particular, if current vacancy rates are above the (time-invariant) natural vacancy rate for the market, labeled V_n, then landlords will reduce rents. If current vacancy rates are below the natural rate, landlords will raise rents. The sensitivity of rental response to vacancy-rate deviations from the natural rate is reflected in the response parameter λ. It is assumed that it takes a year for landlords to respond effectively to changes in the market (perhaps due to the difficulty of accurately observing the market or a sluggish response to the market).

Equation 5f

$$R_t = R_{t-1} \times (1 - \lambda\{[V_t - V_n]/V_n\})$$

The above six equations present a complete dynamic real estate space market system, including market supply, demand, and construction. By quantifying the parameters in the equations, the decision-relevant characteristics of the market equilibrium can be simulated through time. Such a model would be specified and calibrated in a realistic application using econometric techniques. It is also possible to build explicit links to the capital market into the model, for example, by relating the trigger rent, *K*, to capital market parameters such as real interest rates.

To see how such a model of the real estate space market can simulate the functioning of the market over time, consider an office market that starts with an employment level of 70,000, a stock of 20 million SF of built space, a vacancy rate of 10 percent (equal to its natural vacancy rate), and a rent level of $20/SF (equal to the replacement cost rent, *K*). Next, suppose system parameters with the following numerical values characterize this market:

- Supply sensitivity $\varepsilon = 0.3$
- Demand sensitivity $\eta = 0.3$
- Technology $\tau = 200$ SF/employee
- Demand intercept $\alpha = 10$ million SF
- Rent sensitivity $\lambda = 0.3$
- Construction lag $L = 3$ years
- Replacement cost rent $K = \$20$

Exhibit 8-10 shows the 60-year evolution of rents, vacancy rate, and construction in such a market if the employment level grows steadily at 1 percent per year. The left-hand vertical scale in the exhibit shows the equilibrium level of rent (in $/SF), the vacancy rate (in percent), and the level of office employment in the market. The right-hand vertical scale measures the amount of new construction in millions of square feet per year. The graph traces the annual levels of each of these variables, starting from the steady state described earlier.

The cyclical nature of the resulting market dynamics is evident in this model. With the response and lag parameter values cited, this space market has a cycle of approximately 11 years. This real estate cycle exists even though there is no cycle, just steady growth, in the underlying source of the demand for space usage (employment), and even though there is no "lumpiness" in the provision of new space (buildings can be built in any size). The example depicted in Exhibit 8-10 demonstrates several features that tend to characterize real estate space market cycles.

- The real estate cycle may be different from and partially independent of the underlying business cycle in the local economy.
- The cycle will be much more exaggerated in the construction and development industry than in other aspects of the real estate market, such as rents and vacancy.
- The vacancy cycle tends to lead the rent cycle slightly (vacancy peaks before rent bottoms).
- New construction completions tend to peak when vacancy peaks.

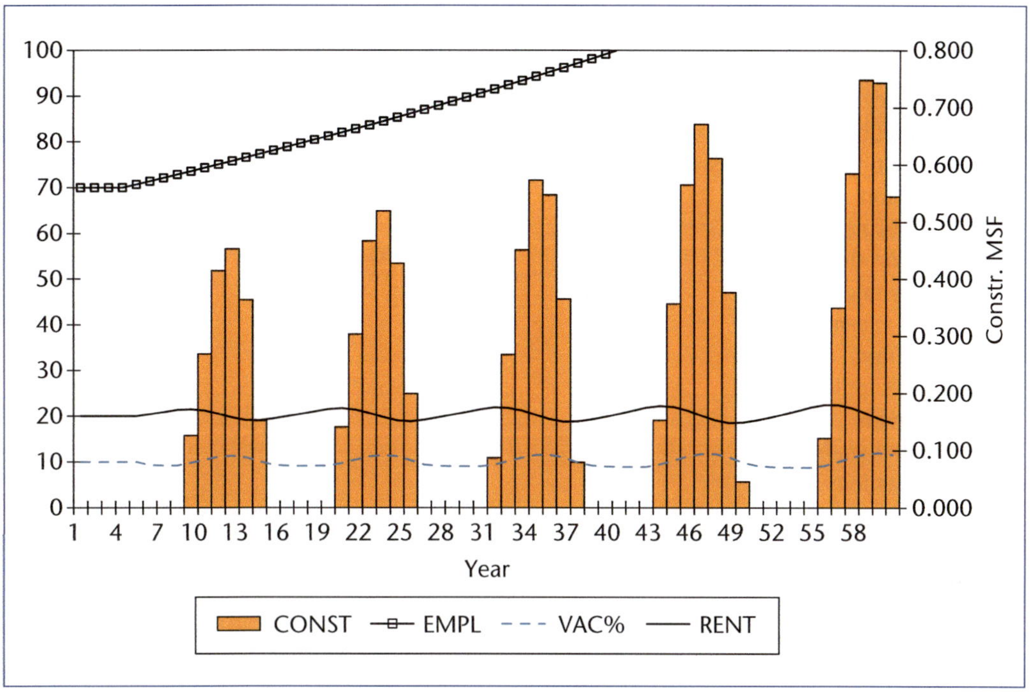

EXHIBIT 8-10 Simulated Space Market Dynamics.

The existence of a "built-in" cycle in the real estate space market, and indeed the specific features of the cycle noted, can result from several characteristics of the model described here. The particular response sensitivities and lags determine the market's cyclicality, and, more fundamentally, the myopic or adaptive nature of the behavior of the market participants tends to produce cyclicality. In this model, the market participants (developers, landlords, and tenants) base their decisions on present and past information rather than on forecasts of the future. Actual behavior in realistic markets is not as simple as this model depicts. Market participants do try to forecast the future, primarily through the role that the real estate asset market plays in the overall system, and also given the prevalence of long-term leases in many markets (though such leases can also exacerbate cyclicality by dampening responsiveness in rental price and space occupancy). Nevertheless, the simple model shown here probably does capture an essential part of real estate market behavior since market participants may not always put as much effort into basing decisions on future forecasts as they should, and even if they did, those forecasts would never be perfect.

8.4 CHAPTER SUMMARY

This chapter presented the basic elements of real estate space market analysis, with a particular motivation and view toward forecasting the economic characteristics that can determine the success of real estate investment, in particular, the prevailing market rent and vacancy levels. The elements and methods used in market analysis are based on the more fundamental urban economic and geographic principles discussed in the previous chapters, but are focused more specifically on practical concerns of real estate investors and developers. In this chapter, we have introduced how an articulated system of supply and demand models of the space market (including the construction industry) can be used to reveal some general patterns in the dynamics of these markets, thereby laying the groundwork for a deeper dive into rent forecasting in the next chapter.

KEY TERMS

- Real estate market analysis
- Market segment
- Construction starts
- Construction completions
- Absorption
- Gross absorption
- Net absorption
- Vacancy rate
- Natural vacancy rate
- Market rent
- Months supply
- Submarkets
- Structural analysis
- Price elasticity
- Lags
- Demand drivers
- Stock-flow model
- Real estate cycle

STUDY QUESTIONS

In Your Own Words

8.1 What is the difference between a micro-level market analysis and a general characterization of a real estate market?

8.2 What are the two dimensions normally involved in defining a relevant real estate market?

8.3 Name and define the major supply and demand variables and indicators of market balance for real estate space usage markets.

8.4 In computing the market vacancy rate, how should one treat space that is leased but unoccupied and available for sublease?

8.5 Why is it normal for there to be some vacancy even in a healthy, well-functioning real estate market?

8.6 What is the relationship among the current market vacancy rate, the natural vacancy rate, and the direction of change in market rents?

8.7 What characteristics of a market are associated with a higher natural vacancy rate?

8.8 Why is net absorption a better measure of demand growth in a market than gross absorption?

8.9 Discuss how you can use the months supply measure of vacant space in a market, combined with knowledge of the typical length of time to complete construction projects, to judge whether the market is likely to be able to absorb additional new construction.

8.10 Describe the major quantifiable drivers of demand for the principal types of real estate.

8.11 What are the major features characterizing cycles in the real estate space usage market according to the basic stock-flow model?

8.12 What is meant by myopic or adaptive behavior by market participants in the stock-flow model?

8.13 Do you think some cycles for a given property type are faster or slower in some markets?

Check Your Knowledge

8.14 What is the main goal of a real estate market analysis?
A) To calculate construction costs
B) To forecast rent and vacancy trends
C) To examine historical rent data only
D) To estimate property management fees

8.15 Which type of analysis focuses on a specific site or user?
A) Macro analysis
B) Market segmentation
C) Feasibility analysis
D) General market analysis

8.16 Which of the following is an example of a Class A property?
A) An outdated office building with few amenities
B) A newer, premium property with high rent and a desirable location
C) A vacant lot zoned for residential use
D) A small, rural apartment complex

8.17 Which organization primarily tracks employment in the United States, helping forecast office space demand?
A) Census Bureau
B) Bureau of Labor Statistics (BLS)
C) Federal Reserve
D) Department of Housing and Urban Development

8.18 Why might the vacancy rate in a real estate market exceed the natural vacancy rate?
A) Supply and demand are perfectly balanced
B) New construction exceeds current demand
C) There is a shortage of rental properties
D) Demand is growing faster than supply

8.19 How does e-commerce growth impact warehouse demand compared to retail demand?
A) Decreases warehouse and retail demand
B) Increases warehouse demand, decreases retail demand
C) Decreases warehouse demand, increases retail demand
D) Increases both warehouse and retail demand

8.20 Suppose a certain market has 1 million SF of currently vacant space, 2 million SF of space under construction, and annual absorption of 1.5 million SF. What is the months supply in this market? If the average project takes two years to complete, would you say this market is oversupplied, meaning that there is no need to pursue any new development projects?

Chapter Case: Office Market Dynamics in Innovia Valley

During the pandemic, many tech companies in Innovia Valley, a major tech hub, adopted full work-from-home policies. "TechNow," one of the leading tech firms in the region, not only transitioned to WFH but also expanded its workforce by 25% to meet rising demand for digital products and services. Despite the increased headcount, TechNow did not expand its office space and maintained its pre-2020 office space.

In 2024, TechNow shifted to a hybrid work model, requiring employees to come into the office 2 days a week. To accommodate the larger workforce within the same office space, TechNow reduced space per employee from 200 square feet to 100 square feet and adopted a hot-desking system, where employees share workspaces.

The shift in office space demand has affected Innovia Valley's commercial real estate market, causing the vacancy rate to increase from a pre-pandemic level of 10% to a current rate of 18%. Office development projects initiated prior to the pandemic are now nearing completion.

In response, landlords in Innovia Valley are offering concessions, resulting in a 15% drop in effective rents compared to asking rents.

Key Market Data

- Natural Vacancy Rate: 12%
- Average Asking Rent: $65 per square foot per year
- Effective Rent: $55 per square foot per year (after concessions)
- Net Absorption: –500,000 square feet (more space vacated than leased)
- Space Under Construction: 3 million square feet, to be completed in the next year
- Total Office Supply: 50 million square feet in Innovia Valley's central business district

Forecast the office space demand in Innovia Valley and answer the following questions.

1. What does a vacancy rate of 18% in the Innovia Valley office market, compared to a natural vacancy rate of 12%, suggest about market conditions?
   A) Strong demand and rising rents
   B) Balanced market conditions
   C) Oversupply, likely putting downward pressure on rents
   D) Shortage of available office space
2. What is one potential challenge TechNow may face if it attempts to sublease some of its office space in the current Innovia Valley market?
   A) Difficulty finding subtenants willing to pay high rents due to high market vacancy
   B) Increased costs due to rising rent rates
   C) Lack of demand for subleased space in a fully remote environment
   D) Overcrowding in its remaining office space
3. What does the negative net absorption (–500,000 square feet) indicate about demand for office space in Innovia Valley?
   A) Demand for office space is increasing rapidly
   B) Demand for office space is decreasing, with more space being vacated than leased
   C) Demand and supply are in balance
   D) Office space supply is insufficient
4. Why might effective rent be a more accurate measure of market conditions than asking rent in a high-vacancy environment like Innovia Valley's?
   A) Effective rent includes concessions, showing the true income landlords receive
   B) Effective rent is always higher than asking rent
   C) Asking rent is always lower than effective rent
   D) Effective rent excludes all concessions
5. How does a sustained high vacancy rate (18%) and high months supply affect development decisions in Innovia Valley?
   A) Encourages new office construction due to rising demand
   B) Discourages new development to avoid further increasing vacancy
   C) Has no impact on development decisions
   D) Increases rental rates for new developments

6. How has TechNow's adoption of hybrid work and reduced space per employee affected the company's office space needs?
   A) It has increased the company's demand for additional office space
   B) It has likely decreased its long-term office space needs
   C) It has led to overcrowding issues requiring immediate expansion
   D) It has no impact on space requirements
7. What long-term effect might the adoption of hybrid work models across the tech industry have on the natural vacancy rate in Innovia Valley?
   A) Decrease the natural vacancy rate
   B) Increase the natural vacancy rate as companies need less space
   C) Stabilize the natural vacancy rate at pre-pandemic levels
   D) Remove the need for tracking vacancy rates
8. What adjustments might landlords in Innovia Valley make to attract tech companies with hybrid work policies?
   A) Increase the amount of dedicated desks
   B) Offer shorter, flexible leases and adapt spaces for collaborative use
   C) Remove all shared spaces
   D) Eliminate concessions and increase rental rates
9. How should Innovia Valley office space that is leased but currently unoccupied and available for sublease be treated in the calculation of the vacancy rate?
   A) It should be excluded from the vacancy rate because it is leased.
   B) It should be counted in the vacancy rate, as it is not being actively used.
   C) It should only be counted if the lease is nearing expiration.
   D) It should be counted as half of the total square footage to reflect partial vacancy.

9 Forecasting The Space Market II

Estimating Cash Flow Growth

CHAPTER OUTLINE

LEARNING OBJECTIVES

After reading this chapter, you should understand:

- How to provide the analyst with a deeper understanding of real estate market analytics and rent forecasts.
- That real estate analysts should use as localized data as possible for the space market.
- How to provide a framework for more advanced statistical approaches to rent forecasts.
- How simulation and sensitivity analysis might be useful tools for risk analysis.
- How to provide the real estate investor with a realistic consideration of real depreciation and how that impacts the DCF proforma and returns, including all components of depreciation, physical, technological, or obsolescence, and locational.
- Renovations of buildings tend to be lumpy when they are upgraded in order to remain competitive.
- That buildings can appreciate from external location sources or depreciate from the same, and those in locations becoming more valuable are lucky and survive a longer economic life.
- That depreciation is non-linear and tends to slow over time for buildings that survive locational obsolescence.
- Among the operating expenses that have grown exponentially are property insurance rates, which are expected to continue to grow rapidly with climate change.

 DOI: 10.1201/9781003643838-11

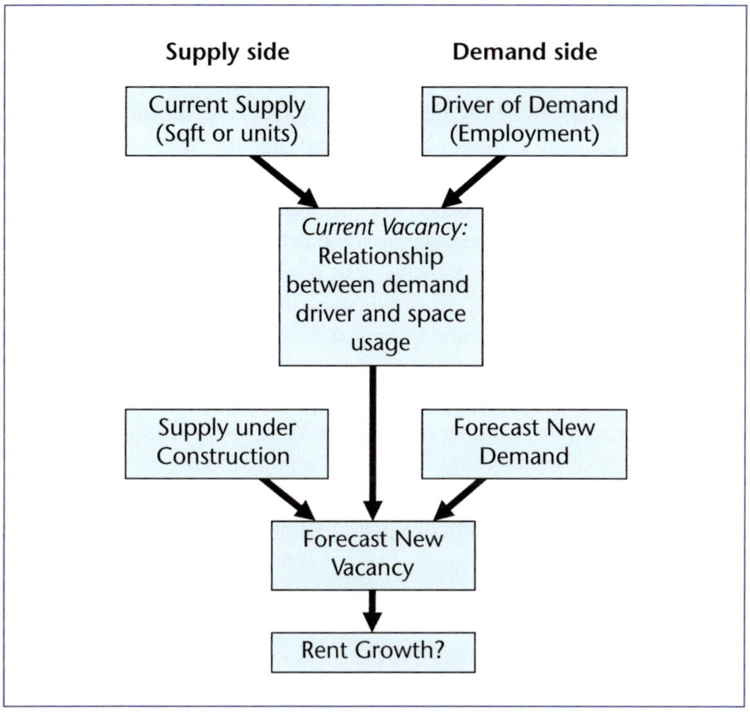

EXHIBIT 9-1 Generic Framework of a Basic Short-Term Structural Market Analysis for Real Estate.

In the previous Chapter, we discussed the main space market fundamentals used for forecasting: rent, net construction, net absorption, and vacancy. We also discussed how these are related in the long run and presented the main drivers of demand for space by property type. In this Chapter, we will take you deeper into the forecasting exercise which is so important for the real estate investor. The aim is to use the basics from the previous chapter to formulate an actual numerical forecast. Broadly, the forecasting expertise we present in this chapter has two purposes. First, we will give you tools you can apply yourself with a basic knowledge of statistics. Secondly, we hope to build your intuition and understanding of modern professional analytical real estate market forecasting, including an appreciation of both the strengths and limitations of these tools. And we will show how the resulting rent forecast is used in our DCF evaluation of a subject property. For this purpose, this chapter will also discuss the real economic depreciation of the property building structure, its impact on the forecast, as well as how to project the potential gross income for a property with multiple (vintage) leases.

9.1 FORECASTING RENTAL GROWTH

Forecasting is difficult but necessary. We start with a simple forecasting exercise that can provide some indication of where the market is going. Subsequently, in a starred Section 9.1.2, we provide a formal regression analysis that provides an actual growth parameter (g).

9.1.1 Simple Structural Analysis

Here, we review the major steps and tasks involved in conducting a structural market analysis at a very basic level, a level that will often suffice for short- to medium-term forecasts of space market conditions (up to about three years in the future). Exhibit 9-1 presents an overview of the tasks involved in a typical analysis of this type. Seven separate tasks are identified. Notice that the tasks involve analysis of both the supply and demand side of the market, with two tasks focusing on each side of the market separately and two tasks integrating across the two sides.

The first steps in the structural market analysis are to inventory the existing supply of space and to identify the fundamental sources of the demand for space usage in the relevant market. Supply inventories are available from local brokerage firms, local planning agencies, and commercial firms specializing in providing this type of data.[1] The fundamental sources of demand are the drivers of the need for space usage in the market, which are discussed in detail in Chapter 8. In the case of office space, we identify office employment as the main driver, for example.

The next step in the structural market analysis is to relate the underlying demand sources to the amount of real estate space usage demand. In some cases, this will be straightforward because of the nature of the market. For example, there should be approximately a one-to-one correspondence between the number of households and the number of housing units demanded (except for special markets such as student housing). However, in other markets, it will be necessary to relate, for example, the number of square feet of space required to the number of employees of a given occupation. This can be done by comparing the square footage of various types of space identified in the supply stock inventory to the number of employees of various occupations identified in the demand side analysis. For example, for Boston office space, we identified the amount of square footage that is going up, currently sitting at 240 square feet per employee, while in Washington, D.C., it is significantly lower and has been trending lower over time. This is why localized data is essential for accurate market assessment.

Next, one must develop forecasts of future demand for and supply of space in the relevant market. On the demand side, the sources of demand previously identified must be projected based on the extrapolation of past trends or judgments about the evolution of the local economic base. In the case of our Boston office example, the BLS expects office jobs to grow at 70 basis points (0.7%) annually in the coming 10 years. This equates to approximately 6,000 office jobs per year. (In 2023, there were 844 thousand office jobs in the Boston metro area.)

On the supply side, this step involves inventorying the construction pipeline, which involves identifying all projects currently under construction and projects in various stages of planning. This information could be found by researching construction permits issued by local governments and public information. Also, local business and financial newspapers typically announce major construction projects that receive financing. However, not all projects that are planned will actually be built, so the quantification of the construction pipeline will involve some judgment or estimation using the percentage of applications that are most likely based on historical analysis. In older neighborhoods or regions, it is critical to add an estimation of the demolition and abandonment of existing occupied space in this step of the analysis. The result of this step is a projection of **new net space** that is expected to be added to the market at various times in the near future. That being said, if we return to our Boston office market, CoStar reports that in 2024, approximately 7 million (net) square feet is under development. Assuming no new construction will occur, all of this square footage will be delivered in three to five years.

The result of a basic structural analysis, as described here, is some projection of the future relationship between supply and demand in the market. In Exhibit 9-2, we put all the numbers together for the Boston office market for the coming five years based on data and projections from the BLS and CoStar. In the first row, we grow the existing stock by the properties under development. (We ignore demolitions and conversions here.) In the second row, we have grown office employment from 844 thousand now to 874 thousand in 5 years (6,000 new jobs a year). If we multiply this by the average square footage by the square feet per employee, we assume a net absorption of over 7 million square feet. As a result, we do not expect the overall vacancy levels to change much. Indeed, the construction pipeline (6.8 million SF) more or less equals the increase in demand for space (7.2 million SF).

In the near term (say, one to three years in the future), this type of analysis can be fairly accurate and result in a quantitative projection of the magnitude of space supply shortfall or surplus. What

[1] For example, CoStar, MSCI, REIS (Moody's), RealPage, Compstak, Atlus and Reonomy.

EXHIBIT 9-2

Example of Short-Run Forecast of Space Market for Boston Office

	Formula	Now	In 5 years	Difference
Net Current Inventory	S + C	223,954,598	230,766,696	6,812,099
Employees	5 years × 6,000	844,000	874,000	30,000
Net Absorption	30,000 empl × 240 sq ft	26,574,343	26,186,442	(387,902)
Vacancy rate	VS/S	11.87%	11.35%	–0.52%

Source: BLS and CoStar.

tends to trip up some such analyses in the real world are unexpected downturns in the underlying economy or the failure to foresee a turning point in a market cycle. Analysts should be on their guard against getting caught up in prevailing conventional assumptions or extrapolations of recent past trends, and conclusions should be elaborated by including sensitivity analyses of the effects on forecasts of changes in underlying assumptions.

With this in mind, market supply/demand balance projections may have various decision implications. For example, it might appear that within three years, there will be a demand for a million more square feet of office space in a certain market than is currently in the construction pipeline. If typical projects are around 500,000 square feet, then this suggests a need for two new such projects. Alternatively, the projection might indicate that excess supply will continue in the market even after three years, with no need for new projects.

In general, the projected tightening of the market (as indicated by a growing space shortfall) should lead to higher rents and lower vacancy rates, and a projected surplus of supply will lead to rising vacancy rates and falling rents. This relates not only to construction and development decisions but also to other types of real estate decisions. Leasing decisions can be enlightened by such a market analysis as well. For example, a landlord may hesitate to commit to a long-term lease at a low rent if the market is projected to tighten. Investment in existing structures will appear more profitable the greater the projected future space supply shortfall (other things being equal, in particular, the price of the property), for this would imply better prospects for future rental growth or greater ease of leasing currently vacant space.

Even though the method described in this section is simple to employ and provides a broad understanding of where rents might be going, it has several drawbacks. The most obvious drawback is that we cannot formulate an exact rental growth expectation (g) using this method; we *need* this number for our DCF. In our Boston office example, the fact that the vacancy remains similar in the coming years may mean rents will grow at a historic rate. In the last decade, office rents in this market grew by 5 percent annually (or 3 percent in real terms). Is it fair to expect such growth rates in the coming years? Another area for possible improvement is that such an approach does not allow for long-term forecasts because it needs to consider the dynamic relationship between the main endogenous variables. Lower vacancies will spur development, which decreases rents, and so forth, as discussed with the Quadrant Model in Chapter 6 and the analytical model of Chapter 8. Both issues can be solved by **regression analysis**. The results of such an analysis are given in Exhibit 9-3. Here, you get an actual growth number (g) plus some formal confidence in your forecast accuracy. This model's (complex) details are laid out in the next (starred) Section, 9.1.2. Even though regression analysis is an advanced topic and, therefore, not for everyone, it is important to acknowledge that it exists and is being used by some of the largest firms serving the real estate investment industry (like CBRE). This model predicts nominal rents to grow by approximately 3.4 percent per annum. The expected inflation during this same period is 2.4 percent (source: Fred), for a modest 1 percent growth in real terms per annum (a third compared to 2012–2022 real growth rate levels). Simple statistical trends can also be used for rent forecasts, but they do not control the nuances as well as regression approaches discussed below.

*9.1.2 A Regression-Based Forecast

Regression analysis is the basic statistical method that can empirically calibrate a dynamic space model system such as the stock-flow model introduced in Section 8.3 of the last chapter. In essence, regression allows you to estimate (linear) relationships between multiple variables. We have multiple related equations in a real estate space market's structural model. The **Vector Autoregressive Model (VAR)** is a popular time series regression model that can produce forecasts for such a system. With a VAR, you relate your variable of interest (rent, for example) to the **lags** of the other endogenous variables, such as new construction and vacancy. The exogenous shock (like employment) is entered contemporaneously. For our purposes, the VAR specification would look something like the simultaneous system labeled as equation (1) below.

Equation 1

$$\Delta R_t = \lambda_1 + \lambda_{11}\Delta R_{t-1} + \lambda_{12}\Delta C_{t-1} + \lambda_{13}\Delta V_{t-1} + \lambda_{14}\Delta D_t + \varepsilon_{r,t}$$

$$\Delta C_t = \lambda_2 + \lambda_{21}\Delta R_{t-1} + \lambda_{22}\Delta C_{t-1} + \lambda_{23}\Delta V_{t-1} + \lambda_{24}\Delta D_t + \varepsilon_{c,t}$$

$$\Delta V_t = \lambda_3 + \lambda_{31}\Delta R_{t-1} + \lambda_{32}\Delta C_{t-1} + \lambda_{33}\Delta V_{t-1} + \lambda_{34}\Delta D_t + \varepsilon_{v,t}$$

Where;

- Δ is the symbol that differences the variables to % change per period t. For example, $\Delta R_t = (R_t - R_{t-1})/R_{t-1}$.
- t is the time period of observation. For example, 2020Q1.
- ΔR is the % change in rent in period t.
- ΔC is the % change in net new construction in period t.
- ΔV is the % change in vacancy rate in period t.
- ΔD is the % change in the demand driver in period t (for example, office employment).
- λ is the "parameter" which relates the variables on the right-hand side of the equal sign to the variable of interest on the left-hand side. For example, if λ_{12} would be –1, it means that a 1% increase in construction levels in the previous period (ΔC_{t-1}) would decrease rents by 1% now (other things being equal). These parameters may be estimated by the basic statistical technique known as ordinary least squares (OLS); see below.
- ε are the "residuals," meaning how "wrong" the model is (in the historical empirical data it is based on) in predicting rent, new construction, and vacancy levels in every period t.

To illustrate concretely, consider the rent equation. We first see a parameter called λ_1. This is a constant and "captures" a long-run trend (if available) in rent. For example, an estimate of 1% for λ_1 would mean that rents grew by approximately 1% per quarter on average on their own (that is, other things equal, without the "help" of the other variables). The second rent parameter, denoted λ_{11}, relates rent changes to their own historic rent change. (This is the "Autoregressive" or "AR" part of the VAR.) If this parameter is negative, rents tend to self-correct (i.e., they are mean-reverting). If this parameter is positive, rents tend to have momentum (rent growth tends to be followed by more rent growth or decline by more decline). The remaining parameters, $\lambda_{12,}$ $\lambda_{13,}$ and λ_{14}, tell the relationship between (past) changes in construction levels, (past) changes in vacancy levels, and (current) changes in demand for space.

The obvious question is: *how do we determine the values for λ?* This is the process known as statistical "estimation." To estimate the λ parameters, we focus first on the residuals, denoted ε. These residuals measure how "wrong" the model is at predicting each of the three dependent variables (ΔR_t, ΔC_t, ΔV_t) in each historical period "t" in the empirically observed on which the estimation is based. We put the word "wrong" in quotes because it is not a question of the model being "right" or "wrong" in some normative sense but rather a measure of how well the model *fits* the historical data.

The idea is to, in effect, try all the possible values of all of the λ parameters, to find the λ values that result in the smallest residual values, the ε values (also referred to as "errors"). We want the λ values that "fit" the model best to the past history.

For example, we could fix all the λ values to be 1. This would probably not be a good model, meaning it cannot describe rents really well with this set of parameters. As a result, the residuals will be large in any given period. Following this logic, we can estimate the (optimal) values for λ by following two simple rules. First, on average, the residuals must be zero. Sometimes, you will overestimate rent growth, and sometimes, you will underestimate rent growth in period *t*. However, the average (*over all t*) should be zero. (This makes the model "unbiased".) Unfortunately, this is not sufficient. For example, say we have two time series observations only. ("Time series" refers to data that spans across time, aka "longitudinal" data.) In model A, the residuals are -1% and +1% in the two periods of time. Next, say that by changing the parameters slightly (model B), we get residuals of -2% and +2%. In both cases, the average is zero. However, we would prefer Model A to Model B because its "errors" are smaller. Therefore, the second condition we impose for finding our optimal λ values is that we also want to minimize the *sum of the absolute values* of the residuals, or more precisely, for the OLS method, we minimize the *sum of the squared* residuals. In this example, the clear winner is Model A, whose sum of squared residuals is $(1^2 + (-1)^2 =)$ 1, whereas for Model B it is $(2^2 + (-2)^2 =)$ 8. Thus, one way to solve the equations and get the most optimal parameters is by naively simulating numerous unique sets of parameters and evaluating the fit per model ex-post. This could take a very long time, as the theoretical combinations are endless. Fortunately, a matrix operation exists that solves for the most optimal set of λ instantaneously. This matrix operation is called **Ordinary Least Squares (OLS)**. Even though the exact operation is outside the scope of this book, most statistical software will have this built-in, including Excel.[2]

Equation (1) is estimated by OLS line-by-line. (The order does not matter for our purposes.) This allows us to forecast rent. For example, say that a change in demand for space (ΔD) would impact rent and new construction one-for-one ($\lambda_{14} = 1$, and $\lambda_{24} = 1$) and vacancy in a negative way ($\lambda_{34} = -0.5$). Before this period, all variables were flat (so there was zero change in any variable beforehand), and the constant is also estimated to be zero for all lines in equation (1). Suppose the demand driver is office employment; suppose in period "t" it changes from 100,000 to 101,000 (a +1% change). In such a setting, according to equation (1), rents would go up in period "t" by 1%, new development (net construction) would go up by 1%, and vacancy would decrease by 0.5%. For the *next* period forecast, we must now consider that the endogenous variables (Rent, Construction, Vacancy) have changed and thus impact subsequent rent through λ_{11}, λ_{12}, and λ_{13}. We will keep doing this iteratively until we reach our intended forecast period. In practice, most software packages will do this for you.

In the above example, we have made several simplifications for ease of illustration. For one thing, model building is not merely an exercise in finding the best λ parameters. It is also a matter of designing the best model in terms of "specification" of the best variables to include. Also, we need to decide on the best lags, which variables should be lagged by how much (e.g., "t-1" or "t-2" or both "t-1" *and* "t-2", and so forth). The lag specification is particularly important for forecasting. In the above example, we only allowed for one lag (and no lag at all on the demand driver variable). Alternatively, you might find that vacancy two quarters ago (ΔV_{t-2}) still impacts rents concurrently. In such a case, you might want to take up two lags in your VAR. As you do not know the ideal lag length ex-ante, you would typically try a few different lag lengths and pick the model that would produce the best fit.[3]

Another complexity lies in the difference operator (Δ). It is quite standard to take up the changes in variables when estimating a VAR, as we did in equation (1). However, it is not always needed. The statistics behind this are rather complex. The gist is as follows: A trending variable must be

---

[2] On our website you can find a primer on regression analysis in Excel. Although we do recommend other, more specialized, software like R or Python, if you really want to become an expert market analyst.

[3] The Akaike Information Criterium (AIC) is a popular of comparing model fit for VAR models.

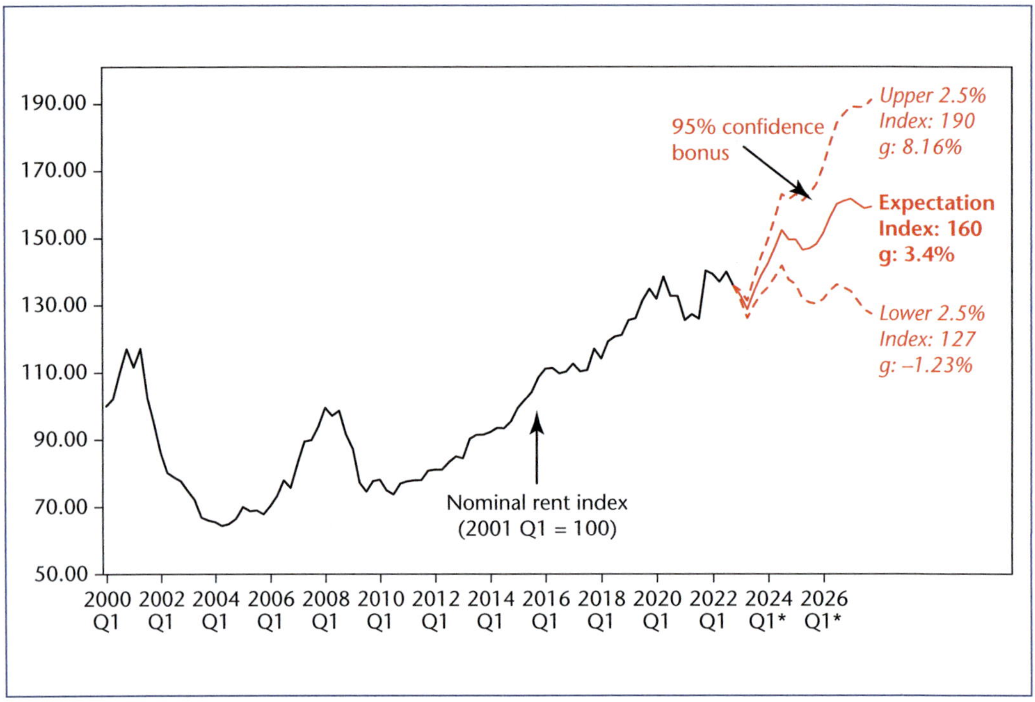

EXHIBIT 9-3 5-Year Forecast of Nominal Effective Rent with Confidence Bounds for Boston Office Market Using a Vector Autoregressive Model (VAR).

Source: Own calculations using: BLS and CoStar data.

differenced *first* before it can be taken up in the VAR. With trending, we mean a variable generally going up or down in our sample.[4]

Finally, what happens if you do not have a forecast for the exogenous variables, in our case, the demand driver variable? In the case of a model of the office market, the BLS has employment forecasts which we can use. However, this might be different for different regions or property subtypes. One solution is to forecast the exogenous variable using the same VAR methodology just described. You just add a line to equation (1) with the exogenous variable on the left-hand side of the equal sign and estimate that model as well. Most of its parameters will be zero if you do not expect endogeneity. However, there might still be a long-run trend or autoregressive component that still yields results, making the exogenous variable forecastable as well. To forecast that variable, you can also run a separate VAR with the particular exogenous variable (such as office employment) and other more relevant variables.

Even though formal forecasting models can be challenging to develop, the results are essential and directly usable by real estate investors. Professional investors are increasingly using such formal forecasting with assistance from various so-called AI (artificial intelligence) programs such as ChatGPT Plus, Co-pilot, Claude, Google Gemini, Hugging Face, and others. Exhibit 9-3 shows an example of an expected growth of 3.4 in rent in nominal terms per annum in the coming five years. (g = [(160 – 136) / 136] / 5 = 3.4%) The exhibit shows the history as a single solid black line. This history provides the empirical data on which the forecasting model is estimated. The solid red line

[4] The exact statistic that would tell you whether a variable is trending or not, is called the Augmented Dickey Fuller (ADF) test. The exact phraseology for a non-trending variable is called stationary. Thus, you only want stationary variables in your VAR. For example, in our case, we found that vacancy levels are stationary on their own, and therefore did not need to be differenced. We still did this anyway to keep everything comparable and relatively simple.

provides the future forecast (beyond the available history). This provides the g parameter needed in our DCF, as described in Chapters 4 and 5. Most statistical software packages will also provide **confidence intervals**, as shown in the Exhibit by the dashed red lines around the future forecast. In this case, the 95% confidence intervals are provided, meaning (based on historic performance) we believe that the forecast will be somewhere between the upper and lower intervals with 95% certainty, with 3.4% per annum growth being the expected value. Note that the width of the confidence intervals increases over time. This makes intuitive sense; errors tend to compound over time. Every forecast error we make in the first year will carry over to the next and beyond. Thus, after 5 years, we predict the rent index will have grown from 136 (in 2022Q4, this is when our rent data ends) to somewhere between 190 and 127 with 95% confidence, while 160 is the average, or "expectation" in probability terms. These confidence intervals can be useful for quantifying the risk in the investment. The next section discusses their use in more detail.

9.2 THE FORECAST IS ALWAYS WRONG

According to our VAR model (Exhibit 9-3), rent is expected to grow on average in the Boston market by 3.4 percent annually over the next five years. Given that inflation is expected to increase by 2.4 percent per year, this could be considered a modest growth (in real terms). It is important to recognize that this is a growth expectation in the market, not for individual existing properties. We will discuss the implications of this difference for constructing a property asset DCF valuation shortly. But first, let us note another fundamental consideration regarding the application of rent forecasting to property investment decision-making. Let us assume for now that the 3.4% forecasted growth rate is indeed the expectation that is relevant in property-level DCF analysis. The traditional DCF methodology treats the growth rate as deterministic. In other words, it is the projected outcome in the DCF with no uncertainty. Of course, in reality, the probability that the rental growth will be *precisely* 3.4 percent is close to zero. What it is, is the *most likely* outcome (according to our forecasting model); hence, we use it as our g parameter for our DCF.[5]

However, returning to Exhibit 9-3, we notice that the confidence bounds are relatively large around the future expectation. To be more precise, there is a 95% probability that the rental growth will average between 8.16% and -1.23% per year, with 3.4% being in the middle. This doesn't sound very precise! If you had heard from the weather bureau that the temperature would be between -10°C and +20°C tomorrow, with 95% certainty, you would still not know what to pack for your field trip.

To understand better what these confidence bounds represent, we must return to our bell-shaped curves introduced in Chapter 3. The bell-shaped curve represents the probability of certain outcomes (annual average rent growth percentage in our case). We plot the full distribution of the implied bell-shaped curve (by the confidence bounds) in Exhibit 9-4A. The horizontal axis gives the outcomes, or rental growth rates in our case, and the vertical axis provides the probability that each such growth rate outcome happens. In Exhibit 9-4A, we find that there is a 68% chance that the rental growth will be between +1 percent and +5.8 percent, and that the probability that the rental growth will exceed 8.2 percent per annum is less than 2.5%.[6] Any future outcome is possible, but with different (un-) certainty levels.

[5] In this specific case, the mean is the most likely outcome. That is, because we assume a normal standard distribution for the forecast error. With more nonstandard, asymmetric distributions, picking the mode of the distribution will provide the most likely outcome. However, with the standard normal distribution, the mode is equal to the mean.

[6] To make such bell-shaped curves yourself, you would need to know the standard deviation of forecast error, which the statistical package tells us is 2.39% in our model. Then you can use a Z-table to compute probabilities at any level, which are readily available online. For example, to compute the 95% confidence, you would have to take the mean (3.4%), and add/subtract 1.96 times the standard deviation (2.39%). The 1.96 comes from the Z-table. To get the 68% confidence, you would add/subtract one time the standard deviation to the mean, etc.

This uncertainty effectively represents the cash flow risk, as discussed in Chapter 4. We also previously discussed that setting the correct discount rate (at the cost of capital) captures this risk. The main point of the cash flow proforma is that the projections should be "unbiased," that is, "most likely" or "expected" amounts. Thus, a fair question would be, *do we care about such confidence bounds*? In the following two sub-sections, we will discuss cases where knowing the distribution of rental growth can be helpful.

9.2.1 Sensitivity and Simulation Analysis

Even though the denominator of the DCF valuation model captures risk, it nevertheless can provide very useful investment decision-making insight in many circumstances to go back and ask questions like: Even though I think it is most likely the market rents will grow on average at 2 percent per year, how would it change my proforma and my valuation if they grow only at 1 percent per year (or zero percent, or even negative 1 percent, for example)? Quantitatively exploring questions like this is called "**sensitivity analysis**," and it can indeed be a useful exercise. Such analysis tends to be most useful for examining specific contingencies, often related to the financial structuring of an investment in a real estate asset. For example, how low a rental growth rate will still enable the property's projected terminal reversion value to exceed a projected outstanding loan balance at that time on a mortgage used to finance the property acquisition.

The confidence bounds from our formal statistical forecast let you pick "bad" and "good" scenarios based on objective, statistical empirically based modeling. Our Boston office forecast found an average expectation of 3.4% rental growth. The confidence bounds from that forecast suggest that a particularly bad outcome would be -1.2 percent, as, based on the normal probability distribution, there is only a 2.5% chance that the rental growth will turn out worse than that. Likewise, a (very) good scenario could be 8.2 percent rental growth. (See Exhibit 9-4A). Say we purchase an office for $1.2 million and make a five-year proforma. The current year's (property) cash flow is $70,000, and the going-out income yield (aka going-out cap rate) is 7%. In the final year, we will receive last year's cash flow plus the sales values (year 6 cash flow divided by the going-out yield). We ignore

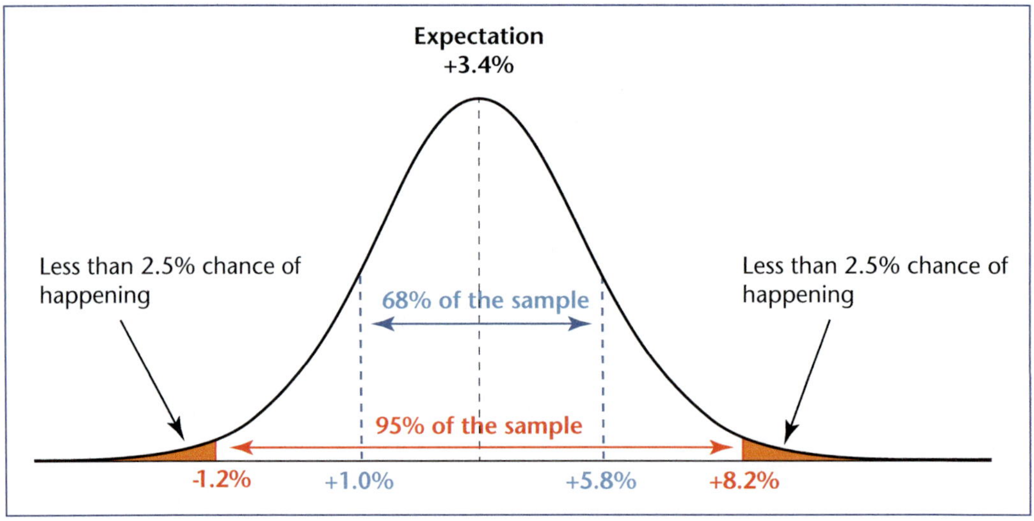

EXHIBIT 9-4A All Possible Outcomes of Rental Growth (g) According to the VAR Model in Exhibit 9-3.

capital expenditures and sales costs for this simple example. Using all three scenarios (average, bad, and good), we get the following IRRs (using the IRR Excel function);

Expected scenario (g = +3.4%)

Cash flows:-$1,200,000 + $72,380 + $74,841 + $77,386 + $80,017 + $1,304,884
Expected IRR:+6.75%

Bad scenario (g = –1.2%)

Cash flows:-$1,200,000 + $69,160 + $68,330 + $67,510 + $66,700 + $996,025
Downside Scenario IRR:+1.24%

Good scenario (g = +8.2%)

Cash flows:-$1,200,000 + $75,740 + $81,951 + $88,671 + $95,942 + $1,708,397
Upside Scenario IRR:+12.55%

Suppose one also attaches subjective probabilities to the possible future parameters (e.g., 40 percent chance the rental growth rate will be 3.4 percent, 30 percent chance it will be negative 1.2 percent, and 30 percent chance it will be 8.2 percent, probabilities that are consistent with an expectation of 3.4 percent growth, though a simplification from the formal assumption of normally distributed growth probability). In that case, the sensitivity analysis can be enhanced to a type of "**simulation analysis**" of the question of interest about the property, in which subjective (ex-ante) probabilities can be attached to outcomes. In Exhibit 9-4B, we perform a simulation analysis for our hypothetical Boston office building, using our forecasts' mean and standard error and assuming normally distributed growth rate probability. (You can find the accompanying Excel file online.)

After simulating all possible IRRs in Exhibit 9-4B, we end up with another bell-shaped curve. On the horizontal axis, we have IRR bins. For example, (6.60% – 7.35%] means an IRR between 6.60 and 7.35 percent. We simulated 2,500 samples for this specific example. Approximately 10% (or 250 of 2,500) are in that IRR bin. (See vertical axis.) This can be interpreted as a 10% chance that the IRR will be between 6.60 and 7.35 percent. According to this analysis, there is only a 1 percent chance that this investment will have a negative IRR. You can calculate this by adding all the samples in the bins below 0% and dividing them by the total sample size.[7] The mean of the IRR distribution is 6.71%, which closely corresponds to the 6.75% IRR found in our base proforma above. The general rule of thumb is that the more simulations you do, the more the distribution average matches the "true" mean (6.75% in our case). (Keep in mind that these are per annum rates over five years.)

Thus, all in all, a simulation (or sensitivity) analysis allows the investor to get a better grasp of the actual risk she is running. It should be reiterated that this does not directly impact the value of the real estate. Fundamentally, the IRR distribution is already embedded in the cost of capital. However, producing distributions as in Exhibit 9-4B can more directly tell you (for example) the probability of a loss of a given magnitude. This, in turn, allows for better decision making (an example is provided in the next starred section). Mortgage providers (and mortgage insurance companies, by extension) are especially interested in such models, as they can show them the likelihood that the property will be worth less than the outstanding mortgage at any given point in time. (See Part V of this book for

[7] Another way to do this more quickly is by using the aforementioned Z-table. The corresponding Z-score is 2.30. In the sense that 6.71% – **2.30** x 2.91% = 0%. The probability associated with this Z-score is 1%.

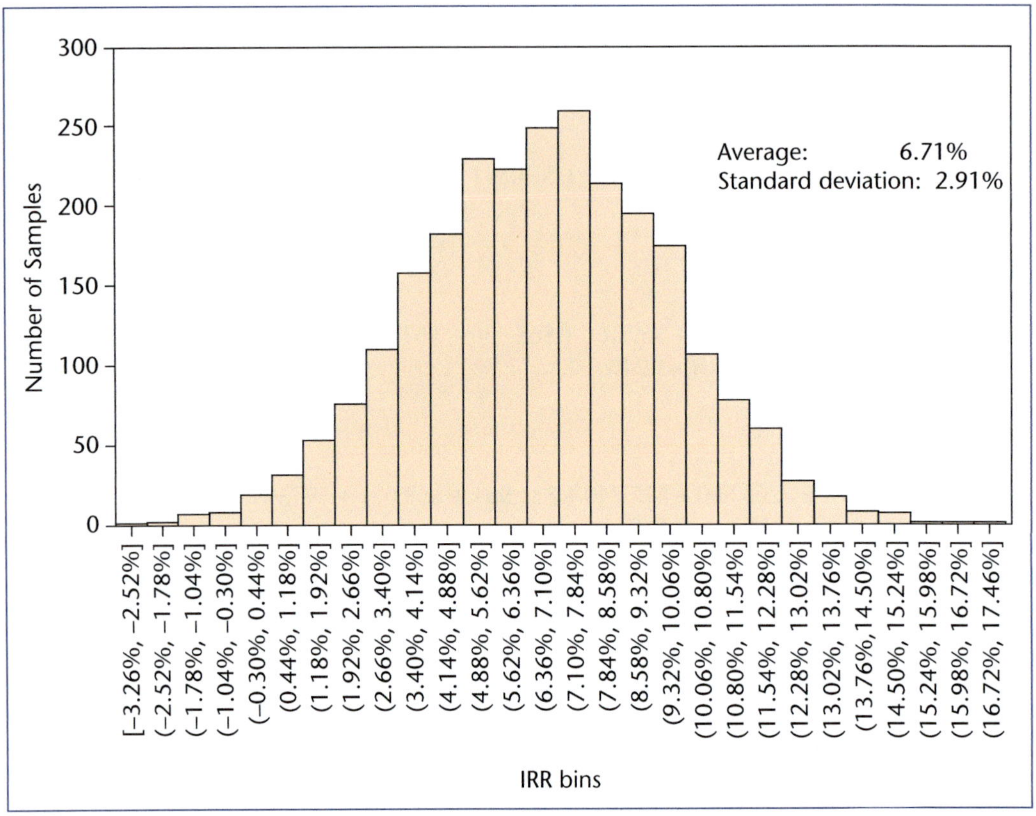

EXHIBIT 9-4B All Possible Outcomes of IRR after Simulating Using the Different Values for Rental Growth (g) in Exhibit 9-4A.

more details on the lenders' perspective.) The probability that the value is less than a specified level is sometimes referred to as **Value at Risk**, or VaR (not to be confused with VAR for forecasting). Suppose a lender will be owed $1,000,000 at a certain time, and the simulation analysis indicates a 2% probability that the value at that time will be $1,000,000 or less. Then, a 2 percent VaR in this context means a 2 percent chance that the property's value will be less than the outstanding mortgage balance.

Our only caveat in using simulation tools is that the generation of impressive statistics based on subjective probabilities and models of the relevant structural relationships (e.g., between rent growth and expense growth and interest rates) can present an appearance of knowing more than you actually do. And while simulation analysis works well with continuous variables like rental growth rates, sensitivity analysis with a few discrete scenarios will often work better to model the uncertainty associated with lumpy variables like new building supply in a market. Don't kid yourself. In the face of real risk and uncertainty, humility is always a virtue, and the parsimony of the fundamental economic valuation model we are working with brings some useful elegance to our analysis. That parsimony is the idea that the discount rate fully captures the valuation implications of the risk and uncertainty, and the discount rate is the opportunity cost of capital, which derives from equilibrium in the capital markets, including the market where the subject asset trades. The capital market cares about risk. Do you know more than the market knows?

9.2.2 The Value of Uncertainty: Resale Timing and Option Value[8]

The classical DCF valuation model implicitly assumes you will sell the property at the end of the proforma, a specified date certain in the future (typically in the U.S. between 5 and 10 years). But generally, the investor is not *required* to sell the property at that time, or any other time pre-set in advance. Property owners have the authority and the discretion to *choose* when to sell. This gives the investor a type of *flexibility*. It is akin to an "option." And options, indeed flexibility in general, have value.

We explained (primarily in Chapter 4) how the end date of the proforma is arbitrary in some sense, an analytical convenience that does not actually affect the property's value. We noted that this is because the property will live on after the proforma horizon, and future buyers will recognize the value generated by its productivity beyond the current proforma. That value will, therefore, be reflected in the resale value of the asset, which is reflected in the reversion value at the end of the DCF cash flow projection. But this does not mean that resale timing flexibility does not have value. In this section, we will show how the uncertainty quantified in the statistical forecast confidence bounds can be used to quantify such value.

To see how **resale timing option value** works, consider the following simplified illustration. Suppose you want to purchase a distribution warehouse on the outskirts of a town called "Geltnerton" in New Mexico (NM). The Federal Government is contemplating developing a large (freight) airport right next to your possible investment. An announcement on the matter is expected by next year. As of now, there is a 50% chance that the airport will be developed there (with a large future increase in cash flows for the warehouse as a result) and a 50% probability that the airport will be developed on the other side of town (which will result in a loss of tenants and rents for the warehouse). You are willing to take this risk and purchase the property for $1 million. According to your proforma, this property is also expected to sell for $1 million in 5 years (no expected growth in nominal property value). That is, $1 million is the expected value at year 5 (the average across the future possible values at that time). To simplify the illustration of the role of uncertainty and resale timing flexibility, suppose that this future expectation reflects essentially two alternative airport scenarios. The value will increase under the positive scenario (airport developed next door) and decrease in value under the negative scenario (no airport next door). In particular, say that in the positive scenario, the property value will increase by $50 thousand a year for 5 years. In the negative scenario, the property value will decrease by $50 thousand a year for 5 years. Note that this is consistent with the $1 million *expected* value in five years as of now (the present) because there is a 50% chance that each outcome in five years will be worth either $1.25 million ($1M + 5 times $50 thousand) or $0.75 million ($1 million – 5 times $50 thousand). If we multiply both possible outcomes by their probability, we end up with an expectation of, indeed, $1 million at year 5 ($1.25 million times 50% plus $0.75 million times 50%).

Upfront, we obviously do not know which scenario will unfold. However, once 1 year has passed, we will know whether we are in the positive or negative scenario for the coming five years, as the airport is being developed (or not) on your side of town in Geltnerton (NM). The resale timing option enables us to act in a value-maximizing way from our perspective. In a year, when the government announces its decision, if we find ourselves in the negative scenario, we could sell the property at that time. The property value will have declined only to $950 thousand before we disinvest and are no longer subject to future price declines. (The $950,000 presumably fully reflected the expected future decline in cash flow due to the unfavorable airport development.) If we find out after the first year that we are in the positive scenario, we hold on to the property for five years to enjoy the full extent of the expected capital gains from the growing location value of the site.

---

[8] This section is mostly based on Chapters 9 and 10 of Geltner and De Neufville's book titled *Flexibility and Real Estate Valuation Under Uncertainty*.

Thus, we end up with a 50% probability that we sell the property for $950 thousand in *1 year* and a 50% probability that we sell the property for $1.25 million in 5 years. Therefore, the property's apparent present value is $1.1 million now ($950 thousand times 50% plus $1.25 million times 50%), ignoring the opportunity cost of capital for the sake of simplicity of illustration. The difference between this number and the original $1 million may be considered a way of quantifying the value of the **resale timing option**, $100,000 in this example ($1.1 million minus $1 million).

Of course, the above example is highly simplified to illustrate the basic point. In reality, uncertainty is much more complex and nuanced. But the essence is the same. The future offers the investor contingent possibilities that can be taken advantage of if the investor has flexibility. And most real estate investments do offer considerable flexibility, especially if they are not greatly encumbered by debt obligations or other constraints or commitments.

It is also important to note that the above example does not imply that the property is actually worth $1.1 million in terms of its market value. We have specified that the property's current market value is $1.0 million. Market value is based on what potential buyers are willing to pay for the property (its opportunity cost). Those potential buyers have just as much ability to take advantage of the value of resale timing options as you do. And the property seller would also presumably have the same flexibility. The $1 million market value must already reflect the value of that flexibility. The example merely illustrates the importance and the approximate magnitude of the value of such flexibility for the investor.

9.3 DEPRECIATION OF CASH FLOWS

By this point, after Chapter 8 and the preceding sections of this chapter, you are developing a sophisticated understanding of rental market forecasting and how such forecasting can enlighten the rational and quantitative valuation and investment decision-making regarding individual properties, what we call micro-level real estate investment analysis. However, we must consider another important aspect of the difference between rental market forecasting and specific property asset-level DCF valuation. The key point is that there is an important difference between *market-level* analysis and individual-specific *property-level* analysis. Market-level analysis applies to entire space market segments, such as office buildings in the Boston CBD. It reflects the *population* of *all* office buildings in that market segment. That population evolves over time. Older buildings leave the population (through demolition or major renovation and rehabilitation or conversion), and newer buildings enter the population (through development or also through major renovation, rehabilitation, or conversion). The average age, or *effective age*, of that *population* of properties, the market segment, does not necessarily increase one-for-one with the passage of time. Indeed, in many viable real estate investment markets, the average age of properties may actually effectively decrease with the passage of time as more new buildings (or more new space, perhaps as larger buildings replace smaller ones) enter the market or more older buildings are removed or converted to other uses. (Revisit Chapter 7.4 as well for the depreciation of whole neighborhoods.)

This is quite different from the way the passage of time affects individual specific buildings. They age one-for-one, 1 year older with the passage of each calendar year (just like people do!). This is a crucial and fundamental fact. Buildings depreciate. As with almost any type of physical capital, the productivity of a given building, as reflected in its net cash flow, tends to decline with age. This importantly affects the realistic cash flow projection in the DCF valuation model. We are speaking here in real terms (net of monetary inflation) and from an economic perspective. Real economic depreciation is not unrelated to but is importantly distinct from what some readers may be more familiar with as depreciation allowances in financial accrual accounting and income tax rules. Real economic depreciation is an important consideration in property valuation and real estate investment, though it is often overlooked or underestimated. Real estate is what has often been and traditionally called a "wasting asset."

Real economic depreciation is perhaps easy to ignore or underestimate because, in nominal (current, inflating) dollars, it is often masked by the fact that the rate of inflation may equal or exceed the rate of real depreciation, especially in terms of total property value including the land value component (as land does not depreciate). The result can often be that the directly observable, nominal property value does not decline over time. Yet, real economic depreciation is occurring nonetheless, underneath that nominal value. And it has an important effect on investment returns.

Real depreciation also underlies the motivation or justification for why, in historic cost-based accrual financial accounting systems (such as what the U.S. income tax law is based on), allowances are permitted for depreciation expense. Tax rules and accounting-based depreciation allowances will be discussed in Chapter 13. The more fundamental and ubiquitous role of depreciation in real estate investment is the type of real economic depreciation that we want to introduce in this section.

Depreciation is important because real estate is a long-lived physical asset. Suppose we produce long-term forecasts based on market-level data. In that case, we should understand that the property (building structure) will age (and, therefore, depreciate in real terms) during that forecast. Market-level average rent growth will generally be greater than your individual property's realistic rent growth (other things equal). Real depreciation has consequences for your bottom line. We will start by simply defining depreciation and all its elements. After this, we will discuss how depreciation impacts the cash flows and, therefore, the forecast.

9.3.1 Components of Rent Depreciation

Recall from Chapter 7, Section 7.4 that real depreciation consists of *three* components. Next, we will discuss in detail how it impacts rents. The first is **physical deterioration**. Physical deterioration is what most people think about when depreciation is mentioned. It is the wear and tear of a building as a property is being used. Paint cracks or colors due to sunlight exposure, carpets get damaged when walked on, and the building structure weakens over (a long) time. Physical deterioration will *always* happen, even if the property is completely vacant, sometimes worse when it is vacant. There can be locational variation, though. Properties close to an ocean will depreciate faster, for example, due to salt exposure. In reality, you will hardly notice physical deterioration when renting space because regular maintenance helps circumvent the most negative impacts for tenants. As a result, you *will* notice it as a *landlord* in your bottom line through increased operating expenses. (See next section as well.)

The second component of depreciation is **functional obsolescence**. Functional obsolescence means that a building is in less demand because technology changes and the style and preferences of tenants change over time. For example, older warehouses from the 1920s through the 1970s had ceilings too low for modern warehouse users of the 1980s or beyond and became obsolete, renting for a fraction of the rent of higher ceiling warehouses. Another example - from the twenty-first century – is that there is more demand for "green" or "healthy" office buildings, for which tenants are willing to pay a premium.[9] A greener or healthier office building will increase workers' productivity, save energy and water, and signal to clients that the company cares about the environment. In the 1980s and 1990s, few companies cared (or knew) about this. Changes in technological innovations also drive functional obsolescence. For example, older homes will have fewer wall plugs and worse access to the internet, as this was simply not (as) necessary a few decades ago. Functional obsolescence is more difficult to "cure" than physical deterioration. Only large-scale renovations, that is, capital expenditures, can help here. Increasing the amount of wall plugs or green retrofitting properties is expensive and time-consuming. Building in such a way that provides flexibility helps prevent

---

[9] A famous example of the opposite is the "sick building syndrome." Many office buildings, especially in the 1970s and 1980s, were built in such a way that you could not open the windows. Combined with poor HVAC systems, this resulted in workers getting physically sick.

functional obsolescence. For example, most hallways of the main MIT building (developed in the early twentieth century) have extra-high ceilings. This was done because the architects understood that more wiring/tubing or whatever else might be invented in the future could be needed in the (distant) future. As a result, no large-scale renovation is required in order to add extra wiring, for example.

The final element of depreciation is what we call **external obsolescence**. External obsolescence occurs when *something* changes near the building or regarding its location, but not to the building itself. An example of external obsolescence can be the development of a new building that blocks the view of your apartment buildings to a river or forest. In such a case, the rent of your property will depreciate. This example is hyper-local. However, more high-level swings in Highest and Best Use (HBU) is also an example of external obsolescence. Say that you purchased a distribution warehouse in a suburban area with little traffic but a good connection to the interstate highway. This location is perfect for such a property. As a result, you can charge relatively high rents. However, over the decades, the city grew to such an extent that your property is now part of the CBD. The heavy congestion that is associated with this change results in less demand / lower rents. It is fair to say that "curing" external obsolescence is next to impossible, other than a complete teardown. Again, flexibility can help, though. For example, canal houses in Amsterdam were built so that they could easily house any type of use. Thus, as the Highest and Best Use changed from office to more residential / hotel, the buildings could easily adapt without being demolished. (Thankfully!)

Keep in mind that land and locations don't systematically depreciate. Depreciation is a phenomenon of the building structure. It is possible for changes in the HBU of a location or site to evolve in a *favorable* direction, actually *increasing* the value of the property while the value of the building structure on it falls. This is because it can become wealth-maximizing to tear down the existing structure and replace it with an entirely new and different building that is better suited to the new HBU. External depreciation is really the only major type of depreciation that purely accrues to the building's structural asset value and not to the productivity of the building per se. That is, the net rent the old building can charge may be rising with prospects to continue rising, yet the value of the building falls, ultimately to nothing. This is because of how much *more* valuable the new replacement (different type or scale) of the building would be. This is the exercise of the landowner's "development call option" exercise, which will be discussed in much more depth in Chapter 16.

An example would be a modest apartment building in a location that has become sufficiently more valuable that a much larger, more upscale apartment, or a retail/office/hotel mixed-use structure, would be much more valuable to place on the site. The wealth-maximizing use (you could say, "fate") of the existing modest apartment structure is to tear it down, which means the building itself has no positive economic value, even though it is still in demand and can still charge high and growing rents.

Finally, it is necessary to discuss other elements of aging, which are not seen as depreciation but are related to it. The first is denoted as the **vintage effect**. Vintage (in this context) means that a combination of materials and designs from a certain era are valued more than others. It is possible to recreate such a style (like "Tudor" style homes in Ohio that mimic medieval England), but typically, tenants will see through this. The original, authentic examples have a caché that imparts extra value. Examples of vintage mostly come from Europe and pertain to housing. However, in the U.S., we know that Jugendstil (also known as "Art Nouvau") office buildings in New York from the 1910s to the 1930s are appreciated more for their distinct style. The most famous examples are the Chrysler and Woolworth buildings, the Rockefeller Center, and the Empire State Building. As a result, tenants are willing to pay more rent, and investors may accept a lower cap rate due to confidence that the property will retain its demand and value in the process. Other examples include brownstone townhouses in New York City and pre-WWII bungalows in Chicago and Los Angeles.

The last element we want to mention regarding statistical and empirical-based analysis of the role of age and history in understanding how property-level rent or value tends to change over time is what is called **survivor bias**. You probably heard the credo "they don't make them like they used to" before. However, what is often forgotten is that the worst (in both an architectural and engineering kind of way) buildings built in, say, 1910 are more likely to have been demolished by now. The same goes for the aforementioned canal houses in Amsterdam. Very few of them are the original houses, but the best are still there. Survivor bias is very important when trying to understand depreciation. For example, you might find that older properties charge higher rents, even for the same location (older buildings tend to be in better sites as well). As a result, you might think that rents do not depreciate in your location. But you might be very mistaken. Unless you are very sure that your building will survive for the ages because it is simply that good, your rents *will* depreciate. According to data from MSCI, only about 20% of all commercial buildings developed 200 years ago still exist in their original form today.

9.3.2 Impact of Depreciation on Rents

In the above discussion, it is clear that depreciation can act either by way of the net rent a building can produce (net of expenses, considered the economic "productivity" of the building) or by way of the building value as a long-lived asset (for example, external depreciation of a building that no longer fits the HBU of a site). In practice, evidence suggests that, at least in the U.S., most real economic depreciation of investment property probably occurs by way of the effect on net rent.

To better understand the impact of depreciation on rents, we plot three time series in Exhibit 9-5. The first is simply the average effective rent per square foot (new leases) for office properties aged between 0 and 120 (horizontal axis), as recorded by Compstak in the U.S. Something curious happens with the average rent per square foot. According to this plan average, rents per square foot for office space decrease from $32 per square foot for newly developed buildings to $23 at 40 years old. This $9 drop indicates rents depreciated by 28% ($9/$32) in 40 years, or about 0.7 percent annually. However, after this, the rents increase quite considerably, to even levels well above that of newly developed properties. How is this possible? Hopefully, the attentive student is aware of what is going on here. There are two factors at play here. First, older properties tend to be in better locations. For example, the average stock in New York is relatively old and large. Thus, New York will dominate the older building stratum. In contrast, Phoenix (AZ) is a relatively young city. Another way to put it is that the average profile shown in Exhibit 9-5 is a mix between (1) the "pure" impact of age on rent and (2) the change in property composition over the different ages. Luckily, there exist statistical techniques to parse out the "pure" age impact and separate it from the composition change. This is the so-called "hedonic" model, which results in a **constant quality** age profile. Even though the hedonic model is outside the scope of this book, it is often used in markets with lots of heterogeneity (like real estate, but also the wine, computer, or used-car market). Thus, getting acquainted with the terminology might be a good thing. If you are hungry for more information on how such models work and how you can do it yourself in Excel, we have placed a primer online, which you can consult. A second issue with taking the plain average is what we discussed above: survivor bias. The older buildings are only the best of those corresponding vintages. Unless you believe your property will be among the best in the future, not accounting for survival bias will result in you overestimating the rents in the (far) future.

Exhibit 9-5 has two other lines. The first (red) is a "constant quality" rent over age. Here, we use the aforementioned "hedonic" approach to ensure the composition of the properties remains the same. The same location, size, etc. The only thing that varies is the age of the building. Here, we find that age – indeed – reduces rents. The rent decrease for the first 40 years is less than the plain average rent decrease. Locational differences probably cause this. Properties developed 20 to 30 years ago are in (less desirable) suburban locations. After 40 years, the rent flattens and subsequently increases. After 120 years, the total decrease is only $2 per square foot compared to a newly developed property (or $30 compared to $32 initially). The final (blue) line is similar to the constant quality rent; however, here, we correct for survival bias as well.[10] This – the most complete representation of

[10] We multiplied the constant quality age profile with the probability of survival for offices in the U.S.

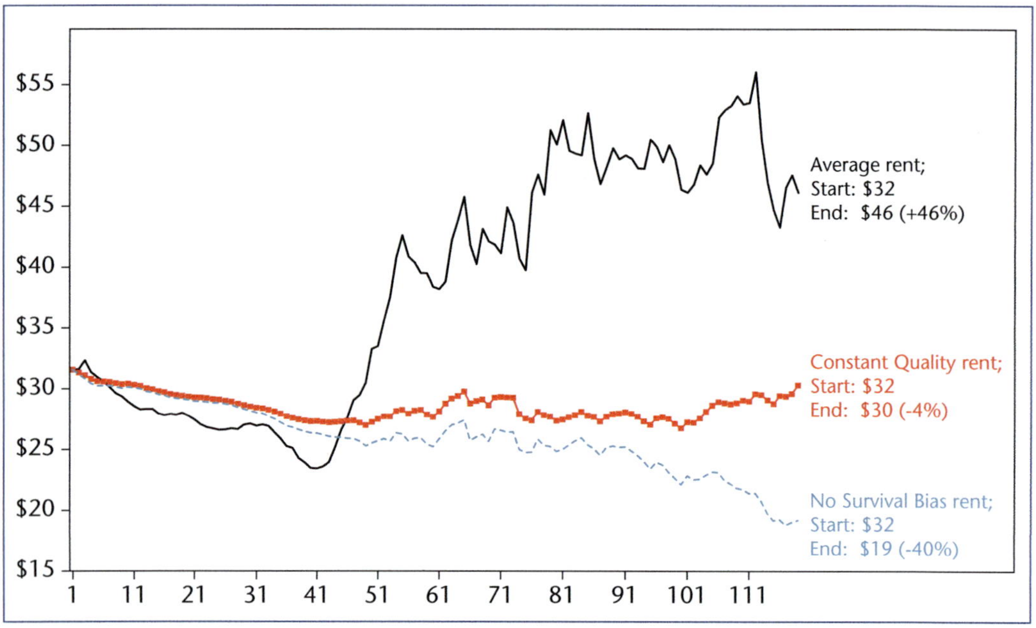

EXHIBIT 9-5 Depreciation of Office (Effective) Rents Aged Between 0 and 120 Years Old.

Source: Own calculation using Compstak and MSCI data.

depreciation - shows that rents decrease at a much higher rate of 40% after 120 years, or 3.26% per decade. We also find a third life cycle here. After 90 years, rents start to drop quite considerably.

Why do we find these distinct life cycles? In the first 30 to 40 years, rents steadily depreciate. This is mostly caused by functional obsolescence, where the property loses its much-revered "A" status, attracting different types of tenants altogether. Between ages 30 and 90, the rents plateau. A "B" class building is a "B" class building; after all, it doesn't really matter if the building is 40 or 60 years old. After 90 years, there are two possibilities. Either you redevelop / heavily renovate the property (reducing the effective age in the process), or you allow the property to depreciate fully (i.e., "terminal stage").

9.3.3 Impact of Depreciation on Operating Expenses, Capital Expenditures, and Vacancy Levels

Much (probably most) depreciation is due to building productivity as opposed to so-called "cap rate creep" (the tendency of the property cap rate, NOI/Asset Value, to increase with building age).[11] However, much of this depreciation is not easily noticeable, especially by the tenants, because maintenance activity (both OpEx and CapEx) partly negates it. As a result, depreciation hurts the landlord's bottom line (PBTCF) more than the top-line rents that are more observable. Operating Expenses *as a fraction of the EGI* will increase only slightly as the property ages, even though maintaining an older property is (much) more expensive. The increase in maintenance spending is partly offset by a reduction in property tax, insurance, and management fees (driven by a reduction in property values). Also, utility bills decrease as vacancy levels increase (see next paragraph). Still,

[11] Based on a study of over 100,000 commercial and multi-family property transaction prices of investment property (over $2.5 million value) spanning 2001–2014, Bokhari & Geltner (2016) found that "cap rate creep" is a minor component of overall property price real depreciation, with real net rent depreciation (building economic productivity) playing the dominant role on average.

we find that (using NCREIF data) the net effect is that operating expenses are approximately 5 percentage points higher after 60 years compared to new developments, expressed as a fraction of EGI. Capital expenditures go up more compared to operating expenses. As mentioned before, renovating properties is both time-consuming and costly.

It should also be noted that the realistic vacancy allowance increases over time as buildings age. (Hopefully, you should see why depreciation gets its own section by now!) Other things being equal, older buildings face a higher likelihood that existing tenants will not renew and/or that there will be a longer vacant period between tenants in a given space. Especially during times of excess supply in the space market, tenants may tend to "move up" from older to newer buildings when their leases expire. For example, Exhibit 9-6 shows vacancy rates between 2010 and 2023 for office buildings in the U.S. office space markets (NCREIF) for two different vintages of buildings over time. Note that both vintages follow – roughly speaking – the same cycle. Vacancy rates were reduced after the Great Financial Crisis but ticked up again after COVID-19 hit in 2020. Perhaps more importantly, the difference in the average vacancy level is approximately four percentage points (12 percent for the 2000s vintage and 16 percent for the 1980s vintage).

To get a sense of the total impact of depreciation on our cash flows, we plot average PGI (which is similar to the rent plotted in Exhibit 9-5), EGI, NOI, and PBTCF per square foot in Exhibit 9-7. For a typical office property in the U.S., we find that vacancy levels go from 5% for newly developed buildings to over 11% at 80 years of age. After 80, we see a small decrease in vacancy levels, driven mainly by the considerable rent reduction. As mentioned earlier, operating expenses stay relatively flat (as a % of EGI), meandering somewhere between 12 and 15 percent. In contrast, capital expenditures vary wildly over age. The average CapEx spending for newly developed buildings is around 20%. Here, CapEx mostly consists of TIs and leasing commissions. As the property ages, more and more building improvements (and even more concessions in the form of TIs) need

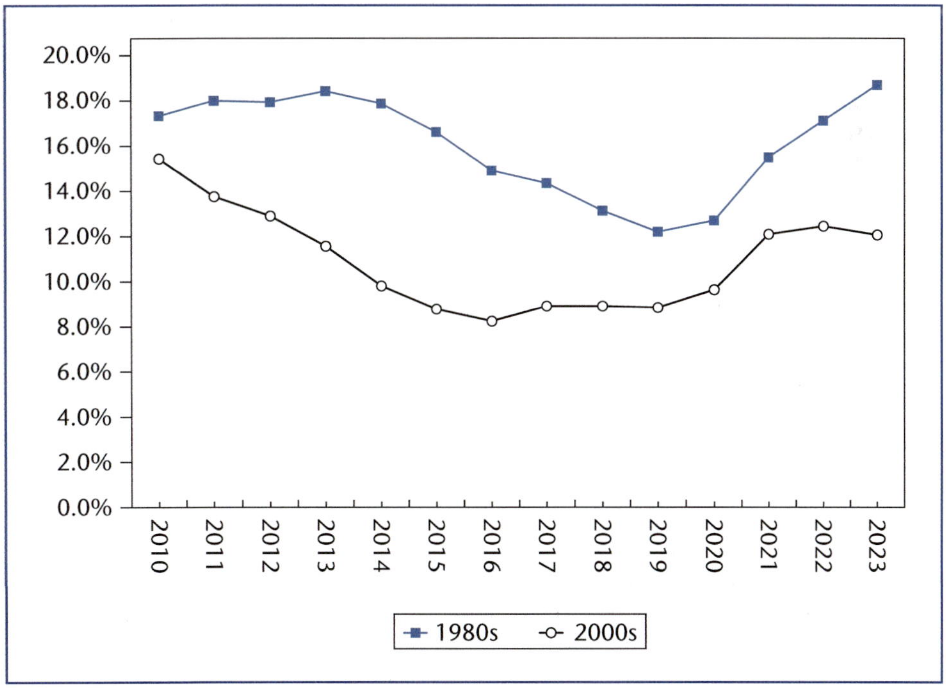

EXHIBIT 9-6 Average Reported Vacancy Among Office Properties, 2010–2023.

Note: We report two separate vacancy rates for two vintages; properties built in the 1980s and properties built in the 2000s.

Source: NCREIF.

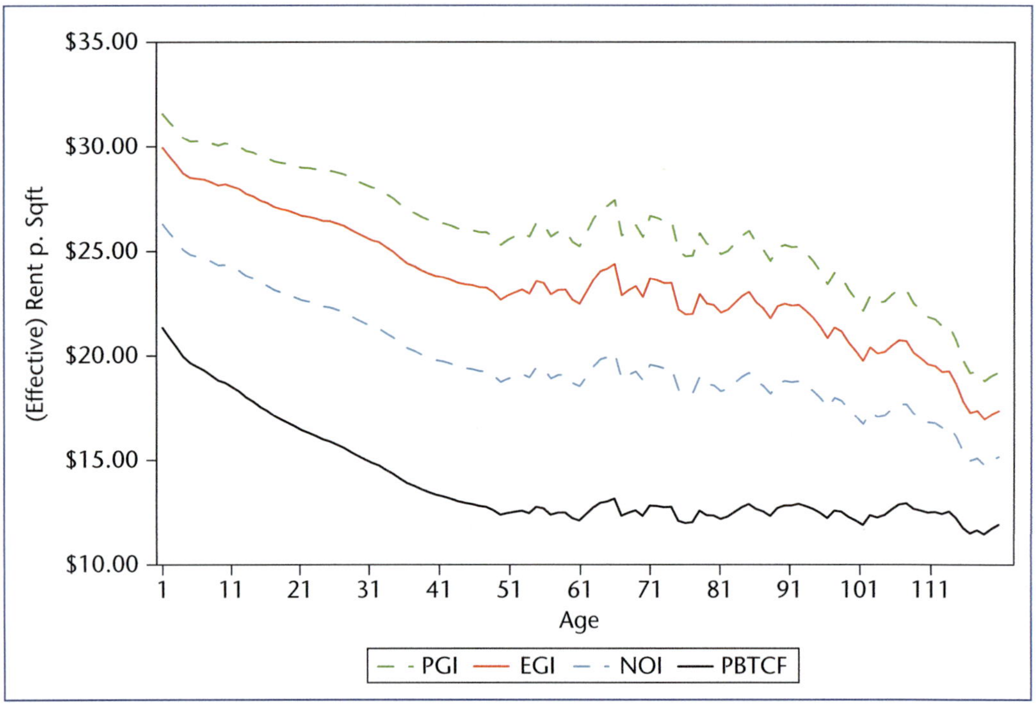

EXHIBIT 9-7 PGI, EGI, NOI, and PBTCF for a Typical Office Property in the US.

Source: Own Calculations using NCREIF and Compstak.

to be considered to offset the impact of functional obsolescence. At its peak, we find that capital expenditures are over 35% of NOI around age 60. We, therefore, also find that the depreciation in PBTCF is much larger compared to the depreciation in rents (PGI) for the first 40 years. More specifically, rents decrease by 16% in the first 40 years, whereas PBTCF decreases by 37%. After a property hits 50 years of age, something interesting happens, though. Here, we find that in the final years of the buildings' life, the PBTCF remains flat. This is partly fueled by the large drop in capital expenditures during this same time period. Obviously, this reduction in capital expenditures doesn't happen in a vacuum. Tenants pay less rent *because* the landlord is not improving the building … and the other way around! Most of the property value with very old buildings is really due to the land and the location value of the site, for which the landlord does not need to expend much capital to make building improvements. (In a fundamental sense, the landlord is reaping value that is produced by society at large, as it shapes the values of locations.) It should be stated here that capital expenditures do not follow such a smooth line in reality on a *property level*. For example, you do not have to install new elevators or HVAC systems every year. As a result, large capital expenditures (building improvements) tend to be concentrated in just one or two years in a 10-year proforma.

9.3.4 Consequences of Depreciation for Rental Growth Forecast

All of the above is important. Cash flows depreciate relative to what top-of-the-line new buildings in the same location could produce as the building's productive capacity diminishes with age. However, we have placed this depreciation discussion in this forecasting chapter for a reason. It is a key understanding and a key step in going from space market forecasting to individual property cash flow forecasting. As noted earlier, the average rents in the space market reflect the average age of the buildings in that market at each point in time, which, unlike any individual actual building, do not generally age on average, certainly not one-for-one year by year.

Say that the market forecast implies that average rents of buildings in the market are expected to increase by 4% per year in the coming 10 years. Unlike the market, the rent in your building will depreciate as your property gets older. Your depreciation will be *relative to the change in market rents*. For example, say you have a newly developed office building (age 0). We know from the above that for the first 40 years, rents will drop by 16 percent or 40 basis points per year. As a result, the rent growth expectation forecast for your specific building will be (4% - 0.4%=) 3.6% (**net of depreciation**). You would want to make similar adjustments to your operating expenses, but especially to capital expenditures. Operating expenses are typically pegged to inflation forecasts.[12] However, you should now be aware that operating expenses as a percentage of EGI can grow in real terms (net of inflation) simply because you need to do more of it (through regular maintenance). Capital expenditures have always been different from those other cash flow line items, as it depends on the state of the building and its components. Naturally, you will find more things to "improve" as your building ages. Evidence exists that for the typical investment property in the United States, total property asset depreciation (including both building and land value), relative to the top of the market, averages between one and two percent per year of age. It tends to be greater in properties with younger buildings and in locations with lower land values and less in middle-aged properties or those in high-value locations.

The exact amount of rent depreciation depends on many factors, including property type, location, and starting age (as well as its architectural and engineering quality). Here is a simple "seat-of-the-pants" way to get a sense of the amount of property-level rent depreciation relevant to your investment. Do a **rent comparable ("comp") analysis** on buildings 10 years older than yours in comparison to yours. In this context, the "comp" approach would consist of two steps. First, you would want to know your property's market rent (per square foot). You can look at the rent in your own building. However, looking at rents charged in similar buildings nearby (of nearly the same age as yours) is also advised. (You want to adjust in case your building has some vintage leases that are too high or low compared to the market overall; see Section 9.4 for more details.) The other (comparable) buildings you look at should be of similar age, property type, size, and class / overall state as your target property. You can move to step two once you have averaged the rent per square foot for all these buildings. The second step is similar to the first step, except that you look at *similar properties nearby that are ten years older*. (Or, you could take 20 years older as the comparables target—or even 30 years. You get the point. Be mindful of any major cycle in your rental market, and how that might relate to when the leases were signed.) The average rent per square foot for the older buildings will likely differ from that of step 1. The difference in rent between these two groups is likely caused by real economic depreciation. Obviously, it is not an exact science. For example, even though you should only look at rents in nearby properties (and of similar size, etc.), it is difficult to correct for survival bias and all the compositional differences in this context. Still, common sense and honest thinking can bring you far here.

TEXT BOX 9.1 RECENT RISE IN CLIMATE-INDUCED INSURANCE FEES

Chapter 28 will detail current challenges in the real estate market. However, in this current chapter on forecasting cash flows, we must mention the recent burgeoning in insurance fees for commercial real estate. Sometimes, a picture says more than a thousand words. In Exhibit 9-8 below, we plot the average insurance fees for office properties per square foot between 2005 and mid-2023, according to NCREIF.

As you can see, insurance fees have doubled on average since 2018. However, the situation is even worse than this graph suggests. The increase is mainly driven by locations impacted by damages through climate-related events, most notably hurricanes and flooding.

[12] There are exceptions to this. Especially when it comes to property taxes. There exist numerous specialized firms that can help with predicting tax rates in the coming years. The other (more recent) exception is insurance premia, see text box.

For example, fees quadrupled in that same period for Florida (source: NCREIF). In some very specific locations, it is very difficult/impossible even to get insurance in the first place (like in floodplains), which is needed to obtain a mortgage. Unlike housing, no federal programs can help in such a case. As of writing in 2024, it is difficult to know where this will be going and if operating expenses will explode due to climate-related damages.

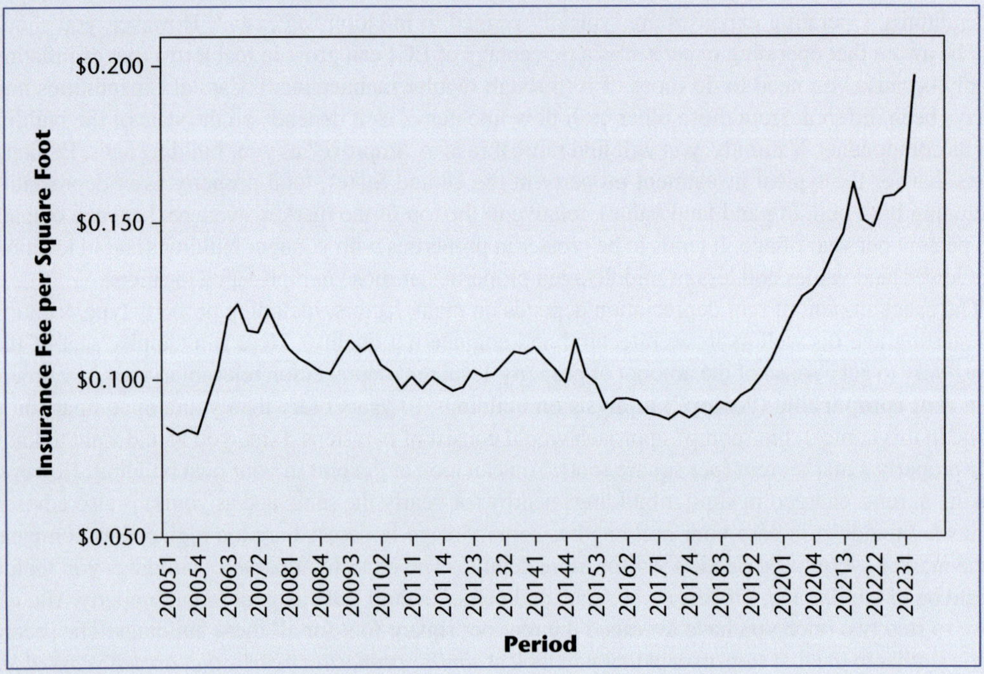

EXHIBIT 9-8 Insurance Fees Over the Years.

Source: NCREIF.

9.4 DETERMINING THE POTENTIAL GROSS INCOME (PGI) AND VACANCY LEVELS

In most properties, particularly those with long-term leases, there is yet another important consideration in going from market-level rent forecasting to the property-level cash flow projection in the DCF valuation model that is so relevant for the investor. In Chapter 5, we treated the Potential Gross Income (PGI) and vacancy as a given. In reality, if your property is in a market characterized by long-term leases, it may have vintage leases and vacancy in it. As a result, your property's vacancy and EGI can be "out of whack." (As compared to the market overall.) We will provide a simple example of how to deal with this in the current Chapter.

Exhibit 9-9 presents a simple example of 10 years of PGI, vacancy, and EGI (used for the proforma) for the "Noname Building," a 30,000-SF office building consisting of three 10,000-SF spaces, each of which rents out separately under a 5-year lease. The building's current and projected market rent is shown in the first row. This top-line market rent in the context of a specific (aging) building should reflect the expected real economic depreciation of the building. In other words, it should include the depreciation discount off the projected rental market growth rate as described in Section 9.3.4. It relates to what a new lease *in the subject building* could be expected to rent for in the space market at the given future date in time. The market rent in year 1 is estimated to be $10/SF,

EXHIBIT 9-9
Calculating the Potential Gross Income, the Example of "Noname Building"

	Year									
	1	**2**	**3**	**4**	**5**	**6**	**7**	**8**	**9**	**10**
Marker Rent/SF:	$10.00	$10.10	$10.20	$10.30	$10.41	$10.51	$10.62	$10.72	$10.83	$10.94
Potential Revenue:										
Gross Rent Space 1 (10,000SF)	$105,000	$105,000	$105,000	$103,030	$103,030	$103,030	$103,030	$103,030	$108,286	$108,286
Gross Rent Space 2 (10,000SF)	$100,000	$100,000	$100,000	$100,000	$100,000	$105,101	$105,101	$105,101	$105,101	$105,101
Gross Rent Space 32 (10,000SF)	$100,000	$101,000	$101,000	$101,000	$101,000	$101,000	$106,152	$106,152	$106,152	$106,152
Total PGI	$305,000	$306,000	$306,000	$304,030	$304,030	$309,131	$314,283	$314,283	$319,539	$319,539
Vacancy allowance:										
Space 1	$0	$0	$0	$51,515	$0	$0	$0	$0	$54,143	$0
Space 2	$0	$0	$0	$0	$0	$52,551	$0	$0	$0	$0
Space 3	$100,000	$0	$0	$0	$0	$0	$53,076	$0	$0	$0
Total vacancy allowance	$100,000	$0	$0	$51,515	$0	$52,551	$53,076	$0	$54,143	$0
Total EGI	$205,000	$306,000	$306,000	$252,515	$304,030	$256,581	$261,207	$314,283	$265,396	$319,539

Notes:

- Rent grows by (g) 1% per annum (net of depreciation)
- The current EGI of space 1 is higher compared to the market average
- Space 3 is vacant at the time of purchase (year 0)
- All leases are expected to expire at the end of the 5th year from signing. Lease 1 was signed 2 years ago; lease 2 was signed recently.

meaning that leases signed today (at the beginning of year 1) would be expected to have this rent. In our illustration, this market rent is then projected to grow at a constant rate of 1 percent per year. Such a projection might be based, for example, on a judgment that the space market is currently in, and expected to remain in, its long-term equilibrium (hence, constant growth rate), with expected real growth of 0.5 percent per year, monetary inflation of 2 percent, and the property's real economic depreciation rate due to the building's aging equal to 1.5 percent per year. This results in a net 1 percent per year expected growth rate for the rent the building could charge on new leases in the rental market (0.5%+2.0%–1.5% = 1.0%).

The next section of the proforma presents the rent roll for the three spaces, totaling to the PGI of the building. Space 1 is currently occupied by a tenant with an existing lease signed two years ago at a higher rent of $10.50/SF. (Perhaps the space market was abnormally tight then, or that tenant negotiated a "bad deal" for themself, or received some free rent or other concession up front when they signed the lease.) This lease is set to run for three more years and will expire at the end of year 3. Space 2 has just leased out in a new 5-year lease at the current market rate of $10/SF. This lease will expire at the end of year 5. Space 3 is currently vacant and not expected to lease up until the beginning of year 2. At that time, the market rent is projected to be $10.10/SF, the projected rent for space three from years 2 through 6.

The proforma calculates the PGI for all three spaces as though each were fully occupied yearly. Note that when a lease is projected to expire, the space "rolls over" at the projected market rent prevailing at the beginning of the next lease period. Thus, for example, after space 1's current lease expires at the end of year 3, the rent roll for that space is "marked to market" as of the next year at the projected year-4 market rent of $10.30/SF. (Actually, this is a rounded estimate. The precise estimate is $10.303, so the PGI for 10,000 SF is projected at $103,030 based on the year-4 market rent.)

The next section of the proforma computes the vacancy allowance that must be subtracted from the PGI to arrive at the effective gross income. Space 3 is expected to be vacant for the entire first year, so its entire PGI for year one is attributed to vacancy allowance. The assumption for the remainder of the proforma is that when leases expire, there is a 50 percent chance the existing tenant will renew, resulting in no vacancy. However, if the existing tenant does not renew, the space is expected to remain vacant for an entire year.

Recall that the proforma is supposed to forecast the expected cash flows, that is, the mean of the subjective ex-ante probability distribution of the possible cash flows for each year. To compute this mean, we multiply the probability of each scenario by the cash flow resulting from that scenario and sum up all the scenarios. In this case, we have two scenarios: the tenant renews, or the tenant does not renew. Thus, we compute the expected vacancy allowance for a given space during the year following its lease expiration as follows:

(1 – Probability of Renewal) x Market Rent x Expected Length of Vacancy if Nonrenewal

For example, the market rent is projected to be $10.51/SF in year 6. Space 2's lease expires at the beginning of year 6. So, the projected vacancy allowance for year 6 for space 2 is:[13]

$$(1 - 0.5) \times \$10.51/\text{SF} \times 10{,}000\text{SF} = \$52{,}551$$

[13] Suppose the renewal probability was estimated to be 75 percent, and the expected vacant period in the event of nonrenewal was four months. Then the projected (expected) vacancy loss for space 2 for year 6 would be:

$$(1 - 0.75)(\$10.51)(10{,}000\text{SF})(4/12\text{mo}) = \$8{,}758$$

It should be noted that in practice conventional wisdom "rules of thumb" are often applied to this calculation, regarding the lease renewal probability and the projected vacancy period downtime in the event of nonrenewal. The industry has not been very "scientific" about this calculation. For example, the most common assumption in the office building market is that leases experience a 75 percent renewal probability.

Obviously, after computing the PGI and EGI, you have to compute the NOI and, finally, the property-before-tax cash flow, as we will do ad nauseam throughout this book. In practice, specialized software often facilitates analysis like this, making it easy to convert lease information into cash flow projections. The most widely used software in the United States in the early 2020s is ARGUS® Software www.altusgroup.com/).

TEXT BOX 9.2 MICRO-LEVEL ANALYSIS OF TENANTS AND LEASES

Forecasting rents over the long term requires market analysis with a focus on the local submarket, yet for a specific property, it starts with the actual leases and tenants in place. A rent roll analysis includes all building leases, the amount of space occupied by each tenant, available space, the lease terms, and each tenant's credit and resiliency.

For example, half of a building might be leased by the US Department of Commerce (DoC), a Federal Agency, for 15 years, with several options for extensions. The cash flow generated from this lease is highly reliable and low risk, affecting valuations and aiding in securing financing. In the event of a COVID-type shutdown or deep recession, the DoC can still pay their rent. Thus, they are not only high credit but also highly resilient to economic or regulatory shocks.

Lease analysis for other spaces in the building should start with existing leases and an assessment of the probability of renewal. The probability of renewal has historically been a function of the degree of space customization, tenant improvements paid for by the tenant, and the type of industry. For example, legal and architectural firms are highly static and resistant to change. At the same time, generic space users like insurance agencies are more prone to move if occupancy savings are possible from lower rents elsewhere. The more generic the space and the more typical the space in size, the more likely a firm would jump to a new space if cheaper rent were offered. Larger tenants tend to be fairly static, and smaller firms tend to be more mobile. Available space and tenants are not likely to renew, which requires assumptions in the proforma based on a statistical analysis of time to lease and expected vacancy. Historically, one of the most biased assumptions by real estate analysts in generating a rental forecast is to assume that empty space will lease up quickly when, in fact, it can take several months for space to lease. We suggest utilizing actual data from recent times to lease when possible.

Finally, sublease space that is empty or for rent is a leading indicator of vacancy. Sublease space availability leads to longer-term vacancy, which in turn leads to rent movements in the market.

9.5 CHAPTER SUMMARY

Chapters 8 and 9 have provided you with a lot of material. It's dense stuff, no doubt a heavy lift if you are trying to follow it all conscientiously. But this is extremely fundamental material that is very basic and important for real estate investors. Investment success or failure depends on what happens in the future, after you buy a property. And the main unifying theme of these two chapters is indeed about forecasting the future. In particular, we are focusing on forecasting the fundamentals that underlie property value: the space market in which the property is located, and the property-level cash flows the asset will generate. Certainly, the capital market and financial considerations are also very important, and we have introduced some of those considerations in Part I and will introduce more in Part III. But fundamentally, property value depends on the cash flow fundamentals, the economic productivity of the asset. This is the level at which real value can be added, the level that really distinguishes real estate from other types of capital assets. That's why Chapters 8 and 9 are so important, and why we have made a point to give these chapters the serious depth and rigor that you have now, hopefully, come to appreciate.

Take a moment here to consider the big picture of both chapters. Chapter 8 starts with space market analysis and then moves into dynamics and forecasting by introducing a simple, formal stock-flow model. Even if you don't want to fully grasp all of the technical details of that formal model (in Section 8.3), understanding the essence is important. Then, Chapter 9 picks up naturally from there with space market forecasting in Section 9.1. As valuable as modern empirical statistical based forecasting is, though, Section 9.2 elaborates how the "forecast is always wrong", how we can quantify the amount of uncertainty that is present, and how investors need not only fear such uncertainty but can, in some ways take advantage of it by use of flexibility. Then Section 9.3 takes the focus from the market level to the individual asset level, the actual investment, focusing primarily and in-depth on the important but often overlooked consideration of real economic depreciation (to be distinguished from accounting depreciation "allowances," which will be addressed in Chapter 13). Finally, Section 9.4 brought in the more mundane and mechanical cash flow forecasting issue of the treatment of vintage and multi-period leases, which, if a bit more mundane and mechanical than the prior material, is nonetheless quite important to complete a conscientious and rigorous property-level cash flow forecast and investment proforma.

KEY TERMS

- Short-term structural market analysis
- Forecasting space markets
- Regression
- Vector Autoregressive (VAR) models
- Ordinary Least Squares (OLS)
- Residuals/errors
- Confidence intervals
- Sensitivity analysis
- Simulation
- Value at Risk (VaR)
- Resale timing option (value)
- Depreciation
- Physical deterioration
- Functional obsolescence
- External obsolescence
- Vintage
- Survivor bias
- Rent growth net of depreciation
- Potential Gross Income and Vacancy in year 1

STUDY QUESTIONS

In Your Own Words

9.1 Explain the purpose of sensitivity analysis in real estate forecasting.

9.2 Explain the three main components of real depreciation in real estate and provide an example of each.

9.3 Describe the "vintage effect" in real estate valuation.

9.4 How does hedonic modeling improve the accuracy of rent depreciation estimates?

9.5 Why might older buildings have higher vacancy rates than newer ones?

9.6 What is survivor bias, and how can it affect depreciation studies in real estate?

Check Your Knowledge

9.7 Why might a property with a strong location experience less functional obsolescence?
- A) Location increases building durability
- B) Location directly impacts only vacancy
- C) Location affects rent more than features
- D) Tenants are more tolerant of older features if the location is desirable

9.8 Why might real economic depreciation be underestimated?
- A) Inflation often masks it in nominal terms
- B) Taxes reduce the observable depreciation
- C) Depreciation applies only to residential buildings
- D) It's always included in property appraisals

9.9 Why is understanding functional obsolescence important in forecasting cash flows?
- A) It directly affects property tax rates
- B) It helps estimate potential renovation needs and future cash flow reductions
- C) It increases tenant satisfaction
- D) It reduces insurance costs

9.10 Why are long-term forecasts especially risky?
- A) Inflation always increases
- B) Market volatility and changing tenant preferences are difficult to predict
- C) Rent growth becomes exponential
- D) Depreciation no longer applies

9.11 Why might hedonic modeling show different depreciation rates across property types?
- A) Different property types may have distinct maintenance costs and tenant preferences
- B) All properties depreciate uniformly
- C) It only applies to office spaces
- D) Residential buildings are excluded from hedonic models

Chapter Case: Renovation Strategies for Bayview Tower

Bayview Tower is a 36-year-old office building located in a global hub's financial district. The building faces increasing challenges with significant impacts on operating costs and tenant retention.

As the property ages, infrastructure, such as HVAC systems, windows, and flooring, is reaching the end of its useful life. This has led to rising maintenance and repair costs, straining the property's net operating income. The rising crime rates in the neighborhood are compounding the issues by increasing tenant turnover and vacancy rates. In addition, nearby properties are offering modern amenities, making Bayview Tower less attractive.

Property Details:

Total Leasable Space: 250,000 sq. ft.
Rent: \$55/sq. ft.
Vacancy Rate: 12%
Operating Expenses: 30% of Effective Gross Income (EGI)
Annual Rent Growth: 1% without renovation; 3% with renovation.

Ping Shen, general manager of Bayview Tower, is evaluating the following strategies to address the building's challenges:

i. No Investment: Accept increasing operating expenses, vacancy, and declining tenant satisfaction.

ii. Targeted Infrastructure Upgrades: Invest $1 million in HVAC, windows, and flooring to reduce operating expenses and tenant dissatisfaction.
iii. Full Renovation and Security Enhancements: Invest $4 million to modernize infrastructure and amenities and add security systems to mitigate crime-related external obsolescence.

1. What type of depreciation is primarily caused by the aging HVAC systems, windows, and flooring at Bayview Tower?
   A) Physical deterioration
   B) Functional obsolescence
   C) External obsolescence
   D) Economic depreciation
2. Which type of depreciation is most difficult for Bayview Tower's management to mitigate?
   A) Physical deterioration
   B) Functional obsolescence
   C) External obsolescence
   D) All types are equally difficult
3. How does functional obsolescence differ from physical deterioration in Bayview Tower's case?
   A) Functional obsolescence results from tenant dissatisfaction, while physical deterioration results from infrastructure wear and tear.
   B) Functional obsolescence increases operating expenses, while physical deterioration reduces rents.
   C) Physical deterioration refers to external factors like crime, while functional obsolescence refers to aging infrastructure.
   D) Both refer to the same concept of wear and tear.
4. How can sensitivity analysis help Ping in evaluating the proposed investment strategies?
   A) By predicting tenant preferences over the next decade
   B) By determining the exact cost of physical deterioration
   C) By assessing how changes in variables like vacancy rates or rent growth impact financial performance
   D) By eliminating all uncertainties in the financial forecast
5. What is the likely long-term impact if Bayview Tower's management fails to address functional obsolescence?
   A) Operating expenses will stabilize over time
   B) Vacancy rates will rise, and rents will stagnate
   C) Tenant demand will remain consistent despite outdated features
   D) Modern competing properties will lose their appeal
6. If Bayview Tower conducts a forecasting analysis, what key factors should it consider?
   A) Rent growth, vacancy trends, and operating expenses
   B) Tax incentives for renovation projects
   C) Changes in local crime rates and population demographics
   D) All of the above
7. Why might Bayview Tower's management decide to invest in a $4 million full renovation instead of a $1 million targeted upgrade?
   A) To address all three types of depreciation (physical, functional, and external obsolescence)
   B) To increase rent growth and stabilize tenant retention
   C) To remain competitive with nearby properties
   D) All of the above

10 Leases and Leasing Strategy

CHAPTER OUTLINE

LEARNING OBJECTIVES

After reading this chapter, you should understand:

- The major characteristics and descriptive terminology used in commercial property leases in the United States.
- What does "effective rent" mean, and how to calculate using an annuitized lease value?
- The major factors determining lease value to the landlord that are left out of the effective rent calculation.
- Some major leasing strategy issues and trade-offs facing landlords and tenants, including occupancy costs and space productivity.

The operating cash flow on which the value of commercial properties is based derives fundamentally from the space market that we explored in earlier chapters of this book. More directly, however, this operating cash flow is mediated by leases, at least on the revenue side. It should immediately be noted that the terms "lease" and "rent" are sometimes used interchangeably, but this would be wrong. A lease involves a (long-term) contract between a holder of property rights and a consumer

DOI: 10.1201/9781003643838-12

or user of at least some of those rights, covering a specified period of time. The property owner or landlord is referred to as the *lessor*.[1] The tenant is referred to as the *lessee*. Normally, the lease gives possession and usage rights but not development or redevelopment rights.[2] The *price* of the lease is normally called *rent* and is typically paid periodically, although up-front payments may be an option for some leases. In addition to possessory rights, the lease normally specifies other rights and duties on the part of the tenant and the landlord, and statutory or common law may dictate certain requirements, especially for residential properties. For example, the landlord may be required to provide a certain type of parking or signage. Lease law is an extensive branch of the law, and commercial lease contracts are usually very complex legal documents.

In residential properties, leases are short-term, typically yearly or month-to-month. In lodging properties, there are generally no leases at all. However, long-term leases of various types are the norm in most other types of commercial property. In all cases, the nature of leases and the major considerations in leasing strategy are key elements in the operational management of commercial properties and important determinants of the investment performance and value of such assets. Without attempting to be fully comprehensive in treating commercial property leases (a topic that would go well beyond the financial economics perspective from which this book is primarily written), we believe that it is nevertheless appropriate in this chapter to introduce some of the basic terminology, analytical tools, and strategic considerations that are important from an economic perspective regarding commercial property leases and leasing.

As a threshold consideration, let us ask a question that may initially seem too obvious: Why does leasing exist? Why don't most users of commercial space build and own the space they use directly themselves? If you go back a while, say before World War II, you will find that owner-occupancy was much more common for commercial space occupants than it is today, and it still is so in many other countries outside the United States. The leasing of commercial real estate in the United States has exploded since the middle of the twentieth century. Why?

Aside from high transaction costs to buy and sell, a major reason, at least in the United States, is income taxes. The particular tax circumstances of tenants and landlords, in the context of both corporate and personal income tax codes, can cause leasing to create the potential for tax arbitrage, that is, to save taxes overall on a net basis across the property investors and the tenants (e.g., if the landlord is tax-exempt and the tenant is subject to double-taxation then the deduction of rent expenses from taxable income can more than offset the loss of depreciation tax shields).

However, there are other important reasons why leasing exists besides taxes. One major reason for leasing is the specialization of skills and expertise and economies of scale. The development, operation, and management of built space have become specialized industries in their own right in the United States and other mature economies. Developers and landlords specializing in this business can do a better job than one-off owner-occupiers who are not primarily focused on developing, operating, and managing built space per se. And there can be economies of scale in applying such special expertise. There may also be free rider or agency problems that leasing can solve. For example, if a single landlord owns all the spaces in which all the shops in a retail center operate, then centralized control can be exercised to optimize the shopping center's functioning as a whole. Common functions with positive externalities, such as the provision of security, become the responsibility of the landlord, who can assess the costs optimally from all of the space users via their rent. Location spillovers and synergies can be optimally managed. Other reasons for leasing can arise from heterogeneity or asymmetry in knowledge about the real estate market, in access to credit, or in preference for avoidance or exposure to specific real estate-related risks.

---

[1] The lessor is not necessarily the underlying property owner. He may be a leasehold owner, for example, the master tenant subleasing space to a subtenant.

[2] An exception to this may occur in the case of very long-term leases of land, often referred to as ground leases.

10.1 COMMERCIAL PROPERTY LEASE TERMINOLOGY AND TYPOLOGY

For a variety of reasons, therefore, leasing has become the dominant way in which most commercial space is occupied and paid for by space users in the United States, at least for the larger and more valuable properties that characterize the professional and institutional real estate investment industry. With this in mind, let's explore some of the basic and typical terminology and characteristics of leases.

10.1.1 Basic Lease Typology: The Responsibility for Expenses

Commercial property leases vary in how the operating expenses of the building are treated. Some leases require the landlord to pay these expenses, some leases require the tenant to pay them, and others provide for various forms of sharing of the operating expenses. By shifting some or all of the operating expense burden to the tenant, the landlord gains the obvious advantage of some protection against inflation or uncertainty in operating expenses. The landlord's reduction in inflation risk and budget uncertainty is offset by an increase in these risks to the tenant. Broadly, the different ways of handling operating expenses are represented in three types of leases: gross, net, and hybrid leases.

- ***Gross Lease.*** In a gross lease, the landlord pays all the operating expenses. This is also called a *full-service lease* because the landlord provides such services as electricity, heat, water, cleaning, maintenance, security, and so on, with no direct expense to the tenant. Generally, telecommunications services are not included even in a full-service lease. Gross leases are the most popular lease type for office properties (Exhibit 10-1). The main reason is that it is difficult, if not impossible, for the landlord to accurately attribute operating expenses to specific tenants in multi-tenant buildings, especially when there is no separate metering. In such a case, it is impossible to accurately know how much electricity every individual tenant uses in a year. In such instances, it is simpler to charge a higher rent amount that covers the operating expenses of every tenant.
- ***Net Lease.*** In a net lease, the tenant is responsible for paying the operating expenses of the building. In a pure net lease (sometimes referred to as **triple net, NNN, or absolute net**), all or almost all operating expenses of the building are charged to the tenant, including expenses that are fixed, that is, not sensitive to the level of occupancy in the building, such as property taxes and insurance costs. However, even with a pure net lease, the landlord may cover some expenses, such as the property manager's fees and costs specifically associated with leasing activities. In multi-tenant buildings, net leases usually provide for all of the building's expenses (even those associated with running the common areas, such as elevators, security, and lighting of lobbies) to be charged to individual tenants on a pro-rata basis, determined by the fraction of the total rentable floor area occupied by each tenant. Typically, an estimate of building operating expenses is derived for the current year based on the past year's actual expense record, and the tenants will pay monthly expense reimbursements based on this estimate. Periodically (typically at the end of the year), the accounts are squared based on the operating expenses incurred, as evidenced in an auditable record. The total payments from the tenants to the landlord thus consist of two components: the net rent payment and the expense reimbursement. NNN leases are mostly popular for properties with single tenants, which is typical for retail and industrial properties (Exhibit 10-1). In contrast to most office properties, the operating expenses are straightforward to attribute to the single tenant in this case.
- ***Hybrid Lease.*** A hybrid lease involves some aspects of both gross and net leases. In other words, the tenant and landlord share the payment of building operating expenses. This may be done in various ways. One common approach is for certain specific expenses to be designated as the tenants' responsibility, while other expenses are the landlord's responsibility. For example, the landlord might pay the fixed costs of property taxes and insurance, as well as utilities and services that cannot be metered separately for each tenant, such as water, building

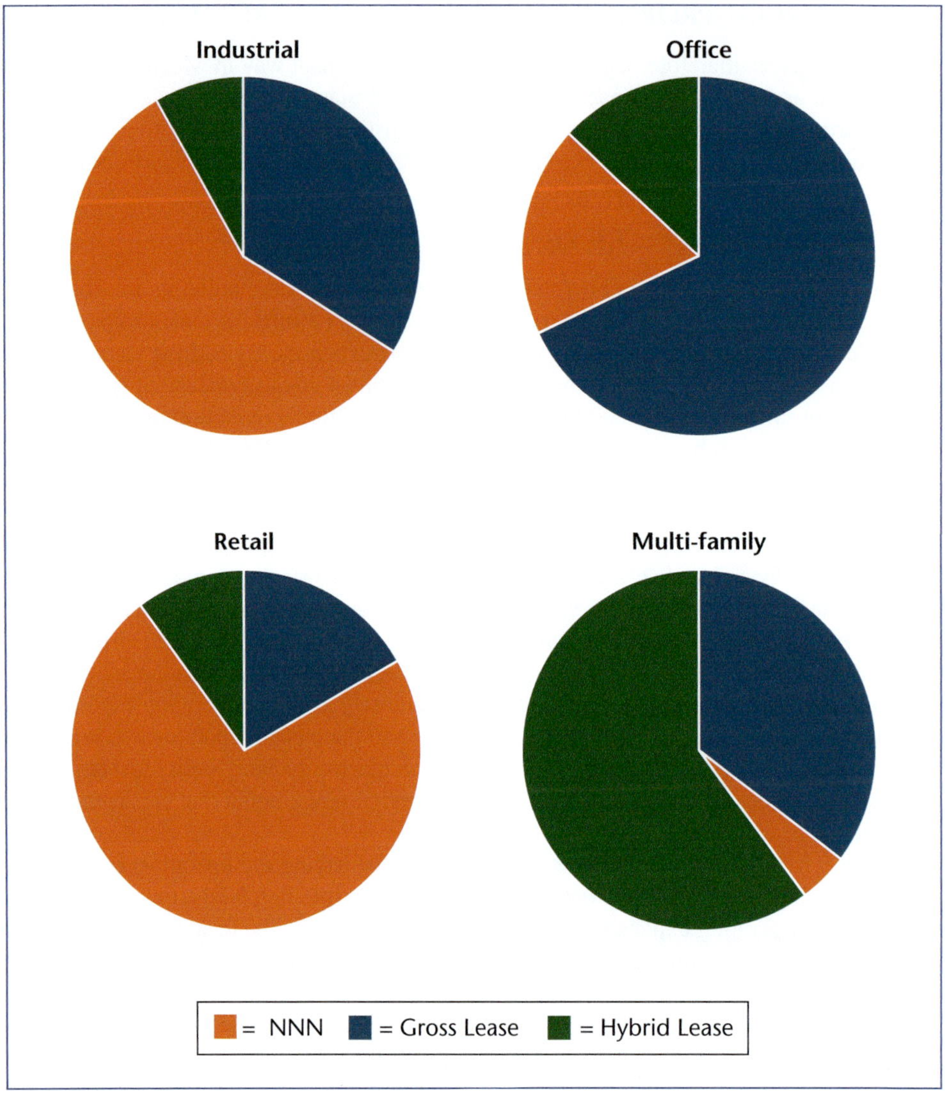

EXHIBIT 10-1 Distribution of Lease Types (by Square Footage) in the US between 2013 and 2023 per Property Type.

Source: Compstak.

security, and common area costs. In contrast, the tenants are responsible for other utility and maintenance costs that can be attributed to each tenant. As shown in Exhibit 10-1, apartment leases are mostly hybrid. Apartments (at least in the US) typically have separate gas and electricity meters per unit, but not for water usage. As a result, the tenant will pay for their electricity and gas separately, but the water bill is part of the rent.

One risk mitigation strategy for landlords sharing expenses is known as an **expense stop**, in which the tenant agrees to pay all operating expenses above a specified annual level known as the "stop." In effect, the expenses for the landlord stop growing at the specified stop level. This technique for sharing expenses is obviously designed to protect the landlord against unexpected inflation in operating expenses, as well as to provide the tenant with an incentive to keep operating costs down while still providing the tenant with something pretty close to a full-service lease. The expense stop is usually set at or near the level of operating expenses at the time the lease is signed, thereby guaranteeing the landlord against any effective increase in operating expenses she will have to pay during the life of the lease.

In multi-tenant buildings, the expense stops are typically negotiated separately for each, resulting in each lease possibly having a different stop amount. The expense stop provision causes tenants to be responsible for making expense reimbursement payments to the landlord based on their individual expense stop levels and a pro-rata assignment of expense responsibility determined by the fraction of the building's rentable space each tenant occupies. For example, suppose a 100,000 SF building has two tenants, tenant A occupying 60,000 SF and tenant B 40,000 SF. Suppose the total operating expenses of the building are $500,000 (i.e., $5.00/SF) and that tenant A has an expense stop of $4.00/SF while tenant B has an expense stop of $4.50/SF. Then, in addition to their rent, tenant A would owe the landlord $60,000 ([$5.00 - $4.00] × 60,000 SF) and tenant B, $20,000 ([$4.50 - $4.00] × 40.000 SF) in expense reimbursements.

10.1.2 Types of Rent Changes in Leases

One of the most important characteristics of long-term commercial property leases that is of interest to investors is how the rent is specified to change over time during the lease contract term. Rent changes serve several purposes. The most basic purpose is to reflect changes in the relevant space market that cause the equilibrium rent to change for new leases being signed in that market. Another purpose in the case of gross leases is to help protect the landlord from inflation in the operating expenses of running the building. A third purpose, which is important in retail leases, is to allow the landlord to share in the tenant's operating profits, as these profits are typically attributable in part to the store location and/or to the landlord's management of the shopping center of which it is a part. The five most common types of rent change provisions in long-term leases in the United States are described here.

- ***Flat Rent.*** The simplest type of lease agreement provides for a fixed, constant rent level throughout the term of the lease; in other words, there is no rent change. Virtually all short-term leases have flat rent, and flat rent is not uncommon in longer-term leases as well, particularly during times of low general inflation.
- ***Graduated Rent.*** The simplest type of lease that provides for a changing rent is called a graduated lease. Such a lease includes specified **step-ups** (or steps) in the rent. In this structure, both the timing and the amount of the rent changes are specified up front in the lease contract. For example, a 10-year graduated lease might start at $15/SF with a provision that at the end of every two years (i.e., after years 2, 4, 6, and 8), the rent will increase by $1 per SF.
- ***Revaluated Rent.*** A revaluation lease also specifies the *times* when the rental payments may change in the lease contract, but it does not specify the exact dollar *amounts* of the rent changes in advance. Instead, the lease stipulates that a professional real estate appraiser will appraise the property (or the particular rental space and rental market), and the rent will be adjusted accordingly. Sometimes, such revaluations call for upward-only adjustments in rent, while other leases allow the adjustment to be in either direction. In the latter case, this becomes a mechanism to keep the rent current with the changes in the local rental market. For example, a 20-year revaluation lease might specify that a certified appraiser will appraise the property after every fifth year, and the rent will be set at one-tenth of the property value per year. Or the lease might call for an analysis of rents on new leases signed on comparable spaces in the local rental market and require the subject rent to be adjusted to the estimated fair market rental rate. Revaluation leases are particularly appropriate for very long-term leases and are traditionally common in the United Kingdom and some other European countries. Since the revaluation can be controversial, some leases will specify peer properties to be used in the sample ahead of time for calculating the appropriate market-based rent.
- ***Indexed Rent.*** Indexed leases call for the rent to be adjusted according to some publicly observable and regularly reported index, such as the consumer price index (CPI) or the producer

price index (PPI). A typical indexed lease might require rents to be adjusted annually at some percentage of the CPI. For example, a 50 percent CPI adjustment would require the rent to be increased by 2.5 percent if inflation had been 5 percent (i.e., if the CPI had increased by 5 percent) during the preceding year. "Full" (i.e., 100 percent) CPI-adjusted leases are not uncommon. Still, often, the adjustment is less than full (50 percent being a typical level) because it may be perceived that building operating expenses typically do not grow as fast as inflation or that the market rents that the building could charge would not grow as fast as inflation.

As a numerical example of how CPI-adjusted rent works, consider a lease that calls for an annual 75 percent CPI adjustment in the rent on the lease anniversary every July, based on the change in the CPI between the previous May and the May before that. Suppose the CPI in May of the prior year was 240, and the CPI in May of the current year was 250. Then there was (250/240) – 1 = 4.17 percent inflation. Seventy-five percent of 4.17 percent is 3.13 percent. So if the rent had been $12/SF per year (paid as $1/SF each month), then the new rent as of July would rise to $12.38/SF per year ($1.0313/SF paid each month), based on $1.0313 × 12 = $12.38.

- ***Percentage Rent.*** Percentage leases also involve changes in rent over time. In this case, however, the motivation and nature of the change are rather different from the foregoing examples, and the application of percentage rent is limited to retail property space. In a percentage lease, the rent is a specified percentage of the tenant's sales revenue or net income in the rented space. Often, the rent will include both a fixed component referred to as the **base rent** (which may or may not have any of the previously described change provisions) plus a percentage component. Sometimes, the percentage component only applies to revenue or profits above a specified threshold amount. Percentage rents are especially common in class A multi-tenant retail spaces, such as shopping malls (and especially for the "in-line" stores rather than the anchor tenants). For example, the rent for a boutique space in a shopping mall might be defined as $10/SF per year plus 5 percent of the gross sales receipts of the store during the preceding year, pro-rated monthly. Obviously, such a lease would require a provision in the contract enabling the mall owner to audit the books of the shop.

10.2 LEASE CHARACTERISTICS AFFECTING VALUE OR RENT

Several characteristics go into determining the rent that the parties agree to in a lease and the value the lease has to the landlord once it is signed. Later in this chapter, we will broadly discuss leasing strategy considerations from both the landlord and tenant perspectives. At this point, however, it may be useful by way of background to call your attention to several characteristics of the space, the tenant, and the lease itself that help to determine either the rent or the lease value (or both).

- ***The Space.*** The most basic and obvious determinant of the value of the space and, therefore, of the rent the landlord can charge is the nature of the product the tenant is getting in return for the rent, namely, the space itself. Obviously, location is an important characteristic of the space. As noted in the early parts of this book, location is important at several levels, ranging from the metropolitan area to the neighborhood to the specific site and even the location of the space within a multi-tenant building. For example, higher floors may command higher rents if views are valued, or prestige is associated with high locations in the building. Rent and rentability are also strongly influenced by the physical and architectural qualities of the building and the specific space being leased. Taller buildings tend to have more structural partitions that impact usable space. (See Chapter 5 as well.) The space's size, shape, and configuration are of great importance in determining its usefulness to the tenant and, therefore, the rent that can be charged. Two spaces in nearly identical locations may command very different rents because they are of different sizes or shapes. In general, rent per square foot (SF) tends to be minimized for space sizes near the most typical or widely demanded space size in the relevant space market, for which multi-tenant buildings are designed, and therefore, supply is greatest.

Particularly large spaces may charge a premium, though occupancy of an entire floor can bring certain efficiencies or benefits to both the landlord and the tenant, which can affect the rent.[3] (See the feature "How Rent Is Related to the Size of the Space Being Rented" on p. 240.)

- ***Tenant.*** Who the lessee is can also be important to the landlord. Some tenants are inevitably more desirable than others due to credit quality, prestige, synergy with other tenants, or parking use intensity. The orchestration of positive externalities among tenants is a key part of the job of shopping mall managers, for example, as certain combinations and spatial positioning of types of shops will lead to greater sales volumes for all. Tenants that rent large blocks of space early in the development of a new building provide a particular benefit for the landlord/developer. High-profile, prestigious tenants whose names may appear on the outside of the structure also bring a particular benefit to the landlord. Two tenants in nearly identical spaces may not pay the same rent for such reasons.
- ***Date and Term of the Lease.*** The length of time covered by the lease (the **lease term**), the time the lease is signed, and when it expires can have value implications for the landlord. Other things being equal, landlords typically prefer longer-term leases or leases that do not expire when many other leases in the same building are scheduled to expire.
- ***Rent.*** Obviously, the level of the rent and the provisions for rent changes during the lease term are fundamental and direct determinants of the value of the lease to the landlord. Indeed, this characteristic of lease value is so basic that we only mention it here to make the point that rent is not the *only* determinant of lease value. Other characteristics and considerations in this list interact with the rent in determining lease value for the landlord. Of course, rent alone only affects the *gross* value of the lease, which is only one part of the NPV of the lease transaction decision, which must also consider the *opportunity cost* to the landlord (what the landlord gives up by entering into the lease agreement).
- ***Concessions.*** Landlords often offer tenants various forms of concessions, such as rent abatements, tenant improvement allowances, moving expense allowances, and so forth.[4] In general, concessions reduce the landlord's net cash flow from the lease, particularly at the outset or during the early stages of the lease. Landlords provide concessions to tenants as "sweeteners" to get them to sign leases that they otherwise would not agree to, with provisions that are beneficial to the landlord or at a time when the rental market is unfavorable for the landlord.
- ***Lease Covenants.*** The value of a lease to a landlord can be influenced by the specific covenants or provisions in the lease contract. In general, such provisions may limit or expand the landlord's and the tenant's rights and duties in ways that affect value. For example, tenants have the right to **sublet** (or assign the use of) their space unless this right is explicitly negated or limited in the lease contract. The ability to sublet the space gives the tenant flexibility and potential value. On the other hand, the landlord may want to control the type of tenant that moves in or share in any increase in rent.
- ***Lease Options.*** Leases often provide explicit options to either the tenant or the landlord. Some such options can importantly influence value. As noted in Chapter 16, an option generally refers to a right without obligation to obtain some benefit, perhaps requiring the payment of some additional sum to exercise the option. Options provide valuable flexibility to the option holder. Still, they may restrict the rights of the opposite party (the option grantor, either the landlord or tenant), thereby reducing value to that party *(ceteris paribus)*. The most common lease options that benefit tenants include the following:
    - **Renewal option**: This option entitles the tenant to renew the space at the end of the lease, either at a specified rent or at prevailing market rents. If it is the latter, this option is similar to a right of first refusal.

---

[3] For example, there may then be no need for a common area on the floor.

[4] While some level of tenant improvement may be considered to be normally provided by the landlord (especially in a new or reconstructed building where the space has not been completely finished out), the provision of extra-large tenant allowances for either tenant improvements or moving may be viewed as a concession.

- **Cancellation option**: This option may be written either for the landlord or tenant and entitles the option holder to cancel the lease prior to the end of the lease term (with specified notice).
- **Expansion option**: This may be in the form of a **right of first refusal** to the tenant for space adjacent to the leased space, or it may be a true lease option specifying a rent at which the tenant has the right but not the obligation to take specified space during some specified window of time.

TEXT BOX 10.1 HOW RENT IS RELATED TO THE SIZE OF THE SPACE BEING RENTED

The chart shows how rent for office and industrial space typically varies by size. The chart is based on average effective rent data from Compstak for the entire US between 2013 and 2023. For office, the effective rents per square foot tend to be lowest for small office space, willing to fill in gaps left over after larger tenants have been accommodated. As tenants require larger and larger spaces, there are usually fewer choices in the market. Such space is also more likely to be provided to an established firm and is often custom-built, pre-leased, or first-generation space customized for the tenant. As such, the cost of tenant improvements tends to be higher. For all these reasons, the rents tend to be higher. (Exceptions can be found for anchor tenants or for leases used by the developer to launch or define the identity of the entire building.) For industrial property, we see the opposite pattern. In contrast to office space, industrial (single-story) property is typically built on the city's outskirts, where space is no issue.

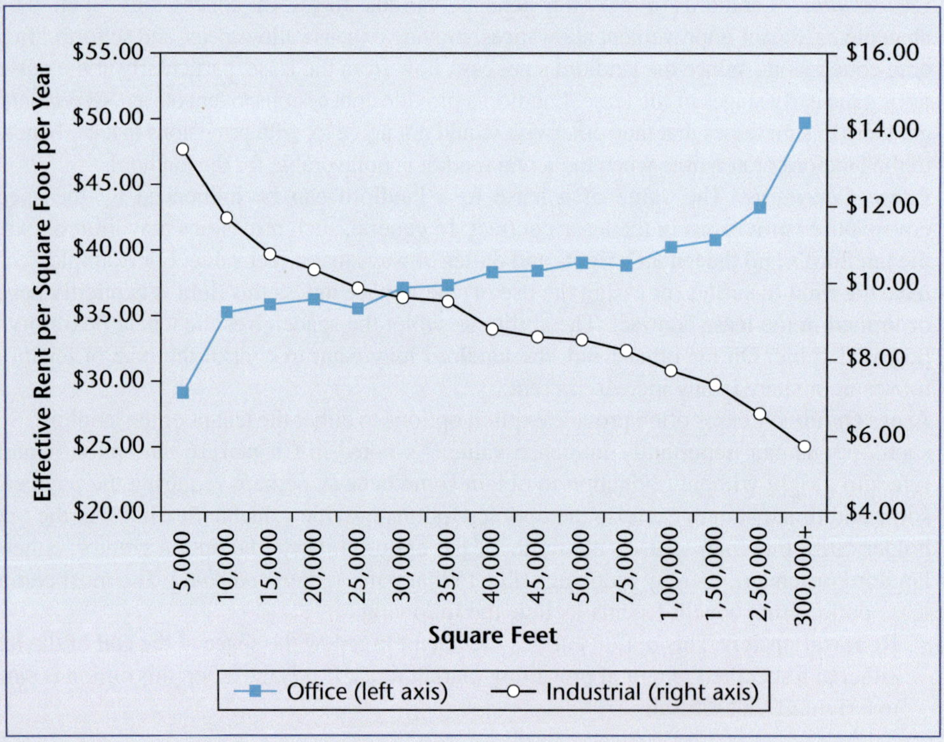

EXHIBIT 10-2 Rent and Size for Office and Industrial Properties.

Source: Compstak.

Additionally, large office buildings tend to have many floors, which industrial properties do not suffer from. Adding floors to real property is more expensive than adding square footage by increasing the footprint (as is the case for industrial properties). The reason is that the load-bearing structure needs to become larger and larger as you increase the number of floors to carry all this added weight. This is more expensive, and the larger load-bearing structure also "eats up" rentable space. As a result, the rent per square foot of the remaining space needs to increase to offset these losses.

10.3 EFFECTIVE RENT CALCULATIONS

The term effective rent is used quite commonly in commercial real estate, but it is often not clearly defined, and people may mean different things when they use the term. Most broadly, effective rent is simply a per annum or per period rental rate that reflects not just the initially stated rent but other aspects of the long-term lease that affect the lease's present value. For example, there may be some free rent given by the landlord to the tenant up front as an incentive to move in. Not uncommonly, there may be rent step-ups at future points within the lease term (as described in Section 10.1.2). The concept of effective rent somehow collapses and reflects all (or some) such considerations into a single per-period rent number.

The simplest way to do this is to just add up all the rental payments provided for under the lease contract (reflecting step-ups or possibly estimates of conditional step-ups), net of or minus any special concessions or incentives provided by the landlord, and then divide by the total number of rental periods in the lease contract.[5] This simplest approach does not attempt to discount time or risk as in a more rigorous present value analysis. This simple definition of effective rent is often how the term is applied in common practice, especially in the leasing brokerage industry. However, there is also substantial (and growing) use of more sophisticated measures of effective rent that do attempt to account for time and present value. We will focus on a more sophisticated or rigorous measure, but to clarify that we are doing so, we shall use the more explicit term **annuitized lease value** (ALV) instead of "effective rent." (But remember that in common parlance, what we will now refer to as ALV may often be called "effective rent" in practice.)

The ALV of a lease is a level annuity with the same present value as that of the expected cash flows of the lease. In current practice, the discounting is often done in an ad hoc manner by applying a constant discount rate for all leases and all tenants (10 percent is probably the most widely used rate). However, ALV can be defined more rigorously based on the economic present value of the lease, which, of course, requires using the economic OCC as the discount rate to compute the annuity. Our focus here will be on the more rigorous, economics-based perspective.

ALV can be computed from either the landlord's or the tenant's perspective. When dealing with long-term leases, the rigorous economics-based ALV construct can aid in comparing alternative lease structures and lease terms. However, one must be careful when making such comparisons. The effective rent typically does not satisfactorily quantify all of the relevant issues to either side. Nonfinancial considerations not captured in the ALV metric may dominate a lease decision, such as exclusive floor access, external signage requirements, exclusive parking access or services,

[5] The data provider used throughout this chapter (Compstak) uses this definition of effective rent. According to their data, rents paid in year 1 are 6.5% higher compared to the effective rent on that lease. The asking rent is even 14% higher compared to the effective rent. The difference between asking rent and eventual effective rent was largest during the GFC, when landlords allowed for a great number of concessions in order to attract tenants.

tenant resiliency during economic recessions or government-mandated shutdowns, or the nature of co-tenants.

ALV is computed in two steps. First, you calculate the present value of the expected cash flow under the lease. We will label this value LPV for lease present value:

Equation 1

$$LPV = CF_1 + \frac{CF_2}{1+k} + \frac{CF_3}{(1+k)^2} + \ldots + \frac{CF_T}{(1+k)^{(T-1)}}$$

where T is the lease term, CF_t is the net cash flow to the landlord in year t, and k is the discount rate.[6] Note that in leases (unlike mortgages and most other financial calculations), payments are usually in advance (that is, at the *beginning* of the period rather than in *arrears*). Thus, the first cash flow is usually at time 0 and, therefore, undiscounted (already in present value).[7]

To compute effective rent from the tenant's perspective, the CF_t amounts should represent the tenant's gross cash outflows due to all space occupancy costs, including payment of whatever building operating expenses are not covered by the landlord (e.g., in a net lease). In the second step of the ALV calculation, you determine the annualized value (or equivalent level annuity payment) of the LPV:

Equation 2

$$Effective\ Rent = \frac{(LPV)k}{(1+k)\left[1-1/(1+k)^T\right]}$$

where k is the same discount rate as previously, and T is again the term of the lease.[8] In Excel, there is also the PMT(rate,nper,PV,FV,1) function, which can help you find the effective rent quite easily, where the rate is monthly for a monthly payment, the number of periods is NPER, in months, FV is usually 0, and the 1 indicates the beginning of the period for the payment.

The second step (calculating the annualized value) might seem redundant (especially from the landlords' perspective). Aren't we supposed to aspire to the highest possible total (present) lease value as the landlord (and the lowest as the tenant)? In reality, a problem arises when multiple options have different lease lengths. In this case, for example, you cannot compare a 5-year lease to a 7-year lease. The reason is that after the 5-year lease expires, you can still rent out this space as the landlord. And from the tenants' perspective, you will still rent after 5 years (either in this space or elsewhere). Thus, even if the 7-year lease provides a larger total present value, you can't compare this directly with the present value provided by the 5-year lease. To make it comparable, you have to make the lease length the same, something you do by annualizing the present value of the lease.

---

6 Here we are depicting annual cash flows for simplicity of illustration, but a more precise calculation would use monthly cash flows for monthly rent, although the ALV is then often quoted in nominal annual terms as 12 times the monthly rent.

7 However, with concessions, this first cash flow may be zero or even negative, for example, if the landlord must pay the tenant's moving costs.

8 Note that in real-world practice the annuity in arrears formula is often used, technically incorrectly, although usually it makes little difference.

TEXT BOX 10.2 ARE RENEWAL OPTIONS "AT MARKET RENT" A CONCESSION?

Lease renewal options often give the tenant the right to renew at the market rent prevailing at the time of lease expiration. There might be a provision for this market rent to be determined by an appraiser if the tenant and landlord cannot agree on the market rent at that time. Especially in a highly efficient ("information rich") rental market (i.e., one in which there is a lot of easily available information about the rents and other terms in the leases being signed and in which there is a lot of leasing activity employing relatively homogeneous leases on relatively homogeneous spaces), this option is effectively no more than a right of first refusal.

Therefore, one might think that a renewal option is not a concession for the landlord. Indeed, if the new lease is at market rate either way (new lease vs. renewal), there is no cost to the landlord. However, two potential "holdup" problems exist that **will** result in a cost for the landlord. (A *holdup problem* is when one party to an agreement can potentially extract an unfair advantage from the other party in the future due to the situation established in the agreement.)

The first "holdup" problem arises especially for tenants that face *large moving costs*. If a tenant has to spend large sums of cash to relocate, and the landlord knows this, the landlord might use this against the tenant to bargain for a higher rent at the end of the lease. In such a situation, the tenant would have to factor in the expected cost of this holdup in the rent they would agree to in the first place. The "at market" renewal option thus facilitates the lease agreement from the tenant's perspective; it may have some slight cost to the landlord because it removes the potential negotiating leverage the landlord could otherwise use to try to obtain a slightly above-market rental rate from the tenant (on the basis that the tenant would save moving expenses). Tenants that experience large moving costs include corporate HQs and many industrial buildings. It is, therefore, not surprising that such tenants will also bargain for longer lease terms in general.

The second problem arises from the tenant "holding up" the landlord. This happens when the landlord wishes to redevelop a property (or at the very least needs the building empty for a large-scale renovation). A redevelopment/renovation could drastically improve the cash flow and, therefore, the property's value. The costs to the landlord could, therefore, be quite large if a tenant uses their option to renew for a specific number of years. If there are only a few tenants (or even only one) that cause this problem, the landlord will typically pay off the tenant for a large sum of cash and will provide an alternative space as well.

Thus, in real estate, a renewal option may have some value to the tenant (and cost to the landlord) even if the option is only for renewal at prevailing market rates and assuming the contract gives the tenant some power over the estimation of what that market rate is (e.g., by giving the tenant a say in the selection of the rent appraiser). Presumably, in equilibrium (in the space market), this value and cost are equated to the rent and other terms agreed to by both parties in the lease.

10.3.1 Discount Rate in the ALV

In the computation of ALV, it is common practice for the discount rate (k) to be approximated rather casually for the typical tenant, using some conventional rule of thumb. For example, 10 percent per year (or 0.833 percent per month) has been widely used. When such blanket rule-of-thumb discounting is used, with the same rate applied to all leases and all tenants and without regard to the current yields and term structure of interest rates in the bond market, the ALV (or in this case probably referred to as "effective rent") calculation is, in theory, little more than a type of shorthand way of quoting rents to account for concessions and landlord capital expenditures (such as tenant improvement expenditures, TIs).[9] ALV used in this way does not measure very precisely the impact of the lease on the market value of the lessor's property rights. While ALV, as defined in this simplified way, does have some practical usefulness, it is not rigorous from a financial economics perspective. In the present section, we will suggest a more correct and sophisticated approach that is still intuitive and easy to apply. We should also note that most of the time, the opportunity cost of capital for tenants tends to be higher than for landlords, as they face different risks and returns with their capital. One might argue that the k for a growing tenant could be quite different from a simple rule of thumb percentage or the rate a landlord might use.

Suppose we are interested in defining the ALV so that it reflects the market value that the lease would have, say, in a lease-obligation-backed security (LOBS) traded in the bond market.[10] Then, the discount rate used in the ALV calculation should reflect the tenant's credit rating and the bond market's current yield curve. In other words, k should equate to the rate at which the tenant could borrow money in an unsecured loan with a duration equal to the duration of the lease cash flows. After all, the lease cash flows are contractual cash flows backed by the tenant's credit, similar to loan cash flows pledged to a lender when the tenant borrows money.[11] In fact, the tenant's borrowing rate is a good rate to use to compute the ALV from the tenant's perspective, at least for a typical fixed-rent lease.

The computation of ALV from the landlord's perspective may be viewed a little differently. The landlord is typically interested in using the ALV to measure the impact of the lease on the market value of his property. For this purpose, it makes more sense to define the ALV based on the present value attributable to the space that is being leased over the period covered by the lease. This present value consists of two components. The first is the value of the lease itself, for example, as it would be valued as a component in a LOBS traded in the bond market, as we just described. To evaluate this component of the landlord's value, the tenant's borrowing rate on an unsecured loan would indeed be the correct discount rate, as we described earlier. But another component to the landlord's value is usually associated with the leased space itself. How does that affect the calculation?

Suppose there is a positive probability that the tenant will default on her lease. In that case, discounting the lease cash flows at the tenant's unsecured borrowing rate will reflect this default probability's impact on the lease's present value. In other words, the lease's present value will be reduced by the probability that the tenant might not be able to pay (some) components of the contractual lease cash flow. These unpaid rents would indeed be losses to the bondholders of a LOBS backed by the lease.[12] However, the landlord probably would not face that much loss in cash flow from the leased space in the event of tenant default during the lease term. In a long-term lease, the landlord would likely be able to evict the defaulted tenant and rent the space to a new tenant before the end of the original lease term. For this reason, a lower discount rate, better approximated by the

[9] As noted, it is not uncommon in practice for discounting to be ignored altogether in the effective rent calculation (effectively assuming $k = 0$).

[10] LOBS, which is like a mortgage-backed security, is discussed briefly in Chapter 4. In actual practice, not all leases are effectively "bondable," and even those that are sometimes are evaluated with a small "illiquidity premium" in their OCC. Therefore, it might be appropriate to add a small extra premium to the debt OCC of the tenant in estimating the OCC applicable to the lease.

[11] If the lease includes revaluation, indexing (such as CPI adjustments), or percentage of sales components, then the lease cash flows will not be exactly like those of fixed interest rate bonds, as they will have some contractual volatility. Such differences could affect the appropriate discount rate in either direction. For example, a CPI-adjusted lease results in the lease being a partial hedge against inflation risk (better than bonds) and, therefore, should probably be discounted at a lower OCC than the tenant's borrowing rate.

[12] Actual LOBS often have default protection provided or paid for by the landlord. For this reason, the yield on LOBS may not be reflective of the appropriate unsecured tenant borrowing rate to use in computing the ALV on a specific lease.

rate at which the tenant could borrow on a *secured* loan, would typically be a more appropriate discount rate to use to compute the effective rent from the landlord's perspective.[13]

10.3.2 ALV Numerical Examples

In this section, we will examine two hypothetical leases from both the landlord's and the tenant's perspectives to illustrate the calculation and usage of the ALV as defined. Both leases are net; the tenant pays the operating expenses.

Lease A is characterized as follows:

- Term: 5 years
- Rent: $20/SF, net
- Concessions: 1-year free rent upfront
- Tenant still pays operating expenses during rent holiday

Assuming a discount rate of 7 percent, lease A's ALV is seen to be $15.44/SF, computed as follows (Equation 1):[14]

$$LPV(\textbf{Option A}, \text{landlord}) = \$0 + \frac{\$20}{1.07} + \frac{\$20}{(1.07)^2} + \frac{\$20}{(1.07)^3} + \frac{\$20}{(1.07)^4} = \$67.74$$

Subsequently, to compute the effective rent, we use the following formula (Equation 2):

$$\text{Effective Rent}(\textbf{Option A}, \text{ landlord}) = \frac{(\$67.74)0.07}{(1.07)\left[1 - \frac{1}{(1.07)^5}\right]} = \$15.44/\textbf{SF}$$

Next, suppose we have an alternative possible lease contract, denoted lease B. Lease B is characterized as follows:

- Term: 6 years
- Rent: $24/SF, net
- Concessions: Two years free rent upfront
- Tenant still pays operating expenses during rent holiday

Again, assuming a discount rate of 7 percent, lease B's ALV is seen to be $14.90/SF, as computed (using the same two-step procedure) here:

---

13 Note that, in principle, the state variable that governs the tenant's lease default event likely has more to do with the net income or value of the tenant's firm than with the market rent or value in the real estate space or asset market in which the building is situated. In the absence of an explicit cancellation option written into the lease, only limited liability and bankruptcy law enable the tenant to have a put option on their leased space, that is, the ability to avoid payment of remaining rents under the lease. More sophisticated approaches to lease valuation based on real options valuation theory can often allow a more rigorous valuation of leases, particularly complex leases involving options of various types written into the lease.

14 Note that the effect of the concession of 1-year free rent causes the first year's cash flow to the landlord to be zero. In the present example, we have ignored leasing costs borne by the landlord, such as tenant improvement expenditures (TIs). In reality, such costs often cause the first year of the lease to have net negative cash flow for the landlord. In any case, it is important to include the effect of landlord leasing costs, such as TIs, in the computation of the ALV from the landlord's perspective for purposes of comparing the value of alternative lease proposals.

$$LPV\left(\textbf{Option B}, \text{landlord}\right) = \$0 + \$0 + \frac{\$24}{(1.07)^2} + \frac{\$24}{(1.07)^3} + \frac{\$24}{(1.07)^4} + \frac{\$24}{(1.07)^5} = \$74.97$$

$$\text{Effective Rent}\left(\textbf{Option B}, \text{landlord}\right) = \frac{(\$74.97)0.07}{(1.07)\left[1 - \frac{1}{(1.07)^6}\right]} = \textbf{\$14.90/SF}$$

Other things being equal, the landlord would prefer lease A because \$15.44 > \$14.90.

Now consider these same two leases from the perspective of the tenant. As these are net leases, the tenant must add the expected operating expenses he will have to pay in order to compute the total ALV from his perspective.[15] This is necessary so that comparisons between alternative leases with different expense provisions can be made on an apples-to-apples basis. Supposing that operating expenses are initially \$10/SF and are expected to grow at a rate of 2 percent per year, we have the following ALV calculations from the tenant's perspective. Note that we will use a modestly higher discount rate of 8 percent instead of 7 percent to reflect the lack of residual value in the event of default, as described at the end of Section 10.3.1.

- Lease A (tenant's perspective):

$$LPV\left(\textbf{Option A}, \text{ tentant}\right) = \$10 + \frac{\$30.20}{1.08} + \frac{\$30.40}{(1.08)^2} + \frac{\$30.61}{(1.08)^3} + \frac{\$30.82}{(1.08)^4} = \$110.99$$

$$\text{Effective Rent}\left(\textbf{Option A}, \text{tenant}\right) = \frac{(\$110.99)0.08}{(1.08)\left[1 - \frac{1}{(1.08)^5}\right]} = \textbf{\$25.74/SF}$$

- Lease B (tenant's perspective):

$$LPV\left(\textbf{Option B}, \text{ landlord}\right) = \$10 + \frac{\$10.20}{(1.08)^1} + \frac{\$34.40}{(1.08)^2} + \frac{\$34.61}{(1.08)^3} + \frac{\$34.82}{(1.08)^4} + \frac{\$35.04}{(1.08)^5} = \$125.86$$

$$\text{Effective Rent }\left(\textbf{Option B}, \text{tentant}\right) = \frac{(\$125.86)0.08}{(1.08)\left[1 - \frac{1}{(1.08)^6}\right]} = \textbf{\$25.21/SF}$$

Thus, the tenant has the opposite preferences to the landlord. *Other things being equal*, the tenant prefers lease B over lease A, because \$25.21 < \$25.74.[16]

---

15 Landlord capital expenditures offered to the tenant as part of the lease package (TIs) need not generally be explicitly incorporated in the tenant's ALV calculation. However, in comparing alternative lease proposals, the tenant needs to consider possible differences between the TIs being offered in the different proposals as they may lead to better quality of space in one location or the other. Obviously, common sense must apply in evaluating an overall lease proposal package. It may make sense for a tenant to pay a higher ALV if in return he receives a TI allowance or build-out from the landlord that makes the space sufficiently more attractive.

16 To facilitate comparisons between alternative lease offers, ALVs should normally be based on net cash flows, that is, *net* rents from the landlord's perspective and *gross* rents from the tenant's perspective.

In reality, where the two parties end up would depend on relative success in negotiation (in part reflecting the current supply-and-demand balance in the space market). That final position would also reflect other considerations important to either party beyond what is included in the ALV calculations described here.

10.3.3 Summarizing ALV and Effective Rent

Although ALV, when properly calculated based on a risk-adjusted discount rate, gives an important indication of the value of a given lease, neither the tenant nor the landlord should necessarily prefer the lease alternative with the best (i.e., lowest or highest, respectively) ALV. The reason is that important strategic considerations are left out of the ALV calculation. This statement applies doubly for less rigorously defined effective rent that is not based on the economic present value of the lease. In the remainder of this chapter, we focus on these broader leasing strategy considerations.

10.4 BROADER LEASING STRATEGY CONSIDERATIONS: TERM LENGTH AND THE SPACE MARKET TERM STRUCTURE OF RENT

Among the most important leasing strategy considerations not present in the ALV or effective rent calculation is the length of the lease term. We will consider this issue in this section from both the landlord and tenant perspectives, including consideration of implications for the resulting equilibrium or normative **term structure of rents**, that is, the way rents should vary in the space market at a given time as a function of the lease term. A good way to approach this question is to consider what is left out of the ALV construct described in the previous section. In other words, why would a landlord sometimes prefer a lease alternative with a lower ALV or a tenant prefer an alternative with a higher ALV?

10.4.1 Releasing Costs

An important consideration in leasing strategy but left out of the ALV or effective rent calculation of Section 10.3, is **releasing costs**. Typically, both the landlord and the tenant face costs associated with releasing. Many of these costs are not included in the effective rent calculation. For example, landlords face expected vacancy and search costs to find a new tenant whenever a lease expires without being renewed. Tenants face moving costs, including disruption of operations.

Because releasing presents potential deadweight costs to both sides in the lease agreement, releasing considerations generally affect both sides of the lease negotiation, landlord and tenant, in the same direction as far as the preferred lease term is concerned. In particular, releasing costs make it advantageous for both sides to prefer longer-term leases, *ceteris paribus.*

The consideration of releasing costs suggests a general bias toward longer-term leases at whatever term structure of rents prevails in the market so as to minimize releasing costs over the long run. However, this bias can be mitigated to some degree by the use of contractual devices to reduce the **holdup problem**, at least on one side. (Remember, a *holdup problem* is when one party to an agreement can potentially extract an unfair advantage from the other party in the future due to the situation established in the agreement.) For example, an option to renew "at market" (equivalent to a "right of first refusal") reduces the ability of the landlord to "hold up" the tenant by threatening to force the tenant to pay moving costs without the landlord giving up the chance to earn market rents.

In some circumstances, holdup costs are potentially particularly severe and cannot be effectively mitigated by contractual provisions. This is most notably the case when the tenant requires a highly customized space that requires substantial unique investment that cannot be recuperated, and where the space is vital to the tenant's operations. Such unique space, in effect, does not trade in a space market: because it is so customized for a particular user, there is no other potential demand for it or supply of it, hence no space market. This makes renewal options "at market rent" difficult to enforce. In such cases, the holdup problem from the tenant's perspective tends to lead to very long-term leases or even to "corporate real estate" in which the user-occupant of the space decides to purchase the property outright in fee simple ownership.

10.4.2 Expectations about the Future Rental Market

Expectations regarding the future trend in spot rents in the relevant space market make the opportunity cost of the lease a function of the lease term, and this is not included in the ALV formula we previously presented. For example, if spot rents are expected to rise, then longer-term leases must have higher ALVs than they otherwise would. This is required for both landlords and tenants to be indifferent between long- and short-term leases. With rising spot-rent expectations, the expected opportunity cost (to the landlord) or opportunity value (to the tenant) of foregoing a strategy of rolling over short-term leases is greater for longer-term leases within the horizon of rising projected spot rents. If, on the other hand, spot rents are expected to fall, then the opposite is the case, and longer-term leases should have lower ALVs relative to shorter-term leases than would be the case otherwise. To the extent that such expectations reflect both sides of the rental market, they will be reflected in the equilibrium lease term structure of rents. This expectation effect overlays the generally slightly downward-sloping equilibrium term structure of rents with constant spot-rent expectations due to the interlease risk effect noted in Section 10.4.1.[17]

Suppose landlord and tenant expectations differ regarding the market's future trend in spot rents. In that case, such differences might be **complementary** or conflicting regarding reaching a negotiated lease agreement. For example, if the tenant believes rents will rise and the landlord believes rents will fall, then expectations are complementary in the sense that it will be easier for the two sides to come to an agreement. If the landlord believes rents will rise and the tenant believes rents will fall, expectations are conflicting because it will be more difficult for the two sides to agree on a rent level. In the event of **conflicting** expectations, if one side or the other (or both) can convince the other to change his or her space market rent expectations, at least partially, in the direction of the other, then the agreement will be facilitated. Suppose space market expectations are conflicting and not reconcilable. In that case, an agreement will be facilitated by reducing the lease-term length, thereby reducing the impact of future changes in market rents on the opportunity cost of the lease.

In effect, shorter lease-term length provides both the landlord and the tenant more flexibility to take advantage of favorable developments in the rental market. Thus, to the extent that there is uncertainty about future market rents such that landlords and tenants can have significantly conflicting expectations, this can lead both landlords and tenants in the same general direction, namely, toward preferring shorter-term leases. In this respect, space market expectations do not carry an overall general implication for the equilibrium term structure of rents. However, rental market uncertainty alone, without conflicting expectations, does not necessarily lead to a preference for shorter lease terms, but it does lead to increased incentive to provide explicit options in the lease for both sides (see Section 10.4.4).

[17] Note that, at least from the landlord's perspective, the spot-rent expectations that matter are those relevant to a given (aging) building, not the average rent in the space market across all buildings currently in that market at each point in time. The age of the average building in the market may not increase with chronological time, as the building stock in the submarket may be renewed. But the opportunity cost of long-term leasing to the landlord is based on what the landlord could rent the space in the given building for in short-term leases rolled over at the prevailing short-term market rent. This is also the relevant opportunity value for the tenant, holding the level of service constant at that provided by the same building over time. It is also important to account for the lease-term length in comparing rental rates across time. As suggested in Section 10.4.1, comparisons of long- and short-term lease rental rates at any point in time will be "apples-versus-oranges."

10.4.3 Uncertainty and the Value of Flexibility and Options in Leases

Certain characteristics of leases and leasing strategies can affect the future decision flexibility of either the tenant, the landlord, or both. Flexibility is valuable because it gives decision-makers options and does not reflect the effective rent calculation per se. We have just noted how shorter lease terms increase a certain type of flexibility for landlords and tenants, namely, the flexibility to take advantage of favorable movements in market rents. Shorter leases can also allow other types of flexibility. Other features of leases, such as explicit options and subleasing provisions, can also be useful in this regard.

- ***Tenant Expectations about Future Space Requirements*** Expectations regarding the tenant's future space requirements influence the ideal lease-term length from the tenant's perspective. For example, if the tenant knows she will need the space for exactly three years, then a three-year lease term would normally be best. If the tenant expects her business to grow steadily, she may prefer shorter-term leases, expecting a future need to expand. Lease options on adjacent or other spaces in the same building can sometimes also help with such expectations. The ability to sublease space also provides flexibility to the tenant. If the tenant needs to abandon the leased space due to a need to downsize or to move to a larger space elsewhere, subleasing can reduce the financial cost to the tenant. In general, the more uncertainty surrounding the tenant's future space needs, the greater the value to the tenant of retaining flexibility in her space commitments and, therefore, the greater the option value to the tenant either in signing shorter-term leases or using options and subleasing rights to provide flexibility.
- ***Landlord's Redevelopment Option*** On the landlord side, a lease encumbers the property owner's normal right to demolish or redevelop the leased building structure. A shorter-term lease reduces the length of time for which this right is relinquished, thereby preserving more flexibility for the landlord in this regard. Once again, the option value lies not in the lease but in the lack of lease, temporally speaking. In the case of very long leases, such as ground leases or the leaseholds that prevail in many European and some Asian countries (but also exist in New York, for example), the impairment of the redevelopment option can be considerable as the lease term approaches. In such cases, explicit redevelopment options written into the lease can add value to the property.

10.4.4 Staggered Lease Expirations and Releasing Risk

The considerations described above regarding optimal lease terms consider each lease separately from the other leases in a building (or portfolio of buildings owned by the landlord). From the landlord's perspective, it may not be desirable to have all (or most) leases expiring at (or near) the same future point in time. If a bunch of leases expire around the same time, the building will be heavily exposed to the vicissitudes of the rental market at a single point in time. The risk or volatility in the building's future cash flow can be reduced by staggering lease expiration dates more uniformly across time. Depending on what the future lease expiration pattern looks like in a given building, this may cause the landlord to prefer either a longer or shorter lease-term length in a given deal than would otherwise be the case.

In some circumstances, there can actually be an advantage to bunching lease expiration times together. The strategic marketing focus of a shopping center depends on the many different stores and the synergy among them. Having all or many of the leases expire near the same time can give the shopping center owner more flexibility to change the center's focus, by assembling a new synergistic collection of tenants.

EXHIBIT 10-3
Typical Lease Terms for Several Property Types

Hotel:	1 day-1 week
Apartment:	1 year
Small retail:	2–5 years
Office:	3–10 years
Anchor retail:	5–15 years
Industrial:	5–20 years
Unique corporate space:	20+ years or user-occupant ownership

10.4.5 Summary: Rent Term Structure and Optimal Lease-Term Length

In Section 10.4, we have raised four considerations of leasing strategy that are not included in the effective rent or ALV calculation: releasing costs, rental market expectations, flexibility considerations, and lease expiration timing considerations for the landlord. The first consideration, releasing cost, implies that both lessors and lessees will prefer longer-term leases and, therefore, carries no general implication for the equilibrium term structure of rents. The flexibility consideration implies that shorter-term leases will be preferred by at least one party, probably by both parties in the lease, though potentially mitigated by explicit options (cancellation or renewal) and subleasing rights in the lease. Again, given this implication, flexibility carries no general implication for the equilibrium term structure of rents. However, there are circumstances where flexibility considerations could lead to either a rising or falling (or "humped") term structure in equilibrium (comparable in principle to the "liquidity preference" or "preferred habitat" theory for why bond yields tend to be upward-sloping on average, that is, in this case, differing relative preferences of landlords and tenants). Finally, the fourth consideration, lease expiration timing, will have implications that could go either way regarding lease-term length depending on the specifics of the situation and, therefore, holds no general implication for the term structure of rents.

The overall result of all of these strategic leasing considerations can, therefore, be reduced to the following general principles:

1. The equilibrium term structure of rents should tend to reflect the general trend in spot market rents (i.e., if rent expectations are sufficiently rising, then the term structure of rents will be upward-sloping), though this general result could be mitigated or even reversed by systematic asymmetrical valuations between tenants and landlords regarding the releasing costs and flexibility considerations noted in (2) below.
2. Optimal lease-term length is largely a trade-off between releasing costs and the value of flexibility.
3. Based largely on (2), specific space submarkets or market sectors (property usage types) will typically have characteristic lease-term lengths that largely prevail within each market.

As a result of point (3), here are some stereotypical characteristic lease terms that prevailed in various types of commercial property space markets.

In general, releasing costs are lowest in hotels,[18] second lowest in apartments, and highest in anchor retail and industrial leases. The need for (and value placed on) lease termination flexibility

[18] This is true from the guest's perspective. In the sense that we treat the guest as the tenant and the hotel as the landlord. However, in reality hotels work differently from many other types of real estate. Indeed, in most cases you can also treat the hotel as the tenant, as the hotel franchise typically doesn't own the real estate itself. The real estate is owned by an investor that leases out the property to any franchise that is interested in operating on that location. Such contracts are long term as well (over 5 years, averaging at 10 years). The same principle works for companies that provide co-working spaces, like Regus or WeWork. They sublet spaces for the short-run but rent themselves from a landlord for the long-run.

is greatest in hotels and apartments and lowest in anchor retail and industrial space. Small retail and typical office space fall midway between releasing cost and the value of flexibility dimensions. Unique space subjects users to potentially high holdup costs that options can't effectively mitigate, and so requires very long-term leases or outright ownership by the user.

10.5 OTHER LEASING AND RENT ISSUES

In addition to the optimal term length and term structure of rent considerations described in the preceding section, several other issues that are not internalized within the effective rent or ALV calculation are important in considering leasing strategy and leasing behavior overall. We will briefly note a few of the most important in this section, including micro-spatial trade-offs and synergies, the use of percentage rents, the use of concessions, and the question of optimal search behavior on the part of landlords for tenants.

10.5.1 Micro-spatial Trade-Offs and Synergies

Micro-spatial considerations refer to issues regarding the design and management of space *within* a single property or project. This includes issues and decisions such as externalities, synergies, and trade-offs across tenants and across leasable spaces, some of the most interesting and important considerations in commercial property management. In many cases, the value of a commercial property can be greatly affected by clever mixing and matching of different types of tenants and spaces. These types of considerations are often particularly important in retail, office, and mixed-use properties. Because they are not reflected in the effective rent or ALV calculation, they explain why a landlord might rationally offer a lease with a lower ALV to one tenant or why a tenant might knowingly choose a lease alternative with a higher ALV. Some examples of micro-spatial considerations include the following:

- ***Optimal Space Size*** There is often an archetypical size of space for any given space usage submarket. Developers tend to target the supply in speculative or multi-tenant buildings for this size, making competition on the supply side greater for the most typical space size. The result is that rents are often the lowest for a space of such a typical size and configuration. Smaller spaces (i.e., greater numbers of tenants for the same total building rentable area) involve higher management costs (per SF) for the landlord and often less efficient use of the building's gross space potentially available (lower **efficiency ratio** in the building, that is, the ratio of rentable space to total space, due to the need for more common areas). Also, finding tenants for particularly small or irregularly shaped spaces is typically difficult. Furthermore, there is some evidence that larger spaces have higher lease renewal frequency. This reduces the effective lifetime cost for the landlord, enabling larger spaces to be rented for less. Space size and configuration issues such as these are particularly important in the design phase of building development or redevelopment. Still, they may also be important whenever long-term leases of large spaces expire, presenting possibilities for subdivision or consolidation and reconfiguration of leasable spaces. Particular considerations apply in shopping centers or other multi-tenant properties where there are interaction effects among the tenants. In such cases, "externalities" must be considered to optimally configure and allocate the space among tenants. Some tenants will cause an increase in the profits of other tenants (positive externalities), and a landlord may rationally allocate more space to such tenants.
- ***Tenant Mix Synergies*** Certain types of tenants generate positive externalities by enabling other nearby tenants to earn higher profits. The opposite may also be true, as incompatible adjacent tenants generate negative externalities. An extreme and important example of positive externalities is what is known **as anchor tenants**. Most prominent in retail development,

a shopping center anchor draws customers who shop at smaller tenants' stores. Anchor tenants in office buildings may add prestige to buildings, perhaps by having the building named after them. The landlord can normally capture a large portion of such positive externalities in the rents charged to the non-anchor tenants. Therefore, from the landlord's perspective (as well as that of the anchor tenant), it makes sense for the landlord to share such externality benefits with the anchor tenant and to use such sharing to help lock the anchor tenant into a long-term commitment to the property. This is one reason anchor tenant leases are often for very long terms and at effective rents favorable to the tenant. In some cases, the anchor tenant may obtain an equity or equity-like position in the property. In retail properties, the landlord may also, in effect, have an equity-like position in the anchor tenant, as the rent may include a percentage component (this reflects the fact that landlord and anchor tenant are often, in effect, equity partners in the retail development). The art of tenant mixing extends to matching the right sort of anchors with the right sort of non-anchor tenants and includes optimal mixing, matching, and location of the non-anchor stores. Using short lease terms and/or renewal and cancellation options on both sides is common in many retail centers. This enables the tenant mix to be constantly optimized in the dynamic retail market where flexibility is particularly important.

10.5.2 Why Percentage Rents? (Consideration of Optimal Rent Structure)

Percentage rents, in which the tenant pays the landlord a proportion of the revenues earned in the rented space, are common in class A retail properties, especially among small tenants in multi-tenant properties such as malls and shopping centers. Usually, the lease calls for a fixed "base rent" component plus an "overage" that equals a percent of revenue over a threshold. There is usually a trade-off between these two: larger base rents are associated with smaller percentage rents and higher sales thresholds. This arrangement often makes sense for several reasons.

- ***Incentive Compatibility*** Percentage rents give the landlord a direct incentive to help maximize store revenues. Landlords have some influence over store revenues because landlords control the tenant mix in the shopping center, and some mixes provide more synergy and positive externalities than others. Without sufficient incentive, landlords might not optimize the tenant mix.
- ***Risk Reduction*** Many retail tenants are small businesses, and rent is typically a larger portion of the total operating expenses of small retail businesses than other types of firms. This makes such firms more sensitive to the leveraging of their business operating risk caused by fixed rents. If rent is proportional to revenue, then this leveraging effect is reduced. This is depicted in Exhibit 10-3, which shows, in a stylized way, the difference in the net income volatility of the tenant's store with fixed versus percentage rent. The difference between the heavy solid gross operating margin line and the rent line (either fixed or percentage, the latter indicated by the dashed line) is the tenant's net revenue stream over time. Notice that with percentage rents, the landlord is, to a degree, like an equity partner of the tenant, sharing in the tenant's operating risk and growth.

In fact, the use of fixed and percentage rent components can be varied so as to produce different effects depending on the nature of the tenant. By increasing the fixed base rent component and decreasing the variable percentage component, the resulting increased operating leverage places the retail tenant under more pressure and more incentive to maximize revenue. The landlord may want to place some tenants under such pressure and incentive if the tenants are financially strong enough to handle the risk and if, by increasing their revenues, the tenants will increase total shopper flow-through in the center, thereby bringing positive externalities to the other stores. This argument will tend to apply more to anchor tenants and tenants that are large national chains.

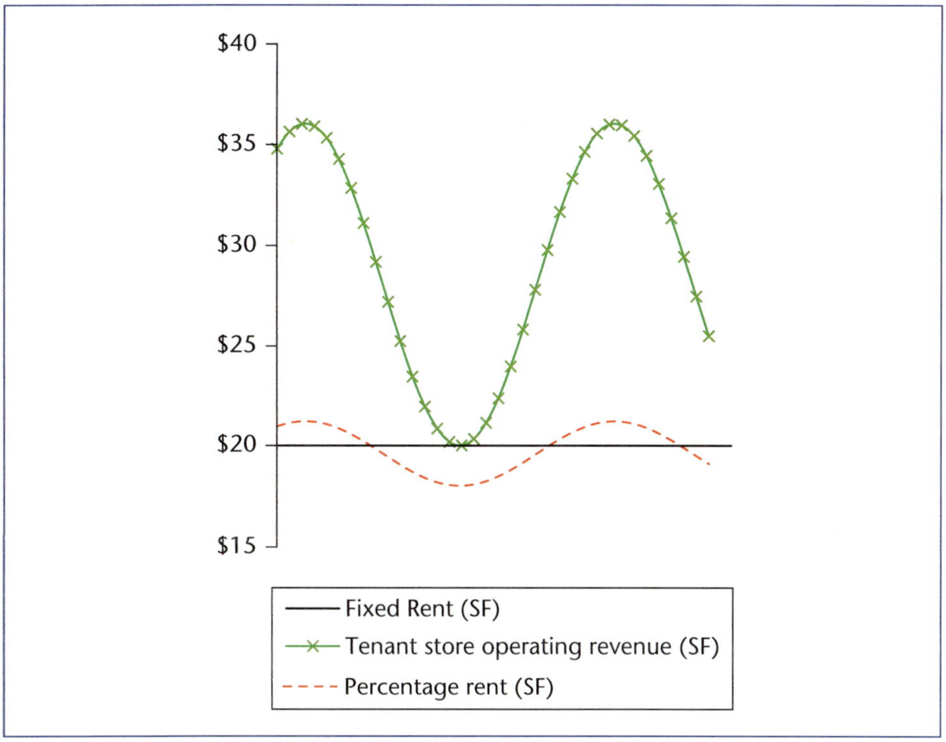

EXHIBIT 10-4 How Percentage Rent Reduces Operating Leverage.

10.5.3 Why Concessions?

Why are quoted rents "stickier" than effective rents? Why do landlords often seem to prefer to give out free rent and generous TI and moving expense allowances up front instead of taking a lower regular rent? For example, in our numerical example in Section 10.3.2, why does the $20/ SF lease A not simply charge the tenant $15.44/SF every year for 5 years starting immediately, rather than take no cash flow at all for the first year? Several reasons are worth pointing out.

- **To ease tenant moving or start-up expenses.** It is not uncommon for a new tenant to be under more financial or cash flow strain when they first move into a new space. They may be just starting up, or expanding, or incurring large moving expenses. Thus, up-front concessions often help to ease this burden, in effect, matching better the timing of rental expenses with revenue generation by the tenant. This argument particularly applies to concessions such as TIs and moving allowances.
- **Strategic timing of cash flow receipts.** There may be some strategy for timing cash flow receipts. Higher future cash flows may make it easier to sell the building at a higher price or to refinance the loan on the building, if these events are more likely to occur in the future than in the near term. This might make sense if the landlord has more liquidity at present than she expects to have in the future. It might also make sense if the property asset market is not fully rational and susceptible to NOI illusions, in which property buyers or lenders are ignorant of the typical use of concessions on the part of property owners and sellers. This does not sound very likely, but even if there is only a small chance of getting away with such an illusion, why throw away that chance?
- **The value of private information in a thin market.** The **quoted rent** (aka **asking rent**, e.g., the $20/SF in lease A) is what gets reported to the public and the other tenants. The

concessions are usually more private between the lessor and lessee. Thus, concessions are a way of concealing from other existing or prospective tenants (and from competing landlords, or perhaps even potential investors) exactly how low a rent the tenant is paying and how soft the demand for the building is. In a thin market with imperfect information, keeping such information private may be valuable in some circumstances.

10.6 CHAPTER SUMMARY

Commercial property leases and leasing strategy are among the most fundamental, important, and complex topics in real estate investment and property management. Understanding long-term leases and leasing strategy is also central to many types of professional real estate careers. This chapter only skimmed the surface, presenting an introduction and overview of the leasing topic. Nevertheless, we covered much of the basic terminology and basic analytical tools relevant to current professional practice for finance and investment-oriented users.

KEY TERMS

- Lease
- Lessor
- Lessee
- Ground lease rent
- Gross (full service) lease net lease
- Triple net (NNN) lease
- Hybrid lease
- Expense stops
- Flat rent
- Graduated rent
- Step-ups
- Revaluated rent
- Indexed rent
- Percentage rent
- Base rent
- Lease term
- Concessions
- Lease covenants
- Sublet
- Lease options
- Right of first refusal
- Effective rent
- Annuitized Lease Value (ALV)
- Releasing costs
- Holdup problem
- Complementary expectations
- Conflicting expectations
- Micro spatial considerations
- Rational expectations
- Efficiency ratio
- Tenant mix synergies
- Anchor tenants

- Quoted (asking) rent
- Optimal asking rent
- Noisy price information

STUDY QUESTIONS

In Your Own Words

10.1 Describe the differences between gross leases, aka "full service" leases, and triple net leases. Which would the landlord and tenant generally prefer?

10.2 Describe the major ways in which commercial leases specify rental changes over time during the lease term.

10.3 Why do landlords usually offer rent concessions, such as free rent up front, rather than just reducing the rent?

10.4 Why do we often see higher rents for large tenants even when there is significant vacancy in the market?

10.5 What is the economic rationale for the existence of percentage rents that are common in retail leases?

10.6 All else equal, the landlord wants the highest possible ALV while the tenant wants the lowest. When might the landlord choose a lease with a lower ALV?

10.7 Why might a tenant or landlord prefer shorter-term leases, *ceteris paribus*?

10.8 What factors would tend to make tenants or landlords prefer longer-term leases, *ceteris paribus*?

10.9 Can you provide some examples of tenants that are more likely to be sticky, that is, stay in the space longer and wish to renew, independent of the lease term?

Check Your Knowledge

10.10 Which lease types usually have the shortest and longest durations?
- A) Retail, Industrial
- B) Office, Retail
- C) Hotel, Industrial
- D) Restaurant, Office

10.11 What is the primary advantage of an "expense stop" clause?
- A) It increases tenant incentives
- B) It protects the tenant from inflation
- C) It limits the landlord's operating expense obligations
- D) It guarantees flat rent for the lease term

10.12 What effect do releasing costs generally have on lease term preferences?
- A) Shorter-term leases are preferred
- B) Landlords avoid leases with renewal options
- C) Both parties may prefer longer terms
- D) Tenants prefer gross leases

10.13 In a net lease, which cost is usually NOT covered by the tenant?
- A) Property taxes
- B) Security fees
- C) Management fees
- D) Rent adjustment fees

10.14 How does a revaluation lease differ from an indexed lease?
   A) Revaluation adjusts based on appraisals, while indexed adjusts based on inflation indices.
   B) Revaluation includes fixed rent changes, indexed includes none.
   C) Indexed leases apply to retail only, and revaluation applies to office spaces.
   D) Revaluation is preferred for long-term leases.

10.15 Why might a landlord offer a lower ALV to a specific tenant?
   A) To meet market demand
   B) To retain or attract an anchor tenant
   C) To match the tenant's revenue fluctuations
   D) To reduce long-term rental obligations

10.16 Why are hybrid leases common for apartment buildings?
   A) They offer full tenant control over utilities
   B) They cover expenses for amenities used by all tenants
   C) They avoid the need for regular rent adjustments
   D) They provide tenants the option to sublet easily

10.17 Calculate the ALV of the following leases from the landlord's perspective, assuming the tenant faces a 10% borrowing rate:
   a. 5-year net lease, $15/SF, 1 year free rent upfront
   b. 5-year net lease, starting at $10/SF, with step-ups of $1 each year
   c. 5-year net lease, starting at $10/SF, CPI adjustments every year equal to 50% of the change in the CPI. CPI change (inflation) is expected to be 5% per year.
   d. 5-year gross lease, $20/SF, expenses expected to be $8/SF initially, growing at 3% per year
   e. 5-year gross lease, $20/SF, expense stop at $8/SF, expenses expected to grow at 3% per year
   f. 6-year net lease, $15/SF, tenant improvements paid by landlord at the beginning in the amount of $20/SF

Chapter Case: Greenville Business Plaza's Lease Strategy

Greenville Business Plaza is a multi-tenant property in a busy urban area. The Plaza's connected buildings house a mix of clients, including corporate offices, high-end retail stores, and popular service providers, making it a local hub for both businesses and customers. The Plaza's anchor tenant, an electronics store, draws substantial foot traffic, increasing the Plaza's visibility.

As leases come up for renewal, the Plaza's leasing strategist team Lily and Kai need to decide on a plan that will maintain tenant satisfaction and the Plaza's financial stability. To navigate these decisions, they consider the specific characteristics of different tenant types and market conditions.

Recently, a high-tech gym with a trendy brand image has shown interest in leasing space at Greenville. The gym plans to feature state-of-the-art equipment and advanced wellness technology. However, the gym faces high moving and initial setup costs, including specialized equipment installation. Corporate office tenants have stable income models. Kai proposes a lease structure that shifts some operating costs onto these tenants, helping the Plaza reduce its exposure to fluctuating expenses. The Plaza's anchor tenant has requested a lease structure that would tie part of its rent to annual sales, citing revenue fluctuations. They propose a base rent along with a percentage applied to sales above a specific threshold. Lily is cautious about this model, as it introduces variable income, while Kai believes it could work well if structured carefully, especially if the tenant's sales are likely to grow.

Addressing inflation risks is also critical. Lily sees an opportunity in an approach that adjusts rent over time in small, regular increments, helping tenants plan financially. Kai recommends a different adjustment model for long-term leases, where rent adjustments would be directly linked to an external measure to stay aligned with broader economic trends.

For future leases, Kai recommends staggering renewal dates to distribute lease expirations over time. For tenants who prefer flexibility, Kai suggests a structure that lets them renew at current market rates, giving Greenville the ability to adjust rent in line with market conditions. Lily recommends offering improvement allowances and other rent concessions to selected tenants.

Answer the following questions and help the Greenville team create a balanced leasing strategy.

1. Which leasing strategy would most likely attract the gym tenants that face high moving and setup costs?
   A) Offering a fixed, short-term lease with no initial discounts
   B) Using a net lease structure
   C) Providing concessions to offset initial expenses
   D) Implementing a high base rent with annual increases
2. Which type of lease would Kai most likely recommend for corporate office tenants at Greenville Business Plaza?
   A) Gross Lease
   B) Net Lease
   C) Percentage Lease
   D) Indexed Lease
3. What type of rent adjustment does Lily consider for long-term leases to provide predictable increases over time and help tenants with budgeting?
   A) Indexed Rent
   B) Graduated Rent
   C) Percentage Rent
   D) Fixed Rent
4. Which rent adjustment method does Kai recommend for long-term leases to align with market trends?
   A) Graduated Rent
   B) Indexed Rent
   C) Percentage Rent
   D) Flat Rent
5. Why might Kai support a rent model that includes a percentage component for its financially strong anchor tenant?
   A) To transfer all operating costs to tenants
   B) To allow Greenville to benefit from the tenants' sales performance
   C) To decrease the Plaza's risk exposure
   D) To provide tenants with a fixed, predictable rent amount
6. Why does Kai recommend staggering lease expirations for Greenville Business Plaza?
   A) To align lease terms with other properties
   B) To reduce the risk of multiple vacancies at the same time
   C) To simplify lease management
   D) To increase rent immediately for expiring leases
7. How might offering renewal options at market rates benefit Greenville for tenants who prefer short-term leases?
   A) It guarantees lower costs for tenants
   B) It allows Greenville to adjust rents based on current market conditions
   C) It eliminates the need for tenant concessions
   D) It ensures all tenants remain for long lease terms

8. Which of the following is a reason Lily suggests offering tenant improvement allowances to key tenants?
   A) It ensures that tenants pay all operating expenses
   B) It incentivizes long-term commitments from key tenants
   C) It reduces Greenville's overall revenue
   D) It simplifies lease termination
9. Why might the Plaza prefer to keep certain rent concessions private?
   A) To prevent influencing market trends
   B) To conceal the property's soft demand from other tenants and landlords
   C) To avoid setting a legal precedent
   D) To simplify the rent agreement
10. If Greenville offers a 5-year lease with a $5,000 tenant improvement allowance, how does Kai incorporate this into the effective rent calculation?
   A) Add $5,000 annually to the rent
   B) Deduct $1,000 per year from the rent
   C) Deduct $5,000 per year from the rent
   D) Increase rent by $2,000 every 2 years

Part III

Completing the Basics of Micro-Level Real Estate Investment and Finance

Part III will now complete our presentation of the basics of the rigorous analysis of micro-level real estate investment. Here, we will build on and extend what you have learned in the two preceding Parts about both financial economics and urban economics. We begin in Chapter 11, considering the very practical exercise of constructing the real estate proforma-based DCF valuation model by focusing on the denominators of that model, complementing and completing the discussion in Chapter 5 of the numerators. We then move to a more advanced level, focusing on the *owner* of the real estate investment, the investor level, rather than just on the underlying property assets per se. That is, we are shifting focus from the property level to the investor level, the individuals or institutions who are considering real estate investments. One implication of the owner perspective is that the issues addressed in Part III sometimes go beyond the consideration of a single property to encompass a broader perspective of the investor's decision-making based upon the investor's overall financial position, which may include a portfolio of many properties as well as different types of investments such as stocks and bonds. Nevertheless, our primary focus in Part III will remain at the micro-level on the analysis of individual properties and deals. (We will reserve most of our treatment of broader, macro-level issues primarily for the online portions of this book.)

After Chapter 11's focus on real estate's opportunity cost of capital (OCC), we move to the important topic of leverage in real estate investment, that is, how does financing the investment by the very widespread use of borrowed money affect the risk and return faced by the investor in the property equity. Then, Chapters 13, 14, and 15 will further enhance the picture by addressing how the interaction of debt financing and income taxes can be rigorously addressed to understand and even quantify the investment decision implications of capital structure. These chapters discuss some issues unique to real estate, issues that begin to bridge the micro- and macro-levels and include fundamental considerations such as market efficiency and valuation philosophy. These topics are at the same time advanced because of their subtlety and complexity, yet still basic because of their omnipresence and importance in making rational real estate investment decisions.

DOI: 10.1201/9781003643838-13

11 Finding the Cost of Capital for Your Real Estate Investment

CHAPTER OUTLINE

LEARNING OBJECTIVES

After reading this, you should understand:

- How to combine space market return estimates with appropriate discount rates in order to value an investment opportunity.
- How one might think about risk in components based on the source of returns.
- How government risk-free debt rates affect required returns.
- How inflation affects nominal discount rates.
- How growth rates and depreciation rates impact discount rates.
- Common mistakes made in DCF analysis or how to game the system to puff an IRR.
- The importance of realistic assumptions and analysis in valuation.

Recall that the DCF valuation procedure consists of numerators and denominators on the right-hand side of the valuation equation (equation (1) in Chapter 4). The preceding part of this book focused on the numerators and the cash flow projection, which fundamentally reflect the space market. To complete the picture, we must pay more attention to the denominators, which fundamentally reflect the asset market. More specifically, we need to consider the "**discount rate**" used in property

DOI: 10.1201/9781003643838-14

valuation, which we labeled *E[r]*. It should be noted that all discussion in this chapter is at what may be called the "property-before-tax" (PBT) level. That is, we are examining valuation (and cash flows, for that matter) at the property (the "asset") level, as distinguished from the level of the owner of the property equity. The PBT level is most appropriate for analyzing the market value of property assets. Thus, the analysis here does not consider funds borrowed against the property, debt service payments, or income taxes, which are matters to be treated in subsequent chapters.

The basic conceptual idea behind the DCF discount rate was already discussed in Chapter 3. The discount rate is the multiperiod, dollar-weighted average total return expected by the investor as a going-in IRR. It is, therefore, an ex-ante (expectation-based) return measure. As a total return, the discount rate includes a risk premium (which we labeled RP) on top of the **risk-free rate** (which we labeled r_f). This risk premium should reflect the amount of risk in the cash flows that are being discounted. There must always be this relationship between the denominators and numerators in a DCF valuation: the denominators must reflect the risk in the numerators. For this reason, we noted that in some cases, it is desirable to separate the property's cash flows into components characterized by different risks, such as existing lease cash flows versus residual cash flows. More often, however, at least in current practice, a single "blended" discount rate is applied to the entire net cash flow of the property, especially if the property has a typical multitenant occupancy and lease expiration pattern. In this Chapter, we want to focus on a more practical level to provide some guidance about determining a reasonable rate to use in the DCF valuation for typical commercial properties.

A good place to begin is to recall the answer to the basic question: Where do discount rates come from? This will be discussed in Section 11.1. Subsequently, we will provide multiple tools for finding the cost of capital for your specific real estate investment property in Section 11.2. In Section 11.3, we will discuss how to find the exit cap rate empirically. This is needed to estimate the property's value at the end of the proforma. The exit cap rate reflects the future expectation of both the numerators and denominators (space and asset markets) beyond the end of the proforma. Finally, at the end of this Chapter, we will have completed the basic proforma (before tax and debt). This makes it a good moment to discuss typical mistakes (honest or not) when developing a DCF for commercial real estate.

11.1 THE CAPITAL MARKETS

From an economic perspective, a real estate investment consists essentially of claims to future cash flows, namely, the rent the buildings can generate for their owners. As such, these real estate assets can be compared to and compete in the capital market with other forms of capital assets, such as stocks and bonds. The net rents generated by a building are analogous in this respect to the dividends paid out by stocks or the interest paid out by bonds, and property competes for investors' capital against these other forms of investments. The real estate asset market must be considered part of the larger capital market, the market for capital assets of all types.

Broadly speaking, capital markets can be divided into four categories, which one can think of as capital resources for an investor. They are equity or debt, and public or private markets. Equity is a

EXHIBIT 11-1
Major Types of Capital Asset Markets and Investment Products

	Public	Private
Equity	Stock	Real estate
	REITs	Equity funds
	Mutual funds	Infrastructure
Debt	Bonds	Bank loans
	MBS	Mortgages
	Money instruments	Venture capital

residual (owner) claim on all returns after servicing the debt first. Remember that debt can also be an investment, as it is for the mortgage lender. (See Exhibit 11-1.) Public markets are those in which small homogeneous units (or "shares") of ownership in assets trade in public exchanges in which many buyers and sellers are generally simultaneously participating in the market with price quotes available for all to observe. The stock market is the classic example of a public capital market. In such markets, transaction prices at which the units of the assets trade are typically reported publicly daily or more frequently. Public markets are characterized by a relatively high degree of liquidity in that it is generally possible to quickly sell units of the assets at or near the last quoted price. This liquidity is both a cause and effect of the fact that in public markets, asset share prices can adjust rapidly to relevant news about their value. This ability of asset prices to respond quickly to relevant news is known as asset market informational efficiency.

In contrast, private markets are those in which the assets are traded in private transactions arranged between individual buyers and sellers who have found each other through some search process, often through the aid of brokers. (Private markets are also sometimes called "search markets.") In private markets, it is common (though not necessary) for whole assets (e.g., an entire company, property, oil well, or mortgage) to be traded in a single transaction.[1] This can mean that the governance or control of the operation of the underlying physical asset is traded along with the ownership and resulting financial claims. The average size of the individual transactions tends to be larger in the private markets than in public capital markets. The focus of the present chapter is on real estate assets traded in the private property market, and that is, therefore, the branch of the capital markets that determines the cost of capital, the discount rates (and terminal cap rates) to be used in DCF valuations of individual investment property assets.

As with all markets, the capital markets consist of a demand side of potential buyers and a supply side of potential sellers. In the case of the property asset market segment of the capital markets, the demand side comprises investors wanting to buy property. The supply side consists of other investors (or developers or owner-users) who want to sell some or all of the property they currently own. Unlike other branches of the capital market, in the property market, some buyers and sellers are not primarily treating the assets as financial investments but rather as factors of production, places to house the operations of their non-real estate companies. This is often referred to as corporate real estate or owner-operator property. While there can be much overlap between such owner-user property and investment property, the key difference is that investment property is owned by investors not occupying and using the properties themselves, and treating the property primarily as a financial investment, comparably and competitively with other forms of investment such as stocks and bonds. Investment property is a large and important component of all commercial and residential rental property and is the focus of this chapter and this book.

Investors in the property market generally fall into a few main types: individuals, smaller entrepreneurial wealth management firms, and larger financial institutions. The major types of institutions include REITs, pension funds, life insurance companies, various types of private equity funds, banks, and other financial institutions. Private individuals invest directly in the property market (typically via partnerships or corporations) and through wealth management funds or syndications. In addition to U.S. institutions, many investors in the U.S. real estate asset market today are foreign individuals and institutions.

In a modern, highly developed economy like that of the United States, the capital markets are highly **integrated** and sophisticated, well-functioning arenas in which vast quantities of money and information are managed and exchanged. The capital markets determine how the wealth and capital resources of the society are allocated, which in turn determines the future growth rate and economic production patterns in the economy. For example, if investors decide that the future earnings potential of artificial intelligence tech companies looks relatively good compared to office buildings, then AI

[1] Someday we may see private markets gain some liquidity by breaking ownership units into tokens that are traded while the underlying ownership entity remains in place.

tech company stock prices will rise, and capital will flow to that industry while office building prices will fall. Developers will struggle to obtain the funds necessary to build new office buildings. For investors, money is money no matter where it is invested and where its returns come from.[2] In this way, the capital markets govern the real physical allocation of the economy's productive resources.

TEXT BOX 11.1 HOW WELL INTEGRATED IS THE REAL ESTATE MARKET INTO THE CAPITAL MARKET?[3]

In the main body of the text, we argue that capital markets are well integrated and that, for example, an industrial property in Dallas competes with an apartment tower in New York or the stock market in general. Indeed, suppose the Dallas industrial properties achieve higher returns than other investments with similar risk. In that case, capital will flow into this market, increase purchase prices, and reduce returns to normal levels. While integration is certainly the case at the big picture level, it should be recognized that significant segmentation exists even in the real estate investment asset market.

The largest segmentation occurs over **price points**. This means that large real estate does not compete much with small real estate (price-wise). There are a few reasons for this. First, small investors do not have the means to purchase large real estate, not in cash or in their borrowing capacity. In other words, there are barriers to entry for this group of investors toward large, expensive investment properties.

The opposite is also true but for different reasons. Large investors do not have the managing capacity to research and manage many smaller investments. In other words, a large $1B sovereign wealth fund would rather buy and manage ten times $100 million properties than 100 times $10 million properties. Researching and managing 100 properties is too costly and time-consuming. As a result, research in the U.S., found that lower-priced properties have a return as high as high-priced properties but with less risk. The market does not "correct" this because of the above-mentioned barriers. Interestingly, research has also uncovered a network channel in this context. For example, if, for whatever reason, a smaller property *does* end up in a large investor's portfolio (perhaps via a portfolio sale), the probability that this smaller price point property will be sold to *another* large investor is relatively high.[4]

The DCF discount rate is meant to be the opportunity cost of capital (OCC) for the subject investment asset. It is the return investors could typically expect to earn (on average) in other investments of similar risk to the subject investment. This is required to get investors to be willing to invest in the subject property. If the expected return on the subject property is lower than that of similar-risk investments in the capital markets, no one should want to invest in it; if the expected return on the subject property is higher than that in similar-risk investments, then there will be a stampede of investors wanting to sell other investments and use the money to buy it, which would drive up the price of the subject property until this price offered a return similar to the other investments. (Recall the inverse relationship between the asset's current price and its expected return.) As "other investments," by definition, are traded in the capital markets (or the asset market), we can, therefore, say that discount rates "come from" the capital markets (including both public and private asset markets).

[2] Contrast this to space markets (Part II), where rents are negotiated for the occupancy and use of buildings. There, any one building cannot necessarily substitute for another. If a tenant needs office space in Boston, industrial space in Boston will not suffice, nor will office space in Miami. The space markets are segmented but in the capital market, all these properties are in direct competition.

[3] This text box is mostly based on: Geltner, D. and Van de Minne, A. (2017), "Do different price points exhibit different investment risk and return in commercial real estate?" in *Journal of Portfolio Management*.

[4] See Cvijanovic D., Milcheva S., and Van de Minne, A. (2022), "Preferences of Institutional Investors in Commercial Real Estate," in *Journal of Real Estate Finance and Economics.*

11.2 ESTIMATING THE COST OF CAPITAL FOR YOUR REAL ESTATE INVESTMENT

This concept of the OCC is all well and good in principle, but what can we say in practice about how to determine the actual numbers to use in analyzing specific real estate investments? Answering this question involves two steps. First, we need to be able to draw empirical conclusions about the typical rates of return investors expect from different types of investments. Second, we need to judge the relative risk of the property we are interested in compared to other investments whose ex-ante returns we can observe empirically.

Two of the characteristics that define a well-functioning asset market are that there is a sufficient volume of asset trading and sufficient information about transaction prices and asset income yields so that investors can make reasonably informed judgments about the ex-ante returns prevailing in the market. Clearly, public stock and bond markets provide a wealth of historical information that helps investors estimate reasonable return expectations. As stocks and bonds are part of the overall investment universe in which real estate competes, information about stock and bond returns is also relevant for forming real estate return expectations. In addition, the private real estate asset market functions sufficiently well to provide direct empirical evidence about expected returns for most real estate types in most places.

It is important to recognize that equilibrium expected returns vary over time in asset markets; therefore, discount rates employed in a DCF valuation should similarly vary over time if one is trying to represent current market valuations. Time-varying return expectations happen in real estate and the stock and bond markets. When asset prices are "high" (in the sense of historically high price/income multiples), then realistic return expectations going forward are "low" (and vice versa). This may be because the real risk-free rate changes over time with the relative supply and demand for capital and government policies, or it may be because investors' risk perceptions or preferences (appetites) change over time. However, stated return expectations may change less than actual, realistic return expectations based on realistic cash flow forecasts.[5]

It is useful to recall what was noted in Chapter 2 about the two ways of breaking out a total investment return r:

1. $r = r_f + RP$
2. $r = y + g$

where;

- r_f = risk-free rate
- RP = risk premium relevant to the subject asset
- y = is the current annual income cash yield payout rate from the asset
- g = is the expected growth rate or capital gain component in the total return[6]

In principle, both perspectives should agree and add up to the same total return rate: r. In practice, breakout (1), r_f + RP, can often be more easily applied to represent a normative or "equilibrium model" of what the expected return should be (realistically), whereas breakout (2), y + g, may be more easily inferred from direct and current empirical evidence about prices and incomes in the asset marketplace. In practice, the two perspectives do not always agree, and when they don't, this can have implications for where one is in the real estate asset market pricing cycle. (More about all of this shortly, and also in Video 1 in the Chapter 11 online supplements.)

[5] We describe in Chapter 11.4 how unrealistic ("rose-tinted") discount rates can be applied to unrealistic ("rose-tinted") cash flow forecasts such that the two errors cancel out in the DCF exercise to arrive at an accurate valuation of the subject asset in the current market. See also Video 2 in the Chapter 11 online supplements.

[6] Since we're generally employing a multiperiod return measure (as real asset investments typically have a multiyear time horizon), the g component may be thought of as consisting of both the cash flow change (CFC) and yield change (YC) components in the IRR attribution breakout components described in the online Supplemental materials for Chapter 4.

Considering the above general considerations, let's try to give you some more specific and practical advice about discount rates.

11.2.1 Computing the Risk-Free Rate

As the OCC consists of two components, the risk-free rate plus the risk premium (r_f + RP), let us begin by considering how we should quantify the risk-free component in the context of a multiyear, forward-looking IRR.

For a short-term investment, the traditional choice to use for r_f is the current T-bill yield, the return expected on investments in the government's short-term debt. Such investments have virtually no interest-rate risk because of their short-term nature (interest rates are not likely to change much over a 30-day horizon) and, traditionally, no default risk (as the Government should, in principle, be able to avoid default on debt in its own currency[7]). See Exhibit 11-2 for an illustration of the 1-Month Treasury bill (T-bill) rate between 2002 and 2024. However, the typical real estate investment is long-term. As noted, the typical DCF analysis will be performed over a 5 to 10-year horizon, with the discount rate being a single, blended IRR representing a long-term OCC. For example, in Exhibit 11-2, you can clearly see that at the end of our sample (2024) and during the GFC (2007), the interest paid on short-run government debt is higher than that of long-run debt (also known as "inverted yield curve"). The difference in yields between short-term (1-month) and long-term (10-year) Treasuries reflects market expectations about economic growth and inflation. A higher 1-month rate can indicate tighter monetary policy by the Federal Reserve (higher interest rates) in the short-term, attempting to control inflation or economic overheating, and/or may indicate the market's expectation of a looming recession.[8]

In this context, the relevant risk-free component for use in a long-term real estate investment's OCC is not the current T-bill yield but rather the average T-bill rate expected over the long-term horizon of the real estate investment. A relevant number in this regard is the current yield on long-term Treasury bonds, especially the 10-year government bond.[9] However, it is important to recognize that long-term government bonds are **not riskless**, and their yields reflect some risk premium in the investment marketplace. While government bonds may have little-to-no default risk, they have interest rate risk (which is related to the differential preferences of borrowers and lenders for short-term versus long-term maturity). This causes the *average* yield on long-term bonds to exceed that of short-term bills. To adjust for this and retrieve a risk-free rate that actually reflects the market's current expectation of the average future short-term yield over a long-term horizon, a simple approach is to subtract from the current long-term Gov-bond yield the typical or average "yield curve effect," that is, the difference between the yield on long-term and short-term government debt that typically prevails in the capital market. This is typically 100–200 basis points between 1-month and 10-year U.S. Treasury securities. The average long-run difference between the two series since 1926 is 1.6%. In Exhibit 11-2, the average difference between 2002 and 2024 sits at 1.6% as well, indicating that the difference is relatively stable over time. Thus, for example, if 10-year government bonds currently yield 4.5 percent, one might subtract about 150 basis points from

---

[7] In the U.S., because of a unique statutory ceiling in the sovereign debt limit, there have been occasional threats of Treasury default in recent years when Congress was controlled by a party different from that of the President. This has led to some minor downgrading of the credit rating of U.S. Government debt. As of writing, however, no default has ever actually happened. In countries that borrow significant amounts denominated in currencies not controlled by that country's own treasuries (such as denominated in U.S. dollars or euros), a default of such foreign debt is much more possible and has occurred occasionally despite international institutions designed to rescue such situations.

[8] Capital flight to the "safe harbor" of U.S. Treasuries actually would depress Treasury yields but can occur in both short-term and long-term Treasuries, though more so typically in the short-term.

[9] Long-run government debt products are called "government bonds" or "treasury bonds". The term "bills" is reserved for the short-term instruments (generally less than 1-year maturity, most commonly 30-day)

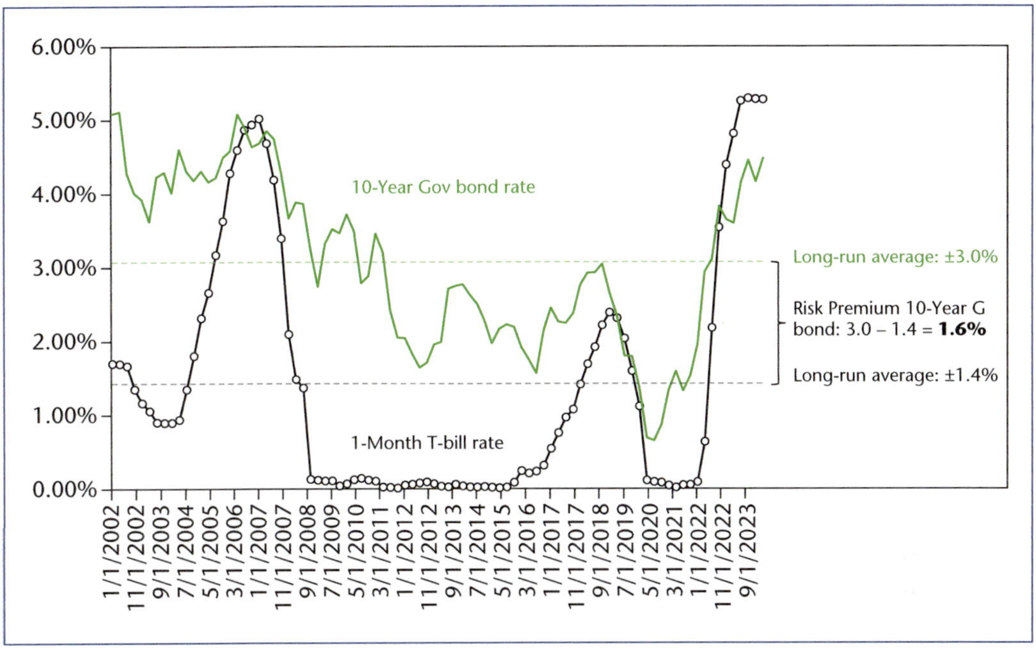

EXHIBIT 11-2 One-Month Treasury Bill (T-bill) versus 10-year Government Bond Yield Rates (Government bonds).[a]

[a] Note that the 30-day T-bill yield is very close to the actually achieved ex-post return on investment (due to the short-term nature of the instrument), whereas the 10-year T-bond yield is the market's forward-looking expected return on the bond investment at the time the bonds are issued (the dates on the horizontal axis). Subsequent ex-post realized returns on the long-term bond investments can vary substantially unless the bonds are held to maturity.

Source: Fred.

this yield to reflect an average expected risk-free rate of about 3 percent during the next 10 years. We can now provide the risk-free rate as follows;

Equation 1

$$r_{f,t} = \text{10-Yr Gov bond}_t - \overline{((\text{10-Yr Gov bond}) - (\text{1-Mth Tbill}))}$$

$$\approx \text{10-Yr Gov bond}_t - 1.5\%$$

Where subscript t represents the fact that the risk-free rate changes from one period to the next, and the bar over the 10-year Treasury bond minus the 1-Month Treasury bills indicates that we take an average of that yield curve effect over a longer period.[10]

[10] While equation 1 reflects sound economic reasoning and will usually work in practice, it must be noted that there have occurred periods when equation 1 gives results that simply do not seem reasonable. This may occur for example if the central bank is applying so-called "quantitative easing", in which the bank buys long-term bonds (in effect, sort of like "printing money") thereby depressing long-term bond yields below what the market alone would provide. The result is long-term risk-free rates per equation 1 that seem unreasonably low, near or even below zero and below current inflation rates even though inflation also is then low. (For example see in Exhibit11-2, the 10-year T-bond yield in 2020.) In such circumstances, in practice investors may fall back onto a heuristically reasonable approach, such as to add 1% to 2% above the long-run inflation target of the central bank. This often results in an applied risk-free rate of around 3%.

EXHIBIT 11-3

Historic Return, Risk, and Risk Premiums, 1970–2022. (Follow up on Exhibit 1-10.)

	Average Total Return	Standard Deviation	Risk Premium
T-bills	4.82%	3.16%	NA
G-bonds	7.30%	3.98%	2.48%
Commercial real estate	9.32%	6.99%	4.50%
Stocks	13.02%	16.46%	8.20%

Note: The risk premium is computed by subtracting the risk-free rate from the returns. The risk-free rate is defined as the (one-month) treasury bill rate.

11.2.2 Method #1: The Structural Approach to Estimate the OCC

We now estimate the total OCC or discount rate, including the risk-free rate and the risk premium. In what may be called the structural approach, we add an estimate of the market risk premium to our estimate of the risk-free rate described above. To estimate the risk premium, a fundamental approach is to build on what we learned in Chapter 1 about the historical returns to different broad classes of assets. This gives a long-term perspective and grounding for estimating the **risk premium (RP)** component within the r_f + RP model of the OCC. Note that we do not observe risk premia directly; there is no data on this. Therefore, we compute historical risk premia by subtracting the long-run risk-free rate from the long-run total returns per asset class. We can't simply use the average total returns directly because, over time, inflation and risk-free rates have varied considerably (as discussed above). However, the average or expected risk premia across the asset classes have remained relatively stable.

Exhibit 11-3 reproduces a part of Exhibit 1-10 and computes the historical risk premiums ("excess returns" over T-bills) associated with the total returns on stocks, bonds, and real estate. This has been done by treating the average return to Treasury bills as the risk-free rate (r_f) and subtracting this from the average annual total returns earned by each of the other three asset classes over the same period.

This exhibit shows that, during the 1970–2022 period, the risk premium on the sorts of institutional-quality commercial properties represented by the NCREIF index averaged 4.50 percent (or 450 basis points). The risk premium on long-term government bonds (10 years) was 248 basis points, while the risk premium on stocks was the highest, at 820 basis points.

Suppose these historical risk premiums represent current expectations. In that case, we can apply them to the projected Treasury bill yield as we described in the previous subsection to derive current expected total returns at the broad asset class level. In Exhibit 11-4, we put everything together for a real estate investment. First, we calculate our 10-year risk-free rate by subtracting 1.5 percentage points from the 10-year government bonds. At the end of our sample (second quarter of 2024), this is almost 3%. Adding our risk premium of 450 basis points suggests an expected total return for institutional-quality commercial real estate of about 7.5 percent going forward in 2024Q2. If T-bond yields were in the 6 to 7 percent range, then the real estate OCC would be more like 5% + 4.5% = 9%–10%.

Of course, it must be recognized with this approach that the historical results in Exhibit 11-3 are **ex-post risk premiums**, not **ex-ante expectations**. They represent the realization of what *did* happen during one sample of time (1970–2022), not necessarily what investors were expecting would happen when they made their investments (in the sense of what was realistically implied ex-ante in the prices they were paying), nor necessarily what investors currently are expecting today. Nevertheless, that 1970–2022 sample reflects over half a century of experience. To the extent that the future is not expected to be too different from the past (or at least that the past is not a biased

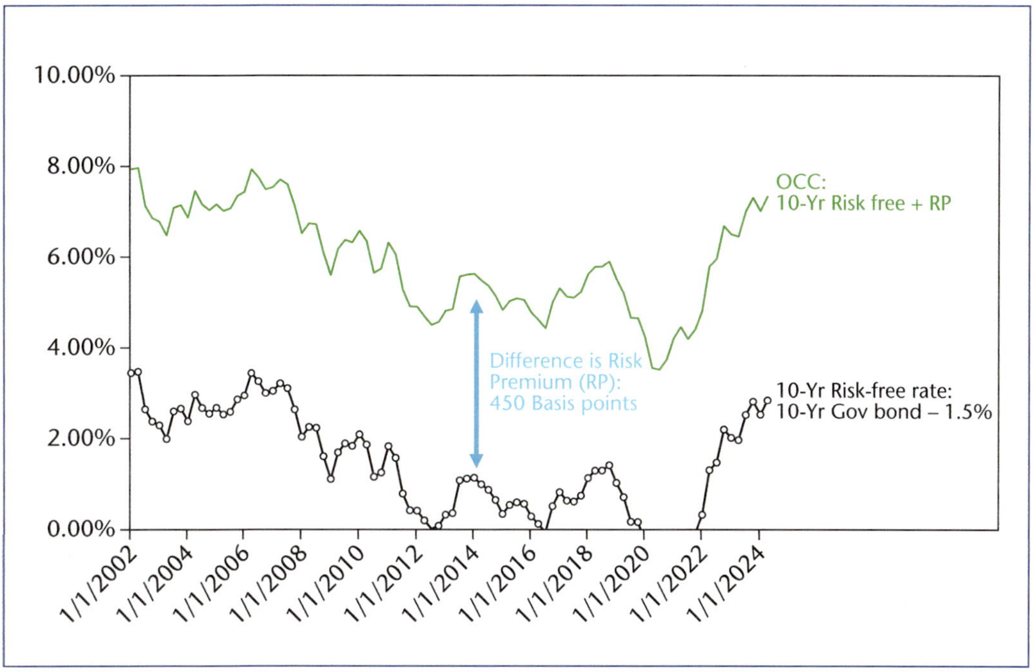

EXHIBIT 11-4 Example of Determining Cost of Capital for Real Estate Investment.

Source: Own calculations using NCREIF and Fred.

indicator of the future), historical results such as those in Exhibit 11-3 provide important information relevant to forming current expectations, regarding the asset class as a whole (the "typical" real estate asset).[11]

Obviously, this is a simple example of all institutional real estate in the United States. In reality, regional and property differences need to be taken into account. For example, the total return for NCREIF Boston office properties during (roughly) the same period was 7%, considerably below the 9.32% national all-property average, indicating a lower historical risk premium. We will provide some more insights into such regional differences in Section 11.4.

11.2.3 Method #2: The Market Approach to Estimate the OCC

The approaches sketched above have provided useful ways to get a general idea about the OCC to apply as the discount rate in property DCF valuation. In this second approach, we drill down to the more granular level of specific property market segments, that is, for particular types of properties in specific geographic locations. We also look at current direct market evidence from recent property sales transactions. We start by observing the prevailing cap rates (or current yields) in the relevant property market. It is easier to objectively and empirically observe the cap rates at which properties trade than to observe the ex-ante total returns investors expect in those trades. Data on transaction cap rates is globally available in many countries using data from MSCI, Moody's, or other sources. This approach of basing the OCC estimation on current cap rate evidence can, therefore, be a way

[11] "Bias" in this context would refer to investors—on average—overestimating, or underestimating, the total return ex-ante. This would seem unlikely, meaning that over the long run, the ex-ante and ex-post total returns should more or less coincide. Additional perspectives on long-term expectations can be obtained from modeling the equilibrium risk premiums in the capital markets, as will be discussed in Part VI.

to apply the y + g model of the OCC suggested at the outset of Section 11.2 as a means of inferring the current expected returns actually (and realistically) prevailing in the marketplace in specific markets.

The cap rate itself is not directly the same as the going-in IRR we need for the DCF denominators (OCC), but the cap rate and the IRR are closely related, as noted in Chapter 4. In particular, we can invoke the constant-growth perpetuity model (introduced in Chapter 2) as an approximation. Recall that this implies that the current yield equals the long-run expected total return minus the long-run expected average growth rate in the property's net cash flow and value. Turning this relationship around, we can derive an approximate indication of the expected total return (or discount rate) from observations about current cap rates by adding realistic growth expectations onto the cap rates:

Equation 2

$$E[r] = E[y] + E[g] \approx 0.7 \times (\text{Cap rate}) + E[g]$$

In the above equation, we multiply the cap rate by 0.7 to reflect that in typical U.S. data, transaction cap rates are based on NOI, not on the PBTCF that reflects actual cash flow net of capital expenditures (as described in Chapter 5). But it is the actual net cash flow yield, the E[y], which matters when computing the *E[r]* in the above formula. Thus, we need to adjust the transaction cap rates downward by about 100 to 200 basis points, or by multiplying them by about (1 – 0.3 =) 70%, to reflect this difference. (On average, in the NCREIF database, capital expenditures are about 30% of NOI.) If the reported cap rate is 7 percent, the relevant *E[y]* rate in the formula above might be 5 percent to 6 percent. The *E[g]* component in the above formula can be estimated from typical market-level rent growth rates in the space market in which the property is situated, net of the property-level "real depreciation" effect discussed in Part II (and recall more fundamentally the principles introduced in Chapter 9).[12]

To provide a numerical example, consider the (real-life) cap rate data in Exhibit 11-4 for offices in Boston. The data is based only on transactions that happened in that market. Two separate lines are presented in the exhibit. One is called the "hedonic" cap rate, whereas the other is simply the average cap rate per quarter. Note that the simple average cap rate is much more volatile than the hedonic version.[13] The main reason is that when comparing averages over time, the composition of underlying properties (on which the average is based) inevitably changes. For example, in one quarter, you might have had a few large class A office buildings sold. In the next quarter, the average cap rate could suddenly be based on a handful of unpopular and dilapidated 1980s properties. As a result, what does a change in cap rates between these two quarters tell us? The change in average is now a mix between (1) the "pure" market change and (2) the change in property composition, similar to our problems when discussing depreciation in Chapter 9. This is a typical problem in real estate, as each asset is unique to some degree, and we do not observe many transactions per quarter in most markets. Hence, a handful of sales can skew the averages. (This is less of an issue in markets with plenty of observations, as the "law of large numbers" will ensure that such outliers do not really impact the averages.) In reality, we are not interested in the impact caused by composition changes

---

[12] The E[g] component should also reflect the effect of likely "cap rate creep," as the going-out cap rate might differ from the going-in cap rate in a long-term investment. In the real world, this impact is negligible for most investments (and especially on the market level). Property-specific exceptions should be made for recently developed properties (where E[g] needs a negative adjustment) or older properties that are up for redevelopment (where E[g] needs a positive adjustment). We will come back to this topic in more detail in Section 11.3.

[13] In fact, the "true" contemporaneous averages are even more volatile. The numbers for the averages in Exhibit 11-4 are already smoothed by taking a rolling 12-month average by the data provider (MSCI).

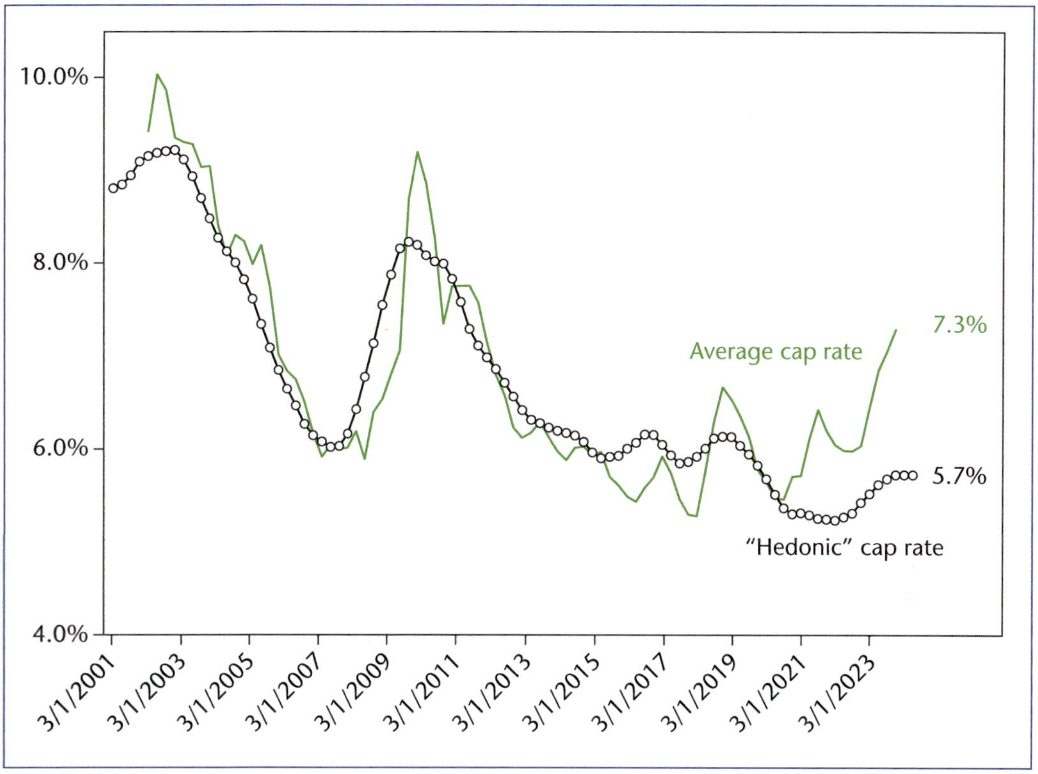

EXHIBIT 11-5 Quarterly Average Transaction Cap Rates for Office Buildings in Boston.

Source: MSCI.

over time. We, therefore, use a "hedonic" cap rate version that keeps the underlying property composition constant over time via regression techniques. (Again, see Chapter 9 for a more thorough discussion on constant quality versus averages.)

We see that offices in Boston were trading at a cap rate of 5.7% at the end of our sample in the first quarter of 2023. Now, assume that rents in that space market are expected to grow over the long term at a projected CPI inflation rate of 2.5% per year (g) for our subject property. Finally, let's assume that, given the age and quality of our subject property, it's reasonable to expect a real depreciation rate of 0.2% (Chapter 9.3). Then, the estimated OCC from equation (2) is:

$$E[r] \approx 0.7 \times (Cap\ rate) + E[g] = 0.7 \times 5.7\% + (2.5\% - 0.2\%) \approx 6.3\% = OCC.$$

One worry you might have with this approach is that your subject property (for which you are making the proforma) might differ from the "average" property in that market, which is reflected in the observed cap rate. In that case, the "market" 5.7% cap rate in Exhibit 11-5 might not be a good starting point for you. For example, you might be interested in a large "trophy" asset: A modern office tower in the CDB with only AAA corporate tenants. As a result, your cap rate is expected to be lower than the market average (less risky). Another example could be if you want to purchase a large 1M+ square foot industrial warehouse. There are not many of those because communities tend to block such large developments (NIMBY), meaning there is excess demand from the space markets for such properties. An average industrial cap rate might not be very informative in this case, either.

EXHIBIT 11-6
Example of Comparable Properties for Offices in Boston

	Property 1	Property 2	Property 3
Location	55 Summer Street	100 Summer Street	141 Tremont Street
Size	130,000	700,000	100,000
Construction year	1970s	1970s	1970s
Cap rate	6.00%	6.50%	9.00%
Year of sale	2023	2024	2009
Adj. cap rate	**6.00%**	**6.50%**	**6.50%**

Alternatively, you can also directly use the transaction data and perform a comparable **cap rate ("comp")** analysis. This analysis is similar in nature to the rent "comp" analysis in Chapter 9.[14] In short, with this methodology, you will try to find transaction cap rates of properties that closely resemble your property of interest. After finding N properties that resemble yours, you can subsequently take an average or weighted average cap rate. For example, we are interested in an office property at 141 Tremont Street in Boston CBD. We want to determine the OCC in the year 2024 using the comp approach. This property was built in the 1970s and is almost 100,000 square feet. After some research, we found the comparable properties presented in Exhibit 11-6.

All properties in Exhibit 11-6 are within walking distance of our target property. The first property is very similar (size and age) to our target property and was sold only a year ago (2023). The second property was sold even more recently but is considerably larger than our target property. As for the final property, this *is* the target property. Nothing is preventing us from using a previous sale as input as well. In this case, our target property was sold in 2009 with a 9% cap rate. In this case, we want to adjust the cap rate by essentially "deflating" it to 2024 levels using the cap rate series presented in Exhibit 11-5. Exhibit 11-5 shows that the overall market cap rates decreased by 250 basis points between 2009 and 2024. Hence, we adjusted the cap rate from 9% to 6.5%. Cap rates did not move much in 2023; thus, we do not need to adjust the first property's cap rate. In our case, all adjusted cap rates are very similar across the three comparables. The average (rounded) expected cap rate for our building would be 6.2%. Using the same expected rental growth rate of 2% net of depreciation as before, the OCC of this property would be (70%) × (6.2%) + 2.3% = 6.6%, slightly higher than if we used the overall market transaction sample as previously.

How many comparable properties should we take? In the example, we used three, but you might have multiple comparable properties (or less). The number will typically be between 3 and 10 in the real world, but no fixed rule exists. And how do you know what a good comparable is and how much weight you should give it? All these questions do not have an exact answer. Again, the point is to gauge what price properties (like yours) are traded for in the market. Sometimes, you might be able to do this comfortably with plenty of comparables, and other times, not so much. In other words, everything depends on specific circumstances. This also makes every real estate investment different—and therefore interesting—from the next. Real estate investment analysis is always a mixture of both "science" and "art."

Specific numbers might differ for specific property markets based on the transaction data. However, note that when inflation is low, say, 3 percent or less per year, the realistic expected total

[14] The main difference is that a cap rate "comp" analysis is more difficult in practice compared to a rent "comp" analysis due to data availability issues. First of all, because a single building has multiple leases (and only 1 cap rate), but also because these rents are quoted periodically (available via REIS or CoStar for example). Cap rates are only quoted when a property transacts (so once every 6–7 years on average), *even if* they are quoted, which is not a given. For example, in the MSCI data set, we only observe a transaction cap rate for approximately 1/3 of all transactions.

return often ends up being very similar to the NOI-based cap rate after considering the effect of capital improvement expenditures and the real depreciation of the property. (In the present example, the resulting OCC happens to be the same as the observed cap rate in both cases.)

Note that this "market approach" to OCC estimation described in this section is essentially the same as the "market method" of appraisal valuation.[15] This is because both perspectives have the same objective, which is to estimate the asset's current market value. The difference is that the multi-year DCF model, which uses the OCC, is a more complete and fundamentally correct financial economic model of asset valuation in the capital market. The multiperiod DCF requires a more explicit and careful analysis of all the components that underlie the property value: current operating cash flow, realistic growth rate in the cash flows, capital expenditure requirements, terminal cap rate, as well as the discount rate, including both its risk-free rate component and its risk premium component. The DCF approach, including OCC estimation, thereby reveals more nuance about the causality of the valuation and more depth of understanding about the valuation. This additional depth can be very valuable for a careful investor. And because the market approach to OCC estimation clarifies that the asset valuation is essentially just an estimate of the current asset market value, we can use this market approach in conjunction with the structural approach to OCC estimation described earlier to gain greater insight into the current asset market and the current appeal of the asset from an investment perspective.

TEXT BOX 11.2 IMPACT OF INFLATION ON DISCOUNT RATES AND CAP RATES

When people talk about inflation and real estate, they usually discuss how rents (and thus income) can be adjusted for inflation. The impact of inflation on discount and cap rates is often ignored. Let's rectify this. Note that the risk-free rate can be broken up into two pieces: the real rate plus inflation. As such, the discount rate can be written down as follows:

$$r = r_f + RP$$

$$r = (R_f + \pi) + RP$$

where r_f is the *nominal* risk-free rate, R_f is the *real* risk-free rate, and π is inflation. It is, therefore, straightforward to see that inflation will directly impact the discount rate "through" the risk-free rate. The only unknown is how (and if) inflation will affect the risk premium. As we said throughout this book, real estate is seen as a good hedge against inflation, as it is a long-lived asset. Therefore, money tends to flow into real estate during high-inflation years, *lowering* the risk premium. The sum effect of inflation is, therefore, not quite one-for-one but slightly less than that, at least on average historically. (Research of PREA shows that a 1% inflation results in a 0.9% increase in OCC.)

And what about the cap rates? As you know by now, cap rates are discount rates minus the expected growth rate (g). Circling back to our earlier discussion on inflation and rental growth, the expected growth rate *also* depends on inflation. Now we get:

$$\textit{Cap rate} = r - g$$

$$\textit{Cap rate} = (R_f + \pi) + RP - (G + \pi)$$

15 With the "market method" in appraising, one tries to find comparable, recently sold, sales in order to appraise a target property. This method is mostly applied to single family housing. You can do this yourself. Look up recently sold houses on Zillow that are comparable to your (or your parents' house), and get a (weighted) average price per square foot. Multiply this with the square footage of your house of interest, and voila, you have an appraised value.

where g is the nominal growth rate, and G is the real growth rate. Obviously, the exact impact of inflation on cap rates depends on many details, like how much the aforementioned risk premium is impacted by inflation and how well rental growth in the actual property can move with inflation (considering possible vintage fixed-rent leases, etc.). Still, the overall picture should be clear from the formulae above: inflation (mostly) cancels out in the cap rate equation! Cap rates tend to be relatively stable during high inflation periods. They fluctuate less than inflation rates and less than interest rates. Also, note that, almost by definition, the cap rate spread (to the risk-free rate) compresses due to inflation. Indeed, during the high inflation period around 2022, it was not uncommon to find properties traded for a cap rate *below* interest rates. But remember, the cap rate spread is <u>*not*</u> the expected investment return risk premium. That is the OCC (total return) spread.

11.2.4 Double Checking: Two Perspectives on the OCC Estimate

We have now suggested quantifying two different perspectives on estimating the OCC for real estate investments. The "structural approach" presented in Sections 11.2.1 and 11.2.2 is given by the $r_f + RP$ sum of the risk-free interest rate plus the appropriate risk premium, which may be based on historical or survey data, which tends to be "big picture," not a specific property market. The "market approach" of Section 11.2.3 is given by the $y + g$ sum of the current realistic income and growth components, in practice relying heavily on empirical observations of current transaction cap rates. By its nature, the structural approach tends to reflect a fundamental normative or equilibrium theory perspective: what the OCC *should* be. In contrast, the market approach more directly reflects the current property asset marketplace, as well as granular space market specifics (property quality, type, and location). In principle, and often in practice, these two perspectives closely agree; they give the same OCC number. However, it is a very useful exercise to try to quantify the OCC from both perspectives. Doing so not only helps to hone the accuracy and reliability of the resulting estimate but also deepens your (the investor's) understanding of a very fundamental question: What is the investment return on the property asset about which you're making an investment decision?

Furthermore, sometimes the two perspectives on the OCC differ, and this can raise a "red flag" (or perhaps a "green flag"). For example, let us look at data typical of what is widely available in the real estate investment industry. Though other sources exist in the marketplace, we will consider data from MSCI for illustrative purposes. According to MSCI, as of August 2007, the peak month of the asset market cycle of the 2000s decade, the nationwide average cap rate among sales of core institutional commercial properties was 6.44 percent. Thus, with rental market inflation expectations running around 3 percent (net of property-level depreciation), the market approach described in Section 11.3 would typically have led to a realistic OCC or going-in IRR estimate for an institutional core property investment of:

$$r = (70\%) \times (6.44\%) + 3\% = \mathbf{7.5\%}$$

At that same time, 10-year government bonds yielded an average of 4.67 percent. Thus, based on the "structural approach" described in Sections 11.2.1&2, and assuming a typical 400 basis points RP assumption (based on historical average institutional real estate performance), we would estimate an OCC of:

$$r = 4.67\% - 1.5\% + 4\% = \mathbf{7.1\%}$$

The two approaches to generating an OCC differ slightly, with the risk premium approach suggesting a lower OCC than the comp or market-based cap rate approach. The difference is not huge, and it could be dismissed, as no doubt it largely was back in 2007 (if it was even noted). After all, there is plenty of fuzziness in many of the numbers and assumptions going into this analysis. But if the difference was real and meaningful, it implied that the then-current (2007) asset prices underlying the observed transaction-based cap rates were providing a realistic expected return going forward, less than what the risk premium model suggested should be the case at that time. In other words, U.S. commercial property prices were, on average, too high. This would imply that they might be in for a fall, which, of course, is what certainly happened shortly after that time.

Now roll the clock forward a couple of years to December 2009, when the bottom of the subsequent trough in asset prices was reached. At that time, the same data source stated an average transaction-based cap rate of 7.88 percent when 10-year government bonds were yielding 3.59 percent. Thus, at that time, the two approaches (holding other assumptions the same) were giving on average:

$$\text{Cap rate market approach: } r = (70\%) \times (7.88\%) + 3\% = \mathbf{8.5\%}$$

$$\text{Risk premium approach: } r = 3.59\% - 1.5\% + 4\% = \mathbf{6.1\%}$$

Once again, the two approaches disagree, but this time in the opposite direction. You might say that inflation expectations in December 2009 would have been reduced below 3 percent in the recession or that the market required a risk premium higher than the more conventional 4 percent assumption due to extreme risk aversion in the aftermath of the financial crisis of 2008. But even so, the suggestion is apparent in the difference between these two approaches that property prices by December 2009 had fallen too low, that they were primed for a rebound, which is exactly what happened in 2010 among the sorts of larger institutional properties measured here.

Our point is not that real estate valuation or investment analysis can be as precise or as easy as this exercise suggests (admittedly with the benefit of hindsight). Our point is simply that it can be useful to go through an exercise like this and to think about the results you get while being mindful of the tendency of the property asset market to be somewhat cyclical (prices overshoot and undershoot the long-term targets). Again, there is never a correct answer in real estate, and you must take all the evidence holistically whenever making an investment.

11.2.5 Alternative Approaches: Survey Evidence and the Corporate Bond Market

In addition to historical empirical evidence and transaction data, another way to get an idea about investors' expected returns on real estate investments is to ask them directly and frequently. Several national real estate information firms regularly survey the investment community and publish the average stated returns investors say they expect in the future. In addition, brokerage and appraisal firms and commercial mortgage underwriters are usually familiar with the discount rates currently used for specific property types in specific locations.

The results of a national survey of investor return expectations, presented in Exhibit 11-7 for the 2013–2023 period, will serve to illustrate this type of survey-based evidence about investor return expectations. Exhibit 11-7 shows the reported values of the Integra Realty Resources (IRR), a national survey-based measure of professional investors' expected total returns (free-and-clear going-in IRRs) on unlevered investments in institutional quality commercial property.

The survey pertains to the same types of property as that of institutional investors in the NCREIF universe we considered previously for the historical record. For comparison purposes, Exhibit 11-7 also shows the historical 20-year trailing total return average for each year indicated in the exhibit. We focus on office, but data on other property types are discussed in Chapter 11.2.6. Thus, Exhibit 11-7's survey results indicate investors' stated expected property-level returns going forward in office investments as of the year indicated. In contrast, the NPI indicates the actual average ex-post property performance as of that same year (in the last 20 years). Exhibit 11-7 also shows current long-term government bond yields and the current inflation rate as of each year. The bond yield, like

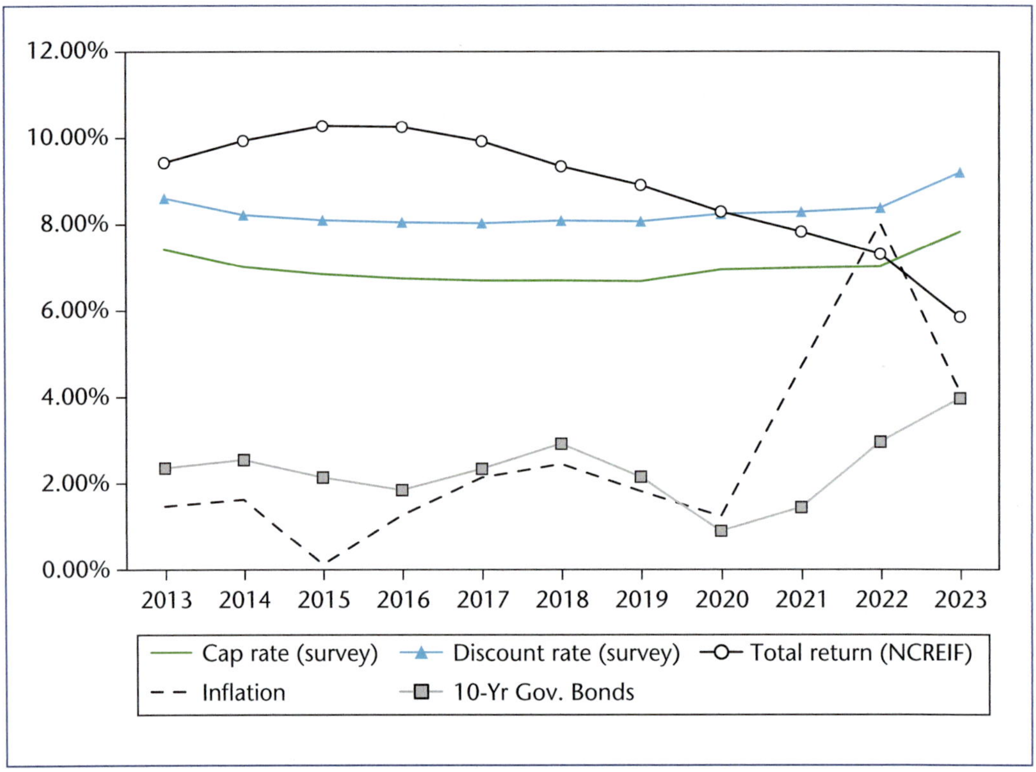

EXHIBIT 11-7 Backward-Looking vs. Forward-Looking Total Returns in the U.S. Institutional Office Market. The NCREIF total return is a 20-year moving average.

the survey, is a current ex-ante measure, although the nature of bonds enables this to be an objective measure based on current bond market prices and the yields to maturity implied by those prices. Inflation was exceptionally high in 2022, caused by the well-documented supply chain disruptions due to COVID-19. Even though inflation is not as high anymore, it did increase the 10-year government bond yields and discount rates for (office) real estate. At the same time, total returns in the institutional office market have been trending downward.

Though the graph shows stated discount rates exceeding historical total returns only near the end of the sample period, in fact, over a longer history, stated implied total return expectations (DCF discount rates) have tended to exceed ex-post actual total returns persistently. Furthermore, the spread between stated total returns and perceived cap rates suggests that the type of "rose-tinted" assumptions we will describe in more detail in Section 11.4.2 is typical of industry DCF proforma practice. If cap rates exceed asset cash yields by some 30% (as noted earlier), then the total return – cap rate spread implied in the surveys suggests long-term average property cash flow growth rates over 3 percent per year (based on the $r = y + g$ model). Such property-level growth would be net of the effect of depreciation, implying typical market rental growth assumptions (which are gross of depreciation) on the order of four to five percent per year. This is well in excess of long-term average inflation, at least for most of recent history. Assuming the surveyed cap rate projections are reasonably accurate (as they are relatively directly empirically observable), this again indicates the "rose-tinted" nature of stated discount rates, that is, implied expected total returns typically at least 100 to 200 basis points greater than realistic unbiased expectations.

TEXT BOX 11.3 RECENT STRUCTURAL CHANGES IN RISK PREMIUM? USE OF SURVEY DATA

Another interesting perspective to help estimate real estate OCC and ex-ante risk premia is by looking at industry surveys of investors' stated expectations. Such surveys have improved in recent years, including a major one done by the Pension Real Estate Association – PREA. The PREA consensus forecast asks its members what they think the NCREIF Property Index will do in the coming years. The NPI reflects actual realized total returns to investment property assets, and the consensus forecast reflects the average of the PREA members' expectations. The PREA forecast is also interesting because it shows how much the forecasts differ across the members at a given point in time. Greater differences indicate more uncertainty about future returns. The number shown in the exhibit below is the standard deviation among these forecasts. This is similar to the standard error in our formal (VAR) forecast of rents in Chapter 9. The difference is that we can visualize the change in consensus over time, and that it is based on the investors' expectations directly through surveys.

What is clear from the Exhibit is that recently (post-COVID), investors are far less sure what real estate values will do in the future. For example, what is the long-term impact of work-from-home (WFH) on commercial real estate? The downside is that this graph does not allow you to infer the cost of capital directly. Still, the change in consensus overnight is striking and worth noting. Also, note that this increase in uncertainty went hand-in-hand with the recent increase in total return requirement, as shown in Exhibit 11-8.

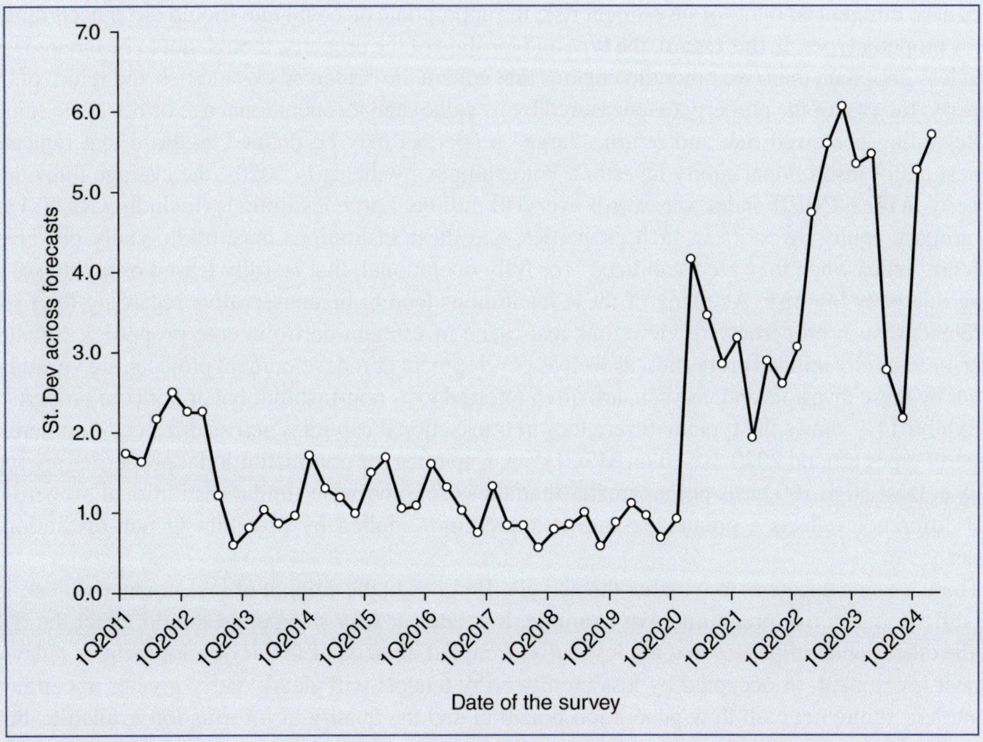

EXHIBIT 11-8 Disagreement Among Investors on the Forecast.

Source: PREA.

A fourth method that can function as a starting point for developing your discount rate is to examine the corporate bond market. This is especially relevant for valuing long-term leases, such as in office properties that house large corporations with long leases. By using the yields on corporate bonds, you can get a sense of the tenants' creditworthiness. If a corporation cannot pay its bondholders, it probably also cannot pay the rent. Per our discussion in Chapter 10, corporate bonds more or less resemble a Lease Obligation Backed Security (LOBS). In fact, real property is arguably slightly less risky than the corporate bonds of the tenants, as a bankrupt tenant may be permitted to pay rent while reorganizing. If they *do* default on the lease, they may be replaced with new tenants. On the other hand, the quoted bond yield is based on contract or coupon rates on the debt, not considering the expectation of losses in the event of default. This causes the expected return on corporate bonds to be less than the contractual yield, yet it is the expected return that is relevant for the OCC and the corresponding discount rate. Considering these two offsetting effects, corporate bond yields can serve as a useful indicator of the OCC for discounting long-term lease cash flows, that is, for the "intra-lease" OCC relevant for valuing existing leases. Overall, the property OCC must then be somewhat greater, as it must reflect the "inter-lease" risk associated with filling vacancies between leases, which reflects the risk in the rental market.

11.2.6 Variation in Return Expectations for Different Types of Property

The preceding sections have explained how to quantify realistic discount rates at a broad-brush level, that is, for typical institutional quality commercial property. This has traditionally been considered to include large, fully operational, income-producing properties of high-quality construction in high-quality locations (so-called class A or premium properties). But, as different commercial property types have different amounts of investment risk, the appropriate discount rate should differ accordingly across property types. In this regard, the type and location of the property, though not to be ignored, are often less important than two other dimensions that govern the perceived ex-ante risk and return of the property: the size of the property (as measured by its value) and its operational age or life cycle status.

Regarding perceived risk and return, "large" properties may be defined as those that typically interest major institutional equity investors. For example, by the early 2020s, the average individual property in the NCREIF index was worth over $40 million. Large institutions (including REITs) are the primary equity investors in such properties, and these institutions have traditionally perceived such properties when they are "stabilized" (or fully operational, that is, fully leased or nearly so) as being relatively low risk. As many of these institutions tend to be conservative regarding their risk preferences, such properties are viewed as real estate investment portfolio core properties. Smaller, older, or less fully utilized properties, as well as development or redevelopment projects, are viewed as riskier by these investors and, as such, are often referred to as non-institutional or noncore properties.

Exhibit 11-9 shows the typical differences in transactional cap rates across different commercial property types around 2020, based on MSCI data. Cap rates for non-institutional properties are typically at least 50 to 100 basis points greater than those for otherwise similar institutional properties. This difference reflects a greater ex-ante risk premium applied by investors in non-institutional property.

There is some debate as to whether the actual difference in the amount of investment risk justifies this differential in risk premiums. For example, it is unclear why size per se should affect the risk. On the other hand, properties that are less fully occupied, in need of major development or redevelopment investment, or occupied by less creditworthy tenants will clearly carry greater uncertainty about their future net cash flow generation potential and the quality of information available about the property. It is also likely that obtaining reliable information about smaller properties is more difficult. Lack of information creates uncertainty, and investors are even more averse to uncertainty than they are to risk. (Risk can be quantified as known unknowns; uncertainty cannot be quantified as unknown unknowns.)

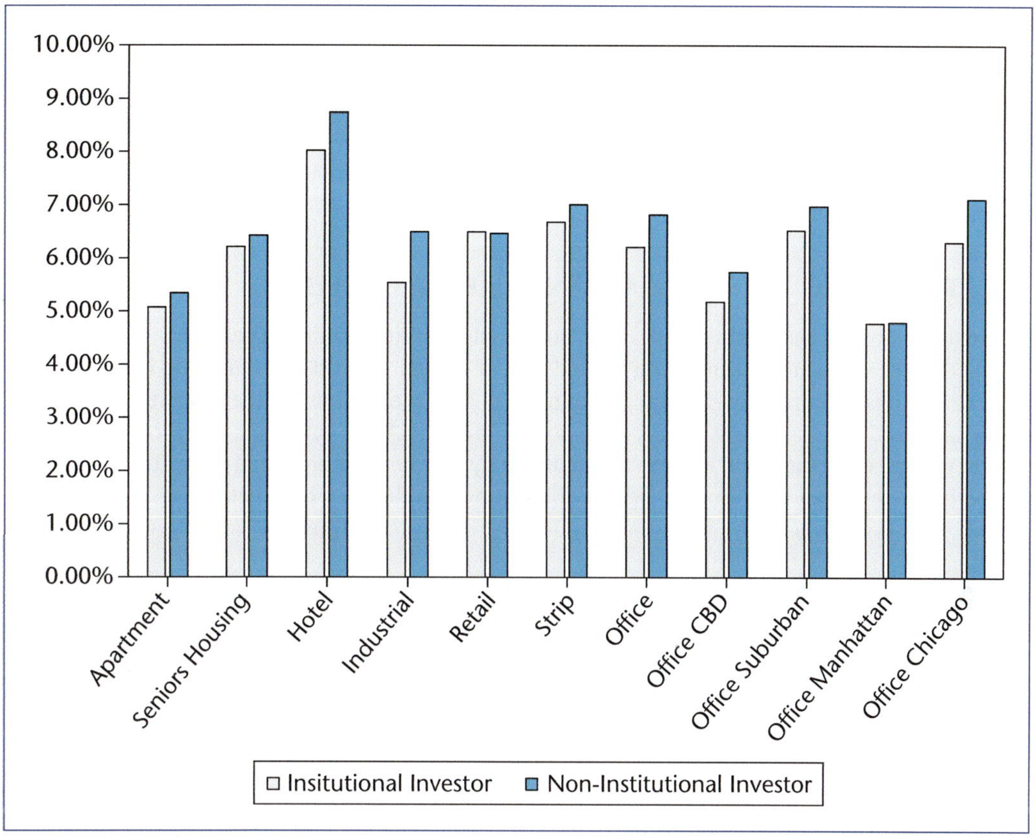

EXHIBIT 11-9 Average Transaction Cap Rates for a Selection of Markets, 201 –2023.

Source: MSCI.

It also seems likely that the private property asset markets are somewhat segmented or characterized by different investor clientele; see also the earlier text box. Smaller-scale individual investors tend to dominate the asset market for the smaller non-institutional properties, while large financial institutions and REITs dominate the institutional asset market. These different investor clientele may have different risk perceptions and preferences. For example, small investors may not be able to diversify their portfolios as well as large institutions can, exposing them to more risk from property investments. Suppose this is so; the typical clientele investors are the marginal investors in each market segment. In that case, asset market prices in that segment will reflect each clientele's risk perceptions and preferences. This could explain higher expected returns for non-institutional properties.[16]

Certain types of property investments are traditionally considered riskier than the major core types of commercial properties portrayed in Exhibit 11-9. For example, hotel properties, especially if they are not luxury hotels in prime locations, will typically command risk premiums 100 to 300 basis points above those of the four major core property types (office, industrial, retail,

16 Another potential difference between small and large investors is that many smaller investors do not charge themselves for managing the property. Therefore, it might seem like smaller investors achieve higher returns, even though in reality this is caused by a difference in reporting standards. As mentioned in Chapter 5, managing fees can be substantial, especially for smaller real estate.

and apartment). This may partly be due to the lack of leases governing their rents. At the extreme for real estate return expectations (on unlevered investments), raw land is reputed to command total return expectations, typically in the 15 percent to 30 percent range. Such real estate generally produces little or no current positive cash flow, and its value depends entirely on the NPV of future construction that can be built on it. As noted in Part II, this gives raw land investment performance characteristics like those of call options, like that of a highly leveraged investment in the underlying asset (the future building on the site).

11.3 THE GOING-OUT CAP RATE AND CAP RATE CREEP

The final component we must discuss is the going-out (or exit) cap rate. The going-out cap rate is an important component of accounting for the cost of capital in property valuation. However, it is related to the cost of capital *and* future operating cash flow projections for the property. In the most widely used and generally best practice method of property DCF valuation, the property's resale value at the end of the analysis horizon is calculated by dividing the projected year 11 net operating income by the exit cap rate. Before we provide some tools that can help determine the going-out cap rate, let's first discuss why the going-out cap rate might be different (or not) from the going-in cap rate.

As we have noted, the cap rate is given by r - g, the OCC minus the estimated long-term average growth rate in the property's cash flows. Now decompose r into the sum of r_f and RP, the risk-free rate plus the risk premium, where both of these apply to long-term averages. And subtract the cap rate in year 10 from the cap rate now (year 0), obtaining the following equation;

$$\Delta_{10}c = c_{t=10} - c_{t=0} = \underbrace{\left(r_{f,t=10} - r_{f,t=0}\right)}_{\text{Risk-free rate}} + \underbrace{\left(RP_{t=10} - RP_{t=0}\right)}_{\text{Risk premium}} - \underbrace{\left(g_{t=10} - g_{t=0}\right)}_{\text{Growth}}$$

Where c is the cap rate. If we assume that the 10-year future long-term average risk-free rate is the same as it is now (probably a typical or average situation), the change in cap rate over ten years is driven by the change in *risk premium* and the change in *rental growth projections*.

Let's start with changes in *g*. Recall from Chapter 9, where we discussed the depreciation of income. We found that the largest loss of income happens in the first few years of the property's life. Just like how a car loses most of its value when you exit the car dealership, a property loses its "newness" quite quickly, and rental income will dwindle. As a result, the expected rental income growth is lower for new developments compared to the broader market average. This drop in expected rental growth will decrease over the years. Indeed, there is no large difference between a 30- and a 40-year property from the space markets' perspective. As a result, the term $g_{t=10} - g_{t=0}$ will be *positive*, especially for newer properties, and will attenuate towards zero in later years. (With exceptions, see below!)

The risk premium tends to *increase* with the properties' age. Older properties are harder to lease (more uncertainty), with increasing vacancies as a typical result, and incur less certain maintenance and repair expenditures, resulting in the risk premium tending to increase with property age. Thus, the $RP_{t=10} - RP_{t=0}$ term will also tend to be *positive*. Therefore, of the three terms on the right-hand side of the cap rate change equation, we have the first one (risk-free rate) of ambiguous sign, the second one of positive sign, and the third of negative sign (since it subtracts a positive). In other words, in principle, the cap rate may change in either direction or not at all as the property ages.

Therefore, let us focus on some data to understand when **cap rate creep** happens. Exhibit 11-10 shows the results of a "hedonic" transaction cap rate age profile model based on MSCI data over the ages 0 to 100. (The hedonic modeling process controls for changes in the composition of the sample at different ages, see the discussion around Exhibit 11-4 as well.)

There are a few lessons to be learned from Exhibit 11-10.

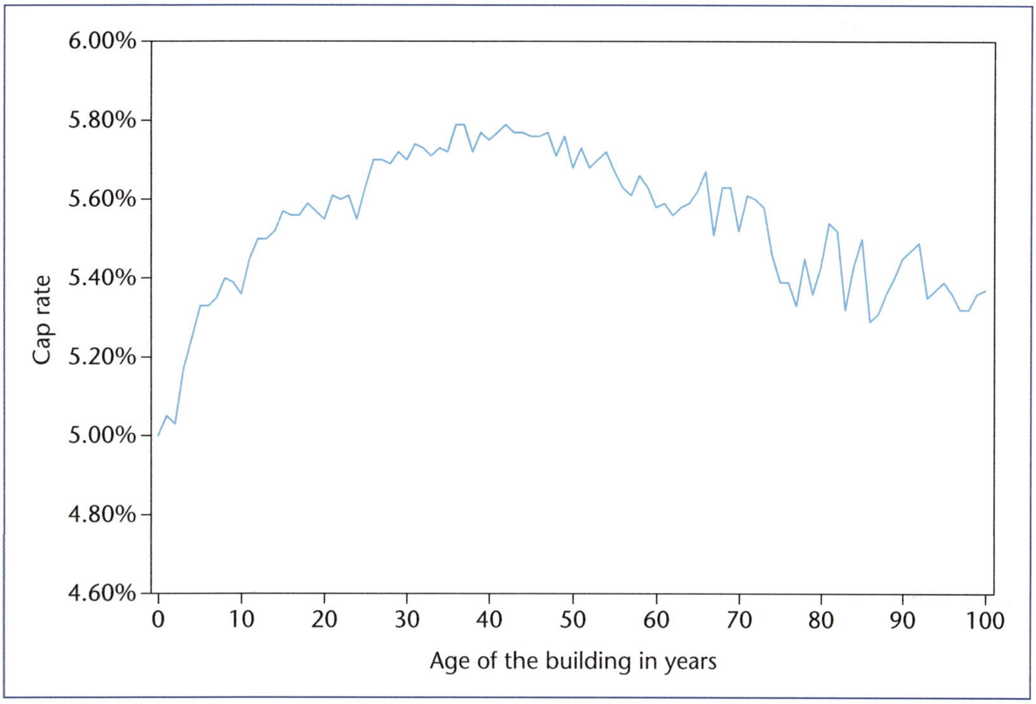

EXHIBIT 11-10 Cap Rate as Properties Age. The Hedonic Model is Estimated on Transaction Cap Rates from MSCI.

- **Cap rate creep.** Younger properties, especially those younger than 10 years, experience cap rate creep, that is, cap rate increasing with age (implying going-out cap rate greater than going-in, other things equal). For younger properties, the risk premium increase seems to outweigh the loss in growth expectations. As a result, when valuing such younger properties, and in the absence of specific countervailing considerations (such as vacancy or vintage lease effects in the Time *0* cap rate), you might want to add around 50 basis points to your going-in cap rate to compute your going-out cap rate. Furthermore, the rapid increase in risk premium as young properties age, suggested by the Exhibit, implies that you might want to subtract a percentage point or so from your cost of capital if the property is newly developed. (Tenants and investors love "newness," partly because new properties embody the latest market preferences in design and construction.)
- **Cap rate compression.** Once the property becomes older, cap rate compression sets in, although at a slower pace compared to the cap rate creep in the first few years of a property's life. After roughly age 50 or so, while the property's risk premium likely still increases, it does so at a slower pace compared to the increase in the expected cash flow growth rate (from the by now lower rent levels in the older property). For example, as a property ages from 50 to 60 years old, the OCC risk premium might increase only from 4.0 to 4.1 percent, while the cash flow growth expectations might increase from 1.0 to 1.2 percent. The result would be that the cap rate would decrease from (4.0-1.0) percent to (4.1-1.2) percent, or from 3.0 to 2.9 percent, that is, a decrease of 10 basis points (holding constant the risk-free rate component of the cap rate). Why would cash flow growth rate expectations (E[g]) increase with age in older properties? Remember that depreciation will substantially decrease the real rents that such properties can charge. The growth <u>rate</u> in the rent is, therefore, from a lower real <u>level</u> of rent. (If we drew an age/real rent profile, the curve of rent over age would be a convex declining

EXHIBIT 11-11
Examples of Comparable Properties that are 10 Years Older

	Property 1	Property 2	Property 3
Location	1 Upland Rd	40 Sylvan Rd	535–545 Boylston St
Size	243,000	348,961	184,643
Construction year	1960s	1960s	1960s
Cap rate	6.50%	6.50%	6.00%
Year of sale	2020	2024	2021
Adj cap rate	**6.80%**	**6.50%**	**6.50%**

Note: See Table 11.1 for the original comparable analysis.

function, with a negative first derivative but a positive second derivative.) Furthermore, as properties age (more precisely, the built structures on the properties age), another consideration comes into play. A larger fraction of the property value becomes the land value rather than the existing structure value. Land values typically do not depreciate, and with an old building on the property, the land value begins to reflect the **redevelopment** option value of the site. The **potential gains in future rental income can be enormous** if a property is ripe for redevelopment. (Greater density or more valuable usage type for the property.) Obviously, not all properties are expected to be redeveloped, which mostly depends on changes in the location's Highest and Best Use (HBU); see Chapter 6.[17]

Overall, Exhibit 11-10 reveals that cap rate creep does occur, but the number is very small on average, and, more importantly, it depends sensitively on the age of the building. Cap rate creep is pretty substantial in young buildings but nonexistent to negative in older buildings.

Now, let's return to this section's original question: How do we compute the going-out cap rate? As mentioned above, you can make small corrections to the going-in cap rate, depending on the age of the structure. But you can also use an **age-adjusted cap rate comparable approach**. The procedure is very simple and should come as no surprise. If the data allows, we can find comparable sales in the transaction data of properties *10 years older*.

Returning to our 141 Tremont Street Boston office building example, we find three comparable sales of properties built in the 1960s. These are presented in Exhibit 11-6. In this case, we find that the adjusted cap rates are higher compared to our going-in cap rate. More specifically, we found a going-in cap rate of 6.2 percent (Exhibit 11-3) and a going-out cap rate of 6.6 percent (Exhibit 11-11). In other words, a difference of 40 basis points.

11.4 TYPICAL MISTAKES IN DCF APPLICATION TO COMMERCIAL PROPERTY

Students and practitioners should be aware of a few mistakes or peculiarities in how the DCF method is often applied to commercial real estate. Generally, the mechanics of the DCF procedure are carried out correctly (that is, the "math all adds up"). But all too often, there is a **GIGO** problem. This stands for "Garbage In, Garbage Out." The point is that a valuation result can be no better than

17 On a more technical note, the model behind Exhibit 11-8 also reveals that cap rates are "harder" to predict as the property ages (higher absolute mean residuals). This makes sense. Not all properties can be redeveloped. So, the cap rate will compress for some properties, and for others, not so much.

the quality of the cash flow and discount rate assumptions that go into the right-hand side of the DCF valuation formula.

Suppose one is trying to use the DCF to develop a realistic and unbiased property value estimate. In that case, the forecasted cash flows and the required return should be realistic expectations, neither optimistic nor pessimistic. In principle, the cash flow forecast should come from a careful examination of the space market in which the property is situated, as described in Parts I and II of this book, as well as consideration of the existing leases and vacant space in the building. The required return (the discount rate) should generally be found by considering the capital markets, including the likely total returns and risks offered by other types of investments competing for the investor's dollar. The required expected total return ($E[r]$), serving as the discount rate, should be considered the opportunity cost of capital and represent the going-in IRR investors could expect from alternative investments of similar risk. In practice, time and resource limitations will often prevent in-depth, formal analysis of these inputs. But why would one use unrealistic or biased numbers, given the available and relevant public information? Let us briefly consider three types of GIGO mistakes prevalent in applying DCF to commercial real estate. The first is intentionally misleading, the second is excessive laziness, and the third is a (perhaps more forgivable) failure to pay sufficient respect to the cyclical tendency of the commercial property asset market.

11.4.1 If Your Case Lacks Merit, Dazzle Them with Numbers

The full-blown DCF procedure might look rather fancy simply because it involves a lot of numbers and mathematical formulas. The procedure itself can sometimes be used as a smokescreen to draw attention away from the underlying assumptions or the reasonableness of the input numbers on the right-hand side of the equation. In fact, the correctness of the math can hide biased assumptions aimed, for example, at making the property look better (more valuable) than it really is. Here are some illustrative examples of such assumptions, which either may not be stated explicitly or may be hidden in the fine print:

- The existing leases will all be renewed with 100 percent probability, implying no need to forecast an expected revenue loss from vacancies between leases and no need to forecast needed capital improvement expenditures to retain or attract tenants.
- Inflation is projected at 3 percent per year, even though recent inflation experiences show that inflation itself can be quite volatile.
- The current market rent applicable for the subject building is based on leases recently signed for other buildings that are nearby but newer than the subject property and which have greater appeal in the space market than the subject property, or the rent projections may be benchmarked on leases either in the subject building itself or other buildings but that contained concessions offered to the tenants at the time of signing that are not reflected in the subject property future cash flow projections.

The point is that it is easy for analysts with a vested interest in one side or the other of a valuation argument to purposely develop their DCF analysis with a view through rose-tinted lenses. The idea is to hide their bias in the sheer mass of numbers and formulas presented in the analysis. The lesson: don't be taken in by this intentional form of GIGO.

11.4.2 Excessive Laziness

A second widespread and implicit form of GIGO in the application of DCF to commercial property occurs when overly simplistic (or downright incorrect) assumptions get taken up into the conventional wisdom and then are applied pretty much as a matter of course in the typical DCF valuation (e.g., We all know cash flows grow with inflation, don't we?). If it would require expensive and time-consuming custom-tailored studies to debunk these assumptions, one could forgive their use in routine work (such as regular appraisal of properties) or the heat of battle (when the pressure is on to "do a deal"). But in many cases, it would take no such expensive or time-consuming studies, just an application of common sense and some basic urban economics (as described in Parts I and II of this book) to improve upon (or debunk) the conventional assumptions.

What is particularly insidious about these types of mistakes is that they could never become widespread or endure so long, except that, on the right-hand side of the DCF valuation formula, the mistakes in the numerators and denominators cancel out! The result is a reasonably accurate indication of the property's present value. This is important because, in a well-functioning property market, DCF assumptions that give unrealistic present values would be easy to spot as silly assumptions: the implied property values would seem unrealistic (for example, by comparison of the implied subject property cap rate with those of other comparable sales or prevailing market yields).

Here is what goes on in a typical form of conventional wisdom GIGO. The property net cash flow in the numerators is forecasted to be either too high on average or grow over time at an unrealistically high rate. For example, forecasted capital improvement expenditures will be unrealistically low, or the projected resale price may be unrealistically high, or the rent the building can charge will be assumed to grow at the expected rate of general inflation. This last assumption is often easy to pass off as being reasonable until you realize that it ignores the likely real depreciation of the building as it ages in its life cycle. Such excesses in the cash flow forecasts would lead to obvious overvaluation of the property, except that they are offset by using an unrealistically high expected total return as the discount rate in the denominators. For example, 3 percent per year expected rent growth and a 10 percent discount rate will typically give about the same property valuation as 1 percent annual growth with an 8 percent discount rate.[18]

So what? you say. If we get the right present value for the property anyway, then what's the problem? In fact, there are two problems, and both are serious. For one thing, investors develop false expectations about returns. The discount rate is the multiperiod expected total return on the investment. If it is unrealistically high, investors live in a fairy tale world where they think they will get higher returns than they actually will, on average. They may also be misled into expecting greater growth in their capital over time than is, in fact, realistic. Unrealistic return expectations could cause investors to make incorrect capital allocations between alternative types of investments or to make financing decisions that do not have the effect they think they will.[19]

A second problem is that the use of "fairy tale numbers" undercuts the credibility of the DCF valuation framework. Market participants and analysts lose faith in the ability of DCF to tell them anything useful because they corrupt it with misinformation. It becomes a "mere proforma" exercise made to satisfy a formality or act as window-dressing. You wouldn't buy a good car and then run it on impure gasoline that will corrode the engine. So, don't use GIGO assumptions on the right-hand side of the DCF valuation equation, even if you can (apparently) get the "right" property valuation. Such a valuation may be "right" only because it seems consistent with the current property market, as observed transaction price cap rates indicate. If the market is currently overvalued, this GIGO-based way of using DCF will not protect you from investing at the wrong time. Recall that one reason for using the multiperiod analysis is to provide some check against the possibility of an overheated asset market that will likely suffer a correction or fall back in the near-to-medium-term future.

---

[18] Recall the constant-growth perpetuity model: $V = CF1/(r - g)$.

[19] Suppose an investor thinks a property presents an expected return of 10 percent, and the investor can take out a long-term mortgage on the property at an 8 percent interest rate. One reason the investor might be interested in the mortgage is because he believes he will have "positive leverage," due to the 200 basis-point spread between the expected return on the underlying property and the contractual cost of the debt. However, the positive-leverage argument is either not realistic or is greatly exaggerated. (The issue of positive leverage will be discussed further in Chapters 12 and 13.)

11.4.3 Watch Out for the Cycle

This brings us to a third major type of mistake in applying the DCF process. It has not been applied effectively in the role noted in that last point above to help prevent investors from overpaying at the peak of the asset market pricing cycle. This is perhaps a more understandable and forgivable mistake than the other two. After all, in a fully rational world and completely efficient asset market, there should not be a predictable asset pricing cycle. Current asset prices should fully incorporate any relevant information, including any predictable future market-wide pricing movements. Until recently, there was not enough hard quantitative data about the history of commercial property prices in the United States to say anything very clearly or strongly or quantitatively about the cyclical tendencies in the market. But we no longer think this is an excuse (especially for institutional real estate investment). Analysts and investors should think carefully about cycles when making projections on the right-hand side of the DCF valuation formula. Both space market cycles (in rent and occupancy) and asset market cycles (in cap rates, as relevant for the terminal cap rate or "going-out" cap rate used in the DCF to project the property resale price) should be noted explicitly in the DCF assumptions.

We admit that accounting for cycles in the DCF analysis is problematic. Space market cycles vary in duration and amplitude and from market to market. Yet, for a given market, one can look at the history, try to judge whether one is near a peak or a trough in the relevant rental market, and then perform market analyses such as we described in Chapter 9. On the other hand, asset market cycles probably tend to be more nationwide in scope (if not global) due to the fungibility of capital (and the asset market cycle may or may not coincide with a space market cycle or economic business cycle). We have seen historically how the private market asset pricing cycle has, at least for the past half-century, been remarkably regular, with a total period of between 15 and 20 years, including a down-phase that tends to be quicker and shorter than the up-phase.[20] The asset market cycle should be considered in the DCF when considering the projected resale price. The horizon of the cash flow analysis might be reconsidered (perhaps a proforma longer than the conventional ten years should be employed if the typical asset market cycle is longer than that). At a more conceptual level, the meaning of the implied DCF valuation should be more carefully and explicitly considered and spelled out as to whether it relates to current market value or long-term investment value; that is, whether it reflects transient cyclical valuation effects or more purely a long-term sustainable valuation (the terms "market value" and "investment value" in this context will be discussed in Chapter 14).

11.4.4 Underwriting Haircuts

Apart from the mistakes described in the previous sections, there is another important peculiarity in how DCF analysis is often employed in the commercial real estate industry. We use the word "peculiarity" rather than the word "mistake" because, in haircutting (or "giving the DCF a haircut"), the analyst is deliberately making conservative assumptions about the projected future cash flows (that is, projecting such cash flows deliberately "erred on the low side"), rather than trying to make unbiased realistic assumptions. More rarely, the analyst may also (or alternatively) deliberately make a conservative assumption about the discount rate (employing a high hurdle rate). The result, quite intentionally, is to come up with a low estimate of the current property value. Low-side estimates of future cash flow may also be objective regarding such "underwriting assumptions" in the proforma.

This type of deliberate "erring" on the downside helps protect against making an investment mistake. It is particularly the province of (traditionally derived from) the commercial mortgage lending industry. (The process of approving and issuing a commercial mortgage is traditionally called "underwriting" the loan.) In the lending industry, the investors (those providing the money

---

20 See Exhibit 1-11 of Chapter 1 for example.

for the loan) generally want to make a conservative (low-risk) type of investment and, as a result, are not asking for a very high return in the form of interest payments. They are generally not in as good a position as the borrower (the equity investor/owner in the property) to know realistically the unbiased expectations for the property's future cash flow and valuation potential. Nor will they have direct control over the operational management of the property. It is natural and appropriate for such investors to want to quantify a conservative perspective on the property value and its future debt servicing capacity (based on its projected operating net cash flow).

While underwriting haircuts are a legitimate and understandable tool and application of DCF, they can raise some problems, primarily because they deliberately seek not to reflect objective, unbiased reality. This can tend to divorce the investment analysis process from rigorous, empirically based, and objective information about the property and the market. The analytical process can "float off" in its own world, in which it can lose its moorings.

Suppose a lender's "underwriting criteria" call for a projected terminal ("going-out") cap rate (to project future property value on resale or loan maturity) no lower than, say, 9 percent and a discount rate no lower than 10 percent. But suppose the real property market provides actual rates of 7 and 8 percent, respectively (i.e., the underwriting criteria are conservative, as they are meant to be). Then, other things being equal (particularly the property's projected cash flows), the underwriting assumptions will imply property value below the current market value. Yet the borrower must pay the market value for the property and is in the market for a loan to help finance that purchase. The lender is, after all, in the lending business; lenders make money from lending, not from not lending. You can see the pressure to ignore the underwriting criteria. Since those criteria are not based on the current reality of the property market, it is hard not to ignore them! If company rules prevent them from being ignored, something has to give. The easiest thing to give might be the cash flow projection in the DCF right-hand-side numerators. The loan will still "pencil out" if the projected cash flows are high enough. And those projections are only estimates anyway. Who is to say the property rents won't grow with inflation (sounds reasonable, after all)? Who is to say the required capital improvement expenditures won't be minimal after all?

You see where we're headed. The underwriting haircut, originally intended to protect the investor from making a bad investment, is starting to simply aid and abet the types of mistakes we described in the previous section: mistakes that actually tend to support careless or sloppy investment or excessive payment for property.

We don't want to imply that underwriting haircuts are a mistake. They certainly have their usefulness. However, they need to be carefully and diligently applied, not with complacency, and not in the absence of rigorous, realistic, objective analysis of the property and the market. Lenders cannot force the market to be as conservative as they might like it to be, but they can operate with transparency and with more explicit knowledge and statements of what the realistic return expectations and risks are. If such knowledge and transparency permeate the system, the industry may be less prone to damaging cycles than it has been.

11.5 CHAPTER SUMMARY

This chapter presented multiple ways to determine the opportunity cost of capital (OCC), a vital input to the DCF. The "structural approach" provides what the OCC *should* be, while the "market approach" gives the current OCC in *the market*. We discussed what it means if you find a different OCC when using a different methodology. The second important topic of this Chapter pertains to estimating a going-out cap rate. The impact of depreciation on cap rates is ambiguous upfront. Luckily, we provide empirical exercises that can help the investor here. Finally, we discussed the different pitfalls when applying the DCF to commercial real estate investment. The many inputs and fuzziness surrounding some of those inputs can easily result in a "bad" DCF, followed by a bad investment decision.

KEY TERMS

- Capital/Asset market
- Reversion cap rate
- Going-out cap rate
- Terminal cap rate
- Resale cap rate
- Going-in cap rate
- Discount rate
- Risk-free rate
- Risk premiums
- Opportunity cost of capital (OCC)
- Ex-post risk premiums
- Ex-ante expectations
- Comparable ("comp") approach
- Cap rate creep
- Cap rate compression
- Redevelopment option value
- Institutional quality commercial real estate
- GIGO

STUDY QUESTIONS

In Your Own Words

11.1 What does it mean that "discount rates come from the capital markets"?

11.2 Why is it more difficult to determine discount rates to employ in valuing assets traded in private markets compared to public markets?

11.3 Outline the three approaches discussed in Section 11.2 to determine the appropriate discount rate or opportunity cost of capital in property valuation. Highlight the pros and cons of each.

11.4 Provide two explanations suggested to justify a higher ex-ante risk premium in the discount rate used to value noninstitutional class property relative to institutional property.

11.5 Why is the 1-month T-bill yield generally unsuitable as the risk-free rate for long-term real estate investments?

11.6 Explain the difference between the structural approach and the market approach to estimating the opportunity cost of capital (OCC) for a real estate investment.

11.7 Why might a going-out (exit) cap rate differ from a going-in (initial) cap rate?

11.8 Why is the market cap rate multiplied by 0.7 when calculating the expected return for real estate investments in the U.S.?

11.9 In the context of DCF analysis, explain the meaning of "GIGO" and how it differs from an underwriting haircut. Why is understanding this difference important in real estate valuation?

11.10 How does inflation affect the discount rate and cap rates in real estate investment analysis?

Check Your Knowledge

11.11 Which market is characterized by high liquidity and publicly available price information?

A) Private markets
B) Public markets

C) Small markets
D) Debt markets

11.12 Why is a hedonic cap rate adjustment useful in real estate analysis?
A) It improves the property's market value
B) It adjusts cap rates for changes in property composition over time
C) It maximizes NOI
D) It increases the risk premium

11.13 Which factor does NOT directly impact the risk premium in real estate OCC calculation?
A) Property location
B) Tenant creditworthiness
C) Maintenance cost uncertainty
D) Monthly utility expenses

11.14 If inflation increases by 1% historically, what is the typical OCC increase?
A) 0.5%
B) 0.9%
C) 1.0%
D) 1.2%

11.15 Which factor might cause a "cap rate creep" in young properties?
A) Increased income stability
B) Higher depreciation risk
C) Reduced growth rate expectations
D) Market demand

11.16 Why might transaction data alone be insufficient in OCC estimation?
A) Limited volume of sales
B) Inaccurate property prices
C) Over-reliance on tenant profiles
D) Limited access to tax information

Chapter Case: Kai Realty Investments and the Union Plaza Project

Kai Realty Investments (KRI) recently acquired Union Plaza, a retail and business center located in a busy CBD. The property generates an annual NOI of $800,000. Senior associate Alex Han and his team need to determine an accurate OCC for this investment.

The team considers several approaches for estimating the discount rate, each reflecting different market perspectives:

1. Ethan subtracts 1.5% from the current 10-year Treasury yield to reflect the property's long-term investment horizon, then adds a risk premium of 3.3%.
2. Thao multiplies the market cap rate by 0.7 and adds the expected NOI growth rate of 2.5%.
3. Sergio collects survey data from institutional real estate investors for additional context on expected returns.

Alex avoids "Garbage In, Garbage Out" errors by verifying rental growth and expense assumptions against historical data. He considers applying an underwriting haircut to create a buffer against market fluctuations. Additionally, Alex anticipates that as the property ages, risks such as increased maintenance, tenant turnover, and reduced competitiveness will impact future performance and the going-out cap rate.

1. What approach was each team member using to estimate the OCC?
A) Ethan: Structural; Thao: Market; Sergio: Survey Data
B) Ethan: Market; Thao: Structural; Sergio: Corporate Bond Benchmark

C) Ethan: Corporate Bond Benchmark; Thao: Survey Data; Sergio: Structural
D) Ethan: Survey Data; Thao: Corporate Bond Benchmark; Sergio: Market

2. Why is it beneficial for KRI's team to use multiple approaches to estimate the discount rate?
   A) To average the rates for a single estimate
   B) To minimize capital expenditures
   C) To capture various perspectives on risk, market conditions, and growth
   D) To increase the NOI
3. Why does Thao multiply the market cap rate by 0.7 in her calculation?
   A) To account for the depreciation of the property
   B) To adjust for capital expenditures, which are typically 30% of NOI
   C) To reflect the expected growth rate of NOI
   D) To align with the Treasury yield
4. What is Sergio's primary objective in collecting survey data from institutional real estate investors?
   A) To determine the average cap rate in the market
   B) To provide context on expected returns from a broad investor perspective
   C) To estimate the NOI growth rate for Union Place
   D) To align OCC with the Treasury bond yield
5. Whose approach is most likely to yield the highest OCC?
   A) Ethan
   B) Thao
   C) Sergio
6. How does an underwriting haircut differ from a GIGO error in DCF analysis?
   A) An underwriting haircut is an error due to poor assumptions, while GIGO improves accuracy
   B) GIGO is a deliberate adjustment, while an underwriting haircut results from poor assumptions
   C) An underwriting haircut is a conservative adjustment, while GIGO results from avoidable errors
   D) GIGO provides more accurate cash flow estimates than an underwriting haircut
7. What should Alex consider when calculating the going-out cap rate for the Plaza at the end of the 10-year holding period?
   A) Only the original market cap rate from the acquisition year
   B) Changes in interest rates and potential property aging effects
   C) NOI growth alone, ignoring cap rate impact
   D) Survey data that reflect only current year trends

12 Use of Debt in Real Estate Investment

The Effect of Leverage

CHAPTER OUTLINE

LEARNING OBJECTIVES

After reading this, you should understand:

- The impact of leverage on risk and return.
- The difference between the Loan-to-Value Ratio and Leverage Ratio.
- The weighted cost of capital, aka "the capital stack" impact on risk.
- The temptation of leverage and the use of other people's money.

The use of debt financing is very widespread in real estate investment. Indeed, real estate is famous as a source of collateral for vast amounts of debt. In the early 2020s, there was over $4 trillion in commercial mortgage loans outstanding in the United States (including loans backing CMBS), as well as additional real estate debt in the form of entity-level bank loans, bonds issued to REITs, and others. Indeed, individuals, taxable investors, and REITs typically use large amounts of debt, and even cash-rich tax-exempt institutions sometimes employ mortgage financing.

In order to help you develop a sophisticated understanding of the use of debt in real estate investment, we will examine this topic in this chapter. Here, we will present the basics of leverage and how it impacts the proforma. Chapter 15 will treat broader capital structure issues, including the use of various types of financing at the project level. All these chapters will consider the role of debt in real

DOI: 10.1201/9781003643838-15

estate investment, primarily from the borrower's perspective, the property equity investor. However, this will occasionally require consideration of what is happening to the lender as well. (Real estate debt, viewed primarily from the lender's or debt holder's perspective, will be the main focus of Part V.)

As noted, the present chapter will focus on the effect of leverage on the investment performance of the equity position. The use of debt to finance an equity investment creates what is called "leverage" in the equity investment because it allows equity investors to magnify the amount of underlying physical capital they control (which may also magnify the risk and return performance of the equity). It is important to understand this effect thoroughly. In this chapter, we will largely ignore income tax considerations related to debt to focus on the pure effect of leverage.

The effect of leverage on equity investment is fundamental to all investment analyses, not just real estate analyses. However, it is particularly salient in real estate investment because of how well-suited real property is to provide collateral for debt and the aforementioned widespread use of debt in real estate investment. The present chapter will start at a very elementary level and take you to a level where you can apply useful analytical tools in real-world practice.

12.1 INTRODUCTION TO LEVERAGE

Before we get into the nuts and bolts of leverage, let's step back for a minute and introduce the use of debt in its broader context in real estate investment to consider the forest rather than the individual trees. Do you recall our point about heterogeneous investors early in Chapter 1? This fundamental fact permeates all aspects of investment, including the issue of debt financing for real estate investments. Indeed, at a broad-brush level, it may be said that the diversity among investors may be a fundamental reason for the widespread use of mortgage debt in income-property investment.

Recall that different individuals, as well as different types of institutional investors, have different objectives and constraints governing their investment decisions. Some investors want growth via property appreciation, while others wish for income via cash flow. Some are willing to take on considerable risk in pursuit of high returns, while others are willing to sacrifice high returns to keep their investments safe and liquid. Some have specific future liabilities for which they are responsible. Also, access to capital and the availability of one's funds to invest vary greatly across investors. This variety among investors results in a need for various investment products, as we call them in Chapter 1.

In this chapter, we will see how leverage provided by mortgage debt allows the same underlying income-generating physical asset to offer very different types of investment products that can satisfy the needs of investors with very different types of objectives and constraints. A moderate-risk, underlying real estate asset presenting moderate growth and moderate yield may support high-risk equity investment with high growth and a low current yield and low-risk debt investment with zero growth and a high current yield. In fact, mortgages are distinguished from real estate equity not only, or not necessarily, by differences in risk and return. Mortgages allow for a relatively "passive" investment, in which the investor does not have to manage the property. Mortgages provide a contractually fixed, finite maturity cash flow stream that may be ideal for an investor with a fixed investment horizon or a future liability to plan for.

Because of the various ways in which mortgages differ from real estate equity from an investment perspective, the pool of investors who are potentially able and willing to invest (directly or indirectly) in real estate (i.e., to provide capital toward the purchase of property) is increased by the use of debt. This tends to increase the efficiency of capital allocation to real estate. At a very fundamental and big-picture level, this is what is happening in the widespread use of debt in real estate investment. At this level, real estate debt and, therefore, the use of leverage, exist in virtually all countries, including many emerging markets. Now, with this in mind, let's get down to the nitty-gritty of understanding how leverage works.

12.1.1 Basic Definition and the Mechanisms of Leverage

A good way to understand the effect of leverage on the real estate equity investor's (that is, the debt borrower's) position is by analogy to the physical principle of the lever. (See Video 1 in Chapter 12 online supplements.) This principle was first explicitly formulated by the ancient Greek mathematician and mechanical engineer Archimedes (287–212 BCE), who lived in Syracuse on the island of Sicily and was famous for his designs of catapults and siege machines, among other clever devices. To illustrate the principle of the lever, Archimedes supposedly made the statement: "Give me a place to stand, and I will move the Earth." He meant this literally, although he would also need an incredibly long-armed lever and a place to put the fulcrum!

In fact, the analogy between financial and physical leverage is very helpful. This analogy is depicted in Exhibit 12-1. The upper panel represents a physical lever. The weight that can be balanced or lifted at the end of one arm of the lever equals the weight at the end of the other arm times the ratio of the two arms' lengths. In the example shown, a 4-pound weight balances a 10-pound weight by standing at the end of an arm two and a half times longer on his side of the pivot point than on the other.

The analogy to financial leverage is direct and provides important insight into the effect on investment. This is represented in the bottom panel of the exhibit. An investor purchases a $10 million apartment property using $4 million of her own money and $6 million borrowed in a mortgage backed by the property as collateral. In this case, the leverage ratio is $10 million divided by $4 million, or 2.5. Just as physical leverage enables 4 pounds of force to lift 10 pounds of weight using a lever with a leverage ratio of 2.5, so financial leverage enables the equity investor to purchase (and "own" or control) an asset whose value is 2.5 times greater than the amount of equity capital invested. With financial leverage, the **leverage ratio (LR)** is defined as the total value of the underlying asset divided by the value of the equity investment:

$$LR = V/E = (L + E)/E,$$

where:

- V is the asset value
- L is the loan value
- E is the equity.

The word **equity** has its roots in the notion of balance and thereby recalls the physical leverage analogy. Investors' equity is their ownership share; in an accounting balance sheet, it equals $V - L$ (assets minus liabilities). Equity normally gives its owners primary governing control over the underlying asset as long as they live up to their requirements under their debt obligation. On the other hand, the debt receives a senior, or preferred, claim on the underlying asset's cash flow and value. As a balancing compensation for giving up that senior position, the equity gets the **residual claim**, the claim to the entire residual value in the investment, or all the remaining cash flow and value after subtracting the debt holder's claim.[1] Thus, equity value equals the underlying property value minus the mortgage value. In the case shown in Exhibit 12-1, the property value is $10 million, and the debt is worth $6 million, so the equity is worth $4 million.

As noted in Chapter 1, this arrangement generally results in a *compatible matching of governance and incentives*. Equity's governance of the asset gives it the greater ability to influence the total value of the underlying asset (e.g., by management actions). At the same time, its residual claim causes any increment in this value to accrue to the value of the equity. If the equity owners manage the property well, they will reap the benefit; if they manage it poorly, they will suffer the loss (at least up to a point). Thus, by giving the equity owner primary management control, the value of the underlying asset (the property) will likely be maximized, thereby maximizing the productivity of the physical capital.[2]

---

[1] We are speaking here of private sector claims on the property. In reality, the government gets the first claim, in the form of property taxes.

[2] Obviously, maximization of the underlying property value is also in the interest of the debt holder, as it minimizes default risk. While the equity/debt incentive alignment works well in normal circumstances (e.g., when the debt is not too large relative to the current property value), there are circumstances in which the incentives can get out of alignment and cause a conflict of interest between equity and debt holders to the detriment of overall underlying property value. Such "agency costs" are ignored in the present chapter but will be treated in Chapter 15.

Physical Lever:

Leverage Ratio = 10 lbs / 4 lbs = 2.5

Financial Leverage:

$4,000,000 Equity Investment

$10,000,000 Property

Equity	= $4,000,000
Debt	= $6,000,000
Leverage Ratio	= $10,000,000 / $4,000,000 = **2.5**
Loan-to-Value	= $6,000,000/$10,000,000 = **60%**

EXHIBIT 12-1 An Analogy of Physical Leverage and Financial Leverage.

Though the *LR* metric is perhaps the most fundamental metric for quantifying leverage, more widespread in common real estate industry usage is another measure, the **Loan-to-Value (LTV)** ratio, where *LTV* = *L/V*. Note that the *LR* and *LTV* are related. A higher *LTV* will automatically also mean a higher *LR*. However, the relationship is not linear:

$$\mathrm{LR} = \frac{\mathrm{V}}{\mathrm{E}} = \frac{\mathrm{V}}{\mathrm{V}-\mathrm{L}} = \frac{1}{\left(1-\dfrac{\mathrm{L}}{\mathrm{V}}\right)} = \frac{1}{1-\mathrm{LTV}};$$

Solve for LTV:

$$LTV = 1 - \frac{1}{LR}$$

To give a numerical example, an *LTV* of 50% corresponds with an *LR* of 2, while an *LTV* of 75% corresponds to an *LR* of 4. Increasing the *LTV* by one-half, in this case, results in a doubling of the leverage ratio. It is important to keep the difference between LR and LTV in mind because leverage is typically spoken in terms of LTV in real estate practice. In contrast, we shall see that equity investment risk and return performance are more directly related to the LR.

12.2 IMPACT OF LEVERAGE ON THE EXPECTED RETURN ON PERIODIC RETURNS

We can see the essence of the effect of leverage on the equity investor's expected return by continuing the previous example for another year. Suppose that by the end of the subsequent year, our $10,000,000 apartment property has increased 2 percent in value to $10,200,000, and meanwhile, it has provided $800,000 in net cash flow during the year. Thus, the underlying property has provided a 2 percent appreciation return or growth and an 8 percent income return for a total return of 10 percent. This is the return applicable to an all-equity investment in the property free and clear of debt, that is, an unlevered investment (LR = 1; LTV = 0).

But what about the levered investor? First, it is essential to recognize that the **debt service** consists of two components: (1) **principal** (or **amortization**) and (2) **interest**. (Where the debt service = principal + interest.) Principal payments reduce the outstanding balance. Thus, if you pay $500,000 in principal payments on a $10,000,000 mortgage, the new outstanding balance will be $9,500,000. In contrast, the interest payment is meant to compensate for the risk that the mortgage provider is taking. In other words, this is the return for the lender. As a result, paying interest does not go toward lowering the outstanding balance.

Suppose the mortgage is an interest-only (meaning no principal/amortization payment is made) loan at 8 percent. At this rate, $480,000 of interest must be paid on the $6 million mortgage (8% × $6,000,000 = $480,000). This leaves only $320,000 cash flow remaining for the equity investor ($800,000 – $480,000 = $320,000). The capital position of the equity investor at the end of the year consists of the asset, which is now worth $10,200,000, minus the $6,000,000 liability still owed (again, no principal payment is made) to the mortgage lender, for a net capital value of $4,200,000. However, the equity investor only invested $4,000,000 of her own money; the rest was obtained from the mortgage. Thus, the return on the leveraged equity investment is 13 percent, consisting of 8 percent in the income component ($320,000/$4,000,000) and 5 percent in the appreciation component (the $200,000 increase in equity value from $4,000,000 to $4,200,000, as a fraction of the $4,000,000 invested).

These results are summarized in the table in Exhibit 12-2. Notice that the substantial leverage used in this case (LR = 2:5; LTV = 60%) substantially increases the expected return.[3] This is because the equity investor has been able to borrow money at an interest rate lower than the expected return on the property (8 percent is less than 10 percent). It is also important to note that, in this case anyway, the increase in the expected return has come entirely in the form of an increased appreciation component, with no change in the income component.

[3] When considering the effect of leverage on the risk and return performance of the investment, we are implicitly holding constant the total amount of capital to be invested by the equity investor. This is why we typically measure the effects of leverage using return percentages rather than absolute dollar amounts. For example, in the case of our apartment building example, we are implicitly assuming, in effect, that the equity investor has a total net wealth of $4,000,000 available to invest at present. Thus, the benchmark of comparison for the equity investor is the levered $4,000,000 investment in the $10,000,000 property versus an unlevered (all-equity) investment in a similar but smaller $4,000,000 property. The expected total return for the unlevered investment is thus 10% × $4,000,000 = $400,000, while that for the levered investment is 13% × $4,000,000 = $520,000.

EXHIBIT 12-2
Typical Effect of Leverage on Expected Investment Returns

	Property	Equity	Debt
Initial Value (t)	$10,000,000	$4,000,000	$6,000,000
Cash flow (t+1)	$800,000	$320,000	$480,000
Exit value (t+1)	$10,200,000	$4,200,000	$6,000,000
Returns			
Income	8.00%	8.00%	8.00%
Appreciation	2.00%	5.00%	0.00%
Total	**10.00%**	**13.00%**	**8.00%**

At first, this sounds great. It sounds like a free lunch: the investor has simply increased her total return expectation by using *other people's money*! But rarely do we get something for nothing in the real world. In fact, this brings us to the other side of the effect of leverage on equity investment.

12.2.1 Impact of Leverage on the Risk on a Single Period Basis

Alas, you know "you can't get something for nothing." Generally, in financial markets, if something increases the expected return on an investment, it probably means that it also increases the investment risk. This is also the case with leverage. If it increases the ex-ante return on equity, then it will also increase the risk of that equity. How does it do this? To answer this question, let us continue our previous numerical example based on the $10 million apartment building.

Suppose that, at the time the investment decision is made, we do not know precisely what the future will bring for this property. This is, of course, a realistic assumption reflecting the fact that the underlying asset is risky. To simplify the picture for illustration, let us say that we can represent the risk in the property by defining two possible future scenarios, each of which is equally likely to occur. We will call the first scenario the optimistic scenario. If this scenario unfolds, the property will increase in value over the coming year to $11,200,000, a 12 percent increase in value (10 percent more increase than the expected growth of 2 percent). The property will also generate $900,000 in net cash flow for the year ($100,000 more than the expected $800,000). The pessimistic scenario envisions a reduction in property value over the coming year to $9,200,000, a decline of 8 percent (which would be 10 percent lower growth than the +2 percent expectation), and the generation of only $700,000 in net cash flow by the building during the year ($100,000 less than expected). These are the only two possible future eventualities. Let us furthermore assume that no matter which of these two scenarios occurs, if the investor has taken out the 8 percent loan, she will still owe $480,000 in interest, with $6,000,000 still outstanding on the loan.

Exhibit 12-3 then quantifies the return components that would prevail in each of the two scenarios under these assumptions, and it indicates the range in these returns between the optimistic and pessimistic outcomes. This range is a way to quantify the risk in the investment. A greater range indicates more uncertainty about future returns, including a potentially worse downside outcome. For example, without leverage, the pessimistic scenario will result in a total return on the property's equity over the coming year of -1 percent. However, with the 60 percent LTV loan, the total return on the levered equity would be -14.5 percent if the pessimistic scenario occurs. Thus, leverage magnifies the downside loss by 13.5 percent in this case. Exhibit 12-3 indicates that the ranges in the equity return components increase by a factor of 2.5 as we move from the unlevered (underlying property) to the levered equity position.

For example, the range in the total return between the optimistic and pessimistic scenarios is ±11 percent with no leverage and ±27.5 percent with the 60 percent LTV loan. The 2.5-factor magnification of the outcome range holds for the total return and each component of the total return (current income and appreciation). The factor 2.5 is also the leverage ratio for a 60 percent LTV loan. It is not a coincidence that the underlying property risk is magnified by a factor equal to the leverage ratio in this case. In this example, the debt is effectively riskless because the debt investor gets the same return (8 percent) no matter which future scenario occurs. When debt is riskless, the risk in the equity return is directly proportional to the leverage ratio (LR).

Of course, debt in the real world, especially long-term debt, is not riskless. We saw in Chapter 1 that long-term bonds might have periodic return **volatility** as high as that of unlevered property equity. However, treating the debt as though it were riskless can often be a useful analytical device from the borrower's perspective to see how the debt affects the risk in the levered equity position. This is because the borrower is contractually obligated to pay the debt service amounts specified in the loan, no matter what happens to the property value or the rent it can earn. Furthermore, the equity investor often intends to hold the property investment and its debt at least until the loan's maturity. In that case, the volatility in the market value of the debt (usually due primarily to fluctuations in interest rates) would not be relevant to the equity investor. The situation the equity investor faces is similar to what is depicted in Exhibit 12-3.

EXHIBIT 12-3

Sensitivity Analysis of Effect of Leverage on Risk in Equity Return Components, as Measured by Percentage Range in Possible Return Outcomes ($ values in millions)

	Property (LR = 1, LTV = 0)					
	Optimistic		Pessimistic		Range	
Initial Value (t)	$	10,000,000	$	10,000,000		
Cash flow (t+1)	$	900,000	$	700,000	$	100,000
Exit value (t+1)	$	11,200,000	$	9,200,000	$	1,000,000
			Returns			
Income		9.00%		7.00%		1.00%
Appreciation		12.00%		-8.00%		10.00%
Total		**21.00%**		**-1.00%**		**11.00%**

	Equity (LR = 2.5, LTV = 40%)					
	Optimistic		Pessimistic		Range	
Initial value (t)	$	4,000,000	$	4,000,000		
Cash flow (t+1)	$	420,000	$	220.,000	$	100,000
Exit value (t+1)	$	5,200,000	$	3,200,000	$	1,000,000
			Returns			
Income		10.50%		5.50%		2.50%
Appreciation		30.00%		-20.00%		25.00%
Total		**40.50%**		**-14.50%**		**27.50%**

	Debt					
	Optimistic		Pessimistic		Range	
Intial value	$	6,000,000	$	6,000,000		
Cash flow (t+1)	$	480,000	$	480,000	$	-
Exit value (t+1)	$	6,000,000	$	6,000,000	$	-
			Returns			
Income		8.00%		8.00%		0.00%
Appreciation		0.00%		0.00%		0.00%
Total		**8.00%**		**8.00%**		**0.00%**

12.2.2 Risk and Return: The Security Market Line

We have now seen, at least for our simple apartment building example, the effect of leverage on both the expected return and the risk in the return for the equity investor.[4] Exhibit 12-4 combines these two effects and demonstrates the effect on the risk premium in the ex-ante equity return under our previous assumption that the mortgage is riskless. Consistent with that assumption, the 8 percent return on the mortgage includes no risk premium. In that case, the risk premium in the levered equity return is directly proportional to the leverage ratio, *LR*. The underlying property asset (or, equivalently, an unlevered equity investment) has a leverage ratio of 1 and a risk premium of 2 percent (the difference between the property's 10 percent expected return and the mortgage's 8 percent return). With the 60 percent LTV loan, the levered property equity investment has a leverage ratio of 2.5 and a risk premium of 5 percent (the difference between the 13 percent expected return on the levered equity and the 8 percent mortgage return), which is 2.5 times the 2 percent risk premium on the unlevered property.

This proportionality of the risk premium and the leverage ratio makes sense when the debt is riskless because, as we saw previously, the equity risk is also directly proportional to the leverage ratio. Thus, the equity risk premium simply remains proportional to the risk.

Note that the expected total return, *E[r]*, does not increase proportionately with the risk. (The 13 percent expected total return on the levered equity is only 1.3 times the 10 percent expectation on the unlevered investment, even though there is 2.5 times the risk.) This is because the ex-ante total return includes the risk-free rate (compensation for the time value of money) and the risk premium (compensation for risk). Only the risk premium component of the total return needs to increase with the added risk brought on by the leverage.

Now let us suppose, more realistically, that the mortgage is not riskless.[5] In this case, the 8 percent interest rate on the mortgage includes a risk premium for the debt investor. For example, suppose that T-bills yield 6 percent, the risk-free rate of return. Then the 8 percent mortgage has a 2 percent risk premium, the 10 percent expected return on the unlevered property represents a 4 percent risk premium, and the levered equity with the 60 percent LTV loan has a 7 percent risk premium, based on the difference between its expected return of 13 percent and the 6 percent risk-free rate. This situation is depicted in the bottom panel of Exhibit 12-4.

When the debt is not riskless, the equity risk premium is no longer directly proportional to the leverage ratio. (The 7 percent risk premium on the levered equity is only 1.75 times the 4 percent risk premium on the unlevered property, even though the leverage ratio is 2.5 times that of the unlevered property.) However, the equity risk premium is still a linear function of the leverage ratio. The exact nature of that function will be discussed in the next section on the WACC formula. The important point is that, regardless of whether the debt is riskless, the ex-ante equity risk premium will normally be directly proportional to the amount of risk in the equity, where risk is defined in how the asset market cares about it. The second horizontal axis indicates this in Exhibit 12-4, parallel to and above the axis measuring the leverage ratio. This top horizontal axis measures risk as defined by the capital markets. By definition, the zero point on this axis corresponds to the 6 percent risk-free rate of return, the rate of return that includes zero risk premium. Suppose we assume that

---

[4] It should be noted that in some types of real estate investment the above-described effects of leverage are inherent in the operational characteristics of the investment even without the use of financial leverage (in the form of debt financing). See, in particular, our discussion of land and development investment in Part IV of this book.

[5] As will be discussed in more depth in Part VI, a mortgage typically has two major sources of risk from the perspective of the mortgage investor. One source is purely related to interest rates prevailing in the capital market. A fixed-interest rate mortgage's present value will vary inversely with prevailing interest rates (that is, the risk-free interest rate, such as that on Treasury bonds), and this makes the mortgage a somewhat risky investment for the mortgage holder. The other source of risk for the mortgage lender is the possibility of default by the borrower on the loan and loss of value in the collateral backing the loan (the property). This source of risk is clearly related to the real estate markets and in particular to the property that is collateral for the loan.

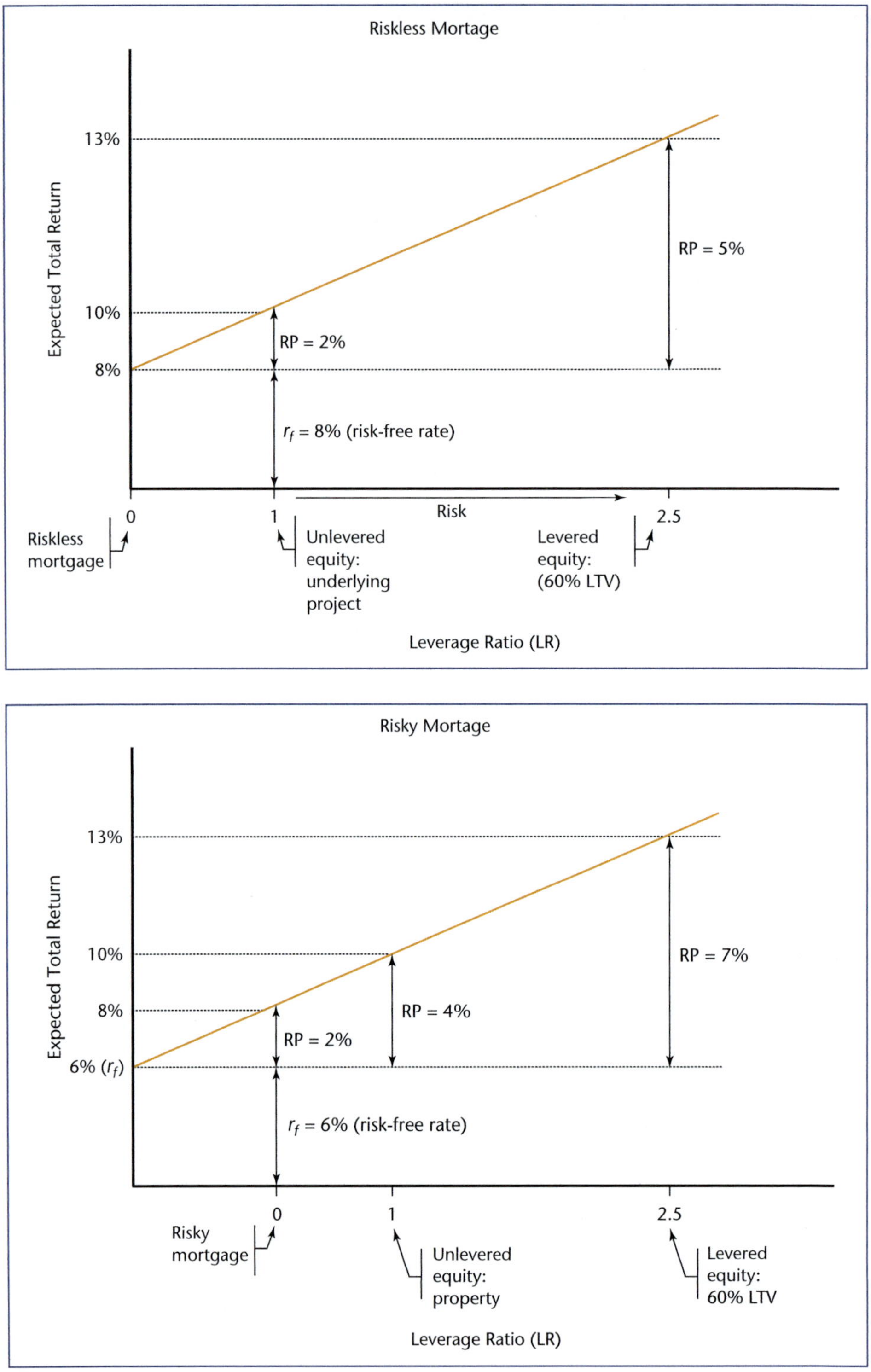

EXHIBIT 12-4 Effect of Leverage on Investment Risk and Return.

the property and debt are both obtained at prevailing market rates of expected return (reflecting the fair market value of the property and of the debt, respectively). In that case, this guarantees that the ex-ante equity risk premium will be directly proportional to its risk as defined by the capital market.

Another way of saying this is to say that the equity ex-ante risk premium per unit of risk (as defined by the capital market) will remain constant no matter how large or small a loan the equity investor takes out to buy a property. This result holds if the loan is unsubsidized and the property is bought at fair market value. By definition, this equity risk premium per unit of risk equals the **market price of risk.**[6] This is another way of saying there is no free lunch in the normal use of leverage. Leverage affects the ex-ante equity risk premium in just such a way that the benefit of the additional expected return is exactly offset by the cost of the additional risk, as evaluated by the capital market.

The relationships between risk and expected return described here and depicted in Exhibit 12-4 reflect what in capital markets theory is called the "Security Market Line" (SML). This function reflects the capital market's price of risk and the relationship between risk and expected return that results from the general equilibrium in the trading among all types of assets in the capital market, including commercial properties. In traditional mainstream investment courses, the SML is primarily applied to and within the stock market, and the capital assets being considered are stocks. In the present context, the "securities" consist of debt (in the form of a mortgage), a property asset (the underlying property collateralizing the loan), and the levered equity investment in the property. These may not be "securities" in the sense that they have not been securitized (broken up into numerous small homogeneous shares or units that are publicly traded on the stock exchange), but they are capital assets that are tradable in the same overall capital market in which stocks also trade. No insurmountable barrier prevents stock market investors from investing in mortgages or property (levered or unlevered). And no insurmountable barrier prevents real estate investors from also (or instead) investing in the stock market or bond market. Hence, assuming a reasonable degree of integration among all these branches of the capital market, the SML that applies to levered equity investment in real property also applies to stock market investment and vice versa.

In Exhibit 12-4, we have not defined exactly *how* the risk on the (upper) horizontal axis is measured or quantified. This is a subject we will address in Chapter 23. In the current context, for practical purposes when analyzing real estate investment risk at the micro-level of individual properties, it may often be useful and legitimate to define a numéraire quantity of risk as that in the subject underlying risky asset, the unlevered property asset, and set this amount of risk (however much risk is in the property) as being equal to "one unit" of risk on the horizontal axis. The levered equity in that underlying asset is essentially a "derivative" of the underlying property asset, with risk essentially like the risk in the underlying asset, only *more* of it.

12.3 THE WACC, A USEFUL SHORTCUT

Before we calculate the impact of leverage on returns over a multiperiod basis (IRR) in Chapter 12.4, we will first introduce the WACC. The WACC is a very popular metric in mainstay corporate finance. Even though its real-life applications to real estate are somewhat limited, the insights it can provide are very useful, nonetheless.

12.3.1 The Weighted Cost of Capital

A formula known as the **weighted average cost of capital (WACC)** is often useful for quantifying the effect of leverage on equity risk and return. The WACC formula is given by:

---

[6] The market price of risk is, by definition, the ex-ante risk premium per unit of risk implied in the market prices of assets.

Equation 1

$$r_P = (LTV)r_D + (1-LTV)r_E,$$

where r_P is the return on the underlying property free and clear; r_D is the return to the property's debt; r_E is the return to the levered equity in the property; and *LTV* is the loan-to-value ratio.[7]

For example, suppose the LTV is 60%, the return to equity is 13%, and the return on the debt is 8%. Then, the previous formula provides a return on the underlying property equal to 10%. Note that these numbers were the same as those used in the preceding text. The "security market lines" in Exhibit 12-4 are a simple graphical expression of the WACC formula. The WACC formula is derived directly from the basic accounting identities and the definition of the simple holding period return (HPR):

Assets = Liabilities + Owners' Equity
Property Cash Flow = Debt Cash Flow + Equity Cash Flow

As expressed in equation (1), the WACC formula shows the return to the underlying asset isolated on the left-hand side of the equation and the LTV and returns to debt and equity on the right-hand side. This is the intuitive way to memorize the formula and the convenient way to apply it when it is easier to empirically observe the return on the levered equity than the return on the underlying physical assets. This is, in fact, the typical situation in corporate finance (including REITs, see the text box), in which we can empirically observe the return on corporate equity by examining the history of the corporation's stock returns.

The WACC, as a simple shortcut, is less usable for real estate investment for two reasons. First, the WACC is only valid for HPR (Chapter 3), including for *simple returns*.[8] However, in practice, the formula is applied over positive spans of time over which a multiperiod return measure, such as the IRR, is used. In this case, the WACC formula holds exactly only if all the variables, the LTV ratio, and the returns remain constant, which is rarely true.[9] This causes the formula to lose exactness in typical applications. It will be less exact when applied over longer periods of time, during which there can be greater fluctuations in the variables. Secondly, in real estate, the return of the property free and clear is an input. We are typically more interested in finding the return on equity.

However, this doesn't mean the WACC is completely useless. First, you can solve the WACC formula for the return on the levered equity. In this way, the more observable parameters are all on the right-hand side of the equation. This is provided by;

---

[7] In many corporate finance texts, the WACC is defined on an after-corporate-income-tax basis, in which the return to the corporation's debt, r_D, is multiplied in the WACC formula by (1 – Tc), where Tc is the marginal corporate income tax rate. However, in most real estate applications, there is effectively no double taxation, either because the real estate investment is made directly without a (taxable) corporate ownership layer (e.g., partnership, LLP, etc.), or because the investment is being made by a corporation that is exempt from corporate-level income tax, such as a REIT. Thus, in effect, Tc = 0 for most real estate applications, so our definition of the WACC is not inconsistent with the corporate finance textbook definition. In other words, we are working here at the before-tax level for the ultimate investor, which is typically equivalent to an after-tax level at the corporate level for most real estate holdings. Taxes will be treated in the next chapter.

[8] That is, where all cash flows and values are registered as of only two points in time, the beginning and end of the "period" (of whatever temporal length) over which the return is defined as the simple ratio of the ending value divided by the beginning value less unity. (See Chapters 2 and 3 for more discussion of return measures.)

[9] For example, the LTV changes as the property's market value and debt change over time. Changes in the LTV also cause changes in the expected returns to debt and equity (*ceteris paribus*), as changes in the LTV affect the relative risk of the equity and debt.

Equation 2

$$r_E = \frac{r_P - LTVr_D}{1 - LTV}$$

For example, suppose we can observe in the property market that the expected total return on a certain type of property is 10 percent and that mortgages are available at 8 percent interest and a 60 percent LTV ratio. Then, the expected total return on the equity invested in such property using a 60 percent LTV ratio mortgage would be 13 percent: 13% = [10% – (0.60)8%]/[1 – (0.60)]. Second, the WACC formula still gives a good back-of-the-envelope *approximation*, especially when combined with common sense.

TEXT BOX 12.1 THE WACC AND REIT COST OF CAPITAL

As expressed in equation (1), the WACC formula can be directly applied to REITs to determine the cost of capital of the underlying real estate (r_P). Indeed, for investors in REITs, it is quite easy to observe empirically their return on levered equity (r_E, i.e., the stock market return), their average LTV, and the interest rate they are paying to service the debt (r_D).

For example, suppose REIT A can borrow at 6 percent, while REIT B must pay 8 percent interest on its debt. Doesn't this imply that REIT A has a lower cost of capital than REIT B? We can use the WACC to answer this question. Suppose REIT A has an LTV of 30 percent while REIT B has an LTV of 50 percent. Suppose both REITs have an expected return to their equity of 15 percent. Then equation (1) tells us:

WACC(A) = (0.3)6% + (1 – 0.3)15% = 12.3%
WACC(B) = (0.5)8% + (1 – 0.5)15% = 11.5%

The weighted average cost of capital for REIT A's assets is 12.3 percent, compared to only 11.5 percent for REIT B's assets. Apparently, REIT B holds less risky property assets than REIT A (or REIT B tends to be less involved in risky development projects, for example). REIT B's debt is more costly, probably because REIT B is more highly levered than REIT A, causing its debt to have more default risk. REIT B's lenders must be compensated for this risk by obtaining a higher interest rate.[10]

Note that if one uses a lower LTV in the previous example, say 20%, one would get a return on the levered equity of 10.2 percent: 10.2% = [10% – (0.20)8%]/[1 – (0.20)]. In other words, in this case, higher debt levels will result in a higher return on equity. (But with an increase in risk, of course!) In real estate, this situation is often referred to as **positive leverage**.

Negative leverage is less widely spoken of (perhaps because it is a less happy circumstance), but it would imply the opposite: leverage decreases the equity investor's return. These terms are often applied in an ex-ante sense, referring to return expectations going forward for the investor. There is also **neutral leverage**, where the amount of leverage will not impact the equity return.

The condition for positive leverage is when $r_P > r_D$. In other words, the return of the underlying property is higher than its mortgage. We have $r_P < r_D$ for negative leverage, and for neutral leverage,

10 REIT B's debt may also be more costly if it has a longer-term average maturity than REIT A's debt and the yield curve in the debt market is upward-sloping. Or perhaps REIT A's debt is largely floating-rate while REIT B's is fixed-rate. Indeed, quantifying the cost of debt capital is a bit more complex than presented in this simple example. The yield curve, default risk premiums, and the relationship between stated yields and expected returns on debt will be discussed in Part IV of this book.

we have $r_P = r_D$. These conditions follow directly from the WACC formula, as seen clearly in the leverage ratio version of equation (2):

$$r_E = r_D + LR(r_P - r_D)$$

The equity return equals the debt return plus the leverage ratio times the difference between the property and debt returns. If this difference is positive (property return is greater than debt return), more leverage will increase the equity return. If this difference is negative, then just the opposite will occur. When the difference is zero, the leverage ratio component will drop out. This is further exemplified in Exhibit 12-5, where we show the three scenarios for different LTV levels.

Investors usually assume that positive leverage will exist in the total return, at least on an ex-ante basis. In fact, such positive leverage is not guaranteed for two reasons. First, the equity investor may overpay for the property. As noted in Chapter 4 (and later in Chapter 14), real estate markets are "thin" and not perfectly efficient, so such pricing mistakes are possible. If the equity investor pays more than fair market value for the property, his realistic ex-ante return (on an unlevered basis) will have a risk premium less than what the market requires and possibly less than that in the mortgage, even though the mortgage may be less risky than the property.

Second, the mortgage can be riskier than the underlying property when the capital markets define risk. It is thus possible for the ex-ante's return on the mortgage to exceed that on the underlying property, even though both the mortgage and property are obtained at market value. Particularly when dealing with more than one asset class (here we have two: real estate and debt), the "type" of risk, or the relevant definition of "risk" as it matters in the capital markets (and hence, as it is reflected in return expectations) is probably not well represented by a one-dimensional measure

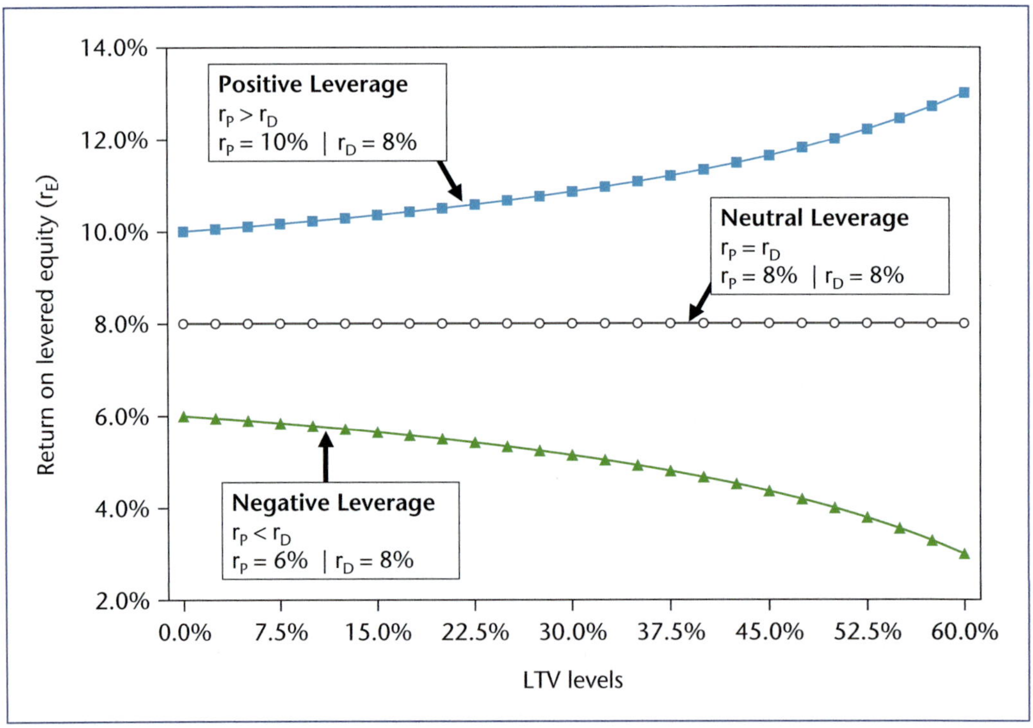

EXHIBIT 12-5 Positive, Neutral, and Negative Leverage for varying LTV levels (x-axis). The return on debt r_D is always 8%.

such as the volatility. The mortgage clearly has different risks from the underlying property, but not necessarily less risk from this perspective. For example, suppose the major source of risk that the market cared about was uncertainty in the future inflation rate. The nominally fixed cash flows in a fixed-rate mortgage would then make such a mortgage riskier, in terms of real (inflation-adjusted) value, than the property whose rent and value will likely be able to adjust to unexpected increases in future inflation. Fixed-income investments are not good inflation hedges, but variable rent leases and short-term leases that move with inflation can make real estate a good hedge.

With those caveats in mind, in general, and on a going-forward basis, most investors view mortgages as less risky than the underlying property, and on an ex-ante basis, mortgage yields usually appear to be lower than realistic IRRs on commercial property, although not necessarily much lower. Ex-ante yields on mortgages are relatively easy to observe, and they typically give long-term fixed-rate commercial mortgages realistic risk premiums on the order of 150 to 300 basis points above T-bills when the yield curve has its most common slightly upward-sloping shape.[11] While realistic ex-ante returns on commercial property are more difficult to observe (as noted in Chapter 11), a typical reasonable range for institutional-quality commercial properties is 400 basis points above T-bills. The ex-ante return spread between property and mortgages (the degree of positive leverage) will tend to be greater in non-institutional property or with shorter-term or adjustable-rate loans.[12] On the other hand, positive leverage will tend to be less when long-run inflation expectations are high or rising, other things being equal.

12.3.2 The WACC and Return Components

The WACC formula can be applied to *any* additive components of the total return, such as the yield (y) and the growth (g), or even the risk premium (RP). You must be consistent, applying the formula to only one component at a time within the equation. For example, if we apply the WACC to the current yield component of the return, then we can obtain the following formula for the **equity cash yield**:

Equation 3

$$y_E = \frac{y_P - LTVy_D}{(1 - LTV)}$$

or its growth/appreciation variant:

$$g_E = \frac{g_P - LTVg_D}{(1 - LTV)}$$

If the current yield on the property (y_P) is 8 percent, and the cash yield (y_D) on the debt is 9 percent, then with an LTV ratio of 50 percent, the initial cash yield on the levered equity investment (y_E) will be 7 percent. This is often referred to as the **cash-on-cash return** on the investment. Note that when applying the formula in this way, the current yield on the loan (y_D) may not be the same as the

---

11 The yield curve reflects the difference between interest rates on long-term versus short-term debt. As will be explained in Chapter 18, realistic ex-ante returns on mortgages are less than their stated or contractual yields or interest rates, as one must consider the probability of credit losses resulting from default. Mortgage risk and ex-ante risk premiums will be discussed further in Part V, but bear in mind that equity investment returns are a function of property asset expected returns and mortgage expected returns, not mortgage contract yields.

12 In principle, the spread should also be increased for sufficiently low LTV ratios, as this should lower the market's required default risk premium in the mortgage ex-ante return.

interest rate on the loan (r_D, used in equation (2)). The loan's current yield is its annual debt service as a fraction of the loan amount, so if the debt service includes amortization of principal (g_D), then the loan's current yield will be greater than its interest rate.[13]

We can also apply the WACC formula to examine the *differential* effect of leverage on the income and appreciation components of the expected return. One major point is that, for typical values of the relevant return variables, leverage *shifts the investor's return relatively away from current income and toward capital gain.* This occurs whether the **cash-on-cash leverage** is positive or negative. With positive cash-on-cash leverage, we mean that $y_P > y_D$, and vice versa. The fundamental reason is that the property-minus-loan differential is usually greater in the appreciation return than in the income return. In other words, usually:

$$g_P - g_D > y_P - y_D$$

This equation typically holds simply because amortization (g_D) *reduces* the outstanding loan balance; in other words, this number will be negative. As a result, the left side of the equation will tend to be larger in most circumstances.

Exhibit 12-6 exemplifies the shift towards capital appreciation for three scenarios: negative, neutral, and positive cash-on-cash leverage. The property in question has a 2 percent growth rate, 8 percent current yield, and 10 percent total return (income + growth). The loan growth rate is the negative of its amortization as a fraction of the current outstanding loan balance. This can be seen as the difference between the loan's current cash yield and its total return as represented by the loan interest rate ($g_D = r_D - y_D$). The current cash yield of the loan is its annual debt service as a fraction of its outstanding loan balance. Initially, this will equal the **mortgage constant (MC)**, the annual annuity factor used to compute the loan payments. In Exhibit 12-6, we have three loan scenarios: one in which the loan interest rate is 6 percent, resulting in *positive leverage* in the cash-on-cash yield for the equity investor; one in which the loan interest rate is 7 percent, or *neutral leverage*, and the final in which the loan interest rate is 8 percent, resulting in *negative leverage*. In all cases, however, the loan is amortized initially at 1 percent per year, as indicated by the difference between the mortgage constant and the loan interest rate. (The 6 percent loan has a 7 percent MC, while the 8 percent loan has a 9 percent MC.) Thus, the initial growth rate differential between the property and the loan is + 3 percent (computed as $g_P - g_D = 2\% - (-1\%) = 2\% + 1\% = 3\%$).

Using WACC Equation (3), we can subsequently compute the income component on equity for all three scenarios for different LTV levels. For example, in the case of a 60 percent LTV with the 7 percent mortgage constant (in case of positive cash-on-cash leverage), we have

$$y_E = \frac{y_P - LTVy_D}{(1-LTV)} = \frac{0.08-(0.6)0.07}{(1-0.6)} = 9.5\%$$

$$g_E = \frac{g_P - LTVg_D}{(1-LTV)} = \frac{0.02-(0.6)-0.01}{(1-0.6)} = 6.5\%$$

13 The loan interest rate (or "yield to maturity") represents the total return to the loan (assuming it is held to maturity and does not default). We can represent the appreciation return component of the loan as the percentage change in the loan balance due. (This is a "book value" definition, ignoring changes in the market value of the debt as might be caused, for example, by changes in interest rates or the LTV.) Therefore, the loan appreciation rate would be *negative* for an amortizing loan. As the appreciation rate plus the current cash yield rate always sums up the total return, an amortized loan's current yield will exceed its contractual interest rate or total yield. For a classical constant-payment amortizing loan, the cash yield is given initially by the "mortgage constant," or annuity factor, introduced in Chapter 2 and discussed in more depth in Part V.

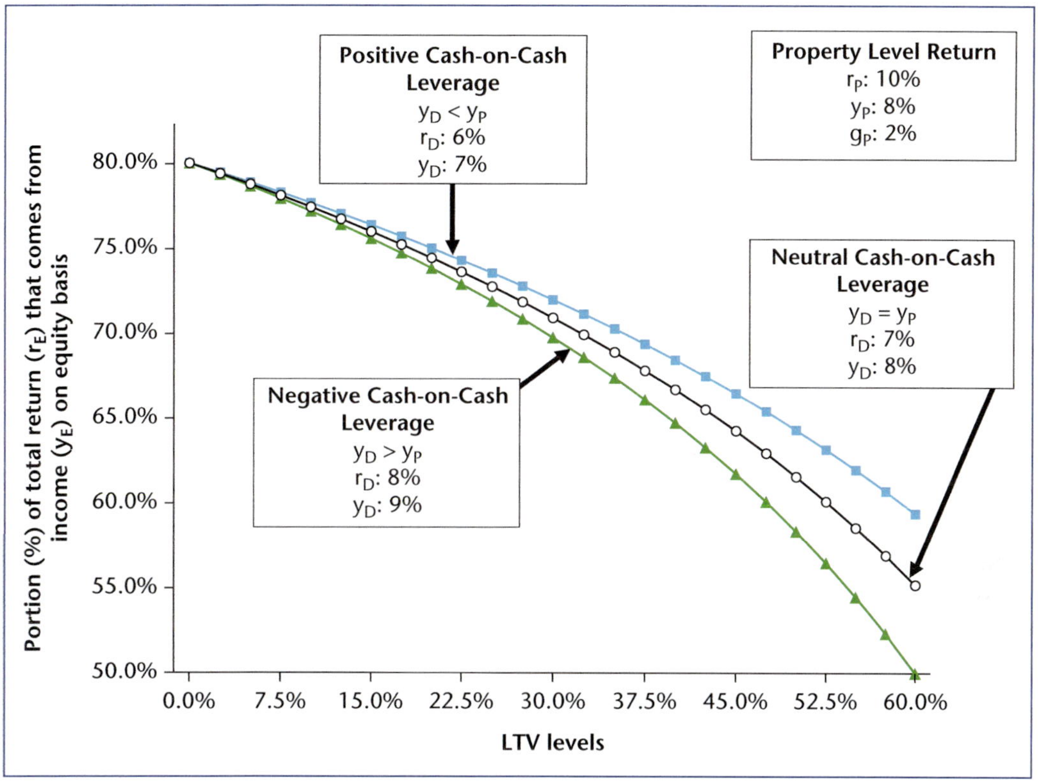

EXHIBIT 12-6 Percentage Contribution of Equity Income Return to Total Return (y_E/r_E, on the y-axis) for Varying Levels of LTV (x-axis).

For example, with no leverage (0% LTV), 80% of the total return comes from income, and the remaining 20% comes from price appreciation.

The levered equity total return is 16 percent, consisting of a 9.5 percent current yield and 6.5 percent growth. In Exhibit 12-6, we subsequently plot the contribution of the income on equity as a proportion of the total income on equity or y_E/r_E. The example above would give us a 62% income contribution to the total return (10%/16% = 62%).

Note that, even in the case of positive cash-on-cash leverage, where the equity yield rises with leverage, the equity appreciation return rises even faster, resulting in a relative increase in the growth component within the equity total return. Thus, leverage shifts the total return relatively away from current income and toward growth, even when income leverage is positive. While this will not necessarily always be the case, it is typical.

12.3.3 The WACC and Risk

As the WACC formula applies to any additive component of total return, we can even apply it to the risk premium (RP). For example, expressing the WACC formula in terms of the leverage ratio instead of the LTV ratio, the ex-ante risk premium in the levered equity investment is given by the following formula:

Equation 4

$$RP_E = RP_D + LR\left(RP_P - RP_D\right)$$

The equity risk premium equals the debt risk premium, plus the leverage ratio times the spread between the property and debt risk premiums. Equation (4) specifies the linear relationship between the risk premium and the leverage ratio noted in our discussion of Exhibit 12-4. It describes the SML relevant to property, debt, and levered equity investment in the present context. Equation (4) also demonstrates that if the debt is riskless ($RP_D = 0$), the equity risk premium is directly proportional to the leverage ratio (Exhibit 12-4), as equation (4) then reduces to:

$$RP_E = (LR)(RP_P)$$

As noted, risk in the equity investment (as measured by the capital market) will be directly proportional to the equity risk premium if both the property and debt are obtained at prevailing market prices, whether the debt is riskless or not.

12.4 IMPACT OF LEVERAGE ON THE EXPECTED RETURN ON A MULTIPERIOD BASIS

As mentioned before, the WACC provides very important insights into the impact of leverage on investor returns. However, its direct and exact usage for a real estate investor is limited. This is mostly driven by the fact that a real estate investment's returns and LTV levels are not constant over time. To find more accurately the impact of leverage on the investors' after-debt IRR, we must return to our proforma and add the cost of debt. (The reader may also find the Chapter 12 Videos 1–3 in the online supplements folder to be helpful at this point.)

12.4.1 Calculating the Debt Payments

After the investor sets its desired LTV ratio, a mortgage will include two important variables: (1) interest rate and (2) amortization. The LTV ratio will determine the total mortgage amount.[14] For example, in Chapter 5 (specifically Exhibit 5-4), we found a property worth approximately \$940K. Combining this with an LTV of 75% would result in an (\$940K x 0.75 =) *initial mortgage of \$700K.* (Rounded.) The interest rate refers to the **contract interest rate** stipulated in the loan agreement, applied as a simple interest rate *per payment period* specified in the mortgage. Thus, if the mortgage specifies monthly payments (which is typically the case), then the applicable interest rate is the simple monthly rate, conventionally defined as the nominal per annum rate stipulated in the loan, divided by the number of payment periods per year specified in the loan. For example, a 12 percent loan with monthly payments applies a simple interest rate of 1 percent, due at the end of each month.[15] Using the notation from Chapter 2: $r = i/m$, where i is the nominal annual rate and m is the number of payment periods per year. The amortization period is when the mortgage is paid in full. This is typically 30 years for residential mortgages and 25 years (= 300 months) for commercial mortgages. The amortization period will impact the principal payment size, which comes on top of the interest payment. A shorter amortization (meaning you have less time to pay off the mortgage in full) will increase the principal payment, and the other way around.

---

14 The typical LTV rate is determined by the investor's risk appetite and cash availability. Therefore, LTVs range between 20% for well-funded pension, sovereign wealth, and insurance funds and 70% for smaller private investors. When originating a mortgage, REITs are typically in the 40% to 50% range. (*Source: MSCI.*)

15 Recall from Chapter 2 that this implies an effective annual rate (EAR) of $(1.01)^{12} - 1 = 12.68\%$, compounding the simple monthly rate at the monthly frequency. See Part V in the online portion of this book for more depth and detail about loan payments, alternative loan structures, computation of loan yields and expected returns, and underwriting of commercial mortgages.

With all this in place, we can now calculate our monthly mortgage payments using the following rules:[16]

- Outstanding balance (OLB). The outstanding balance at the end of the month (OLB_t), is the outstanding balance at the beginning of the month (OLB_{t-1}) minus the principal payment ($AMORT_t$). The outstanding balance at the start of the month equals the outstanding balance at the end of the month in the preceding period, except for the first month, where it simply equals the initial loan amount (L). Or $OLB_0 = L$.
- Total debt service (PMT). With the monthly interest rate (r), outstanding balance at the start of the month (OBL_{t-1}), and the months left until maturity (N_t), you can calculate the monthly payments using the annuity formula in arrears;

Equation 5

$$PMT_t = \frac{OBL_{t-1} \times r_t \times (1+r_t)^{N_t}}{(1+r_t)^{N_t} - 1}$$

You can also use the PMT() formula in Excel.

- Principal payments (AMORT). You can calculate the monthly principal payments by subtracting the interest payments (INT) from the debt service (PMT). Thus, $AMORT_t = PMT_t - INT_t$. The interest payments are calculated by multiplying the interest rate by the outstanding balance at the start of the month. Thus, $INT_t = r_t \times OLB_{t-1}$.

Note that we used the following abbreviations;

- L = initial contract principal amount (the loan amount)
- r_t = contract simple monthly interest rate applicable for payment in period t.
- INT_t = interest owed in period t.
- $AMORT_t$ = principal payment in period t.
- OLB_t = outstanding balance at the *end* of period t.
- PMT_t = total loan payment, also known as the debt service (principal + interest).
- Nt = periods left to amortization.

In most conventional cases, the *payment and interest rate are assumed to be constant over time* in the proforma, although they could change in reality; see the text box as well. Such a mortgage is called a **Constant Payment Mortgage (CPM)**. Other variants are discussed in Part V of this book, but in reality, the CPM is used in most, if not all, cases when developing a proforma.

With this information, we can now calculate the monthly interest and principal payments and the outstanding balance in any month. Using our previous example, we need a $702,670 loan (75% LTV) for this property. Next, say that the nominal yearly interest rate is 5% for a loan that amortizes in 25 years. Note that because we are assuming a CPM, the total payments can be calculated using a simplified version of equation (5):

$$PMT = \frac{L \times r \times (1+r)^{N}}{(1+r)^{N} - 1}$$

[16] See Videos 4–6 in the Chapter 12 online supplements folder to see how to set up mortgage payment and balance tables in Excel.

EXHIBIT 12-7A

Example of Monthly Loan Payments Over the Course of 25 Years (300 months)

INPUTS

Loan amount	$ 702,670
Interest (Yearly)	5.00%
Interest (Monthly)	0.42%
Amortization period (Years)	25
Amortization period (Months)	300

Month	OLB (begin)	PMT	INT	AMORT	OLB (end)
1	$ 702,670	$ 4,108	$ 2,928	$ 1,180	$ 701,490
2	$ 701,490	$ 4,108	$ 2,923	$ 1,185	$ 700,305
3	$ 700,305	$ 4,108	$ 2,918	$ 1,190	$ 699,115
4	$ 699,115	$ 4,108	$ 2,913	$ 1,195	$ 697,921
5	$ 697,921	$ 4,108	$ 2,908	$ 1,200	$ 696,721
...	...	...	...	...	...
296	$ 20,284	$ 4,108	$ 85	$ 4,023	$ 16,261
297	$ 16,261	$ 4,108	$ 68	$ 4,040	$ 12,221
298	$ 12,221	$ 4,108	$ 51	$ 4,057	$ 8,164
299	$ 8,164	$ 4,108	$ 34	$ 4,074	$ 4,091
300	$ 4,091	$ 4,108	$ 17	$ 4,091	$ 0

If we take r = 5%/12 = 0.42% and a maturity of N = 300 months (which equates to 25 years), we will find monthly payments of *$4,108*. Note that there is no subscript *t* anymore, indicating the payments are time-invariant. The interest rate paid in the first month will be INT_1 = L x r = $702,670 x 0.0042 = *$2,928*. To calculate the interest paid (INT) in the following months, we will use the outstanding balance at the start of the month (OLB_{t-1}) instead of L, in words: $INT_{t>1} = OLB_{t-1}$ x r. The difference between the payment and the interest is the principal payment. Thus, AMORT = PMT– INT = $4,108– $2,928= *$1,180.*[17] The principal payment reduces our outstanding balance. Thus, $OLB_t = OLB_{t-1} - AMORT_t$ = $702,670– $1,180 = *$701,490*. After this, we can start again for the following month. If done correctly, you will get what is shown in Exhibit 12-7A (we only show the first 5 and last 5 months). Note that the outstanding balance at the end of the final month (300) should be zero. (Shown in the bottom right of Exhibit 12-7A).

Where:

- OLB (begin) = outstanding balance at the beginning of the month
- PMT = debt service (interest plus amortization), calculated using equation (5)
- INT = interest payment
- AMORT = principal payment
- OLB (end) = outstanding balance at the end of the month (OLB (begin) – AMORT)

You will find that even though the payments (PMT) stay the same over the full 300 months, the underlying components will change (INT and AMORT). This is shown graphically in Exhibit 12-7B.

[17] Per usual, the numbers shown here are rounded. As such you might find small deviations. For full reference and transparency, you might want to look up the Excel file found online.

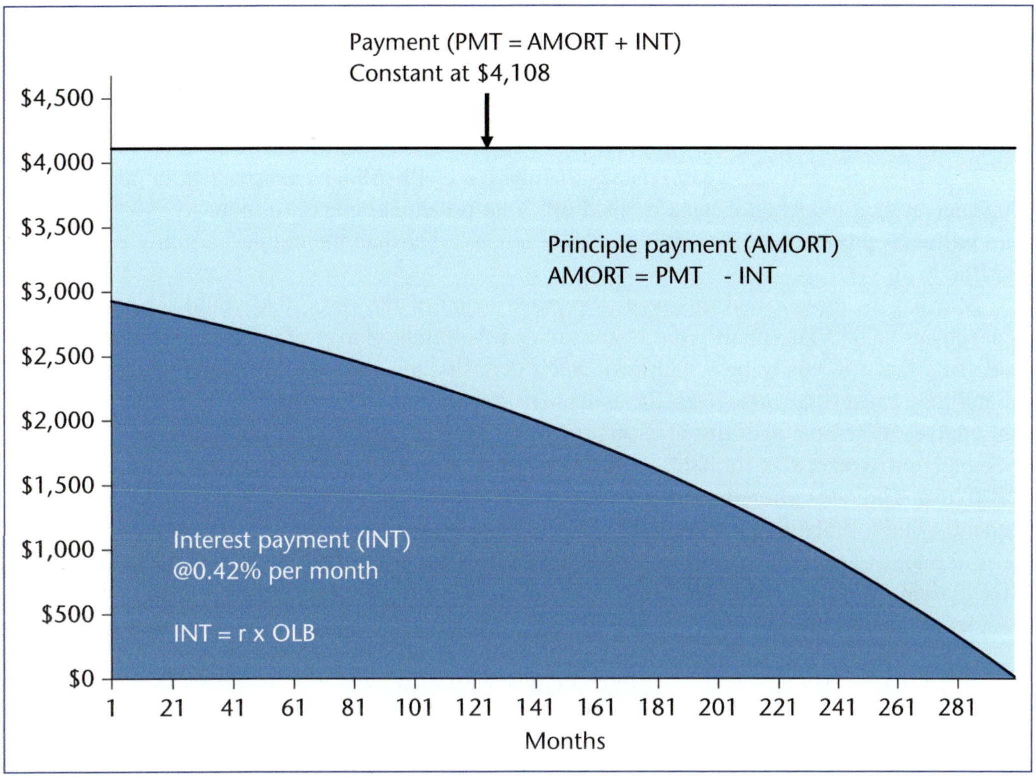

EXHIBIT 12-7B Full Payment Scheme over 25 years (300 months).

The investors' payment will predominantly go toward interest in the first few months. In the final months, almost all payments go towards paying the outstanding balance. This makes intuitive sense. At the start of assuming the mortgage, the outstanding balance is at its highest. Thus, the interest payment will be equally high. Over time, as the investor slowly pays off the outstanding balance, the interest paid on the mortgage will equally reduce.

TEXT BOX 12.2 LET'S GET REAL. WHAT DO MORTGAGES ON COMMERCIAL PROPERTY REALLY LOOK LIKE?

The most popular commercial mortgage types in the United States are 1/4, 1/6, or 2/8, with an amortization rate of 25 years. A 1/7 has a fixed mortgage rate for one year and will adjust for the following six years. The mortgage "**matures**" (must be paid off) and must be *refinanced* (or replaced with additional equity) after (1 + 6) = 7 years. The adjusting interest rate (mortgages with interest rates that change at pre-specified discrete intervals, such as annually, are called **ARMs: Adjustable-Rate Mortgages**) is determined by negotiating an index upfront, which both parties cannot influence. A popular option (internationally) is the LIBOR (London Interbank Offered Rate). Other indexing options include Inflation (CPI) and Government bonds. The ARM will adjust *periodically* by changing the interest rate based on how much the LIBOR changed during that same time window. For example, if the LIBOR went up 50 basis points in the past year, the interest rate will also increase by that much. A 5% interest rate would adjust to 5.5% in this case. The 2/8 mortgage will have a fixed interest rate for the first two years, then adjust for the final eight years, etc. Note that the payments are still calculated using the 25-year amortization rate for the mortgage (that is, the principal payments are based on fully amortizing the loan, paying the balance down completely over a 25-year horizon). The fact that the loan matures at a horizon shorter than the amortization rate (e.g., 5, 7, or 10 years versus 25 years) means that the loan will still have an outstanding principal balance at the time when it must be paid off. That principal balance at maturity is known as a **"balloon" payment** because it is typically much larger than the regular monthly payment on the loan.

Mortgages are designed this way to remove many of the risks that would otherwise be placed on banks. The main issue is **maturity mismatch**. Banks are financed (mostly) by deposits that can easily be withdrawn. Such deposits are, therefore, effectively short-term liabilities. However, banks invest these deposits in long-term mortgages (among other things, of course). When the maturity of assets is greater than the maturity of liabilities, this creates a dangerous type of risk for banks, which, in effect, is a type of leveraging up of risk as well as return. The rates offered on deposits must track short-term interest rates, which vary frequently due to inflation, economic conditions, and monetary policy, for example. However, if the interest rate (known as the "coupon rate") on long-term assets such as mortgages is fixed, then the banks could find themselves in immediate trouble when short-term rates rise, something banks cannot control. The ARM structure safeguards banks from such scenarios by allowing them to raise the interest rate on their assets to match the increases they must pay on their liabilities. This also means that the interest rates themselves can be relatively low, as at least this one major type of risk faced by banks (known as "interest rate risk") can be largely mitigated.

But what about the investors? How does it change the equity proforma? The ARM itself could increase the risk from the investors' point of view. Indeed, if interest rates increase over time, the payments will also increase. This could get the real estate investor in trouble, especially if rents do not rise at the same rate. (Though, if the increase in short-term interest rates is related to current inflation, it might be possible for the property investor to raise nominal rents.) Of course, greater loan payment risk could increase the loan default risk, other things equal, which wouldn't be good for either the lender or the borrower. But this is why the equilibrium result is for ARM interest rates to typically be lower than fixed-rate mortgage (FRM) interest rates, other things equal. Borrowers want (need) lower interest rates to get them to be willing to take on more payment risk. Also, lenders are willing to accept lower interest rates to reduce their maturity mismatch interest rate risk and the loan payment default risk.

As regards how the property investor sets up their equity proforma, the use of adjustable loans does not much affect the mechanics, as the proforma is done ex-ante, and the general base-case assumption is that future interest rates will stay the same (known as the "random walk" theory of interest rates). Furthermore, investors can hedge against interest rate swings (albeit with some cost, paying the differential between FRM vs. ARM rates).

Finally, you might have noticed that the 5-to-10 years to refinance coincides with the typical 5-to-10-year proformas discussed throughout the book. Many long-term rental leases are also in this same time frame. This is no coincidence! Investors adjust their proforma based on the time to refinance, as the banks require this for their own underwriting procedures. As mentioned in Chapter 4, the actual end date in the proforma should not impact the computation of the value of the real estate in a DCF valuation, considering the asset's terminal value at the end of the analysis horizon.

12.4.2 Annualizing the Mortgage Payments

Note that two large discrepancies exist between the mortgage example in Exhibit 12-7 and our proforma from Chapter 5. First, the proforma is yearly, whereas our mortgage payments are monthly. Second, the mortgage payments go on for 25 years, whereas a typical proforma is limited to 5 or 10 years.

To solve the first issue, we must sum up all the payments intra-year. Thus, all debt service (PMT) and its underlying elements (INT and AMORT) are summed between months 1 and 12 for year 1, between months 13 and 24 for year 2, etc. This will give us the expected payments per year. The outstanding balance is treated slightly differently. The outstanding balance at the end of year 1 is simply the outstanding balance at the end of month 12, the outstanding balance at the end of year 2 is the outstanding balance at the end of month 24, etc. For the second issue, we assume a large **balloon payment** at the end of the proforma, which pays off the entire outstanding balance at once. Just like we assume that we sell the property at the end of the proforma (even though that does not need to be the case), we also assume that we use the sales proceeds to pay off the outstanding balance at the bank first. Only after paying the bank first can we enjoy whatever is left of the sale of the property.

After annualizing Exhibit 12-8 for 10 years (and pivoting the table so it will fit more nicely with our proforma), we get the following extra line items for our proforma;

Used for **operating** cash flows

Cash Flow Items	Year 1	2	3	4	5	6	7	8	9	10
OLB (begin)	$ 702,670	$ 688,181	$ 672,952	$ 656,943	$ 640,115	$ 622,426	$ 603,833	$ 584,287	$ 563,742	$ 542,146
PMT	$ 49,293	$ 49,293	$ 49,293	$ 49,293	$ 49,293	$ 49,293	$ 49,293	$ 49,293	$ 49,293	$ 49,293
INT	$ 34,804	$ 34,063	$ 33,284	$ 32,465	$ 31,604	$ 30,699	$ 29,748	$ 28,748	$ 27,697	$ 26,592
AMORT	$ 14,488	$ 15,230	$ 16,009	$ 16,828	$ 17,689	$ 18,594	$ 19,545	$ 20,545	$ 21,596	$ 22,701
OLB (end)	$ 688,181	$ 672,952	$ 656,943	$ 640,115	$ 622,426	$ 603,833	$ 584,287	$ 563,742	$ 542,146	$ 519,445

Used for **reversion** cash flow

EXHIBIT 12-8 Adding Debt Payments to the Proforma.

12.4.3 Calculating the Equity-Before-Tax Cash Flow (EBTCF) and its IRR

To find our **Equity-Before-Tax Cash Flows (EBTCF)**, we must (1) subtract the debt service from our operational Property-Before-Tax Cash Flows (PBTCF) and (2) subtract the outstanding balance at the end of our proforma from the PBTCF reversion cash flow. In other words, the investor pays the debt service using the free cash flow when holding the property. When we sell the property at the end of our proforma, we immediately pay off the outstanding balance at the bank (the "balloon" payment noted earlier). For example, with the investment introduced in Chapter 5, we have a PBTCF of $61,800 in year 1. The debt service in that same year is expected to be $49,293. As a result, the EBTCF will be ($61,800 - $49,293 =) $12,507. Similarly, when selling the property in year 10 (after selling costs), we are left with (PBTCF =) $1,232,833. The outstanding balance at this same moment (OLB at the end of year 10) is $519,445. The EBTCF on reversion is calculated by subtracting the two: EBTCF = $1,232,833- $519,445 = $713,388. If done correctly (expending on the proforma from Chapter 5), we get Exhibit 12-9. (Note that you must subtract the debt payments from the PBTCF, *not the discounted PBTCF*. This is a common mistake among students.)

There are a few things to note here. First, while the PBTCF is expected to grow over time (g), the debt payments are assumed to be constant. As a result, the EBTCF grows at a higher rate than the PBTCF (when there is positive leverage, of course). In fact, the PBTCF was 30% higher in year 10 than in year 1, whereas the EBTCF grew by over 150% during that same time period. However, because the bank payments are fixed, the negative cash flow in year 7 (caused by capital expenditures) will be exacerbated. Not only is the investment expected to provide a negative $27K cash flow on its own, but we also must pay $49K in debt service, resulting in a negative EBTCF of almost $77K. This further stresses the point that the timing of (large) capital expenditures must be carefully planned upfront.

Now that we have calculated the EBTCF of this investment, we can also calculate its IRR (see Chapter 3, equation (7)). To calculate this IRR, we must calibrate the discount rate so that the sum of the discounted EBTCF equals the PV of this investment. The PV on an EBTCF basis is equal to the *equity*. The equity investment is the purchase price of the investment minus the initial loan amount, or $936,893 - $702,670 = $234,223 in our example. In math, this is represented as follows;

$$Equity = \frac{EBTCF_1}{1+IRR} + \frac{EBTCF_2}{(1+IRR)^2} + \ldots + \frac{EBTCF_T}{(1+IRR)^T}$$

The EBTCF in the final year will equal the operational cash flow of year 10 *plus the reversion cash flow* on an equity basis. Filling in the equation with the numbers used above, we get;

$$\$234,223 = \frac{\$12,507}{1+IRR} + \frac{\$14,361}{(1+IRR)^2} + \ldots + \frac{\$31,342 + \$713,388}{(1+IRR)^{10}}$$

You can solve the equation above by trial and error or using the IRR() function in Excel. The correct IRR (EBTCF) equals **15.03%**. Note that the IRR on the property level (PBTCF) is 8.60%. In other words, leverage increased the investor's expected IRR.

Finally, Exhibit 12-10 recalculates the IRR on equity for this investment at different typical LTV levels and interest rates. Even though all options result in positive leverage ($r_P > r_D$), the difference in potential outcomes varies drastically at higher debt levels. With no debt (LTV = 0), the return

EXHIBIT 12-9
Example of Proforma with Debt Service

Property	
PGI year 1	$ 100,000
Selling costs	5.00%
Going-out cap rate	8.00%
Going-in cap rate	8.00%
r	8.60%
g	3.00%

Loan	
LTV	75.00%
Interest (Y)	5.00%
Maturity (Y)	25

EXHIBIT 12-9 (Continued)

A. Property-level (Chapter 5)

Operating Cash	Year										Reversion	
Flow Items	1	2	3	4	5	6	7	8	9	10	11	10
PGI	$ 103,000	$ 106,090	$ 109,273	$ 112,551	$ 115,927	$ 119,405	$ 122,987	$ 126,677	$ 130,477	$ 134,392	$ 138,423	*Sales price* $ 1,297,719
Vacancy	$ 5,150	$ 5,305	$ 5,464	$ 5,628	$ 5,796	$ 5,970	$ 6,149	$ 6,334	$ 6,524	$ 6,720	$ 6,921	*Selling cost* $ 64,886
OpEx	$ 20,600	$ 21,218	$ 21,855	$ 22,510	$ 23,185	$ 23,881	$ 24,597	$ 25,335	$ 26,095	$ 26,878	$ 27,685	
NOI	$ 77,250	$ 79,568	$ 81,955	$ 84,413	$ 86,946	$ 89,554	$ 92,241	$ 95,008	$ 97,858	$ 100,794	$ 103,818	
CapEx	$ 15,450	$ 15,914	$ 16,391	$ 16,883	$ 17,389	$ 17,911	$ 120,000	$ 19,002	$ 19,572	$ 20,159		
PBTCF	$ 61,800	$ 63,654	$ 65,564	$ 67,531	$ 69,556	$ 71,643	$ (27,759)	$ 76,006	$ 78,286	$ 80,635		$ 1,232,833
PV(PBTCF)	*$ 56,906*	*$ 53,972*	*$ 51,189*	*$ 48,549*	*$ 46,046*	*$ 43,671*	*$ (15,581)*	*$ 39,284*	*$ 37,258*	*$ 35,337*		*$ 540,264*
SUM:DCF	**$ 936,893**											

B. After-Debt (Chapter 12)

Operating Cash	Year									Reversion	
Flow Items	1	2	3	4	5	6	7	8	9	10	10
OLB (begin)	$ 702,670	$ 688,181	$ 672,952	$ 656,943	$ 640,115	$ 622,426	$ 603,833	$ 584,287	$ 563,742	$ 542,146	
PMT	$ 49,293	$ 49,293	$ 49,293	$ 49,293	$ 49,293	$ 49,293	$ 49,293	$ 49,293	$ 49,293	$ 49,293	
INT	$ 34,804	$ 34,063	$ 33,284	$ 32,465	$ 31,604	$ 30,699	$ 29,748	$ 28,748	$ 27,697	$ 26,592	
AMORT	$ 14,488	$ 15,230	$ 16,009	$ 16,828	$ 17,689	$ 18,594	$ 19,545	$ 20,545	$ 21,596	$ 22,701	
OLB (end)	$ 688,181	$ 672,952	$ 656,943	$ 640,115	$ 622,426	$ 603,833	$ 584,287	$ 563,742	$ 542,146	$ 519,445	
EBTCF	$ 12,507	$ 14,361	$ 16,271	$ 18,238	$ 20,264	$ 22,350	$ (77,052)	$ 26,713	$ 28,994	$ 31,342	$ 713,388

Where;

- PMT = Debt service (calculated using equation (5))
- INT = Interest payment (from monthly schedule)
- AMORT = Principal payment (Debt service minus interest payment)
- OLB (end) = Outstanding balance at the end of the year.
- EBTCF = Equity-Before-Tax Cash Flow. For the operating cash flow: (6) – (8). For reversion: line (6) reversion minus year 10 outstanding balance (end of the year)

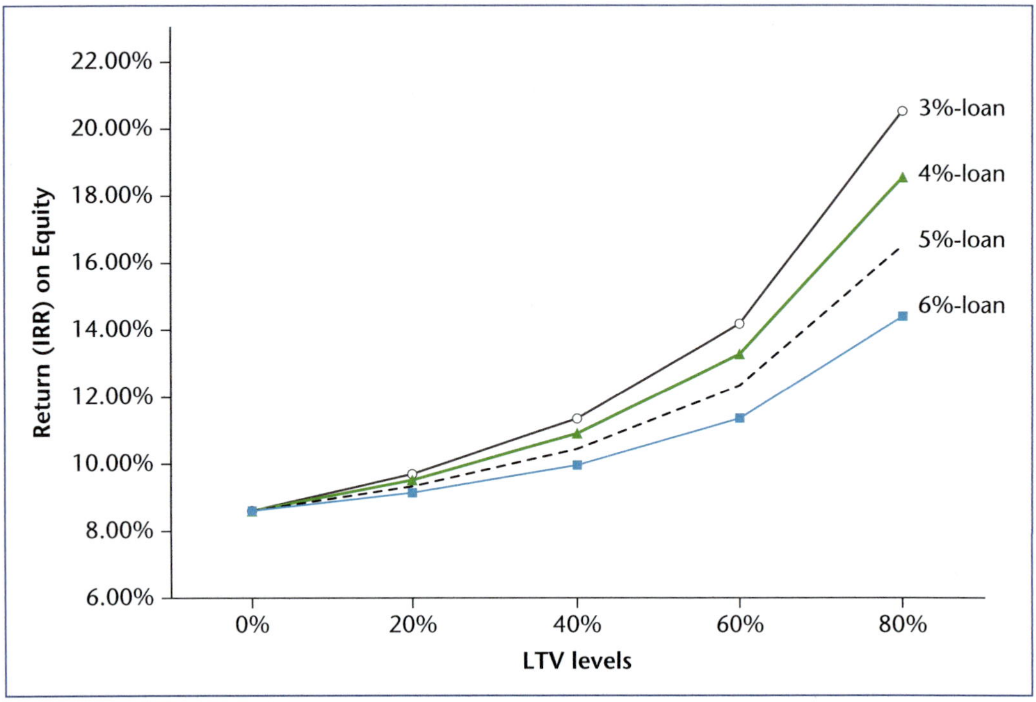

EXHIBIT 12-10 Expected Return on Equity for different LTV levels and Interest Rates using the proforma example of Exhibit 12-9.

on equity will be the same for all options, namely 8.60% (the return on the property). In contrast, at 80% LTV, the return on equity will be 20.51% for a 3%-loan and a much lower 14.39% for a 6%-loan.

In summary, the impact of leverage on multiperiod returns (IRR) is similar to the impact of leverage on simple returns (WACC). In both cases, leverage will increase the (ex-ante) return on equity. However, in practice, the impact of leverage on the IRR is somewhat attenuated compared to using the WACC. This attenuation occurs due to two reasons: (1) the amortization of debt and (2) the IRR is a per annum rate covering a multi-year duration. The first (amortization of debt) decreases the outstanding debt as we hold the investment over multiple years, reducing the leverage in its wake as well. As for the second point, the IRR itself is attenuated as a multiperiod return is annualized. As a result, the impact of leverage on the return will also be weakened.

One final point is important to note. In this chapter, we have been speaking of leverage as though it is achieved through the use of a traditional mortgage. But in fact, in the twenty-first century, there are various ways that real estate investors effectively achieve (or we could say, incur) leverage besides just borrowing a single classical type of commercial mortgage from a bank. Frequently, in particular, with larger properties, there may be multiple layers of financing. Possibly more than one mortgage, other types of debt financing, or quasi-debt arrangements such as preferred equity. The sources of such capital may be traditional banks and insurance companies. Still, they might alternatively include non-bank sources such as REITs, private equity funds, other types of investors, or even the use of derivatives. We will explore some of these interesting possibilities in subsequent chapters, but the key point to remember is that, well, "leverage is leverage." It doesn't matter if the vehicles providing financing are technically mortgages, debt, or whatever. What creates leverage is the seniority of the claims and the relatively fixed nature of the claims that the ultimate equity investor must pay. This increases the risk the equity investor faces and also what (in normal circumstances) creates the higher expected (total) returns for the equity investor, the essential investment effects of leverage, as we have discussed in this chapter.

12.5 CHAPTER SUMMARY

Under the typical assumption that the loan is less risky than the underlying property, leverage will increase the ex-ante total return on the equity investment by increasing the risk premium in that return. Under that same relative risk assumption, leverage will increase the risk of the equity investment, normally proportionally with the increase in the risk premium. Leverage will usually (if we assume non-negative price appreciation and non-negative amortization) shift the expected return for the equity investor relatively away from the current income component and toward the growth or capital appreciation component.

TEXT BOX 12.3 FINAL THOUGHTS: LEVERAGE CAN BE TEMPTING, BUT WATCH OUT!

You can see how tempting leverage can be for the property equity investor. You do get to use "other peoples' money" to buy something you largely control, from which you can take all the profit (after you pay what you owe to the lender). But look back at that picture of the physical lever we showed at the beginning of the chapter: It is like a highly off-center seesaw offering a different ride for each side. The person riding on the long-arm side (the property equity investor) will bounce wildly up and down; the person on the short-arm side only bounces a little. The person riding the long-arm side of the seesaw can crash onto the ground with devastating force. In real estate investment, excessive use of leverage is the leading cause of excessive losses and bankruptcy.

Leverage is also tempting for lenders as well. The money they're lending you is probably also borrowed mainly from depositors, bondholders, insurance policyholders, or even the government! The temptations of leverage are not limited to commercial real estate but extend to housing and throughout the capital markets for corporations and funds of many types.[18] As a result, capital markets tend toward maximum use of leverage and toward "systemic" risk caused by interconnected chains of debt through which a failure in one part of the system can rapidly propagate to other parts at first seemingly remote.

Governments and the investment industry itself attempt to police these tendencies, for example, by requiring banks to restrain the amount that they borrow (ceilings on their own leverage ratios). But the capital markets are such a fast-growing, dynamic, technologically changing, and entrepreneurial arena that the system sometimes, inevitably, gets out of control. This happened with devastating results in the GFC of 2008-2009, which is only one of history's many financial crises. Commercial property asset markets have suffered more localized "crashes" at least once every couple of decades in the United States. In each case, excessive leverage has played a major role, and it claimed the latest crop of equity investor victims.[19] In recent years, following the shocks of the GFC and COVID-19 pandemic, there has, in fact, been a tendency of at least some real estate investors to take on less leverage and for traditional lenders to supply loans only with shorter maturities and with adjustable interest rates (as we shall see in Part V).

---

[18] There may be additional issues associated with use of leverage by homebuyers. This text is focused on commercial and investment real estate as a business enterprise, not on home buying or consumer finance. Homeowners potentially risk not only equity investment losses, but personal bankruptcy or loss of their home, and they may lack the type of expertise and financial knowledge that investors do (or should) have. And owner-occupied housing is a much larger segment of the national wealth and of the demand underlying the national economy (the GDP), implying greater spillover effects or systemic risk.

[19] A good starting point might be Jim Clayton's 2009 article in the *Journal of Real Estate Portfolio Management*. Excessive leverage in the housing sector was arguably the largest single cause of the great financial crisis of 2008 and subsequent recession.

In future chapters, we will explore the use of debt and leverage in more depth. Leverage can indeed bring various advantages besides the higher expected returns we focused on in this chapter, such as potential owner's income tax advantages (Chapter 14) and inflation protection (Chapter 15). However, it also brings additional concerns besides increased volatility, such as loss of valuable flexibility in a world of uncertainty where "the forecast is always wrong" (Chapter 9).

KEY TERMS

- Leverage
- Heterogeneous investors
- Leverage ratio (LR)
- Equity
- Residual claim
- Loan-to-value (LTV)
- Management incentive effects
- Default risk
- Weighted average cost of capital (WACC)
- Risk premium (RP)
- Equity cash yield
- Cash-on-cash return
- Positive leverage
- Negative leverage
- Mortgage constant (MC)
- Equity-before-tax cash flow (EBTCF)
- Principal payment
- Interest payment
- Outstanding balance
- Amortization versus maturity

STUDY QUESTIONS

In Your Own Words

12.1 How does the use of fixed cost debt financing create "leverage" in the equity position of an income-property investment?

12.2 What is the difference between the leverage ratio (LR) and the loan-to-value ratio (LTV)? How much greater property value can be purchased with a 75% LTV than with a 50% LTV? What is the LR associated with each of those two LTVs?

12.3 What is the relationship between the leverage ratio (LR) and the loan to equity (L/E) ratio?

12.4 What is meant by the preferred or senior claim of debt?

12.5 How does the equity investor's ability to control property management align the interests and incentives of the debt and equity investors in normal circumstances, so as to maximize total property value? (Hint: What are the implications of the fact that equity has the "residual" claim on property value?)

12.6 What is wrong with the following statement: Only a fool would invest in real estate without financing most of the purchase with a mortgage; borrowing allows you to increase your expected return by using other people's money!

12.7 What is the relationship between the leverage ratio and both the risk and the risk premium in the equity investor's return, assuming that debt is riskless?

12.8 Without assuming riskless debt, what is the relationship between the ex-ante equity risk premium and the amount of risk in the equity investment, measuring risk as it is defined by the capital markets and assuming that both the property and debt are obtained at market value? How is this relationship affected by the degree of leverage (amount of debt)?

12.9 a. How does leverage affect the equity investor's ex ante risk-adjusted return, or the expected risk premium per unit of risk, assuming the property is bought at fair market value and the debt is unsubsidized?

b. How does leverage affect the NPV of the equity investor's investment if the property is bought at a price *different from* its fair market value, assuming the loan is at the market interest rate and the investor has unlimited equity capital available to invest?

12.10 Identify what is wrong with the following statements: Real estate investors who use debt financing have a significant advantage when interest rates are low. The cheaper cost of debt allows these investors to outbid pension funds and other investors who typically do not employ financial leverage for property acquisitions.

12.11 Why doesn't the equity investor's expected total return increase proportionately with risk?

12.12 John Clapp has $1,000,000 of his own equity capital available to make a real estate investment. He finds a bargain, a property with a market value of $1,100,000 that he can buy for $1,000,000.

a. By how much can John enhance his net wealth by leveraging his purchase of this bargain property using borrowed money to finance at least part of his investment?

b. Now suppose the bargain property is twice as large, worth $2,200,000, and John can buy it for $2,000,000, but he still has only $1,000,000 of his own capital available. In these circumstances, how much more can John increase his net wealth by using leverage, assuming he could borrow at least up to a 50% LTV ratio?

12.13 Derive the WACC formula in terms of first-year property, equity investor, and lender yields (i.e., current income yield components of return). (Hint: Start with the identity *Property cash flow = Debt cash flow + Equity cash flow*, which you can write as PBTCF = DS + EBTCF. Divide each side by V, and then multiply DS by (L/L) and EBTCF by (E/E). You should have no trouble finishing from here.)

12.14 Discuss the following statement: There is *always* positive leverage with respect to the *total* return (ex ante).

12.15 With respect to the *income component* of the before-tax ex-ante return, when will there be positive leverage, and when will there be negative leverage?

12.16 How is the expected income return component related to the LTV ratio, the property cap rate, and the mortgage constant on the loan (on a before-tax basis)?

12.17 Suppose you want to increase the income component of your return from your real estate equity portfolio, but you do not want to sacrifice the appreciation component. What must you look for? If you can't find a loan with positive leverage in the equity yield, what trade-off must you accept?

12.18 How does leverage usually affect the relative magnitude of the income and appreciation components in the equity investor's expected return?

12.19 Does increasing leverage (borrowing a larger fraction of the property value) usually primarily increase the expected income component of the return or the appreciation component? Why? (Hint: Use the WACC formula and assume that $E[g_D]$ is usually either zero or negative, less than $E[g_P]$, while $E[y_D]$ is usually positive and around the same magnitude as $E[y_P]$.)

12.20 How does leverage enable the same underlying asset to serve the investment objectives of different types of investors? What are the two types of investment products that result from the use of debt financing for real estate investment?

Check Your Knowledge

12.21 Why is leverage riskier in thin real estate markets?

A) Thin markets have more predictable prices

B) Property values may be mispriced, amplifying losses

C) They offer lower debt limits
D) They restrict equity growth

12.22 What is a balloon payment?
A) Monthly interest-only payment
B) Large final payment to settle the debt
C) Initial down payment
D) Final payment to the equity holder

12.23 Why might an investor prefer a fixed-rate mortgage over an adjustable-rate mortgage?
A) To reduce debt payment
B) To avoid changes in payment amounts
C) To increase leverage
D) To maximize short-term returns

12.24 Why does debt amortization reduce the leverage ratio (LR) over the holding period of a real estate investment?
A) Because it increases property value faster than debt payments
B) Because it decreases the outstanding debt balance over time
C) Because it increases property appreciation rates
D) Because it lowers the LTV ratio but not the LR

12.25 Suppose you expect that one year from now, a certain property's before-tax cash flow ($PBTCF = NOI - CI$) will equal only $15,000 per year under a plausible pessimistic scenario or as much as $25,000 per year under a plausible optimistic scenario. If you borrow an amount such that the loan payments will be $10,000 per year (for certain), then what is your *range* of expected income return component (equity yield) under the no-leverage and leverage alternatives, assuming that the property price is $200,000 and the loan amount is $100,000?

12.26 If the cap rate on a certain property is 12% and loans are available at an 11% mortgage constant (where MC = DS/LOAN), then what is the expected income component of your before-tax return (i.e., first return on equity or cash-on-cash return) if you borrow 80% of the property price? What if you only borrow 50%?

12.27 A property is being acquired today for $100. The cap rate, or return on assets, is 7.5%, and the investor can obtain a mortgage for 75% of the property purchase price with an annual mortgage constant (MC) of 6.25%.
a. What is the leverage ratio associated with this transaction? What is the loan-to-equity ratio?
b. What is the investor's expected first-year return on equity (cash-on-cash return)? Compute these two different ways: (i) directly using the definition of equity cash yield = EBTCF/E; and (ii) using the WACC formula approach.

12.28 An investor is considering the purchase of a property for $1 million. Based on the $1 million price, the property has a cap rate of 10.5%. The investor can obtain an interest-only mortgage loan at 8.0%. Suppose the investor borrows 75% of the price to acquire the property. What is the maximum price the investor could pay for the property before debt financing has a neutral effect on the equity cash yield?

12.29 If the cap rate on a certain property is 12% and loans are available at an 11% mortgage constant. Assume the loan interest rate is 10% and the expected total return on the property is also 10%. What is the growth component of the equity return if you borrow 80% of the property price? What if the property cap rate were 9% instead of 12%?

12.30 The figures in the following table depict the before-tax cash flow projection for a typical 10-year holding period for a levered investment in a property whose current market value is $5 million, for which a $3 million interest-only 10-year mortgage would be the typical financing mechanism at a market interest rate of 8%. What is the market's implied required going-in 10-year IRR for the levered equity investment?

Year	0	1	2	3	4	5	6	7	8	9	10
Prop. Inc.		450,000	454,500	459,045	463,635	468,272	472,955	477,684	482,461	487,286	492,158
Debt Svc.		–240,000	–240,000	–240,000	–240,000	–240,000	–240,000	–240,000	–240,000	–240,000	–240,000
Prop. Sale	–5,000,000										5,523,111
Loan	3,000,000										–3,000,000
Equity CF	–2,000,000	210,000	214,500	219,045	223,635	228,272	232,955	237,684	242,461	247,286	2,775,269

12.31 Assuming riskless debt, if the loan-to-value ratio is 80%, approximately how much more risk will there be in the equity return than if the LTV ratio were 60%? Put another way: If the return to equity can vary per year within a range of ± 20% with a 60% LTV ratio, then within what range can it vary with an 80% LTV ratio? How much larger should the market's required risk premium be in the required return to equity with 80% debt as compared to 60% debt?

12.32 Kai Estate Limited Partnership (LP) advertises that it has a target of matching the stock market in total return for its limited partner investors, before taxes. (Suppose that the stock market risk premium is expected to be 7%.) The conservative office and warehouse properties that the partnership plans to acquire typically command risk premiums in their before-tax expected returns of about 3%. Assuming riskless debt, what loan-to-value ratio must the LP plan to maintain in its property investments in order to have a good chance of meeting its stated target?

12.33 Answer the above question, assuming the risk-free interest rate is 5% and the debt would have an interest rate of 7%.

Chapter Case: Shattuck Square Financing Strategy

Brittany Jones, an experienced real estate investor, is evaluating financing strategies for the purchase of Shattuck Square, a mixed-use commercial property located in downtown Berkeley, California. The property has a purchase price of $8 million, with projected annual property income growing at 3%. Shattuck Square offers strong investment potential. However, property income may fluctuate with economic cycles.

To prepare her proforma, Brittany is analyzing three 25-year fully amortizing constant payment mortgage (CPM) options with varying loan-to-value (LTV) ratios and interest rates:

Low Leverage (50% LTV): 5% interest rate
Moderate Leverage (70% LTV): 6% interest rate
High Leverage (85% LTV): 7% interest rate

1. How much equity would Brittany need to invest if she chooses the high-leverage option?
   A) $1.2 million
   B) $4 million
   C) $1.5 million
   D) $2 million
2. If Brittany takes out a fully amortizing loan with a 25-year term, what is her total number of payments?
   A) 240
   B) 360
   C) 300
   D) 180

3. If Brittany chooses the moderate leverage option to finance the investment, what is the annual debt service?
   A) $36,080
   B) $432,970
   C) $536,666
   D) $34,722
4. If rising interest rates is anticipated, which of the following loan types might carry the most risk?
   A) Fixed Rate Interest-Only Loan
   B) Fixed Rate Fully Amortizing Loan
   C) Adjustable-Rate Mortgage
   D) All options carry the same risk
5. If Brittany's goal is to maximize her return on equity (ROE), which leverage option would likely provide the highest potential ROE, assuming the property's return exceeds debt costs?
   A) 50% LTV
   B) 70% LTV
   C) 85% LTV
   D) All provide the same ROE
6. How does choosing a higher LTV (85%) affect risk and expected return on equity in the investment?
   A) Decreases both risk and return on equity
   B) Increases both risk and return on equity
   C) Only increases risk, with no effect on return
   D) Has no effect on risk and return on equity
7. If Shattuck Square generates $500,000 in annual PBTCF and has a debt service of approximately $280,000, what would be the EBTCF for the year?
   A) $220,000
   B) $280,000
   C) $500,000
   D) $780,000
8. What happens to the EBTCF if debt service payments increase while PBTCF remains constant?
   A) EBTCF increases
   B) EBTCF decreases
   C) EBTCF stays the same
   D) EBTCF becomes negative
9. If the PBTCF grows by 3% annually due to income growth, and debt service remains fixed, what will happen to the EBTCF over time?
   A) EBTCF will increase
   B) EBTCF will decrease
   C) EBTCF will remain the same
   D) EBTCF will be eliminated

13 After-Tax Real Estate Investment Analysis

CHAPTER OUTLINE

LEARNING OBJECTIVES

After reading this, you should understand:

- How to calculate annual estimates of after-tax cash flow.
- How to calculate annual taxable income.
- How depreciation postpones taxation.
- How resale gains are taxed.
- How to run an after-tax cash flow proforma through to sale.
- How to utilize the proforma to analyze the impact of leverage.

In the last chapter, we began to step beyond pure property-level analysis to investor-level analysis by considering the effect of leverage on equity investment. This chapter extends this progression by considering how the owner's income tax obligations may affect the owner's cash flows net of those taxes, that is, at the after-tax level. We will see how income tax effects interact with the possible use of debt financing in the expected total return faced by the equity investor.

This chapter focuses on the basic mechanical level of quantifying cash flows and forecasting investment returns. Deeper and broader considerations of opportunity cost and valuation, and after-tax capital budgeting in the context of the asset market equilibrium are deferred to the next chapter. This chapter is divided into three sections. Section 13.1 focuses on the operating cash flows, that is, cash flow during the investor's expected holding period. Section 13.2 considers the after-tax reversion cash flows at the time of resale. Finally, Section 13.3 focuses on the ex-ante after-tax investment returns. Along the way, we also introduce an innovative way to structure the presentation of both the operating and reversion cash flows so as to facilitate investment analysis, which we call the Cash Flow Components format, and which will be useful in the next chapter.

It should be noted that many of the specific considerations in this chapter are relevant, particularly regarding the income tax and accounting provisions in the United States. Indeed, they reflect the specific provisions prevailing as of the time of writing the current edition of this book. Tax laws and accounting conventions change from time to time, and the decade of the 2020s promises to

DOI: 10.1201/9781003643838-16

be a particularly dynamic period. Other countries, of course, have different rules on depreciation, capital expenditure immediate expense write-off limits, and different tax rates and laws. However, at a more general level, this chapter's basic principles and process should be broadly applicable in other countries, even as specific provisions, such as the calculation of depreciation, can differ.

13.1 IMPACT OF TAX ON OPERATING CASH FLOWS

To begin with, it is important to understand how a property owner's income tax obligation increases or reduces the net after-tax cash flow received by that investor each period and how certain non-cash expenses can provide a tax shield for taxable investors. To see how this works, we must consider the difference between property-level before-tax cash flows (PBTCF) and owner-level after-tax cash flows (EATCF).

This requires considering some basic differences between accrual and cash flow accounting. Accrual accounting is designed to register income and expenses when they are "accrued," that is, when they are legally owed.[1] On the other hand, cash flow accounting is designed to register cash inflows and outflows when they *actually* occur for the property owner. Even though, as always, we primarily care about cash flows, the owner's accrual-based income statement is relevant because in the United States, the owner's income tax obligation on commercial property income is based on accrual accounting, and income taxes are themselves, of course, a cash flow item. In other words, the investors' cash flow is not directly taxed, but the net income, according to tax regulation, is, and that affects the investor's cash flow. Net income can diverge significantly from net cash flow at times.

Recall first from Chapter 5 that the typical property-level before-tax cash flow statement identifies the net operating income (NOI) from the property each year, as well as a bottom-line property-level before-tax net cash flow (PBTCF), which consists of the NOI less any capital improvement expenditures. At reversion, we subtract the selling costs from the expected selling price to obtain our property-level before-tax net cash flow. Such a cash flow statement differs from the accrual statement on which the owner's income tax obligations are computed. Three differences are usually the most important: (1) depreciation expense, (2) capital expenditures, and (3) debt amortization.

1. **Depreciation Expense.** Depreciation expense is not deducted from the cash flow bottom line because depreciation expense is not a cash outflow but reflects (in theory) the presumed accrual of losses in property value over time. While in actual fact property often does not lose value over time in nominal terms (that is, in current dollars, typically due largely to the effect of monetary inflation), U.S. tax rules still allow property depreciation expenses related to the built structure on the property to be subtracted from taxable income to compute the owner's income tax obligation each year. Generally offsetting this to some extent, however, at the time of property resale, the capital gains income tax obligation will be based on the net sale price minus the **book value** of the property (referred to in U.S. tax rules as the "adjusted basis" of the property), with the latter being net of the **accumulated depreciation expenses** taken during the period of ownership.[2]
2. **Capital Expenditures**. Capital expenditures are deducted from the cash flow bottom line because these are cash outflows. In contrast, on an accrual basis, such expenditures would not usually be fully charged as expenses in the year they are made. Still, they would be capitalized into the asset's book value and then depreciated (or "amortized") gradually over the life of the improvement. Thus, capital expenditures do not (much) reduce the

[1] You can view accrual accounting as simply the standard type of accounting taught in basic accounting courses and used in corporate accounting. Many of its fundamental procedures and principles famously originated in the Italian Renaissance, mainly in Florence and Venice, where merchants popularized the use of double-entry bookkeeping.

[2] Note, however, that the capital gains tax may be deferred by using the sale proceeds to buy a similar type of property within a limited period of time (referred to as a section 1031 "like-kind" transfer).

income tax obligation of the property owner in the year they are made, even though they do reduce the owner's net cash flow that year (though this may be mitigated by financing the improvements with borrowing). Note that many capital improvements can be written off more quickly than the building as a whole, using cost segregation rules that allow for an economic life related to the specific improvement component. For example, a new water heater might be written off over 10 years or, in some cases, based on first-year write-off allowances, written off entirely in the first year. Such a more aggressive approach usually requires the help of an accountant or tax lawyer and will not be covered here.

3. **Debt Amortization**. Suppose the owner has financed the property by taking out a mortgage or debt associated with the acquisition. In that case, the cash flow to the owner is reduced by the entire amount of the debt service payments to the lender, including both the interest component of the debt service and the debt amortization component (repayment of principal). From an accrual perspective, however, *only the interest portion of the debt service payment is charged as an expense against the owner's taxable income*, as any portion of the debt service that is used to pay down the principal is viewed as a reduction of the owner's debt liability, which is not an expense.[3] Another perspective is that all principal debt repayments are now part of the owner's equity share and are available when the property is sold, so no write-off of this cash flow deduction is permitted.

All three general effects of income taxes and debt on the property owner's operating cash flow are depicted in Exhibit 13-1. The exhibit shows two branches of further calculations starting from the property NOI. The right-hand branch is accrual-based, and the left-hand branch is cash-flow-based. In the right-hand branch, the owner's income tax obligation is calculated based on taxable income, which removes the accrual items of debt interest and depreciation expenses from the NOI. The income tax obligation thusly calculated from accrued income is itself a cash outflow item, which is removed from the NOI along with the entire debt service (principal amortization as well as interest) and any capital improvement expenditures to arrive at the equity-after-tax cash flow (EATCF) at the bottom of the left-hand branch in the diagram. The EATCF is the bottom line of ultimate interest to the property owner.[4] The right-hand branch shows how the tax item is computed.

Note from Exhibit 13-1 that the depreciation expense (DE) is an important determinant of the investors' taxable income. Depreciation of the property value over time is not considered an operating expense (and, as noted, may not actually occur in nominal value levels for a properly maintained building in an environment with even modest inflation). However, the IRS allows depreciation expenses to be charged against taxable income (*IRS publication 527*). To calculate the allowed depreciation expense, we need to take the following two steps;

1. **Depreciable Cost Basis.** IRS rules allow only the property's building structure, equipment, and fixtures to be depreciated, *not* the land component of the property value. The rationale behind the non-depreciation of land is that land does not physically "wear out" as a structure does, and "location value" (as described in Part II) is traditionally considered to be at least as likely to increase as decrease over time. The land value component of the property value is typically allocated (by the IRS) based on reasonable assumptions (often consistent with property tax assessment). However, formal appraisals can also be made for larger properties. The depreciable cost basis is subsequently determined by subtracting the land value from the acquisition price. The land value as a percentage of the purchase price in the

---

[3] This point still sometimes confuses students. Why wouldn't principal payments be an expense to me? Look at it this (simplified) way: If I gave you $100 and you gave the $100 back in a week, returning that money would not be seen as a profit to me or a loss to you. Only if I charge interest on the $100 will there be seen any profit to me and expense to you.

[4] As Professor Stewart Myers once said in a 1984 class when explaining why cash flows are more relevant for investment analysis than accounting-based income: "You can't buy beer with accrued net income."

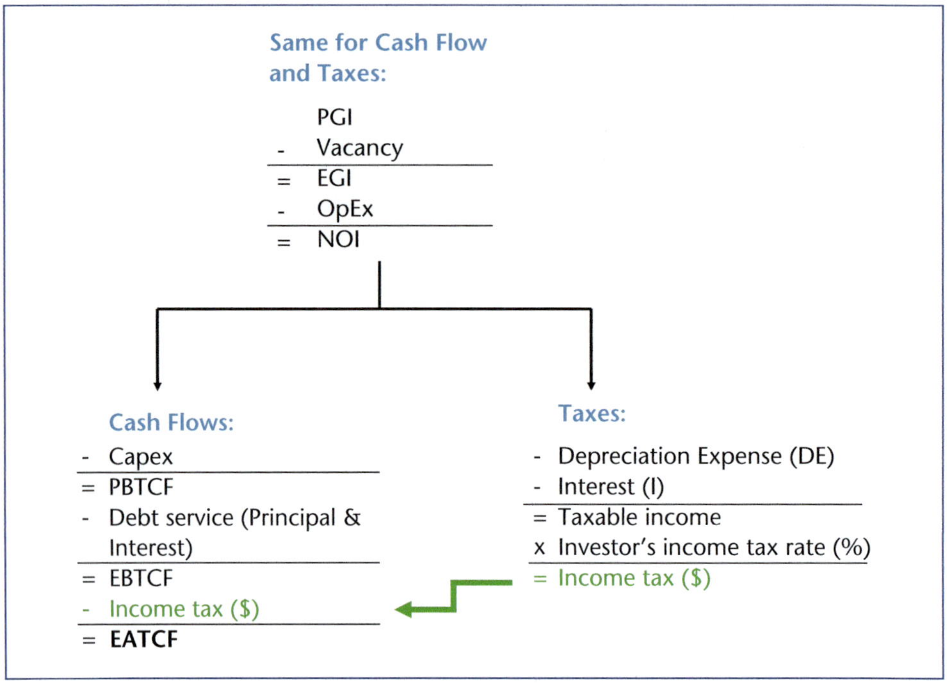

EXHIBIT 13-1 Numerical Example of Capital Gains Tax for Three Scenarios.

U.S. has typically been in the range of 20%–30%, though this can vary greatly with location and, in recent times, has tended to increase in many urban areas.[5]

2. **Lifetime of the Building.** As of the early 2020s, the IRS rules for income property require **straight-line depreciation** based on a 27.5-year lifetime for residential structures and 39 years for non-residential property.[6] Note that a shorter lifetime for tax purposes is a good thing from the investors' point of view (all things equal), as this allows you to depreciate your property at a higher rate, deducting greater expenses from taxable income and thus lowering your tax bill. The yearly depreciation expense is found by dividing the depreciable cost basis by the minimum permitted lifetime.[7]

---

[5] Recent research indicates that for the average commercial property in the U.S., land value equals about half of the total property value. It should be noted that if the property asset that was purchased is only a leasehold (also called a "ground lease," as distinct from a perpetual "freehold" of the property), then in most circumstances, the entire purchase price could be depreciated under U.S. tax law (not just the structure value). In other words, in effect, the leasehold is presumed for tax purposes not to include land value. See the online supplemental materials for more discussion of the treatment of leasehold properties.

[6] Capital improvements, such as roofs or heating/cooling systems, made to the building can usually be depreciated over a different lifetime than the building, often 5 to 15 years. Investments that help a building attain a LEED rating, such as photovoltaic solar cells, new lighting systems, or raised floors, could be eligible for faster write-offs. Depreciation of the leasehold in the case of ground leases is over the lesser of either the structure depreciation lifetime (27.5 or 39 years) or the remaining lifetime of the lease. In the interest of simplicity, we have ignored this in the present numerical example. So-called "cost segregation" can be a method to reduce the tax obligation of the property. Cost segregation can apply not only to new capital improvements but also to existing components of the building. Usually, 5 percent to 20 percent of the building value can be separated for faster write-off than the building's 27.5- or 39-year life. Consult a tax lawyer or accounting expert.

[7] Most closing costs incurred in the property acquisition (ignored in this example) can be written into the depreciable cost basis (including loan "points," which can be amortized over the life of the loan). Some components of the property equipment, such as HVAC or kitchen appliances, may be depreciated more rapidly than the building life. Tenant improvement expenditures paid by the landlord to finish out or improve spaces associated with specific long-term (multiyear) leases are "amortized" (depreciated) over the maturity of the building (27.5 or 39 years). Still, they may be completely written down when/if the tenant leaves or terminates the lease. Some leasing costs, such as broker commissions may be amortized (depreciated) over the life of the lease. All these subtleties are ignored for to clarify the position in this example.

For a simple numerical example, say you purchased a property for $1,000,000, with a cost basis of $800,000 ($200,000 land value).[8] If the property is residential, our yearly depreciation expense (DE) would be $800,000 / 27.5 = $29,091. You can deduct these depreciation expenses until the entire cost basis is depreciated (27.5 years in this example). The depreciation clock is reset for the new owner whenever the property is sold (regardless of the age of the building). In other words, if I sell a (residential) property after owning it for 20 years, the new investor can charge the depreciation expense for another 27.5 years (and not just the 7.5 years as I would have).

With all of the above in mind, let us consider how we calculate the operational EATCF for the investment introduced in Chapter 5 and expanded upon in Chapter 12.[9] The operating cash flow projection in Exhibit 13-2 picks up where our description of property cash flow proformas left off in Chapter 12. In this example, the NOI of the property is projected to start at $77,250 in the first year and then grow at a rate of 3 percent per year to a level of $100,794 in year 10. Chapters 5 and 12 described this NOI as a property-level operating income figure net of all operating expenses, including property taxes and management expenses. The proforma in Exhibit 13-2 assumes that the investor will take out a loan to finance 75 percent of the property's purchase price (at $936 thousand). This $702 thousand mortgage will have an interest rate of 5 percent and must be paid in full in 25 years. As shown in Chapter 12, in year one, this results in an interest payment of $35K and a principal payment of $14K.

We calculate our "accrued" net income for our tax obligation as follows (Exhibit 13-1): net income = NOI – INT – DE. The NOI and interest payments (INT) follow directly from the proforma.[10] Thus, determining our depreciation expense (DE) is the only thing left to do. First, we subtract the land value from the purchase price to obtain the depreciable cost basis. Assume that the depreciable cost basis is 80% of the purchase price. This gives us ($936,893 x 0.8=) $749,515 in depreciable costs. If this property is a small **apartment** building, we are allowed ($749,515 / 27.5 years =) $27,255 in depreciation expenses (DE) annually. (Remember, for other property types, we would have to divide the depreciable cost basis by 39 years, resulting in a lower depreciation expense annually.) Our accrued net income for tax purposes is now $77K (NOI) – 35K (INT) – $27K (DE) = $15,190 in year 1.

TEXT BOX 13.1 WHAT HAPPENS IF I HAVE NEGATIVE TAXABLE INCOME – TAX SHIELDS AND SHELTERS

In our Exhibit 13-2 example, we achieved positive accrual-based taxable income for all years. Good for us! However, this is not necessarily a given in the real world. Achieving negative accrual-based taxable income is possible, especially at higher interest rates and high LTV levels. What would happen with our proforma and tax obligation in such a year? Would taxes due be

---

8 The allocation for land is typically 10% to 30% but may be higher in some markets. One defendable allocation is based upon the ratio used in property tax assessments. Tax accountants will know the permitted ratios in each market, not likely to raise a red flag by the federal income tax auditors.

9 The example presented in this chapter will use a classical single mortgage and make specific tax rate assumption, purely to illustrate the mechanics of after-tax levered equity analysis. As noted, tax rates and taxation policies vary over time and in different jurisdictions (states) and countries. The specific numbers used here, though probably not untypical in the U.S., should not be taken to represent any actual real-world situation. Furthermore, as noted at the end of the previous chapter, financing vehicles used in the twenty-first century, especially for larger properties, can be multi-layered and varied, even for a single property investment. But the essential and typical after-tax investment effects of leverage will be well illustrated, even if simplified, by the example presented in this chapter.

10 If the property were a leasehold (instead of freehold as in the present example), and if the ground lease required regular ground rent payments, then those rental payments could also be deducted entirely from the property owner's taxable income, similarly to the interest on the loan. Indeed, such ground rent payments imply that the ground lease is acting in the role of providing some financing for the property purchase, similar in this respect to a loan (assuming relatively fixed ground rent not based on the property net income, and with resulting leverage implications as discussed in the Appendix to this chapter).

zero? The answer is **no**. The property owner typically has other positive taxable income from other appropriate sources. This **tax loss** can be deducted against other income, thereby reducing the owner's overall taxable income. This will save the owner income taxes in the amount of her income tax rate times the taxable income deduction. This is referred to as a **tax shield** or **tax shelter** because it allows other income that would otherwise be taxable to avoid paying taxes. This negative tax income should be part of the property's proforma, as this investment creates this cash flow. As a result, the proforma will have "negative taxes." Tax losses can also be carried forward from one year to the next when the investor's total taxable income is negative.

As a small side note and history lesson, such tax shields, together with generous depreciation schemes, created a bona fide real estate crisis in the late 1980s. The tax incentives created by the Reagan Administration and easy access to credit due to the deregulation of banks in that same period created a large run to commercial real estate by wealthy investors. By the mid to late 1980s, the huge, accumulated flow of capital to commercial real estate had stimulated a building boom of historic proportions. The development industry converted financial capital into physical structures, especially office buildings, shopping malls, and hotels. Much of this development was driven or supported by tax incentives that distanced the investor from the underlying economic costs and benefits of the physical real estate that was being built, resulting in many bad projects that found themselves with few tenants. Furthermore, the savings and loan and commercial banks that financed much of the new construction operated in an environment of "moral hazard," in which government deposit insurance divorced their source of capital from the risks of their investment.[11] In 1986, a sweeping tax reform act removed virtually all the special tax incentives that had benefited real estate. Commercial real estate prices took over a decade to reach 1985 levels again.

We multiply the taxable income by the tax rate to compute our tax obligation. A reasonable assumption (in the early 2020s) in the U.S. is an ordinary (income) tax rate on income of 35% on average. As mentioned earlier, municipal property taxes are already embedded in the operating expenses (Chapter 5). Our taxes due in year 1 are now $15,190 (taxable income) x 35% (income tax rate) = *$5,317*. The final step is subtracting the tax obligation from our EBTCF to obtain our EATCF. In year 1, this would give us $12,507 (EBTCF) – $5,317 (taxes) = **$7,109 (EATCF)**.

We also provide the **Property-After-Tax Cash Flow (PATCF)** calculated by subtracting the tax obligation on the property level (free of debt) from the PBTCF for completeness in Exhibit 13-2. The PATCF will come in handy later. Given that we assume no debt is on the property (so no interest rate deduction), we calculate the property-after-tax cash flow as: PATCF = PBTCF – 0.35 × (NOI - DE).

In summary, calculating the operational EATCF involves the following steps;

- **Depreciation expense (DE).** DE = Depreciable cost basis / Lifetime of asset.
- **Taxable income (TAXIN).** TAXIN = NOI – INT – DE.
- **Taxes due (TAX).** TAX = TAXIN x ordinary tax rate.
- **Equity-After-Tax Cash Flows (EATCF)**. EATCF = EBTCF – TAX.

Where NOI is the Net Operating Income, INT is the interest paid on the mortgage, and the tax rate is based on the investor's income tax bracket. EBTCF is the equity-before-tax cash flow as calculated

[11] The term moral hazard was coined in the insurance industry to describe a situation in which one party controls the risks (in this case, the financial institutions). In contrast, another party pays the price of the downside outcome from a risky decision (in this case, the U.S. government via the Deposit Insurance Corporations).

in the previous chapter. Calculating the property-after-tax cash flow (PATCF) is similar to the steps above, with the exception of the second line (TAXIN). In this case; TAXIN = NOI – DE. (We assume no debt.)

If done correctly, you should get an after-tax proforma like that in Exhibit 13-2. A few interesting observations should be made before calculating after-tax reversion cash flows. First, in our case (after taking out the large projected year 7 capital expenditures), the before-tax cash flows (EBTCF) are relatively similar to the accrual-based net income. For example, the first year's before-tax cash flow is approximately $13K, whereas the accrual-based net income is $15K, which is a small difference.

While the cash flows are generally similar to the net income in our case, this will not always be the case, depending on how much depreciation allowance is available and especially on how much leverage is used and at what interest and amortization rate on the debt. Note also that even under the illustrative assumptions, the before-tax cash flows are less smooth over time than the accrual-based income numbers. As noted in Chapter 12, this is because of the effect of capital expenditures, which tend to be "lumpy," occurring in large amounts at irregular and occasional points in time. However, this lumpiness effect is magnified in the equity bottom line because debt adds financial leverage to the operating cash flow of the building. In the case of our example apartment building, the cash flow proforma reveals a year (7) in which the equity owner will experience substantial negative net cash flow, much larger negative amounts in a single year than appear in the accrual-based net income figures. The owner must plan for and budget for such negative years, and the lender should also be aware of the stress such years can put on the borrower's ability to service the debt unless adequate precautions and preparations are made. While some capital expenditures are somewhat discretionary and can be postponed, financed with loans, or paid for gradually, others cannot be delayed and must be paid upfront. For example, the expiration of long-term leases may require major expenditures to bring in a new long-term tenant. It should not be surprising that certain investors are very keen to "sell" capital expenditure items as operating expenses to the IRS. Operating expenses lower the NOI and thus lower the taxable income, whereas capital expenditures do not.[12]

Finally, we have presented an alternative method of calculating the same cash flows, dubbed the Cash Flow Components format, in Exhibit 13-3. This cash flow components format is simpler than the traditional format in some respects and illustrates more clearly the components of the after-tax cash flows. This presentation explicitly highlights the tax shield components of the cash flow, including separating the portions of the tax shields attributable to depreciation and interest expense. In this approach, the EBTCF is calculated first, directly from the PBTCF and the debt service (like before). Then, the income tax, as if there were no tax shields, is computed by applying the ordinary income tax rate (at 35% in our case) to the NOI. Finally, the depreciation tax shields (DTS) and interest tax shields (ITS) are directly and separately computed and added back in to arrive at the EATCF. Note that the bottom lines of PBTCF, EBTCF, and EATCF are identical between the traditional format in Exhibit 13-2 and the components format in Exhibit 13-3. For operating cash flows, the DTS equals the depreciable cost basis divided by the depreciable life, times the owner's ordinary income tax rate. The ITS equals the loan interest expense times the owner's ordinary income tax rate. This cash flow components format can be useful for analytical purposes because each line item is a cash flow stream, and some of these components have different risk characteristics.

---

12 Interestingly, most tax-exempt investors try the reverse. NOI is widely available and is often used as a (unofficial) benchmark of sorts. Thus, if an investor can artificially move certain OpEx towards CapEx, it will seemingly increase the property's NOI. This might make the manager look particularly good at their jobs. See this as a warning when looking at and using data provided by investors, as they might be creative with their numbers.

EXHIBIT 13-2
Proforma. Operational Cash Flows on an After-Tax Basis

A. Property-level (Chapter 5)

#	Operating Cash Flow Items	Year 1	2	3	4	5	6	7	8	9	10
1	*PGI*	$ 103,000	$ 106,090	$ 109,273	$ 112,551	$ 115,927	$ 119,405	$ 122,987	$ 126,677	$ 130,477	$ 134,392
2	*Vacancy*	$ 5,150	$ 5,305	$ 5,464	$ 5,628	$ 5,796	$ 5,970	$ 6,149	$ 6,334	$ 6,524	$ 6,720
3	*OpEx*	$ 20,600	$ 21,218	$ 21,855	$ 22,510	$ 23,185	$ 23,881	$ 24,597	$ 25,335	$ 26,095	$ 26,878
4	*NOI*	$ 77,250	$ 79,568	$ 81,955	$ 84,413	$ 86,946	$ 89,554	$ 92,241	$ 95,008	$ 97,858	$ 100,794
5	*CapEx*	$ 15,450	$ 15,914	$ 16,391	$ 16,883	$ 17,389	$ 17,911	$ 120,000	$ 19,002	$ 19,572	$ 20,159
6	*PBTCF*	$ 61,800	$ 63,654	$ 65,564	$ 67,531	$ 69,556	$ 71,643	$ (27,759)	$ 76,006	$ 78,286	$ 80,635
	PV(PBTCF)	*$ 56,906*	*$ 53,972*	*$ 51,189*	*$ 48,549*	*$ 46,046*	*$ 43,671*	*$ (15,581)*	*$ 39,284*	*$ 37,258*	*$ 35,337*
	SUM:DCF	**$ 936,893**									

B. After-Debt (Chapter 12)

#	Operating Cash Flow Items	Year 1	2	3	4	5	6	7	8	9	10
7	OLB (begin)	$ 702,670	$ 688,181	$ 672,952	$ 656,943	$ 640,115	$ 622,426	$ 603,833	$ 584,287	$ 563,742	$ 542,146
8	PMT	$ 49,293	$ 49,293	$ 49,293	$ 49,293	$ 49,293	$ 49,293	$ 49,293	$ 49,293	$ 49,293	$ 49,293
9	INT	$ 34,804	$ 34,063	$ 33,284	$ 32,465	$ 31,604	$ 30,699	$ 29,748	$ 28,748	$ 27,697	$ 26,592
10	AMORT	$ 14,488	$ 15,230	$ 16,009	$ 16,828	$ 17,689	$ 18,594	$ 19,545	$ 20,545	$ 21,596	$ 22,701
11	OLB (end)	$ 688,181	$ 672,952	$ 656,943	$ 640,115	$ 622,426	$ 603,833	$ 584,287	$ 563,742	$ 542,146	$ 519,445
12	EBTCF	$ 12,507	$ 14,361	$ 16,271	$ 18,238	$ 20,264	$ 22,350	$ (77,052)	$ 26,713	$ 28,994	$ 31,342

(continued)

C. After-Tax (Chapter 13)

	Operating Cash	Year									
	Flow Items	**1**	**2**	**3**	**4**	**5**	**6**	**7**	**8**	**9**	**10**
13	DE	$ 27,255	$ 27,255	$ 27,255	$ 27,255	$ 27,255	$ 27,255	$ 27,255	$ 27,255	$ 27,255	$ 27,255
14	Taxable Income	$ 15,190	$ 18,249	$ 21,415	$ 24,693	$ 28,086	$ 31,600	$ 35,238	$ 39,005	$ 42,906	$ 46,947
15	Taxes due	$ 5,317	$ 6,387	$ 7,495	$ 8,643	$ 9,830	$ 11,060	$ 12,333	$ 13,652	$ 15,017	$ 16,431
16	PATCF	$ 44,302	$ 45,345	$ 46,419	$ 47,525	$ 48,665	$ 49,839	$ (50,504)	$ 52,293	$ 53,575	$ 54,896
17	EATCF	$ 7,190	$ 7,974	$ 8,775	$ 9,595	$ 10,433	$ 11,290	$ (89,386)	$ 13,062	$ 13,976	$ 14,911

Where:

- EATCF = Equity-After-Tax Cash Flow = (12) – (15)
- PATCF = Property-After-Tax Cash Flow = (6) – 0.35((4) – (13)).
- DE = Depreciation expense = (0.8V)/27.5
- Ordinary tax rate on income is assumed to be 35%.

EXHIBIT 13-3
Cash Flow Components Format

Cash Flow Components Format

Operating Cash Flow Items	Year 1	2	3	4	5	6	7	8	9	10
NOI	$ 77,250	$ 79,568	$ 81,955	$ 84,413	$ 86,946	$ 89,554	$ 92,241	$ 95,008	$ 97,858	$ 100,794
- CapEx	$ 15,450	$ 15,914	$ 16,391	$ 16,883	$ 17,389	$ 17,911	$ 120,000	$ 19,002	$ 19,572	$ 20,159
PBTCF	$ 61,800	$ 63,654	$ 65,564	$ 67,531	$ 69,556	$ 71,643	$ (27,759)	$ 76,006	$ 78,286	$ 80,635
- PMT	$ 49,293	$ 49,293	$ 49,293	$ 49,293	$ 49,293	$ 49,293	$ 49,293	$ 49,293	$ 49,293	$ 49,293
EBTCF	$ 12,507	$ 14,361	$ 16,271	$ 18,238	$ 20,264	$ 22,350	$ (77,052)	$ 26,713	$ 28,994	$ 31,342
- Tax on NOI	$ 27,038	$ 27,849	$ 28,684	$ 29,545	$ 30,431	$ 31,344	$ 32,284	$ 33,253	$ 34,250	$ 35,278
+ Tax on DE (DTS)	$ 9,539	$ 9,539	$ 9,539	$ 9,539	$ 9,539	$ 9,539	$ 9,539	$ 9,539	$ 9,539	$ 9,539
+ Tax on INT (ITS)	$ 12,182	$ 11,922	$ 11,649	$ 11,363	$ 11,061	$ 10,745	$ 10,412	$ 10,062	$ 9,694	$ 9,307
EATCF	$ 7,190	$ 7,974	$ 8,775	$ 9,595	$ 10,433	$ 11,290	$ (89,386)	$ 13,062	$ 13,976	$ 14,911

13.2 IMPACT OF TAX ON REVERSION CASH FLOW

During years when there is a reversion cash flow (e.g., typically when the property is sold), the owner pays **capital gains tax (CGT)**. Note that this Chapter only considers properties that were held for more than 1 year. If a property is held for less than that, all proceeds (capital gains) are taxed at normal income rate levels, which tend to be higher than the capital gains tax. Before we show how to calculate the capital gains tax, it is vital to be able to distinguish between the following definitions;

- **Net Sales Proceeds (NSP)**. This is essentially the sales price minus any costs of selling the property. We previously called this the Property-level Before-Tax Cash Flow (PBTCF) at reversion.
- **Gross Book Value (GBV)**. The gross book value is computed by adding all the capital expenditures to the purchase price (P).[13] The GBV, therefore, represents the total gross investment in a property. Or: GBV = P + ΣCapEx.
- **Adjusted (Cost) Basis (AB).** It is also referred to as the net book value. The AB is calculated by subtracting all the claimed depreciation expenses (DE) from the GBV. Or AB = P + ΣCapEx – ΣDE.
- **Capital Gain / Loss.** According to the IRS, the investor achieves a capital gain if the net sales price exceeds the adjusted basis, or: NSP > AB. In this case, the investor is subject to capital gains tax. A capital loss (again, according to the IRS) means the opposite, or: NSP < AB.

Thus, the investor will be taxed whenever the investor's net sales price is higher than the adjusted cost basis. Based on current law, the projected capital gains tax (CGT) owed upon sale consists of two tax regimes: (1) "pure" capital gains and (2) depreciation recapture.

[13] Technically, also all the costs of purchasing the property should be included, like a broker's fee and mortgage points.

EXHIBIT 13-4A

Equity- after-Tax Cash Flows from Operations

	(I) Good		(II) Neutral		(III) Bad	
Net sales price (NSP)	$	1,500,000	$	1,150,000	$	900,000
Purchase price	$	1,000,000	$	1,000,000	$	1,000,000
+ Total capital expenditures	$	150,000	$	150,000	$	150,000
Gross Book Value (GBV)	$	1,150,000	$	1,150,000	$	1,150,000
- Total depreciation expenses	$	300,000	$	300,000	$	300,000
Adjusted basis (AB)	$	850,000	$	850,000	$	850,000
NSP – AB	$	650,000	$	300,000	$	50,000
	Determining Taxes					
"Pure" capital gain = NSP - GBV	$	350,000	$	-	$	(250,000)
Tax due (@15%)	$	52,500	$	-	$	-
Depreciation recapture	$	300,000	$	300,000	$	50,000
Tax due (@25%)	$	75,000	$	75,000	$	12,500
Total capital gains tax	**$**	**127,500**	**$**	**75,000**	**$**	**12,500**

1. **"Pure" capital gains**. The first capital gains element is the difference between the resale price (net of projected selling expenses such as broker and legal fees) and the gross book value (aka original cost basis). Let's assume that this portion of the capital gains (net resale proceeds minus the gross book value) is taxed at 15%.[14] Thus, this portion of the capital gains tax is calculated as 0.15 × (NSP – GBV). If the net sales price is below the gross book value, the investor is not subject to this 15% tax rate.
2. **Depreciation recapture**. The second component of the CGT consists of the accumulated depreciation recapture. Any *portion* of this accumulated depreciation expense that is recovered in the resale price will be subject to the "recapture tax" at a rate of 25%. If the net sales price exceeds the gross book value (original cost basis), then the entire accumulated depreciation will be taxed at the recapture rate: 0.25 × ΣDE. If the property sales proceeds are below the gross book value but above the net book value (adjusted basis), the recapture portion of the reversion tax is 0.25 × (NSP – AB), where "AB" is the adjusted basis.

We look at three scenarios in Exhibit 13-4 to exemplify the workings of reversion taxation. In all scenarios, the property is bought for $1 million, the investor claims $300,000 in depreciation expenses (ΣDE), and the total capital expenditures are expected to be $150,000 (ΣCapEx) during the operating period. The only difference is the expected sales price (net of projected selling expenses such as broker and legal fees), which is $1.5 million (good scenario), $1.15 million (neutral), and $900,000 (bad scenario). (We ignore any depreciation/amortization of the capital expenditures.) Note that all the way to the Adjusted Basis (AB), the numbers are similar between the three scenarios.

In the first scenario, we have NSP > GBV. The "pure" capital gains are $350,000 (= NSP – GBV = $1,500,000 - $1,150,000). This portion of the capital gains is taxed at 15%, or $52,500. Given that the net sales proceeds are above the gross book value, the total depreciation is recaptured,

[14] In reality, the tax rate will typically go up, as higher gains are achieved (i.e., progressively taxed). Consult a tax expert if you want to know your exact tax bracket.

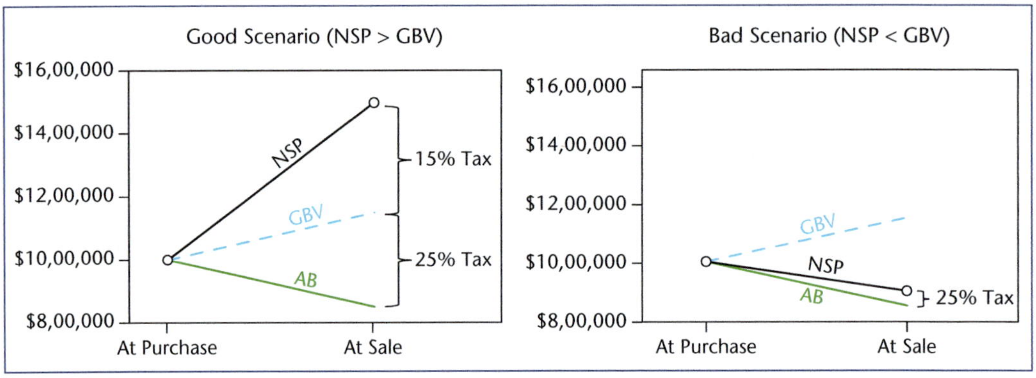

EXHIBIT 13-4B Graphical Example of Capital Gains Tax for the Good and Bad Scenario.

meaning $75,000 (= 0.25 × $300,000) in additional capital gains tax. Therefore, this scenario's total capital gains tax is $75,000 + $52,500 = **$127,500**.

In the second scenario, we sell the property for exactly the gross book value or NSP = GBV. In this case, we are not taxed at the lower rate, as NSP – GBV = 0. However, we still fully captured the $300,000 in depreciation expenses. Thus, we owe the IRS **$75,000** (0.25 × $300,000) in capital gains taxes.

In the final scenario, we sell the property for less than what we bought it for (NSP < P), even if we disregard the capital expenditures. Perhaps counterintuitively, we are still subject to capital gains tax because we, in essence, claimed too much in depreciation expenses. The adjusted basis for this property is $850,000 (= $900,000 + $150,000 - $300,000). The net sales price is $900,000. Thus, $50,000 in depreciation is recuperated at 25%. In other words, the capital gains tax is **$12,500** for this scenario.

But what happens if we achieve a **capital loss**? For example, what if we sold the property for $700,000 in the previous example, such that NSP < AB? In case of a loss, we can offset capital gains in other assets or use them to lower our taxable income (for multiple years). Therefore, depending on the investor's specific circumstances, the exact tax rate is a bit ambiguous. Many limitations are also put in place based on your corporate structure. Still, this means that "negative taxes" (like in the case of operational cash flows, see text box) can be achieved in a real estate proforma for the reversion cash flows as well.

If we return to our proforma from Chapter 12 and Exhibit 13-2, we can calculate the expected capital gains tax using the above-mentioned procedures. In this example, the property will sell for more than the gross book value, and thus, the depreciation is fully recaptured by the resale price, making the calculations rather simple;

- **Gross Book Value (GBV).** GVB = Purchase price + ΣCapital Expenditures. This equals (rounded) $1.2 million.
- **"Pure" capital gains tax**. Calculated as: 0.15 × (Net Proceeds – GBV) = *$17,271.*
- **Deprecation recapture**. Calculated as: 0.25 × (ΣDepreciation Expenses) = *$68,138.*
- **Total Capital Gains Tax** = *$70,728* (= $17,271+ $68,138).

Once the CGT is determined, the reversion cash flows are straightforward to calculate. The before-tax reversion for the equity owner is simply the projected property sale proceeds of $1,232,833 (net of any selling expenses) less the projected outstanding loan balance on the mortgage, which in this example is $519,445 (the original $702,670 loan amount less 10 years' worth of annual amortization payments). This leaves an equity-before-tax reversion cash flow of $713,388. (We also did these calculations in Chapter 12.) If we subtract the projected capital gains income tax obligation of \$70,728 (as calculated above), we arrive at the equity-after-tax reversion cash flow just shy of \$643 thousand (rounded).[15]

It is important to note that under current IRS rules (**section 1031**), payment of the capital gains tax can be deferred (but not exempted) by using so-called "like-kind exchanges," in which the investor invests the proceeds of the property resale into a new "like-kind" investment. In this context, "like-kind" means other real estate (including land), but it doesn't have to be a similar property type.[16] In fact, you can use it to purchase multiple new properties. There are a few rules that an investor must follow. First, the investor must name a third-party facilitator who helps manage the exchange process. They hold the proceeds from the relinquished property sale and ensure that the exchange meets IRS requirements. Second, the new investment(s) value must be equal to or greater than the old investment. Also, the investor is under time pressure to make the like-kind exchange, as current IRS rules (as of the early 2020s) only allow 180 days to close the exchange (and only 45 days to identify the exchange, with the investor not allowed to take possession of the original property resale proceeds in between the two investments). You can keep making these like-kind investments multiple times, meaning you can keep deferring such capital gains tax for a long time. Still, this doesn't mean that you should not include the capital gains tax in your proforma, as eventually, the capital gains tax will have to be paid (perhaps by your heirs).

13.3 CASH FLOW COMPONENTS ANALYSIS AND PROJECTED TOTAL RETURN CALCULATIONS

Now that you are familiar with the basic mechanics of after-tax proforma construction, we can begin to do some investment analysis. A good way to start this is to recast and expand the proforma cash flow projection as we have done previously in Exhibit 13-3, only now transposed from rows to columns in Exhibit 13-5 and enhanced to also include the reversion cash flows and the capital values for both the initial investment at year 0 and the presumed or projected resale at the end of year 10. Note that comparing the "horizontal" Exhibit 13-3 and the "vertical" Exhibit 13-5, the bottom line cash flows are identical (for example, the EATCFs for years 1 and 9 of \$7,190 and \$13,976, respectively).

The Exhibit 13-5 enhancements can help with investment analysis. Investment cash outflow components corresponding to the subsequent cash inflow components are indicated as negative amounts in the "year zero" (investment decision time) row at the top of the columns. Reversion and operating cash flows are combined in the terminal year-10 row so that we can apply a spreadsheet IRR function directly to the cash flow range in each column to compute the IRR associated with any cash flow component.

Separating the investment cash flows into components in this manner can be helpful for investment analysis because it highlights the different sources and nature of the various cash flow components, and it groups the cash flows into component streams of similar risk. For example, the unlevered property-based cash flows in columns (4), (5), and (7) contain moderate risk. The contractual or debt-like cash flows in columns (6), (9), (10), and (13) contain relatively less risk. The levered equity cash flows in columns (11) and (12) contain the most risk. When we compute the going-in IRRs presented by each of these columns, you can see that the lower-risk cash flows present lower expected returns (apart from the effect of income taxes).

15 The Property-After-Tax Cash Flow (PATCF) on reversion is simply the Property-Before-Tax Cash Flow at reversion minus the capital gains tax. Note that unlike with the operational cash flows, there is no interest rate shield in place at sale.

16 As of writing, it is possible to defer capital gains tax while using proceeds from other non-real estate investments to purchase real estate. But you can only purchase real estate in opportunity zones (i.e., designated areas that are economically behind the state average), and your projected capital expenditures must be at least the same amount as the purchase price. This "opportunity zone" program was introduced in 2017 and will be phased out in 2027.

EXHIBIT 13-5

Cash Flow Components Investment Analysis of the Example Property

	(1)	(2)	(3)	(4)	(5)	(6)	(7)	(8)	(9)	(10)	(11)	(12)	(13)
							(4) - (5) + (6)				(4)-(8)-(9)	(4)-(8)-(10)	
year	Property value	NOI	CapEx	PBTCF	Tax w/o shields	DTS	PATCF	Loan Balance	Loan DS	ITS	EBTCF	EATCF	LATCF
0	$ 936,893			$ (936,893)			$ (936,893)	$ 702,670	$ (702,670)		$ (234,223)	$ (234,223)	$ (702,670)
1	$ 988,129	$ 77,250	$ 15,450	$ 61,800	$ 27,038	$ 9,539	$ 44,302	$ 688,181	$ 49,293	$ 12,182	$ 12,507	$ 7,190	$ 37,111
2	$ 1,042,167	$ 79,568	$ 15,914	$ 63,654	$ 27,849	$ 9,539	$ 45,345	$ 672,952	$ 49,293	$ 11,922	$ 14,361	$ 7,974	$ 37,371
3	$ 1,099,160	$ 81,955	$ 16,391	$ 65,564	$ 28,684	$ 9,539	$ 46,419	$ 656,943	$ 49,293	$ 11,649	$ 16,271	$ 8,775	$ 37,643
4	$ 1,159,269	$ 84,413	$ 16,883	$ 67,531	$ 29,545	$ 9,539	$ 47,525	$ 640,115	$ 49,293	$ 11,363	$ 18,238	$ 9,595	$ 37,930
5	$ 1,222,666	$ 86,946	$ 17,389	$ 69,556	$ 30,431	$ 9,539	$ 48,665	$ 622,426	$ 49,293	$ 11,061	$ 20,264	$ 10,433	$ 38,231
6	$ 1,289,530	$ 89,554	$ 17,911	$ 71,643	$ 31,344	$ 9,539	$ 49,839	$ 603,833	$ 49,293	$ 10,745	$ 22,350	$ 11,290	$ 38,548
7	$ 1,360,051	$ 92,241	$ 120,000	$ (27,759)	$ 32,284	$ 9,539	$ (50,504)	$ 584,287	$ 49,293	$ 10,412	$ (77,052)	$ (89,386)	$ 38,881
8	$ 1,434,428	$ 95,008	$ 19,002	$ 76,006	$ 33,253	$ 9,539	$ 52,293	$ 563,742	$ 49,293	$ 10,062	$ 26,713	$ 13,062	$ 39,231
9	$ 1,512,872	$ 97,858	$ 19,572	$ 78,286	$ 34,250	$ 9,539	$ 53,575	$ 542,146	$ 49,293	$ 9,694	$ 28,994	$ 13,976	$ 39,599
10	$ 1,297,719	$ 100,794	$ 20,159	$ 1,313,468	$ 35,278	$ 9,539	$ 1,217,001	$ 519,445	$ 568,738	$ 9,307	$ 744,730	$ 657,571	$ 559,431
IRR				**8.60%**			**6.05%**		**4.94%**		**15.03%**	**11.17%**	**3.21%**

Where:

- Property value is assumed to grow linearly between years 0 and 10
- PBTCF/PATCF is the Property Before/After-Tax Cash Flow
- EBTCF/EATCF is the Equity Before/After-Tax Cash Flow
- LATCF is the Loan After-Tax Cash Flow
- Tax without shield is calculated as NOI x income tax rate (35%)
- Loan DS is the loan debt service.

Using the net cash flow figures in the proforma, it is possible to calculate the overall projected internal rate of return (IRR) for the investment in our target property. Assuming an up-front investment of $936 thousand in cash and ignoring the debt-based components of the cash flow projection, one can calculate the unlevered returns, also known as property-level or free-and-clear returns. At a before-tax level, this is done by applying the IRR function to the PBTCF stream in column (4) of Exhibit 13-5. This indicates that this asset presents a property-level before-tax (PBT) going-in IRR of 8.60 percent per year over the projected 10-year holding period. This shouldn't come as a surprise, as this *number should equal our assumed cost of capital* (r). However, computing the PBTCF IRR this way is still useful for flagging any mistakes. At the after-tax level, we apply the IRR function to the PATCF stream in column (7), which reflects the cash flow after income taxes without any debt on the property. The result is a property-level after-tax going-in IRR of 6.05 percent.

To calculate the levered equity return based on the $234 thousand up-front cash investment and the $702 thousand loan, we use the EBTCF and EATCF streams in columns (11) and (12) of Exhibit 13-5 for before-tax and after-tax returns, respectively. The result is levered equity-level going-in IRRs of 15.03 percent and 11.17 percent before and after tax, respectively. Note that the before-tax returns are higher than the after-tax returns because income taxes take away some of the investor's investment earnings.[17] The levered equity returns are higher than the unlevered property-level returns because of positive leverage (as described in Chapter 12). Note, however, that the after-tax return expectation for the levered equity is not as much reduced below the before-tax return as is the case without leverage. This reflects the leveraging of the tax shield effects, primarily from the depreciation tax shields. In this case, without leverage, the after-tax return is 75 percent of the before-tax return (6.05%/8.60%), reflecting an "effective" tax rate of 25 percent in the 10-year going-in IRR. This effective 30 percent tax rate is a blend of the 35 percent ordinary income tax rate, the 15 percent capital gains tax rate, and the 25 percent recapture rate. The effective tax rate on the IRR reflects the fact that some of the total return is achieved through the receipt of ordinary income and some through the realization of capital gain. It also reflects the effect of the depreciation tax shield and the length of the projected investment horizon (10 years). In part, because the IRR is expressed as a per annum rate, the IRR impact of the payback of the recapture is reduced the longer the horizon until the resale.

With leverage, the effective tax rate is reduced in this example to only 26 percent (1 – [11.71%/14.34%]). This reduction in the effective tax rate occurs for two reasons. For one thing, the leverage shifts the composition of the investor's IRR relatively away from ordinary income and toward the capital gain component, which is more lightly taxed (15/25 versus 35 percent). More importantly, however, is that leverage magnifies the effect of depreciation tax shields. If we aggressively increase our LTV level to 90%, the effective tax rate drops to 24% (Exhibit 13-6). It should also be kept in mind that the lower effective tax rate on the levered investment does not necessarily imply that the use of debt financing brings any positive NPV in itself. Remember that leverage brings added investment risk to the equity, which can easily offset the greater return expectation, viewed from a before-tax or after-tax perspective. (The relationship between debt financing and NPV will be discussed in depth in the next chapter.)

Up to this point in the chapter (and, in fact, the entire book), we have explicitly *and* implicitly used the cost of capital on the property level before-tax cash flow as an input. This allows us to forecast the cash flows and investment returns at the equity-after-tax level of micro-level real estate investment. However, it should be noted that, in principle, any cash flow line items could be used as a starting point. For example, we could discount the projected equity-after-tax bottom line from the after-tax proforma (the EATCF row column (12) in Exhibit 13-5). This results in an estimate of the

[17] This is typical, but in real estate, it does not always have to be the case, as sufficient tax shelter can sometimes be provided to cause after-tax returns to exceed before-tax returns. That would be most common in cases where tax incentives are provided to subsidize the investment, such as with affordable (or "social") housing or historical preservation properties or properties able to take advantage of government programs of financial stimulus for alternative energy or energy efficiency.

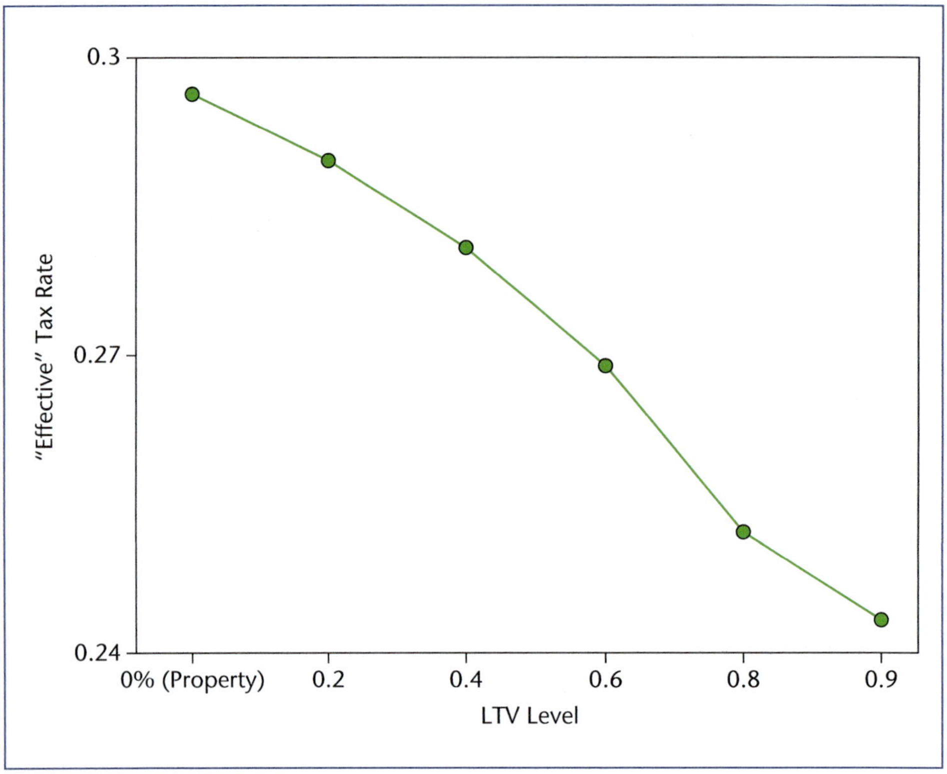

EXHIBIT 13-6 Impact of Leverage on the Effective Tax Rate of the Example Property.

present value of the investor's levered equity in the property, including consideration of the income-tax-shield effects. (Be sure to include the after-tax equity reversion in the terminal year.) Add this equity present value to the amount of any loan the equity investor will receive for the property purchase to arrive at an estimate of the total value of the property to the equity investor. In evaluating the investor's equity in this way, it is important to be consistent in the treatment of the numerator and denominator within the basic DCF operation. The following rule must be heeded carefully:

Discount equity-after-tax cash flows at the appropriate equity-after-tax discount rate.

Correctly quantifying the effect of equity leverage and the effect of income taxes on the opportunity cost of capital can be quite difficult in practice. We know that the amount one must add to the before-tax risk premium in the required expected total return is usually greater, the greater the leverage. *But how much greater*? We know the after-tax required return is likely lower than the before-tax required return for a taxable investment. *But how much lower*? For example, the effective tax rate on the total return is a function of the proportion of the return that will be received as ordinary income as opposed to capital gains income and of the likely holding period of the investor. It is often difficult in practice to account explicitly and properly for all these considerations to estimate an appropriate after-tax discount rate for the levered equity cash flows.

Of course, the investor cannot just "make up" any discount rate he likes without invalidating the realism of the entire investment analysis. No investor can "make the market." We all must deal in the market of the real world, which reflects the equilibrium between many investors on the supply and demand sides. For this reason, it is also not rigorous for the investor to use a "personalized" OCC as the discount rate for determining property values. The OCC comes from the capital market, not from any particular investor. The OCC must reflect the capital market's price of time and risk because any investor can always access the capital market to trade investment payoffs in the time and risk dimensions. This OCC will reflect the after-tax perception and preferences for time and risk of investors in the relevant part of the capital market, in this case, the subject property asset market.

However, if this is the rigorous approach in principle, it is nevertheless difficult to implement in practice because it is difficult to empirically observe after-tax returns to equity. Such information is proprietary and varies across individual investors. This makes levered after-tax returns much more difficult to observe than the property-level returns (before accounting for debt or taxes). Property-level returns can be inferred at least to a reasonable approximation from widely available market information and then used to compute market value, as shown in Chapter 11.

Using the property's before-tax cost of capital as an input is doubly sound for explicitly estimating the value of a property. Not only is this approach simpler, but by avoiding the need to estimate the marginal tax rates, holding periods, and leverage of the property market investors, it avoids the danger of making mistakes in estimating these parameters. In a well-functioning property asset market, it is generally easier to make reliable empirical observations regarding the market values of the before-tax numbers (both the cash flows and the expected returns), so mistakes are less likely at the property before-tax level.

Now, even though it might seem a *fait accompli* (after-tax cash flows are "merely" an output), we will come back to this point in much more detail in Chapter 14. Especially when making capital budgeting decisions, after-tax considerations can play a significant role.

13.4 CHAPTER SUMMARY

Chapter 13 extended the basic micro-level investment analysis and evaluation framework from the previous chapters to the equity-after-tax level, covering PBTCFs to EATCFs. While equity-after-tax analysis is, in principle, a straightforward extension of the framework present in previous chapters, in practice, it is often complicated to know exactly the correct cash flow and discount rate assumptions to apply. Fortunately, the widespread existence of a well-functioning property market often makes it possible in real estate practice to take a shortcut around these difficulties by working at the PBT level and deriving the other cash flows from there. Furthermore, this chapter showed how leverage and taxation interact.

KEY TERMS

- Equity-after-tax cash flow (EATCF)
- Property-after-tax cash flow (PATCF)
- Depreciation expense
- Book value
- Adjusted cost basis
- Depreciable cost basis
- Accumulated depreciation
- Capital gains tax (CGT)
- Straight-line depreciation
- Tax loss
- Tax shield or tax shelter
- Depreciation tax shield (DS)
- Interest rate shield (ITS)
- Depreciable life
- Ordinary income tax
- Effective tax rate

STUDY QUESTIONS

In Your Own Words

13.1 How does depreciation shield real estate investors from taxation?

13.2 How can your after-tax cash flow be higher than your before-tax cash flow in a real estate investment?

13.3 Why is the distinction between operating expenses and capital expenditures an important one from the IRS's perspective?

13.4 Two rookie real estate investors, Megan and Sean, are having a heated discussion about how to calculate annual equity after-tax cash flow (EATCF) on an income-property investment. The two agree that EATCF = EBTCF – income tax, and that income tax = (taxable income) × (tax rate), but are at odds over the calculation of taxable income. Megan believes that taxable income = EBTCF + principal + CI reserves – depreciation, whereas Sean feels this is incorrect and argues that taxable income = NOI – interest – depreciation. Who is correct? Explain.

13.5 What are the two components of "taxes due on sale" for a taxable investor selling an income property? Explain how each is determined.

Check Your Knowledge

13.6 How does debt amortization affect cash flow calculations?
- A) It is treated as an operating expense
- B) It does not affect cash flow
- C) It reduces cash flow, but is not an expense for tax purposes
- D) It increases the taxable income

13.7 When is a capital gains tax applied to the sale of a property?
- A) When the property is sold below the purchase price
- B) When the net sales proceeds exceed the adjusted basis
- C) When depreciation has been fully claimed
- D) When the gross book value is zero

13.8 What does the Adjusted Basis represent in real estate tax calculations?
- A) Purchase price minus accumulated depreciation
- B) Purchase price plus all capital improvements minus accumulated depreciation
- C) Purchase price plus land value
- D) Purchase price plus operating expenses

13.9 What is the depreciable cost basis?
- A) Total purchase price of property
- B) Property value minus land value
- C) Property value minus improvements
- D) Adjusted Basis after depreciation

13.10 If the Net Sales Proceeds (NSP) are less than the Gross Book Value but above the Adjusted Basis, what tax is incurred?
- A) No tax is incurred
- B) Only depreciation recapture tax
- C) Only capital gains tax
- D) Both capital gains and recapture tax

13.11 Why are capital expenditures not fully deductible in the year they occur?
- A) They are not considered expenses
- B) They must be capitalized and depreciated over time
- C) They are deducted only upon sale
- D) They increase taxable income

13.12 How does the effective tax rate on levered returns compare to unlevered returns?
- A) Higher for levered returns
- B) Lower for levered returns due to increased deductions
- C) No difference
- D) Higher initially, then decreases

13.13 The NOI is $850,000, the debt service is $600,000 of which $550,000 is interest, the depreciation expense is $350,000, and the income tax rate is 35%.
- a. What is the before-tax cash flow to the equity investor (EBTCF) if there are no capital improvement expenditures or reversion items this period?
- b. What is the after-tax cash flow to the equity investor if the income tax rate is 35%?

13.14 A nonresidential commercial property that costs $500,000 is considered to have 30% of its total value attributable to land. What is the annual depreciation expense chargeable against taxable income?

13.15 Determine the acquisition cost of an apartment property if the annual depreciation deduction will be $170,000, assuming 20% of the cost is allocated to land and 80% to structure at the time of purchase.

13.16 Consider the following information for the first year of a proposed property acquisition: effective gross income (EGI) is estimated to be $1.5 million; operating expenses are $450,000; $25,000 will be put into a capital improvement reserve account; the investor has a 35% marginal tax rate. The property is going to be acquired with a 65% loan-to-value ratio mortgage, interest-only with a 10-year term and 6% interest rate. The acquisition cost implies an 8.4% going-in cap rate, based on first-year NOI. It is anticipated that 25% of the acquisition cost will be allocated to land for tax purposes. Depreciation is straight-line over 39 years. Determine the first-year equity after-tax cash flow (EATCF).

13.17 Ten years ago, an investor acquired a property for $14 million. At the time of acquisition, the land value was estimated to be $2.1 million. The depreciation (cost recovery) period for the building is 27.5 years, with depreciation being straight-line. Each year since she acquired the property, the investor has set aside $100,000 in a capital reserve account. The estimated current market value of the property is $20 million. If the investor were to sell the property today, what would be her total federal income taxes due at sale assuming that depreciation recapture is taxed at 25% and capital gains at 15%? For simplicity, assume that the entire amount in the capital reserves account would be spent now, immediately before the property sale. Selling expenses will be 4% of the sale price.

Chapter Case: Durant Apartments

Jones Property Group is considering the acquisition of Durant Apartments, a 200-unit apartment complex located in a college town with easy access to major metropolitan areas. This location has made land highly valuable, with the land component appraised at 30% of the purchase price. Durant Apartments serves primarily university students and has maintained full occupancy for the past five years due to high demand for off-campus housing.

The property's purchase price is $20 million, and Jones Property Group plans to hold it for 10 years and anticipates selling the property for $24 million at the end of the holding period. To finance the investment, Jones Property Group is currently selling Shattuck Square, another building in its portfolio, and plans to reinvest the proceeds into Durant Apartments using a 1031 tax-deferred exchange.

Based on what you learned in this chapter, answer the following questions:

1. What is the depreciable cost basis of Durant Apartments?
   - A) $20 million
   - B) $14 million
   - C) $6 million
   - D) $10 million

2. What is the annual depreciation deduction for Durant Apartments if it remains classified as residential property?
   A) $727,273
   B) $509,091
   C) $512,821
   D) $358,974
3. If Durant Apartments is reclassified as commercial property, what would the annual depreciation expense be?
   A) $727,273
   B) $509,091
   C) $512,821
   D) $358,974
4. Why might a Jones Property Group prefer a shorter depreciable life for tax purposes?
   A) It reduces annual deductions
   B) It increases taxable income
   C) It allows larger deductions each year, reducing taxable income faster
   D) It only affects property value
5. Why is land excluded from the depreciation schedule under IRS rules?
   A) Land is considered a commercial asset.
   B) Land is not a "wearing-out" asset and does not depreciate over time.
   C) Land depreciation is included in the building's depreciation.
   D) Land depreciation only applies to certain property classifications.
6. If Durant Apartments is sold after 10 years, how will depreciation recapture taxes apply?
   A) The recapture tax will apply to the total amount of accumulated depreciation at a rate of 25%.
   B) The recapture tax will apply to the total sale price of the property.
   C) Depreciation recapture taxes are deferred indefinitely if the property is residential.
   D) Depreciation recapture taxes only apply to commercial properties.
7. What must Jones Property Group do to qualify for a 1031 exchange when selling Shattuck Square?
   A) Identify a replacement property within 45 days and close on it within 180 days.
   B) Identify a replacement property within 90 days and close on it within one year.
   C) Reinvest the proceeds into a property with a lower purchase price.
   D) Use the proceeds to pay off any outstanding debt from Shattuck Square.
8. Compared to a rural university town where land is less expensive, how does the high land value impact the depreciation calculations for Durant Apartments?
   A) It increases the annual depreciation deduction.
   B) It extends the depreciation schedule for the property.
   C) It reduces the depreciable cost basis to 70% of the purchase price.
   D) It eliminates depreciation deductions for the property.
9. What happens to its depreciation clock when Shattuck Square is sold?
   A) It continues based on the previous owner's schedule
   B) It resets for the new owner
   C) It continues for the remaining depreciable years
   D) Depreciation is no longer allowed
10. What happens to depreciation recapture taxes if Jones Property Group uses a 1031 exchange to sell Durant Apartments after 10 years?
    A) They are waived entirely.
    B) They are deferred until the replacement property is sold.
    C) They are taxed at the ordinary income tax rate.
    D) They are recalculated based on the replacement property's value.

14 Advanced Topics I

Investment Value in Property Investment and Debt Financing

CHAPTER OUTLINE

LEARNING OBJECTIVES

After reading this, you should understand:

- The difference between market value and investment value.
- How investment and market values may influence the bargaining process within the real estate market.
- The concept that marginal investors set equilibrium prices.
- The impact of debt and tax rates on the marginal investor's valuation of a property.
- How marginal values and intramarginal investors can both exist in the same market.

The preceding chapters have introduced you to the basics of investment analysis and evaluation at the micro-level of individual deals or transactions involving commercial property. Most of this material is essentially standard corporate finance and investment principles and methods applied to real estate. However, to be a more sophisticated investor in the real estate arena, you should be aware of some additional issues and concepts relating to the unique attributes of real estate. Real estate investment assets are often not owned by or held through publicly traded corporations, but real estate assets trade directly in the private property market. Among the fundamental considerations that are unique to real estate as distinct from corporate finance and mainstream investments, nothing could be more basic and important than the notion of *value* itself, and this is the subject we turn to in the present chapter.

Whether we have explicitly said so or not, up to now, we have been defining and measuring value, including the net present value in our NPV investment evaluation rule, based on the conception of value

DOI: 10.1201/9781003643838-17

referred to as "market value." In particular, our analysis has been focused on, or based on, the *market value* of the assets involved in the deal, where market value is defined as the expected price at which the assets would sell currently in the private real estate asset market. This reflects the fundamental economic principle of basing rational decision-making on "opportunity cost," what one foregoes or gives up in selling, or what one has to forego or give up to obtain the investment position. We noted that using market value in a construct such as NPV is possible and practical because real estate asset markets generally function well for the assets in question. But now, we need to think about this in more depth.

We have treated real estate asset values like stock market analysts treat publicly listed equity values.[1] But unlike stock investors who can buy and sell quickly and easily at very low transaction costs without assuming any management burden of the assets they purchase, real estate investors typically hold onto a given property for a much longer period, and they can (indeed, must) manage the operation and marketing of that asset. This is not a short-term game; it's a long-term commitment that requires patience and strategic planning. The average holding periods for institutional investors are typically between 5 and 10 years and often longer, highlighting the gravity of the decisions in real estate investing.

In this respect, real estate investing is more like corporate capital budgeting than stock market investing. Corporations allocate their capital to long-lived projects to produce real goods and services over a long period, such as a new microchip plant or a line of consumer products. However, corporate capital budgeting is different from real estate investment because for the industrial corporation, there is typically no well-functioning direct market for the underlying assets the corporation is investing in, and because in real estate, there is typically no liquid market for the equity vehicle itself that holds the underlying investment asset (akin to the public market for the equity stock of the industrial corporation).

Given that real estate straddles these two worlds (securities investments and corporate capital budgeting), it's crucial that we carefully apply the classical principles and methodologies from these fields, basing ourselves squarely on fundamental economic principles. And this is where and how a second conception of value becomes important, different from, though related to market value. The subject of the present chapter is what we will refer to as *investment value*. We will introduce the concept and discuss its general application in real estate investment analysis and evaluation in the first part of the chapter. Then, in Section 14.2, we will consider how the investment value concept relates, in particular, to the evaluation and use of debt in real estate by investors or investment vehicles facing different income tax rates. Finally, we discuss the slightly different but related topic of market inefficiencies in the supplemental online materials. While most of the material in this chapter is not found either in traditional real estate finance and investments texts or in mainstream corporate finance books, it simply represents a straightforward application to real estate of the basic economic tenets of mainstream financial economics as applied to corporate finance and investments as taught in advanced MBA programs worldwide.

14.1 INVESTMENT VALUE AT THE PROPERTY LEVEL

First, let us clarify what we mean by **market value** (which we typically abbreviate as **MV**) and why this concept is important and useful in real estate investment analysis. Market value is the expected price at which the asset can be sold in the current property market without pressure or distress (like foreclosures).[2] In other words, if we put a property up for sale, we don't know exactly what price we can get. It partly depends on who we find as the opposite party in the deal. We may find someone particularly enthusiastic about the property, or, on the other hand, we may have to deal with a tough negotiator.

[1] The stock market analogy helps us understand why the NPV of a typical deal is zero. When investors buy and sell stocks, such trading is not generally perceived as involving positive or negative NPV for the participants.

[2] Within appraisal texts, the definition would include the notion of informed buyers and sellers, whereby no one has inside information, and no one has unique circumstances. Appraisers seeking market value are statistically seeking the most probable price resulting from the most typical buyer and most typical seller.

The market value can be considered the most likely price at which we will make a deal before a deal is done. It is the ex-ante expectation (or the mean of the probability distribution) of the possible prices.[3]

As thusly defined, the market value is a very important and useful measure of value because it reflects the current opportunity cost or **opportunity value** of the investment in the asset. Any investor can purchase or sell the asset for a price close to its market value (and with the actual ex-post transaction price as likely to be above as below the market value) at any time. In effect, as well as any single number can represent, the investor gives up the opportunity to retain or receive the MV in cash when she decides instead to purchase or continue holding the asset.

Although the market value and an NPV estimation based on MV are always useful and fundamentally important in decision-making, one can conceptually define and measure commercial property value in another way and calculate an NPV based on this second concept of value. In the real estate profession, this second definition of value is called the **investment value** (which we sometimes abbreviate as **IV**).[4] A property's investment value is its value to a particular owner, who would own and operate the asset for a long period of time and is explicitly not planning to sell the asset for a long time. As IV is defined concerning a specified investor, and investors differ in their ability to generate and use future cash flow and value from the asset, IV values may differ for different investors for the same asset at the same point in time. In contrast, the MV is, in principle, the same for a given asset for all investors at a given point in time.[5] You can think of the distinction between MV and IV in rough terms as follows:

IV = a private or subjective valuation of a party
MV = an objective value exogenous to any one party, in principle, based on the prototype of a typical buyer and seller.

IV is a private or subjective valuation of a party; MV is an objective valuation exogenous to any one party, in principle.

To make the point livelier, let's think of a few (somewhat related) scenarios where the private valuation (IV) of a specific investor for a real estate investment opportunity is different from how other (e.g., "the Market") investors would perceive it:

- KrazyLoPrices Inc. Discount Warehouse has built a booming business at its store at 9999 Consumption Boulevard and now needs expansion space and more parking capacity. It would also hate to see its main competitor, EvenLowerPrices Ltd., open up one of its megastores across the street. In such a situation, the vacant lots adjacent to and across the street, at 9997 and 9998 Consumption Boulevard, are likely worth more to KrazyLo than any other party. In other words, IV > MV for those lots for KrazyLo.
- A large sovereign wealth fund owns the majority of apartment buildings in Santa Monica (Los Angeles County). Santa Monica is unique in that it is a highly desirable area, conjoined with

---

[3] The concept of market value also must entail a commitment to sell (or buy) the property reasonably quickly, regardless of the current market conditions. Otherwise, we could make MV out to be unrealistically high (or low) and say we will wait as long as it takes to find someone willing to pay (or accept) that price. In effect, we would say that we will wait until the market moves in our favor (if it ever does). This would be analogous to a stock market investor placing a "limit order" to sell (buy) a given stock at a specified price above (below) the current market price of the stock. The real estate concept of MV is meant to be analogous to the market price of the stock, not some investor's limit order price.

[4] Investment value is especially well defined in the appraisal profession, closely related to other definitions of value as "inherent value" or "usage value." The appraisal industry carefully distinguishes these concepts from those of market value (or "exchange value"). Another term sometimes used as investment value is "intrinsic value." Like inherent value, intrinsic value highlights the value placed on real property by users of the property, in contrast to investment value, which highlights the value of the property more explicitly for a nonuser owner (an investor). However, there is considerable overlap in meaning across all the "i" valuation concepts: inherent, intrinsic, and investment. (See Chapter 14A.3 in the online supplemental materials for further elaboration on concepts of value.)

[5] Although two people may disagree in their estimate of MV, conceptually, only one true MV exists at any given time.

the fact that new development is difficult because of the mountains to the north, the ocean to the west, and the city of Los Angeles in the other directions. Every apartment property for sale will be worth more to this investor as it can strengthen its (quasi-) monopolistic hold on this area, allowing the sovereign wealth fund to increase rents and use its market power to block new developments elsewhere.[6]

- Boston Real Estate REIT owns an apartment complex in downtown Boston. A vacant lot next to its apartment tower is available for sale, and its Highest and Best Use (Chapter 6) is an apartment complex as well. As a result, the MV of the vacant lot will be based on an apartment complex.[7] However, Boston Real Estate believes a retail complex next door could create more synergy with the existing apartment complex. Thus, the combination of retail and apartments maximizes wealth for this specific investor (and *only* this investor) compared to other investors who would be only interested in an apartment building there.
- After studying this book, one of our more entrepreneurial students (could be you!) invents a new "super-senior housing" formula for a fast-growing demographic segment with latent demand for such a product. This allows you to make a bundle, at least for a while (until other copycat developers build enough competing units to drive rents and prices down to the normal profit level).

As you can see from the list above, the predominant source of positive investment value NPVs comes with operational advantages in controlling the real productive capacity of the property.[8] These factors play a significant role in determining the investment value of a deal. Often, the latter source involves some quasi-monopolistic position that gives the investor some advantageous market control. For example, due to synergy and spillover effects, a developer's ownership of adjacent sites might give it the unique ability to profit from a certain type of development on a given parcel of land. Another typical type of potentially profitable situation occurs when the owner of the property is also the primary user of the property, and the property has a unique fit in the real productive process of this owner (as in our KrazyLo example earlier). In fact, the type of uniqueness associated with substantially positive NPV opportunities often requires some construction or redevelopment of a property. The market tends to reward, at least temporarily, those who are first with a good idea.

Compared to classical corporate capital budgeting, because there is typically no well-functioning market for the underlying physical assets, IV is the only way to measure the value of the relevant assets and the *only* basis to calculate the NPV of proposed projects, even though the IV terminology may not be used.[9] In real estate, the property market also quantifies the MV perspective (for individual physical assets). However, we can also define the IV perspective for real estate deals. Indeed, some real estate deals involve assets or financial arrangements that are so unique that it would be exceedingly challenging to estimate the relevant market values accurately. Even when we can estimate MV accurately, the IV perspective remains a crucial factor in investment decision-making in real estate, as we will explore in the following sections.

---

[6] It should be noted here that, as usual, things are more complex than this. For example, on a portfolio level, the investor does not want to be exposed to even more apartments. However, we will only introduce such portfolio considerations in Part VI of this book. Also, if rents are increased too much, the tenants might decide to move to other areas in LA County.

[7] As we will explore in Part IV, the price of the vacant lot also depends on the costs to construct it property and on the price uncertainty during development. However, we will ignore these things for now in this example and assume it is similar for all the available options.

[8] There may also be circumstances in which the financing arrangements for a deal generate advantageous results for one or more parties to the transaction, apart from anything related to the underlying physical productivity of the asset. This will be discussed in the next Section, 14.2. A third possible source, "quasi-arbitrage," between the market for REIT shares in the stock market and the private (direct) market for property assets, will be discussed in Chapter 26.

[9] Classical capital budgeting theory assumes that IV at the level of the corporation's underlying assets will be reflected rapidly in the MV of the corporation's stock due to the informational efficiency of the stock market. Thus, for a publicly traded firm, IV at the firm's level is traditionally considered virtually equivalent to MV at the level of the firm's investors. While this classical conception ignores such issues as asymmetric information between managers and investors, it probably provides a useful approximation of reality for most publicly traded firms most of the time (including REITs).

14.1.1 How to Measure Investment Value

One should use the multiperiod DCF technique described in the previous Chapters to quantify investment value. Indeed, in practice, the multiperiod perspective is often more important in quantifying IV than MV. Although, in principle, multiperiod DCF analysis underlies the determination of MV at a fundamental level, estimating the current MV for a given type of property may often be done by a number of shortcut methods, such as simply observing the transaction prices of similar assets (essentially the cap rate "comps" analysis laid out in Chapter 11) and dividing the cap rates into the NOI of the subject property. However, IV, based on the assumption that the asset will be held for a long period, can only be determined through a full long-term projection of net cash flows.[10]

Because IV is specific to a particular owner or user of the asset, the cash flows should reflect how that owner or user would manage and operate the asset, including synergy or spillover effects with the owner's other assets and operations and the owner's particular income tax situation. Thus, the actual cash flow amounts forecasted on the right-hand side of the DCF formula may differ from one investor to another in computing IV. In principle, the investor's after-tax cash flows are discounted at market after-tax discount rates.

In theory, the discount rate applied in the denominators of the DCF calculation may also differ from one investor to another in the computation of IV. However, care must be taken not to abuse this theoretical possibility in practice. Discount rates for computing IV should not be "pulled from the air" or made up ad hoc on the claim that a given investor has "unique risk preferences." Remember that discount rates reflect the time value of money and the price of risk. All investors have access to the capital markets, and so all investors face the prices of time and risk available in that market. Going beyond the market is stepping out on very soft sand.[11] Therefore, as a matter of good practice, even when computing IV, discount rates should still reflect an opportunity cost of capital (OCC) based on the capital market.[12] Thus, we should always analyze the capital market (including the property market itself) to determine the relevant price of risk and time value of money. Only if the investor would (realistically) uniquely operate the subject property so that the capital market would perceive its cash flows to be of different risk than that of the typical operation of such a property can one legitimately employ a different discount rate risk premium than the property market would apply. Such a situation is rare and difficult to quantify with rigor. Thus, the main focus in questions of IV differing from MV should normally be on the *numerators of the DCF valuation and the expected future cash flow generation* rather than on the denominators.[13]

---

[10] An exception to the need for a long horizon in the analysis sometimes occurs in the case of raw land and development projects. It is sometimes appropriate for an IV analysis horizon to end with a projected sale of the completed new structure.

[11] For example, to apply a "personalized" risk premium, it is necessary to quantify the investor's utility function or risk preferences, given his overall wealth portfolio and consumption patterns. Such analysis is rare in practice and usually considered beyond the reasonable scope of the definition of investment value. Indeed, there is fundamental theoretical ambiguity about aggregating preferences across the different owners for an investment entity with more than one individual owner. (Economist Kenneth Arrow won a Nobel Prize in part for his discovery of an "Impossibility Theorem," which states that individual preferences cannot be aggregated into a rational "social welfare function" describing aggregate utility.)

[12] In general, this implies that the relevant OCC for determining MV and IV will reflect the risk and time preferences of the marginal investors in the relevant part of the capital market, based on the market model presented below in Section 14.1.3 and Exhibit 14-1. This point will be made more concrete in Section 14.2.2 in our discussion of after-tax investment valuation.

[13] In traditional corporate capital budgeting, the investment decision-making entity is a publicly traded corporation acting on behalf of its shareholders. In such circumstances, the derivation of the appropriate discount rates purely from the capital market is obvious because the capital market will determine the corporation's share price, and hence, its shareholders' wealth impacts any corporate investment decisions based on the market for the firm's equity shares. This same argument applies in real estate to the case of investment by publicly traded entities such as REITs. However, in real estate investment, property assets can be held directly by individuals or private entities. In such circumstances, personalized IV discount rates can be contemplated, at least theoretically. For example, a private investor whose personal wealth is uniquely and necessarily tied to Chicago apartment property may place a low investment value on purchasing an additional Chicago apartment due to its failure to diversify its constrained portfolio. An additional Chicago apartment is a riskier investment to her than the typical investor. However, such considerations are normally addressed at the macro-level of investment strategy as part of the investor's portfolio policy, as they are difficult to quantify at the micro-level regarding the investment value of specific assets. (Portfolio theory will be addressed in Chapter 22.)

More specifically, the size of the IV will be driven by the net cash flows in general in the numerators of the DCF, as often simplified by the growth rate parameter g. For example, if you believe you can purchase a standard apartment building and convert it into "super-senior housing," you would expect higher net cash flow or cash flow growth than other market participants when developing a DCF. However, note that the DCF should *also* include the synergy/spillover impacts (if applicable) to the investors' portfolio and not only consider the target investment itself. The question is, how much wealth is created *in total* for this investor? Let's look at a simple numerical example to buttress this point further.

Let's return to the example of Boston Real Estate (BRE), the REIT that owns an apartment complex in downtown Boston. Assume that the current plot is called plot A. The (projected) property-level before-tax cash flow of the current apartment building is $100,000 yearly (no growth), and the property is expected to sell for $1,000,000 in year 10. Assuming an OCC of 6%, we would get the following (market) value of these cash flows;

$$MV(Apt,\ plot\ A) = \frac{\$100{,}000}{(1.06)} + \frac{\$100{,}000}{(1.06)^2} + \ldots + \frac{\$1{,}100{,}000}{(1.06)^{10}}$$
$$= \$1.3\ \boldsymbol{million\ rounding\ from}\ \$1{,}294{,}403$$

Remember that the final year's cash flow is the reversion cash flow ($1 million) plus the operating cash flow in that same year ($100,000). According to the DCF, the current property would sell for $1.3 million in the market as is. Plot B is owned by Boston Landowners (BLO), and two possible scenarios are possible for this plot of land. The first option is an apartment building, and the second is a retail property. The projected cash flows of an apartment property on plot B would be exactly the same as plot A's. As a result, the MV for an apartment on plot B would also be $1.3 million. The retail property would generate $80,000 (property before-tax) annually and sell for an expected $800,000 in year 10. Assume that retail is a slightly riskier proposition than apartment, with a cost of capital of 8%. In that case, we would get a market value for retail on plot B of;

$$MV(Ret, plot\ B) = \frac{\$80{,}000}{(1.08)} + \frac{\$80{,}000}{(1.08)^2} + \ldots + \frac{\$880{,}000}{(1.08)^{10}}$$
$$= \$900{,}000\ \boldsymbol{rounding\ from}\ \$907{,}361$$

In this example, the apartment costs $500,000 and the retail $400,000 to develop. In that case, plot B's highest and best use is evidently an apartment building. The market value of the land (using the residual theory of land from Chapter 6) would be ($1.3 million - $500,000 =) $800,000. (Compared to $900,000 - $400,000 = $500,000 for retail.) Thus, any other (marginal) investor would purchase the land for $800,000 (competitive 0-NPV bid price) and develop an apartment complex for $500,000 construction cost in this location.

However, BRE expects that the retail complex will allow for positive spillover effects to its apartment building on plot A. In other words, apartment rents on plot A are expected to grow (more) when retail is developed next door, compared to yet another apartment building there. In fact, the extra competition of another apartment building might even reduce rents in our current building (although we will disregard this possibility for the example)! If a retail property is developed next door, the PBTCF of the apartment building on plot A is expected to grow by 5% annually (to $150,000 in year 10), and the (net) sales price is expected to increase to $1,350,000 (resulting in a year 10 cash flow of approximately $1.5 million). The market value of the apartment property on plot A in this parallel universe would be:

$$MV(Apt,\ plot\ A)^{*} = \frac{\$100{,}000}{(1.06)} + \frac{\$105{,}000}{(1.06)^{2}} + \ldots + \frac{\$1{,}505{,}133}{(1.06)^{10}}$$
$$= \$1.7\ \textbf{\textit{million rounding from}}\ \$1{,}658{,}170$$

(Note that the cost of capital remains the same.) In this scenario, the retail property will increase the value of the neighboring real estate by $400,000 ($1.7 million - $1.3 million). For BRE, the IV of plot B will, therefore, be the MV of the land (with retail), plus the increase in value of its apartment building on plot A. The MV of land with retail is ($900,000 - $400,000 =) $500,000, resulting in an *IV for plot B of $900,000* ($500,000 + $400,000), compared to a $800,000 market value (i.e., IV > MV for BRE).

An obvious follow-up question is: How much is the land exactly worth to BRE in this example? Should they spend only up to $800,000, or all the way up to $900,000, on purchasing the land? We will tackle this part of the puzzle in the next section.

14.1.2 Joint Use of IV and MV in Decision Making

As it is common in real estate to be able to compute reasonable estimates of both IV and MV, we need to consider how these two perspectives of value relate to each other in making rational investment decisions. Recall that the basic investment decision rule is to maximize your NPV across all mutually exclusive alternatives and never to do a deal with a negative NPV. But when applying this rule, should you use the NPV based on market or investment value?

To answer this question, you first need to compute the NPV both ways, so you know what sort of situation you are facing. If the deal passes both NPV criteria, then there is no philosophical issue. However, it is still useful to know both values, as they can be useful in negotiating the deal and understanding how to "create value."

Suppose you are interested in buying a particular asset or project and differ from the typical marginal investor in the market for such assets. Then your IV can differ from the MV of the asset, and in this case, you can face one of two interesting situations that require some thought:

$NPV_{MV} \gg 0 \gg NPV_{IV}$, or;
$NPV_{IV} \gg 0 \gg NPV_{MV}$

where ">>" means "substantially greater" (net of transaction costs).

In the first situation, the deal makes sense from a market value perspective but not from an investment value perspective. This implies that you could do the deal and then reverse it almost immediately in the marketplace and almost certainly make some money. As noted in Chapter 4, such situations are no doubt rare in practice and must be presumed to result from some "error" or lack of information on someone's part. The wealth-maximization principle would suggest that you should go ahead and do the deal even though, from your personal perspective, it has $NPV_{IV} < 0$. However, apart from the importance of looking at such "gift horses" very carefully "in the mouth," there is an important business strategy question here. The fact that $NPV_{MV} > NPV_{IV}$ by a significant margin suggests that the type of deal in question here is not the type you specialize in or have a particular expertise in. It is, by definition, a kind of deal for which you are not as well suited as the typical marginal investor in the market (as such, marginal investors determine the MV). In other words, this is not the type of deal that conforms with what is (or should be) your main business strategy. In such a circumstance, you need to think carefully about whether it really makes sense for you to get distracted by pursuing the deal. (Perhaps you can pass it on to someone else who specializes in "flipping" assets in return for some share of the positive NPV without spending much of your own firm's resources on the deal?)

Now consider the second interesting situation, in which the deal makes sense from an investment value perspective but not from a market value perspective. For example, let's assume for a minute that the land was offered to Boston Real Estate at $850,000, even though we previously established that the land's MV was $800,000. This feels like we are being ripped off! On the flip side, we also established that the IV of the land for Boston Real Estate (and *only* for them) is $900,000. In other words, from an IV point of view, we achieve *positive* NPV. Should you make such a deal?

Two philosophies answer this question. For convenience, we can term one the "conservative philosophy" and the other the "liberal philosophy" (though these terms have no implications regarding political philosophy). The conservative philosophy says "no," you should not make the deal. You should never pay more than MV for something (or sell for less than MV) because, after all, why should you? MV means that you should be able to buy (or sell) at that price. For example, suppose the seller does not sell to you. In that case, he cannot expect to get more than MV for the asset from anyone else, so why should you reward him with a windfall just because you can do something unique with the property or use it in some particularly advantageous way because of your unique circumstances? Bargain the seller down to where his price equals MV ($NPV_{MV} = 0$), or walk away from the deal.

On the other hand, liberal philosophy says "yes" to making the deal, even if necessary, at NPV_{MV} 0, as long as the deal meets the investment decision criterion on an NPV_{IV} basis. Since this rule does require you to obtain as high an NPV as possible (across all mutually exclusive alternatives), it presumes that you will bargain the seller down to as low a price as possible (or, if you are the seller, bargain a purchaser up to as high a price as possible). Once you have done that, the idea is that it would be foolish (not wealth-maximizing) to walk away from a deal that presents a positive NPV from your investment value perspective (that is, based on what you realistically can do with it or on what your unique circumstances are).

Of course, there may be a considerable gap between your IV and the MV for the subject asset. Even under the "liberal" philosophy, should you really be willing to pay up to your IV for the asset? The NPV rule says you should try to get the asset for as low a price as possible, but how low is low enough? The answer to this question, from a rational or normative perspective, is the subject of a field of economics known as "optimal search theory." According to this theory, logically enough, the answer depends on how sure you are or how well you can determine the actual MV of the asset, and of course, it also depends on how desperately you want the asset, how costly it is for you to continue searching for alternative assets, and so forth. Optimal search theory suggests that you may think about how high you are willing to pay (up to a maximum of your IV for the asset) in terms of a "reservation price" that you set privately (secretly for yourself), below which you will stop searching or negotiating and buy the asset. In general, the less certain you are about the MV of the asset, the lower (more conservatively) you would set your reservation price (farther below your IV). On the other hand, the more certain you are about the MV, the closer to that perceived MV (less above it) you will set your reservation price (assuming your IV remains above the MV).[14]

Real estate deals can have substantially positive (or negative) NPV when computed from the IV perspective. This could occur even though the deal is at market value, so it has a zero NPV from the MV perspective. Indeed, viewed from the IV perspective, a deal can produce a positive NPV for both sides of the transaction due to unique circumstances affecting one or both parties. This is because IV is personal in that it relates to a specific owner or investor and is divorced from the market. After all, the asset is presumed to be held off the market for a long time. Finding situations where the IV-based NPV is positive for both sides of the deal is one of the main objectives of much real estate investment activity.

---

[14] We will note optimal search theory again in the online supplemental materials, and we gave a simple example of a particular optimal search model (for landlord–tenant search) in the supplemental materials of Chapter 10.

Generally, when IV > MV, buying, building, or holding (whichever is relevant) makes sense. On the other hand, when IV < MV, it makes sense to sell if you already own and not to buy if you don't yet own the property, as would be the case, for example, if KrazyLo somehow lost its ability to make a profit at the Consumption Boulevard location.

An important difference between real estate and securities is that unique, whole assets are traded in the property market (along with their governing authority and operational responsibility). This creates a certain "lumpiness" in the property market and makes it difficult to know exactly what the MV is of a given asset at any given time.[15] With this in mind, a notion often used in practice to help conceive of MV and relate it to IV is that of **the second-most-motivated buyer**. The maximum price this buyer would be willing to pay (the IV to this buyer) is taken to be the MV for the property. The most motivated buyer is the one who has the highest IV for the property. For example, the most creative and entrepreneurial developer with the greatest expertise regarding using a given site (or the most ability to profit, like KrazyLo in the previous example) can probably purchase that site for a positive NPV viewed from his own IV-based perspective. The IV of the site for this "best" developer is greater than it is for any other developer and, hence, greater than the MV of the site.

Suppose there is not much heterogeneity or uniqueness in the properties or the potential investors. In that case, the IV of the most-motivated and second-most-motivated buyers will be very similar. But suppose the most-motivated buyer would place a much higher IV on the property than would the second-most-motivated buyer. In that case, it may be possible to sell the property for more than its market value (based on the "liberal" philosophy noted above).

One implication of the difference between IV and MV is that you need to be aware that the opposite party in a transaction may have some idea about the magnitude of your IV in the deal. They will naturally try to negotiate a price above MV, closer to your IV, to take advantage of this knowledge if they can. For example, the owner of 9997 and 9998 Consumption Boulevard will certainly know that her lots are worth more to KrazyLo than to anyone else, that is, more than their MV. The question is: *How much more*? This is where careful investigation and negotiating skills can pay off (on either side). If you deal with unique assets or financial arrangements, you may have little recourse to competing players as alternative opposite parties. However, the other side may have little recourse as well. It is important to keep IV information confidential and to apply sound negotiation principles when dealing with such a situation.

This brings us back to our starting point about the difference between real estate and securities investment on the one hand and between real estate and corporate capital budgeting investment on the other hand. The more lumpiness and uniqueness there is among assets and investors, the more difficult it will be to estimate market values accurately, and the more likely it will be that investors' IVs could greatly differ from any estimate that could be made of MV. This is the situation in which real estate investment analysis converges toward corporate capital budgeting analysis in some respects, and IV tends to become the only relevant value perspective. The more homogeneous the assets and the investors are, the easier it will be to estimate market values, and the less likely it will be that IV differs much from MV for most active market participants. This is where real estate investment analysis converges toward classical securities investment analysis, and MV becomes the dominant valuation perspective. Much commercial real estate investing occurs somewhere between these two extremes.

---

[15] Real estate fractional ownership shares or tokens that will trade in an open market may evolve over time require scale and significant market informational efficiency, but may someday reduce the lumpiness of real estate.

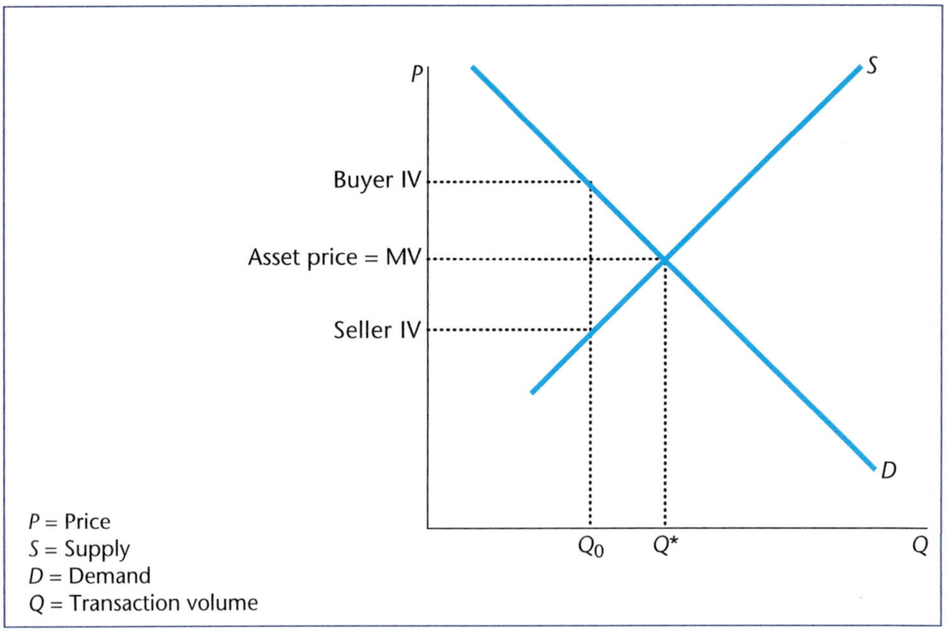

EXHIBIT 14-1 Relation between Investment Value (IV) and Market Value (MV) in a Well-Functioning Asset Market.

Where;

- Q_0 = Volume of transactions by investors with more favorable circumstances, hence, would enter the market at less favorable prices (i.e., intramarginal market participants, e.g., investors with different tax circumstances than marginal investors in the market.
- Q^* = Total volume of property transactions, including marginal investment (investors on margin are indifferent between investing and not investing in property.)
- Note: Prices and market values (MV) are determined by the IV of the marginal investors (investors for whom NPV = 0 on both an IV and MV basis).

14.1.3 The Asset Market Model with Marginal and Intramarginal Investors: How to Get Positive NPV

We noted that the difference between the MV and IV of the asset for the investor typically determines the investment value NPV of a given deal for a given investor. Examining how these two valuation measures operate in a well-functioning property market can deepen our understanding of both IV and MV and provide additional practical insight. A useful concept in this regard is the distinction between **marginal** and **intramarginal investors** in the market.

The chart in Exhibit 14-1 presents a schematic picture of a well-functioning property market.[16] The horizontal axis represents the annual trading volume in the asset market (e.g., number of properties bought and sold). The vertical axis represents the prices of properties (e.g., per square foot). The downward-sloping demand function shows the amount of assets potential buyers want to purchase based on their perceived investment values. Investors with the highest IVs would first become active in the market, even at relatively high prices. At lower prices, additional buyers would enter the

16 A deeper understanding of the nature of this asset market model can be obtained by reading online supplemental materials for this chapter.

market. So, the demand function is downward sloping. The upward-sloping supply function shows the amount of assets that potential sellers (existing owners of the assets) would like to sell based on their perceived investment values. Only a few sellers would be willing to do deals at low prices. More sellers enter the market at higher prices that exceed more owners' investment values, producing the upward-sloping supply function shown in the chart.[17]

Market value is determined by **asset transaction market equilibrium**. The equilibrium price is that which equates or balances the supply and demand. This is the price at which IV is the same for buyers and sellers on the margin. By definition, the equilibrium market price (the expectation of which is the MV of the assets in this market) produces NPV = 0 computed on both an IV and MV basis for the marginal participants in this market. Exhibit 14-1 shows how the IV of the marginal investors determines or underlies the market prices. MV equals the IV of the marginal participants in the asset market.

IV will differ from MV (which will enable positive NPV deals to be done, measured based on IV, by trading at MV prices) only for intramarginal market participants, those to the left of the equilibrium point in the diagram. These are market participants for whom (and deals in which) the IV for the buyer differs from the IV for the seller for the same asset. By definition, this requires that the sellers and buyers in these deals are different from each other in some way that is important to the investment value of the asset.

We can distill from this analysis some practical conclusions about how you can know whether you are likely to be able to do a substantially positive NPV deal, measured based on your IV, in a well-functioning market. We see that positive NPV deals are intramarginal deals. Intramarginal investors face positive NPV from an IV perspective on one side of the market (either demand/buying or supply/selling) and negative NPV on the opposite side of the market (either supply/selling or demand/buying). Our market model gives us a way to recognize such intramarginal deals. A necessary characteristic of intramarginal deals is that the principal parties on the two sides of the deal must be different in some important way regarding their ability to profit from the asset, at least going forward and on an after-tax basis. This type of difference is a necessary, although not sufficient, condition for positive investment value NPV deals. (Such a difference by itself is insufficient to ensure a positive NPV because you still must ensure you are not making a pricing mistake in negotiating the deal.)

14.2 INVESTMENT VALUE THROUGH DEBT FINANCING

It is a cliché often attributed to Benjamin Franklin that the only certainties in this world are death and taxes. For financial economists, Merton Miller's paraphrase of this cliché in his famous "Debt and Taxes" 1976 AFA Presidential Address is perhaps more relevant. (He demonstrated that in equilibrium, the value of a firm is independent of whether or how much the firm borrows, except when affected by such real-world considerations as income taxes, among other things.) And you now have enough background to usefully explore the "debt and taxes" question in the analysis and evaluation of real estate investment. It turns out that the investment value concept that we elaborated on in the previous sections bears directly on how to understand and value the use of debt in real estate investment. And this, of course, also figures prominently in the analysis and evaluation of micro-level real estate investment from an after-tax (investment value) perspective.

---

[17] As described in the Chapter 14A3 online, the demand and supply functions may be influenced by search behavior including the setting of "reservation prices" (at which parties will stop searching and consummate transactions). This can cause the demand and supply functions to be "flatter" and more price-elastic than would be implied by the underlying investment values, and this price-elasticity may vary over time (sometimes quickly and radically). But fundamentally, the demand and supply functions reflect the investment values potential buyers and sellers place on the individual properties potentially in the asset market. There is evidence that prices and trading volume are interconnected in the private property market in a manner that suggests a lack of perfect price-elasticity (i.e., the demand is downward-sloping and supply upward-sloping supply, as indicated in the exhibit). In private property markets, trading volume and prices tend to move together, with changes in volume slightly leading to changes in prices.

We have previously noted that large amounts of debt financing are often used to finance real estate investments, and we pointed out that using debt to finance a real estate investment does not automatically bring any positive NPV component to the investment. We said that the effect of positive leverage gearing up the total expected return to equity is offset by the increased risk in that return. Now, we can qualify and elaborate upon this point by using the investment value construct. In fact, the point about the zero NPV impact of debt financing will always be true only from the *market value* perspective and from an investment value viewpoint (after-tax) only for real estate investors who happen to face the same marginal income tax rate as the marginal investors in the debt market. From an investment value perspective, more generally, the use of debt to finance a real estate investment may be either positive or negative in its NPV impact on the investment, depending on the investor's tax situation and how well they can exploit tax shields provided by real estate investments.[18] This will be the topic of Section 14.2.

When we introduced the DCF method and the NPV decision rule, we were implicitly taking the property before-tax (PBT) perspective, or what you now know as the market value perspective, that is, before or without considering debt and income taxes.[19] Based on the market model introduced in the previous section, you now know that if you are a *marginal* investor, the MV will equal your IV. In that case, in principle, PBT level analysis provides a kind of shortcut. In doing capital budgeting or investment evaluation at the micro-level, you can work with property-level before-tax cash flows (PBTCF) rather than equity-after-tax cash flows (EATCF), greatly simplifying the analysis. You can also use the property-before-tax level OCC as the discount rate you apply to the PBTCF for evaluation purposes. In fact, this shortcut approach is widely used in real estate investment practice, implicitly (if not explicitly) assuming that the investor is marginal in the real estate asset investment market and, therefore, that IV = MV (or else that the analyst cares only about the MV perspective). Let's label this "shortcut" the **property-before-tax (PBT) approach**. Although the PBT approach is handy and widely applied, remember that, in principle, it applies in general only to market value and, therefore, to investment value only for a typical marginal investor in the market for the type of property in question.

But how can you know if you are a marginal investor regarding income taxes and leverage in the relevant property asset market? If you are not, how can you analyze and evaluate the investment from an after-tax IV perspective? This is especially important when the investor faces an income status different from that of typical participants in the market and/or if debt financing is being considered. On an after-tax basis (considering the investor's income tax status), debt cash flows associated with the levered property investment will differ across different investors or different types of investors (such as taxable individuals, taxable corporations, and tax-exempt institutions).

In principle, we must use the investor's own personalized cash flows in the numerators of any DCF evaluation. And as described above and in Chapter 11, we also must use an appropriate OCC from the relevant capital market. The relevant capital market for real estate cash flows is the property market. However, the relevant capital market for debt cash flows is the debt market, the market for fixed-income investments. The principle is always that the relevant OCC for a stream of cash flows is the expected return faced by marginal investors in the market for investments that produce cash flows of similar risk to the stream you are evaluating. Because real estate cash flows and debt cash

---

[18] The statement and the analysis to follow in this section presume that the investor does not borrow "to excess." That is, we assume that the capital structure is not sub-optimal in the sense of borrowing so much that financial distress or agency costs detract from the value of the overall investment. The question of optimal capital structure will be discussed in Chapter 15.

[19] Corporate finance textbooks apply DCF valuation and capital budgeting analysis at the after-tax level. However, in the typical corporate context, the taxes being considered are corporate-level income taxes only. The typical textbook application is at a before-tax level from the perspective of the ultimate investors, the corporation's shareholders. In real estate, taxed corporate-level entities rarely hold the property, so our before-tax presentation in Chapter 12 was consistent with the typical corporate finance textbook presentation viewed from the perspective of the ultimate investors.

flows differ in their risk (and therefore in their OCC), it makes sense to separate out those cash flow streams for evaluation, and this can facilitate the IV evaluation of levered investments. We consider the nuts and bolts of this procedure in the following subsections.

TEXT BOX 14.1 HOW ARE PENSION FUND CONTRIBUTIONS EFFECTIVELY TAX-EXEMPT?

Consider \$1,000 of pretax (i.e., gross) income at time zero. You must first pay taxes on this income at time zero before you can do anything with it. If the tax rate is 30 percent, you have \$700 of disposable income left over to invest. Suppose you can invest at a pretax rate of return of 10 percent (e.g., you buy a government bond that yields 10 percent). If your investment is not tax sheltered, then you must pay taxes of 30 percent each year on your investment earnings that year. This makes the effective after-tax rate of growth of your money 7 percent [(1 - 0.3) x 10% = 7%], not 10 percent. Therefore, after N years, you will have \$700(1.07)N of disposable cash to spend, with no more taxes owed then. On the other hand, if you could have invested your \$700 time-zero disposable income in a tax-sheltered vehicle, then you would have been able to earn the entire 10 percent return without paying taxes, so your disposable cash in year N would have been \$700(1.10)N, which is greater than \$700(1.07)N (and this difference is more, the greater is N).

Now, consider the way pension fund contributions work. We start with the same \$1,000 pretax gross income at time zero. If you put that in a pension fund at time zero, you won't have to pay taxes because pension contributions are deductible from your taxable income. So, you can invest the entire \$1,000 rather than just \$700. Furthermore, earnings in the fund are tax-exempt if you leave them in the fund. Your money will grow at the full 10 percent rate during the N years, after which time you will have \$1,000(1.10)N in the fund. However, when you take your money out of the pension fund in year N, you *will* pay taxes on all the money you withdraw from the fund. In other words, your after-tax disposable cash in year N from your pension investment is (1 -0.3) x \$1,000(1.10)N = \$700(1.10)N, which is the same as if you had been able to make a time-zero investment of your regular after-tax disposable income in a tax-sheltered vehicle that did not have to pay taxes on its investment returns. Thus, the combination of tax-deductible contributions up front, plus tax-sheltered growth while the investment is in the fund, makes pension investments effectively exempt from tax, as though the investment returns were not taxed.

14.2.1 Value Additivity and the APV Decision Rule

This section introduces a simple and intuitive procedure for dealing with the interaction of investment and financing decisions at the after-tax level. Recall when we introduced the cash flow components format of the equity after-tax proforma projection in the previous chapter in the bottom panel of Exhibit 13-3: we suggested that this type of parsing of cash flow by component could be helpful for investment analysis because different components of the future cash flow stream have different risk characteristics. This components format was carried forward into Exhibit 13-5 (only transposed). Now, we will extend and formalize this approach by giving it the name of the *Value Additivity* principle, the idea that the property's value must equal the sum of the values of all the components of the property's cash flows.

Perhaps the simplest and most basic (and most widely used) application of this principle is to break out and value separately (and then add back together) the value of the property cash flows, and the debt cash flows (or any external financing-related cash flows) associated with a levered equity investment. In this case, the value additivity approach dovetails nicely with the PBT shortcut described above. In this context, value additivity underlies an investment evaluation procedure taught in corporate finance, often called **adjusted present value, or APV**. The APV decision rule can be as applicable for real estate investment analysis as it is for corporate capital budgeting.

The APV procedure extends the basic NPV analysis procedure described in Chapter 13. APV allows the NPV procedure to include explicitly the effect of financing in evaluating a levered real estate investment deal. From the equity investor's perspective, the deal may be considered the combination of the property purchase as if it were free and clear of debt, and the financing arrangements. More formally, the APV of a deal is defined as follows:

Equation 1

$$APV = NPV(Property) + NPV(Financing)$$

In equation (1), *NPV(Property)* is the NPV of the property transaction as if there were no debt. *NPV(Financing)* is the net value of the financing arrangements to (from the perspective of) the property equity investor. Typically, financing involves the use of debt or debt-like instruments.

The APV investment decision rule states that the traditional NPV decision criterion should be applied to the APV, that is, to the NPV of the overall deal, including its financing component (the sum on the right-hand side of Equation (1)). This APV must be maximized across all mutually exclusive alternatives and always be nonnegative for the deal to make sense from a wealth-maximization perspective. As with NPV, in markets where debt financing is common, equilibrium tends to drive the typical APV to zero when evaluating deals from a market value perspective *and* also from an investment value perspective for the marginal investors in that property market.

As the debt market is usually rather competitive and efficient, the *NPV(Financing)* term will usually have a value of zero from an MV perspective, assuming unsubsidized, market-rate financing of typical "commodity-like" debt products (as would typically be obtained, for example, from a bank or other private financial institution, or by issuing bonds in the public market). In these conditions, therefore, the NPV of the equity investment (using debt) is the same as the NPV of an all-equity investment in the property without using debt, evaluated from the perspective of market value, that is, $APV = NPV(Property)$. This is the condition or perspective in which the PBT shortcut described earlier is typically applied (MV perspective or IV perspective for marginal investors).

On the other hand, *if* subsidized financing is involved in the deal, such as some seller-provided loans or government-assisted funding, then the NPV of the financing part of the deal can be substantially positive to the buyer/investor, even viewed from a market value perspective.[20] In this case, the APV can exceed the NPV of an all-equity investment in the property. The PBT shortcut may still be useful for quantifying the *NPV(Property)* component of the APV. Still, the *NPV(Financing)* component must be valued separately and added to the *NPV(Property)* to obtain the total deal value for the equity investor.

It is important to note that the APV procedure (like the NPV) can be applied from either the MV or IV perspective. From the IV perspective, one needs to consider whether the investor (for example, the property purchaser) is marginal or intramarginal not only in the property market for the subject asset but also in the debt market for the financing aspect of the deal. Positive or negative net value can occur in either component of the overall deal, particularly from an IV perspective, because of

[20] Obviously, the flip side of this point is that a seller should offer cut-rate financing only if it would otherwise be impossible to sell the property at as high a price (in the same period of time). From an MV perspective, the value of the *NPV (financing)* term in the APV formula is the same magnitude for the seller as for the buyer, only the opposite in sign; as for the seller financing, the two parties are simply on the opposite side of the same before-tax cash flows.

differential income tax effects. This raises a very important topic in real estate investment and perhaps misunderstood in some current practices in the United States: the after-tax valuation of debt financing from the point of view of the property investor (borrower).

14.2.2 After-Tax Valuation of Debt Financing

In this section, we want to consider how to rigorously evaluate the use of debt financing for real estate investors from a market value and investment value perspective, both before-tax and after-tax. This allows us to calculate *and understand* the *NPV(Financing)* component of the APV decision rule in equation (1).

Consider a simple stylized hypothetical debt market. All loans are perpetual in this market, and the prevailing market interest rate on mortgages is 4 percent. For every \$100 you borrow to finance a property acquisition, you will forever pay \$4 interest at the end of every year. In addition, there is a market for tax-exempt debt, such as notes issued by state and local governments ("municipal bonds" or "munis"), where the prevailing market interest rate is 3 percent. Because equilibrium must exist across the markets for mortgage investment and municipal bond investment, the market interest rates in these two markets tell us that marginal investors in the debt market (marginal lenders) face an effective tax rate on mortgage interest income of 25 percent. This tax rate leaves debt investors indifferent between a 4 percent return before tax in the mortgage market and the 3 percent return they can get tax-free in the municipal bond market. Thus, we can readily observe that the OCC is 4 percent before and 3 percent after-tax in the mortgage market.[21]

First, consider how we would represent a mortgage's market value (MV) in this market framework using DCF valuation. The market value of \$100 worth of debt would be, by definition, \$100, based on the following DCF equation, which discounts the before-tax cash flows of the mortgage at the market's before-tax OCC of 4 percent (recalling the perpetuity formula):

$$MV = \frac{\$4}{1.04} + \frac{\$4}{1.04^2} + \ldots = \frac{\$4}{0.04} = \$100$$

Let's consider how this MV compares to the investment value (IV) of the debt liability obligation associated with this mortgage for three intrepid real estate investors who want to borrow \$100 to help finance a real estate investment. The first investor is Mary. Mary is like the typical marginal investor in the debt market, facing a marginal tax rate of 25 percent on her investment income. To compute Mary's investment value of her mortgage interest obligations, labeled IV_M, we discount her after-tax cash flows at the market's after-tax OCC of 3 percent:

$$IV_M = \frac{(1-0.25)\$4}{1.03} + \frac{(1-0.25)\$4}{1.03^2} + \ldots = \frac{\$3}{0.03} = \$100$$

Mary can deduct the \$4 of interest expense each year from her taxable income, saving \$1 in taxes yearly because she borrowed the mortgage (25% × \$4 = \$1, leaving her an after-tax interest cash outflow of only \$3 each year). Mary's IV_M exactly equals the MV of the mortgage because Mary is like the marginal investor in the debt market.[22] Thus, the loan for her is a zero-NPV transaction,

[21] In the real world, it is typical in the United States for municipal bonds to be priced at yields about three-quarters the yield of similar-maturity, similarly rated taxable income corporate bonds, although this ratio does vary somewhat over time and should logically reflect changes in tax policy and tax rates.

[22] We are ignoring the standard deduction option in these examples for simplicity.

giving her \$100 of cash upfront in return for a future interest liability obligation with a present IV_M value of exactly \$100.

We use the OCC from the debt market, not from the property market, even though Mary is investing in the property market, because as you recall, the basic principle is that the OCC comes from the market in which assets trade that have cash flows of similar risk to the cash flows the discount rate (OCC) is being applied to (the cash flows whose present value you are evaluating).

The next investor is Abner. Abner is "tax-advantaged." He faces only a 20 percent marginal income tax rate on investment earnings instead of the 25 percent rate faced by Mary and the marginal investors in the debt market. (Perhaps this is because Abner has a lower taxable income or lives in a state/country with little to no income tax.) Of course, Abner faces the same market value as Mary or anyone else, so he will also receive \$100 in upfront debt. However, Abner's investment value of the subsequent loan liability, labeled IV_A, differs from Mary's because of his tax status. Abner's IV_A value of his obligations is computed by discounting his "personalized" after-tax cash flows of the loan at the market's after-tax OCC:

$$IV_A = \frac{(1-0.20)\$4}{1.03} + \frac{(1-0.20)\$4}{1.03^2} + \ldots = \frac{\$3.20}{0.03} = \$107$$

(Rounded from \$106.67)

Recall that, for IV, while we take the OCC (discount rate) from the capital market, we apply that OCC to the cash flows of the subject investor whose IV we are computing.

From Abner's perspective, he can only save \$0.80 in taxes yearly by borrowing the mortgage, because his tax rate is only 20 percent, leaving him with after-tax interest payments of \$3.20 per year. Thus, Abner's borrowing to finance his real estate investment is *a negative NPV deal.* He obtains \$100 cash upfront but incurs an obligation with an investment value of negative \$107 for an IV-based NPV of negative \$7.

Just the opposite case is provided by our third investor, Clarence. Clarence is tax-disadvantaged as an investor, perhaps not unlike a profitable "C corporation," which in effect subjects its investors to double taxation on investment earnings, once by the corporate income tax and then by the personal income tax that is applied to realized investment income. For simplicity in this example, let's say Clarence faces a 30 percent tax rate. Thus, the investment value of the loan payment obligations Clarence incurs, labeled IV_C, is given by:

$$IV_C = \frac{(1-0.30)\$4}{1.03} + \frac{(1-0.30)\$4}{1.03^2} + \ldots = \frac{\$2.80}{0.03} = \$93$$

(Rounded from \$93.33)

Thus, for Clarence, borrowing to finance his real estate investment is a *positive NPV proposition.* Apart from whatever leverage objectives he may have or other reasons to want to use debt to finance his real estate investment, the debt financing by itself provides a positive NPV viewed from Clarence's investment value perspective, even though it is unsubsidized (market rate) debt.

What we have just discovered is summarized graphically in our asset market model framework, originally introduced in Exhibit 14-1, here for the present debt market example in Exhibit 14-2. Mary is a marginal borrower, while Abner and Clarence are both intramarginal, on opposite sides of the debt market. Borrowing to finance a real estate transaction normally is zero-NPV from a market value perspective (unless the debt is subsidized, nonmarket rate). From an investment value perspective, there is also zero-NPV for investors who face a marginal tax rate like that of marginal investors in the debt market (which we suggested has traditionally

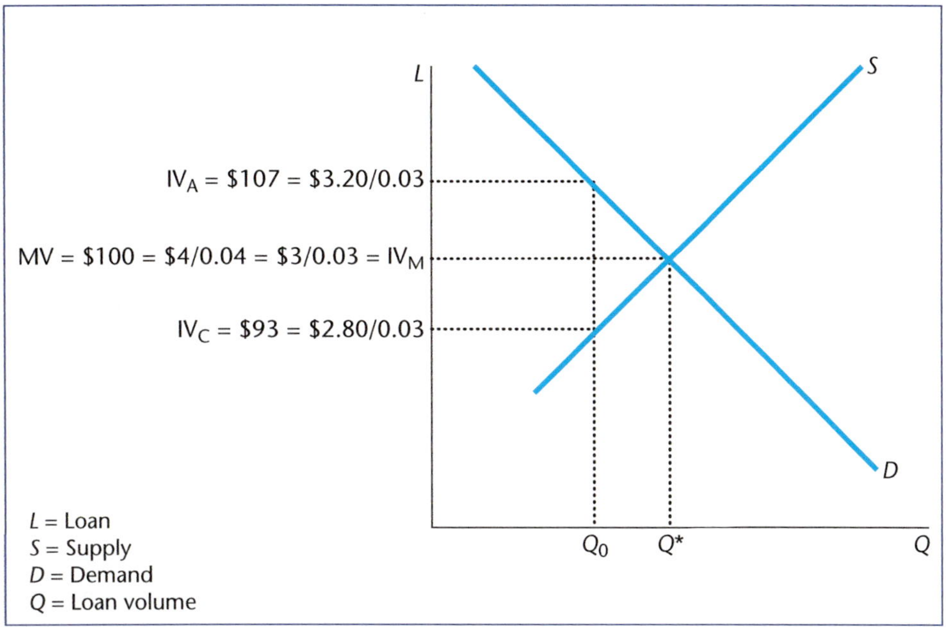

EXHIBIT 14-2 Market Value and Investment Value of Debt for Marginal and Intramarginal Investors, based on Tax Bracket.

been around 25 percent in the United States). For investors facing a lower tax rate, such as our tax-advantaged investor Abner, borrowing is a negative NPV. (For example, this might be true for many lower- or moderate-income home purchasers.) However, for investors facing an effectively higher tax rate than the marginal investors in the debt market, borrowing is itself a positive NPV transaction.

Now, consider how this framework applies in the case of a subsidized loan. Suppose, for example, that a property seller offers a below-market rate loan at 3.5% instead of the market rate of 4%. From an investment value perspective, the subsidized loan NPV calculations are shown below for all three of our previous borrowers (rounded answers to the nearest whole number):

$$NPV\left(IV_M\right) = \$100 - \left(\frac{(1-0.25)\$3.50}{1.03} + \frac{(1-0.25)\$3.50}{1.03^2} + \ldots\right)$$
$$= \$100 - \frac{\$2.63}{0.03} = \$100 - \$88 = +\$12$$

$$NPV\left(IV_A\right) = \$100 - \left(\frac{(1-0.20)\$3.50}{1.03} + \frac{(1-0.20)\$3.50}{1.03^2} + \ldots\right)$$
$$= \$100 - \frac{\$2.80}{0.03} = \$100 - \$93 = +\$7$$

$$NPV\left(IV_C\right) = \$100 - \left(\frac{(1-0.30)\$3.50}{1.03} + \frac{(1-0.30)\$3.50}{1.03^2} + \ldots\right)$$
$$= \$100 - \frac{\$2.45}{0.03} = \$100 - \$82 = +\$18$$

This tells us that subsidized financing can bring positive NPV from borrowing, even to more tax-advantaged investors, although it depends on *how* tax-advantaged they are (and how big the subsidy is). In the above example, an interest rate subsidized down to 3.5% from a market rate of 4% would not be sufficient to make borrowing positive NPV for an investor who was completely tax-exempt or facing effectively zero income taxes. That would require a rate below 3%.[23]

14.2.3 Debt and Taxes and Equilibrium in the Property Investment Market

Now consider the implications of Sections 14.2.1 and 14.2.2 viewed from the perspective of equilibrium in the property asset market, where investors buy and sell real estate. In equilibrium in that market, the APV of the **property-plus-loan deal** will be driven by competition down to zero, including from an IV (after-tax) perspective for the marginal investors *in the property market.* (Recall that the defining characteristic of the marginal investors in any market is that they are indifferent between buying and selling, that is, investors for whom APV = 0 from both an MV and IV perspective.)

We should note that although real estate asset markets tend to be well integrated (more so than space markets), there may nevertheless be some market segmentation, including by different sizes and types of investors on the margin. It is possible that tax-exempt or at least tax-advantaged investors may be on the margin in some market segments. However, it is very likely that the marginal investors in many real estate markets are investors facing rather high personal marginal tax rates. (This may be particularly true in the market for smaller investment properties.)

On the other hand, much of the investment in the debt market is done by tax-exempt institutions. It is therefore quite possible for the marginal investors in a typical real estate asset market to face higher marginal income tax rates than those faced by the marginal investors in the debt market. In that circumstance, the marginal investors in the real estate market are like Clarence in our simplistic example in Section 14.2.1.

Clarence faces a positive NPV from borrowing equal to $7 per $100 of debt. Suppose that the typical marginal investor on the property market (like Clarence) uses 50% LTV leverage. Then, for every $200 of property they buy, they would obtain $7 of positive NPV from the loan. But we know from the previous sections in this chapter that in equilibrium on the margin, APV = 0. In other words, property prices must be driven to the point that, in equilibrium, the marginal investors face zero APV, considering both the property asset and the loan. In equilibrium, competition among buyers on the margin would, therefore, drive the property asset price above $200, in fact, to something more like $207 (or even a little more, assuming the 50% LTV ratio would be applied to the equilibrium price, implying a loan slightly greater than $100).

The property market would be characterized on the margin in equilibrium by pricing and evaluation as follows (from equation (1), per approximately $200 of property value):

$$\begin{aligned} APV &= NPV(Property) + NPV(Financing) \\ &= (IV_C(property) - Property\ Price) + (Loan\ Amount) - IV_C(loan)) \\ &= (\$200 - \$207) + (\$100 - \$93) \\ &= -\$7 + \$7 \\ &= 0. \end{aligned}$$

[23] Note that some government programs allow real estate projects to be financed using tax-exempt municipal bond debt. It should also be noted that for finite-duration loans, the NPV of subsidized loans will be less than what is implied in the present perpetuity example and, from the IV perspective, will differ from the MV perspective, even for the marginal borrower. As the loan term becomes short, the NPV of a subsidized loan from an IV perspective converges toward (1-T) times the NPV of the loan from an MV (before-tax) perspective, where "T" is the borrower's tax rate.

Where IV_C refers to the investment value from the perspective of Clarence (the marginal investor in the property market).

In other words, the prevailing price for property in the market would be a bit higher ($207) than what it would be ($200) if the marginal investors didn't face income tax rates higher than the marginal investors in the debt market (as evidenced by the yield spread between otherwise equivalent taxable vs. tax-exempt bonds) and/or if the marginal investors in the property market did not in fact use leverage in their real estate investments. The market's observable, prevailing property price (the $207 in the above example) then becomes the market value in the market where investors like Clarence are on the margin.[24]

14.2.4 Example Application of APV to Marginal Investor

Let us combine the points from the preceding subsections to see how they can be applied in a more realistic, typical investment property market. Consider again our apartment property example from Chapter 13. In Section 14.2.1, we discussed how we could estimate the market's after-tax OCC for the levered equity investment from knowledge of the property's market value and assumptions about the characteristics of the typical marginal investor. Assuming the cash flows in Exhibit 13-5 are representative of the marginal investor in the market for our apartment building, which has a market value of $937 thousand, our estimate of the equity after-tax OCC was 11.17 percent for the 10-year IRR, resulting in the $234 thousand valuation of the equity.

Now, while this investor is indeed marginal in the property market, she is intramarginal in the debt market. In particular, let's suppose that our apartment property investor is in a higher marginal income tax bracket than the marginal investor in the debt market. This will make our apartment investor intramarginal on the "sell" (i.e., borrow) side of the debt market, not unlike Clarence in the example in the previous section, obtaining some positive NPV from borrowing. To be more specific, let us suppose that by comparison of market yields in the municipal bond market and the corporate bond and mortgage markets, we can ascertain that the marginal investor in the mortgage market faces an effective tax rate of 15 percent on investment income. This compares with the 35 percent tax bracket for ordinary income that our marginal real estate investor faces, which is relevant for evaluating debt interest tax shields. Exhibit 14-3 shows how we can use this knowledge of the after-tax OCC of debt, combined with our APV = 0 equilibrium condition, to derive the implied investment value for the marginal investor of the property itself without any debt. Note that only four cells have changed compared to Exhibit 13-5. The year 0 PATCF (column 7), LATCF (column 13), and the corresponding IRRs. As a reminder, PATCF is property-after-tax, and LATCF is loan-after-tax cash flows.

First, we compute the NPV of the loan component of the marginal investor's deal. If the loan's interest rate is 5 percent, the implied after-tax OCC for this debt investment is $(1 - 0.15) \times 5\% = 4.25\%$. If a tax-exempt municipality issued the mortgage, it would presumably trade at a 4.25 percent yield in the municipal bond market. We discount our apartment investor's personalized after-tax debt service cash flows (reflecting her 35 percent tax rate) shown in column (13) of Exhibit 14-3. Discounted at the 4.25 percent OCC, we determine that the present value of the loan obligation payments is $649,767 from the IV perspective of this investor. Thus, the investor obtains $702,670

[24] Obviously, this is a simplified stylized example to illustrate the key underlying principles. Even in that context, the values are approximate because we have not iterated through to the final equilibrium condition (for example, if the MV has become $207, and Clarence wants 50% LTV, then he would borrow $103.50, not $100, and that would provide him with $7.25 worth of positive IV-based NPV from borrowing, instead of just $7.00, and so on). Note also that this result does not necessarily imply that tax-advantaged investors (e.g., pension funds) should not be buyers in the market. Although they cannot benefit from leverage on an after-tax basis, their tax advantage benefits them in their IV evaluation of the property asset itself.

cash upfront from the loan (column 8) in return for a liability with a present value of $649,767, resulting in an IV-based NPV of the loan of positive $52,903.

In general, the magnitude of the positive NPV from debt financing will not be very large compared to the size of the loan (as is the case here), even for high-tax-bracket investors. It will be much less than the value of the interest tax shields (ITS) associated with the loan. For example, if we sum the discounted cash flows from the tax shields in column (5) using a discount rate of 4.25%, we get $246 thousand, much larger than the $52,903 NPV from the debt itself. The difference is caused by taxes paid by the marginal lender in the debt market. Only the net effect of tax shields that remain in the private sector reduces the investment value in the private sector.

That being said, given that the apartment investor portrayed in Exhibit 14-3 is marginal in the property market, we know that the deal's APV must equal zero. Hence, the NPV of the property component of the deal without any debt must be negative $63,072. Because the property's market value is $1,116,981, the property's investment value to the marginal investor must be $1,053,909 without any debt.

$$
\begin{aligned}
\text{APV} &= \mathit{NPV(Property)} + \mathit{NPV(Financing)} \\
&= (\$883{,}990 - \$936{,}893) + (\$702{,}670 - \$649{,}767) \\
&= -\$52{,}903 + \$52{,}903 = 0
\end{aligned}
$$

Knowing that the property alone, without any debt, is worth $883,990 to the marginal investor in the property market implies that the market's after-tax unlevered OCC is 6.79 percent. The IRR of an investment of $883,990 returns the property-level after-tax cash flows shown in column (7) of Exhibit 14-3. This compares to the property-level before-tax OCC of 8.60 percent in column (4).

Note that this does not imply that one could buy the property for $883,990 without taking out a loan. The property's market price is $936,893, its equilibrium value in the marketplace. The implication is that if you face a personal tax rate above 15 percent on your marginal income (from such a property investment), the acquisition at market value will be negative NPV from your IV perspective unless you take out a loan.

This information can now help us dissect the apartment deal for the typical marginal investor using valuation by components and value additivity. First, we need to group our cash flows into two categories: first, those that are relatively risky because they are subject to the volatility of the property and rental markets, and second, those that are relatively safe or fixed because they are essentially contractual or statutory. The former category includes the PBTCF and the tax without shields in columns (4) and (5). The latter includes the depreciation tax shields and the loan cash flows in columns (6) and (13). Together, these two categories add up to the total after-tax cash flows of the equity investor. The example is given in Exhibit 14-4.

To value the investment by components, we discount each type of cash flow stream at the market OCC appropriate for its type of risk and then add the resulting component present values. We use after-tax discount rates because we deal with after-tax cash flows. Assuming the investor is typical on the margin in the market, the IRRs shown at the bottom of the cash flow columns in the exhibit are the market's after-tax OCC rates appropriate for each cash flow component. Thus, the relatively risky cash flows are discounted at the 7.16 percent rate, which is the IRR on the PATCFs in column (7),[25] while the relatively safe cash flows are discounted at the 4.25 percent rate, which is the IRR

[25] Indeed, for the reasons noted in the previous section, it will often be easier and less prone to error to quantify NPV(Property) and NPV(Financing) separately and add these two components rather than attempting to quantify directly the NPV of the levered equity. At a minimum, the APV approach provides a good check on any direct quantification of the levered equity value. In particular, direct evaluation of NPV(Equity) should not generally imply a violation of the APV = 0 rule for MV-based valuations unless there is a clear reason to believe this rule does not apply.

EXHIBIT 14-3

Apartment Property Example Valuation by Components for Marginal Investor

	(1)	(2)	(3)	(4)	(5)	(6)	(7)	(8)	(9)	(10)	(11)	(12)	(13)
							(4) - (5) + (6)				(4)-(8)-(9)	(4)-(8)-(10)	(9)-(10)
year	**Property value**	**NOI**	**CapEx**	**PBTCF**	**Tax w/o shields**	**DTS**	**PATCF**	**Loan Balance**	**Loan DS**	**ITS**	**EBTCF**	**EATCF**	**LATCF**
0	$ 936,893			$ (936,893)			**$ (883,990)**	$ 702,670	$ (702,670)		$ (234,223)	$ (234,223)	**$(649,767)**
1	$ 988,129	$ 77,250	$ 15,450	$ 61,800	$ 27,038	$ 9,539	$ 44,302	$ 688,181	$ 49,293	$ 12,182	$ 12,507	$ 7,190	$ 37,111
2	$ 1,042,167	$ 79,568	$ 15,914	$ 63,654	$ 27,849	$ 9,539	$ 45,345	$ 672,952	$ 49,293	$ 11,922	$ 14,361	$ 7,974	$ 37,371
3	$ 1,099,160	$ 81,955	$ 16,391	$ 65,564	$ 28,684	$ 9,539	$ 46,419	$ 656,943	$ 49,293	$ 11,649	$ 16,271	$ 8,775	$ 37,643
4	$ 1,159,269	$ 84,413	$ 16,883	$ 67,531	$ 29,545	$ 9,539	$ 47,525	$ 640,115	$ 49,293	$ 11,363	$ 18,238	$ 9,595	$ 37,930
5	$ 1,222,666	$ 86,946	$ 17,389	$ 69,556	$ 30,431	$ 9,539	$ 48,665	$ 622,426	$ 49,293	$ 11,061	$ 20,264	$ 10,433	$ 38,231
6	$ 1,289,530	$ 89,554	$ 17,911	$ 71,643	$ 31,344	$ 9,539	$ 49,839	$ 603,833	$ 49,293	$ 10,745	$ 22,350	$ 11,290	$ 38,548
7	$ 1,360,051	$ 92,241	$ 120,000	$ (27,759)	$ 32,284	$ 9,539	$ (50,504)	$ 584,287	$ 49,293	$ 10,412	$ (77,052)	$ (89,386)	$ 38,881
8	$ 1,434,428	$ 95,008	$ 19,002	$ 76,006	$ 33,253	$ 9,539	$ 52,293	$ 563,742	$ 49,293	$ 10,062	$ 26,713	$ 13,062	$ 39,231
9	$ 1,512,872	$ 97,858	$ 19,572	$ 78,286	$ 34,250	$ 9,539	$ 53,575	$ 542,146	$ 49,293	$ 9,694	$ 28,994	$ 13,976	$ 39,599
10	$ 1,297,719	$ 100,794	$ 20,159	$ 1,313,468	$ 35,278	$ 9,539	$ 1,217,001	$ 519,445	$ 568,738	$ 9,307	$ 744,730	$ 657,571	$ 559,431
IRR				**8.60%**			**6.79%**		**4.94%**		**15.03%**	**11.17%**	**4.25%**

- **Step 1:** Calculate after-tax OCC of debt at (1-0.15)5% = 4.25%
- **Step 2:** Discount cash flows years 1 through 10 of column (13) using 4.25%
  - *This gives the IV of the loan at $744,644 (Year 0, column (13))*
- **Step 3:** Calculate NPV(Finance) = $702,670– $649,767 = +$52,903
- **Step 4:** According to APV rule: NPV(Property) = -$52,903
  - *Value of property-after-tax (colum n (7)) is, therefore: $936,893 – $52,903 = $883,990*

EXHIBIT 14-4
Apartment Property Example Cash Flow Components Grouped by Risk Category

	(4)–(5)		(6)–(13)	
	Risky		Fixed	
year	Cash flows	DCF (@6.79%)	Cash flows	DCF (@4.25%)
1	$ 34,763	$ 32,551	$ (27,572)	$ (26,448)
2	$ 35,805	$ 31,395	$ (27,831)	$ (25,608)
3	$ 36,880	$ 30,280	$ (28,104)	$ (24,805)
4	$ 37,986	$ 29,205	$ (28,391)	$ (24,037)
5	$ 39,126	$ 28,168	$ (28,692)	$ (23,301)
6	$ 40,299	$ 27,167	$ (29,009)	$ (22,598)
7	$ (60,044)	$ (37,903)	$ (29,342)	$ (21,926)
8	$ 42,753	$ 25,272	$ (29,692)	$ (21,283)
9	$ 44,036	$ 24,374	$ (30,060)	$ (20,668)
10	$ 1,278,190	$ 662,492	$ (549,891)	$ (362,674)
SUM(DCF)	$ 853,002		$ (573,349)	

on the loan after-tax cash flows in column (13). The risky cash flows thus have a present value of $853,002. The relatively safe cash flows have a value of $573,349, negative to the investor. The net difference of (rounded) $270 thousand is essentially the same as the value of the equity that is implied by discounting the EATCFs directly lumped together at their market after-tax levered OCC of 11.17 percent, as we saw regarding the investment value for the marginal investor described in Section 13.3 and Exhibit 13-5.

When we are dealing with market value, or investment value for marginal investors, the value additivity and valuation by components approach of Exhibit 14-4 or 14-3 should, in principle, produce the same equity value as the direct valuation of the equity as represented in column (12) of Exhibit 13-3 and the market value as discussed in Section 13.3. If there is a discrepancy between these two approaches, this suggests some disequilibrium or "supernormal" profit opportunity across the markets for property and debt. In reality, of course, real estate valuations cannot be determined so precisely. Combined with trading costs, this prevents minor valuation discrepancies from being immediately "arbitraged" away. Nevertheless, the two approaches are useful as a cross-check on one another to determine normative valuation. Furthermore, this valuation by components procedure can be applied in more complex circumstances to evaluate more uniquely structured financial arrangements, for example, with more than one layer or type of debt, provided one can come up with a reasonable estimate of the appropriate OCCs to apply as discount rates.

TEXT BOX 14.2 CORPORATE REAL ESTATE: THE OWN-VERSUS-RENT DECISION

In the real estate investment industry, "corporate real estate" refers to real estate owned by non-real estate corporations or companies, that is, firms that are not primarily in the business of real estate development or investment. This includes a large amount of commercial and industrial property in most countries. A very important question in corporate real estate management is the buy-versus-lease (or, more generally, own-versus-rent) decision. Broadly, this is the question of how much space and which space the company should own instead of rent. A corporation may face this question from either the buy or sell side, as the possibility of engaging in sale-leaseback transactions for space the company already owns enables consideration of the sale of corporate property without giving up the necessary usage and control of the space.

There are many considerations in answering the own-versus-rent question, both at a macro policy level and at the micro-level of specific space decisions. Many of these considerations are beyond the scope of this text. However, there is an important financial economics component to the buy-versus-lease question. Whatever other considerations are important in a given own-versus-rent question is also a micro-level real estate investment decision. Should the corporation invest in a given real property asset (that it would use) or not (and therefore rent the space)?

Viewed from this perspective, we hope it is clear that the after-tax levered equity investment analysis framework presented in this chapter is relevant to analyzing the corporate own-versus-rent decision. Indeed, from this perspective, holding the underlying real estate investment economics neutral (i.e., assuming market value pricing), the decision's impact on the corporation's value will be driven by the particular income tax situation that the corporation's investors face. Assuming that the real estate in question would be purchased (or sold, in the case of a sale-leaseback) at fair market value (zero NPV transaction from a market value perspective), the NPV from an investment value perspective will essentially equal the negative of the change in the present value of the future tax revenues the government can expect to receive because of the property tenure status. When applied to a corporate own-versus-rent question, the framework presented in this chapter will show this impact. The details of the application of this methodology in this context are presented in the online Appendix. Here in the text, we will content ourselves with enumerating the key guiding principles of the own-versus-rent evaluation:

- Discount after-tax cash flows at after-tax discount rates to compute NPV.
- Include both levels of taxation: corporate and personal.
- Discount cash flow components at OCC rates reflecting their risk (not always at the corporate WACC).

These principles can be applied using the valuation by components and adjusted present value (APV) procedures described in Section 14.2. This will provide a coherent framework that ensures consistency of the own-versus-rent evaluation with equilibrium (market) pricing within and across the three asset markets relevant to the decision: the property market, the bond market, and the stock market in which the corporation's shares (do or could) trade. The inclusion in the analysis framework of both levels of taxation, corporate and personal, is more obviously necessary in the case of real estate than other types of corporate assets because real estate assets trade directly in a well-functioning asset market in which the marginal participants typically face less overall taxation than investors in profitable taxed corporations. (Recall our analysis of the bond market in Section 14.2 in which we likened our "tax-disadvantaged investor" to a corporation that results in double-taxation to its investors.)

When these principles are applied to the typical own-versus-rent decision of a profitable taxed corporation in the United States under the tax rules prevailing in the early 2020s, the result is typically that the corporation should lease rather than own, from a tax perspective. However, the magnitude of the value impact is typically rather small when one also considers the effect of property ownership on the corporation's debt capacity (recall that borrowing is a positive NPV transaction for the tax-disadvantaged investor). There are particular circumstances where the evaluation can turn out the other way, depending on the specific parameters of the micro-level decision, such as the duration of the anticipated corporate usage of the space, the magnitude of depreciation allowances that can be used, the price/ rent multiple in the current property market, and both the expected capital gains and capital gains tax rates (among other factors). It is also important to recognize that other considerations besides the narrow tax-based financial considerations can be important in the final decision about corporate ownership of a given space. If a corporation should decide that it wants to reduce its exposure to real estate market investment risk while continuing to own its corporate real estate, a new mechanism for accomplishing this is beginning to be marketed in some countries, in the form of real estate index return swaps, an investment derivative product that allows hedging of commercial real estate property market risk.

14.3 CHAPTER SUMMARY

You can now unfasten your seatbelts. We have landed. Chapter 14 dealt with some intense and subtle issues. This is the kind of thing you must read more than once and think about it for a while. We sympathize. However, the topics addressed here are obviously important and fundamental. Although they are of academic interest, they also carry important implications for real-world investment decision-making. Furthermore, some of the most exciting opportunities in real estate investment can be found in these unique characteristics of real estate investment. If you study this chapter carefully, you should come away with a deeper and more accurate understanding of and insight into micro-level real estate investment decision-making and how real estate asset markets work. Smart people can make use of such a level of knowledge in the real world!

KEY TERMS

- Market value (MV)
- Opportunity value
- Investment value (IV)
- Opportunity cost of capital (OCC)
- Second-most-motivated buyer
- Marginal investors
- Intramarginal investors
- Entrepreneurial profit

STUDY QUESTIONS

In Your Own Words

14.1 Why is market value (MV) an important way to conceive of and measure asset value for investors in commercial real estate?

14.2 Why is investment value (IV) an important way to conceive of and measure asset value for investors in commercial real estate?

14.3 Suppose a certain site has a McDonald's restaurant on it (equipped with the usual golden arches, etc.). As a McDonald's, the site can generate $50,000 per year, net cash. In any other use, it can only generate at most $40,000 per year, and it would cost $20,000 to remove the golden arches. Assuming a 10% required return:

a. What is the market value of this property?

b. What is its investment value to McDonald's? (Hint: Use the perpetuity formula: V = *CF/r.*)

14.4 In the previous question, assume that the property is currently owned by McDonald's.

a. What is McDonald's expected NPV from selling the property, evaluated from an MV perspective?

b. What is McDonald's expected NPV from selling the property, evaluated from an IV perspective?

14.5 Now assume that the property described in Question 14.3 is owned by someone other than McDonald's, a "typical" real estate investor by the name of Bob.

a. What is Bob's expected NPV from selling the property, evaluated from an MV perspective?

b. What is Bob's expected NPV from selling the property, evaluated from an IV perspective?

c. What if Bob tries to sell the property to McDonald's?

14.6 What are the general (and defining) characteristics of marginal participants in an asset market?

14.7 What are the general necessary conditions for a real estate investment transaction to involve substantial positive NPV for at least one side of the deal without involving negative NPV for the other side?

14.8 Name at least three sources or causes of real estate transaction prices deviating from the market value of the asset.

14.9 What is meant by the adjusted present value (APV) approach to extending the NPV rule to encompass project financing? What is the relationship of the APV technique to the value additivity principle?

14.10 In valuing income property rigorously with discounted cash flow analysis, is it necessary for "marginal" investors to use after-tax cash flows? Why or why not? What about "intramarginal" investors?

14.11 Explain whether the following statement is true or false and why: One reason to borrow money to finance a real estate investment is that you obtain valuable interest tax shields that save you from paying some taxes you would otherwise owe.

14.12 Why do the interest tax shields associated with debt financing have a positive value for the typical profitable corporation but not for the typical taxed individual investing directly in the property market?

14.13 If income taxes were the only consideration, would you expect to find profitable taxed corporations owning much of their own real estate? Why or why not?

Check Your Knowledge

14.14 Which of the following best illustrates a scenario where IV > MV?

A) A property is located in a high-demand area.

B) An investor owns adjacent land that increases value with the acquisition of the property.

C) The property is newly renovated.

D) A competing investor underbids on the property.

14.15 What is a primary advantage of using the liberal approach to purchase decisions when IV > MV?

A) It allows for better negotiation tactics.

B) It enables acquisitions based on unique investor-specific value.

C) It avoids paying any premium on MV.

D) It minimizes financing costs.

14.16 How does an investor's tax rate impact the NPV of debt financing?
- A) A higher tax rate decreases the NPV.
- B) A higher tax rate increases the NPV of debt due to tax shields.
- C) Tax rate has no effect on NPV.
- D) It lowers the IV of the property.

14.17 Which of the following cash flows are considered risky?
- A) Fixed mortgage payments.
- B) Maintenance expenses.
- C) Capital appreciation of property.
- D) Annual Depreciation.

14.18 How does competition affect property prices in a well-functioning market?
- A) It drives prices below equilibrium.
- B) It forces MV to increase.
- C) It brings prices to equilibrium based on marginal investors.
- D) It results in speculative pricing.

14.19 If a certain property is put up for sale, there is a 50% chance it will sell for $900,000 and a 50% chance it will sell for $1,100,000.
- a. What is the market value of this property?
- b. What is the standard deviation of the random noise in this property's price as a percentage of its market value?
- c. If the property sells for $900,000, what was the ex-post NPV from the market value perspective for the seller and the buyer?
- d. If the property sells for $1,100,000, what was the ex-post NPV from the market value perspective for the seller and the buyer?
- e. What is the ex-ante NPV from the market value perspective?

14.20 Consider an apartment property that costs $400,000, of which $300,000 is structure value (the rest is land). Suppose an investor expects to hold this property for five years and then sell it for at least what he paid for it (without putting any significant capital into the property). If the investor's marginal income tax rate is 35%, and depreciation recapture is taxed at 25%, what is the present value, as of the time of purchase, of the depreciation tax shields obtained directly by this investor during the 5-year expected holding period (including the payback in the reversion)? Assume taxes are paid annually, with the first tax payment due 1 year from present, and assume that DTS for this investor is effectively riskless, and the investor's after-tax borrowing rate is 5%.

14.21 Consider a commercial (nonresidential) property that costs $1 million with an initial before-tax yield of 9% (based on NOI) and an expected growth rate of 2.5% per year (in income and value). Ignoring capital improvements and selling expenses, develop a 10-year proforma for before-tax and after-tax property and equity cash flows. The relevant tax rates are 35% on annual operations, 15% for capital gains, and 25% for depreciation recapture. Assume mortgage financing of 75% of the property price with a 10% interest-only loan, and that land is worth 20% of the property value.
- a. Use the proforma to determine the ex-ante before-tax IRR of the unlevered property investment.
- b. Use the proforma to determine the after-tax IRR of the unlevered property investment.
- c. Use the ratio of the ATIRR calculated in (b) divided by the BTIRR calculated in (a) to determine the after-tax borrowing rate for the investor (by applying this ratio to the loan rate).
- d. Apply the after-tax borrowing rate you just calculated to determine the present value of the DTS during the projected 10-year holding period (including the payback of the DTS in the reversion).

e. Compute the implicit PV (DTS) component in the reversion resale price of the property by treating the present value of the DTS you computed in (d) as a constant-growth perpetuity that recurs once every 10 years with a growth rate of 2.5% per year and a discount rate to present value equal to the ATIRR you calculated in (b).
f. Add the answers to (d) and (e) to arrive at the total component of DTS in the value of the property, as a percentage of the property value.
g. Compute the before-tax ex ante IRR of the levered investment in this property.
h. Compute the after-tax ex ante IRR of the levered equity in this property.
i. Compute the ratio of the AT/BT in the levered IRR, and note the difference between this ratio and the unlevered equivalent. Do you think this is an argument for debt financing for this property investment for this investor?

14.22 (APV Decision Rule) A seller has offered you a $1.5 million interest-only 7-year loan at 6% (annual payments), when market interest rates on such loans are 7%. You face a 35% marginal income tax rate.
a. Basing your decision on market values, how much more should you be willing to pay for the property than you otherwise think it is worth, due to the financing offer?
b. Answer the same question only now basing your answer on investment value rather than market value. You may assume that the investor is typical of the marginal investors in the property market, and faces a tax rate similar to that of marginal investors in the bond market.

Chapter Case: Kai Real Estate's Development Options

Kai Real Estate is evaluating a downtown property with potential for two different uses. The site is priced at $3 million, which reflects the amount a typical investor would pay in the current market. Kai Real Estate is weighing two development options:

1. Residential Complex: The residential project would generate an annual PBTCF of $250,000 for 15 years, with a terminal value of $2 million at the end of the project. The OCC for residential development is 6%.
2. Mixed-Use Commercial and Retail Space: Following the current zoning regulation, this development would generate a PBTCF of $350,000 for 15 years and a terminal value of $3 million. Kai Real Estate has secured special development rights from the local government that reduce zoning restrictions and allow for higher density construction. This advantage is exclusive to Kai and enables them to add 20% more leasable space in the mixed-use project, increasing its PBTCF by $70,000 annually. However, this project is riskier, with an OCC of 8%.

Both projects qualify for annual depreciation tax deductions. Kai plans to finance 60% of the project cost with a 4% interest loan, while the corporate tax rate is 35%.

1. What is the market value (MV) of the property for Kai Real Estate?
   A) $2 million
   B) $3 million
   C) $4 million
   D) $5 million
2. What is the annual PBTCF for the mixed-use project, including Sapphire's unique development advantage?
   A) $250,000
   B) $350,000
   C) $420,000
   D) $490,000

3. Why does Kai Real Estate's IV for the mixed-use project exceed its MV?
   A) Sapphire's exclusive development rights increase the leasable space and PBTCF.
   B) The market value includes financing benefits.
   C) Kai can reduce depreciation costs.
   D) Sapphire's OCC is lower than the market average.
4. How does the property-before-tax (PBT) approach simplify Sapphire's analysis of these projects?
   A) It excludes financing and tax effects, focusing only on PBTCF.
   B) It incorporates financing effects like tax shields.
   C) It calculates net cash flows after taxes.
   D) It evaluates projects based on market value.
5. What is the primary factor contributing to Sapphire's entrepreneurial profit in the mixed-use project?
   A) The $70,000 annual PBTCF increase from special development rights.
   B) The lower OCC compared to residential development.
   C) The depreciation tax shield.
   D) The loan's interest tax shield.
6. What assumption is true for a marginal investor in this scenario?
   A) Their IV equals the MV of $3 million.
   B) Their IV is higher than $3 million due to unique synergies.
   C) They are unwilling to buy the property.
   D) They only consider the residential project.
7. Why is Kai Real Estate considered an intramarginal investor in this case?
   A) They have no competition for the property.
   B) Their IV exceeds MV due to their unique development rights.
   C) They only consider low-risk projects.
   D) They are willing to sell below MV.
8. Why does the mixed-use project have a higher OCC (8%) compared to the residential project (6%)?
   A) Mixed-use projects involve lower risks.
   B) Retail and commercial properties are more volatile than residential properties.
   C) Mixed-use projects guarantee higher returns.
   D) Residential projects are always preferred by marginal investors.
9. If Kai Real Estate finances the mixed-use project with debt, what adjustment would the APV method make?
   A) It would increase NPV by including tax shields on interest payments.
   B) It would reduce PBTCF due to financing costs.
   C) It would eliminate the OCC calculation.
   D) It would ignore synergies and entrepreneurial profit.
10. What is the primary role of marginal investors in determining the market value (MV) of the property?
    A) They set the equilibrium price where investment value (IV) equals market value (MV).
    B) They negotiate for exclusive development rights to enhance property value.
    C) They achieve entrepreneurial profit through strategic synergies.
    D) They purchase properties at prices lower than market value.

15 Advanced Topics II
Capital Structure

CHAPTER OUTLINE

LEARNING OBJECTIVES

After reading this, you should understand:

- Gain an understanding of human capital versus debt or equity capital.
- Gain an understanding of how human capital might enhance investment value and NPV.
- How debt capital enhances diversification.
- Passive versus active investor objectives in terms of control and governance.
- How debt can be viewed as a disciplined force for investors.
- How leverage can enhance incentives for investment managers.
- How liquidity provides strategic advantages.
- How the cost and probability of financial distress are priced into mortgage loans.
- Only unexpected inflation will benefit borrowers at the expense of lenders.
- Expected inflation benefits neither, even if it is historically high.
- How mortgages and equity positions can be differentiated in terms of priority and risk positions.
- How Mezz debt is used.
- How general partners and limited partners are paid.
- How multi-tiered capital stacks can provide risks and returns that match the preferences of various investors.

Chapter 15 continues our exploration of the role of debt in real estate equity investment, which began in Chapter 12. It moves beyond simple debt to consider other typical types of finance vehicles used in real estate project finance. In this chapter, we will consider both the big picture of why

DOI: 10.1201/9781003643838-18

different types of investors might want to (or not want to) employ debt and other similar vehicles to finance their real estate investments, as well as examine more "nuts and bolts" of how micro-level capital structure (project finance) is typically done in the global institutional real estate investment business. These questions are traditionally considered in corporate finance under **capital structure**, which is classically defined as the relative use of debt versus equity financing of publicly traded corporations, including the closely related question of how much financing should be externally sourced versus internally generated from retained earnings. The present chapter examines this topic from real estate investment and investors' perspectives. (Additional discussion relevant particularly to REITs' capital structure will be addressed in Chapter 26.)

As usual, some of the peculiar aspects of real estate and the context in which real estate investment typically occurs bring some unique considerations regarding capital structure. For example, much real estate investment is made directly, that is, by **ultimate investors** themselves or via relatively passive pass-through vehicles such as partnerships or funds. Thus, we will focus here primarily on the micro-level of individual deals or projects, which is the level at which capital structure and financing are often addressed in the real estate investment business. Also, the nature of the underlying physical assets—which are relatively easy for outsiders to observe, understand, and evaluate (thanks in part to a well-functioning direct market for these assets)—has implications for using secured debt and other such project financing vehicles. It is interesting to see how various types of investors and investment vehicles can be combined to structure the financing of complex deals, such as large-scale real estate development projects, to allocate to each class of investor the type of risk and return they are seeking for their investment in combination with the kind of control and incentives that will facilitate the successful investment outcome of the overall project. Finally, we will briefly address how typical deal financing structures have evolved recently with changes in the financial system and investment industry.

The plan of attack in Chapter 15 is first to survey the major issues relevant to using debt in real estate investment and then focus on the nuts and bolts of more complex capital structures. We have already discussed some of the important issues regarding the use of debt in our discussion of leverage in Chapter 12 and our analysis of equity after-tax investment in Chapter 13. There, we noted that real estate equity is a very different investment product from real estate debt, and some of these differences are magnified by leverage. For example, using debt financing will typically increase the risk and average total return in the equity investment, especially the growth component of that return. These characteristics may be appealing to certain investors. Our discussion in Chapter 14 also treated the classic mainstay of corporate finance capital structure analysis at the micro-level, the relationship between debt financing and the investor's income taxes, suggesting that the tax-based value of debt financing may be less than is often believed.

In this chapter, we will introduce some further considerations. We will begin by considering the implications of **equity capital constraints**. This topic is often skipped or lightly passed over in corporate finance textbooks. Large publicly traded corporations do not usually face a constraint on their availability of equity capital for financing good investments. However, this topic is worthy of consideration for many real estate investors. Next, we will introduce several other important issues, such as the costs of financial distress and the roles of liquidity, management incentives, and inflation. Finally, we will zero in on the nuts-and-bolts level again, this time presenting typical complex capital structures that gained prominence for project-level finance in the institutional investment world in the twenty-first century, including more types of capital than just traditional pure equity and pure debt.

15.1 DEBT WHEN THERE IS AN EQUITY CAPITAL CONSTRAINT

Large publicly traded corporations can almost always raise capital rather easily to finance positive NPV investment opportunities, and they usually have a choice of raising either equity or debt. For example, equity capital can be raised in the public markets through new stock issuance, or it can be raised privately through joint ventures. On the other hand, individual investors and tax-exempt institutions may not have this kind of freedom. If they want to expand their investments beyond what their own equity can provide, debt may effectively be their only alternative. Even their ability to borrow money may be sharply constrained unless the debt is secured by tangible assets such as real estate.

In such cases, debt financing represents a way to break through an equity capital constraint. But why would this be valuable? Why should investors want to invest more capital than they already own? Apart from the leverage issue already discussed (i.e., to move up and out along the security market line to an investment position of greater expected return but greater risk), there are two reasons: (1) to take advantage of positive NPV investment opportunities and (2) to diversify their holdings of risky assets. Let's consider each of these in turn.

15.1.1 Debt to Obtain Positive Equity NPV

Although positive NPV opportunities may be rare when evaluated from a market value (MV) perspective, we suggested in Chapter 14 that they may be available from an investment value (IV) perspective for entrepreneurial or tax-advantaged developers and investors. Furthermore, the "lumpiness" of real estate investment, typically requiring the purchase of "whole assets," often presents investors with capital requirements greater than their available equity. In short, they would have to forgo positive NPV opportunities if not for debt financing.

Related to this point is a consideration that is often particularly important at the level of small-to-moderate-scale individual real estate entrepreneurs. This is the possibility of leveraging the investor's own "human capital." For some investors, the effect of leverage can extend beyond the leveraging of their financial capital invested in commercial property. It can also leverage its human capital through its property management or development abilities.

In general, the term **human capital** refers to the productive abilities and skills, or valuable expertise, that individuals acquire that can be used to generate income. The "return" on human capital is typically in wages, salaries, or other earned income. Still, it may come in any form of wealth enhancement. Some individuals possess human capital in their ability to analyze opportunities, creatively add value through better tenant mixes and relationships, and use their skills to improve property, and manage or develop commercial property. Perhaps your human capital will be enhanced by absorbing the material in this text? For such individuals, acquiring property is not only an investment of their financial capital but also a means to obtain a return on their human capital. By owning or developing property, they effectively guarantee themselves some degree of employment as property managers or developers. With the previously noted constraints and difficulties in acquiring equity capital, using debt financing allows such individuals to purchase larger physical quantities of property than would otherwise be the case. This allows them to perform more property management or development services and thereby obtain more return on their human capital.

Although small companies are most likely to face a capital constraint, larger entities can also use debt to leverage property management or real estate development human capital within the firm. Real estate operating companies (REOCs), some private equity funds, and vertically integrated REITs that are quite large in scale often argue, in effect, that their unique real estate skills enable them to "create value." Some might claim they are better at design, others at tenant mix, others at more efficient operations, and tenant retention.

How would the leveraging of human capital show up in the quantitative DCF and NPV mechanics we described in previous chapters? In practice, it may be difficult to distinguish this component. However, in principle, the present value of the return on human capital should be a component in a positive NPV calculation of an appropriate deal at the micro-level, evaluated from the IV perspective. Investors' human capital gives them a unique ability to profit from a given investment. One way to account for this is to define multiple "profit centers" for the investment entity, some of which derive from entity-level operations as distinct from passive asset-level investment. Thus, the property "operating expenses" that are pure cash outflows from the asset-level investment perspective may contain an element of profit from the entity-level operational perspective. This is most obvious when the firm engages in third-party property or development operations "for a fee" for other property owners. Still, it may also be a component of investment profitability for particular investors on their own account.

Recall from our discussion of IV and MV in Chapter 14 that the NPV of a property acquisition equals IV — MV when evaluated from an IV perspective. And recall that, at the level of individual deals, it is often most practical to think of MV as being determined by what the second-most-motivated buyer is willing to pay. In this circumstance, the human capital of the first-most-motivated buyer may elevate her IV above the MV cost of the acquisition. In this framework, the cost of acquiring the relevant human capital has already been paid (i.e., it is a "sunk cost" in economics terminology). Thus, the return on this capital in the form of the unique ability to earn additional income from the property investment represents a positive component in the investor's NPV.

Assuming this human capital return (measured in dollars) is proportional to the property investment's physical size or dollar value, the positive NPV component due to human capital will be greater the larger the underlying property investment. Hence, to the extent that equity capital availability is constrained below the level of exhaustion of the investor's human capital, debt financing enables additional positive NPV to be realized.

15.1.2 Debt and Diversification

It can be valuable to break through a capital constraint on real estate equity investment for another important reason. Debt financing may be the only way equity-constrained investors can *diversify their real estate investments*. Due to the previously noted lumpy nature of direct real estate investment in the private property market, where whole assets must be purchased, even a moderately large amount of equity capital may only be sufficient to purchase one or a few individual properties. However, mortgages can typically be obtained for large fractions of the total value of the underlying property, enabling debt capital to stretch the investor's equity significantly and facilitating diversification across a greater number of individual properties. For example, without debt, $10 million worth of equity can only purchase two $5 million properties. With a 75 percent LTV ratio, the same $10 million equity can be diversified across eight different $5 million properties.

Diversification is a desirable part of any investment strategy, no matter how risk-averse or aggressive the investor is. It is a rare phenomenon in economics because it offers a "free lunch." Diversification allows you to increase your expected return without increasing your risk, or vice versa, to reduce your risk exposure without reducing your expected return.[1]

An important point should be considered regarding the diversification argument for using debt. Any diversification financed by debt should generally be in the form of equity investments in risky assets, such as property or stocks. It generally does not make sense to finance "diversification into bonds" using debt. Do not "borrow in order to lend." If you simultaneously borrow money to finance a real estate investment while investing in bonds or mortgage-backed securities as well, you cancel out one position with the other while paying the **banker's spread** (the difference between the borrowing and lending interest rate).

15.1.3 Limitations on the Equity Constraint Argument for the Use of Debt

Clearly, there is a powerful argument for using debt financing in real estate equity investment if that is the only way the investor can realize a positive NPV equity opportunity or diversify his equity investments. But how widespread are genuine constraints on the supply of equity capital, particularly when positive NPV equity investment opportunities are available? The existence of such constraints reflects a shortcoming in the capital markets. Getting rid of such shortcomings provides profit opportunities in the investment industry. Has somebody missed an opportunity here?

---

[1] This will be discussed in more depth in Chapter 22.

In fact, constraints on equity capital are not as widespread as is often assumed in real estate, even for relatively small individual investors. Comingled real estate investment funds, limited partnerships, tenancy-in-common funds, and syndications of various types, in addition to private and public REITs, are among the many vehicles widely used to funnel equity capital into commercial real estate. Real estate entrepreneurs are adept at setting up partnerships, funds, and corporations of various types, including limited partnerships in which the "outside" equity capital providers have very little control over property or asset management. This may be difficult for very small individual investors just starting. Still, once a successful investment track record can be demonstrated, it is much easier to obtain equity partners.

REITs and large publicly traded firms are not the only ones with virtually unconstrained access to equity capital, especially if positive NPV equity opportunities are available. Indeed, access to equity capital may depend more on the seeker's track record than on how its equity is traded. However, there is probably a bias in favor of larger-sized entities. Unsuccessful REITs have little ability to raise equity by issuing new shares, but large firms can make more small mistakes before investors sour on them.

Nor is it necessary even for small real estate investors to use debt to diversify their real estate investments across numerous individual properties. Diversified real estate equity investment vehicles, from publicly traded REITs to private unit trusts and partnerships, exist as alternatives to debt-financed diversification. Therefore, the diversification argument for debt financing is not a "pure" argument favoring using debt. It must involve other considerations, such as control or information sharing, or the type of income tax considerations described in Chapters 13 and 14. This again suggests that positive NPV equity opportunities and human capital considerations will likely be involved.

To summarize, equity capital is rarely completely constrained in an absolute sense when positive NPV opportunities are available. Rather, there may be management control and governance issues, and information revelation and sharing that may convince some investors not to look for additional equity partners when facing a positive NPV opportunity. This may be perceived as an "effective equity constraint." In other circumstances, however, an absolute equity constraint may indeed be said to exist. Pension funds may be an important example.

15.2 OTHER CONSIDERATIONS REGARDING THE ROLE OF DEBT IN REAL ESTATE INVESTMENTS

In addition to the previously described considerations of leverage and risk/return preference matching (Chapters 1 and 12), income tax considerations (Chapters 13 and 14), and dealing with capital constraints or management control concerns (this chapter), several other considerations are important in the overall picture of the role of debt in real estate investment. Some of the major considerations will be described in the present section.[2]

15.2.1 Debt as an Incentive and Disciplinary Tool for Management

One argument for using debt in real estate investment is that leverage can be a tool to help give incentives or discipline to property asset managers (management incentives). This argument differs fascinatingly from our previous discussion in that it is based on human behavioral considerations beyond the classical economic assumption of rational behavior. In particular, the idea is that real estate equity investors, as owners/managers of property, behave irrationally (or sub-optimally) when faced with lower levels of risk and reward in their investment. Here is how the argument goes.

[2] Some prominent considerations in corporate finance are left out of the following discussion, such as the possible "signaling" role of the use of debt finance and the resulting "pecking order" theory suggesting a preference for debt finance over external equity. It is unclear that such considerations are as important for real estate due to the different tax and investment holding environments, as discussed earlier.

You have seen how debt increases the risk and return potential in the property equity owner's position. Indeed, as it is typically possible to borrow large fractions of the underlying property value, risk and reward can be greatly magnified through debt. At least as an approximation, an equity investment with a 75 percent LTV loan will have four times the risk and reward potential of an unlevered position in the property and twice the risk and reward even of a 50 percent LTV investment (100 percent debt/equity ratio). Yet property investments with 75 percent LTV ratios are not considered abnormally risky, and they are not uncommon in the real world. If such highly leveraged equity is not abnormally risky, imagine how little the risk is in the underlying property assets free and clear of debt. Without debt, much commercial property presents a very low risk, with correspondingly low reward potential.

The property's low risk and reward potential is particularly noticeable compared to other productive underlying physical assets that require active management, such as the typical industrial or technology and service corporations that trade on the major stock exchanges. Furthermore, the argument continues that it is relatively straightforward to manage properties. Compared to managing, say, a high-tech firm or multinational industrial corporation, there is limited scope for the creative possibilities of what can be done or how the income-earning capability of the underlying assets can be made to grow. Managers can't usually make major mistakes besides doing obviously stupid things. Indeed, this characteristic of real estate is probably a major reason lenders are willing to loan such a high percentage of the underlying asset value in real estate.

In short, in the absence of leverage, real estate from a management perspective may actually be perceived, consciously or subconsciously, as a bit boring. Properties alone are not likely to attract the most creative management talent, people willing to work hard and take risks to advance a long-term career path. With so little risk and scope for management impact, this argument suggests that property owners/managers could get lazy over time. They may let opportunities to improve the profitability of the underlying properties slip by. They might not notice or pursue an opportunity that only improves property cash flow by 1 percent or overlook or fail to correct a mistake that reduces asset value by only 1 percent. They may take the attitude of "Why fix something that is not broken," leading to less experimentation and innovation.

However, sufficient leverage can change this picture, according to the argument. Leverage (and lots of it) can make these stodgy underlying assets interesting or even exciting. As we have seen in Chapter 12, sufficient leverage can turn low-risk, low-growth underlying assets into high-risk, high-growth investments from the perspective of the equity owner/manager of the property. This can turn those 1 percent impacts into 4 percent impacts (e.g., with a 75 percent LTV ratio debt). Little things start becoming more noticeable. Managers face much more incentive to pay attention to details and opportunities. If you "borrow to the hilt," gearing the equity up to leverage ratios of three or four, those cozy cash flow margins become much thinner. Managers must stay on their toes and occasionally get quite creative to make the necessary profits and avoid losing their equity by default. In other words, debt makes real estate exciting (at least for fully operational, up-and-running properties)! This excitement makes property owners/managers do their jobs more efficiently and effectively. This, in turn, enhances productivity and the value of the underlying real physical assets. In short, through debt, real value is potentially created. If the amount of debt is right, not too little or too much, this could increase the size of the total pie for both debt and equity investors.

This argument in favor of debt applies in principle to small individual entrepreneurs, large corporations, and institutions such as REITs. It is relevant to managing individual property assets and portfolio assets at both the property management and asset management levels.

15.2.2 Debt and Liquidity

We have shown how the WACC (weighted average cost of capital) model can be used to quantify how debt increases the risk of equity investments. But there is another cost of debt that is closely related to the increase in risk, but more difficult to quantify, although it is no less real. Debt generally results in a loss of liquidity for the equity investor.

Why is this a problem? Well, it may not be for an investor who is very liquid overall or for one who only borrows a small fraction of the underlying property value. However, it is often possible to borrow large fractions of the value of income-producing properties. Such debt can result in a serious loss in liquidity for the borrower. **Liquidity** in this context refers to one's ability to quickly convert one's net worth into cash without suffering a loss of value. Investors have liquidity when the value of their assets, especially their readily marketable assets such as cash and securities (sometimes called "liquid assets"), comfortably exceeds the value of their liabilities. *Liquidity is desirable for investors because it provides* **decision flexibility**.

In general, lack of liquidity, or illiquidity, is one of the major concerns about direct real estate investment compared to stocks and bonds, for example. While the typical investor can sell stocks or bonds virtually immediately at full value, selling a commercial property at full value may take months (remember from Chapter 1 that the average time to sell for commercial property is 6 months). However, provided you have *not already borrowed much against a property you own*, you can generally convert much of the equity value of a real estate investment into cash relatively quickly and at relatively little transaction cost without selling the property at all by taking out a mortgage on it. Thus, one way to at least partially "cure" the illiquidity problem in real estate investments is not to lever the initial purchase of the property, holding the debt capacity "in reserve" for a time when it is more needed. In other words, *you can borrow later if you don't borrow now*. Thus, keeping debt as low as possible gives the investor strategic and tactical decision flexibility and control. This is particularly important in the face of inefficiency in asset markets.

In previous chapters, we noted how property market prices sometimes "bubble up" above their fundamental values and sometimes "crash" below their true value. Such cyclicality may make property markets more predictable than security markets. As noted in the supplemental materials of Chapter 14, there are dangers and opportunities in the real estate asset market, such as inefficiency and predictability. Those who maintain liquidity are likely to be more able to take advantage of the opportunity and are less likely to fall victim to the danger. The principal danger is that one may pay too much for a property and then be forced to sell it at the bottom of the cycle. The most likely reason an investor would be forced to sell when the market is bad is that his creditors are demanding payment, and the investor lacks sufficient cash (i.e., liquidity) to come up with the money owed. On the other hand, a more liquid investor will be able to take advantage of bargain buys when the market is down. Indeed, this point applies even apart from cyclical opportunities in real estate markets. Favorable investment opportunities in the form of individual positive NPV opportunities do not tend to wait long, and even with the use of debt, the investor must typically come up with some equity cash. Taking advantage of such opportunities requires liquidity. This, in turn, requires keeping indebtedness low.

While the liquidity argument against the use of debt applies to all investors in principle, it is certainly less important for investors who, by their very nature, tend to be highly liquid, such as pension funds of growing corporations, for example. Also, this argument may not be as applicable to individual investors making real estate investments via relatively liquid vehicles such as REITs. On the other hand, the liquidity argument applies at the entity level of the REITs themselves, as they invest directly in the relatively illiquid private property market.

While flexibility argues for minimizing the use of debt as a general policy, there is another side to the coin in the relationship between debt and liquidity in real estate investment. The illiquidity of the property itself, combined with the ability to borrow secured debt at high loan-to-value ratios, enables debt to play a useful role in allowing investors to partially liquefy their real estate investment holdings without actually selling these equity investments. Mortgages can be a useful vehicle to "cash out" a large portion of the capital gains an investor has incurred over the years in property investment while still holding onto the investment. However, it must be remembered that this practice brings with it the leverage and loss of flexibility (i.e., the ability to do the same thing later) previously discussed.

15.2.3 Cost of Financial Distress

The argument in Section 15.2.1 about the incentive benefits of debt suggests that human behavioral characteristics may cause debt to actually add real value to the underlying property investments. This is a controversial idea because it is difficult to quantify or prove and goes against the classical economic assumption of rational human behavior (in some sense). On the other hand, another argument, which is much less controversial, points out that debt, at least at a sufficiently high LTV, brings deadweight costs onto the underlying property investment. This potential cost of debt is often referred to as the **cost of financial distress**, or **COFD** for short.

There are two fundamental sources of COFD. One is the deadweight burden of **third-party costs**, such as legal and administrative fees, in the event of default, **foreclosure**, or **bankruptcy** caused by the existence of the debt. These legal and administrative costs potentially burden both the equity and debt investors. The second source of COFD is the **agency cost** associated with conflicts of interest that can arise between equity and debt investors at high LTV ratios. This cost is well described in most corporate finance texts. Because of the existence of **limited liability**, equity investors with highly levered positions face little downside risk from high-risk investments on the part of the corporation, thereby exposing the corporation's debt holders to most of the downside. The result can be a skewing of incentives to the detriment of the firm's overall value (that is, to the sum of debt and equity value). In the case of real property, for example, equity investors may lose their incentive to seek good long-term tenants and to maintain or upgrade the property optimally.

The third-party costs of default, foreclosure, and agency costs arise in an expectational or probabilistic sense well before they materialize. The mere possibility of their occurrence affects the present value of the debt and equity. Although such costs fall largely on debt holders ex-post (when and if they ever actually occur), their ex-ante impact at the time a loan is taken out falls on the equity investor, as lenders factor in the expected COFD in the interest rates and origination fees they charge for issuing debt.

As a result of these considerations of the cost of financial distress, we can say for certain that 100 percent debt financing (even if it were possible) would never be optimal, even for the borrower (at least in a well-functioning debt market).[3] How much less than 100 percent is the optimal level of debt depends on the relative strengths and importance of the likely costs of financial distress and the other pros and cons of debt we have been discussing in this chapter.

In this regard, it is important to note that fully operational commercial real estate assets (so-called "stabilized" or "core" assets) can probably take on higher levels of debt than other more management-intensive or more volatile underlying assets without raising a significant expectation of financial distress costs. As noted in Section 15.2.1, fully operational real estate assets are relatively low in volatility, and their management is relatively straightforward, presenting managers with relatively little opportunity to make major mistakes. The relative simplicity of property and asset management also makes it easy for outside investors, such as debt holders, to observe and monitor the quality of such management. This transparency reduces the potential conflict of interest between equity and debt investors and enables a larger fraction of underlying asset value to be borrowed before COFD becomes significant.

---

[3] In real estate investment circles, one sometimes hears stories about "100 percent debt financing." In fact, 100 percent debt financing for individual projects is generally a sort of illusion. Either a significant (hidden) equity contribution is, in fact, being made (perhaps "in kind"), or the lender is counting on recourse to the borrower's other assets and income-earning ability. Otherwise, why would the lender accept relatively low debt-like returns for an investment that contains at least as much risk for the lender as an all-equity position in the underlying asset, which offers higher risky-asset return expectations? If the apparent 100 percent financed project displaces borrowing capacity on the part of the owner of the project, then effectively only a portion of the project debt is backed by the project itself; the borrower/owner of the project backs the rest. In this sense, the financing is not 100 percent.

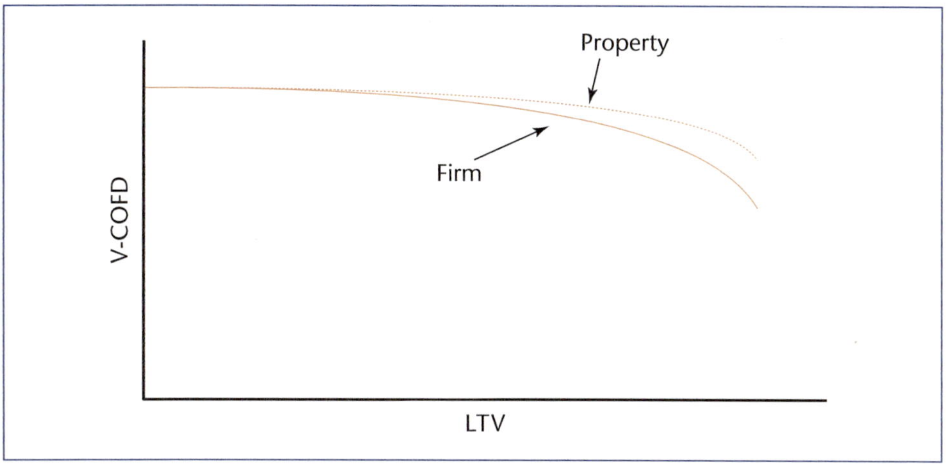

EXHIBIT 15-1 Effect of Expected Costs of Financial Distress (COFD) on the Value of the Firm and Property Value.

This is the major reason debt/equity ratios or effective leverage ratios are higher for various forms of debt secured by real property than for debt backed by the typical publicly traded industrial or service corporation. This point is illustrated in Exhibit 15-1, which traces the total "value of the firm" (or value of the underlying asset) as a function of the ratio of debt value divided by the total firm value (or LTV ratio). The solid line represents the typical industrial or service corporation traded on the stock exchange, while the dashed line represents a typical fully operational real property asset. The firm's value equals the underlying asset value free and clear of debt, minus the present value of any expected future costs of financial distress: V - COFD.

Real estate typically allows a greater LTV ratio before the COFD factor becomes important. Traditionally, commercial mortgages have often been made at LTVs up to 75 percent. In contrast, the debt-to-asset ratios of most publicly traded corporations (other than financial institutions) tend to remain around or below 50 percent, except because of corporate distress.

15.2.4 Debt and Inflation

We already discussed the general impact of inflation on rents and the cost of capital; however, many misconceptions exist regarding inflation and debt. Popular "get-rich-quick" literature on real estate investment touts the benefits of debt financing to make money off inflation. The more you borrow, the more money you make just from inflation, and real estate provides more ability to borrow than any other type of investment. After all, when you borrow money in an inflationary environment, the dollars you pay back to the lender are worth less than the dollars you originally borrowed because inflation is eating away at the purchasing power of the dollars.

You probably already see the fallacy in this argument. Like the simplistic conventional wisdom about the tax advantages of debt, no matter the borrower's tax rate, this inflation-based argument for debt ignores the lender side of the debt market. It implicitly assumes that lenders are stupid or cannot forecast inflation like borrowers. Neither of these assumptions is true. Lenders factor the expected inflation rate into the interest rate at which they are willing to lend. The total dollars you pay back to the lender are more than the dollars you borrow due to the interest you pay. The interest rate in the debt market, whether for mortgages or bonds, is sufficient to cover the expected level of inflation and still provide lenders with a real return.

This is especially true when a fixed-rate loan is made (most residential and a portion of CRE loans such as multifamily loans). Indeed, if inflation turns out to be higher than expected, the borrower will be rendered better off and the lender worse off. But this is ex-post, not ex-ante, and the borrower cannot control or influence the subsequent inflation rate. Inflation is just as likely to turn out to be lower than had been expected when the loan was made, making the borrower worse off and the lender better off.[4] The ex-ante expectations are relevant for deciding on the use of debt, and those expectations do not favor the borrower or the lender in the debt transaction.

Nevertheless, it is important to understand the effect of inflation on the borrower's ex-post position and how this alters real estate's natural inflation-hedging ability. In general, rents and property values tend to move with inflation. When inflation turns out to be greater than expected, rents and property values can be greater than they would be, *measured in nominal terms*. This makes real estate act as an inflation hedge, protecting the investor against unanticipated increases in inflation.[5]

This inflation-hedging quality of real estate equity is magnified using fixed-rate debt to the point that inflation can become a positive risk factor in the levered equity. That is, unanticipated surges in inflation may improve the levered equity real estate return net of inflation. This can have a valuable effect on investors who are particularly exposed to possible harm from unanticipated increases in inflation. For example, if the investor is likely to lose her job because of a surge in inflation or if her wealth is trapped in assets that tend to be particularly negatively affected by inflation, then the "inflation-reversing" effect of financing real estate investment with fixed-rate debt could be attractive.[6]

Of course, the inflation effect cuts the other way when inflation turns out to be less than expected. Then, nominal real estate equity returns may turn out to be lower than previously expected, and using fixed-rate debt will magnify this effect, leading to a lower real return than expected.

These effects are illustrated numerically in Exhibit 15-2. The exhibit portrays a property initially worth $100 in an environment in which inflation over the next year is anticipated to be 2 percent, and the property is expected to depreciate 1 percent in real terms. The third column reflects these ex-ante expectations. The two other columns show alternative inflation scenarios, one in which inflation turns out to be 2 percent less than anticipated and the other in which inflation turns out to be 2 percent greater than anticipated. The property itself is assumed to be a "perfect" inflation hedge in that it retains its same real value no matter what happens to inflation. The exhibit shows the effect on the levered equity with a 60 percent LTV ratio 1-year loan whose principal is payable at the end of the first year.[7]

Notice that the property value grows 1 percent less than the inflation rate in all scenarios, producing a -1 percent real return. The real deviation of the ex-post return from the ex-ante expectation is zero in all scenarios for the unlevered property, as seen in the second-to-last row in the table. This reflects our "perfect hedge" assumption. On the other hand, property growth is magnified in the levered equity, allowing it to provide a slightly positive real return under the ex-ante scenario and magnifying its positive covariance with inflation. The levered equity will lose 2.5 percent in real value if the low-inflation scenario materializes or gain 3.5 percent if the high-inflation scenario occurs. In real terms, the levered equity loses (or gains) when inflation turns out to be lower

[4] The borrower may be able to refinance and take advantage of the lower inflation depending on prepayment penalties, otherwise they are worse off if inflation turns out lower than expected.

[5] Remember: real estate is a risky asset, even measured in real terms, net of inflation. Thus, real estate is not a "perfect" hedge against inflation. Real estate returns in the private property market tend to be positively correlated with inflation, but not perfectly correlated. Also, keep in mind that unanticipated changes in inflation are usually correlated with events in the real macro economy and in monetary policy. These events often have an impact on the real value of property. For example, an unanticipated upsurge in inflation may trigger tighter monetary policy and signal slower-than-anticipated future real economic growth. Such "news" would be negative for most real estate values in real terms.

[6] On the other hand, don't forget our dictum: Don't borrow in order to lend, as the net result is the payment of the banker's spread. If the investor's portfolio is overly sensitive to inflation due to heavy concentration in long-term fixed-rate bond investments, reducing the bond exposure would generally make more sense rather than borrowing money while still holding onto the bonds.

[7] We may assume the loan interest is paid from the property's operating cash flow, which is not depicted in the exhibit.

EXHIBIT 15-2

One-Year Example of the Impact of Inflation on Ex-Post Levered Returns in Nominal and Real Terms

Scenario	Colum (I) low inflation	Column (II) high inflation	Column (III) *expected* inflation
Inflation	0.00%	4.00%	2.00%
Depreciation	1.00%	1.00%	1.00%
		Values	
Property Values			
Year 0	\$ 100	\$ 100	\$ 100
Year 1	\$ 99	\$ 103	\$ 101
Debt balance			
Year 0	\$ 60	\$ 60	\$ 60
Year 1	\$ 60	\$ 60	\$ 60
Equity			
Year 0	\$ 40	\$ 40	\$ 40
Year 1	\$ 39	\$ 43	\$ 41
		Appreciation (%)	
Nominal			
Property	-1.00%	3.00%	1.00%
Equity	-2.50%	7.50%	2.50%
Real			
Property	-1.00%	-1.00%	-1.00%
Equity	-2.50%	3.50%	0.50%

(or higher) than anticipated, even though the real return of unlevered property is invariant across inflation scenarios. The levered equity's real deviation from its ex-ante expectation is approximately ± 3 percent, positively correlated with the inflation outcome.[8]

Thus, the example in Exhibit 15-2 shows how leverage can increase the covariance between the ex-post nominal return and inflation and introduce a positive correlation between the ex-post real return and inflation. This **reverse-inflation risk** may be useful to some investors or a needless increase in risk to other investors. It is a factor to consider, but not a general argument for debt financing applicable to all investors.

15.3 PROJECT-LEVEL CAPITAL STRUCTURE IN REAL ESTATE

As noted, much real estate finance occurs at the micro-level of individual investments in properties, projects, or "deals." As a result, much of the "capital structure" in real estate occurs at this micro-level. This is partly because much real estate investment is still done directly by individuals or small entrepreneurial firms. However, it is also because of the nature of real estate assets. As we

[8] Note that the results portrayed in Exhibit 15-2 are well approximated by the WACC formula described in Chapter 13. Slight deviations from this formula reflect that a positive span of time (1 year) is covered in Exhibit 15-2. During this time, the LTV ratio changes, which makes the WACC formula an inexact approximation.

have pointed out before, the relatively simple, tangible, and "transparent" nature of property assets as investments and the fact that they trade in generally well-functioning markets makes them ideal candidates for secured debt and other types of project-level financing in which external investors need to feel confident that they know what is going on in the investment even if they don't have direct management control or highly specialized expertise. The law governing real property rights also facilitates this type of finance, at least in Anglo-Saxon "common law" countries.

In general, the prevalence of project-level finance does not alter the basic principles and considerations raised in the preceding chapters and sections of this chapter regarding capital structure and the use of debt. The classical micro-level real estate finance deal consists simply of an equity-owning investor taking out a mortgage loan secured by the property, and our previous discussion in this chapter and the analysis framework presented in Chapters 12-14 can be applied to this model. In recent years, however, the capital markets have become more sophisticated in custom-tailoring investment vehicles to a more diverse range of investors. Combined in some cases with a growing prevalence of larger, more complex property investment projects, such as those including development phases and/or multiple individual assets, the result has been a growth in more complex capital structures, even at the micro-level. Financing considerations peculiar to development project investments will be addressed in Chapter 18, and mortgages will be addressed from an investment perspective in Part V. Here, however, it will be worth our while to point out some of the major types of financing and capital structures and vehicles currently or recently used for real estate investments in the United States and indeed, internationally within the global institutional investment community.

Broadly speaking, the additional financing arrangements consist of investment vehicles that are intermediate or "hybrid" between the classical first-lien mortgage and the classical pure undifferentiated residual equity. These include both subordinated debt and preferred equity vehicles (with and without "convertibility" or equity call option features), as well as differentiation among "classes" of investors within the residual equity ownership entity itself. The overriding purpose of developing these types of more complex capital structures is to facilitate two related objectives:

1. To match the risk and return (and holding horizon or liquidity) preferences of different types of investors, thereby attracting capital from more or larger pools of investors; and
2. To match appropriate investment performance incentives with the governance structure of the operational control and authority in the project to optimize the project's management, thereby minimizing agency costs and maximizing underlying project value for all parties.

15.3.1 Enriching the Traditional Capital Structure Plate

Some of the more widely used vehicles and mechanisms of project-level capital structure include subordinate types of debt (often called "mezzanine"), preferred equity, and differentiated residual equity classes with investment return "hurdles" and "promotes."[9] These are described below.

- **Multiple-Note Mortgages**. It used to be that a mortgage was always a single undifferentiated note. While this is still largely the case, the twenty-first century has witnessed the advent of multiple-note mortgages. Typically, they originate from very large first-lien (senior) mortgages. Splitting a mortgage into two or more separate notes allows separate investors (or owners) of the same mortgage. The splitting may be done either "horizontally" or "vertically." With horizontal splitting, the two notes are identical regarding seniority and interest ("pari passu"). Sometimes, one note will be securitized and the other held privately, or the two notes

[9] Another hybrid vehicle, "shared responsibility mortgages." In brief, a shared responsibility mortgage, often a first-lien note, gives the debt holder some participation in the collateral property's equity cash flow, property value appreciation, or at least the upside thereof, in return for a lower base interest rate or other considerations for the borrower.

will both be securitized but put into different CMBS (commercial mortgage-backed securities) pools, as the entire loan might be too large for any one pool. In the case of vertical splitting, there may be an "A-note" and a "B-note", with the former having precedence in claims over the latter. The B-note becomes much like a "second mortgage" or subordinate debt, though it is structured as a note on a single underlying mortgage. Sometimes, the A-note will be securitized, and the B-note will be held privately. While an important innovation, multiple-note mortgages do not fundamentally affect the equity investor as much as the other vehicles listed below.

- **Mezzanine Debt.** So-called "mezz debt" is a somewhat vaguely defined term whose meaning can vary. It refers to an investment vehicle structured as a loan and senior to equity but subordinated to other debt that is senior to it. In some cases, mezz debt is secured directly by real property assets. It includes a "lien"[10] on the underlying property but subordinated to other specified senior investment vehicles (typically including a first mortgage that might be a construction loan for a development investment and/or a permanent loan for a stabilized investment); in this case, mezz debt is essentially like a "second mortgage" or subordinated mortgage. However, in the early 2000s, the term "mezz debt" came to be applied particularly to loans not necessarily secured directly by property assets but rather made to an investment entity (which in turn owned property assets encumbered by senior mortgage debt). Generally, mezz debt investors are not entitled to receive a return on their investment until senior debt holders are fully compensated for what is owed to them. On the other hand, if not all capital is invested at once, mezz debt capital is typically "drawn" or placed into the investment before the senior debt capital. In this way, the mezz debt investment provides a buffer of capital exposure that helps protect senior debt investors. There may be more than one layer of mezz debt in large, complex deals. Mezz debt typically carries interest rates considerably above those of first mortgages. Usually, the interest not paid out currently accrues and accumulates with compounding (interest is earned on interest not yet paid out).
- **Preferred Equity**. Preferred equity is like mezz debt, providing a contractually stated dividend or yield payment as a "guaranteed" return. However, preferred equity is normally subordinated to debt on the property or investment entity (including mezz debt). Preferred equity normally has no formal lien on the underlying real estate. On the other hand, as the name implies, preferred equity precedes common (or residual) equity in the priority of claims. Preferred equity obtains its returns usually 100% in a preferred dividend (no appreciation of principal or capital paid in). Sometimes, the preferred return not paid out currently accumulates with (or without) compounding, as with debt. In capital structures with both mezz debt and preferred equity, the preferred equity usually goes in before. It comes out after the mezz debt capital, and the preferred equity return is higher than the mezz debt interest rate. While mezz debt typically has a maturity or explicit principal payback horizon, this is not generally the case for preferred equity. The preferred equity holder may or may not have some say in whether or when the underlying assets will be sold (leading to the investment principal's payback).
- **Common (or Residual) Equity**. This is normally the property ownership entity with the operational management responsibility and primary governing control of the project, at least unless and until there is a default of the senior obligations. (Under its lien and loan covenants, secured senior debt can take over control in the event of default.) Common equity has no guaranteed or contractual return and receives only the residual cash flow, generally after the other

[10] A "lien" is a construct of Anglo-Saxon common law that gives a creditor potential real property ownership right, for example, in the event of default on the loan enabling the creditor to take ownership of the property. More than one lien may be attached to a property, in which case the liens have a priority normally based on chronological order. Still, it can be subordinated to subsequent liens, as in the case of mezz debt that might be arranged before a permanent first-lien mortgage. Classical mortgage terminology and covenants will be discussed in Part V.

senior investment vehicles have been paid their preferred returns. (However, various specific arrangements are possible; for example, common equity is sometimes entitled to return its paid-in capital with zero return before preferred equity is paid its preferred return.)

- **Differentiated Equity Partners (Classes)**. It is typical, particularly in larger real estate investments, for the common equity ownership entity to have more than one investor, organized as a partnership or corporation. In such a "**joint venture**," it is common for the investors to be differentiated according to what they bring into the deal and what they want to get out of it. For example, an entrepreneurial investor may bring operational management ability and the deal itself (e.g., in development, the land with entitlements and permits, and the project design). In contrast, a money partner brings most (or sometimes all) of the required equity cash but lacks the ability or desire to manage the operation of the project or property. Defining different "classes" of partners or stockholders in the ownership equity entity makes sense to reflect such differing contributions and investment objectives. A typical arrangement will grant operational management control primarily to what we will label the "**general partner (GP)**" (or "manager"). In contrast, the "**limited partner (LP)**" often retains primary control over major capital decisions (financing and asset buy/sell decisions). The GP may or may not subordinate some of its equity claims to that of the LP (though the GP may also take a service fee). A very common arrangement splits the equity entity's overall cash flow (net of fees) among the partners on a "**pro-rata pari passu**" basis (proportionately relative to their capital contributions) up until the equity entity achieves a certain "**preferred**" or "hurdle" return (specified either on a cumulative current or a look-back IRR basis, or both); beyond that hurdle return, the cash flow split is differentiated to provide the GP with a proportion greater than its capital contribution (either on a current or back-end basis). This is called a "**promote**" and surpassing the preferred return hurdle is called "earning the promote."[11] Such structures incentivize the partner charged with operational management to make the project successful. As such, success benefits not only the managing partner but all the investors in the project, it is crucial to provide this kind of incentive. The promote structure may also provide some degree of "reward" for putting the deal together in the first place.

One of the characteristics of project-level capital structure is that two investment management considerations are to some extent blended: that of capital structure per se (in particular, the nature and degree of leverage) and that of project management and governance, including the very important considerations of incentives compatibility and mitigation of potential conflicts of interest among the various investors. The structuring of the equity partnership vehicle is more about the latter considerations. In contrast, using extra intermediate or hybrid finance vehicles with claim priority between the traditional first-lien mortgage and traditional equity is more about the capital structure issue. In general, both mezz debt and preferred equity vehicles evolved to ever greater degrees of leverage in property investment during the mid-2000s "bubble." On top of traditional first-lien mortgages, they brought in new types of real estate capital providers, typically from the nonbank financial sector

[11] Typical preferred return hurdles have been in the range of 6 percent to 12 percent, with the promote share to the GP typically ranging from 10 percent to 50 percent. There may also be "claw-back" or "hold-back" provisions that allow the LP to retrieve some promote that had been paid to the managing partner if subsequently the deal performance turns out badly after it had previously been good enough to provide some promote. Another type of arrangement gives the LP a senior position ahead of the manager up until the preferred return is earned but then allows the manager to have a "catch-up" period in which he gets all of the cash flow until he also has made the preferred return, followed then by a promoted split structure. Yet another structure is more complex, in which there may be two (or more) hurdles. This is more typical in business entities that are not just for the purpose of a single investment but allocating money to a portfolio of several properties. Project-level finance and joint ventures typically specify hurdles based on IRR metrics. However, in the case of co-mingled funds with many investors and many properties, it is generally presumed that the manager does not have control over investment timing, in which case hurdles and promotes are typically based on time-weighted returns (see Chapter 3).

(such as private equity funds). They allowed ever-thinner slices of real estate equity investment to buy and control underlying property assets with very little cash investment. After the financial crisis and property crash of 2008–2009, the use of these types of vehicles diminished in favor of a simpler structure that was more transparent (and more traditional). However, intermediate financing did not cease altogether, as it can provide valuable benefits. While extra layers in the capital structure probably tend to be driven by the desire for greater leverage, the overall degree of leverage can be kept down by reducing the LTV of the first-lien mortgage and reducing the "thickness" (amount of financing) in the intermediate layers, thereby keeping the overall LTV to a safe level (including all layers of financing other than the residual equity). One lesson from the crash, however, was that complexity itself can have a cost, as it can obfuscate the picture of the investment and confound the control of the project. Too many layers of finance can be like too many cooks in the kitchen!

15.3.2 Numerical Example of Multi-Tiered Project Capital Structure

To see more concretely how this type of project-level capital structure and joint venture equity structuring works, let us return to our simple apartment property example from Chapter 12. (We will be ignoring tax in this section.) Only now will we consider not just the simple first-lien mortgage and undifferentiated equity considered there but also some of the vehicles and arrangements noted in the previous section.

We will continue with our apartment example, which is used throughout the book. Remember, the property was bought for approximately $937,000, with a 75% LTV. The first-lien mortgage of approximately $703 thousand has a 5 percent interest with a 25-year amortization rate (Chapter 12). The resulting EBTCF is displayed in Exhibit 15-4 at the very top (item 0, Panel A). The total equity invested in this property is approximately $234 thousand.

Let us assume that this project's equity investment and ownership will consist of two differentiated partners. A relatively passive limited partner (say a German pension fund) will contribute 90 percent of the equity cash requirement ($211 thousand of the $234 thousand purchase price equity at year 0). In contrast, a (local) general partner will contribute the rest of the cash and have operational management control of the stabilized apartment property in Boston. The arrangement between these two partners specifies that the money partner will receive an annual preferred return of 5.5 percent on (not of) invested capital, with any unpaid current return accumulating with annual compounding. Any positive net operating cash flow from the property (after the debt service has been paid) will go first to provide the money partner with that preferred 5.5 percent return (as current as possible). Any extra operating cash flow beyond that will be split 50/50 between the two partners, even though the limited partner contributes 90 percent of the equity capital and the general partner only 10 percent. Reversion cash flow from net resale proceeds (after debt repayment) will first provide the limited partner with their preferred 5.5 percent return (now of, as well as on, their investment). Any remaining reversion cash available upon termination will go first to pay back the general partner for their capital contribution (with zero return) and will be split 50/50 between the two partners afterward.

Note that the arrangement described in this illustration does not provide a pro-rata pari passu split of residual cash flow up to the earning of the 5.5 percent preferred return, as has been typical practice. Thus, this structure combines the senior/subordinate aspect of the "preferred equity" intermediate capital structure layer (between the mortgage and the residual equity) described in Section 15.3.1 with aspects of the return hurdle-with-promote joint venture arrangement described at the end of that section. This hybrid structure has consequences for the general partner, which we shall see shortly. Exhibit 15-3 visually depicts the cash flow "waterfall" implied by the arrangement. The exhibit highlights both the "horizontal" splitting of cash flows in the senior/subordinate arrangement characteristic of capital structure slices or "tranches," as well as the "vertical" cash flow splitting characteristic of residual equity classes. It also shows graphically how the arrangement is slightly

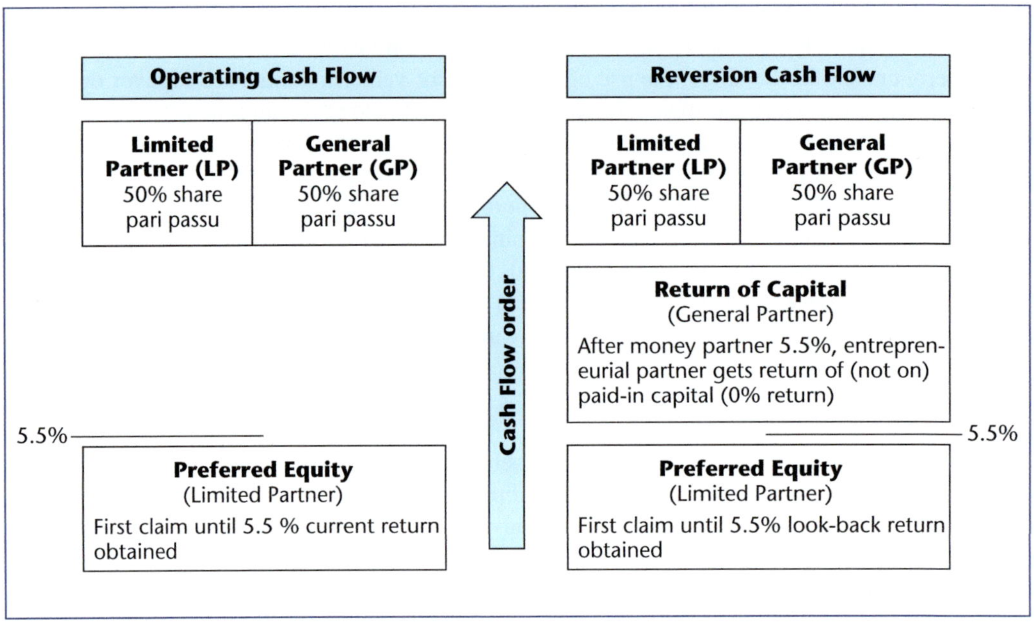

EXHIBIT 15-3 Apartment Example Waterfall Illustration.

different in this example between operational and reversion (asset sale proceeds) cash flows, with an extra layer of horizontal splitting in the reversion to give the managing partner some priority in at least getting their capital investment back.[12]

Exhibit 15-4 summarizes this investment's projected operating cash flows quantitatively at the before-tax level for a 10-year holding horizon. (Negative cash flows, or cash outflows, are indicated by parentheses.) We start with the (undifferentiated) equity-level-before-tax cash flows (EBTCF) in the top row (Item #0), after payment of debt service. In the remainder of this section, we will go through all the rows in Exhibit 15-4 in greater detail.

We track the LP's capital account balance in the Item #1 line of Panel A in Exhibit 15-4.[13] This information is needed to calculate the preferred return (and the reversion cash flow later). In this case, the capital balance at the start of the first year is simply the invested equity by the LP of $211 thousand. The GP provides the rest of the capital (Panel B, Item #1). Given that the LP's equity investment in year 1 is $211 thousand, its preferred return is 5.5% times the $211 thousand, or *$11,594* (see Item #3). This return can be paid to the LP in full, plus the LP gets an additional residual claim because the property is projected to provide $12,507 (Item #0) after the first-lien mortgage is paid, which is greater than the 5.5% preferred amount. This residual is calculated as 50% times the difference between the EBTCF and the preferred return ($12,507 - $11,596), which equals $456. The GP gets the other half of the residual or also $456, in year 1.[14]

[12] While the structure described here could well exist in particular circumstances in the real world, we are using it here more for pedagogical purposes (not suggesting that it would be very typical). We are doing this in order to make a point about fairness and incentive considerations in cash flow split arrangements and in order to demonstrate capital accounting for the senior and intermediate portions of the capital structure. In effect, the LP in this deal has assumed two roles, that of a preferred equity investor and that of a joint venture partner, taking much of their joint venture partnership return through their preferred equity vehicle.

[13] As with mortgages, in the real world, this type of accounting would typically be done at a monthly frequency.

[14] Although, as noted earlier *and* later, the GP will get a property management fee, which shows up in the operating expenses, not here (assuming they will act as property manager). The GP may also get entity level fees, though we have not specified any such here.

EXHIBIT 15-4
Operating Income and Balance for Limited and General Partners. The EBTCF was calculated in Chapter 12

Capital Structure	
Share of LP	90%
Preferred Return (%)	5.50%
Equity LP	$ 210,801
Equity GP	$ 23,422
Residual claim	50.00%

Panel A. Limited Partner

#	Flow Items	Year 1	2	3	4	5	6	7	8	9	10
0	**EBTCF**	**$ 12,507**	**$ 14,361**	**$ 16,271**	**$ 18,238**	**$ 20,264**	**$ 22,350**	**$ (77,052)**	**$ 26,713**	**$ 28,994**	**$ 31,342**
1	LP balance (begin)	$ 210,801	$ 210,801	$ 210,801	$ 210,801	$ 210,801	$ 210,801	$ 210,801	$ 291,742	$ 281,075	$ 267,540
2	Addition LP investment	$ -	$ -	$ -	$ -	$ -	$ -	$ 69,347	$ -	$ -	$ -
3	Preferred Equity	$ 11,594	$ 11,594	$ 11,594	$ 11,594	$ 11,594	$ 11,594	$ 11,594	$ 16,046	$ 15,459	$ 14,715
4	Preferred Equity (Paid)	$ 11,594	$ 11,594	$ 11,594	$ 11,594	$ 11,594	$ 11,594	$ -	$ 16,046	$ 15,459	$ 14,715
5	Preferred Equity (Unpaid)	$ -	$ -	$ -	$ -	$ -	$ -	$ 11,594	$ -	$ -	$ -
6	Pay off Accrued LP Balance	$ -	$ -	$ -	$ -	$ -	$ -	$ -	$ 10,668	$ 13,534	$ 16,627
8	LP balance (end)	$ 210,801	$ 210,801	$ 210,801	$ 210,801	$ 210,801	$ 210,801	$ 291,742	$ 281,075	$ 267,540	$ 250,913

Panel B. General Partner

#		Year 1	2	3	4	5	6	7	8	9	10
1	GP balance (begin)	$ 23,422	$ 23,422	$ 23,422	$ 23,422	$ 23,422	$ 23,422	$ 23,422	$ 31,128	$ 31,128	$ 31,128
2	Additional GP investment	$ -	$ -	$ -	$ -	$ -	$ -	$ 7,705	$ -	$ -	$ -
3	GP balance (end)	$ 23,422	$ 23,422	$ 23,422	$ 23,422	$ 23,422	$ 23,422	$ 31,128	$ 31,128	$ 31,128	$ 31,128

Through years 2 to 6, the property's cash flows (after debt) are sufficient to pay the LP its preferred return. As a result, the LP's invested capital remains stable throughout these years (Item #7). This changes in year 7, when additional equity capital "draws" are projected due to the negative EBTCF in that year, which was caused by the projected need for major capital expenditures. Those draws will add to the cumulative preferred equity balance carried forward for the money partner. A special provision will call for excess cash flow over the current preferred return to be used *first* to pay down *only any such LP equity contributions subsequent to the initial (year 0) LP investment* before the normal 50/50 split of excess operating equity cash flows.

For example, the projected entity-level EBTCF in year 7 is negative $77,025. Ninety percent of this amount, $69,347 (Item #2, year 7), will be drawn from the LP and added to her preferred equity account balance along with the current preferred return in year 7 that cannot be paid that year, and which therefore also accumulates in the capital account balance. Subsequently, any excess cash flow (over the preferred return) will go towards paying off any of the unpaid previously earned returns as well as any capital contributions subsequent to the year 0 initial investment, prior to the 50/50 split with the GP. Thus, item #6 represents the difference between the EBTCF and preferred return. This money will be subtracted from the LP's capital account until it reaches the original investment amount of $211 thousand. *Only after this* will any remaining cash flows again be split between the LP and GP on a 50/50 basis. We are now able to calculate the full outstanding capital account balance at the end of the year by adding the unpaid preferred return (item 5) and additional "draws" (item 2) and subtracting (if applicable) any additional cash that can be used to pay off previously unpaid preferred return to the LP (item 6) to the outstanding balance at the start of the year (item 1).

By the end of the 10-year holding period, the capital balance projected in the LP's preferred account is projected to be $250,913. This represents the limited partner's share of the initial equity capital outlay of the joint venture, as well as an as yet unpaid amount of the subsequent draws of operating capital expenditure requirements in year 7 (and any previously earned unpaid current returns still not paid off by that time). This balance is net of current returns paid from operations. Based on this deal's hybrid senior/subordinate structure, the LP's preferred equity gives her a senior position to claim this balance upon resale of the property. The limited partner will thus have the first claim on the reversion cash flow projected in year 10 until her projected preferred capital balance of $250,913 is fully paid off, including her 5.5% preferred return on her total investment. The intended result of the preferred equity capital account rows in Exhibit 15-4 Panel A is to pay the LP her 5.5 percent preferred return currently insofar as possible with priority over the GP's receipts, except that the original year 0 LP investment is not meant to be repaid until/except out of the reversion when the property is sold. Any proceeds from the subordinated 50/50 split during the operating phase will not pay down the LP capital balance. As the projected reversion EBTCF in year 10 is $713,388, it is expected that the preferred capital balance will indeed be paid off at that time (as would typically be the case in a forward projection at investment inception).

The next claim on the partnership's reversion cash flow in the terminal period is that of the GP's original and subsequent capital investment (with zero return) of $31 thousand (including his original $23 thousand investment plus his share of the negative equity cash flow in year 7 due to major capital improvement investments), see items #2 and #4 in Exhibit 15-4 Panel B. In the present agreement, this amount is to be paid as much as possible from the reversion cash flow. The total reversion projected for year 7 minus the LP's projected capital balance is ($713,366 - $267,540 =) $462,476, far more than the $31 thousand that must be paid to the GP. Therefore, the GP expects to be paid back their full $31 thousand capital contribution from the reversion in year 10. To complete the reversion cash flow for our two types of investors, we split the remaining cash 50/50. After the GP's balance is paid off, we end up with ($462,476 - $31,128 =) $431,348. Thus, each investor will receive an additional $215 thousand (rounded) from selling the property in year 10.

Exhibit 15-5 adds all cash flows for all the parts of the capital structure, including the effect on the equity partners of the differentiated splits reflecting the promote for the GP. In years 1 through

EXHIBIT 15-5
Going-in IRR for All Components of Capital Structure

#		IRR	0	1	2	3	4	5	6	7	8	9	10
0	EBTCF	**15.03%**	$ (234,223)	$ 12,507	$ 14,361	$ 16,271	$ 18,238	$ 20,264	$ 22,350	$ (77,052)	$ 26,713	$ 28,994	$ 744,730
1	LP	**11.84%**	$ (210,801)	$ 12,051	$ 12,978	$ 13,932	$ 14,916	$ 15,929	$ 16,972	$ (69,347)	$ 26,713	$ 28,994	$ 497,929
2	GP	**29.30%**	$ (23,422)	$ 457	$ 1,384	$ 2,338	$ 3,322	$ 4,335	$ 5,378	$ (7,705)	$ -	$ -	$ 246,802

10, the LP receives their (paid) preferred return (Exh.15-4 Panel A Item #4) plus any cash used to pay off any accrued non-paid preferred return and capital contributions subsequent to year 0 (item 6) minus any additional capital draws (item 2). Any additional cash beyond that will be split equally between the LP and GP. In year 10, both the LP and GP get back their full outstanding capital balance (in that order) from the expected sales price of the property (minus the mortgage), plus 50% of any outstanding amount after the LP and GP's equity investment is paid off.

Consider first the LP. They contribute 90 percent of the initial equity investment (and 90 percent of the subsequent capital improvement cash requirement). On that investment, they obtain an 11.84% expected return. This is not as high as the 15.03% return on overall (entity level) equity (EBTCF), but the LP assumes less risk due to their preferred position. It still provides the LP with a higher expected return than a property (asset) level investment, unlevered, which we saw would be 8.60 percent, and it provides a much higher expected return than an investment in the mortgage, which only yields 5 percent. (The mortgage, of course, is much safer, as it has overall seniority.)

The bottom row of Exhibit 15-5 provides the GP's cash flows and return. As the GP is the residual claimant, his cash flows may be easily calculated as the difference between the undifferentiated equity entity level EBTCF minus the LP cash flows described in the preceding paragraphs. In our example, we see that the GP gets no intermediate cash flows in years 7 through 9 and very little in the earlier years. At first, this might seem like a bad deal for the GP. However, as noted earlier, the GP will receive a management fee for operating the property. In fact, many GPs prioritize this management fee side of the deal, as it provides a stable source of income, with seniority. It allows the GP to pay its bills and employees, especially during uncertain times. However, it should also be noted that the GP gets an expected IRR on their financial investment of 29%, much higher than the LP. It is appropriate that the GP receives the highest going-in returns because his investment is in the most junior, riskiest position, and the payoff does not happen largely until the property is sold.[15]

As noted, the arrangement in our apartment project example here does not provide for the classical hurdle-with-promote structure, in which all equity cash flows are shared pro-rata pari passu until the specified hurdle return. Nevertheless, the 50/50 sharing after the preferred return does provide the GP with a strong incentive to achieve superior performance in the project. In fact, the example structure combines a sort of "stick" with the usual "carrot." The "stick" is that the GP does not earn any return until after the LP makes her 5.5 percent, and most of the GPs return comes from the value of the property at the time of reversion. The "carrot" is that, beyond the LP's 5.5% preferred return, the 50/50 split with the GP having invested only 10 percent of the equity capital enables the GP to make a very high return if the project performs sufficiently well, thus providing a type of "promote" incentive for the GP.

The question now naturally arises as to whether these expected returns are *fair* to all the parties in this capital structure and whether they provide appropriate incentives to both parties under a range of possible scenarios.[16] Should the general partner receive expected returns so much higher than the limited partner? On the other hand, has the GP given away too much to the LP, perhaps by

---

[15] It is common in joint ventures between a money partner and a developer that there will be provision for the developer to exit the venture upon completion and lease-up of the property, if the developer wants to, obtaining their share of the stabilized property value at that time. The split might be based on an appraised value, or on a "buy/sell" agreement in which either party may buy out the other party for a price at which the triggering party would be willing (and able) to either buy or sell their share of the property.

[16] For simplicity, we will ignore the debt component, assuming that any loans are at market interest rates in a competitive debt market, implying that the debt's expected return is fair and that using such debt does not alter the fairness of the equity returns. This is a reasonable assumption from a market value perspective, but recall our discussion in Section 14.2 of Chapter 14 regarding after-tax investment value. If the two equity partners face different income tax situations (e.g., the LP might be a tax-exempt institution, and the GP might be a taxable corporation), then from an IV perspective, the two partners might not benefit equally from the debt. Nevertheless, we will assume that the borrowing decision has already been made and for whatever reasons (e.g., perhaps related to our discussion in earlier sections of the present chapter) is agreeable to both parties.

excessively exposing himself to downside outcomes through the "stick" referred to earlier, by not taking a pro-rata share until the money partner earns a 5.5 percent return? The following section will present a simple approach to examining this question.

15.3.3 An Example Application of Sensitivity Analysis

In principle, we know how to examine the question of the fairness of project finance and capital structure arrangements such as that described for our apartment example in the previous section. Each investor or class of investors (each of which might involve a combination of components or investment entities or "vehicles" in the capital structure) should earn an expected return going into the investment equal to the market opportunity cost of capital (OCC) for investments with similar risk characteristics to what that investor faces. As discussed in depth in Chapter 14, the market OCC provides a zero net investment value for the marginal investors in the market. The result will provide each investor with an expected return risk premium directly proportional to the relative amount of risk their position in the capital structure exposes them to, as the capital market perceives and values such risk.

In practice, however, it may be very difficult to ascertain the appropriate market OCC for any complex and unique capital structure component, such as the preferred and residual equity components and splits in our previous apartment example. There may not be a functioning "market" for unique pieces of privately held project-level capital structure; hence, there is no way to observe "market" return expectations. The problem is compounded if the underlying property asset itself is very unique from a financial economic perspective, such as many development projects. Nevertheless, some insight can be obtained using artful and honest sensitivity analysis.

Fundamentally, the idea is to use the fact that the various pieces of the capital structure of investment in the same underlying asset can often be mainly viewed as derivatives of the underlying asset. Thus, their investment performance is highly correlated with each other and with the underlying asset so that the relative amount of risk in each piece, as the capital market would view and evaluate such risk, can be ascertained by modeling the performance of each piece as a function of the performance of the underlying asset. It may therefore be possible to construct a sort of synthetic security market line (SML) relevant for the pieces of the capital structure. We offer the following scenario analysis as a simple example of such an approach.

Returning to our apartment investment example from the previous subsection, recall that ex-ante we expect a rental growth (g) of 3%. With sensitivity analysis, we want to consider what happens to our IRRs if the growth is, ex-post, lower than we expected, or higher? We therefore redo the analysis of Section 15.3.2 only now reducing (and increasing) the growth (in effect, ex-post) by steps of 100bps, from pessimistic scenarios down to $g = 1.00\%$ up to a top optimistic scenario of $g = 5.00\%$. Note that our ex-ante expectation is in the middle of that range. On the x-axis of Exhibit 15-6A, we provide the range of ex-post growth outcomes. On the vertical axis the graph lines show the sensitivity of the resulting hypothetical ex-post IRRs for each level or component of the capital structure, and thus for each investor. In Exhibit 15-6B we perform a similar test on the IRR sensitivity to the ex post going-out cap rate. Again, we changed the going-out cap rate in steps of 100bps from pessimistic (10.00%) to very optimistic (6.00%), with our ex-ante expected going-out cap rate in the middle (8%). More importantly, in Exhibit 15-6C we combine both dimensions of ex post performance. The rent growth and the exit cap rate outcomes are not likely to be independent of each other. If rental growth is lower than expected, the going-out cap rate will probably also be higher, etc. Thus, Exhibit 15-6C provides the IRRs in the most pessimistic scenario to the left (growth 1.00%, going-out cap rate 10.00%[17]) and the most optimistic scenario to the right (growth 5.00%, going-out cap rate 6.00%) and all scenarios in between.

---

17 In full disclosure, setting the growth rate at 1.00% results in an error in the IRR function, as this will result in only negative cash flows. We therefore set the pessimistic growth rate at 1.05% for Exhibit 15-6C. You can play with the online Excel file yourself in the online supplemental resources of this text, to see what inputs "break" the proforma.

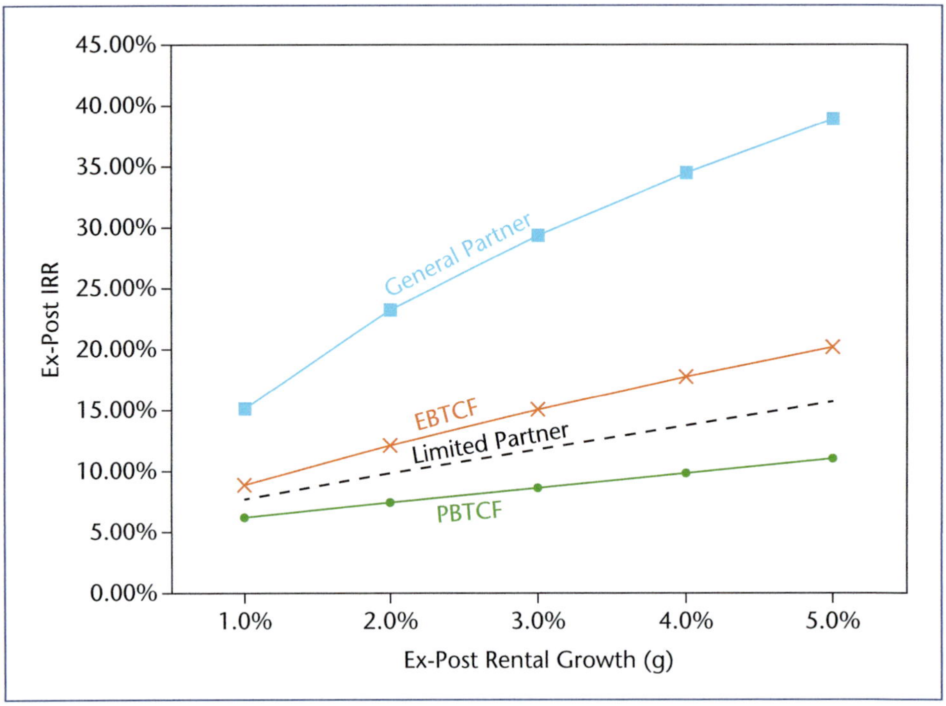

EXHIBIT 15-6A Sensitivity of Achieved IRR on Ex-post Rental Growth for Each Investor Class.

Exhibit 15-6C shows us that even in the most pessimistic scenario (1.00% rental growth and 10.00% exit cap), the LP still gets an IRR of 4.74 percent, whereas the GP will face an investment disaster with a negative 22 percent per year IRR.[18] On the other end of the spectrum, if we enjoy 5.00% rent growth and achieve a 6.00 percent going-out cap rate, the LP "only" gets a 19.07 percent IRR, whereas the GP makes a whopping 44.67 percent IRR. Compare these results to the ex-ante IRR of 11.84% and 29.30% for the LP and GP, respectively.

To relate the risk implied by these two extreme scenarios to the expected returns of each party going into the investment, we need to subtract the risk-free interest rate from the going-in expected returns to compute the expected risk premia. For example, supposing the risk-free interest rate (e.g., as proxied by the T-bill yield) is 4 percent, this implies that the limited partner faces a 7.84 percent risk premium (computed as 11.84% - 4%). In comparison, the general partner faces a 25.30 percent risk premium. Taking the absolute range between the scenario upside and downside outcomes as a measure of relative risk, the LP and GP face a risk of 14.33 percent (computed as: 19.07% - 4.74%) and 66.59 percent (computed as +44.67% minus -21.92%), respectively. Dividing the ex-ante risk premia by these simulated relative risk magnitudes, we get a risk premium-to-risk ratio of 0.55 (computed as: 7.84/14.33) for the limited partner and 0.38 (computed as 25.30/66.59) for the general partner.[19]

[18] Such a negative IRR over a 10-year horizon would effectively mean a total loss of the GP's financial investment, though project operational management fees would presumably still have been earned. (In reality, in the face of such poor performance, it is possible that the GP would not be retained as manager for the entire 10 years.)

[19] You can also compute the risk ratios for the PBTCF and EBTCF this way. You will find that this ratio is approximately 0.52 *for both* (that is, with or without leverage). This makes sense if the debt is at market interest rates, as market rate debt has zero NPV and therefore should not change the risk ratio for an investment in an asset that is also priced at market value.

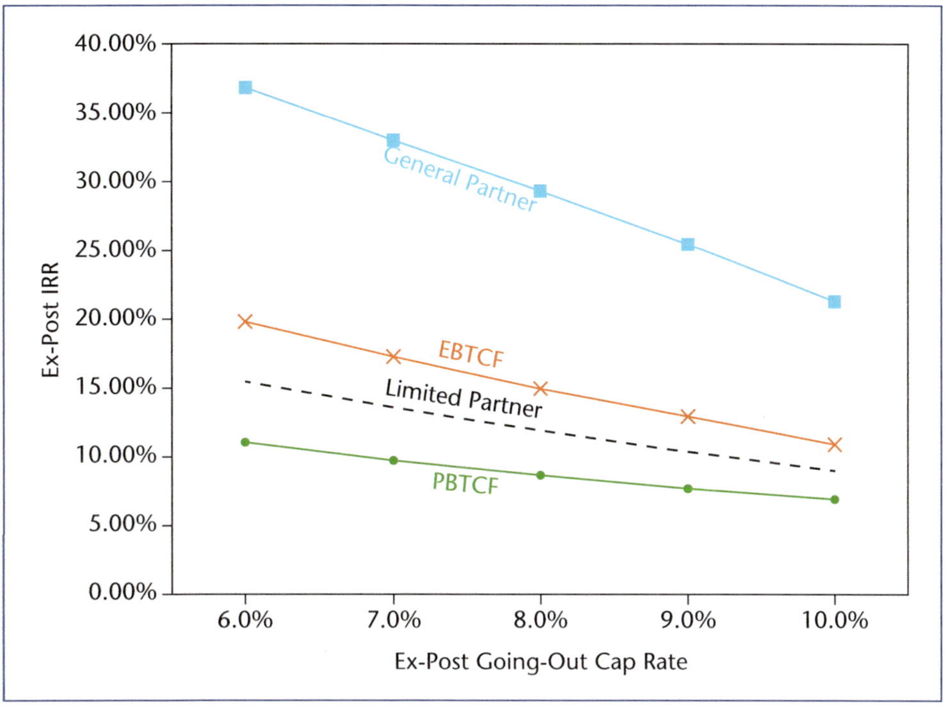

EXHIBIT 15-6B Sensitivity of Achieved IRR on Ex-post Going-out Cap Rate for Each Investor Class.

In principle, at least as a starting point, these two ratios should be approximately equal, implying the same expected return risk premium per unit of risk across the two partners (equal "risk-adjusted" returns, providing a common "price of risk"), at least if the risk model implied by our scenario sensitivity analysis is a reasonably complete and unbiased representation of the relative amount of risk that matters in the capital markets. If that is the case, then these risk ratios can be thought of essentially as synthetic "Treynor Ratios", measures of risk-adjusted returns, at least relatively speaking within the context of the subject investment. In our example, the general partner seems to get the short end of the deal by this measure. Its Treyno Ratio is lower than that of the limited partner. This might be taken as suggesting that the proposed capital structure is not "fair".

This idea is depicted qualitatively by the graph in Exhibit 15-7. In that Exhibit, the sloped straight line represents the Treynor Ratio of the entity-level levered equity investment (slope = 0.52 units of ex-ante IRR per units of risk measured by ex-post IRR spread, which is also that of the underlying unlevered asset, since the debt is a zero-NPV market value loan). The ex-ante risk-adjusted return (Treynor Ratio) of the LP is above that line, while that of the GP is below. (Lines drawn from the risk-free rate on the vertical axis through the risk and return points of the LP and GP would have slopes of 0.55 and 0.38, respectively.) While the GP's going-in IRR is substantially greater than the LP's, the implication is that it is *not enough* greater to compensate for the greater risk. Perhaps the lack of a pro-rata pari passu provision before the 5.5 percent hurdle, in combination with the height of the 5.5 percent preferred return hurdle (along with the 50/50 residual cash flow split provision), puts the general partner at too much of a disadvantage.

However, it is still possible that the GP's investment position is nevertheless a "fair" one, in the sense of non-negative NPV, going in. This could be the case if the underlying asset (in this case, the unlevered property or development project) has been priced at below market value (or the parties face sufficient *investment value* in the asset), such that there is sufficient positive NPV in the joint venture (at least on an investment value basis), so that the GP's position is non-negative NPV even

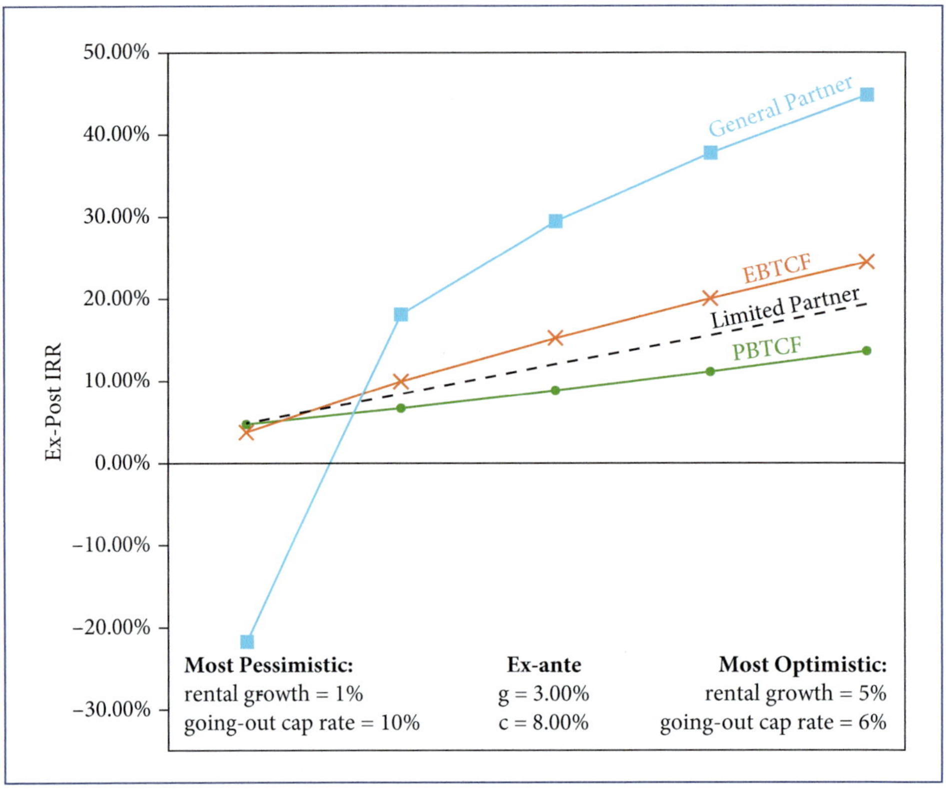

EXHIBIT 15-6C Sensitivity of Achieved IRR on Both Ex-post Rental Growth and Exit Cap Rate for Each Investor Class.

though its Treynor Ratio is below that of the LP. In other words, the GP's dot in the graph could be above the Security Market Line (SML), even though it is below the Treynor Ratio of the equity JV (the sloped line).[20]

Of course, this sensitivity analysis risk premium-to-risk ratio measure is only suggestive, not a definitive analysis, because aspects of risk and the investors' objectives and concerns are not included in the above model and analysis. As mentioned earlier, in practice, it is common for the general partner, assuming they are serving effectively as the operational manager of the investment, to take "asset management fees" (or "developer fees" if it is a development project) on top of any equity cash flow to the joint venture. These fees may be structured in various ways and, for institutional investment, are typically on the order of 1 percent of the invested capital per year. While such fees should be interpreted at least in part as a fee for service (not a return on financial investment), they increase the revenue and reduce the risk position of the managing partner. They may effectively represent a separate "profit center" for the GP firm.

Finally, it should be noted that an additional dimension to analyzing capital structure is the incentive ramifications for the various participants. This is particularly true regarding joint venture arrangements and their implications for equity partners. It is important to consider what incentives each party will face under various scenarios, including substantial upside and downside outcomes that differ sharply from the initial expectations. This can be particularly important in the event of

[20] For example, income tax advantages from borrowing might accrue to a taxable GP that a tax-exempt LP might not be able to obtain (per Chapter 14).

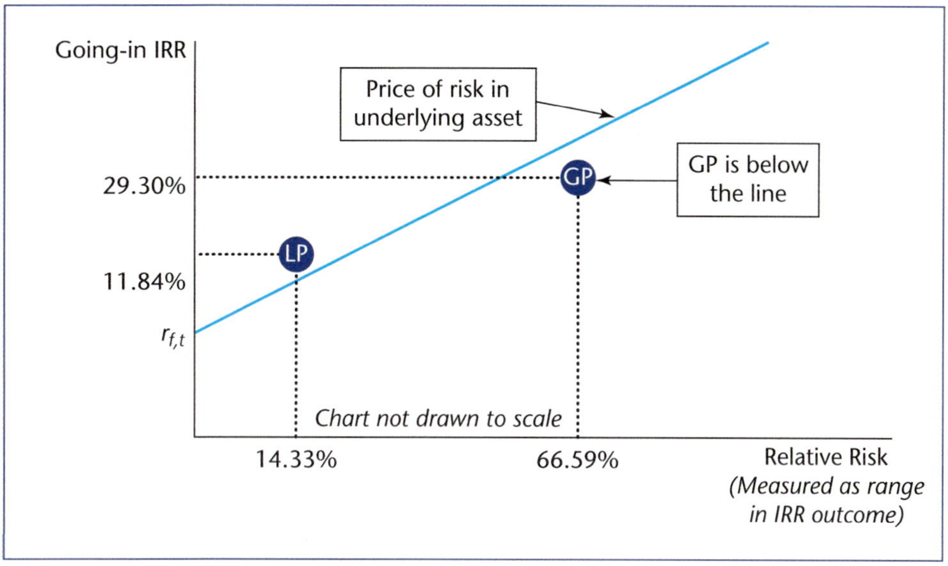

EXHIBIT 15-7 Framework for Evaluating Fairness of Capital Structure Terms.

downside outcomes, especially in the case of development projects, which will depend on the general partner continuing to perform to bring the project to a successful conclusion even though things have not worked out as originally anticipated and hoped. While such incentive considerations are not unrelated to the "fairness" considerations noted above, they present an important additional type of consideration. For example, incentive considerations no doubt underlie much of the rationale for the widespread use of pro-rata pari passu arrangements, which give the managing partner equal returns to the money partner in downside scenarios even though the managing partner receives a promote that gives him much higher returns in the upside.

In summary, scenario sensitivity analysis along the lines illustrated in this section can offer interesting insights and sometimes help in the negotiations among partners trying to put together capital structure arrangements. Such analysis also helps to highlight the risky nature of property investment.

15.4 CHAPTER SUMMARY

This chapter reviewed the value of debt financing of real estate equity investments from the equity investor's perspective. In this chapter, we broached the question of optimal capital structure (the share of debt versus equity) in real estate investment. Still, we did not attempt to offer a definitive answer to this question. Instead, we sought to clarify the major issues and considerations that are important for designing finance strategies for various types of real estate investors. These issues lie on both sides of the argument for the use of debt and affect different types of investors in different ways. The treatment of capital structure in this chapter should be viewed in combination with our discussion of leverage in Chapter 12 and of tax considerations related to the value of debt from the equity investor's perspective in Chapters 13 and 14.

The obvious overall result of a comprehensive consideration of the pros and cons of debt is that, on balance, some investors find it more profitable to borrow. In contrast, others find it more profitable to lend. This result applies both to real estate investors and to investors at large. The debt market equilibrates these two positions in the aggregate with the resulting interest rates and yields observed in that market. (In Part V, we will consider mortgages from the lender's perspective.)

To summarize Chapter 15 and Part III, clearly, no single "correct" capital structure exists for all real estate investments or all investors. However, it does appear likely that relatively "transparent" and stable, low-volatility investments, such as most income-producing properties, can optimally support higher levels of debt than can more managerially complicated and challenging, higher-risk underlying assets, such as many industrial, technology, and service corporations. The widespread use of large amounts of debt in real estate investment (over $5 trillion outstanding for commercial mortgages in the United States) suggests this. On the other hand, casual empiricism suggests that the major reason real estate investors get into trouble usually involves excessive debt (at least, with the advantage of hindsight). Both the equity investors (borrowers) and the debt investors (lenders) suffer in this repeating play. Perhaps the conventional wisdom "hypes up" the advantages of debt a bit more than is really warranted. So, be careful!

KEY TERMS

- Capital structure
- Ultimate investors (individuals)
- Equity capital constraint
- Human capital
- IV-based NPV
- Diversification (and debt)
- Banker's spread
- Control and governance issues
- Management incentives
- Liquidity
- Decision flexibility
- Costs of financial distress (COFD)
- Third-party costs
- Foreclosure
- Bankruptcy agency costs
- Limited liability ex-ante costs (probabilistic expectations)
- Inflation
- Hedging inflation risk
- Real returns
- Reverse-inflation risk
- Multiple-note mortgages
- Mezzanine debt
- Preferred equity
- Common (or residual) equity
- Differentiated equity partners (classes)
- Joint venture
- Entrepreneurial partner
- Money partner
- Pro-rata pari passu
- Promote (hurdle and preferred return)
- Capital account
- Cash flow splits
- Sensitivity analysis

STUDY QUESTIONS

In Your Own Words

15.1 What is "human capital," and in what sense does debt financing allow small- to moderate-scale real estate entrepreneurs to "leverage their own human capital"?

15.2 Why does the ability to leverage positive-NPV opportunities and the ability to diversify property investments make an argument in favor of borrowing for investors that face a constraint on their supply of equity capital but not for investors that are not so constrained (such as REITs or open-end funds)?

15.3 Discuss the following statement: One reason to borrow money to finance a real estate investment is to reduce your risk exposure. If you borrow $80,000 and put up only $20,000 of your own money to buy a $100,000 property, you have less of your own money at risk, particularly if you take the extra money that you would otherwise have put in the property and put it in a safe investment such as CDs or Treasury bonds instead.

15.4 What types of investors or investment entities are likely to truly face a serious equity capital constraint? How does the issue of governance and control of the underlying asset interact with the capital structure question so that it may appear to some investors that they face an equity constraint?

15.5 Explain why constraints on equity capital are probably not as widespread as is often assumed in real estate, even for relatively small individual investors.

15.6 How can it make sense for a pension fund, which is tax-exempt, to borrow money to finance a real estate equity investment?

15.7 Describe the management incentive argument for the use of debt financing in real estate. Why might this argument be more relevant for understanding the use of debt by equity real estate investment trusts (REITs) than for project-level finance decisions by private real estate entrepreneurs? [Hint: Why might REIT investors (i.e., shareholders) want REIT managers to employ debt financing?]

15.8 What is the relationship between debt and liquidity, and why is liquidity valuable for investors? Are there considerations peculiar to real estate that affect the value of liquidity? If so, what are they?

15.9 Describe the two fundamental sources of the costs of financial distress (COFD). How is the COFD related to the ex-ante cost of debt capital faced by the borrower at the time of the financing decision?

15.10 Is the expectation of future inflation a reason for real estate equity investors to borrow money to finance their real estate investments? Explain why or why not.

15.11 (Putting it all together). Chapters 13 through 15 provide a comprehensive exploration of the role of debt financing in equity real estate investment. Based on the material presented in these three chapters, discuss the pros and cons of borrowing to finance real estate investments. As part of your answer, describe at least two considerations that would always be a negative for debt for any investor, and at least two considerations that would always be positive for virtually any investor. In addition, explain how leverage, taxes, liquidity, and inflation considerations might lead some investors to prefer borrowing and others to avoid borrowing.

15.12 What is mezzanine debt? Why is mezzanine debt referred to as an intermediate or hybrid part of the project-level capital structure or capital stack?

15.13 What does each partner bring to the deal in a typical real estate development joint venture arrangement between a local entrepreneur and a national capital source? What does each partner expect to get out of the deal?

15.14 Describe the pro-rata pari passu arrangement with a "promote" for determining the allocation (or split) of overall equity cash flows to the equity partners. What is the purpose of the "promote"?

Check Your Knowledge

15.15 In a joint venture structured with a "promote" provision, the general partner would receive:
- A) A guaranteed fixed return before the limited partner (LP) achieves their preferred return
- B) An increased share of profits only after achieving a specified hurdle rate for the LP
- C) Equal cash flows to the LP at all return levels
- D) No return unless all debt is paid off

15.16 The concept of "reverse-inflation risk" in levered equity means:
- A) Levered equity returns decrease if inflation is lower than expected
- B) Equity returns increase predictably with lower inflation
- C) Levered equity returns are immune to inflation rate changes
- D) Reverse-inflation risk only applies to unlevered investments

15.17 Which characteristic most often differentiates preferred equity from mezzanine debt in real estate finance?
- A) Mezzanine debt has priority over preferred equity in claims.
- B) Preferred equity usually includes a lien on the property.
- C) Mezzanine debt cannot be used in real estate investments.
- D) Preferred equity does not involve a guaranteed return.

15.18 Which situation would most likely lead to a higher preferred return hurdle in a joint venture structure?
- A) Low management fees
- B) High-risk investment with low transparency
- C) Stable asset with long-term income potential
- D) High liquidity in the underlying market

15.19 The "promote" structure in a joint venture aligns the interests of:
- A) Limited partners only
- B) Debt holders only
- C) General partners with limited partners by providing performance-based incentives
- D) Property managers only

15.20 Which of the following is a primary drawback of using excessive layers in a project-level capital structure?
- A) It reduces debt coverage ratios.
- B) It increases transparency for equity investors.
- C) It can obscure true investment risk and complicate control.
- D) It lowers the incentive for the general partner to perform.

15.21 Which of the following best explains how debt enhances diversification for equity-constrained real estate investors?
- A) It allows investors to purchase a larger number of high-risk properties with minimal equity.
- B) It reduces the overall portfolio risk by enabling purchases across different asset classes.
- C) It stretches equity capital across multiple properties, allowing for risk distribution without full ownership.
- D) It provides tax benefits that lower the cost of borrowing, allowing for more investments.

15.22 In a scenario where inflation exceeds expectations, which of the following best explains why fixed-rate debt benefits the borrower?
- A) The real value of debt repayments decreases, effectively lowering the real cost of borrowing.
- B) The fixed interest rate will automatically adjust to inflation, aligning with market returns.
- C) Fixed-rate debt is exempt from any adverse effects of inflation.
- D) Inflation only impacts equity returns, not debt obligations.

15.23 A project with high debt and low liquidity could face which of the following primary risks during a market downturn?
- A) Increased cash flow from higher rental demand
- B) Difficulty in meeting debt obligations due to reduced operational flexibility
- C) Greater ease of refinancing due to lower market rates
- D) Increased tax benefits from depreciation

15.24 In a capital structure with both mezzanine debt and preferred equity, preferred equity typically:
- A) Has a higher claim on cash flow than mezzanine debt
- B) Offers guaranteed returns in the event of project failure
- C) Sits below mezzanine debt in the capital stack but above common equity
- D) Requires payment only if mezzanine debt has been paid off in full

15.25 Which of the following best describes the concept of "reverse-inflation risk" in real estate leveraged equity?
- A) It is the risk that levered equity returns decline when inflation is unexpectedly high.
- B) It refers to the risk that lower-than-expected inflation decreases the real returns on levered equity.
- C) It reflects the benefit of inflation in increasing property values.
- D) It is the risk that inflation causes an increase in interest rates on fixed-rate loans.

15.26 Believe it or not, Bob has amassed quite a lot of human capital in the form of his property management expertise. For every 100,000 SF of property Bob manages, he can earn $20,000 per year of net "wages," over and above what he could earn doing anything else with his time. Over Bob's expected remaining active lifetime, these earnings amount to a present value of $200,000 for every 100,000 SF he manages permanently. Bob has the capacity to manage up to 1,000,000 SF of property at any given time. However, Bob likes to work on his own, and so he prefers to manage his own properties rather than hiring himself out as a third-party manager. (This is more efficient and allows Bob more freedom and flexibility to use his expertise to the maximum.) The types of properties Bob knows how to manage cost $50/SF and come in buildings of 100,000 SF each. Suppose Bob has access to over $100 million of equity capital, consisting of his own wealth and that of some partners whom he feels comfortable with and that he knows they will not interfere with his property management practices.
- a. What is the value to Bob of being able to borrow up to 80% of the value of any properties he buys?
- b. Now suppose Bob can access only $10 million of equity without jeopardizing his ability to control management. What is the value to Bob of being able to borrow up to 60% of the value of any properties he buys? What is the value to him of being able to borrow up to 80% of property value?

15.27 Consider the numerical example of a multi-tiered capital structure in Section 15.3.2. Suppose that the time zero cost of the land is not $200,000 but $220,000 and that the relatively passive equity money partner contributes 85% of the equity cash requirement rather than 90%. These are the only two parameters of the deal that change. Recalculate the figures in the preferred equity capital account as well as the cash flows to the preferred and subordinated equity partners in years 1 through 4. That is, revise the numbers in Exhibit 15-3 for these years. Do this first by hand, and then check your answers using the Excel worksheet for this chapter on the accompanying CD.

15.28 (Hybrid Financing with a "Lookback" IRR) An investor acquires a property with expected operating cash flows (PBTCF) shown below. In addition to a senior permanent mortgage loan, the capital structure includes a mezzanine loan with the following features: $15 million loan, 10-year term, 1% upfront fee, 7% annual interest and annual payments. Payments are interest-only payments in years 1 through 5. Principal payments, in addition to interest, start in year 6 and are specified as a function of PBTCF as follows: year 6 = 10% of property operating PBTCF, year 7 = 20%, years 8, 9, and 10 = 25% of PBTCF. In addition, at the end of year 10, the investor must make a lump sum payment such that the mezz lender receives a 14% internal rate of return on the mezz loan investment. This lump sum includes the principal or balance owing on the loan plus a bonus to bump the expected total return to 14%. Based on this information and the property cash flows, show the expected loan cash flows and determine the size of the lump sum and the bonus that must be paid. (Hints: Answer this in Excel either using trial and error with the "=IRR()" function or alternatively using the "Solver" tool. Note that the mez lender's initial time zero investment is $14.85 million because of the upfront 1% fee, though interest payments are based on the full $15 million principal amount.)

	1	2	3	4	5	6	7	8	9	10
PBTCF	6,746	9,894	10,505	11,283	11,780	12,348	12,920	13,438	14,201	14,694

Index

Note: Page numbers in *italics* refer to exhibits. Page numbers followed by 'n' refer to notes. Page numbers in **bold** refers to Tables

E

M

Q

R

T

U